MOBILE MARKETING
MANAGEMENT

Case Studies from
Successful Practices

MOBILE MARKETING MANAGEMENT

Case Studies from
Successful Practices

HONGBING HUA

Routledge
Taylor & Francis Group

A PRODUCTIVITY PRESS BOOK

Project Director: Qin Lide
Project Coordinator: Zhang Kun

First edition published in 2019
by Routledge/Productivity Press
52 Vanderbilt Avenue, 11th Floor New York, NY 10017
2 Park Square, Milton Park, Abingdon, Oxon OX14 4RN, UK

© 2019 by Hongbing Hua

Routledge/Productivity Press is an imprint of Taylor & Francis Group, an Informa business

No claim to original U.S. Government works

Printed on acid-free paper

International Standard Book Number-13: 978-0-367-14246-9 (Hardback)
International Standard Book Number-13: 978-0-367-14105-9 (Paperback)
International Standard Book Number-13: 978-0-429-03087-1 (eBook)

Library of Congress Cataloging-in-Publication Data

Names: Hua, Hongbing, author.
Title: Mobile marketing management : case studies from successful practices / Hongbing Hua.
Description: New York, NY : Routledge, 2019. |
Identifiers: LCCN 2018048377 (print) | LCCN 2018050700 (ebook) | ISBN 9780429030871 (e-Book) | ISBN 9780367141059 (pbk. : alk. paper) | ISBN 9780367142469 (hardback : alk. paper)
Subjects: LCSH: Internet marketing--Management. | Mobile commerce.
Classification: LCC HF5415.1265 (ebook) | LCC HF5415.1265 .H83 2019 (print) | DDC 658.8/72--dc23
LC record available at https://lccn.loc.gov/2018048377

Visit the Taylor & Francis Web site at
http://www.taylorandfrancis.com

Preface

It has been only 50 years since humanity entered the information society, and it was the Industrial Revolution that took humanity from the Agricultural Age into the Industrial Age in the past 400 years. Both in the industrial society and in the information society, enterprises and markets have been the main drivers of economic growth. What, then, is the driver that lies behind enterprises and markets?

The knowledge that takes enterprises as its subject study is referred to as Enterprise Management, while the knowledge that studies markets is referred to as Marketing.

The three most influential books in the past century are Peter F. Drucker's *The Practice of Management*, Philip Kotler's *Marketing Management*, and Jack Trout's *Positioning*. Drucker is revered as "The Father of Modern Management", while Kotler is known as "The Father of Modern Marketing", and Trout was called "The Father of Positioning". These three "godfathers" are all from the U.S. This is not surprising given that the U.S. has been not only the locomotive of the global economy in the past century, but also the testbed for market and management innovation.

Let's first talk about Drucker, the Father of Modern Management. In 1954, he proposed the epoch-making concept of Management by Objective ("MBO"). This is one of the most important and most influential concepts invented by Drucker. One of the influences of this concept is the separation of management from economics, metrology, and behavioral sciences to become an independent discipline for research in colleges and universities. The schools of business administration established by colleges and universities are the result of Drucker's efforts. Successors of Drucker, including Tom

Peters, Champy, Hamel, Collins, and even Kenichi Ohmae from Japan have emerged in succession within management circles; however, it was only after Drucker passed away in 2005 that people discovered there would be no new Drucker. Wu Xiaobo, a Chinese scholar, asked, "Who will be the next one to reflect on the management for us after he has gone?".

Next is Kotler, the Father of Modern Marketing. Before him, market management comprised the marketing mix of the 4Ps (product, price, place, and promotion). Kotler has expanded the concept of marketing from the mere sales work in the past to the more comprehensive communication and exchange processes, and even national marketing. His *Marketing Management*, which is regarded by marketers in 58 countries as the "Bible of Marketing", has become the most widely used marketing textbook worldwide. The greatest contribution of this book, now in its 15th edition, is turning marketing into a science and an independent research discipline in colleges and universities.

Third is Trout, the Father of Positioning. In 1969, Jack Trout was the first to introduce positioning, and in 1981 he published his academic monograph *Positioning*. The Positioning Theory was rated as "the most influential idea affecting American marketing in the history" by the American Marketing Association in 2001, prevailing over the theories of both Philip Kotler and Michael Porter. Trout was praised by Morgan Stanley as a better strategist than Michael Porter, and revered as "The Father of Positioning". The key breakthrough of the Positioning Theory is the concept that enterprises have only two tasks: the first is to find a decisive "position" in the heads of users outside of enterprises, and the second is to allocate all internal resources of enterprises as oriented by this "position" to conduct operations management so as to create the best operation results. Put simply, with the application of Positioning Theory, one could seize the mental resources of customers and dominate over one's competitors. The Positioning Theory was the first theory to break through enterprise management boundaries: in the past management was viewed internally, while the Positioning Theory stresses centering on external view. This has changed the research methods of science of business administration not only in the U.S. but across the whole world.

Despite the innovations in business administration theories, there has been no masterpiece that could rival those of the three masters over the three decades since the 1980s. The main reason is that the basic economic structure of the industrial economic society has not changed. We entered the mobile Internet era in 2012, and a new world came into sight.

Connecting everything – The mobile era, holding the banner of "connecting everything", has completely broken down management boundaries. The organizations based on traditional MBO have been replaced by self-propelled self-organizations, with each self-organization connecting to others via mobile networks to generate a new combination form. Key performance indicator (KPI) assessment is failing, and the traditional management is at a loss when confronted with this situation.

The Wooden Barrel Theory, for example, prevailed from 1980s to 2000. The volume of water a barrel can hold depends on its shortest plank. Likewise, the direction of management is to find the shortest plank and extend it to a long one; however, the shortest-plank principle did not work in the information economy era from 2000 to 2012, and only the long-plank principle held true: it was not the mission of an organization to extend the shortest plank because they could find a long plank directly. This is the Anti-Barrel Theory of the information revolution.

Since 2012, the world has been in the mobile era which cannot be summarized as an information era but an era where the 4.0 industrial revolution, which includes

artificial intelligence (AI), life sciences and 3D printing, choruses with mobile Internet. "Barrels" disappear, as every home has "tap water", and everyone accesses the Internet and connects via smartphones. There is no need to find the shortest or the longest plank because the barrels themselves are no longer needed. Jack Ma said, "Young people will not be able to find a job in another three decades." This is possible because by then, robots will operate in factories, people will go to see a doctor at intelligent big-data hospitals, and intelligent robots will teach in schools; robots will farm in the countryside, intelligent robots will babysit at home; not even packages will be sent by people, but are directly delivered to your balcony by unmanned helicopters ... Every one of us should be thrilled to be a part of this trend! The sentence which summarized the trend of the period of the planned economy was: a year of famine does not starve a craftsman. The period of the market economy time can be summarized as: only by doing business may you become rich. The era of the sharing economy time may be characterized as: how many people you help equals how many people will help you, and what matters from now on is big data, not oil or coal!

Fast iteration – The second banner held by the mobile Internet has revolutionized the mass base of the Positioning Theory oriented by competition. The Positioning Theory proposes to first build a mental model in people's minds and then launch new products, all of which is a positioning process that takes some time to complete. However, in the mobile era, "being fast" is the first; "transient advantage" is emphasized above long-term advantage, industry boundaries become increasingly blurred as the market changes are increasingly accelerating, crossover ravagers emerge in an endless stream, and enterprises should not continue to depend on certain core competences to keep their single competitive advantage. Instead, they should transform with changes, rapidly innovate, and build successive transient advantage. The "decoring" of transient advantage leads to an increasingly short time for enterprises to retain their core competences.

Users first – This is the third banner, fluttering in the sky of the mobile era. The Marketing Theory of 4Ps born in the age of the industrial economy starts with products. The mobile era, on the other hand, proposes a shift of the power center from "enterprise products" to users. Users' participation soars to unprecedented heights, and the theory of serving users is deep in the minds of people.

China entered the mobile era in 2012 and is now a major country in the application of mobile Internet technology. With a wealth of experience accumulated through trial and error in the practices of mobile-DNA management innovations and market innovations, it is the original intention of this *Mobile Marketing Management* (firstly published in 2017 and secondly in 2018) to summarize such practical experience of enterprises, and outline the market and management laws for the next 30 years. The mobile marketing management is one of the world's toughest problems. Therefore, on publication this book was termed the pioneering work of the mobile marketing management discipline in China.

Before publishing *Mobile Marketing Management*, the author spent more than ten years in creating seven reprints of one book entitled *Mobile Internet Panoramic Cogitation*. He is at the forefront of the era, and has established that the basic attributes of the mobile Internet are to be "people-oriented, evolutionary, and open". Because of this book, the author has been recognized as "The Founder of Mobile Internet Theories" in

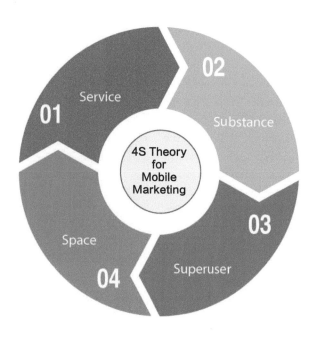

China. Over the past ten years, all his books, which are not for sale, have been donated to 1,200 libraries.

In spring 2019, the English version of *Mobile Marketing Management* was published. It establishes the four pillars in the new marketing world: Service, Substance of content, Super user, and Space. They are known in short as the "4S Theory".

In light of "users first", all products will be services, and the future market competition will not be the competition of products, but the competition of the productization of the service idea. In light of failure of mass communication, the competition among all services will be the competition of substance differentiation; in light of popularization of self-organizations, the trend will be to develop markets through working with people (Super users) instead of companies; and in light of blurred market boundaries, the ultimate task for enterprises will be to optimize their own living space and evolve their own development space.

Behind the 4S Theory are over 100 successful global cases taken from the past ten years. Following the publication of the new book, its practical application has been followed by a large number of micro, small and medium-sized enterprises, excluding conservative academic lecturers and industry giant enterprises that are too big to turn around. This might well be the natural law in the forest: it is difficult for humanity to predict or completely extinguish forest fires. Each forest fire leaves in its wake the destruction of towering trees, and yet new seeds under these big trees or in the soil would not obtain the nutrition necessary for growth and the chance of survival if the forest fire did not naturally eliminate the big trees.

What is the correlation among science, art, philosophy, literature, economy, and politics? They were independent disciplines mutually influencing but not directly correlating with each other before the book *Mobile Marketing Management* was published. However, the basic principles of the mobile marketing have promoted crossover cooperation between the six disciplines. Each discipline has also had to separately establish its own "transient advantage" with the help of the mobile marketing management. The mobile application that "speed connects everything" has changed the construction period of each discipline. The construction period of a discipline's revolutionary results often took decades. During the previous centuries, even more than a century. However, when the mobile Internet enables the discipline specialties to horizontally correlate, professional transient advantages of disciplines will be built in a short time, and the transient advantage that is accumulated and evolved bit by bit will eventually become the revolutionary results of each discipline.

Presently, the turning point for the Lazy Economy has come. Users prefer to "stay at home" and shop via their cell phones. Such a consumer preference stimulates the rapid development of the delivery business. The delivery business is making progress, and the lazy become even lazier. All one needs is a cell phone installed with the "Taobao Home Delivery" app. Users stay in the comfort of their own home and wait for their home deliveries, which might range from fresh fruit, vegetables and flowers to medicines and housekeeping services, anything you expect. In addition to third-party logistics companies, the shop assistants of each terminal store serve both visiting and home customers. Everybody is a courier. Users sit back and enjoy the fruits of such a developed logistics network. All consumption is conducted on a mobile terminal.

The turning point of SF-Express reminds us that the mobile marketing's spring is coming. On opening this book, you will find not only a strategy or tactic, but also a convincing system of mobile marketing. This book contains 107 knowledge points related to marketing innovation and they form an all-new and convincing marketing system. The spring for mobility, science and system has arrived.

The purpose of this book is to help readers to find out, summarize and apply the pattern. As the second largest economy in the real world and the largest economy in the mobile network world, China has rich experience and lessons in mobile marketing, which will be beneficial to the scholars' research.

The technological trend is good for those who understand it and bad for those who ignore it. In January 2017, when Master, Google's internet chess player, successively beat 61 grandmasters from China and other countries, and achieved an incredible performance of 60 wins and one draw, people were suddenly enlightened and realized that the era of artificial intelligence has arrived. In the past, artificial intelligence was something we read about in scientific fiction or research literature as it had not been sufficiently developed to catch our eye. Today, it has crossed that border and stepped into the arena. Before we knew it, the chess game has become a competition between an intelligent robot and its assistant and another chess player and his intelligent robot assistant. How to conduct cultural and sports marketing in the world of chess? Overnight, the marketing society has found that even its objects of marketing are robots. Maybe the marketing society itself will be replaced by intelligent robots. Who knows?

3D printing joins in the fun. The means of production has changed. Some life science research argues that human beings can live up to the age of 500 years, provided that the research and development (R&D) of new materials is highly optimistic, and aged and decayed internal organs of human body can be replaced with 3D-printed organs made of suitable materials. The train of the 4.0 Industry Revolution quickly rumbles through the traditional marketing society, carrying away nothing but the grievance of the latter.

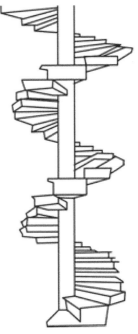

New technologies, environments and tools are constantly emerging. The 90 million population of China's marketing society needs to be redeemed and the marketing textbooks of colleges need to be innovated. Students in classrooms shall absorb nourishment from new textbooks. When leaving school, marketing students shall not be in the dark when it comes to marketing, as you never fight your enemy who holds a machine gun while you only have a spear in your hand.

Helical symbols appear throughout this book, carrying the meaning that the development of everything follows a spiral ascending pattern. Human brains and organs contain large quantities of helical structures, and the 4S marketing theory is just like the helical brain of mobile marketing. In buildings, spiral stairs are space-saving and aesthetic, reminding us of the circularly ascending reading logic in mobile marketing learning of each chapter of this book.

Common twining plants are typical of the spiral form. A morning glory with a series of trumpet flowers climbs clockwise around a rod, while a *Periploca calophylla* grows upwards counterclockwise. Pine cone seeds and sunflower seeds grow in spirals along inversed patterns. We can see the spatial theory proposed by mobile marketing from these plants, that the terminal channels in modern marketing are the spirals of online and offline as well as virtuality and reality in two opposite directions, which ultimately present the spiral growth of mobile marketing. Inspired by spirals in nature, Fibonacci, the mathematician who invented the Fibonacci sequence, found that the spiral is more close to the golden ratio (0.618). The optimization method is extensively applied in all chapters of this book. Nature has its preference and its strong love of beauty. Marketing activities of human beings must follow the principle that man is an integral part of nature and must continue to pursue the harmonious and health development of mobile marketing.

Through the thinking of the Zen and the Tao, we realize that our life is full of twists and turns. For an enterprise, the growth is destined to be a spiral rise out of failure.

Readers should know that in this era, knowledge learning is the new trend. We should pay homage to traditions and explore the unknown world to create a tomorrow of infinite possibilities. I have to say that experience is a negative asset in this era. While many people are stuck in their successful experience, we would see that the more successful a person used to be, the more difficult it may be for him to make changes. This is like the teacher who stresses the empty-cup mentality, i.e., how could one accept new things, new knowledge, and new experience when one's mind is filled with things of the past? Change is the eternal truth of the world. The Chinese theory of "copinism" through the years has hindered innovative thinking among Chinese. Only disruption can live up to innovation. The rapid development of China has drawn worldwide attention but has also endangered the owners of the Chinese small- and medium-sized enterprises! Nobody knows how many people have stumbled and how many people have been held back.

Mobile Marketing Management is a theoretical book about successful market practices and management activities in China. We hope that more people will learn and borrow from it.

China's experience is here for the world to draw on.

-Thomas Qin on July 31, 2017 in Beijing, China

Contents

Preface   **V**

Part 1

Evolution Theory of

Marketing   **1**

Chapter 1

Evolution of Mobile Marketing   2

1. What is Mobile Marketing?   3
2. Marketing Environment in the Age of
   Transformation   5
3. Background of Evolution of Mobile Marketing 14
4. Path of Evolution of Mobile Marketing   20

Chapter 2

4S Mobile Marketing Theory   27

1. Proposal of 4S Mobile Marketing Theory 28
2. Principles of Economics for 4S Mobile
   Marketing Theory   29
3. Tool Kit - 4S Mobile Marketing Theory   34

Part 2

Service   **37**

Chapter 3

Overview   38

1. All Products Involve Services   39
2. Five Models Redefining Product Service 41
3. App Service Operation   48

Chapter 4

Seven Thinking Models for

Developing Services   54

1. User Thinking   55
2. Socialized Thinking   63
3. Extreme Thinking   70
4. Big-Data Thinking   73
5. Open Thinking   75
6. Micro-innovation Thinking   77
7. Story Thinking   82

Chapter 5

Service Marketing Mode   90

1. Studio Service Mode   91
2. Personalized Service Mode   93
3. User Participation Service Mode   95
4. 3D Printing Service Mode   98
5. Integrated Service Mode   103
6. Industrial Service Mode   105

Chapter 6

Service Value Marketing   108

1. Value Goal Orientation   109
2. Price Strategy Operation   111
3. A Good Product Spreads Itself   117
4. Tipping Point-Hot Sale Model-Hot
   Sale Item   118
5. Tool Kit - 16 Methods for Service Upgrade 122

Part 3

Substance   129

Chapter 7

Redefining Substance Marketing   130
1. The Three Directions of Mobile Substance
   Marketing   131
2. Redefining Substance Marketing   134
3. Presentation Forms of "Content Prevails"   139

Chapter 8

Substance Management:
Mobile Brand Management   146
1. What Is Brand?   147
2. Mobile Brand Building   149
3. Mobile Brand Identity System   157
4. Substance Dissemination of Mobile Brand   171

Chapter 9

Deep Substance of Management   181
1. Three Renaissance Movements   182
2. IP-based Substance Marketing   185

Chapter 10

Big Data Substance Marketing   193
1. Knowing About Big Data   194
2. Big Data Marketing   200
3. Tool Kit - 22 Methods for Substance of
   Content Marketing   204

Part 4

Super User   213

Chapter 11

Vital Few   214
1. Focusing on 1%   215
2. Value of 1%   220
3. From 1% to 99%   226

Chapter 12

Behavioral Characteristics of
Super Users   231
1. The Rise of Communities   233
2. Brand Communities   237
3. Community Leaders   243

Chapter 13

Application Principle of Super User:
Sharing Economy   252
1. Principle of Sharing   253
2. Consumer Business   255

Chapter 14

The Marketing Law of Super Users   258
1. Psychological Cognition Rules of
   Common Users   259
2. Psychological Cognition Rules of
   Super Users   264

5. Application of 4S Theory in New Retail   374
6. Tool Kit - Mobile Marketing Space Spread   383

Part 5

Space   273

Chapter 15

Introduction of Marketing Space   274
1. The Evolution of Marketing Channels   275
2. Age of Market Space 3.0   285
3. Operational Tools   288

Chapter 16

Network Marketing Space   297
1. E-commerce Marketing   298
2. Cross-border E-commerce   315

Chapter 17

Marketing Space 4.0 - Mobile End-to-end Marketing   320
1. Mobile Space for Virtual Reality   321
2. Artificial Intelligence - A New Scene for Holistic Marketing   322
3. Blockchain - Creating a New Space for Trust   331
4. Augmented Reality（AR）Space   340

Chapter 18

Mobile Marketing Space Spread   346
1. Field under the Boundary Theory   347
2. Scene   351
3. Scene-based Marketing   356
4. New Retail in the Context of Mobile Internet   362

Part 6

Global Marketing   391

Chapter 19

Global Marketing - A Viewpoint from China   392
1. Reinterpreting Four Industrial Revolutions   393
2. Age of Conflict 4.0   403

Chapter 20

Spiral Economics   407
1. Spiral Economics   408

Bibliography   415

Definition and Interpretation   423

Postscript   443

About the Author

Hongbing Hua

Founder of Basic Theories of
Mobile Marketing in China

Hongbing Hua is a well-known and highly recognized brand marketing professional in China and founder of the academic discipline of mobile marketing. For the past 29 years in his career, he has been dedicated to implementing the innovative practices and services in fields of branding, marketing and consulting services. He has provided training and consulting services to 160 companies of diversified industry sectors, among them 45 companies are public companies. From 2008, he started in-depth studies and research in the field of mobile marketing and published a book entitled *Mobile Internet Panoramic Cogitation*, which was reprinted for seven times with updated input. He has been regarded as the founder of basic theories of mobile marketing by academia in China.

The Chinese version 1.0 of *Mobile Marketing Management* was published in 2017 and Chinese version 2.0 was published in 2018. The book has systematically elaborated the fundamental theories of international mobile marketing and has become the bestseller among books of the same field.

Based on many case studies and field practices, Hongbing Hua has created the 4s theorical system of mobile marketing. He has built up a comprehensive knowledge system of mobile marketing from four dimensions, namely, service, substance, super user and space. He has filled in the blanks in the mobile applications of global marketing theories.

Collection of Major Works

Mobile Marketing Management; Mobile Internet Panoramic Cogitation; Chinese-style Marketing: Hua's Ideas; 54 Golden Keys to Unlock Your Marketing Potential; Chinese-style Marketing: 54 Golden Keys; Enterprise Management in China: Big Marketing, Big Planning; One Degree Strategy; Reverse Marketing; Strong Brand and Strong Marketing; Profit Explosion; Top-level Design; Secrets of Marketing.

Part 1

Evolution
Theory of Marketing

Chapter 1

Evolution of Mobile Marketing

Topics:

1. What is Mobile Marketing?
2. Marketing Environment in the Age of Transformation
3. Background of Evolution of Mobile Marketing
4. Path of Evolution of Mobile Marketing

With the rise of the Internet and big data in the 21st century, mobile marketing has become a standard practice in enterprise marketing. It is like an "evolution" where, thanks to mobile media, the entire marketing industry is witnessing a continual "replacement" and ultimately "metamorphosis". In the long run, it will be only one of the stages of "marketing evolution". In the future, the marketing industry will inevitably continue "evolving" along with the change of the "media".

The insipidness of marketing may just be the beginning of the evolutionary progress. This is worthy of our acclaim.

The change of marketing from instant progress to evolutionary progress can indeed be called a watershed. When the age of "Terminal War" has become history, many marketing people are in search of a new messianic marketing mode. Therefore, "innovation" and "reform" have become the direction of their exploration. Instant progress may ultimately become history, but evolutionary progress is bound to "quietly predominate".

The next age is the age of mobile marketing which will satisfy various demands and serve the masses.

What Is Mobile Marketing?

Mobile marketing refers to the act of delivering personalized instant messages directly and accurately to the target audience on a mobile terminal (cellphone or tablet PC), so as to achieve the goal of marketing via information interaction with consumers.

In the early stages, mobile marketing was known as interactive marketing on handsets or wireless marketing. It obtains cloud marketing content via mobile terminal with the support of powerful cloud services to deliver personalized instant messages accurately and effectively to each consumer, achieving "one-to-one" interactive marketing.

Conceptually, mobile marketing realizes information spreading based on certain network platforms which could be either mobile communication network or wireless local area network, and the corresponding access means or equipment includes cellphones, personal digital assistants, portable computers or other special access devices. The information delivered is meant to achieve "one-to-one" communication between the enterprise and the consumer. The purpose of this communication is to improve brand awareness, collect consumer information, increase the possibility of purchase, improve the credibility of mobile marketing, and increase

enterprise income. Seeing the development trend of mobile terminal in terms of intellectualization, the cellphone is no longer merely a means of communication; instead, it has developed into a living platform integrating Internet services such as communication, information acquisition, commercial trade, and network entertainment. The cellphone has already transcended its original significance to become a part of our life. In the future, to understand your cellphone is to understand the world. Controlling mobile portals will be the most important step in mobile Internet marketing. To study mobile marketing, you need to understand mobile equipment application platforms and platform tools.

Among the numerous mobile equipment platforms in the market, there are three major ones, i.e., Apple's IOS, Google's Android, and Microsoft's Windows Phone.

1. IOS

The IOS platform is a mobile equipment operating system developed by the American company Apple Inc. Originally designed for iPhones, and named iPhone-OS, it was successively applied to other Apple products such as the iPod touch, the iPad, and the iPad mini. It was renamed IOS at the Apple's Worldwide Developers Conference (WWDC) on June 7, 2010.

The development of IOS is the most successful and the most stable among the three platforms. By February 2012, there had been 552,247 applications on the platform, with game apps, book apps, and entertainment apps ranking at the top. IOS also has diversified application functions including: map app, Siri, Passbook, Facetime, and Appstore. The IOS interface is rigorous and innovative. It has more applications than the other two platforms, with thousands of apps in each category, each of which is exquisitely designed. This is because Apple Inc. provides plenty of tools and APIs for third-party developers to ensure their applications have full access to the advanced technology contained in each piece of IOS equipment.

2. Android

The Android operating system was originally developed by Andy Rubin, and the first Android smartphone was released

	Icon Function	ios	Android	Windows Phone	Comments
1	Search	Q	Q	Q	Entrance
2	History (or recently used)	⊙	⊙		Easy to find
3	Collection (or favorite)	★	★	★	Easy to find
4	Group (iOS: followed)	👥	👥	No social contact limitation	Social attributes
5	Picks (or share)	User feature	👍		Lazy mode and show-off supported
6	Download	⊙	↓		Information exchange, medium function
7	Contacts	👤	👤	No social contact	Social contact, communication
8	Settings	Existing	⇶	⚙	DIY: satisfying user habit
9	More	●●●	⋮		Thinking for the user
10	SD card	Included	💾		Easy to store
11	Write	🖊	✏	✏	Access to input and expression
12	E-mail	Included	✉		Social contact, delivery
13	Camera	📷	📷	📷	Integrated, multifunction
14	Bookmark (tag)	📖	🏷		Easy to store
15	Like		♥	♥	Catering to the user
16	Add	+	⊞	⊕	Function
17	Dustbin	🗑	🗑	🗑	Clearing up
18	Administration		▬	▬	Administration
19	Reply	←	↩		Intercommunication
20	Stop	✕	✕	✕	Function
21	Refresh	↻	↻	↻	Function

Figure 1-1   Comparison of Toolbar Icons across the Three Platforms

in October 2008. Android has expanded to tablet PCs and other fields such as televisions, digital cameras, and game consoles.

The competition of Android goes beyond the imaginable. In January 2011, Google declared that the daily new users of Android equipment had reached 300,000, and by July 2011, the number had increased to 550,000, with the total number of Android system equipment users numbering to 135 million. At that time, the Android system was the system with the largest market share in the smartphone field at that time. On August 2, 2011, Android cellphones accounted for 43% in the smartphone market, ranking number one in the world.

3. Windows Phone

Released by Microsoft in 2010, the Windows Phone platform is a mobile equipment operating system which integrates Microsoft's Xbox Live games and Xbox Music as well as unique video experience. Compared with IOS and Android, Windows Phone has its own distinct features with a series of radical operations such as desktop icon dragging and sliding control.

Although the design specifications and meanings of the toolbar icons of the three platforms differ slightly, they are broadly similar. We have compared some of the toolbar icons of these platforms so that their differences and similarities can be seen directly. See Figure 1-1.

Marketing Environment in the Age of Transformation

I. The Age of Screens

In 2012, Google pointed out in its The New Multi-screen World study that interaction via all kinds of screens, including emerging digital media such as smartphone, PC, tablet PC, and TV, had already been the major part of the daily media interaction of consumers. Compared with traditional newspapers and broadcasting as well as magazines, the interaction via these emerging digital media accounts for 90%. People use various screens for 4.4 hours every day,

excluding usage during working times. See Figure 1-2.

In the age of transformation, consumers and the market are always faster than the enterprises. The great changes of the market propel the upgrading of competition, the reform of the enterprise supply side[①], and the entry of marketing science into "the age of screens". Nowadays, the consumers have become "digital-first". Digital has penetrated the whole process of consumers' purchase behaviors and decision-making.

> ①
>
> *Supply side: relative to demand side. Supply in economics refers to the certain amount of commodities or labor service the producer is willing and able to provide in a certain period at a certain price level.*

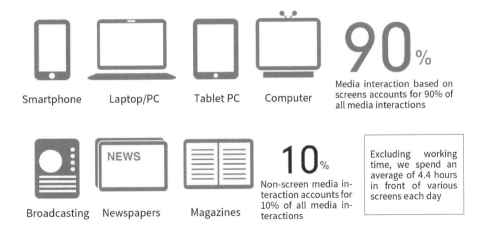

| Smartphone | Laptop/PC | Tablet PC | Computer | 90% Media interaction based on screens accounts for 90% of all media interactions |

| Broadcasting | Newspapers | Magazines | 10% Non-screen media interaction accounts for 10% of all media interactions | Excluding working time, we spend an average of 4.4 hours in front of various screens each day |

Figure 1-2 People's interaction with digital media vs. traditional media.
Source: Google, The New Multi-screen World. August 2012

Definition

- Preferential use of smartphones to acquire necessary information when making purchase decisions
- Not limited to "digital natives"
- Applicable to B2C, B2B, as well as O2O

Features of Digital-first Consumers

- 90% of consumption is in front of screens
- 90% use multiple screens continuously
- 65% conduct their first-time shopping online
- 63% use mobile payment
- 61% use social media on smartphones
- 59% conduct their first-time money management on smartphones
- 58% rely on search engine when making personal finance decisions

"The current marketing is different from that of 30 years, 10 years, and even one year ago. The changes of consumer expectation, technology, and competition have made the market environment change with each passing day."

Cristene Gonzalez Wartz, Associate Partner of IBM

II. Connection Is More than Anything

In the age of mobile Internet, the primary task of marketing is connection. What is to be connected? Who is to be connected? How shall it be connected? In terms of 4S marketing theory, it means connecting the super user with rich substance sharing to achieve the mobile connection of products.

1. Connection

If the development process of Internet is divided by typical historic stages, it can be summarized as four evolutionary stages: the first stage is digitization, which started at the birth of the real network using packet switching technology in 1969. In this stage, single computers were connected in a few organizations. The second stage is digital media, starting in the 1990s. Since the introduction of Netscape Browser in

1995, we witnessed the ever-increasing interconnection of approximately 500 million computers based in workplaces and households in the next decade. The web portal Google emerged as a professional information search tool, making the transfer and capture of information easier. The Internet was more of a tool of information revolution in this stage. The third stage, digital commerce, then followed. In 1994, Jeff Bezos, the founder of Amazon, proposed 20 commodities which he believed were suitable for marketing in virtual reality; these included books, music products, magazines, and PC hardware and software. In the end, he chose books. Twenty years later, Amazon had become a super e-commerce company, the net sales of which reached USD 74.45 billion in 2013. The fourth stage is mobile network. It actually started approx-

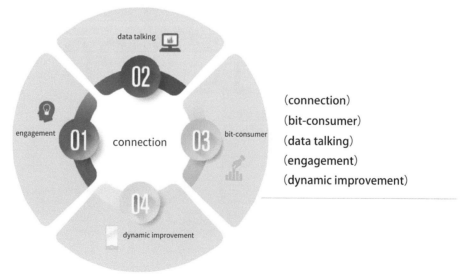

(connection)
(bit-consumer)
(data talking)
(engagement)
(dynamic improvement)

Model of Digitization Degree. Source: KMG Research

imately at the same time as the second and the third stages of the Internet, including Facebook, Twitter, China's domestic website Kaixin, and the current Microblog and WeChat. Internet in this stage is more often empowered by cellphones, so the stage is also known as "the age of the mobile Internet". Clay Shirky, the columnist of *WIRED* magazine, calls it "Here comes everybody". And now we have already entered an age of "social business". Enterprises can now carry out commercial activities in the environment of developed and mature social media. In a sense, social commerce (s-commerce) is just mobile marketing based on communities. It can deepen customer relations and even engage the customers in enterprise creation and operation.

It is not difficult to see that there is a common thread which runs through the history of the evolution of the Internet. If one word can summarize that thread, it is "connection". In this evolution process, people are connected together, ever more closely, quickly, widely, deeply, and fully. At any time, site and thing are connected on the path of evolution, breaking the spatio-temporal boundaries and forming the existence ecology of all of mankind. The age of pure commodity promotion has come to an end. See Figure 1-3.

2. Bit–consumer

In the age of digital marketing, all consumer behaviors can be recorded and tracked. In the overwhelming age of big data, the marketing process can be transparent through the collection and analysis of big data and use of that big data in decision-making. Digitizing, and then tracking and analyzing one's consumers and customers, would appear to be crucial. Many retail stores have affixed new-type bar code tags to their clothes, with which information relating to when the clothes were picked up, put down or tried on can be recorded precisely and delivered to the background management system. All those data will be analyzed to provide accurate direction to enterprises for next-step product development, design or purchase.

3. Data Talking

One of the cores of digital marketing is the birth, collection, and application of data. Data are generated in real interactive behaviors. These data include user attributes, views, clicks, and interactions based on the users, and advertisements, behavior surveillance, and effect feedback based on the enterprises.

Data talking is the digitization of operational decision-making. In the stage of data accumulation and exchange, digital operation is not urgently needed; however, when the data source is established and user-centered cross-screen intercommunication is realized, how to analyze and realize intelligent and visual data presentation becomes crucial. A data talking system shall be established above the subjective judgment of the decision makers and the managers. Data talking has changed the strategic model of operational decision-making, transferring the decision-making bases of the 4P marketing theory, i.e., consumer behavior, consumer psychology, and consumer preference, from the heads of marketers to cellphones and computers.

4. Engagement

Consumers are allowed to engage in enterprise marketing strategies. Enterprises and users are interpreted as Party A and Party B in marketing science, but now this logic has changed. Consumers should have

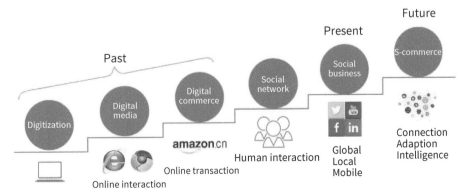

Figure 1-3   Development of the Internet. Source: Philip Kotler, Lecture Notes at Kellogg School of Management: KMG Research

Figure 1-4   Personal Charisma of Enterprises.
Source: Peter Walshe

vital right of speech in the marketing process of enterprises. The consumers can be regarded as external employees that are out of the control of the enterprises but can ensure the normal and efficient operation and propel the decision-making of the enterprises. By participating in enterprise operation in terms of product design, brand promotion, event planning, and channel selection, and so on, the consumers will have a sense of belonging to the enterprises.

5.   Dynamic Improvement

Since consumer data are updated extremely frequently nowadays, enterprises need rapid progress and dynamic improve-

ments while adjusting strategies in order to ensure their current digital marketing strategy can match the existing consumer behaviors. The emergence of dynamic improvement requires marketing science to adapt to the fast-changing market. This has led to the appearance of agile management.

The biggest change in the mobile age has appeared in people, i.e., entrepreneurs and consumers. The mobile age is "an age of subversion". In this age, we can see that the charisma of enterprises has turned toward the two dimensions of "challenge" and "change". An enterprise drawing close to one dimension may show little charisma with elaborate planning, but an enterprise approaching to both dimensions may probably enjoy an "infinite charisma". As shown in Figure 1-4, the "fun" of Logic Show and "rebellion" of Tesla just correspond to the "funny person" and the "rebel" at the cross of the two indicators. Donald Trump's election as the President of the United States was not accidental: it was an inevitable choice of this age.

Traditional Customer Relation Management (CRM) strategies can no longer adapt to the current social media. A new CRM system should make comprehensive use of digital technology, automatic and synchronous sales and marketing, customer service, and technical support. It should allow the core products and technology managed by the company to intercommunicate with current and future customers.

As Figure 1-5 shows:

1) Users in the mobile age do not want to "be managed".

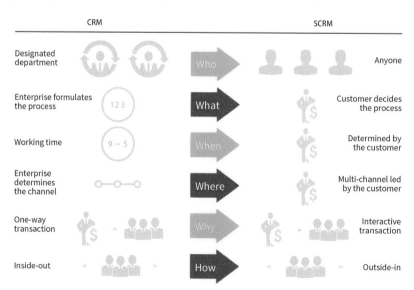

Figure 1-5   Customer relation management evolving toward socialization.

2) The boundary between internal and external management of an enterprise is becoming obscure.

3) Users do not consume "at set sites and set time"; this creates a big problem for the marketers.

What is the consumer persona? From the proposal of user persona to the big data consumer persona of today, marketers have never stopped exploring methods for observing their customers.

The concept of persona was firstly proposed by Alan Cooper, "the Father of Interactive Design", in the 1980s. Personae are user models formed with the characteristics and attributes extracted from real user behaviors. They represent different user types and corresponding attitudes and behaviors, and they are virtual portraits. The personae are used for studying the behavioral characteristics of consumers according to their preference and psychology.

Personae are usually used together with the concept of market segmentation in marketing. They represent the typical customers of a certain market segment, helping enterprises or the government better understand the users and their demands and communicate with them effectively. In the age of mobile marketing, the means of persona is needed when a product is targeted at a market segment. Please see Figure 1-6.

JD.COM has listed over 300 tags for its users by means of consumer persona, while the consumer persona of the Haier Group is a user data tag system diagram containing seven tiers, 143 dimensions, and 5,228 nodes. See Figure 1-7.

Figure 1-6 User Portraits

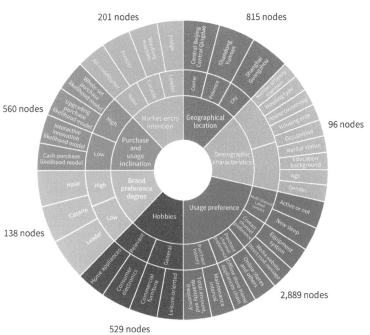

Figure 1-7 "User Portraits" from Big Data. Source: Sun Kunpeng, "User Portraits" from Big Data

III. Marketing in Mobile State

The behavioral transformation of consumers is also shown in that the users can have contact with marketing at any time and in any place. Such marketing includes mobile searches, mobile positioning, mobile navigation, mobile booking, and mobile payments. Marketing can be said to be omnipresent in this age. See Figure 1-8.

It is not difficult to see from the customer travel map provided by Lego in Figure 1-8 that the customer cannot live without the smartphone. The main battlefield of marketing has transferred from traditional stores and PC websites to cellphones. This change is profound and unprecedented.

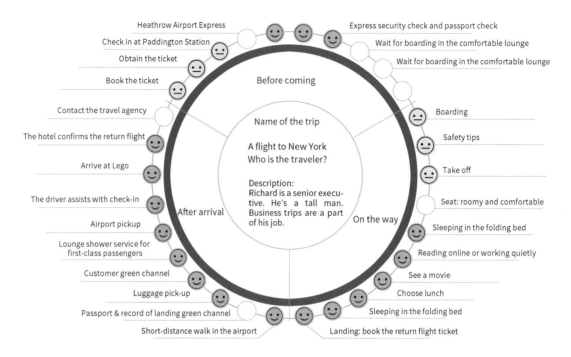

Figure 1-8   Customer Journey Plan. Source: Lego

IV. Internet Geography

When talking about the basic conditions of mobile marketing, online information geography, we should firstly understand the Internet application mode and infrastructure. In 2002, sub-Saharan Africa had only six million Internet users, and India had just 16 million (compared with the 130 million of 2012). Many notable disparities in Internet applications are caused by the actual geographical distribution differences of Internet infrastructures. For example, in 2009, some regions in the world were more closely connected than other regions, but there were still some regions without any Internet connection with the outside (East Africa is one of the last regions that are connected to the outside via optical network). The absence of an optical

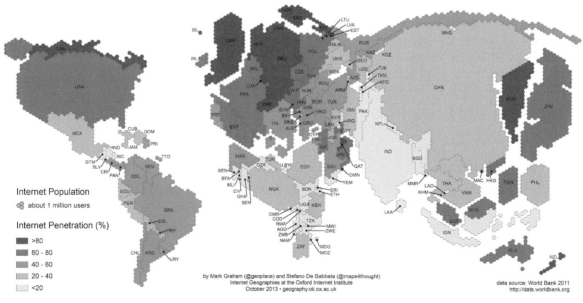

Figure 1-9   Percentage of Internet Penetration. Source: Internet Map of Oxford Internet Institute

network means slow Internet surfing and higher cost than that of other regions. We can, therefore, say that cost and efficiency restrict Internet applications.

However, such restriction of infrastructure has been overcome. Currently, there are only a few regions not connected to the global network. Internet penetration and mobile growth have seen rapid development in poor countries. By the end of 2011, there were six billion mobile devices around the world (See http: //data.world-bank.org, accessed January 9, 2013), which means 85% of the world population were interconnected via mobile Internet terminals. There were still over 2.5 billion Internet users, and most of those Internet users are living in underdeveloped countries.

As shown in Figure 1-9, the poorer one is, the more willing one is to connect with the outside world via the Internet. For the impoverished population, connecting with the outside may mean much more. The free flow of Internet information is often regarded as "an important equalizer". Hamadoun Toure, Secretary General of the International Telecommunication Union (ITU), repeated that point many times in his speech in 2012. He pointed out that once the world divided by territories is closely connected via Internet, people around the world will have the chance to approach infinite knowledge and to freely express themselves, and this can better help people build and enjoy the knowledge society.

V. The Differentiated and Innovative Application of Brand Design in Apps

With the trend in recent years for mobile Internet entrepreneurship, apps have grown increasingly mature. IOS and Android devices have been standardized, and technically and visually designing an app is not difficult. If one picks at random some mainstream commercial apps and compares their interface designs, one will find only slight differences beyond their icons. The homogenization of apps is growing increasingly serious.

To design an app with a unique brand gene different from other competing goods has become a pressing requirement for many large enterprises. Internet companies have a clear division of labor; the usual process one where the User Interface (UI) designer discusses the plan for each version with the product manager and the interaction designer, roughly drawing out the process in lo-fi forms during the discussion, after which the UI designer completes the interfaces for later review; the standard documents after the review are transferred to the development engineer. This is the standard process where there is little space for the imagination of and execution by the designer. App designs produced from the standard process are not likely to have bugs, but they are very likely to be homogenous. The only way of improving the app design level is to introduce the brand design, to make brand-new designs from the source of the brand culture. Leaving users with a deep and effective impression through brand building will render more possibilities for the improvement of the overall design quality of the app.

1. The Extraction of the Brand Visual Symbols

The extraction of the brand visual symbols of an app is similar to the logo design process in graphic design. The design of the app is also a visual extension of the enterprise brand. The first thing is an in-depth exploration of the brand, understanding the brand orientation, extracting brand-related key words, and searching for pictorial material using the key words. This procedure can be completed through team brainstorming. Extract the core visual symbol for visual impact and memorability, to enable the app to quickly attract users. Create big memory points with unique small visual symbols; this can be called "little symbols, big memories".

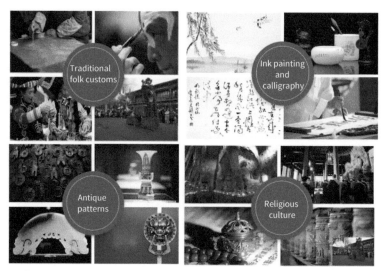

Extraction of the Brand Visual. Source: Wang Xianggui, DEM UED INC.

Extraction of Key Words

By collecting relevant materials relating to Chinese traditional folk customs, ink painting and calligraphy, antique patterns, and religious culture, the four key phrases as shown in Figure 1-10 are extracted based on the app orientation of Zhongyiyoumei, and the style design, tone selection, and so are carried out accordingly.

Figure 1-10   Extraction of Key Words. Source: Wang Xianggui, DEM UED INC.

Extraction of Visual Symbols

Visual symbols are extracted through the four key phrases of concise, clean, Chinese style and culture, and these visual symbols will run through the whole app design process and will even be extended to the design of the main banner, promotion pictures for the app store, and so on.

Visual Symbols. Source: Wang Xianggui, DEM UED INC.

2. Brand Internalization Demonstrated by the Main Style Design

As everyone knows, the two camps of IOS and Android are the source of apps. It is very challenging to introduce Chinese cultural elements and give them international features based on the standards of these two application systems.

Oriental Artisan obtained tens of millions of Round A+ investment on

February 6, 2017, and Treasure Hunt obtained CNY 3 million of angel investment on April 1, 2015. These two apps have numerous active users, including ethnic Chinese across the world.

Chinese culture is well known for its diversity, extensiveness and depth. The Chinese style details and the international vision will surely bring a worldwide trend for Chinese style. Clever application of traditional Chinese elements in the design can often create visual elements with unique oriental artistic charms. Classical works can only be designed based on a profound understanding of the traditional national culture connotation and the smart combination with modern design philosophies.

Different from traditional print media, apps are carriers that support short videos and animations. Therefore, a more user-friendly interactive experience can help improve the design quality of the apps.

3. The Differentiated and Innovative Design for the Bottom Navigation Bar of the App

Due to the limited width of a cellphone screen, there are usually 4 to 5 function items on the bottom navigation bar of an app. The function items are usually composed of icons and characters; the latter is for making the meaning clearer. The icon for the home page is often a "small house" or the logo.

东家·守艺人

Starting Page

Homepage

"Oriental Artisan" App. Source: Wang Xianggui, DEM UED INC.

寻宝之旅

Starting Page

Homepage

"Treasure Hunt" App. Source: Wang Xianggui, DEM UED INC.

"Oriental Artisan" App. Source: Wang Xianggui, DEM UED INC.

The bottom navigation bar of "Oriental Artisan" is very identifiable. It combines the Song typeface with concrete graphics. The Song typeface has thin transverse strokes and thick vertical strokes, with decorations at the ends (i.e., the "foot" or "serif"); the

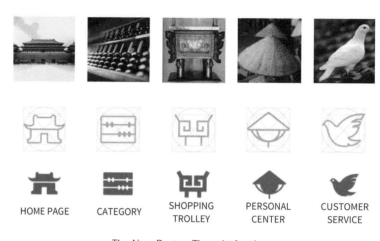

The New Design Thought for the
Bottom Navigation Bar of Zhongyiyoumei App 2.0.
Source: Wang Xianggui, DEM UED INC.

dot, the left stroke, the right stroke, and the hook stroke all have tips making it a serif font. The Song typeface derived from the Suzhou area during the reign of Hongzhi in the Ming Dynasty, and came to be used commonly in countries such as Japan, North Korea, and Vietnam.

When the brand design is introduced into an app design, it helps to build an identifiable and uniform style for the app, thus facilitating subsequent marketing. An effective brand design can benefit the upgrading of the app.

Background of Evolution of Mobile Marketing

The mobile Internet implies an unprecedented market potential which means that various economic entities in social life will "have no choice but to" change their Internet thinking and daily operations, and build a mobile Internet development strategy based on their own actual situa-

tions, so as to take a share of benefit from the huge market of mobile Internet. At this stage, China's mobile Internet industry has formed a dynamic development pattern: the traditional Internet company giants (like Tencent, Alibaba, and Baidu) have been conducting mergers and reorganization; governments and public institutions at all levels have been building various platforms; small and medium-sized Internet enterprises have been developing various applications; and traditional industry enterprises (such as Suning and Wanda) have initiated their online layout.

Similarly, the mobile Internet has empowered the O2O industry with a strong

"O2O" (Online To Offline)

vitality and more powerful features. Mobile technologies, such as mobile positioning, mobile applications and mobile payment, have made a great contribution to the O2O industry, and have been promoting the realization of transferring commercial values to major vertical circulation links in the O2O industry.

O2O has built-in advantages on the access to online and offline circulation links, including comprehensive user information and diversified publicity and promotion channels, which provide good ground on which the mobile Internet can land. The mobile O2O with the complementary advantages will become the development trend of the future mobile Internet and O2O industry, promoting the process of mobile information industry in China. This is shown in the above figure.

As a product of mobile terminal, mobile communication and mobile information technology, the mobile Internet has been in the Chinese market for 18 years.

On November 10, 2000, CMCC launched its Monternet Plan① which aimed at creating an open, cooperative and win-win industrial value chain from the very beginning. The Monternet Plan has gone through four stages: GPRS period (e.g., images and ringtones), WAP period (e.g., mobile news, novels, and music), Functional Application period (e.g., mobile QQ and mobile search) and the mobile Internet period based on LBS (e.g., mobile map, Sina microblog, and WeChat). Now it provides a more convenient user experience, richer applications and more accurate user positioning which are favored by many users. With its user quantity, market size, hardware shipment, Internet user coverage and penetration surpassing the traditional PC Internet market, Monternet has become an important driving force for the development of the Internet industry at this stage.

① *Monternet Plan: a unified mobile Internet brand of CMCC. CMCC (China Mobile Communications Group Co., Ltd.) will step out of the traditional frames of operators, and provide a platform for numerous applications content/application service providers. It will provide open and fair access, and bridge the application service providers and users through gathering customers.*

The 5G Age of Huawei: not only the Connection between People

Huawei has invested USD $600 million in the research and innovation of the 5G standard, and will definitely invest more afterwards in the R&D of 5G products.

Huawei has summarized the demands of 5G users, basically including: (1) the 5G age is not only for the connection between people, but the full connection between people and things, and between things; (2) some virtual reality games are required for 5G, so that the peak speed of 5G should reach 10Gbps, thousands of times of the 4G network speed; and (3) the time delay should reach several milliseconds.

On November 18, 2016, during the 87th RAN1 session of 3GPP held in Reno, Nevada, 3GPP finally confirmed the channel encoding technical scheme for 5G eMBB scenarios after several rounds of technical discussions between company representatives, in which Polar Code was taken as the encoding scheme for control channels and LDPC for data channels.

This time, the result that the Polar Code promoted by China with Huawei as the core representative was adopted by 3GPP as the standard scheme for 5G eMBB control channels is an important progress of China in 5G mobile communication technology research and standardization.

Then what on earth is the Polar Code scheme of Huawei? Why is it so influential? And what is 5G? What influences can it exert on the world? Let's talk about these questions now.

What Is 5G?

You must be very familiar with the cellphone parameters that support the 2G, 3G, and 4G networks of China Mobile and China Unicom. 5G is just their next generation. G stands for the English word "generation", and 5G means the 5th generation mobile communication technology.

What Is the Polar Code Scheme of Huawei? What Is Its Meaning?

The Polar Code of Huawei is a channel encoding scheme of 5G short code block. It defeated the American LDPC scheme and the French Turbo2.0 scheme at the 87th RAN1 session of 3GPP held in Reno from November 14 to 18, 2016 to be the final scheme for 5G control channel eMBB scenario encoding.

What Is the eMBB Scenario?

Three 5G scenarios were defined in the 3GPP session: eMBB, mMTC, and URLLC.

Figure 1-11   The leaflet of Rongchang e-Bag Laundry

"Lazy economy" has been well received by investors since the end of 2014, and life apps have ushered in an age of explosion. From taxiing, laundry, housekeeping, to take-away, every detail of life is covered by the Internet. You can always find a considerate app for your "lazy" life. Recently, Rongchang has promoted the "Rongchang e-Bag Laundry" that standardizes the laundry service. Customers can pay the cleaning fee per bag, book via the mobile terminal, and enjoy laundry collection and delivery at their doors. It has successfully solved the problems of scarce parking at the laundry, troublesome handover time, and unmatched business hours, as shown in Figure 1-11.

The success of e-Bag Laundry is actually a successful practice of the O2O business mode in the housekeeping market segment. In fact, Diaoye Sirloin, Rongchang e-Bag Laundry, Order a Duck, and Dejiner Abalone all overturn the traditional industry with Internet thinking and cling to the right customers with better and more convenient service, combining online and offline business and solving the consumption pain spots of the customers. Lu Wenyong, CEO of e-Bag Laundry, once said, "With the rise of the middle class, the demands for service have seen unprecedented growth. This is the best age for the entrepreneurs." Then what is the next venture opportunity of the service industry?

The case source quoted from: chinaz.com2015-02-26
http://www.chinaz.com/manage/2015/0226/385969.shtml

eMBB: 3D/UHDV and other large-flow mobile broadband services;

mMTC: large-scale services of Internet of Things;

URLLC: services that require the connection of low time delay and high reliability, e.g., manless driving and industrial automation.

In the 5G eMBB scenario, the Polar Code of Huawei has become the uplink and downlink encoding scheme for control channels, while the uplink and downlink short code scheme for data channels is the LDPC of Qualcomm.

In short, the Polar Code of Huawei can be understood as an encoding scheme for control channels under the 5G technology.

What Changes Can 5G Bring Us?

The news that the 5G encoding of Huawei was adopted has again brought "5G" to the spotlight. It seems that 5G is around the corner right after 4G has been just popularized. Then what changes can 5G bring us? Do we really need it?

Based on the technical development of the mobile communication network, 5G is necessary. There was once this joke on the Internet:

An uncle went to the service hall and asked the assistant, "What is good about 4G?" The female assistant answered, "Uncle, with 2G you can read the novels of Sora Aoi, with 3G you can watch her pictures, and with 4G you can watch her videos." "Young girl, stop talking nonsense. Who is Sora Aoi? You just give me a 4G card right now!"

So 5G is not just about videos. The current research of various countries on 5G technology have shown that it has the following advantages: fast speed, wide coverage, large flow, and low cost.

The peak rate of 5G technology will grow tens of times, from the 100Mb/s of 4G to dozens of Gb/s, which means one can download over 10 Japanese movies within one second. It will also have a wider coverage, providing networks for the sites of weak signals such as metros, underground stores, and remote areas. Besides, it is available for multi-device connection, supporting one million sets of devices within one square kilometer.

The 5G technology can utilize more spectrum resources. With richer resources, the cost will naturally reduce. Maybe someday 1G flow will only cost CNY 0.1. Li Zhengmao, Vice President of China Mobile, once said that as the data transmission cost of the 5G age would reduce, the price of communication equipment would decrease accordingly. He said, "From the 4G age to the 5G age, the transmission cost of unit bit has decreased by 1,000 times, so we hope the price of telecommunication equipment can also reduce by 1,000 times. The cost is the key to the profitability of operators in the data age."

Different from the multiple standards of the 3G and 4G ages, 5G is expected to have a uniform global standard. That means in spite of China Unicom, China Mobile, and China Telecom, as long as your cellphone supports the 5G function, you can use the phone card of any operator. You will never worry about the versions of iPhones that support certain networks any more. It also saves the cellphone manufacturers from the network adaptation for different operators, thus reducing the manufacturing cost to some extent.

The popularization of 5G is the real advent of the age of Internet of Things.

In addition to the fast speed, wide coverage, and large flow mentioned above, 5G technology still has the advantages of low time delay and low power consumption. All these advantages together constitute the real age of Internet of Things.

The 3G and 4G ages connect people and information, while 5G connects objects. Thanks to its advantages, 5G can realize the Internet of Everything more easily and better use the cloud service. Just as the Chromebook of Google is based on the cloud concept, our devices do not need strong operational performance anymore; the terminal is only responsible for receiving and sending signals, and data processing is all completed on the server.

The advantage of low time delay can make the Internet of Vehicles be better applied. It can connect various vehicles via the network and the devices can mutually obtain the road environment and navigation data for real-time data analysis, road condition forecast, etc. It is not difficult to achieve manless driving in the future by means of big data and artificial intelligence (AI).

The mobile Internet, as a newly emerging business gaining services via intelligent mobile terminals and mobile wireless communication, is the collective term of the combination and practical activities of the technology, platform, business mode, and application of the Internet and the mobile communication technology. The complete industrial ecosystem of the mobile Internet includes nine aspects, e.g., the most visualized mobile terminals (cellphones, tablet PCs, etc.) and operating systems (Android, iOS, Symbian, etc.) to the users, the intermediate mobile operators (China Telecom, China Mobile, China Unicom, etc.) and retailers, and the "invisible and impalpable" distributing and delivering level.

 **Case Study** Feeds

Figure 1-12 WeChat Ads of BMW China

"Ads can be a part of life." On January 21, 2015, the WeChat team quietly posted a promotion message to test the advertising function of the moments. On January 25, the first batch of WeChat moments ads, "BMW China", "vivo", and "Coca Cola", were posted and became a hot issue that night. Such ads are feeds in the WeChat moments, similar to the original messages you see in your moments. They are composed of texts and pictures, available for likes and comments. You can see the comments of your friends and interact with them. See Figure 1-12.

Feeds are not new. They have been seen in Facebook, Twitter, Sina Microblog, QQ Space, etc. By the advanced Substance matching technology, the feeds system can turn mobile ads into useful information, and since the feeds are directly placed into the visual focus of the users, they can hardly be ignored. The WeChat moments, as the No. 1 flow portal of the mobile Internet nowadays, can never let go of this great opportunity; but of course, whether the user experience can be ensured or not remains to be seen. However, this move of WeChat may facilitate the popularization of the native advertising market, establishing a brand-new mobile Internet advertising ecosystem under the cooperation between the advertisers and the platform providers.

The case source quoted from: chinaz.com2015-02-26
http://www.chinaz.com/manage/2015/0226/385969.shtml

① *Mobile marketing: the act of directly and accurately delivering personalized instant messages to the focus target audience on the mobile terminals (cellphones or tablet PCs), thus achieving the purpose of marketing via the information interaction with the consumers.*

The mobile Internet has taken in the network interconnection of WEB1.0 and the social advantages of WEB2.0, and has really realized the intelligent connection between information. Relying on the "anytime and anywhere" feature of the mobile communication technology and the open and interactive functions of the Internet, it provides multiple services including accurate positioning and mobile e-commerce anytime, anywhere for the users with more diversified access terminals, more stable and rapid transmission technology, and more convenient and human-oriented user experience. The mobile Internet has taken good care of the feelings of the "lazy people".

As the product of the integration and interaction of mobile technology and Internet technology, the mobile Internet has inherited the industry characteristics of both technologies, which are mainly shown in accuracy, convenience, and expansibility.

The friendly user interface of the mobile Internet (with more pictures, weakening the function of texts in publicity) can help the enterprises accumulate great numbers of users in a short time, and the strong and convenient functions (content pushing and utility functions) can help the enterprises stimulate the investors' confidence in the field. So the enterprises have rapidly accumulated popularity among users in both global and domestic mobile Internet markets. Some social apps are filled with ads, too.

According to the 2013 Information Society Analysis issued by ITU of the UN in the second half of 2013, the global netizens reached 2.7 billion in 2013, with over two billion mobile netizens and over 6.8 billion mobile Internet connections. The scale has been very close to the overall scale of the global population.

According to the areal distribution, among the 2.7 billion mobile netizens, there are 460 million American users and 895 million Asian users, with a CAGR of 45%. The Asian areas, especially the developing countries of Asia, have been a major driving force of the mobile Internet user growth at present, among which the most crucial forces are China and India.

In this age, mobile marketing① has been a standard configuration of the enterprises, and some Internet companies even regard it as all of their marketing. It is like an "evolution" where the whole marketing industry keeps "progressing" with the mobile media till the final "transformation". In the long run, it is only one stage of the "marketing evolution". The marketing industry will surely keep "evolving" with the change of the "media" in the future.

According to the data published by the Ministry of Industry and Information Technology in January 2016, there are nearly 1.3 billion mobile phone users and nearly 900 million mobile Internet users in China. The total number of mobile phone users has reached 1.29 billion households in China, with the popularity rate of 94.6 per 100 people. The rate of the 10 provinces and regions of Beijing, Guangdong, Shanghai, Zhejiang, Fujian, Inner Mongolia, Jiangsu, Liaoning, Ningxia, and Hainan has exceeded 100 per 100 people. Chinese marketers have been more and more aware of the fact that we can no longer break away from the development track of the mobile media.

Case Study | **The Current Situation of Brand Marketing of Mobile Internet Terminal Manufacturers—Taking Apple as an Example**

Apple's success comes from a perfect product chain on which every product is the driving force for constant innovation and improving of brand image. Apple's products mainly include the Mac, iPod, iPhone, iPad, and iTunes.

I. Brands and characteristics of Apple products

1. The Mac

The Mac is different from the computer equipped with the Microsoft Windows system. The Mac OSX is

IMAC G3

a Darwin-based core system which enhances the stability, performance and responsiveness of the system. The Mac has always had a transparent in appearance, which gives it a sense of elegance. Among others, the IMac G3 has adopted an epoch-making design that fully integrates the computer host and the monitor. Coupled with a colorful and translucent appearance, it instantly swept around the world.

2. The iPod

The iPod is a large capacity MP3 player introduced by Apple which has a maximum capacity of between 10 and 160 GB which can store 2,500-10,000 MP3 songs. It has a sound management procedure and innovative operation mode as well as uniquely creative appearance.

iPod

It is also one of the few Apple hardware products which can be used on both PC and Mac platforms. In addition to being an MP3 player, the iPod can also serve as high-speed mobile hard disk which can display contacts, calendar and tasks, read text e-books and play audio books and podcasts.

3. The iPhone

iPhone is a 4-band GSM cellphone which supports EDGE and 802.11b / g wireless Internet access as well as e-mail, mobile calls,

iPhone

SMS, web browsing and other wireless communication services. The iPhone has no keyboard, and introduces the innovative multi-touch screen. In terms of operability, it leads other brands of cellphone. It is also a handset combining camera phone, personal digital assistant, media player and wireless communication.

4. The iPad

The iPad is a tablet PC launched by Apple in 2010

iPad

with the positioning between the iPhone and a laptop. Its whole body has only four buttons and the same layout as the iPhone, providing such functions as browsing the Internet, sending and receiving e-mail, reading e-books and playing audio or video.

5. iTunes

iTunes is a digital media player application for playing and managing digital music and video files.

iTunes

II. Current status of Apple's brand marketing

1. Hungry Marketing

The reason why Apple products are so popular is largely due to its control of the market supply; that is, Apple keeps the market in a relatively "hungry" state. It contributes to maintaining the stability of product prices as well as the control over product upgrading. The iPhone is definitely representative of this kind of sales strategy. Since coming into the market, Apple has insisted on the policy of limited supply, no matter how great the market demand is. Naturally, this kind of marketing has also brought doubts to Apple. Apple's marketing attitude is also meant to reinforce its product style of dominance, pride and being a maverick.

2. Experience Marketing

For the promotion meeting of each new product, Apple will choose a mysterious theater and promote its products in the form of multi-act play, which arouses strong curiosity among the public. For example, Steve Jobs usually spent only 10 minutes to show a new product or new features in a very entertaining way. When introducing the iPhone at Macworld, he showed how to use Google Maps on the iPhone. In the meantime, Apple has established numerous experience stores around the world to further cultivate consumer brand awareness.

3. Cultural Marketing

The Apple computer has left a distinctive imprint in the minds of consumers with the characteristics of superior performance, special shape and perfect design. The Apple computer means maverick, cool industrial design and fashion. Jobs sought to make innovative products in line with the Apple cultural imprint in the minds of consumers. With each Apple device,

Jobs has brought an ecstasy of delight to consumers: This is my Apple! Coca-Cola has taken the top rung on the Coke ladder, thus representing an American value, and Jobs also made Apple top the list of innovative products and creative cultures.

4. Word-of-mouth Marketing

Marketing must be entertaining, so that the public will participate voluntarily and joyfully. In the increasingly popular trend of microblog, iPhone also acts as a fashion tool to entertain the public. Popular entrepreneurs and celebrities intend to post entertaining information on their microblogs, and the post will be marked with the tag "From an iPhone User". Therefore, more microblog users may want to show this tag in their own posts, which will naturally deepen consumers' awareness of Apple products.

The case source quoted from: Internet Marketing Teaching Website 2012-11-18
https://wenku.baidu.com/view/c276e7543b3567ec102d8a41.html

Path of Evolution of Mobile Marketing

In the beginning of mobile marketing, each node has a corresponding coordinate for a marketing hero. From 2009 to 2016, marketing major events has driven the great era of mobile marketing in 2017, as shown in the below figure.

I. Mobile Marketing 1.0: Viral marketing is growing vigorously

Viral Marketing. Source: Jianshu.com

In March 2006, Evan Williams, founder of pioneering Blogger established an emerging company called Obvious and launched Twitter. Twitter brought the world into a smaller world known as the microblog. Seventy-three of the Global Top 100 companies have registered Twitter accounts, and Dell was among the earliest of Twitter users. Since March 2007, Dell's Twitter account has gained more than 1.5 million followers. There are more than USD $6.5 million of personal computers, computer accessories and software sold through Twitter, and more than 100 Dell employees communicate with customers on Twitter. Many Chinese entrepreneurs saw the business opportunities from Twitter's popularity in foreign countries.

In August 2009, Sina, the largest portal site in China, launched a beta version of Sina Microblog, and became the first website in China to provide professional microblog services. This officially marked the entry of the microblog into the mainstream among Chinese Internet users. The new term "Microblog" has also become the most popular word in the world. In terms of enterprise microblog, there are more than 130,000 enterprises that have registered official microblogs in Sina Microblog, and more than half of the individual users have followed enterprise microblogs. On the microblog, enterprises can have a dialogue with consumers in a more humanized manner, and consumers can directly file complaints and protect their rights through the enterprise microblog. At present, the daily average peak interaction time for both buyers and sellers has reached 12 hours.

On Sina Microblog alone, there are enterprise users from 22 industries who have initially registered their accounts, and the five highest amount of enterprise users are food and beverage, automobile transportation, business services, e-commerce and IT. Among the 130,000 enterprise microblog users, there are 143 Global 500 companies and 207 China Top 500 companies. In terms of geographical distribution, enterprises from Beijing, Shanghai and Guangzhou, with average enterprise microblog users of more than 17,000, have topped the geographical distribution list. Since then, the era of mobile marketing has begun.

As a new form of mobile media, the microblog has caused a strong impact on the content and organization of traditional media:

(1) Compared with the declining traditional blog, microblog is more convenient, and the 140 words can be sent instantly;

(2) Microblog is more suitable for users to browse in computers, cellphones and other platforms. The posted information can spread faster, and new technologies make it easy for users to comment and reply, thus forming an interactive relationship;

(3) User Generated Content (UGC) mode and fan mode with low threshold can bring users a sense of vanity and presence, so that Internet users feel for the first time that they are speakers rather than listeners. Therefore, these advantages have popularized microblog rapidly.

At this stage, the viral marketing brought by the revolution is in full swing. However, it does not bring too much substantial benefits to the enterprises, because browsing does not mean consumption, so only the conversion rate can bring about substantial economic benefits.

II. Mobile Marketing 2.0: Precision Marketing

In 2012, the WeChat public platform came into being, which not only means the formation of a brand new media format, but also means that mobile marketing was getting started.

WeChat public platform is positioned as providing valuable services and eliminating geographical constraints and intermediaries, and the system can really decentralize itself and build an ecosystem. It is under the influence of this concept that the WeChat public platform, which has a more mature form than the earlier microblog, has challenged the declining microblog. Thus, many microblog users with large numbers of followers began to settle in the WeChat public platform, so in this case, mobile marketing also began to undergo substantial changes.

Firstly, enterprises began to build their own official channels in social media, and gradually settled on Sina Microblog and the WeChat public platform.

Secondly, the conventional thinking of "diversion" began to be abandoned. Entrepreneurs started to take their Official WeChat accounts as a place to speak in social media, and learned to use it to develop PR value or to form brand value.

Finally, in terms of content output, it was no longer used to present content in a simple and crude manner, but began to implant soft content or to give the brand personality. Acting cute is a kind of skill most Official WeChat accounts learned during this period.

At this point, the new form of mobile marketing has gradually stabilized and formed. The core essence of mobile marketing is revealed more clearly in front of the business community: creativity and content are surely important carriers of visitor traffic, but the brand-related traffic from everyone is the real media with a large scale, a high certainty and the most potential.

From the perspective of narration, the "substance of content" includes at least five elements—who is to say (Who), what to say (What), how to say it (How), to whom to say it (Whom,) and which one to say (Which). For the traditional media, "To Whom" is generally unknown or even ignored. Even known or noticed, it is often out of imagination and assumption. In this framework of narration, we can see three new aspects in the new media:

The first aspect is the "new subjects". If there is no microblog on the Internet, or no WeChat on the mobile Internet, they can only count as semi-new media. This is because in the past, even there are forums

On July 8, 2014, when the World Cup was turning white-hot, a group of French celebrities and beauties including the French actress Elsa Couturier and the international model Mathilde Vernon launched the performance art of "The Most Beautiful World Cup" in Paris. They exclaimed "We are the best" and called on the men to reflect on the social problems caused by the World Cup and to shift their attention from the World Cup to their partners. The top color jewelry jointly produced by the leading brand Chenim and the French celebrity club, "The Most Beautiful World Cup", worth tens of millions of Euros, was also released.

On July 9, the campaign took Paris Fashion Week by storm, and even won support from Chinese star Carina Lau. The European Times, Yahoo, and other authoritative media reported it with headlines, focuses and features, rapidly creating a worldwide sensation.

On July 10, Xinhua News Agency issued the "French Beauties Launch 'The Most Beautiful World Cup' to Call on Men to Pay Attention to Their Partners", which was widely reported by the media in China. According to official data from Sina Microblog, the topic #The Most Beautiful World Cup# shot into Top 3 hot topics and had over 50 million followers in only two days. It became one of the hottest topics for that July.

From July 12 to 14, many beauties appeared in the streets of cities such as Beijing, Shanghai, Guangzhou, and Qingdao to support "The Most Beautiful World Cup". Thus, Chenim's "The Most Beautiful World Cup" successfully won the attention of society. The topic was becoming increasingly popular and the costly jewel also became a highlight.

Chenim then declared that Carina Lau would participate in the debut of "The Most Beautiful World Cup" jewelry at the "Chenim Color Jewel Fashion Show" from August 15 to 17, drawing the attention of the public from "The Most Beautiful World Cup" to the Chenim brand and its annual big show. The marketing ignited by the global public relations, the surprising creative idea, and the outstanding control on the three key points made "The Most Beautiful World Cup" one of the most eye-catching cases in 2014.

According to Mr. Liu Dongming, expert of the Network Marketing President Class of Tsinghua University and Pecking University, the routine-breaking public relations method, the global operation, and the smart utilization of the "World Cup" were highly commendable in this marketing battle. Countless brands made big investments in the football field, football stars, and sponsorship during this most influential sports event; it was a white-hot marketing battlefield. However, Chenim developed another "World Cup for women" which stood out in the world of men, passion and sports, coming into the spotlight of society. Chenim's formula of "fashion week + famous models + superstars + priceless jewelry + World Cup + love + controversy" finally came to the unique perspective of the social problem caused by the World Cup, which made sense when it had a huge response in society.

The case source quoted from: Sina Microblog 2016-06-03
http://blog.sina.com.cn/s/blog_161e1a5d20102wusu.html

and blogs on the Internet, the agenda setting is still dominated by the unilateral selectivity of traditional media. The great contribution of microblog and WeChat lies in the creation of a new mass communication subject of scale, that is, "who's to say" has changed from a single subject to diversified subjects and from few subjects to a wealth of subjects. A content market with diversified subjects, diverse forms and multi-dimensional narration is being inexorably generated. In consequence, the truth view in the industrial age will be subverted. In the traditional view, "the truth is just the truth", and "this is the truth" prevailed.

But in the new media environment of the Internet era, "everyone has a microphone" and "Everyone is a We Media", meaning that everyone has the power of interpretation. The truth may seem to change with different perspectives, but ultimately in most cases, the truth depends on the use of language and is easily influenced by the context in which people live.

The second new aspect is new audiences. The new media has pulled in the "To Whom" and closed the loop of narrative dynamics, so that narratives and audiences are drawn into an unprecedented intimate relationship and tied together. Since "To Whom" enters the process of narrative, the unspecified audiences in the past have turned into specific audiences. It is both an incentive and a constraint that will reshape "what to say" and "how to say", for example, the new media and the traditional media often have significant differences in language styles.

Case Study iQiyi: Improving video value with technologies

How can we reconstruct the original advertising scenes in the videos that have been shot or broadcast, and achieve the integration of the ads and the plot?

On February 5, 2015, iQiyi officially announced the commercial use of "Video out" technology, an upgraded version of the visual chain. This technology can identify video objects rapidly and accurately through intelligent algorithms, and guide the large-scale purchase operation. Data shows that the click rate of "Video out" goods ads has increased by over ten times than that of the traditional ads.

Both Video in and Video out technologies are major reforms to the video marketing value. The intro-duction of "Video in" dynamic advertising implant is a revolutionary subversion to the form of ads implant. Without limitation in the filming cycle of videos, advertisers can implant their products into the video at any time as needed. Relying on its unique video recognition algorithms, Video out technology has technically realized the dream that goods within the video are what you buy. Video out technology has seamlessly connected the video substance with the purchase, so that the video is no longer merely a pure entertainment tool, but also an important channel for consumers to obtain shopping information.

The case source quoted from: chinaz.com2015-02-26
http://www.chinaz.com/manage/2015/0226/385969.shtml

It is important to emphasize that specific audiences will not stand at a certain place waiting for a match, but need to be created. For example, fans of Logic Show① are not matched but created. Its creativity derives from insights into "the grammar of life".

Of course, "To Whom" or specific audiences are currently still largely vague, its clarity and identification in reality require data capabilities, i.e., the further use and exploration of fan management software will involve the knowledge, emotions and values of specific audiences. This is not so much opening to specific audiences as opening to a subtle sensation, which will promote the generation of subtler observation and narration closer to life.

The third new aspect is new media. Speaking of media, we must mention Marshall McLuhan's view that the medium is the message, which means that the media is a material dynamic mechanism:

1) The media itself is a kind of space-time interface;

2) Space-time interface itself is a kind of constraint (material and cost);

3) The constraint itself is to invite innovation.

New media is named from new intermediaries that break the speech hegemony of traditional media. The lower cost of communication will also continuously create new subjects, new audiences and new contents.

In the industrial age, news has concentrated on informational attributes, that is, the information on "important facts" identified by industrialist views based on static structures, while the knowledge substance is provided by the educational system. However, in the Internet era, the sequence of important facts formed in the industrial age will surely be expanded and reconstructed with the uprising of life narration and the rapid iteration of knowledge, and the knowledge substance is bound to increase greatly. For example, the new media will integrate in some way with online education. This is certain to require some time.

① *Logic Show is currently a large Internet knowledge community, of which the interaction forms include Official WeChat account, knowledge-based talk show video and audio, membership system, WeChat mall, Baidu Post Bar and WeChat group, mainly servicing post-80s and 90s generations with a strong demand for love, wisdom and truth. The slogan of Logic Show is "Persevering, Interesting and Pragmatic". It is a model of marketing in China, which advocates independence and rational thinking, promotes liberalism and Internet thinking, and gathers ambitious and free young people in pursuit of love, wisdom and truth and with sound personalities.*

Case Study The WeChat public marketing of Natural Workshop

As the WeChat ecosystem has become a tool for people to access information, many media professionals have joined the emerging We Media industry. They have attracted concerns and attention from readers through their strong original capabilities, their extremely professional background and precise posi-tioning, and high-quality substance and stable output have provided a brilliant spiritual input for the present times.

The official WeChat account of Natural Workshop is just like an uncontrollable dark horse which has bolted from its stable, and has drawn the attention of many people in the community, including Internet professionals. Only five months since its launch, the official WeChat account of Natural Workshop had been followed by more than four million members. Why is Natural Workshop so popular? Why has every article on its official WeChat account been read by more than 100,000 users, and mostly within just an hour? How are these miracles created? What are the underlying causes behind these miracles? After carefully analyzing its enterprise gene and reading the essence of its articles, it is not difficult for us to find its recipes of success.

Solution 1: Feelings, big love, environmental protection, health and perfection

Many people may ignore feelings and big love. However, with the ramping material desire and the accelerated pace of life, feelings not only never perish and are respected from the deep hearts, like a cure to aspiring for and cultivating the heart and soul. The official WeChat account of Natural Workshop has displayed a good interpretation of these values through numerous graphics and videos. Through thousands of years of vicissitudes, the Chinese civilization has formed a splendid culture, and feelings and big love are among its essence. With the mission to inherit traditional cultures and relying on the innovative Internet-based thinking, Natural Workshop has spread and integrated feelings and big love into real life. This has attracted a large number of fans with common values and members with very high viscosity. It is difficult for many other marketing platforms to achieve this.

Many people may just think about such important things as environmental protection and health. Though people may have some kind of awareness on environmental protection and health in their daily life, most of people regard them as macro-events that are not directly related to them, or think they are not urgent matters. With this attitude of just thinking but not caring, macro-events have turned into irrelevant issues, thus environmental protection and health has become increasingly serious. Born with high-quality health genes, Natural Workshop shares a strong sense of environmental protection and an ultimate pursuit for life, work and products. Each of its articles has a readership of 100,000+, and this proves that many people are taking action in support of environmental protection and health. They have realized that health and happiness are not purely physical and material things but a kind of spirit and culture. They are promoting environmental protection with practical actions, and start to protect the environment from changing the habits of using tissue papers. Unity is strength, and the sand can accumulate to ultimately form a pago-

da. These people who share a common philosophy of environmental protection and health have created the miracle that is Natural Workshop.

Solution 2: Substituting the traditional model with the Internet model

If a decade ago a dozen founding members had used just a single yellow tissue, what would have happened? It can be summed up as a miserable death. People may be deeply troubled and overwhelmed by a series of cumbersome things, such as development, production, marketing, channel establishment, distribution, logistics and payment. Can an article attract 100,000+ readers within an hour 10 years ago? It is nothing but fiction.

This is the best era—the mobile Internet era. This era brings up Natural Workshop, and Natural Workshop conforms to this era. When all people are using WeChat, the relationships between people are more closely connected in the mobile Internet ecosystem like WeChat, and the consumers can be converted into consumer businesses more easily. Natural Workshop has seized the opportunity of the era to integrate Internet resources, and immerse Internet technologies into life, thus making them more convenient and fast. Natural Workshop has also integrated the ecosystem of social attributes, and made full use of WeChat.

In the mobile Internet era, universal mobile consumption will inevitably promote the universal marketing, so that everyone can be a spokesperson for a brand, just like universal brokers. In Natural Workshop's mechanism, a participant can turn into an initiator, thus forming the fission of fans. Therefore, a miracle can be created by way of the Internet within a few months, and everything happens without extra effort.

Solution 3: The coming of the consumer business era

The reasons why the articles and videos from Natural Workshop can spread dramatically within WeChat Moments not only results from the big love, perfect products and mechanism innovation of the Internet era. The consumer business era is another important factor. Under the macro-background of universal entrepreneurship, it is bound to become a trend that people will spend money as needed and try to earn money which could not previously be obtained. Therefore, when the consumer business era sweeps through, it will bring new opportunities. It will offer others products as well as opportunities, while how to seize the opportunity created by the era and transfer consumers into consumer businesses will depend on whether we can blend in and grasp the rhythm of the era. The consumer business era has begun and entered into our life rapidly, and Natural Workshop is a good example, and the readership of 100,000+ are the best witness and beneficiaries. The advent of the consumer business era is an irresistible trend. Are you ready?

In the era of full flow of overwhelming information, numerous entertainment accounts and fashion accounts with a single "100,000+ article" within the whole WeChat ecosystem have been generated, while few enterprise accounts can reach 100,000+ readers for each and every article. Natural Workshop, however, is among this short list. Unlike others, Natural Workshop is a consumer business official account with great feelings and the core values of promoting environmental protection and healthy life. If a platform can quickly create a series of short-term miracles, can get followed by millions of readers and can generate consumption, this is not accidental but inevitable! When a group of people carry feelings and big love, and constantly strive for the cause of environmental protection and healthy life, it is no doubt that their articles can reach 100,000+ readers.

Naturally, 100,000+ is an infinite space, and they are only the first seed readers and users or super users of Natural Workshop. In the future, Natural Workshop will reach more than 100,000+ readers and four million members. At the current pace of development, Natural Workshop may reach more than 10 million readers for every article and 30 million members. This would surpass your wildest imagination.

The case source quoted from: Natural Workshop2017/04/11
http://www.360doc.com/content/17/0411/20/39337473_644758148.shtml

III. Mobile Marketing: Live broadcast Marketing

The mobile Internet live broadcast began in 2016 and reached its peak in that mid-summer. There are various live broadcast platforms in China, including Tencent Douyu TV and Now TV, Baidu Ucloud, Sina Yi TV and Panda TV founded by Wang Sicong.

However, the live broadcast industry in China is mostly concentrated on the customer terminal services mode featuring cyber celebrities and games, and are dominated by digital media, while there is a relative lack of live broadcast marketing by enterprises. As a new tool, the live broadcast has advantages on scene immediacy, sensory empathy and interactive participation, which can inject vitality into the enterprise substance marketing. If only used for seeking novelty on cyber celebrities, it is a little pity.

Papi Jiang[1], a Chinese comedian, was able to gain rapid popularity because she caught the blowout opportunity for UGC contents and integrated her television expertise in creating content. She designed outstanding topics from life, to entertainment and to gender relations, told stories in a down-to-earth manner, and combined it with current events. She arranged various complaint points which mattered to young users in a short video, which more directly met the needs of entertainment videos for the young groups. Therefore, She successfully stood out in the ecological environment where there is a lack of interesting content.

Papi Jiang has expressed clear values in her videos, such as striving for authenticity, abandoning hypocrisy, teasing all pretentious behavior and advocating individual freedoms, which are the common pursuit of the younger generation. That is why videos from Papi Jiang can resonate so widely.

That being the case, how can Chinese enterprises conduct their marketing through the live broadcast model?

The live broadcast substance marketing of leading international enterprises which have surpassed cyber celebrities, variety shows and games focuses on the following aspects: first, to satisfy the curiosity of consumers; second, to reduce the sense of distance between the brand and audiences; third, to create an immersion sense like actually being there; fourth, to tell the story and foundation of products; and fifth, to embrace the live broadcast, lead the commercial front and get rid of stereotypes.

1. To satisfy the curiosity of consumers

For some more complex and abstract products and services, such as B2B and healthcare, consumers may be more or less curious about how the product is made. Substance marketing can resolve any doubts. The pure text description is somewhat cold, and pictures, while they may be beautiful they are just a frozen moment in

[1] Papi Jiang: In 2016, the comedian appeared before the public as an older young woman and became a "cewebrity" through short videos which featured assertive personalities and vicious complaints. She was called China's Top Cewebrity in 2016 by Chinese netizens.

time. Videos may be much more vivid, but the live broadcast is more fresh and alive as if one is actually present at the scene.

2. To reduce the sense of distance from products

Many high-end brands, such as luxury goods, may seem mysterious, strange and distant to users who have never known them before or are still in the process of cultivation. Can a God-like brand be less proud and get closer to potential buyers?

3. To create an immersion sense for users

In today's world, the experience economy takes the lead. Challenged by the virtual e-commerce, it is more pressing than ever for an enterprise to create a desire and pursuit for a non-physical experience. Dubai has built the world's largest indoor alpine skiing resort, but no matter how rich Dubai Tyrant is, the physical experience will be constrained by the physical space. To expand the radiation scope of experience, we should create a sense of immersion so that the consumers outside the experience space can also feel a sensory empathy and enjoy every fun.

4. To taste the product story

Everyone, young and old, knows that the story is the key of substance marketing. An old photograph (such as the stage photo of Titanic) and a brand symbol (such as the Nike Swoosh) are all concentrated stories. Many brands often follow the trend to post corresponding poster on festivals, and these measures on substance marketing will bring benefits. However, if the story is more complex and nuanced, and lays more groundwork, the story may be expressed in a more vivid manner when carefully savored.

5. To send a signal for transition

Where an industry has a long history with a profound tradition, this may from another perspective be regarded as a burden of stereotype. How can a brand demonstrate its determination to depart from the stereotype and embrace a new life? The live broadcast substance marketing with the new media is a perfect way to send the signal of transition!

4S Mobile Marketing Theory

Chapter 2

Topics:

1. Proposal of 4S Mobile Marketing Theory
2. Principles of Economics for 4S Mobile Marketing Theory
3. Tool Kit - 4S Mobile Marketing Theory

Proposal of 4S Mobile Marketing Theory

Figure 2-1   Marketing flow process of the 4S mobile marketing theory. Source: 4S Mobile Marketing Theory Model Diagram

In the era of the mobile Internet, marketing is undergoing a revolutionary evolution and development in light of new technology. As long as enterprises grasp the basic rules of mobile marketing, they can make significant profit by applying the new marketing principles to their individual development.

Mobile Internet is now transforming the marketing science, so the marketing strategy in this new era becomes even more important.

4S Mobile Marketing Theory is the basic marketing law composed of the marketing elements in the mobile Internet era. It includes the four elements of Service, Substance, Super user and Space as well as the marketing flow process composed by these elements (see Figure 2-1).

4S Mobile Marketing Theory

The 4S mobile marketing theory is based on the following principles:

(1) Designing and delivering better products and services to meet the needs of users is the cornerstone of mobile marketing success. All good services have two basic characteristics: (i) the pursuit of the optimization and humanization; and (ii) the joint creation with users.

(2) Mobile marketing has less association with the integrated marketing of mass media, where, product selling point, and words and celebrity endorsement which are the three major communication weapons have been replaced with the word "content." Therefore, good content is the next crucial factor for mobile marketing, and the only standard for judging the content as good or bad is whether or not users are willing to share this content actively.

(3) Traditional marketing is to communicate through mass media by selecting high-quality customers from mass users and dividing them into different classes, and it is a marketing logic in which the marketing relationship is determined according to transaction relationship. Mobile marketing is just the opposite. Mobile marketing starts from the trust, participation and the word of mouth of very few key users to form customer strong relations and super users, then spreads into mass ordinary users. It is the marketing logic determined based on interpersonal relationship.

(4) In the traditional marketing cognition, marketing channels include offline outlets and PC end stores, and the relation between offline and online is contradicto-ry. During the 12 years from 2000 to 2012, the word "destruction" could frequently be heard from the mouths of online marketing experts. Mobile marketing advocates achieving product experience, user sharing, and service compatibility connectivity in a tradable space. No word can describe mobile marketing more appropriately than "space" (also known as "spatial connectivity"). There are three ways to connect mobile space: the marketing relationship connection between offline space and online space; the experience of real space and virtual space; the organic connection between the four marketing elements of service, substance, user sharing and transaction exchange.

In short, the 4S mobile marketing model is not only a theoretical prototype for exploring the general law of mobile marketing, but also a combination of application tools for practicing the special new method of mobile marketing.

Based on the users' demand for the extremely good in mobile Internet era, the first thing that mobile marketing shall do is to provide services which comply with mobile user consuming habit with respect to product-in-process quality, quality concept and product experience; the second is to make service culture, service feeling and service concept centered on users' demand for users to obtain more and wider consumption information; and the third is to discover and cultivate super users.

What are super users?

The characteristics of Super users: they love both advantages and disadvantages of your products, and treat a defect of your product as a beauty. They buy your products whenever you request, and also convince their friends to buy them. They spread good word regarding your products without any reason, nor do they share any profit, as long as the spirit in your products supports their lifestyle. They are your consumers and also investors. The relationship between your products and them is a marriage rather than a one-night stand.

The fourth step of mobile marketing is to discover or develop a mobile marketing space, and plant service, substance, user and payment into one mobile space for completion. This space may be a mobile network app interface, or a smart terminal device embedded with mobile payment software, or an interactive experience space integrated with mobile Internet software and physical experience store.

4S mobile marketing can also be realized through a set of smart terminal devices.

4S mobile marketing can also be realized through "Internet + physical" convergence model. For example, the CNY 10 billion acquisition of YHD.com by Jingdong was actually an acquisition by Jingdong of YHD.com in order to complete the "Internet + Wal-Mart" network convergence model; the advancement of this model lies in transforming Internet space and physical store space into an advantage complementary eco-space from originally standalone marketing spaces.

In conclusion, mobile Internet is now transforming the marketing science, and the evolution from 4P Theory to 4S Theory is inevitable.

Principles of Economics for 4S Mobile Marketing Theory

4S Mobile Marketing Theory is about a new marketing space generated by the collection of three new marketing elements: service, substance and super user, and this space collects enterprise R&D, operation[①], sales and service into one; simply speaking, 4S is a collection space.

We have mentioned the word "collection" many times, and the use of the word "collection" in marketing science is a major invention, since originally this word is a concept of modern mathematics. One collection is the integration of different objects or elements.

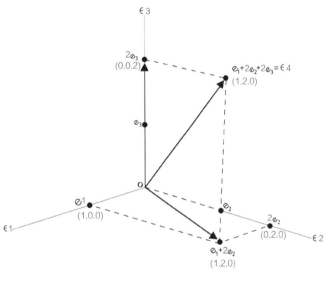

Figure 2-2   Mobile 4S Marketing 3D Space Diagram

4S Theory is the collection of finite elements. To facilitate the consideration of the value of 4S model from economics perspective, the members of the collection are represented by the symbol ∈ (a letter from the Greek alphabet, the variant of epsilon's initials), assuming that the service, substance and super user space are respectively denoted by ∈ 1, ∈ 2, ∈ 3, ∈ 4, then the 4S model is a 3D vector space (see Figure 2-2).

According to the analytical method of Mathematical Economics[②], two linearly independent vectors E1 and E2 generate a

two-dimensional space, which can also be said to form a basis for multi-dimensional space. If expressed by Internet language 0 and 1, the unit vectors of E1 and E2 are (10) and (01), service (E1) is 1, the value of marketing is the addition of 0 after 1. The more you add 0, the more revenue an enterprise may have, and the more valuable the marketing will be; Substance (E2) is 0, the value of marketing is to add service culture, thinking and value and other contents from 0 to 1 onto service, and the role of substance marketing is making service say what consumers like to hear. Super user (E3) is a unit vector from 0 to 0 then

① *Operation: this refers to the planning, organization, execution and control of operation process; operation is the general term for any or all management work closely relating to product manufacturing and service creation. From another perspective, operational management can also refer to the design, operation, evaluation and improvement of systems that produce and deliver the company's main products and services.*

② *Mathematical Economics: a branch of discipline that uses mathematical methods to present and study economic theories. In economic history, scholars engaged in this research are called mathematical economists, and classified as the school of mathematical economics, and simply called mathematical school.*

$$\in 1 \equiv \begin{bmatrix} 1 \\ 0 \\ 0 \end{bmatrix} \qquad \in 2 \equiv \begin{bmatrix} 0 \\ 1 \\ 0 \end{bmatrix} \qquad \in 3 \equiv \begin{bmatrix} 0 \\ 0 \\ 1 \end{bmatrix}$$

Figure 2-3   The 3D Vector Space

1, and the value of marketing is a process from zero user awareness, non-acceptance and then acceptance and purchase of products (see Figure 2-3).

The 3D vector space is the full collection of E1, E2 and E3 unit vectors. Although it is difficult to draw a 3D diagram, we still can imagine a 3D space generated by all the linear independent E elements. Each vector, as an ordered innumerable group, represents a point in 3D space, or a directional line segment extending from the origin to that point. The distance between two vector points represents the index of marketing innovation; the distance between each vector and the origin represents the depth and intensity of marketing.

The following three types of unit vector changes represent three imbalances in corporate marketing:

Imbalance I

This is an enterprise which has services and super users, but the substance created for communication and sharing is its shortcoming, and the enterprise profit space is insufficient (see Figure 2-4).

Imbalance II

This is an enterprise with super users, the capability to produce product communication substance but poor service quality, which causes its marketing and profit-making space being confined (see Figure 2-5).

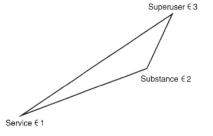

Figure 2-4   The 3D Vector Space—Imbalance I

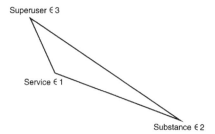

Figure 2-5   The 3D Vector Space—Imbalance II

Imbalance III

This is an enterprise having good service and substance but with insufficient super users, which narrows its marketing and profit-making space (see Figure 2-6).

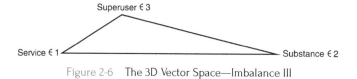

Figure 2-6   The 3D Vector Space—Imbalance III

Case Study   The Mobile Marketing of Samsung

1.   Sports Marketing

For the Beijing Olympics in 2008, Samsung had made a marketing plan very early. From 2002 to 2007, it provided CNY 1 million to the Beijing Olympic Committee every year as the funds for the "Olympic Training Program", and USD $120,000 every year for planting the "Forest of Hope" of the Beijing Olympics. By actively participating in these events, Samsung organically combined the brand connotation with the

Olympic spirit of "Higher, Faster, and Stronger", further increasing the internal value of the brand.

2.   Campus Marketing

In modern Chinese society, college students are a new force in the consumption field, who to some extent are guiding the future consumption. This feature perfectly conforms to the product orientation of the Samsung. For that reason, Samsung often visits various campuses nationwide during marketing, unconsciously influencing the college students. For example, it sponsors various computer contests and sci-tech invention competitions, providing funds and electronic equipment for the students; it has also set up Samsung digital experience halls in the computer cities on many campuses to let the students experience the charisma of Samsung products. According to the latest statistics, Samsung invests over CNY 10 million in Chinese campuses every year.

3.   Celebrity Endorsement

As public figures in society, the stars can greatly influence the consumer behaviors and the fashion trend with what they say and what they do, so choosing them to speak for the enterprise not only can effectively deliver the inherent meaning of the brand but also can drastically increase the brand value. Samsung has used stars like Rain to expand its reputation and publicize the brand image of "High-end, fashionable, and the leader of digital products".

4.   Cultural Marketing

In recent years, with the popularity of Korean movies, TV plays, network novels, and FLASH animations, the Korean culture has been a fever across China. In this situation, Samsung timely promoted a series of cultural events such as the "Korean Trend Month". For example, it organized the "TOKEBI STORM" percussion event which represented the new Korean trend in Beijing, Shanghai and Tianjin, to increase the brand awareness and the "Fashion and High-tech" brand image of Samsung.

5.   Cause Marketing

Repaying society has always been a basic operating principle of Samsung, for it believes that an enterprise can never develop without the care and support of the entire society. So Samsung never forgets its social role and responsibilities as an "enterprise citizen" during daily operation. It organizes the employees in Beijing to do cleaning jobs in Xiangshan; it helps the life of the handicapped in Huizhou City, Guangdong, as far as possible; and it has established the Samsung Scholarship in 17 key universities in China to fund the excellent students. By those public benefit activities, it delivers to the Chinese consumers that Samsung is not only a large transnational corporation providing high-tech digital products, but also an enterprise trying to repay society.

The ads of Samsung can be seen at every airport in both developed countries and emerging market economies; you can always hear the name of Samsung on TV no matter which country you are in. Investing a huge amount for publicity and gaining a large sales volume is the secret of the leapfrog development of Samsung. However, behind its powerful marketing strategy is the relatively weak R&D. With the continuously swelling marketing expense, it has seen little growth in the R&D expense, which has led to its deficiency in product innovation. The battery explosion of Note7 put Samsung into a passive position in smartphone product strategy and made it miss many opportunities.

The Note7 incident has not fundamentally harmed the Samsung users' confidence in the brand and the products, and they will go on supporting the Samsung products. But it has brought a negative impact on the brand reputation for those who are not Samsung users. Samsung users are still highly loyal to the brand, while those non-Samsung-users are suspicious about the brand. Among the Samsung users, 54.2% of the original Note7 users are willing to buy Samsung cellphones again, and 53.6% of the users of other Samsung products have expressed the same will.

The case source quoted from: mbalib.com2016/11/13
http://doc.mbalib.com/view/df52058a720b8f82288fc9f2fc11d312.html

Modern marketing is a science about choice and configuration. Typically, when reaching a specific economic goal, enterprises have multiple options and paths available for realizing a certain level of output, among which there is one option or path being the best. As proved by Mathematical Economics methodology, the essence of optimum solution is to obtain the sets of selected variables which can achieve extreme values of target functions. From a purely mathematical point of view, the extremum is the extreme value; from the marketing management point of view, the extremum is the control expenditure to the minimum, the income to the maximum. For instance, if an enterprise is pursuing profit π to the maximum, i.e., the difference between the maximum total income R and the total cost minimum value C, assuming the operating level of the enterprise is Q, then the formula shall be:

$$\pi (Q) = R (Q) - C (Q)$$

This formula constitutes the target function of mobile marketing, π is the maximum target, then Q is the only selected variable, and the key of the optimum solution lies in the highest output level Q which makes π maximized. Q is the EQ and IQ of the business management team in utilizing mobile marketing. The mobile marketing of a high-Q enterprise makes the configuration of 4S marketing elements to a balanced state of selected configuration, and thus makes 4S mobile marketing gain the maximum enterprise profit.

The configuration standard for a balanced state is an equilateral triangle, thus making its marketing space and profit space to be maximized.

In practice, 4S Mobile Marketing Theory requires enterprises to change their organizational structure by changing their traditional marketing managed ads, business planning, marketing and customer service functional management design to R&D center, service center, substance center and user center mobile marketing basic functional management model, in which, a user center is also known as partner center.

Since 2012, 4S mobile marketing model has been widely used by many emerging growth enterprises, producing unprecedented mobile capability. The fire of marketing innovation has been ignited all over the world. Why are emerging companies so happy to adopt 4S new marketing model? As remarked by Elon Musk, CEO of Tesla US, "mature big companies are not willing to take the risk in making new things, so many great innovations come from entrepreneurial firms." Tesla is just the company which has completed its marketing innovation in the four aspects of service, substance, super user and space, starting from brand innovation and technical innovation.

💡 Case Study Elon Musk and Tesla automobile

Elon Musk adored Nicola Tesla (1856-1943), a Yugoslav-American physicist, and regarded him as his spiritual idol, naming his business Tesla. More than 100 years ago, Tesla accurately sketched out the life of wireless communications, predicted the possibility of videophones, electric vehicles, and interplanetary communications technology. In 1898 he produced a radio-controlled ship and invented the X-ray camera technology, solar-powered engines, fax machine, vacuum tube, electronic clock and other products, and founded robot engineering principles. Elon Musk named his business after Nicola Tesla, illustrating that the corporate brand has infused the brand name of "Crazy Man" since its naming. Tesla automobiles insisted on technological innovation from the very beginning. In February 2008, Tesla launched the world's first pure electric vehicle equipped with state-of-the-art Li-ion battery series, and the energy regeneration system installed in Tesla automobile is able to recharge the battery while the automobile is decelerating, such that the automobile is compensated with energy while it is driving, and historically Tesla automobile realized the record of 350 km continuous driving after a recharge. Tesla produced its ModelS in 2012, Model X was then manufactured, and became profitable in 2013, and its stock price went up from USD $33.87 in Q1 to USD $100 at the end of Q2. Just before the advent of new products, Musk constantly was working on substance marketing, Musk's phrases became the hot-spot during 2012-2013, such as: the automotive industry for too long had no fresh things; there was no revolutionary change in the past 100 years; doing business is just like gazing into the abyss of death; I am not afraid of failure, and can expect failure, even if only 10% success rate exists, I will try; I basically do not read textbooks, what I read all are other books......

The substance marketing of Musk received returns with a large number of purchase orders came in flakes, and most of those who placed the purchase order were young innovative elites who placed the order directly online without seeing the sample car, because all of them were influenced by Musk's golden phrases. Tesla deeply understands the role of super-user's praise for marketing promotion. In March 2009, Tesla household Model S prototype electric vehicle was piloted, and then Musk invited Steven Chu, the U.S. Secretary of Energy, and Barack Hussein Obama II, the President of the United States, to visit Tesla's factory. In June of the same year, Musk obtained a sum of low-interest loan USD $465 million from the Department of Energy (required to be repaid before December 2022) for the batch production of Model S.

Tesla decided to enter the Chinese market in early 2013. At the 2013 China International Forum on Auto Industry held in September, Wan Gang, the Minister of Science and Technology of the People's Republic of China praised Tesla, and Zhang Guobao, the Director of National Energy Administration of China, openly praised Musk as an unusual innovative talent. Thus Tesla easily opened the door of China's market. In the construction of its network marketing channels, Tesla completely abandoned traditional automobile 4S exclusive agency mode and removed middlemen, instead, it adopted direct marketing mode, and received purchase and service orders online, and Tesla managed the after-service and constructed its own charging piles and experience rooms.

In 2013, Tesla built a network of "super charging stations" across the United States. In addition, the company also developed successfully express battery exchange station, which enabled battery unit replacement within one minute without electricity. In addition to Tesla Electric Motor Company, Musk also created three other companies: Solar City (the largest private solar energy supplier in the US) and online payment company Paypal and Spacer; Musk organized the design and successfully launched aircraft to space station.

Musk is not only a technology innovation product manager, but also a marketing master who skillfully uses 4S Mobile Marketing Theory.

The case source quoted from: Baidu Tieba

100 Questions for the Innovators

Questions about personal qualification

1. Are you somebody who tries to break through and surpass? ·················· Yes ( ) No ( )
2. Do you have any interest in research?······························· Yes ( ) No ( )
3. Does your mind diverge without limitation? ······················· Yes ( ) No ( )
4. Are you confident? ······································· Yes ( ) No ( )
5. Are you brave enough to put creative ideas into practice? ············ Yes ( ) No ( )
6. Are your logical thoughts rigorous? ···························· Yes ( ) No ( )
7. Do you have the ability to learn from one instance? ················ Yes ( ) No ( )
8. Do you have a grounded mind? ······························· Yes ( ) No ( )
9. Do you have a wide range of knowledge? ························ Yes ( ) No ( )
10. Can you cross-use the knowledge that you have learned from different fields? ······ Yes ( ) No ( )
11. Do you have a habit of critical thinking? ······················· Yes ( ) No ( )
12. Are you flexible enough? ································· Yes ( ) No ( )
13. Do you have enough willpower to stick around? ·················· Yes ( ) No ( )
14. Do you have a strong curiosity? ···························· Yes ( ) No ( )
15. Do you have sharp insight? ······························· Yes ( ) No ( )
16. Do you have plenty of imagination? ·························· Yes ( ) No ( )
17. Do you have deep learning skills? ··························· Yes ( ) No ( )
18. Do you have self-driving force without relying on others? ············ Yes ( ) No ( )
19. Do you have the ability of thinking ahead? ····················· Yes ( ) No ( )
20. Do you have a strong enough ambition? ······················· Yes ( ) No ( )

Questions about knowledge

21. Do you agree with such an argument that people cannot enter into the
    same river twice? ··
    ·· Yes ( ) No ( )
22. Do you think sometimes consciousness also determines matter? ·············· Yes ( ) No ( )
23. Do you understand the principle of game theory?····················· Yes ( ) No ( )
24. Do you understand the lever principle in economics? ················ Yes ( ) No ( )
25. Do you understand the principle of economic equilibrium? ············ Yes ( ) No ( )
26. Do you understand the marginal effects of economics? ·············· Yes ( ) No ( )
27. Do you understand the basic principles of cost accounting? ············ Yes ( ) No ( )
28. Do you understand the basic principles of quantum physics? ·········· Yes ( ) No ( )
29. Do you understand the principle of inflation? ···················· Yes ( ) No ( )
30. Do you understand the theory of relativity? ····················· Yes ( ) No ( )
31. Do you understand Darwin's Theory of Evolution? ················· Yes ( ) No ( )
32. Have you read more than three philosophical works? ··············· Yes ( ) No ( )
33. Do you understand the comparative history of the British historian Toynbee?········ Yes ( ) No ( )
34. Have you studied three or more logical monographs? ··············· Yes ( ) No ( )
35. Have you studied more than three psychology monographs? ··········· Yes ( ) No ( )

36. Do you master the principles of statistics? ·· Yes ( ) No ( )

37. Do you master the theory of probability in mathematics? ··························· Yes ( ) No ( )

38. Do you master the principles of geometry in mathematics? ······················· Yes ( ) No ( )

39. Do you master the space and the mathematical principles in mathematics? ··········· Yes ( ) No ( )

40. Can you answer the basic principles of more than three chemical reactions? ········· Yes ( ) No ( )

Questions about personal manners

41. Can you tolerate the moment? ·· Yes ( ) No ( )

42. Can you still live a life after seeing through life? ································· Yes ( ) No ( )

43. Can you afford to face life? ·· Yes ( ) No ( )

44. Can you put down the pain? ··· Yes ( ) No ( )

45. Can you bear your responsibility rather than shifting it to others? ·············· Yes ( ) No ( )

46. Can you do anything without avoiding it? ·· Yes ( ) No ( )

47. Can you be trustworthy? ·· Yes ( ) No ( )

48. Can you stick to your values when frustrated? ······································· Yes ( ) No ( )

49. Can you remain optimistic when you are frustrated? ······························· Yes ( ) No ( )

50. If you failed 100 times, will you try the 101st time? ······························ Yes ( ) No ( )

51. Can you quietly listen to the advice of others? ····································· Yes ( ) No ( )

52. Can you still be calm when people around you laugh at you? ···················· Yes ( ) No ( )

53. Do you have concentration? ··· Yes ( ) No ( )

54. Are you somebody who never gives up? ·· Yes ( ) No ( )

55. Will you communicate sincerely with your users? ·································· Yes ( ) No ( )

56. Will you communicate effectively with your boss? ································ Yes ( ) No ( )

57. Do you have the empathy and think from the other person's position? ·············· Yes ( ) No ( )

58. Have you ever meditated? ·· Yes ( ) No ( )

59. Are you gossiping about people when you are free? ······························· Yes ( ) No ( )

60. Can you do what you say? ··· Yes ( ) No ( )

Questions about personal ability

61. Do you have organization and commanding ability? ······························· Yes ( ) No ( )

62. Do you have strategic decision-making skills? ······································ Yes ( ) No ( )

63. Do you have the ability to know, choose and use people? ······················· Yes ( ) No ( )

64. Do you have communication and coordination skills? ···························· Yes ( ) No ( )

65. Do you have social skills? ··· Yes ( ) No ( )

66. Do you have language skills? ·· Yes ( ) No ( )

67. Have you mastered at least one foreign language? ································· Yes ( ) No ( )

68. Do you have strong critical thinking skills? ··· Yes ( ) No ( )

69. Do you have the ability to convince others? ··· Yes ( ) No ( )

70. Are you a bold but cautious person? ·· Yes ( ) No ( )

71. Do you have commercial sensitivity? ··· Yes ( ) No ( )

72. Do you have the ability to convert technology into application? ················ Yes ( ) No ( )

73. Do you have the ability to stand pressure? ··· Yes ( ) No ( )

74. Do you have the ability to establish and improve business management systems? ··· Yes ( ) No ( )

75. Do you have the ability to collect, analyze and process information? ··············· Yes ( ) No ( )

76. Do you understand the market research methods and means? ······················ Yes ( ) No ( )

77. Do you have the ability to read and analyze financial statements? ················· Yes ( ) No ( )

78. Do you have the ability to negotiate business? ································· Yes ( ) No ( )

79. Do you have the ability to deal with corporate crisis? ························ Yes ( ) No ( )

80. Do you have the ability to manage your own physical health? ·················· Yes ( ) No ( )

Questions about miscellaneous issues

81. Have you ever experienced a failed business? ····························· Yes ( ) No ( )

82. Do you have any unsuccessful innovation learning? ························· Yes ( ) No ( )

83. Have you ever been in love and seriously loved someone? ·················· Yes ( ) No ( )

84. Are you somebody with idea and spirit? ································· Yes ( ) No ( )

85. Are you somebody who is not satisfied with your current situation? ··········· Yes ( ) No ( )

86. Do you love your family and your life? ································· Yes ( ) No ( )

87. Do you like poetry and write love letters? ······························ Yes ( ) No ( )

88. Do you like a sense of humor? ··· Yes ( ) No ( )

89. Do you believe that hardwork can make success? ························· Yes ( ) No ( )

90. Do you believe that the more diligent you are, the luckier you will be? ········· Yes ( ) No ( )

91. Do you know how to get along with yourself? ····························· Yes ( ) No ( )

92. Can you overcome the sense of fear? ···································· Yes ( ) No ( )

93. Do you have like-minded partners? ····································· Yes ( ) No ( )

94. Can you tell stories to shape your own intellectual property (IP)? ············· Yes ( ) No ( )

95. Do you have the ability to attract investment for a bold vision? ·············· Yes ( ) No ( )

96. Are you sensitive to state-of-the-art technologies? ······················· Yes ( ) No ( )

97. Do you have the good habit of reading books? ··························· Yes ( ) No ( )

98. Do you have a grateful heart? ··· Yes ( ) No ( )

99. Have you mastered the way technology integrates with art? ················· Yes ( ) No ( )

100. Do you understand yourself? ··· Yes ( ) No ( )

You will get one point when you check "Yes" in the bracket or 0 points when you check "No"; score yourself to see how you rate.

0-30 points	Beginner
31-50 points	Intermediate
51-70 points	Advanced
71-90 points	Super advanced
91-100 points	Perfect! You are Steve Jobs!

Part 2

Service

Chapter 3

Overview

Topics:

1. All Products Involve Services
2. Five Models Redefining Product Service
3. App Service Operation

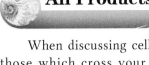
All Products Involve Services

When discussing cellphone brands, those which cross your mind may be Apple, Samsung, Huawei, MIUI and Meizu. What may surprise you is that a brand you have never heard of has occupied 40% of the market share in Africa, far more than occupied by Apple and Samsung. With sales of 80 million cellphones, it was China's biggest cellphone export in terms of volume in 2016.

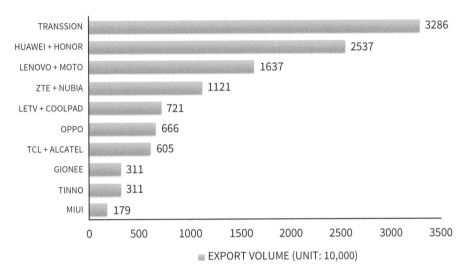

The sales lists of China Mobile Export in the first half year of 2016.
Source: China Customs Statistics for the First Half of 2016

The enterprise which is quietly making its fortune is Transsion from Shenzhen in China. It has three types of smartphones: TECNO, itel and Infinix. According to research, here are the reasons Transsion is developing so rapidly in Africa:

Firstly, Transsion always knows the "pain spot" of African people. For example, the famous TECNO solved the issue of selfies for Africans. Before the introduction of TECNO, the selfies of African people looked like the upper two pictures in Figure 3-1.

Faced with this, Samsung and Huawei did nothing, but TECNO made its move. It collected a great number of pictures of local people and analyzed their facial outline features and the imaging effect of exposure compensation, and then used eyes and teeth for shooting positioning. Then there came the camera phone Camon C8 for the Africans. Comparison is a good way to highlight their excellence.

Anyone can make products targeted at "pain spots", but nowadays, a product with only one feature can never win customers. As for African customers, Transsion still has another highlight satisfying their "special need". Transsion found that on average each African would have more than two SIM cards, so it made its phones able to support four cards. Four must be enough!

Grasping the pain spot and having a highlight are still not enough. A brand can only dominate in a continent by "digging" the culture of that continent and providing the screaming point for the local people. The African people are good at singing and dancing, so Transsion introduced the Boom J8 music phone, sold with a customized headset as a gift. This was a great coup.

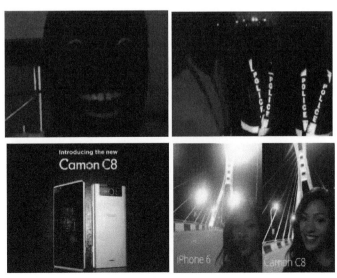

Figure 3-1   Photographs of User. Source: SOHU.com

Transsion Boom J8 Music phone. Source: SOHU.com

It is not that Transsion has no competitors in Africa: it does, and they are all well-known brands. At that time, the African market was controlled by Nokia, with Samsung in second place. Both adopted the distribution system. The system has three short comings: poor service, late feedback of user demand, and poor adherence between products and users. Transsion has not only set up R&D centers for localization in Lagos in Nigeria, the most populous country in Africa, and Kenya's capital city Nairobi, but it also established a large number of customer service centers. Service has helped the users better understand the product functions and increased the adherence between the brand and the users.

What does the adherence between users and products mean? It means the formation of consumer preference and the ability of continuous consumption of the brand. If the pain spot corresponds to expectation, the highlight to appearance, and the screaming point to excitement (all the three belong to psychological cognition of the users), the adherence point (i.e., the adherence of the users to the brand) contributes to the formation of consumer preference. Taking Transsion as an example, when Camon C9 was released, it sold like hot cakes.

Transsion was founded in 2006, with little brand awareness compared with Nokia, the cellphone leader at that time. Transsion's strategy is to cultivate local technical workers, solve the problem of local employment, and build the local trust in the brand. Transsion makes much mention of social responsibility in its advertisements in Africa, thus achieving brand differentiation. Nokia has popularity, while Transsion has credibility. Obviously, "users trust the brand" is the highest state in mobile marketing. In 2016, the South African business magazine *African Business* released the "Top 100 Favorite Brands of African Consumers 2015",

where two brands of Transsion were listed. TECNO ranked No. 16, after Samsung, Nokia, and Apple, and ahead of Sony, GUCCI and Microsoft, etc. In 2017, Transsion took the second step of its globalization strategy, "Think Globally, Act Locally", i.e., local implementation of global perspectives.

The success of Transsion is not an isolated case. Since 2012, all cases of successful marketing seem to have adhered to this rule: forget products; everything in the future is all about service.

In the article "Evolving to a New Dominant Logic for Marketing", Stephen L. Vargo and Robert F. Lusch introduced a new marketing mode which they call "service-dominant logic", i.e., fundamentally changing the marketing philosophy of enterprises and making it a process of fostering customers. In their opinion, the product is not the ultimate purpose, but the means of providing service. The customers are cooperative producers, and knowledge is the foundation of competitive edges.

In the product-dominant logic, production is the core process of value creation, while customer service belongs to the cost which must be minimized. But in the service-dominant logic, the product is the cost, and service becomes the core process of value creation.

What, then, is product and what is service? And why do we need the subversive change mentioned above?

What is product? It appears to be a simple question. All the things you eat, wear, use and play with are products. But we still need a managerial definition. One statement is that a product is an object or an intangible carrier used to satisfy the needs and wants of human beings. In a word, a product is anything that can be provided to the market, used and consumed by people to satisfy their certain needs, including tangible objects, intangible services, organizations, concepts, or a combination of the above. That is, however, only the definition of product in the industrial age. What then is service? Literally speaking, service means to perform some task or engage in some business. In Chinese-speaking regions as well as countries such as France, it also means to work for the public or others. In other western countries and regions, it is an economic term, covering all the intangible industries satisfying the customers with their utility and leaving no goods after the transaction. That is the so-called "tertiary industry" to which British economist Colin Clark refers in the "Fourastié Clark Theory".

In modern society, the connotation of service is growing increasingly wider. It is a type or a series of intangible activities which can bring people certain benefits or satisfaction, available for transfer with compensation. Service is usually intangible, and it is the result of at least one activity between supplier and customer.

The provision of service may involve:

(1) Activities completed on the tangible product provided by the customer (e.g., a car to be repaired);

(2) Activities completed on the intangible product provided by the customer (e.g., the income statement for a tax return);

(3) The delivery of intangible products (e.g., information provision for knowledge instruction);

(4) Creating an atmosphere for the customers (e.g., in a hotel or restaurant).

We find that the cost of products is very high, requiring a large amount of R&D investment, factory construction and carrying out of production activities in the early stage. Only after that will income be generated. In addition, in the age of the mobile Internet, products are lifeless, and the cost invested during production will only see returns after a certain period of time. However, in that period, the demand of the customers may change rapidly. The ability to respond quickly to fast-changing user demand is the core competence of an enterprise which can only be acquired from service.

Investing in service can make an enterprise more flexible. By not betting all property on a long-cycle product, the enterprise can better respond to new demands from customers.

Many people have grown accustomed to the product-dominant enterprise mode,

so this subversive mode may make them feel unnatural and uneasy, like a cigarette held back to front.

Fortunately, however, there are now more and more service-type enterprises like Transsion, and many enterprises devoted to service improvement are earning more money and getting more competitive.

The brand-new mobile car rental concept initiated by Daimler AG, the "car2go" car-sharing program, is aimed at providing an easy and convenient way of improving individual mobility. They put the small "smarts" at the "car2go" carports in location such as railway stations and airports for one-way rental, which greatly facilitates the car rental of the users who can borrow and return the cars any time after valid registration. The "car2go" program innovatively transferred selling vehicles (the product) to selling the solution to individual mobility (the service), treating manufacture as a kind of service. The program is well received for such unique features as the absence of fixed car rental site, the one-way mode, self-service, open service and the transparent pricing scheme.

In fact, any innovation may face great collisions.

Leo Tolstoy once said, "There are two most difficult things in the world. One is to put my ideas into your head; the other is to put your money into my pocket." "Putting my ideas in your head" is for the purpose of you "putting your money into my pocket". That is traditional marketing where concepts, fear appeals, USP consumption points[①] and benefits are explored, and the numerous classical marketing cases at home and abroad are developed.

However, the trend of mobile marketing is like a bolting horse: you will never overtake it but can only go with it by riding on its back. Driven by the two wheels of service orientation and value orientation, the traditional product concept needs to be redefined. That is to say, all products involve services.

①
USP: in 1960, the famous American advertiser Rosser Reeves proposed the renowned USP theory in his book The Reality in Advertising - USP, i.e., the "unique selling proposition". Its basic points are:

1. Each advertisement must "tell a proposition" to the consumers, making them understand what specific benefits they can get by buying the product in the ad.

2. The proposition emphasized must be something the competitors cannot achieve or provide. Its uniqueness must be advertised with unparalleled brand and message.

3. The proposition emphasized must be powerful and focused on one point to touch and attract the consumers to buy the product. For this, the concept of USP is adopted in the traditional marketing.

Five Models Redefining Product Service

Since the 1990s, Philip Kotler et al. have tended to use five levels to describe the whole concept of product, deeming this to be more profound and accurate. The whole concept of product requires

the marketers to consider the five levels of customer value they can provide while planning the market supply. The five basic levels of the whole concept of products are as follows:

(1) Core product: the basic utility or benefit of the product provided for the customers. Basically, every product is produced to solve a problem in nature. Therefore, any product sold to the customers must have the basic utility or benefit that reflects the core demand of the customers.

(2) Actual product: the form through which the core product is realized, comprising five features, i.e., quality, style, characteristics, trademark and packaging. Even pure service has similar features in form.

(3) Expected product: a whole set of attributes and conditions closely related to the product that the buyer wants to have when buying the product.

(4) Augmented product: the sum of various benefits attached when the customer buys the actual product and expected product, including product instructions, warranty, installation, maintenance, delivery and technical training. The success of many enterprises at home and abroad to some extent owes to their better awareness of the important role of service in the whole concept of product.

(5) Potential product: the existing product (including all the augmented products) that has the potential of developing into an ultimate product in the future. The potential product indicates the possible evolution trend and prospect of the existing product [See Marketing Management by Philip Kotler].

According to Kotler, "Professor Jerry McCarthy first put forward the 4P theory in his *Marketing* (first edition, published around 1960). However, as soon as he obtained his doctorate from Northwestern University, his advisor, Richard Clewett, had used the theoretical framework centered on 'Product, Price, Distribution and Promotion'. Jerry changed 'Distribution' into 'Placing', accomplishing the so-called '4P' theory. (People think I pushed the popularization of the 4P theory. My major contribution to this theory should be that I explained that 4P is for tactics and must be carried out after the strategic decision-making on STP, i.e., Segmentation, Targeting and Positioning)."

It is obvious that the product is the starting point of the 4P marketing theory. However, the above definition of product can no more adapt to the age of the mobile Internet. The label on the gate of the new world says: Everything is about service.

In the past, people were used to calling tangible products the commodity and intangible products the service. In the future, the product attribute will decrease while the service attribute will increase, resulting in tangible and intangible services. The former creates the brand value of service for the users via the carrier of concrete commodities, while the latter creates experience value of service for the users via the carrier of abstract substance.

Sometimes, the two values combine.

How to bring out strong competitiveness from service? We may as well try the five-force model of Porter first.

The five-force model was proposed by Michael Porter in the 1980s. According to the model, there are five forces deciding the competition scale and degree in the industry, which together influence the attraction of the industry and the competitive strategy decisions of existing enterprises.

The five forces are the competitiveness of competitors in the industry, the entry ability of potential competitors, the substituting capacity of the substitutes, the supplier's bargaining power, and the buyer's bargaining power.

Porter five-force model

Competition between Existing Competitors

The object of study here is the existing brand enterprises in the industry, i.e., the price, products, and market share of the enterprises. Compare them with yourself and find out your strengths and weaknesses.

Threat from New Entrants

The main problems faced by new entrants are the entry barriers and the attacks from existing enterprises in the industry. Any new enterprise will face these problems. Consideration shall be given to the scale economy of the enterprise, the rejection of other enterprises, capital and technical support, and so on.

Threat from Substitutes

Substitutes are products having the same properties as your product that can also satisfy customer demand. The products of enterprises in the same industry shall be analyzed and compared in terms of the advantages in technology, price, quality and service.

The Buyer's Bargaining Power

Bargaining of the buyer means the influence of your product in the market. If your product is leading in the industry, such power of the buyer will be low; but if your product has ordinary performance in the market, the buyer can definitely choose the products of other manufacturers for the most favorable price.

The Supplier's Bargaining Power

The means of threat of the supplier is mainly to increase the supply price or decrease the quality of the product and service supplied.

It mainly starts from the raw materials for the product you need, plus the uniqueness of the supplier's raw materials, so undoubtedly, the supplier's bargaining power will increase. Otherwise it may decrease, based on your dependence on the supplier's raw materials.

Porter believes that the fact reflected by the five competitive forces, i.e., the threat of entry, the threat of substitutes, the customer's bargaining power, the supplier's bargaining power and the competition of existing competitors, is that the competition of an industry far exceeds the scope of the existing participants.

The customers, suppliers, substitutes and potential entrants are all "competitors" of the industry, showing their importance to a greater or lesser extent according to specific circumstances as shown in Figure 3-2. This generalized competition can be called "expanding competition", where the five competitive forces together determine the intensity of the industry competition and the industry profit rate. The strongest force or forces dominates the competition and plays a crucial role in terms of strategy formation.

In the competition of the five forces, there are three basic strategic methods that may make your company the industry leader: ① overall cost leadership, ② differentiation, and ③ focus.

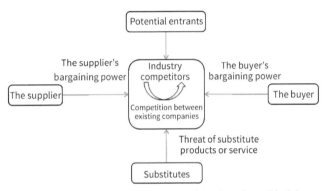

Figure 3-2   Schematic Diagram of the Five-force Model

Porter's competition theory opened up a new perspective of the strategic field, developing his own school of thought which dominated in the 1980s. This theory has its rationality in the environment of the 1980s. By the 1990s, however, as the business environment changed, the limitations of the theory became clear.

Porter's research on competition theory was carried out among existing industries; i.e., he chose industries based on incumbent firms. Since the information revolution in the 1980s, constant technology innovation has resulted in industry transformation; the industry boundaries have become increasingly blurred, and it has been more meaningful to focus on future industries and relevant strategy construction. There are some defects in the discussion about how to most effectively face industry transformation and establish long-term competition. As the market environment is changing more frequently and it is more and more difficult to develop the plans, the five-force model advocates enhancing the detection and control over the possible trends and potential in the environment; however, it is hard to predict the actual environment. Therefore, new strategists have proposed that enterprise strategies, in addition to guiding the competition in the existing industry, need to compete in building the future industry structure, so as to help the enterprise continuously create and seize new business opportunities. Its effect directly depends on the enterprise's ability in predicting the future industry development in the formation stage of the industry and depends on whether the enterprise can obtain the technical expertise required for the future in the fastest and the most economical way to gain the first-mover advantage. In this case, importance must be attached to resources and ability construction while emphasizing the significance of opportunities.

In Porter's opinion, every company must be clear about those three strategies,

because companies which hesitate have poor implementation and inconsistent requirements. The realization of overall cost leadership relies mainly on mass production which produces standardized products in batches and cannot satisfy the diversified consumer demands. Differentiation in the industry requires giving up the efforts toward low cost. Differentiation strategy means the expensive "customization" for specific customers, usually including the privilege price and the excess profit.

Porter's model looks even more obsolete and exhausted in the mobile Internet age of the 21st century. Porter's five-force research begins with competition and ends with competitiveness, but none of the successful cases in the age of the mobile Internet starts with competitor research: they actually start by exploring the pain spots of the users. Mobile marketing takes user demand as a basic starting point for consideration, while the competitor element is at most a side point for reference and not a basic point.

Porter's five forces have lost their efficacy, and the five-value rule of mobile marketing has come into being:

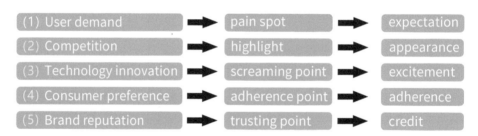

(1) User demand	➡	pain spot	➡	expectation
(2) Competition	➡	highlight	➡	appearance
(3) Technology innovation	➡	screaming point	➡	excitement
(4) Consumer preference	➡	adherence point	➡	adherence
(5) Brand reputation	➡	trusting point	➡	credit

The Five-Value Rule of Mobile Marketing

The service chain is constituted by the five kinds of value (discovering the pain spot, showing the highlight, making the user scream, making the user adhered, and making the user trust) from the beginning to the end without stopping.

The highest marketing model of service is to establish a user self-driven system. "digg" is translated into Chinese as "Jue Ke (digger)" or transliterated as "Ding Ge", the originator of which is digg Company from the US. "Digg" is a latest network term. There are over one million people gathering at digg reading, commenting on, and "digging" about 4,000 messages

every day. You can be a digger by applying for an account at a digg website, just like applying to be a blogger at a blog website.

In October 2004, the American Kevin Rose founded the first digg website, which gained renown in March 2005. The website was initially oriented at digging scientific news. Since its third revision in June 2006, it has included other categories, enjoying soaring network flow afterwards. Now digg has been the No. 24 public website in the US, easily winning over Fox News and drawing near *The New York Times* (No. 19). The Alexa ranking of digg is No. 100 in the world. There are over one million people gathering at digg reading, commenting on and "digging" about 4,000 messages every day.

A digg website is an article voting and commentary site, integrating bookmarks, blogs, really simple syndication (RSS) and non-grade comment control. Its uniqueness lies in that it has no professional web editor and the website is completely edited by the users. Users can submit articles at will and the readers will judge whether the articles are useful. The more people add an article to their favorites, the more highlights the article may have. If the users think an article is good, they may dig it; when the digging number reaches a certain amount, the article will be topped at the home page or other pages.

It seems like that the popular phrase, "Have you blogged today?" will be changed to "Have you digged today?".

User-driven mechanism is adopted for digg. It has a buffer for the news resources. The news submitted by the user first enters the buffer and appears on the digg page if approved by enough readers; otherwise, it will be excluded out of the buffer.

The root cause for the rise of digg is that it represents a massive network development direction, i.e., content evaluation.

If search service means content searching, digg represents a higher level, i.e., content evaluation, both of which are necessary basic modes for solving the problem of information matching in the age of Internet information explosion. Therefore, the future and direction represented by the digg mode is massive and profound, a brand-new business prospect second not even to search engine - we can give it a more proper name that can better reflect the same significance and prospect of it as the search engine, i.e., evaluation engine.

The evaluation engine and search engine must have some crossover region in technology and service, but the two are fundamentally different in information processing. When the search engine searches information for the user, the starting point of the user is a clear target; but when the digg evaluation engine searches information for the user, the starting point of the user is only a general direction, without a specific target. Therefore, the evaluation engine not only can search information for individuals, but also can process, evaluate, and sort the network information as a whole. It is a new application that really propels the ultimate network goal of "Information serves the people".

The "evaluation engine" is the new hinge of the 2.0 Era, a new opportunity second not even to the search engine. In particular, such opportunity is still in the early stages of development, which means it is still not late for the entrepreneurs to gain the first-mover advantage in this field.

1. SWOT is a scientific analytical method identifying the strengths, weaknesses, opportunities and threats of the enterprise so as to organically integrate the enterprise strategy with its internal resources and external environment.

2. Michael Porter's "five-force" analysis is the static profile scanning of the profitability and attraction of the enterprise, showing the average profitability in the industry. It is, therefore, a measuring indicator for the industry trend rather than enterprise competence.

3. Michael Porter's Value Chain Model divides the internal and external value adding activities into basic activities and supportive activities. The former involves production, selling, inbound logistics, outbound logistics, and after-sales service. The latter involves human resources, finance, planning, R&D and purchase. The two constitute the value of the enterprise.

4. The SCP model was proposed, Bain and Scherer, by authorities in industrial economics from Harvard University, in the 1930s. This model provides a Structure-Conduct-Performance industrial analysis framework which covers the specific links and has a logic system.

5. The McKinsey Matrix is a management model for business portfolio of the enterprise's strategic business units. It is also known as GE Matrix, Business Assessment Array and GE Business Screen.

Five Analysis Models

Analytical Tools

1. MECE

2. Cross quadrant

3. 5W2H

MECE means "Mutually Exclusive, Collectively Exhaustive", i.e. to carry out classification of a significant issue without overlap or omission and to effectively grasp the core of and solution for the problem.

Cross quadrant can replace the simple algorithm of the summation formula. It is a graphic method, especially suitable for mixture calculation of two sums and two relations, for calculating the ratio of two constituents in a mixture.

The inventor asks rhetoric questions with five English words starting with the letter W and two words starting with the letter H to find clues of the solution, seek invention ideas, consider design concepts, and work out new inventions. That is the 5W2H method. (1) What? (2) How? (3) Why? (4) When? (5) Where? (6) Who? (7) How much?

Analytical Tools

More excitingly, the "evaluation engines" including Digg are still in the early exploration stage. This growing mode representing the general future still has many things unknown, and there has not been any big gap between the first-movers and the late entrants, which brings great dreams for those courageous adventurers.

To examine the mobile Internet thinking in products, you may employ the following tools and modes:

In the age of the mobile Internet, the dimensions of product concept have seen great changes. The dimension inside the product is called quality, that outside the product is brand, and that above the product is content. The definition of product is being Internet-based. In addition to products and service, an independent app is often called a product.

🔎 Case Study   Nestlé: from Selling Products to Selling Services

In September 2017, Nestlé's "SENSE CAFE" pop-up store opened in Beijing. This is Nestlé's first pop-up café in China in almost 30 years.

Previously, Nestlé announced that it had obtained the majority interest of Blue Bottle Coffee (a high-end professional coffee roaster and retailer) by acquisition, formally declaring its involvement in the fast-growing super high-end coffee chain market segment.

At the same time, the WeChat business of Nestlé-related products was also launched, selling notebooks, vacuum cups, backpacks, and so on.

As a prudent and conservative foreign-funded enterprise representative in the Fast-Moving Consumer Goods (FMCG) industry, under the overall background of consumption upgrade, Nestlé has begun to try a series of cross-boundary business in the Chinese market.

Do Pop-up Stores Make the Brand More "Fashionable"?

"We hope to be more engaged and interactive with young consumers in the future through some new means. No matter whether by the pop-up café or other forms, we just want to get as close as possible to the consumers," said Guven, the Senior Vice President of Nestlé Greater China Coffee Business.

The name of pop-up shop or temporary store has the meaning of "pop out" in English, referring to setting up temporary shops in commercial areas. This type of business often has no large-scale publicity in advance; the shop will suddenly appear somewhere, rapidly attract consumers, run for a short time, and soon disappear.

In 2003, the first pop-up store in the world appeared in the SOHO area of New York. It was opened by the footwear brand Dr. Martens, with brilliant sales performance. Since then, pop-up stores have shown up around the world, arriving in China in 2015. Such famous brands as Hermès, Chanel, Adidas, and Nike all spend heavily inviting renowned designers and stars for pop-up store experiential marketing near the landmarks of first-tier cities.

According to the new generation report of Bain, traditional content marketing is no longer effective. More than 3/4 of the "new consumers" (including the millennial generation born after 1980) are interested in live feelings and real-time experiences.

As the largest instant coffee manufacturer in the world, Nestlé naturally wants to rid itself of its "middle age" tag and actively pursue a younger and more fashionable brand image. "There have been great changes both online and offline in the recent three to four years. We've been facing great pressure," said Guven. He hopes that Nestlé can keep its current advantages and turns into a lifestyle.

According to a Mintel report, coffee consumption in China has an annual growth of about 15%, much higher than the 2% of the international market; students and white-collar workers are becoming the main consumers. Currently, the proportion of instant coffee, ready-to-drink coffee, and fresh ground coffee in the Chinese market is approximately 7:2:1, while fresh ground coffee accounts for over 87% in the aggregate consumption around the world. In developed countries, when the per capita GDP and the consumption level rise, people would gradually turn from instant coffee and cafes to fresh ground coffee.

Although coffee consumption in China enjoys robust growth, the market of instant coffee has seen a shrinking trend. Nestlé has the highest market share of instant coffee in China, but Guven admitted that the market share of Nestlé's instant coffee in China has seen the growth declined to single digit this year despite its yearly increase in the past three years. The annual sales volume of the Greater China in 2016 was CHF 6.54 billion (about CNY 44.1 billion), with a year-on-year decrease of 7.4%.

Besides, other foreign-funded chains like Starbucks and Costa are accelerating to open stores in China. The Chairman of UBC Coffee of Japan, Kamishima Changzuolang, said, "The Chinese coffee market has great potential. The growth rate of coffee consumption is startling. In the near future, China will not only be a country of tea, but also a country of coffee."

Zhu Danpeng, a Chinese food industry analyst, expressed that Nestlé was trying to touch the young consumers by purchasing Blue Bottle Coffee and opening pop-up stores, etc. "Most century-old enterprises are experiencing the problem of brand and product aging. Upgrading and activating the product line, duly adjusting the mid- and long-term strategies, enhancing the right of speech in the coffee field, and catering to different consumers with products of various forms and levels are what Nestlé is doing right now," said Zhu.

How to Solve the Problem of Consumption Upgrade Problem?

Obviously, one can never make all young consumers fall in love with you simply by opening a pop-up store. Consumption upgrade is a required question for all FMCG enterprises.

In fact, Nestlé has accelerated its transformation by successively completing several acquisitions and collaborations in the capital market.

In June 2017, Nestlé purchased a take-out company dedicated to healthy food, Freshly; in September, Nestlé purchased a newly established food company, Sweet Earth, and sold some snack and candy businesses.

On September 19, 2017, the chocolate brand Chaobii under Hsu Fu Chi declared its upgrading to Nestlé Chaobii, which will be released in the market this fall. This is the first-time that there have been large-scale integration and effort toward the Chinese middle-end and high-end candy market after Nestlé's purchase of Hsu Fu Chi in 2011.

Furthermore, after purchasing Blue Bottle with USD 500 million, Nestlé declared in a joint statement that it planned to open 55 new stores by the end of this year. Now Blue Bottle Coffee has more than 50 branches and has won the investment from Morgan Stanley and Fidelity, etc. The management of Starbucks once said that independent fashionable cafes are the biggest threat to their business. Insiders believe that as Blue Bottle Coffee has been purchased by Nestlé, it will hopefully be a good weapon of Nestlé to compete against Starbucks.

It is worth mentioning that, on September 19, 2017, Nestlé declared the launch of its smart home nutrition and health assistant with speech recognition together with JD Group. Chairman and CEO of Nestlé Greater China, Rashid Qureshi, stated that the Chinese market changes so rapidly that Nestlé has to upgrade its orientation and strategies every two to three years. Through the cross-boundary layout, Nestlé wants to attract more consumers and collect more user information for more solutions by means of smart products.

Zhu Danpeng said that many Fortune Global 500 enterprises including Nestlé, Danone, and P&G are now transforming, turning toward middle- and high-end high-margin products on the one hand, while studying the future layout on the other hand. The current consumer demand is changing, too. Old consumers are loyal to the brand, but young consumers are inclined to a mode dominated by the product and supplemented by the brand and price. The series of actions of Nestlé are apparently aimed at maximum extension of the brand, and big data support is also considered. It will perfect its data platform, so as to support its future product line layout in the Chinese market with enough data.

P&G chooses "simplification", Nestlé tries to be "fashionable", and Danone continues cooperating with Chinese enterprises. The answers of these transnational enterprises to the consumption upgrade of the Chinese market still need to be tested by the time.

The case source quoted from: Hou Juan, China Economic Weekly 2017/11/06
http://finance.sina.com.cn/roll/2017-11-06/doc-ifynmvuq8987444.shtml

App Service Operation

I. What Is an App?

App is an abbreviation of "application", referring to the software installed on cellphones for improvement and individualization. It is a significant manifestation of the mobile Internet products. (See Figure 3-3.) Mobile platform systems supporting App software include IOS and Android.

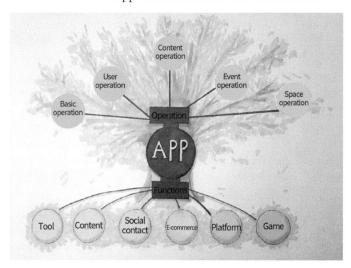

Figure 3-3   Functionality and Process of APP

1.   Functionality of Apps can be divided into the Following Six Categories:

(1) Tool: products solving some problem of the users, e.g., Moji Weather, and Baidu Map.

(2) Content: the core of the products is the content on the websites/app, e.g., Tencent Video and YYlive.

(3) Social contact: mainly designed for interpersonal communication, e.g., Facebook, and Momo.

II. App Operation

Having entered the age of the mobile Internet, many enterprises want to make money from it. The potential app development demand of millions of enterprise websites in China has seen explosive growth. When the app is developed and released, it enters a key stage - the stage of operation and promotion. There has been a serious problem of homogeneity of the mobile Internet products in recent years. Many good products would be met with a number of competitors

(4) E-commerce: mainly designed for various transactions on the mobile Internet, e.g., Taobao, Tmall and Amazon.

(5) Platform: some comprehensive mobile Internet products, supporting tools, content, and social contact at the same time.

(6) Game: a virtual 2D world, e.g., "Onmyoji", and "Arena Of Valor", which can be turned into a virtual 3D world with VR.

2.   Cellphone App Development Mainly Comprises iOS, Android and html 5:

App development process:

(1) The project leader leads the team to carry out user research, study the user demand, and work out the framework and flow of the app.

(2) The product manager (PM) produces the draft sketch and line drawing according to the framework and flow.

(3) The interaction designer (UI) produces the prototype according to the draft sketch and line drawing, usually via AXURE.

(4) When there is no experience problem, the designer makes Hi-Fi renderings according to the prototype, usually via Photoshop.

(5) After the above steps, the programmer develops the app.

(6) After the developed app has been repeatedly tested by the tester and adjusted by the programmer, it can be released for download.

following release. In addition to real value and excellent product experience, app promotion and operation is an important element that decides whether the product can stand out. The operator tries everything to let the users see, know and use the product via the access to the Internet (websites, wireless application protocol [WAP], app, and smart equipment). To see is the primary stage, to know is the further stage, and to use the product is the ultimate purpose of promotion.

1. App Promotion Channels

Firstly: the first step of promotion is to launch the product online. That is a basic condition. There is no need for money, only coverage in the maximum range, such as in various download markets, app malls, large platforms and downloading sites.

Download markets: Android, Gfan, Anzhi, AppChina, 91, Mumayi, Nduo, eoe, Anmarket and FLMobile etc.

App malls: Google Play, HTC mall, LIQU, Crossmo, Kaiqi, Aimi, Wochacha, Flyme, Lenovo Developer Community and oppo App Store, etc.

Large platforms: MMarket, Wostore, 189store, HUAWEI App Market and Tencent App Center, etc.

Client-side: Wandoujia, 91 cellphone assistant and 360 software manager, etc.

Wap sites: Paojiao, WAPTW.com, Lexun and Easou, etc.

Downloading sites: skycn.com, Onlinedown.net, CRSKY.com and DownG.com, etc.

Secondly: promotion takes place through forums, microblogs and advertorials.

Forums: Zhihu, Jianshu, Gfan, Android and Anzhi, etc. You can see many industry forums at the bottom of relevant websites.

Microblogs: Yixieshi.com, 36Kr, Tech-Web, Guokr.com, Tech2IPO, etc.

Microblog promotion has great potential. Marketing is limitless. The cost here is the lowest but, if successful, the effect may be surprising.

Advertorials: digi.tech.qq.com, digi.sohu.com and ZOL.COM.CN, etc. If your advertorial is well written, it will be reposted by many sites following release.

Thirdly: paid promotion.

Paid promotion includes built-in paid promotion, payment by amount, and advertisement network paid promotion.

Promotion methods are only patterns. Successful promotion requires the promoter to find the promotion point, target users, and the profit model of his App so as to make precisely oriented promotion strategies.

2. App Promotion Skills and Strategies

Firstly, confirm the primary promotion purpose: Downloads or exposure?

The download of the app will not rely on app markets only. In addition to the product itself, the download is the most important. The download is determined by exposure. That is to say, the app may be downloaded by 10 people when released in one app mall, by 25 people when released in two app malls, and by 50 people in three app malls, on the premise that the download is the same in every app mall.

The reason is simple: a user may not like your app when he sees it in an app mall, and he may go to another app mall; when he sees your app again, he may find it ok, and then becomes your user. That is the effect of exposure, especially concentrated exposure in the early stage. Is it not cool that the users always see the name of your app in a certain period? Then how to achieve concentrated exposure?

Secondly, pay attention to the release time and description in app stores/downloading sites.

Let's first look at the app stores/downloading sites with good effects.

(1) Android Market: excellent download in the early stage, fast approval, the place of first release.

(2) HiMarket: fewer actual users than download, lower conversion rate than Android Market, fair approval speed.

(3) Gfan Market: fast approval.

(4) AppChina: similar download to that of Gfan Market.

(5) Sohu Download: long time for application.

(6) 3G Portal Download: favorable download in the early stage.

(7) Mumayi Market: stable but not high.

(8) 91sc.com: ordinary, there may be too many competitive apps.

(9) StarAndroid: ordinary, but with convenient background.

While being familiar with the ranking, you should still pay attention to the release time. Not all apps are suitable for release on Fridays, because many high-quality apps are updated on that day. Therefore, grassroots developers would do better to choose Wednesday or Thursday for update.

Thirdly, quickly accumulate positive comments in the app stores.

When an app has just been released, it often needs some time to gain valuable comments. Try to invite your friends to download and use it and encourage them to give positive comments based on their true feelings. That would give your product a good start. You can also remind the users in the app to grade and comment on it in the app store. Such reminders would usually pop up when the user has used the product for several times, so as to ensure he has a basic understanding of the product. Please do not give such reminders too early or too frequently, or it may arouse a negative feeling of the user.

Fourthly, report all malicious or invalid comments.

If you receive malicious or invalid blank comments, report to the app store as soon as possible.

3. App Operation Process

How do you make the users use your app and finally make revenue? What do the operators need to know in this app operation process?

(1) App operation objective: to have revenues or profits, increase new users, and improve the activeness of old users. Activeness usually means the online time and login frequency of the users of an online product.

(2) The three elements of app operation: the user, the product and the space. Despite the former two, the so-called app operation space refers to the channel connecting the product and the user.

(3) The content of app operation mainly includes: app operation planning, BD①, media, activity marketing, data analysis and market monitoring. Confirm the direction and update of the product by constant app operation planning, establish favorable communication with the channel placing parties by BD, advertise the product to the users by various media, increase active users by activity marketing, and lay the foundation for next app operation planning by data analysis and market monitoring.

(4) Classification of app operation:

Basic operation: the most daily and the commonest work to maintain the normal operation of the product.

User operation: maintain the users, increasing the number of users and improving their activeness.

Content operation: direct, recommend, integrate and promote the content of the product, provide text materials for app event operation personnel, etc.

Event operation: plan the events according to demand and the goal and monitor the event effect and properly adjust the event by data analysis, thus improving key performance indicators (KPI) and promoting the product. Some app event operation tools are usually adopted for assistance during the event operation.

Space operation: promote and output the product by business cooperation, product cooperation, and placing cooperation, etc.

If you want to have good performance in app operation, you need to combine operation, product and users. The product must have good quality to give the users favorable experience. Carry out app operation and promotion targeted at the demands of the product and the users; and satisfy the user demands such as self-expression and identity when designing the activities.

① BD: means to formulate and implement cross-industry development plans based on the company situation, establish smooth cooperation channels places with upstream and parallel partners, and communicate with relevant governments and associations to seek for support and resources. "BD" can be understood as "generalized marketing" or "strategic marketing".

💡 Case Study | OPPO Cellphone

Launched in 2004, OPPO was previously a sub-brand of BBK together with its sister brand Vivo, and later became independent of BBK. According to statistics from the authoritative data institution IDC, OPPO became the number one brand in terms of shipments in the Chinese cellphone market in 2016. There are now more than 200 million young people around the world using OPPO camera phones. For over a decade, OPPO has focused on cellphone technology innovation: it started the era of selfie beautification with cellphones, and creatively introduced the world's first motorized rotating camera, Pure Image, and so on to furnish young people in over 20 countries and regions with an excellent cellphone photography experience. It is an up-rising star among Chinese cellphone brands.

I. Analysis of placing strategy for OPPO cellphones: Based on offline placing, supplemented by online placing

Compared to the model of Huawei and Xiaomi which are based on online sales, OPPO's offline placing is relatively strong: it has over 200,000 offline experience stores in China which bring better experiences to users and contribute most sales of OPPO every year. This is the weapon with which OPPO catches up and surpasses Huawei and Xiaomi.

In the meantime, online sales of OPPO are not inferior to other brands: OPPO ranked fifth by cellphone brand sales of Tmall during the Double Eleven Shopping Festival in 2015, and its R7s was the sales champion among cellphones in the CNY 2,000-3,000 price bracket; OPPO R9 also enjoyed very good sales on Tmall and Jingdong on the 6.18 Online Shopping Festival in 2016, and was the sales champion among cellphones in the CNY 2,000-3,000 price bracket.

The offline placing of OPPO, therefore, is apparently the foundation of its sales while its online placing well supplements its offline placing. The two are complementary and inseparable, and one thing that Internet manufacturers, which lack or pay no attention to offline placing, are unable to match.

Share benefits with the placing: OPPO's relationship with agents can be traced to 2008 when OPPO started to enter the cellphone market. Friendship begins with the bundling of interests. Some of OPPO's early agents have even become its shareholders, sharing common interests, and bearing losses when cellphones are unsalable.

II. Analysis of publicity strategy for OPPO cellphones: sticking to selling points, celebrity endorsement, and high key and fashion

1. Distinctive, catchy, memorable and easily spread slogan

OPPO U701 (2012, OPPO's first selfie cellphone): Ultimate selfie snapper.

OPPO R1 (2013, cellphone featuring night shot): Capture all, even in the dark.

OPPO N1 (2013, cellphone with rotating camera): Return to Innovation.

OPPO N1 Mini (2014): Unique rotating camera, Unique shooting experience.

OPPO R3 (2014): World's thinnest 4G LTE smartphone.

OPPO Find 7 (2014): Versatile 4G LTE Flagship.

OPPO R7 (2015): Style in a flash (all-metal, camera, and VOOC).

OPPO R9 (2016): Charge for five minutes, talk for two hours.

OPPO R11 (2017): Beauty made clearer, dual 20MP cameras.

We can see that the slogan for each product well reflects its main features: from selfie, night shot, rotating camera, to 3G-to-4G period, products were rapidly and widely publicized through the highly refined and catchy slogans.

The "Charge for five minutes, talk for two hours" of the R9 spread all over China and is known by everyone.

2. Celebrity endorsement, KOLs, and fan economy to strengthen the brand influence

With regard to the star spokespeople selected by OPPO, from Leonardo DiCaprio, who made USD $5 million, Song Hye-kyo who made USD $15 million, to Li Yifeng, Yang Yang, Yang Mi, and TFBOYS who were invited when R3 was launched in March 2016 and for whom the custom models were introduced, the emphasis has been increasingly on their strong attraction to their fans, both offline and on social media.

3. Pervasive TV commercials to aim at target customers

OPPO expands its brand awareness in the form of commercials in prime time of each satellite TV channel, product placement on hot variety shows, and celebrity endorsements and celebrity custom models, which are welcomed by consumers and users and lead to better sales and reputation of OPPO cellphones. OPPO advertised in prime time on CCTV-5 during the 2016 Olympics; during UEFA Euro 2016, it not only advertised but also launched its FC Barcelona Edition cellphone engraved with the signatures of Messi, Neymar, Suárez, Rakitic, and Iniesta. OPPO's changes in marketing have shown the upward pursuit of the brand and served its strategic change from villages to cities.

III. Analysis of product strategy for OPPO cellphones: in-depth exploration of user demands and solving user pain spots

The root cause of the rise of OPPO is its deep understanding of users, and how it reflects user demand in its product by design and planning at the time of project approval, so that every product has distinctive selling points before it appears on the market and the selling point is based on user demand instead of the technology it has.

1. OPPO's grasp of user demand for fast charging

As the flagship product launched in March 2016, OPPO R9 exceeded sales volume of 7 million units in 88 days after being launched, amount to one unit per 1.1 second, with the slogan of "charge for five minutes, talk for two hours" and the first selling point of fast charging!

The standby time of smartphones is generally about one day, this cannot match the three days of feature phones. Many users have an inexplicable anxiety when seeing low battery, and the standby time is a pain to smartphone users. The proud Apple and Samsung have chosen to ignore this problem, and Huawei has chosen to increase battery life, while OPPO has chosen fast charging.

When thinking about what led to the different choices of Huawei and OPPO, there was speculation that Huawei's engineers and decision-makers started from their own usage habits; the habit of most office workers several years ago was that they went to work in the morning with phones fully charged and went back home with phones in low battery; the battery life could not last a whole day for heavy use, and caused more difficulties during business travel, therefore, naturally, they came up with the idea of increasing battery capacity.

However, many OPPO users were not office workers, did not stay out all day, and seldom took business trips. Therefore, fast charging better met their demands. Regardless of the reasons for the different choices, seen from the results, the battery lives of most smartphones in the market are currently not substantially improved, but fast charging does bring genuine sales to R9 as a selling point.

2. OPPO's grasp of user demand for beautification and selfies

Looking back through the history of OPPO, the "selfie beautification" concept was first proposed by OPPO in China, the inspiration for which came from one product designer of OPPO. A girl enjoyed taking selfies with her Casio selfie snapper (TR100) and told her colleagues in the project team about female users' feelings, "We don't care about how clear the photo is. We only want to look beautiful in it."

Based on this understanding of user psychology, OPPO soon developed the U701, the first cellphone with beautification and selfie function in 2012, and later developed the big-screen camera phone N1 with rotating camera, which achieved a sales volume of 3 million units. OPPO then continued to explore this demand and launched the night shot phone R1 at the end of 2013, which achieved a sales volume of 4.60 million units.

3. OPPO's grasp of user demand for stylish appearance

As a life necessity, whether a cellphone is beautiful or not has increasingly become an important selection criterion for consumers, when cellphones are not much different in terms of functionality. Grasping this psychology of consumers, OPPO launched the R9, including the medium- to low-end A59 and A37, all of which bear a strong resemblance to the iPhone, because the iPhone represents and leads the trend and fashion of cellphones.

4. OPPO's grasp of users' pain spot of "lag"

One year after use, smartphones become slow and lagging as apps increase and become bigger, fragments consume more memory, and the Android system itself causes problems. This greatly affects the user experience. Especially for the first generation of users who shifted from feature phones to smartphones, as the smartphones they initially bought were cheap, the running speed became even slower. According to research, slowing down and lagging has become the number one reason for users to change cellphones.

Targeted at the "lagging" pain spot of users, OPPO was the first to launch the "4G big RAM" cellphone at the beginning of 2016, with the slogan "big RAM, no lagging" easily understood and accepted by users.

5. Patents of core technologies

Patent is also one of OPPO's weapons. According to the State Intellectual Property Office of China on January 14, 2016, OPPO ranked fourth in the "number of applications for invention patents of enterprises accepted in 2015". R&D is the reliance for an enterprise to achieve sound and long development. OPPO, a brand focusing on the cellphone field, has been valuing R&D; for example, it has a high-quality patent portfolio for the rotating camera and VOOC flash charging.

In summary, OPPO did not emerge suddenly, and there are many reasons for its rise. OPPO has become another industry trend changer at present because it has seized the new industry opportunity of consumption upgrade, worked hard over the years in the middle- and high-end market, and perceived the consumer demands. The soaring market share has made OPPO a national focus, however, while its product strategy that has long favored offline placing over online placing enables it to complete layout in third-tier and fourth-tier cities, OPPO should not only depend on placing and advertising that put marketing first, but also adhere to investing more energy in product quality, industrial design, and manufacturing process if it wants to occupy the consumer market of first- and second-tier cities.

The case source quoted from: ifeng.com2017/6/5

http://www.docin.com/p-1942658027.html

Chapter 4

Seven Thinking Models for Developing Services

Topics:

1. User Thinking
2. Socialized Thinking
3. Extreme Thinking
4. Big-Data Thinking
5. Open Thinking
6. Micro-innovation Thinking
7. Story Thinking

From PC Internet to mobile Internet, the Internet era has entered its second half. The mobile Internet thinking of products can be analyzed from seven dimensions, namely user thinking, socialized thinking, extreme thinking, big-data thinking, open thinking, micro-innovation thinking, and story thinking (see Figure 4-1).

Internet thinking was first proposed by Robin Li, the Founder of Baidu, Inc., in 2011 when he was discussing development issues with bosses and entrepreneurs in traditional industries in a large-scale activity of Baidu. He said, "We entrepreneurs should possess the Internet thinking from now on. Your business may not relate to the Internet, but you should gradually think about issues from the perspective of the Internet." Lei Jun started to frequently mention a relevant phrase—Internet thought—in 2012, and he had been trying to sum up the differences of Internet enterprises from the rest over the years. In 2013, with the growing of visibility of Lei Jun, some We Media figures like Luo Zhenyu started to frequently mention Internet thinking, and some TMT[①] industry reporters also started to use the phrase. Pony Ma, the Founder of Tencent, also ended with this phrase in a speech on November 8, 2013.

The Internet has changed industries such as music, game, media, retail, and finance,and in the future, the spirit of the Internet will change every industry. Traditional enterprises must possess Internet thinking even if they have yet to figure out how to combine with the Internet. Several years after it was proposed, this idea has been gradually recognized by more and more entrepreneurs, and even people in every

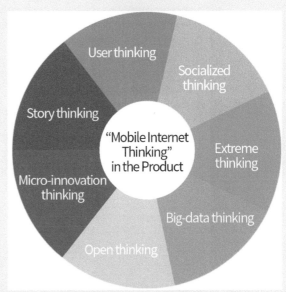

Figure 4-1　"Mobile Internet Thinking" in the Product

walk of life and every field outside enterprises, and the phrase Internet thinking has evolved to have several different explanations.

The way of thinking in the Internet era is not limited to Internet products and Internet enterprises, and the Internet here is not the desktop Internet or mobile Internet, but the pan-Internet, as the future network form must be across various terminal devices like desktops, laptops, tablets PCs, cellphones, watches, and glasses. The Internet thinking refers to the way of thinking that re-examines the market, user, product, enterprise value chain, and even the entire business ecosystem against the background where the mobile Internet, big data, cloud computing, and so on are constantly developing.

From the perspective of marketing, changes brought by the mobile Internet to products are mainly reflected in the following types of mobile Internet thinking.

① TMT is an acronym for technology, media, and telecom. The TMT industry is in fact the backdrop where the trend of convergence of future (Internet) technology, media and telecommunications, including IT, happens.

 User Thinking

User thinking is the first and most important of mobile Internet thinking, the core of mobile Internet thinking, and the foundation of other types of thinking. Without user thinking, there will be no other types of thinking.

What user thinking focuses on is "people" instead of "objects" only: not focusing on the mechanized production mode, but the users themselves at the time of product creation; it is a thinking model that creates products by mainly centering on the overall demand of users and meeting the user demand diligently, and it has the following features:

(1) Humanization. The thinking model is based on a specific user, and

directly shows care, trust, respect, and other humanized elements relating to that user.

(2) Individualization. This means that it meets user demand, and is not limited to the popularized demand, but more likely the individualized demand.

(3) Diversification. This means that it meets user demand on multiple levels and in multiple formats. Product and service are only a material level of diversification. Diversification is more about culture, feeling, spirit, and thought.

Enterprises have evolved from focusing on the pure brand and placing to focusing on products, but this is far from enough today.

When making the product, one will only achieve the better and not the best, but after having the users participate in the making, they will have their expectations at each stage, you only have to exceed their expectations, and your product will constantly iterate and advance with their opinions.

It is truly sad when people talk about which companies are Internet companies today, because within three to five years every company will become an Internet company. Everyone will do things via the Internet, with Internet thinking, using the execution capacity of the Internet. It is essentially the same thing, regardless of whether you are selling alcohol, tea, or cellphones.

I. Focusing on User Experience

User experience is a purely subjective feeling in the process of using a product by a user; however, the commonality of user experience for a well-defined user community can be recognized through well-designed practice. Regarding the new competitiveness, as referred to in the "Internet Marketing Foundation and Practice", the development of computer technology and Internet is enabling the transformation of the form of technological innovation, the user-centered and people-oriented ideas are drawing more and more attention, and user experience is thus called the essence of the Innovation 2.0 model.

In the past, the determination as to whether a product is good or not depended on the project leader's requirements for the product; however, as people may understand the Tragedy of Hamlet from different points of view, everyone has their own judgment of a product. Therefore, if the project leader is not capable of grasping the product quality, it will turn out

terrible. Internet users in the past were forced to accept the function design of a product; therefore, product managers seldom or even never considered the product experience of users when designing the product, so that there were many "anti-human designs". Today, however, with the productivity development and competition intensification, users have more and more options in a product, and they start to realize something out of the experience, and instinctively select the most humanized design. It will be difficult for a product to stand out if the user experience is not considered at the design stage.

The field of user experience was established to cover the holistic analysis and perspective of how a person feels about using a system. The research focus is on pleasure and value brought by the system rather than on performance of the system. The exact definition, framework, and elements of user experience are still evolving and innovating.

🔆 Case Study   NetEase Cloud Music: Listen to the Good Times

Born in 2013, NetEase Cloud Music is a music product developed by NetEase. At that time, the music player market of China was already occupied by QQ Music, Kugou Music, Baidu Music, and so on; however, NetEase Cloud Music broke this siege and achieved something in the music player market. By the beginning of July 2016, it had over 200 million users, pro-

duced over 100 million playlists, and included more than 10 million high-quality copyrighted songs, with average daily 420,000 playlists created.

In July 2015, NetEase Cloud Music announced that its users had exceeded 100 million, showing that the number was doubled only in one year, with growth reaching 100%, and NetEase Cloud Music became

NetEase Cloud Music App. Source: tech.ifeng.com

the fastest growing music platform. The success of NetEase Cloud Music lies in its focus on users and meeting of users' high-level demands, to which all its three core functions relate. The unique advantages of NetEase Cloud Music include:

1. Playlist. NetEase Cloud Music is the first music app with the playlist as its architecture. The playlist is the collection of songs. In NetEase Cloud Music, users can create a playlist of their favorite songs which can be viewed, added to favorites, commented on, and shared by other users. This makes NetEase Cloud Music different from others. The reason for such comment of users is in fact the personalized recommendation gives them exactly the music that they need.

Apps. During the interaction, the playlist creators feel the results they have created are appreciated and they will have the desire to create better content, and even package names and covers of the playlists to attract more attention. This slowly forms a virtuous cycle: everyone creates something, something is shared by others, and content is created by users ceaselessly through interaction and communication on the platform with the playlist as the carrier. Not only has playlist-based architecture stimulated users' creation desire, provided more possibilities for product operation, and made the entire product operation model very individualized and creative, but also it has provided possibilities for the individualized playlist of the 3.0 version.

2. Personalized recommendation. Personalized recommendation refers to the personalized recommendation actively made for users upon collecting their feature data and according to their characteristics like interests and preferences. NetEase Cloud Music provides the personalized recommendation function by using unique recommendation algorithms and according to users' preferences in listening to songs. Such personalized service indeed hits the "pain spot" of users in this age when personality is overemphasized. The private FM, daily recommended playlist, similar song function, and similar singer function keep you discovering songs that you have never listened to before but you will like. Those functions of NetEase Cloud Music have been repeatedly recommended and have turned many music fans into loyal fans.

Some users have commented, "NetEase Cloud Music knows me better than my boyfriend/girlfriend, my mom, and myself."

3. Comment sharing. There have been over 200 million music comments produced in NetEase Cloud Music by 2016, but in fact, the comment function was not prominent during the 1.0 version of NetEase Cloud Music; then the number of comments gradually increased, and the content thereof was shared to Sina Microblog and Zhihu. After discovering this, Zhu Yiwen's team firstly placed comments in the most visible position, with the number of comments displayed, for example, don't you want to click to read the comments when the icon says there are 999+ comments? Secondly, the team opened the "like" function for comments. After these adjustments, the comment area became hot, with even more than one million comments left under Jay Chou's Sunny Day; the comment area is not only the platform for users to exchange feelings, but also becomes a reference for users when they listen to unfamiliar music, and gradually has users form the habit of commenting while listening to music, and it has also enjoyed good reputation.

"Five Hundred Miles" is a song I like very much. There is some special sadness every time when I listen to it. When I read the comment, "The melody is about wandering, the lyrics are about sadness, and when I listen to it, I feel like I am on a journey", it touched me very much, and thereafter, I would read comments when I listen to music, and sometimes, share something.

The case source quoted from: Reorganized from materials on tech.ifeng.com 2016/12/08
http://tech.ifeng.com/a/20161208/44510423_0.shtml

II. Caring for user needs

We must have found certain needs before defining a product. Then we make a product to meet said needs. So what is need? Maslow proposed the need hierarchy theory in his "A Theory of Human Motivation Psychological Review" published in 1943.

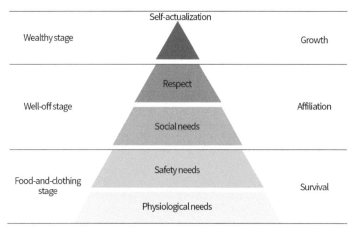

User Need Hierarchy Theory from Maslow's (A Theory of Human Motivation Psychological Review) Source: Baidu Baike

Maslow's theory divides demands into five sets of goals from lower to higher levels: physiological needs, safety needs, social needs, respect and self-actualization.

1. Physiological needs

Physiological needs are the most fundamental condition for human beings to survive, which covers every aspect of daily life of human beings: clothing, food, accommodation and traveling.

Human beings cannot survive without these needs satisfied. Maslow believed that only when these most fundamental needs were sufficiently met for survival that other needs could become new incentives, when these needs are relatively met then there would no longer be incentives.

2. Safety needs

Human beings need to guarantee their own safety, get rid of the threat of losing wealth, get harsh supervision off their backs, etc. According to Maslow, each living being was a mechanism constantly pursuing safety. The perceptive organs, effector

organs, intelligence and other energies of human beings were tools used to seek safety, and we could even regard science and the outlook on life as a part of our safety needs. Obviously, once relatively satisfied, these demands will no longer be incentives.

3. Emotional needs

Needs at this level include two aspects. Firstly, there are needs for friendship, i.e., everybody needs friends, harmony or the maintenance of friendship and loyalty; everybody hopes to love and to be loved. Secondly, there are also affiliation needs, that is, people hope to belong to certain groups, becoming a member of them, in which they care about each other. Emotional needs are more particular than physiological needs, which are related to individual physiological characteristics, experiences, educational background and religion.

4. Needs for respect

People always expect stable social status and the acceptance of personal capability and achievements by society. There are two parts of respect: internal respect and external respect. Internal respect means that no matter in what situation one can still keep his capacity and be competent, confident and independent. In sum, internal respect means self-respect. External respect means that one hopes to achieve the social status and own the prestige. He or she can be respected, trusted and highly apprised by others. Maslow believed that the satisfaction of the need for respect can make people fully confident, be full of enthusiasm for society and realize their own use and values.

5. Needs for self-actualization

Self-actualization stands at the top of the pyramid of needs, meaning the realization of personal ideas, the full play to one's ability and the accomplishment of all things matching one's capability. That is, people must do what they are good at to enjoy the greatest happiness. Maslow came up with the idea that the path for self-actualization varied with each individual. Driven by the needs for self-actualization, people explore their potentials to the maximum degree and make themselves become whom they have expected to be.

User Need Hierarchy Theory from the Author. Source: Baidu Baike

We believe that, in the era of mobile Internet, in addition to the five levels of needs proposed by Maslow, there is the higher need — the need for belief and soul affiliation. By defining the need for belief and soul affiliation, we believe that it is a firm belief in and execution of the unique truth about everything.

Warren Buffett ranked 3rd on *Forbes* World's Billionaires list in 2016, a globally established investor and having an estimated fortune of around USD $68 billion. To our surprise, he currently still lives in an ordinary house that was bought at a price of USD $31,500 (about CNY 200,000) in 1958. He has no bodyguards or servants. He drives an ordinary-looking and old car to his 20m^2 office in a small and old building with no fancy decor. However, being a Christian, he has beliefs and his soul gets its place. In his letters to shareholders each year, he always quotes the Bible; as he believed, all his fortunes are entrusted to him by God, and upon his departure from the world, the fortunes must be returned to God for better use.

As early as ten years ago, Buffett had signed a letter of intent, determined to donate 85% of his wealth, approximately USD $37.5 billion, to five charity foundations. This is the largest charity donation in the United States and the world.

6. How to identify needs

Now that demands are so important, shall we satisfy every demand of our users? No. We need to identify their real needs from those that are unreasonable such as, "I'd like to stay at home and earn money without working" and other pseudo-needs.

(1) We need to know that what users want is not necessarily what they need. It is need that often drives them. We need to identify unreal demands and shall never satisfy all of their needs without

justification. Even the needs driving the users are not always to be satisfied. Users whimsically expect the best services for free. They hate promotions and propagandas, in the meantime hoping not to run around. All these are needs. But the question is, can you satisfy all of these needs? How can your company earn money if so?

Take YY Language for example. It was nothing but a communication application in the the early days aiming to provide free group chat. Then it found that it was necessary to add some live streaming and entertaining elements to develop live broadcast communities, which was objected to by many users. People constantly made complaints to the user services, wanting the original version. YY brushed these complaints aside. YY noticed these user needs but did nothing. Today, it has become the largest live streaming platform and has been listed on NASDAQ.

Not every user need shall be satisfied, even if such need is proposed by massive loyal users. The problem here is that the so-called pseudo-needs are not so easy to identify. Bill Gates, founder of Microsoft, once said that it was a steal that users obtained software free of charge. It is true. Isn't it a pseudo-need to obtain technical products at no cost? Rising Antivirus said the same thing later, that "Free virus killing is nothing but bullying", and then it was defeated by 360, which was for free.

(2) Needs usually hole up in search engines. We need to find out the essential needs instead of blindly following users' descriptions. Users' search terms reflect their needs. One of the key paths for targeting user needs is to analyze search characteristics and look up the Baidu Index[①]. Baidu Index tells you about the search scale of a certain key word in Baidu, the trend of search of such word and the changes in public opinions relating to the word, the specific groups that are concerned about the word, where are they and what else have they searched. All these efforts help our users optimize their digital marketing plans.

For example, you search cellphones from Baidu Index, the affiliated hot words are Huawei, iPhone, AceDeceiver and 360. From Baidu Index, you can also look up

①

Baidu Index: a data-sharing platform based on massive netizen behaviors in Baidu, one of the key statistical and analysis platforms during the Internet era and even the whole data era, becoming an important basis for enterprises to make marketing decisions since the date of launching.

and search the number of people searching said key words as well as their gender and age constitution. Why should we review users' search behaviors? We need to analyze the consistency between users' anticipations and search results by tracking their search behaviors. If difference occurs, we need to conduct particular analysis on the difference by other means. There is an interesting case from a social network. A user inputted a key word—"apple". You can hardly know the user's real intent because "apple" can point to many things: a kind of fruit, a digital brand, or a movie popular at the time.

The user did not generate a valid click but searched a combination of words: "apple, Fan Bingbing". It is obvious that the user was searching a film named "Apple" which was popular at that time. But what is the user's purpose? to locate a cinema nearby? For behind-the-scenes look? To search the online video of the film? It is still unknown. However, it is clear that the user did not obtain what he/she wanted when searching "apple".

Then, the user searched another combination of words: "apple, Fan Bingbing, sexy". Now the user's intent is obvious. Nevertheless, such research will definitely achieve no result. At that time, Apple was completed from the Internet due to some pornographic pictures in the film. The user then changed from one key word to another, from Baidu web search to video search and then tried some other key words. Finally, the user searched "Yahoo" and then left.

Put ourselves in the position and figure out why the user searched "Yahoo". It is not difficult to image that the user was disappointed at Baidu search and turned to Yahoo to continue the searching. It was funny though. In 20 minutes, the user came back and continued to search key words and all that. What does that mean? He failed two in Yahoo search and finally gave up.

(3) Understand what users want better than they do. Many years ago, Henry Ford[1] said, "If I had asked people what they wanted, they would have said faster horses." Many user needs are merely the self-righteous needs, not the real needs. User needs require proper guidance. Users did not know their need for Facebook before it came out. User needs require

exploration, not only listening to their own descriptions.

Facebook is a U.S. social network website that went online on February 4, 2004, mainly founded by Mark Zuckerberg, an American.

Currently, Facebook is a world-leading photo sharing site. According to financial report of 2016 Q1, the scale of monthly active user (MAU)[2] reached 1.65 billion. Even such a globally established company has faced continuous user protests in the evolution process. We shall remember that in March 2009, Facebook released a large-scale revision that was based on status updating to compete with Twitter. According to the revision, information could be updated in real time and highlighted on the right of the screen. However, the revision triggered unprecedented protests from users. A total of 1.7 million users requested Facebook to abandon the revision.

Facebook made some minor adjustments to comfort its users, but the new design still went on. In October of 2009, Facebook redesigned the main page. It promoted an algorithm to sort status updating so that status updating would not be sorted only by time. Some designs removed earlier on came back, e.g., the acceptance of a friend request and the current status of relationship. In other words, Facebook did stretch a point to protests from users in March 2009. However, users were still unsatisfied. Over one million Facebook users requested that the original page design be restored. Some even asked Facebook to re-apply time-based sorting to the News Feed.

For each revision, similar disputes came as usual. Many people criticized Mark Zuckerberg's ignorance of user needs. According to the latter, changes are always accompanied by support and objection. Be it support or objection, it is always a beneficial feedback for Facebook from users. We can find out those we have never heard of and make adjustments accordingly. Such objection shows users' attachment to Facebook. That is why they propose advices. In some sense, the stronger the objection is, the more they care about the application. Silence, however, is different. Silence often means the downheartedness and despair, and the intent to leave.

① *Henry Ford (July 30, 1863-April 8, 1947): American automobile engineer and entrepreneur, founder of Ford Motor, first producing automobiles through production lines in the world. Ford's mode of production enabled the mass popularization of automobiles, not only revolutionized the mode of industrial production, but also greatly influenced modern society and culture.*

② *Monthly active user (MAU): users logging into a website/App/game, etc. at least once in a month, i.e., the de-weighed number of users instead of the summary of certain numbers.*

Zhihu: Share with the World Your Knowledge, Experience and Opinion

Zhihu is a real Internet Q&A community where the atmosphere is friendly and rational, the elites from all walks of life are connected, and the users share their own expertise, experiences and opinions to continuously provide high-quality information to the Chinese-language Internet. In May 2016, only five years after the launch of Zhihu in 2011, Zhou Yuan, founder of Zhihu, announced the latest achievements of Zhihu at the Zhihu Salt Club: 13 million daily active users, 5 billion monthly page views, a per capita visit length of 33 minutes, 10 million questions, and 34 million accumulative answers.

It is not difficult to see the target users of Zhihu from its name which in Classical Chinese means "Do

ZhiHu Program. Source: Zhihu Interface

you know?". The primary audience of Zhihu was disclosed in the Zhihu Salt Club: experts, college students, white-collar employees, entrepreneurs, and people who like to study, show themselves through their words, and make friends with big fish.

Zhihu has no incentive mechanism or material reward in any form, but user engagement is relatively high, with users including many real-name Internet elites, such as WeChat founder Zhang Xiaolong, and executives from the likes of Xiaomi and Baidu.

If Microblog and WeChat meet people's social needs, then Zhihu meets their two highest needs: esteem and self-actualization. In this elite community, in particular, where "there is no unlearned common man", when the questions answered are "liked" and "thanked" by elites and celebrities, the strong sense of satisfaction of higher level needs will be more effective than any other incentive.

The core function of Zhihu is sharing, and the premise of sharing is high-quality questions, preferably questions that will provoke your desire to answer and that you will repeatedly modify when answering, like writing an academic paper. You will get spiritual rewards from answering: it will build your reputation, and the more and better your answers are, the more people approve them, the more knowledgeable you will look. This is an exact match of the top need in Maslow's pyramid: self-actualization.

Source: Missed by Baidu,
What Does Zhihu Intend to Do after Obtaining
a Huge Amount of Finance?, Taishan Capital

III. Enhancing the sense of participation

Participation means to allow users to really get involved. Lei Jun, founder of MI, once said that "it is the sense of participation that MI sells to its users, which is the real secret behind the success of MI." There is always an empty chair at board meetings of Amazon. It is for their customers, who are believed to be an important member and shall be invited to take part in decision-making of the enterprise.

Li Wanqiang, joint founder of MI, mentioned in The Sense of Participation① that "in private, some friends often asked me what kind of magic MI had played to rapidly win reputation from socialized media? My answer was: firstly, the sense of participation; secondly, the sense of

participation and thirdly, the sense of participation. Word of mouth is the core of Internet thinking, which is in nature user's thinking and embodied by the participation of users. Then, why do we call general product consumers the users while those of MI the fans? The key is the sense of participation!"

In short, the actualization of the sense of participation depends on the following conditions.

(1) We need to develop and maintain product influence to gradually build up confidence of our users, who will believe that their products will be continuously improved. Such effort should be progressive. The participation in and witnessing

①

The Sense of Participation: prefaced by Lei Jun in his own hand and written by Li Wanqiang, joint founder of MI. The book reveals the concepts, approaches and cases behind the miracle of MI: 60 billion in four years. It is the most authoritative, thorough and comprehensive book on MI so far.

the growth of a product is extremely vital and attractive to our users.

(2) The lower the cost for users to participate, the better the result will be. Low-cost means include voting, making comments, following, etc., while downloading APP, QR code scanning, binding account to a cellphone number, etc. cost more.

(3) Give a reason for users to participate. There must be the value of participation, i.e., the satisfaction of a certain need of the user. There is always a reason for participation, whoever he or she is.

(4) The value and attraction of the product itself decide the willingness of users to participate. In consumption

 Case Study Bilibili: Danmaku

Bilibili is now the largest pop culture and entertainment community of young people in China. It was created on June 26, 2009 and is also known as "B site".

The greatest thing about Bilibili is the real-time comments overlaying videos which are called "danmaku" by fans. Viewers can comment and "tsukkomi" on any video at any time.

Such a unique sense of participation enables the real-time danmaku to overcome the time and distance constraints and construct a fantastic synchronistic relationship, forming a virtual tribal viewing atmosphere and making Bilibili a pop culture and entertainment community full of interaction and sharing, and secondary creation.

The case source quoted from: Baidu Baike2016/12/12
https://baike.baidu.com/item/bilibili/7056160?fr=aladdin

Case Study Baidu, Inc.

Baidu (NASDAQ: BIDU) is the world's largest Chinese search engine and Chinese website established by Robin Li in Zhongguancun, Beijing in January 2000 and committed to furnishing people with a "simple and reliable" means of information acquisition. Baidu takes its name from the "...Hundreds and thousands of times (the literal meaning of Baidu), for her I searched in chaos..." in The Lantern Festival Night to the Tune of Green Jade Table by Song-Dynasty poet Xin Qiji. This stands for Baidu's persistent pursuit of the Chinese information retrieval technology.

Baidu is a high-tech company that constantly innovates and makes its mission "to provide the best and most equitable way for people to find what they're looking for".

Baidu's mission: Provide the best and most equitable way for people to find what they're looking for.

Baidu's core values: Simple and reliable.

As the world's largest Chinese search engine, Baidu, upon the strong netizen search database, can have a clear insight into the consuming willingness and consumption pattern of netizens and becomes the ROI media platform that "knows consumers best" in China.

With the unique advantages of Baidu marketing platform, Baidu's brand marketing always centers on consumers, formulates the best Internet marketing solutions for customers, and strives to have the advertisements marketing appeals directly reach minds of consumers during the process of serving custom-

ers, to thus maximize the marketing ROI.

A Wall Street analyst said, "Despite impacts of the snow disaster around the Spring Festival, Baidu could still maintain excellent performance, which once again shows the scalability of Baidu's business model and that the Chinese enterprises regard Baidu as the online marketing platform for promoting products and services. In terms of Internet promotion and online marketing, Baidu's operating income has surpassed other competitors and it becomes the well-deserved king of Internet marketing in China."

According to Long Yongtu, former Secretary-General of the Boao Forum for Asia, Baidu has made important contributions to China and the world no matter in terms of the information retrieval for common netizens or the marketing for enterprises, "Chinese entrepreneurs can look for more partners of shared interest and even form a competitive community of shared interest via Baidu, which will guarantee the long prosperity of our Chinese enterprises and China's economy."

Shu Xun, Baidu's former Director of Enterprise Market Department, also shared his interpretation of the marketing way of search engines, "Baidu marketing can help enterprises better understand, find, and win customers; it brings enterprises a profound but silent marketing revolution, and is improving the marketing efficiency and marketing ability of tens of millions of enterprises to an unprecedented height."

The case source quoted from: Baidu Wenku2013/6/18
https://wenku.baidu.com/view/5000fe68a26925c52cc5bfd1.html

activities, value is measured by price. On many occasions, price affects value. MI has practiced the Daoruoji rules for brand building: affordability, utility, comparison and even some pride. Why would users wait if the product is just affordable?

The key is "comparison". Users of MI 3 may feel as proud as those using the gold version of the iPhone. For users, it is a pride to obtain something that is hard to get. This is the sense of glory that reflects from the participation of users.

 ## Socialized Thinking

I. What is socialized thinking?

Socialized thinking is a product of the mobile Internet era during which enterprises rapidly develop relationships with their users to promote their products through open platforms. In China, WeChat, Microblog and various forums are common social platforms. Whatever the product is, you only need to open an account on a certain social media, where you can release information about the product to attract potential users or interact with those interested in you. This is socialized thinking. In an age like this, when traditional enterprises are opening up to the Internet, great challenges are faced regarding how to enhance social attributes and functions in product design, user experience, marketing and other business activities.

II. How important is socialized thinking?

(1) Socialized thinking establishes brand reputation and value. We can present an amicable and communicable image on social media, build communities based on strategies customized to our "audiences" and discover and encourage brand supports to become "preachers" of the brand.

 ## Case Study   U.S. Presidential Election

The candidate who can maximize the potential of the Internet will stand out in the next presidential election.

—Eric Schmidt, former Google CEO

Twitter President: U.S. President Donald J. Trump posted the following tweet on November 9, 2016:

Such a beautiful and important evening! The forgotten man and woman will never be forgotten again. We will all come together as never before.

Trump posted the following Tweet on November 10, 2016: Happy 241st birthday to the U.S. Marine Corps! Thank you for your service!!

Source: Screenshot of Trump's Twitter Account

Trump posted the following Tweet on November 10:
A fantastic day in D.C. Met with President Obama for first time. Really good meeting, great chemistry. Melania liked Mrs. O a lot!

Trump's releasing news on Twitter has revolutionized the method of former U.S. presidents doing so by means of the present's press conference. Trump explained, "I can directly communicate with voters by releasing news on Twitter." Releasing news with social media is apparently a kind of disruptive innovation of the conventional press conference, and fully shows the revolutionary influence of social media on the president's external communication in the era of mobile Internet.

Source: Screenshot of Trump's Twitter Account

The case source quoted from: Huanqiu.com2016.11.14
https://news.sina.cn/gj/2016-11-14/detail-ifxxsmif3013224.d.html

(2) Socialized thinking creates greater value for consumers and improves sales performance of the enterprise. On social media, we actively listen to and monitor various dynamics, take remedial measures and provide convenience for consumers. High praise from existing consumers brings more customers, thus to cultivate a loyal consumer population at the same time of improving sales performance.

(3) Socialized thinking improves operation efficiency. It shortens the time span between production and selling, reduces production costs and offers the opportunity for try and fall.

(4) Socialized thinking enhances morale and creates company culture. We provide employees with social media training, allowing the latter to act as the "advocator" on social networks. We also feed consumer opinions back to our employees to improve their service quality. The biggest obstacle for a socialized enterprise is to allow the management at each level to really understand the significance of socialization for the enterprise.

III. Social networks & word-of-mouth marketing

Word-of-mouth marketing is a process in which the word-of-mouth concept is applied to every aspect of the field of mobile Internet marketing. That is, a word-of-mouth product simultaneously attracts attention from consumers, media and the public, who actively spread the brand or the product in a positive manner that describes features or advantages of the brand or the product. Meanwhile, the brand or the product is widely recognized by the public and becomes the topic of conversation among consumers. It is a bilaterally interactive act of spreading that, through third parties, transfers in an expressed or implied way the information about a specific product, brand, enterprise culture[①], manufacturer, dealer or any organization or individual suggesting aforesaid objects, so that the audience receives relevant information, changes his attitude and even his purchasing behavior. Word-of-mouth marketing delivers value through the chain of trust. It is a marketing mode and process that enterprises, by adopting varied means, lead the public to discuss about their products, services and enterprise images and encourage them to introduce and recommend products to their relatives and friends.

Word-of-mouth marketing sees big things from small ones, utilizing powerful momentum in operations—natural laws, policies and regulations, emergencies and even momentum from competitors. This mode of marketing is known for its high success rate and credibility.

Before the Internet, simultaneous word-of-mouth communication was considerably restricted in both speed and dimension. On one hand, word-of-mouth communication was often confined to secondary communication—your personal experience and information heard from friends (the so-called acquaintance world), which was a point-to-point form of communication; on the other hand, word-of-mouth was usually passive and subject to the stimulation in a specific context. For instance, a crowd of men are drinking together, and topics naturally come from one bar to another. In contrast, you will be puzzled if someone leaves you a message on WeChat at the office, telling you about a bar.

However, in the era of mobile Internet, social media undoubtedly becomes the main battlefield of brand marketing. The chain communication goes around so fast that enterprises today have to seriously consider the role of social media. Foodies share everything they think delicious into WeChat and Microblog, with some comments. Their friends, relatives and fans see such information, and those who are not friends with them may also search and find the information.

This is the value of the mobile Internet for word-of-mouth marketing. WeChat, forums, communities and Microblog have rapidly broken the traditional acquaintance world relied on by word-of-mouth in the past. In the traditional environment, word-of-mouth marketing could at the most influence those very close to you. When the open and interactive era of mobile Internet comes, your voice, theoretically, can influence netizens of the world.

① Enterprise culture: the spiritual wealth and material form with characteristics of the enterprise developed during the production, operation and management of the enterprise under certain conditions. Enterprise culture consists of cultural concepts, values, enterprise spirit, ethics, conduct norms, history, rules, cultural environment and products. Values are the core of enterprise culture.

IV. Popular social networks in China

Name	Website	Introduction
Sina Microblog	www.Microblog.com	A mainstream and very popular microblog product in China
Renren	www.renren.com	A real social network
Douban	www.douban.com	A network recommending, commenting and comparing prices of books, movies and music products as well as sharing unique cultural life in different cities
Tencent Microblog	t.qq.com	A Twitter-like website offering microblog services developed by Tencent
Qzone	Qzone.qq.com	A large social network in China and one of the core social platforms of Tencent
51.com	www.51.com	An influential blog community in China that provides personal blog and zone services
DATE	www.jiayuan.com	A dating platform aiming to establish serious relationships
Kaixin001	www.kaixin001.com	An online community to help you keep in touch with your friends
NetEase Microblog	1.163.com	Adhering to the idea of enabling everyone to become the center of attention and China's pulse
TAOM	www.61.com	A comprehensive interactive and entertaining platform for Chinese children

Popular social networks in China. Source: Compiled from O2O

1. Lay a solid foundation for your enterprise, brand and product via "endorsement" by authoritative media and celebrities

Authoritative media and celebrities should be those active on social media and blogs who can help to promote your information and brand. Jay Baer, a marketing expert, makes a good explanation of it and says, "Real influence not only raises prestige but also triggers actions." In today's world, consumers trust third parties more than enterprises themselves. It is a brand-new mode of marketing to transfer correct information to influential people. If operated in the right way, your enterprise may see an explosive growth.

 Case Study Wolf Warrior 2 Film

According to a successful person, every successful brand must have gone through careful marketing planning. The most successful planning can evoke people's emotions and is the emotional marketing.

In my opinion, the Wolf Warrior 2 film achieves success because it does best in emotional marketing!

According to recent information on Wolf Warrior 2, the film has achieved CNY 1.757 billion box office earnings by 19:00, August 2, 2017, 7 days after it was released. The film has broken many records in the history of Chinese cinema and made many A-share listed companies light up with pleasure.

Analysis on brand marketing planning of Wolf Warrior 2:

1. Momentum Borrowing Marketing

People who watched Wolf Warrior 1 know that it was a successful film with very good revenue, and many people wanted to watch it again, including me.

The success of Wolf Warrior 2 borrows the momentum of Wolf Warrior 1, as Wolf Warrior 1 would lead to association of Wolf Warrior 2 and make people who like it look forward to Wolf Warrior 2. As the saying goes, success is built upon success!

Momentum borrowing marketing is one of the brand marketing strategies of many big brands, and is nothing surprising; for example, Transformers and Kungfu Panda used such marketing.

2. Emotional Marketing

In my opinion, the most important factor for the success of Wolf Warrior 2 lies in the emotional marketing. Wolf Warrior 2 is very good at emotional marketing which is the cleverest marketing strategy.

Both Wolf Warrior 1 and Wolf Warrior 2 promote the patriotism of Chinese soldiers; however, the difference of the latter is that it is about how Chinese soldiers protect the people overseas, which is the sublimation of the emotional marketing of Wolf Warrior 2.

Who would give you the best protection if you were in foreign countries and your lives were threatened? Your motherland! You will be very proud when there is a strong motherland standing behind you.

In Wolf Warrior 2, when the people enter the Chinese Embassy, other armed forces stop advancing and attacking. Why is that? Because they enter the Chinese Embassy and there is a strong motherland behind them.

I believe that many people felt the same way and resonated when watching the episode as it stirred up the emotions of all the Chinese people.

Any successful marketing strategy cannot do without emotional marketing. If one can stir up the emotions of everyone, one will achieve the most success in the marketing.

3. Momentum Building Marketing

People who watched the trailer from director Wu Jing would hear the sentence, "filmed at the risk of his own life!" It is this sentence that has given many people a different perception of Wolf Warrior 2.

In the trailer, Wu Jing said of the crew's selection of a slum for the film location, "You would stumble across people pointing an AK47 at you in that place!"

Wu Jing's crew was robbed when filming there, and they risked their lives as they would be shot dead if they were not careful. In order to shoot the film, Wu

Ultrahigh Box Office Earnings of Wolf Warrior 2

"Almost Perfect Film" Hot in Cinemas and Public Opinion Field

✓ CNY 5.7 billion box office earnings, number one among the earnings of Chinese films

✓ CNY 357 million earnings reached in one day, a new record in the history of Chinese cinema of exceeding CNY 1 billion

✓ Nearly 90% of reviews positive or neutral, and 29.3% of Douban reviews five-star

Model for Chinese-produced war films / Total devotion of the international team / Superhero IP / Exciting theme

Negative 11.28%
Positive 45.16%
Neutral 43.56%

● Positive ● Neutral ● Negative

Source: Investment Data

Jing hired fully armed local security guards.

He really was risking his life when shooting the film. This is why, after watching the trailer, many of us are moved and want to support him.

The film has been quite a success, and is considered by many to be the best film of the past decade. In all seriousness, this is the best film I have ever watched.

To achieve a realistic effect, many scenes of the film were shot without use of any special effects, which making people feel it is perfect. This was the most important thing of the brand marketing planning. Its box office earnings have exceeded CNY 5.6 billion and are constantly increasing.

The case source quoted from: Sohu.com, Fan Zhe
http://www.sohu.com/a/161930801_571085

2. Optimized search marketing enables favorable information to appear on the homepage and thus enhances consumer confidence.

Properly edit Baidu Baike, 360 Baike (baike.so.com), Hudong Baike (baike.com), community contributions, Q&As, Microblog optimization, etc. to make favorable content appear on the homepage when a consumer is searching the key word of your products. More and more consumers are used to search for real information on Baidu. Thus the optimization of information on Baidu has become a popular method for an enterprise's word-of-mouth marketing.

If you want to buy something you are not familiar with, will you still buy it if negative information about the product—e.g., the product does not work; the product is of no use; service attitude is poor, etc.—appears on Baidu or other search engines?

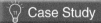 **Case Study**   SF Express

Established on March 26, 1993 in Shunde, Guangdong, China SF Express is a Hong Kong-invested express enterprise mainly operating international and domestic express business. Its business during the early days was same-day express business between Shunde and Hong Kong, and its service network extended to Zhongshan, Panyu, Jiangmen, and Foshan as customer demand increased. SF Express is one of the companies delivering the packages the fastest within China's express industry, and there is a saying, "Choose SF if you want packages to move fast".

If you searching for "how is SF?" on Baidu, the first result indicates that SF is currently the best express company in China both in terms of speed or service. Will you be more confident in their product when you see such information?

Source: Baidu Tieba

J&J: The Key to Overcoming a Crisis is a Product that Satisfies the Users

Some Johnson's baby products. Source: Official Website of J & J

In March 2009, a test report issued by a U.S. non-profit consumer organization said that the baby bath products of many companies including J & J and Pampers contained toxic substances such as formaldehyde and 1, 4-dioxane.

Soon, a netizen revealed in a post titled "J & J almost disfigured my 1.5-year old daughter" that her daughter's face was covered in a rash after the baby used J & J's moisturizer, and posted photos as evidence, which caused great response from parents all over China who claimed that their kids had the same situation. The child of a Changchun resident suffered anaphylaxis after using J & J's baby moisturizing

cream. The parent said, "The kid's face is swollen" and intended to sue J & J.

However, J & J had been stressing that the product had no safety warning issued and said that the product would not be removed from Mainland China shelves for the time being. According to relevant reports, the interviews at Beijing Walmart and Merry Mart found that there were few customers in front of J & J shelves.

According to a salesperson, few people had bought J & J's products since the report. Instead, many parents were asking about whether this brand's products were safe.

A consumer said that she used J & J's products herself and knew nothing about the harmful ingredients of J & J's products. After learning about the issues, she was surprised and immediately removed the body wash from her shopping basket, and said, "If J & J's products have problems in foreign countries, their products must be even worse in China. I'd better not use them." The online survey of ce.cn showed that 90% consumers were affected in terms of confidence, and nearly 50% consumers said that they would no longer buy J & J's products.

In the face of this product crisis, J & J failed to give a reasonable explanation to the netizens, so that there was intense questioning and criticizing from consumers which caused a negative impact to J & J's image in the Chinese market.

The case source quoted from: ifeng.com2011/1/13
https://wenku.baidu.com/view/4bed9e8b6529647d272852e2.html

3. Providing quality services to customers

A 2015 report shows that the probability for selling products to existing customers is 60–70% while for new customers, the figure is 5–20%. Thus enterprises shall put forth effort in customer services and transform them into fans who always speak of the brand. Presents and promotions are not sufficient for this. You need to consider how to treat your customers who have been supporting your business as well as how to communicate with them.

The procurement of a commodity by a consumer is not the end of the transaction. It is also the start of the "fan mode". After the first transaction, the user accepts and appreciates the product in the process of use and become attracted to it when enjoying associated services. Good services are often beyond consumers' expectations. Pre-sales consultation or after-sales services and maintenance, all play a vital role in affecting consumers and transforming

them into fans. Fans are affectionate. You never liked a person or a thing unconditionally unless there is emotion. Enhanced user services can emotionally conquer the fans who continuously create income for the enterprise.

4. Letting people comment

In word-of-mouth marketing, the nightmare is that consumers find it hard to leave any comments and suggestions or to communicate with others about your brand. Enterprises shall streamline the interaction between customers and the brand.

Word-of-mouth communication is the oldest form of advertisement, also the most effective one, being a critical information promoter in today's Internet-based and quick-pace world. It is different now, however. You need to think about how to attract customers with your products without the face-to-face contact.

When a marketing plan fails, you need to know what people talk about, what

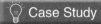

Like: a network term, means "approval" and "fond". The term comes from the "like" function available on online communities.

the latest news discuss about and what people share on social media. Whatever advanced technologies we have, brand owners need to know that it is people who they are dealing with. In other words, casting aside the number of fans, the number of likes[①] and other things that are pursued by everyone, we need to look at a deeper level—what are people talking about, and know well about people who can promote your business.

Case Study — Samsung Cellphone Explosion

Samsung cellphones mainly refer to the smartphones developed by Samsung Group. The A-series cellphones enabled Samsung cellphones to start to sweep the world. According to the market data counted by Canaccord Genuity, the sales volume of Samsung smartphones accounted for 23.96% of the total world sales in 2015, ranking first, followed by Apple with sales volume accounting for 17.2% of the total; in terms of profits, Apple still dominated with 90%, with the rest occupied by Samsung: the pattern of the two giants did not change.

Samsung launched its core product Note7 on August 2, 2016 in the U.S.

Several photographs of suspected Note7 explosions were posted on a well-known South Korean cellphone forum on August 24 which was then followed by at least 35 spontaneous combustion events of Note7 around the world.

On September 2, Samsung announced its recall of the 2.5 million Note7 cellphones sold across the world, but this excluded China.

On September 14, after being interviewed by the General Administration of Quality Supervision, Inspection and Quarantine of the P.R.C., Samsung announced the recall of 1,858 Note7 cellphones from China.

On September 18, a Note7 of the edition sold in China exploded, and Samsung said that the explosion was caused by external heating.

On September 29, a statement was released on Samsung's official website apologizing to Chinese consumers for not fully considering their feelings.

On October 11, Samsung recalled all the SM-N9300 Galaxy Note7 digital mobile phones sold in Mainland China, totaling 190,984 units (including the 1,858 units in the first recall announced on September 14, 2016).

For Samsung, one of the oldest smartphone manufacturers in the world and one of the few large manufacturers to have survived (the only third force that used to rival Nokia and Motorola), why did such a major product safety accident occur? This might be the worst accident throughout the history of smartphones. With more than 70 explosion and spontaneous combustion events around the world, and the serious heat, and burns caused to consumers, we could imagine what that meant to consumers: the cellphone did not simply affect consumers' use or cause monetary losses, it even threatened the safety of their lives.

Samsung started the global recall that was called the biggest disaster in the history of smartphones so far by Forbes, but its recall in Mainland China was 40 days later than other countries and regions. This sparked much furor. On the one hand, Samsung emphasized that it took the same measures for the Chinese consumers; but on the other hand, it acted differently.

For example, in the U.S., Samsung would contact consumers at the first opportunity and immediately compensate and pacify them. They stated that they would cooperate with investigation by the relevant U.S. department. In China, however, users who suffered the fourth explosion and fifth explosions of Note7 sold in China were still treated coldly by Samsung China. In the first recall, Samsung recalled cellphones sold in countries other than China.

According to the 2016 Q3 financial statement issued by Samsung Electronics on October 27, 2016, its net profit was down by 16.8% and overall operating profit was down by 30%; while three months ago, its Q2 financial statement showed that Samsung Electronics achieved the highest quarterly operating profit over the two years. Samsung's market share also fell out the top 5 in China. According to data of Gartner, the global smartphone shipments reached 373 million units in Q3, growing by 5.7% year after year, with the growth mainly contributed to by Chinese manufacturers, including Huawei, OPPO, and BBK (including Vivo and OnePlus). According to data from IDC, in terms of global market growth, Huawei, OPPO, and Vivo became the minority to achieve rapid growth in the market, far ahead the 1% growth of the overall market share in the world.

A netizen shared an experience on the Internet the other day: At a counter selling Korean juicers in a department store, a woman aged about 50 was looking at juicers and she asked the salesperson, "What is the brand?" "Korean brand. All our products are imported from South Korea, with guaranteed quality," answered the salesperson.

The woman was astonished and said with a disgusted expression, "South Korea? Will they explode like the Samsung cellphones?" The salesperson was lost for words.

Good reputation can spread all over the world in the era of the mobile Internet, so can a bad one. In this product recall event of Samsung, the product's spontaneous combustion itself firstly had a very negative impact on consumers; and secondly, Samsung treated Chinese consumers differently in its global recall of the defective product, severely hurting the feelings of the Chinese people, and directly leading to the repeated decline of the market share of Samsung cellphones in China.

Source: Samsung China is Said to Lay off 20% Employees, Note7 is Called the "Worst PR Case"

5. Promoting virus-like spreading through topical events

By nature, topical events are information worthy of disseminating or having high entertaining value planned by brand owners themselves or by entrusted planning companies based on brand/product characteristics, which is spread on social platforms and ultimately in a virus-like scale.

6. Keep participating in communities

People never stop talking about Red Bull because the companies are always organizing activities for them to take part in. For example, Red Bull's Wings Team drive an eye-catching car with the mark of Red Bull and distribute samples to people on streets, aiming to promote the reputation at the same time of creating fun; Student Manager New Star Competition—a campus brand of Red Bull—sponsored activities of students around the campus so as to establish the reputation of the brand; Red Bull's Dormitory Band Program organized various shows to exhibit talents of students and establish relationships with students; Red Bull's Reporter Program sponsored students majoring in news and movies to create stories and thus to popularize Red Bull's brand.

These activities allowed people to participate and improved public praise for the brand, making it a real leader in the market.

📖 Case Study   Nike's Response to Liu Xiang's Withdrawal

The Chinese athlete Liu Xiang fell and withdrew from the 110-metre hurdles in the London Olympics. Within half an hour of this, Nike rapidly responded through its microblog by taking the opportunity of the Chinese people's collective grief for Liu Xiang's failure. Within 24 hours of being posted, this microblog was reposted 130,000 times and received more than 26,000 comments. Nike's highly creative response was very timely and much accorded with the feelings of the Chinese people. Liu Xiang's sponsors included Nike, Coca-Cola, Amway Nutrilite, Yili, Lenovo, and Tsingtao Beer. After that event, Coca-Cola and Tsingtao Beer passed positive energy on their official microblog accounts: the attention they gained, however, was less than Nike. This was because Nike had been well prepared: it launched the complete marketing program "Find Your Greatness" in the world in that summer.

The brand information contained in the "Find Your Greatness" was quite flexible since athletes are "great" regardless of whether they win or lose.

This simple but powerful brand information is designed only for encouragement. Both this brand positioning and the spokespeople selected could stimulate the resonance of consumers and encourage them. Nike succeeded in enhancing the brand image and good reputation with this event of Liu Xiang's withdrawal.

An enterprise which pays no attention to good reputation will be defeated by bad reputation. The characteristic of good reputation communication is that products of poor quality will have no market, and only fine products, therefore, will win out. Enterprises should depend on the masses, conduct constant iteration and improvement, and achieve the ultimate for the products to win a good reputation and users, and to thus form the positive cycle; otherwise, it will be a vicious circle that leads to loss of users, good reputation, and everything.

The case source quoted from: iwebad.com2012/8/10
Case address: http://www.100ec.cn/detail--6102275.html

Extreme Thinking

Product extremity is the precondition for successful mobile marketing. We may start from mottos of some famous entrepreneurs to understand the concept of extreme thinking. Steve Jobs's motto is "Stay Hungry, Stay Foolish". Tian Suning, a Chinese entrepreneur, interprets it in a more Chinese way. Lei Jun, CEO of MI advocates that "to do extremity means to drive yourself crazy and others to death".

I. Craftsmanship spirit

Craftsmanship spirit

Source: People's Daily online forum

In 2016, the term "craftsmanship spirit" became very popular in China with the convening of the Two Sessions. For the first time, "craftsmanship spirit" appeared in the Government Work Report. In the Report, it said that "three aspects shall be highlighted in improving product and service supply: quality of consumer products, upgrading of the manufacturing industry and acceleration of the modern service industry. Enterprises are encouraged to carry out customized and flexible production to increase the variety, quality and brand reputation through the cultivation of the excelsior craftsmanship spirit."

What is craftsmanship spirit? The term of "craftsmanship spirit" reminds me of the Zhaozhou Bridge designed and built by Li Chun, a famous craftsman during the Sui Dynasty. The bridge has just one large span (37.4m), being the longest stone arch bridge at the time and having a history over 1,400 years. The bridge has survived eight earthquakes, eight wars, pedestrians and vehicles coming and going, numerous floods, countless snows and rains.

The craftsmanship spirit is indispensible for such a great achievement. By definition, craftsmanship spirit is the combination of industry, dedication, modesty, capability, obedience, scrupulousness, adhering to principles, meticulosity and excellence.

Why do we call the craftsmanship spirit? Rand had spent two decades in tracking 500 world-famous companies, finding a common virtue among those surviving a hundred years: in value, human beings exceed things, the common exceeds the individual, the society exceeds the profit and the user exceeds the production. Man is the subject of creating social wealth and pushing the wheel of the history. Man is the core factor for an enterprise, and the path to getting out of trouble in sales is to cultivate the "craftsmanship spirit". Craftsmen continuously polish their works and improve their techniques, enjoying the sublimation of their efforts to the products. Enterprises pursuing the "craftsmanship spirit" see the process of continual improvement and perfection of their products and ultimately exist in a form that meets the stringent requirements of themselves. Statistics show that there are 3,146 Japanese enterprises having survived over 200 years, followed by Germany (837), Holland (222) and France (196). Why do these enterprises get together in these countries? They all have inherited one sprit—the craftsmanship spirit. Craftsmanship spirit is not just a slogan. It lies in every one. For a long time, our personal paths of growth were bumpy and rugged and our enterprises stumbled because we lacked the adherence to, pursuit of and accumulation of quality. Such deficiency makes it extremely difficult to continuously innovate. Ever green enterprises are thus a rare breed. In modern times when resources are increasing scarce, the raking up and re-development of the craftsmanship spirit is our only way to survival and development.

Case Study   Hermes Spirit of Craftsmanship

Originally a harness shop specializing in making the exquisite supporting ornaments for carriages on the street of Paris, it has now become a world luxury brand with 14 product ranges.

It has adhered to handwork and delicate work for over 170 years and is still interpreting traditional beauty and precision.

It is Hermes, a family luxury brand passed down through six generations, which has conquered the world with classics and high quality.

The legend of Hermes began in 1837 when carriages were the main means of transport. Hermes was a horse lover who understood horses and harnesses. He saw the value in making harnesses and thought that decorating horses of the nobility with superior leather would be good business. Hermes opened a small shop named after him on the busy Parisian street of rue Basse-du-Rempart. His harness workshop made various delicate accessories for carriages, with Hermes harnesses seen on the most beautiful wagons in Paris at that time. Hermes craftsmen worked on every product with the great care of artists, leaving behind them many masterpieces. Hermes won first prize in the 1867 Exposition Universelle for exquisite craftsmanship.

For more than 170 years, six generations of Hermes have devoted all their energies and zeal to leather, undertaking the deepest exploration in the world of leather, making quality leather glow with a poetry and elegance through professional handicraft, and persistently adhering to the handicraft family's pursuit of perfection.

Hermes and Guo Meimei became famous in China overnight. The leather bag with prices from CNY 80,000 to more than CNY 1 million became a means of showing off wealth on Microblog and appeared in many "showing off" microblogs besides that of Guo Meimei. A photograph with Birkin bags of different colors placed on a flight of stairs was even widely circulated.

Why does Hermes so fascinate and drive people crazy? It is because of the spirit of craftsmanship.

Every style of Hermes bags is taken full charge of by a craftsman, from the selection of leather, to cutting, sewing, hardware mounting, and finally to the unique code engraved on each bag.

The leather selection before manufacture is extremely rigorous. Even a tiny bitten wound that is hard to distinguish will lead to rejection of the leather by the craftsmen.

In terms of detail, Hermes would make 10 straps from the same colored leather, and select the best one for the bag, with a good strap generally requiring 3.5 hours to make. Each Hermes bag has a code containing a letter and an Arabic numeral on the back of the metal bag buckle: the former indicates the year of production and the latter indicates the identifying code of the craftsman who made it.

There are more than 90 colors and materials available for the Birkin bag. Different kinds of leather ranging from rare leather such as alligator skin, lizard skin and ostrich skin, to common calfskin and goat skin are used on bags.

In terms of craftsmanship, Hermes sublimates the original leather into the art of life by tanning, laundering, finishing, repairing, and sewing. Every Hermes leather product undergoes over 200 complex processes. It displays its charm to anyone who touches it through its unique, elegant and ingenious design, tough and precision sewing, and soft and delicate feel.

Source: New Channel

II. Best services, another form of marketing

Best thinking means to achieve the ultimate for products and services and provide the best user experiences that are far beyond their expectations. In competitions of the era of mobile Internet, the winner takes all. Only extreme good can win over the consumers and their loyalty. Behind the best product, there are enormous efforts and inputs. Every piece of such product is thoroughly tempered.

 **Case Study**   Differentiated Services of Haidilao

Why are so many people attracted to Haidilao? Is it because of the unparalleled taste? No, Haidilao hotpot tastes great, but this is not the main reason for its popularity, and in an industry like the hotpot industry where everyone has different tastes, it is very difficult to become the number one in the mind of everyone. Many people feel that the hotpot of Shujiuxiang and Spice World tastes better than that of Haidilao, and it is only the latter's better service which makes it the industry benchmark. As we know, many other companies in the service industry have organized their employees to experience Haidilao. Haidilao only does something that is not seen in its industry, i.e., differentiated services such as manicure, shoe shining, and complimentary snacks before the meal. Satisfying customers can be called a good job for many enterprises, but Haidilao does not stop there. For them, reassuring customers is third-level service, satisfying customers is second-level service, and moving customers is the first-level service. Only by moving customers can these customers become fans of the enterprise and always support it. Service

Source: Official Website of Haidilao

is its biggest when the market competition becomes so increasingly fierce that the quality and variety of many products reaches extreme homogeneity, what else can lead to the differentiation between enterprises? What else can an enterprise differ from others? Only service can achieve this.

What is the biggest competition in the 21st century? Some say it is the competition of talents, some say it is the competition of products, while others say it is the competition of knowledge, but Haidilao tells us that service alone is the biggest competition in the 21st century, because only the service can create the biggest differentiation.

Zhang Yong insisted on capturing he hearts of customers with a sincere attitude in his early years operating Haidilao.

As Zhang Yong sees it, service is the biggest weapon for Haidilao's success and the most powerful weapon in his competition with its rivals. In fact, Zhang Yong eventually achieved the appearance of Haidilao across China because of his adherence to the purpose that only service can satisfy and move customers, with "service paramount" being the foundation of Haidilao through the years.

The highest level of service: from satisfaction to moving.

Before entering the store: queuing.

After entering the store: there is an iPad with a self-ordering system on every table which will automatically display the menu and total price after customers order, with the data transmitted to the waiter/waitress via a real-time network. Completion of ordering is very easy.

Netizens have summed up the service of Haidilao as, for example, the waiter/waitress will kindly remind you that you have ordered enough when you order too much; they will suggest you order half a portion if you do not have many people eating with you; waiters/waitresses are quick and ready to answer any questions; if you dine in a private room, there will be a designated waiter/waitress to serve you; if there is a pregnant woman in your party, a Haidilao waiter/waitress will specially compliment a dish of pickle with a big serving; when a customer mentions that he particularly likes certain free food of the store, the waiter/waitress will immediately box up an individual serving for him to take away... These services do not only satisfy Haidilao customers but also surprise and move them as they are not available in other restaurants.

There is a joke in the Internet that there were some people who did not finish the fruit bowl with watermelon that was served to them after they finished dinner. They asked the waiter whether they could take away the watermelon they had not eaten, but the waiter said no. This is in fact a common practice in restaurants; however, this waiter ended up giving away an entire watermelon after the people checked out, saying that it was unhygienic to take back the cut watermelon. He, therefore, gave them the entire watermelon. This is why every time I dine at Haidilao, I want to...

Source: You Can't Copy Haidilao, Huang Tieying

III. Simplicity, another name of extreme good

Google is a seemingly simple website, once mocked by society after launching that it was a waste of the precious homepage, as most Internet enterprises paid much attention to their homepages. As they believed, a simple homepage design as that of Google would never escape the fate of failure. However, visitors who have long been surrounded by multicolored websites are attracted to it, for it is visually simple and operationally convenient. The simpler the website, the more power the users will feel from it. It is such a wonder that you can search for hundreds of millions of websites within 0.1 second on such a simple page.

As simple as the website appears, there are astounding databases and technical support standing behind: internationally advanced and unique operation search technology, dozens of billions of website data in databases, and the support from thousands of up-to-date high-performance servers.

Sometimes, a simple appearance implies a complex and precise inside. Simplicity means to highlight what should be highlighted and weaken what should be weakened and to visually indicate the significance of high-priority tasks by proper grouping and layering. Anyone who has dealt with Apple can say that a "simple" method is usually not simple. To achieve simplicity, people need to spend more time, money and energy. Simplicity is never crudeness or being mindlessly understood as "less". Complexity has origins in

MUJI. Source: Official Website of MUJI

Founded in Japan, MUJI means "no-brand quality goods". Although downplaying brand awareness, all its products, which are produced by following the unified design idea, interpret MUJI's brand image, and the natural, simple, and plain lifestyle is highly praised by people with high taste.

One of the biggest characteristics of MUJI is minimalism. Its products have no trademark, unnecessary design, or unnecessary processing and colors, and are so simple that they have only materials and functions. It is difficult for customers to find its brand mark on all MUJI items, except the brand signboard and mark on paper bags. Customers hardly see any bright colors except the red "MUJI" box, as most products have a dominant color of white, beige, blue or black.

The design idea of MUJI inherits the traditional simplistic aesthetics of Japan. Its design is so simple, plain, and peaceful, and production is so elaborate that nobody needs to worry about the bad influence on them when using its product in public.

Instead, MUJI becomes a carrier for them to honestly demonstrate their attitude toward life.

Cores of simple thinking:

1. Concentrated, less is more

Be concentrated with product line planning. This means concentrating efforts on achieving a breakthrough in a certain period to accomplish one thing. Concentration is also required for brand positioning. You just need to give the consumers a single reason to choose you.

2. Simplicity is beauty

Subtract in terms of product design: the appearance should be simple, and the internal operation process should be simplified.

The case source quoted from: Reorganized based on materials on MUJI's official website
https://www.muji.com.cn/

simplicity, as that "intelligence emerges" when the simple accumulation like the swarm of bees or the shoal of fish reaches a certain degree. An extremely simple guidance can create incomparably complex and delicate systems through evolution.

Big–Data Thinking

Faced with rapid technological development, more and more enterprises have realized that continuous wealth only comes from the acquisition of correct data and the thorough understanding of what's behind these data. The Era of Big Data comes, leading the new pace of the world with sonorous and powerful rhythm.

I. What is big data?

In *Big Data: The Next Frontier for Innovation, Competition, and Productivity* by McKinsey Global Institute, the definition for "big data" is given as below: big data refers to the rapid growth of data that is beyond the ability of traditional databases and software tools in terms of data acquisition, storage, processing, and usage.

Big data, by definition, is the data set that cannot be acquired, managed and processed with traditional software within a specific period of time, a kind of massive, highly growing and diversified information asset which needs new processing modes to actualize powerful decision-making power, perceptivity and process optimization. In *Big Data* of Viktor Mayer-Schonberger and Kenneth Cukier, big data implies the abandon of the shortcut method (the random analysis method, i.e., spot check[①]) and the processing of all data. Big data are usually characterized by 5Vs (proposed by IBM): Volume, Velocity, Variety, Value and Veracity.

The strategic significance of big data does not lie in the obtaining of massive

① Spot check: a means of non-comprehensive research that takes certain objects from a whole group objects of research and estimates and infers information of the latter based on partial examination.

information, but in the professional processing of these meaningful data. In other words, by comparing big data to an industry, the key to realizing profits of the industry is the improvement of data "processing capability", that is, to "add the value" of data through "processing".

II. Big data are essentially the estimate on the direction of product development

What is the role of big data? According to the definition given by Claude Elwood Shannon, the fundamental purpose of data is to provide the basis for decision making and minimize uncertainty. Both individuals and organizations are facing uncertainties for the future and in unknown areas. Despite such uncertainties, individuals and organizations have to make decisions on a daily basis. Due to such uncertainties, some decisions are obviously wrong in the current view. Nowadays, people make decisions mostly based on feelings, following the trend and personal experiences. Only a few of them base their decisions on objective data analysis. Massive data provide us with a more reliable basis for decision making. If there is a magic wand that can eliminate all uncertainties and thus minimize the errors in decision making, how much will it be valued? Big data estimate the possibility of events by applying mathematical algorithms to meaningful data. For example, it estimates the possibility of a mail being discarded as junk mail or the possibility of misspelling "teh" for "the". In the near future, many areas currently depending on man's judgment will be changed by big data. In today's world, JD recommend books for us, Baidu ranks associated websites, Toutiao delivers to us our favorite news, Microblog knows about our preferences and Taobao, which is even stronger, knows about the consumption trend of China.

III. What composes the value chain of big data?

By source of value (data, skills and thinking), big data companies are usually divided into three categories.

Some companies have their own massive data and are capable of extracting data value and thus nursing new ideas, e.g., the Alibaba Cloud big data and Tencent big data analysis.

Some other companies are founded based on data. They own, or at least are capable of acquiring, massive data. However, they are not the optimal either in extracting data value or in nursing new ideas. Take Twitter as an example. Twitter

---

 Case Study

Unbelievable: Few Chinese Know China's Consumption Tax Rate

Table of Consumption Tax Rates:

I. Cigarettes: Fixed tax rate for each standard case (50,000 pieces) is CNY 150; for the standard carton (200 pieces), the tax rate is 45% for those with transfer price above CNY 50, and 30% for those with transfer price below CNY 50; the tax rate is 25% for cigars; tax rate of 45% is applicable to other imported cigarettes and hand-rolled cigarettes, etc.; the tax rate is 30% for cut tobacco.

II. Wine and alcohol: the tax amount standard for every 500g of grain spirit is: CNY 0.5 + ex-factory price x 25%; of potato spirit is: CNY 0.5 + ex-factory price x 15%; tax amount standard for yellow rice and millet wine is: CNY 240 per ton; tax amount standard for beer is CNY 250 if the ex-factory price is above CNY 3,000 per ton, and is CNY 220 if the ex-factory price is below CNY 3,000 per ton; the tax rate for other kinds of wine is 10%; the tax rate for alcohol is 5%.

III. Cosmetics: the tax rate is 30%.

IV. Skin and hair care products: the tax rate is 8%.

V. Gold and silver jewelry: the tax rate is 5%; other jewelry and gems: the tax rate is 10%.

VI. Fireworks: the tax rate is 15%.

VII. Gasoline: the tax amount per liter of unleaded gasoline is CNY 0.2, and of leaded gasoline is CNY 0.28.

VIII. Diesel oil: the tax amount per liter is CNY 0.1.

IX. Automobile tires: the tax rate is 10%.

X. Motorcycles: the tax rate is 10%.

XI. Automobiles: the tax rate is separately 3%, 5%, and 8%.

This is what is so awesome about big data.

The case source quoted from: Baidu Tieba 2011/02/24
http://china.findlaw.cn/jingjifa/caishuifa/cszs/swzs/45099.html

owns massive data, but such data will be authorized to two other companies for use. The rest are technology-based companies, usually in the fields of consultation, technology supply or analysis. Such companies are professional but have no massive data. For example, Teradata is a large data analysis company whose marketing data come from two retailers: Wal-Mart and Pop-Tarts.

Case Study
Tencent Issued the 2016 Internet Entrepreneurship and Innovation White Paper

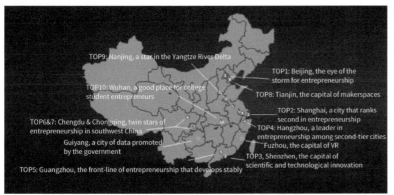

The Map of the Top 50 Cities. Source: tech.qq.com

Tencent Research Institute and Tencent Open Platform issued the 2016 Internet Entrepreneurship and Innovation White Paper in 2016 Tencent Global Partner Conference, which is 160 pages and nearly 100,000 Chinese characters in length, acquired authoritative data of the industry and Tencent Company, and comprehensively analyzes the current situation and future picture of global innovation and entrepreneurship as well as results in promotion of China's "mass entrepreneurship and innovation" from five dimensions: entrepreneurship economy, global entrepreneurship situation, situation of mass entrepreneurship and innovation in China, 2016 Tencent opening strategy and developer ecosystem, and Internet entrepreneurial drive mechanism. The White Paper forecast that the number of makerspaces possibly exceeds 4,000 in China by the end of 2016. The map of the Top 50 cities by entrepreneurial energy in China was issued, wherein, Beijing, Shanghai, and Shenzhen ranked among the "first-tier".

The White Paper also forecast that the number of makerspaces would possibly exceed 4,000 in China by the end of 2016; the scale had developed from over 50 to over 2,300 during 2014-2015 alone, growing by 46 times. In terms of positioning, makerspaces are mainly divided into education and training type, investment and financing service type, new real estate type, media extension type, industrial ecological resources sharing type, and government-led type, evolving from single services to multidimensional services, and gathering resources and services like basic service, enterprise service, policy resources, development funds, social platform, growth guidance, platform technology, network traffic, and media resources, to create total-element entrepreneurship service ecosystem horizontally and vertically.

The White Paper summarized the ripple model and innovation interaction system that would promote implementation of the mass entrepreneurship and innovation strategy, covering over 30 elements on four layers: entrepreneurship subject layer, service operation layer, innovation ecosystem layer, and policy environment layer. It showed the innovation interaction system with makerspace as the platform and gathering subjects including the state and local governments, big enterprises, operation enterprises, and start-ups; this system has the core objective of growth of entrepreneurship subjects, paves ways for entrepreneurs' development by service operation, sets up the growth environment for the construction of innovation ecosystem, and further solidifies the foundation by using the policy environment, to gather strength for mass entrepreneurship and innovation.

The case source quoted from: tech.qq.com, Shanyun Liu 2016/09/22
http://tech.qq.com/a/20160922/026189.htm

Open Thinking

At the entrance to mobile Internet are humanism, evolution and openness. An ecological circle has been formed, the root of which is an open mind. Earth will change once you open your mind. Just as Apple encourages music fans to "select, edit and burn[①]", self-makers also start to "select, modify and create". They conduct 3D-scanning on materials, modify them with CAD formula and then make the products using 3D printers. This is what an open mind can lead to.

①

Burn: to record (also burn) data to a disc using a recorder. Currently there are two types of discs: CD and DVD.

I. Traffic priority

Phil Libin, CEO of Evernote, once said that the simplest way of making one million people pay is to obtain one billion users. Said one billion users must be free users. This is where the value of Internet traffic lies. It is obvious that traffic realizes information spreading and thus resulting in traffic deals. Traffic means mass, and mass means component.

"Where the eyes are laid, wealth follows." Traffic is the money, the entrance.

The value of traffic is self-explanatory. QQ, a chatting application of Tencent, owns hundreds of millions of users because it is free, which leads to the income from Q-coins and varied memberships. It is the early-stage free services that bring revenue through further transformation. Therefore, a huge traffic means a great value. There must be sufficient users to guarantee a great purchasing power.

II. Crossover cooperation

Cross-border marketing is an emerging mode of marketing that integrates and extends seemingly unrelated elements based on the generality and connection between industries, products and consumers having different preferences, so as to demonstrate a different attitude towards life, aesthetic sentiment or concept of value and thus to win favors of targeted consumers and maximize both market share and profit as a cross-border enterprise. Cross-border marketing means the breakdown of traditional marketing thinking patterns, avoidance of sole competition and seeking for non-industry partners so as to achieve the coordination among brands of different categories. In nature, cross-border is the explanation of characteristics of the same user based on multiple brands and from multiple perspectives.

With the development of Internet and high technologies, pure physical economy starts to integrate with pure virtual economy, leading to more and more ambiguous boundaries between industries. Internet enterprises are getting in by every opening including the fields of retail, manufacture, books, finance, telecommunication,

entertaining industry, traffic, media, etc. Cross-border marketing, an overturn phenomenon for Internet enterprises, is essentially the combination of lower efficiency by higher efficiency, which includes structural efficiency and operational efficiency.

When Internet crosses the border to the clothing industry, we see HSTYLE; when Internet crosses the border to roasted seeds and nuts, we see Three Squirrels. Under the influences of cross-border thinking, the only thing that will ultimately appear is Internet enterprises, because by that time, all enterprises will have been Internet enterprises.

Cross-border products of well-known brands always drive the fans crazy. Have a cup of coffee at Versace; buy some clothes at Starbucks; have a dinner with friends at Chanel's restaurant; take a yacht trip with Armani; drive an LV sedan... It will no longer be asking for the moon with more and more brands extending their businesses into other fields.

On the strategic cooperation news conference of Tencent Game Carnival on December 9, 2016, CrossFire officially announced the IP cross-border cooperation with Zippo, an internationally recognized artwork and collection brand and launched the first CF-authorized and customized Zippo lighter. As the most popular gun shooting game in China, CrossFire has over 500 million registered users, with the peak on-line population exceeding 6 million, having long reached the top of the pyramid in China's domestic game market. Lying behind the cross-border cooperation with Zippo is the unique advantage due to the IP authorization open-cooperation mode by CrossFire and the long-term development and maintenance of its own IP value.

Crossover Cooperation. Source: China Public Security (CPS)

CrossFire has made a good start by cooperating with Zippo. Attributed to the open-cooperation IP strategy, there will be more authorized partners joining the progress of enhance IP value of CrossFire. It is not only a protection for IP, but also an enjoyment for players at different game culture levels. Since then, China Merchants Bank introduced the Tencent Game joint credit card, aiming at users fond of games.

Some luxury brands are also attempting cross-border operations and flock together into mass consumption fields such as hotel, restaurant, café, etc. Gucci has opened two cafés, separately in Florence, Italy and Tokyo, Japan. Chanel also opened its Beige restaurant in Japan's Ginza. Hermes has set up a café in Seoul, South Korea. From architectural style to tissues, everything at the café conveys the sense of design consistent with the brand. At the end of 2008, Prada opened its Double Club near Angel Subway Station in London.

Core contents of cross-border thinking are

(1) Have the users in hand to oppress other enterprises. Why can these Internet enterprises participate in and even win cross-border competitions? The answer is simple: users. On one hand, they possess massive user data; on the other hand, they think like their users. No wonder why they can have the users in hand to oppress other enterprises. The application for banking business by Alibaba and Tencent, the manufacture of cellphones, TV sets, rice cookers, etc., are done in the same way.

In the decade coming, China's business industry will see massive "robbing". The "granary" of large enterprises may be faced with such "robbing". Faced with fundamental changes in people's lifestyle, those who cannot keep up with the situation and carry out reform will meet their predestinated fate.

Ma Yun once said, "if banks do not change, then we change the banks." On June 17, 2013, Alipay—a brand under Alibaba—officially launched Yu EBao in cooperation with Tianhong Asset Management. By buying this product, Alipay users transfer money into the product, which means they have subscribed for Tianhong Zenglibao fund and will enjoy the profits from this monetary fund. Users can transfer their funds from Yu EBao or directly pay with Yu EBao, considered the redemption of corresponding shares of Zenglibao fund. Besides, funds in Yu EBao can be used for online shopping, charging the phone and making transfers at any time. As of June 30, 2016, Yu EBao had attracted over 300 million users. According to Wang Dengfeng, Fund Manager, as of December 18, 2016 (i.e., three years, six months and 6 days since the foundation of Tianhong Yu EBao), the daily net redemption of the product never exceeded 1%. During the "Double 11" Online Shopping Festival in 2016, Yu EBao achieved net subscription, of which the "stability" went beyond the expectation. As the fund manager of Yu EBao, Tianhong and Ant Financial have their own large-scale data analysis team that constantly analyzes the flowability of Yu EBao funds and estimates the subscription and redemption behaviors in the next month. The estimate error is constrained to around 1%.

(2) Innovate boldly and subversively with Internet thinking. Both traditional and Internet enterprises need to actively embrace changes and innovate boldly and subversively, which is an inevitable requirement of the times.

A genius individual must have cross-border thinking where he can find his own coordinates at the junction between science, technology and culture. A genius enterprise must possess user and data resources, have its maneuvers, and dare to make cross-border innovations.

By not crossing the border, someone will cross the border to rob you; by not crossing the border, someone will make you "derail".

Micro-innovation Thinking

Zhou Hongwei, CEO of 360 Security Guard, brought up a clear direction on the Forum on Internet Grassroot Entrepreneurship and Employment during the 2010 China Internet Conference, "innovation of user experience is the key to the popularity of an Internet application. This is micro-innovation."

① Micro-innovation: the 2010 Forum on Dreamer-Internet Grassroot Entrepreneurship and Employment, a secondary forum of the 2010 China Internet Conference, was held at Beijing International Convention Center on the August 19th. Zhou Hongwei, CEO of 360 suggested on the forum that Internet grassroot entrepreneurs be dedicated to "micro-innovation". "All companies shall base themselves on 'innovation'. For entrepreneurs, innovation is critical. So how to understand 'innovation'? Some say that I'm a small player, I'm grass-rooted, therefore I have no breakthrough technologies or the capability of overturning the industry. I personally learned recently that a new mode of innovation have appeared, that is, micro-innovation. It may be something valuable for grassroot entrepreneurs. I believe that micro-innovation is a key approach to product innovation in the future."

Micro-innovation① leads the new trends and waves of Internet. 360 has experienced a series of micro-innovations during its development: anti-hooligan software, junk file cleaning, user's definition for infamous software, replacement of Trojan killing by patching, etc. Each of these functions was highly demanded in the market at that time. However, no one except for 360 was willing to realize them because "lacking impressive technology", and 360 seized the opportunity. Zhou Hongwei explained micro-innovation in a specific product saying that "micro-innovation means to continuously make minor improvements with user experiences in consideration. Maybe such minor improvements have no immediate effects. If you insist on it, if you improve by 1% and even 0.1% on a daily basis, the effect will be great after a quarter."

I. Product life cycle

1. Product life cycle (PLC) is the market life of a product, i.e., the entire process from the entrance of the product into the market to its elimination from the market. The theory of product life cycle was first proposed by Raymond Vernon, a professor of Harvard. Vernon believes that just like man, a product has its own life. Each product experiences the stages of exploration, growth, maturity and senility, as shown in Figure 4-2.

(1) Start/exploration: sales grow very slowly when the product starts in the market. There is almost no profit due to the enormous cost for the product to enter into the market.

(2) Growth: the product is rapidly accepted by the market and the profit increases significantly.

(3) Maturity: sales growth slows down because the product has been accepted by

Regarding micro-innovation of 360 Browser, minor improvements are made continuously so that those not good at computers feel free to use the browser without difficulty.

"For example, what can Youjiantong, :Microblog Prompt, E-Bank plug-in do for users? On one hand, there are things that are impossible for users to find out in time, and we need to make sure they do; on the other hand, let's talk about plug-ins②. Take the E-bank plug-in for example. Many users are not used to it and even ignore the yellow warning at the top of the browser. For them, the plug-in become useless. Later we developed a new function. Once the E-bank homepage appeared and no plug-in was detected, a dialog box was popped up, asking the user if one-click installation was required. The user only needed to confirm and those necessary were installed."

most potential buyers. In this stage, increasingly fierce competition leads to gradual stability and even reduction in profit.

(4) Senility: sales show a stronger declining trend and profits keep falling.

Philip Kotler provides us with a diagram about a product life cycle in *Marketing Management*. When we speak of product life cycle, we usually mean the following four aspects:

(1) A product's life is limited.

(2) Product sales experience several stages, each bringing different challenges to the seller.

(3) Product profits fluctuate in different stages of a product life cycle.

(4) A product requires different marketing, financial, manufacturing, purchasing and manpower strategies in different stages of a product life cycle.

② Control: the encapsulation of data and methods. Control can have its own attributes and methods. Attributes are simple visitors of control data. Methods are some simple but visible functions of control.

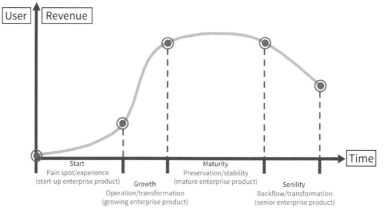

Figure 4-2　A product's life cycle. Source: Marketing Management, Philip Kotler

He further explains that semi-automatic washing machines are eliminated due to the emergency of fully automatic washing machines.

However, this view of point is being challenged in the era of mobile Internet. If a product inevitably heads toward a decline, I wonder, considering the highly precise electronic watch timers produced by Japan, when will Swiss watches such as Rolex, Omega, etc. that are not so precise step down from the stage of history? Drinks emerge endlessly, then when will Coca Cola and Pepsi retire? KFC and McDonald's have been selling a few popular products for decades, when will they leave the stage?

Actually, in most cases, it is these outdated theories that bad-mouthed the product and the brand. As shown in the following figure, a complete product life cycle consists of product R&D and market development, growth, maturity and instability stages (instability may imply both decrease and increase). Innovation is the only way to maintain the growth in the stability stage.

Continuous innovation and the following of trends in the era of mobile Internet make an enterprise survive and continue to grow even in the maturity period.

2. A product may die, but innovation never will. We are often caught off guard by changes in the era of mobile Internet. It is not a literary exaggeration or a psychological feeling, but the objective reality. Changes, rises, upheavals, eliminations, all are too fast for us to perceive. A cellphone bought this year becomes an antique in the next year. Today's emerging industries become traditional ones tomorrow. Stronger and stronger technical advancements will greatly speed up the life cycle of a product, that is, the "close to zero" of product life cycle. We can figuratively speak of it as "with birth there is death; with death there is birth". Think about our first three cellphones. What is their average life of use? How about the last three cellphones? This phenomenon is well explained in The Innovator's Dilemma. Technical advancements are shortening product life cycle, then what will happen if a product life cycle is "close to zero"?

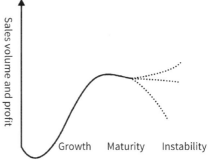

Product R&D and Market Development.
Source: Hongbing Hua, One Degree Strategy

As Zhang Xiaolong said, "Products are in continuous evolution. We'll never know what they look like in six months. All plans are cheaters." Zuckerberg said something similar, that "Products are never completed." Thus we view products more like a continuous process. Since the Internet emerged, we have seen too many updates and eliminations. Hundred-year enterprises fell apart in just a few years. And this may be just a beginning. In years coming, the world will see unprecedented industrial restructuring, during which traditional enterprises will be impacted in an unheard-of manner. Emerging enterprises will not take the lead for decades with only one trick. Elimination occurs in a single day if we ignore and stop innovation. Enterprises emerge continuously, but innovation never ends.

II. Product iteration

"When you're finished changing, you're finished", said Benjamin Franklin. Lei Jun, CEO of MI, once mentioned that "On the path to success, we need rapid iteration and continual error testing. This is the dominating rule of the Internet era." Iteration thinking adapts us to changes of the Internet based on something remote. That is, the product iteration process applies to every product. Fastness makes one remain invincible. Products have their own shortcomings after coming out, which need continuous improvement in the following stages.

Aim and shoot. Keep improving. Fail fast and fail cheap. Enterprises shall establish an inclusive culture that treats failure friendly and properly.

Traditional business thinking focuses on comprehensive and thorough control. Decision-makers usually take full consideration of every aspect of a problem and resort to all resources, which makes "fastness" impossible. Traditional enterprises conduct R&D, launching and updating of products round by round. Consumers can hardly remember a brand or product without several years' experience. In contrast, trotting and rapid iteration are features of the Internet era. Decisions are made on a weekly basis.

III. Overturning innovative thinking

Overturning innovative thinking leads to the process from quantitative change to qualitative change, from gradual change to ultimate overturn and from existing pattern to a brand-new mode and chain of value on the basis of traditional innovation, disruptive innovation and micro-innovation.

China Merchants Bank (CMB) is the first joint-stock commercial bank completely held by an enterprise entity in China, founded on April 8, 1987 by China Merchants Group, currently being the sixth largest bank in mainland China and one of the "Eight Banks and Five Insurance Companies" listed at HKEx, headquartered in Futian District, Shenzhen. On April 9, 2002, A-shares of CMB were publicly listed at SSE. On September 8, 2006, CMB went public in Hong Kong, during which a total of about 2.2 billion H-shares were offered, collecting a capital of HKD 20 billion. On September 22, CMB was listed at HKEx. It has a net capital of more than CNY 290 billion and total capital of more than CNY 4.4 trillion.

CMB has set up 113 brands and 943 sub-branches in over 110 cities across mainland China, 1 branch-level specialized institution (the Credit Card Center), 1 representative office, 2,330 self-service banks, one branch in Hong Kong (Hong Kong Branch), one branch and one representative office in New York, one branch in Singapore and representative offices in London and Taipei. In mainland China, CMB wholly owns CMB Financial Leasing Co., Ltd. and China Merchants Fund, holds 50% equity of CIGNA & CMB Life Insurance Company Limited and wholly owns Wing Lung Bank and CMB International in Hong Kong.

In March 2013, CMB launched the credit card WeChat customer service. In July of that year, CMB launched the first "WeChat Bank" in China, which extends the scope of business from credit card services to all-customer comprehensive services including debit card and credit card. The platform provides the functions of transfer, cellphone charging, appointment, etc. The WeChat service of CMB nearly replaced 90% of the conventional customer service functions of the bank and greatly relieved the stresses of customer service that annually increases by 50%. Besides, the hit rate of auto reply from the WeChat official account of the bank has reached as high as 98%. Within just two months, the number of WeChat followers of CMB exceeded one million. The WeChat official account of CMB also topped the list of seven WeChat accounts officially recommended by WeChat. As of the end of March 2014, CMB WeChat had served over 10 million users. The number of WeChat friends exceeded 8 million, which is still growing today.

Consumers can rapidly handle their businesses through WeChat. It may only take half a minute, such half a minute is fragmented and consumers can handle businesses whenever they want. Every consumer enjoys efficiency and convenience, which perfectly embodies the instantaneity of WeChat. Besides, the WeChat official account is operated based on artificial intelligence interaction. Man can never achieve the precision of a computer. Such smart and precise operation guarantees point-to-point services and eliminates errors usually occuring in manual services and thus avoids lots of complaints. We can use the words of "convenience, fastness and precision" to correctly describe CMB's WeChat services. When these factors are considered and realized in the best way, the loyalty to and utilization rate of the WeChat official account are consequentially high. Thus, it makes sense that there are as many as a million customers who prefer the WeChat services.

China Merchants Bank Website. Source: Information publicized on CMB's official website

Regarding cost saving, the WeChat official account is the most valuable for CMB.

Regarding cost saving, the WeChat official account is the most valuable for CMB.

In recent years, CMB and other service enterprises are witnessing rapid growth in their customer population and volume of transaction, but their own manpower remains the existing structure. In this environment, existing manual services can no longer meet customer needs. Service staff receive more calls as the result of increased transactions. Business development necessarily brings tress to services.

In addition, when China's demographic dividend dribbles away, increased manual cost leads to higher service cost. All these factors are enormous resistance for the development of an enterprise.

According to statistics, the quantity of call service of CMB is about 60 million each year. As for the banking industry, the cost for one service call is about CNY 5 (including manual cost, site cost, water and electricity fees and communication fee).

It is easy to calculate that the expenditure of CMB on call services is more than CNY 300 million each year. If the WeChat official account undertakes 30% of the business, a total of nearly CNY 100 million can be saved. The cost for text services can be saved as well. CMB has about 20 million credit card users, each of whom receive over 20 service text messages each year. The payment for each text message is CNY 0.03 for large companies such as CMB who has cooperative relationship with communication carriers. Thus, the bank can save nearly CNY 10 million each year with the introduction of the WeChat official account.

 **Case Study** | **P&G**

Founded in 1837 and headquartered in Cincinnati, Ohio, the U.S., Procter & Gamble (P&G) is one of the largest consumer goods companies in the world and is a joint-stock company with nearly 110,000 employees around the world. It is a Global 500 firm and occupies half of the Chinese market of the daily chemical industry.

There are different products under P&G, from soap, toothpaste, mouthwash, shampoo, conditioner, softener, and detergent, to coffee, orange juice, baking oil, cake mix, and potato chips, to toilet paper, facial tissue, sanitary napkin, cold medication, and stomach medicine, crossing over cleaning supplies, food, paper products, and medicines.

Its marketing and brand strategies have been included in various textbooks. P&G is in fact a classical product of the big industrial age. The so-called big industrial age was an age in which people's demands were uniform, and products were all neatly planned from material procurement, to design and production, to advertising, to placing, and to after-sales customer service, and then penetrated every corner of people's lives through standardized mass production.

P&G is the product of the "big production + big retail + big placing + big brand + big logistics" of the industrial age; like the Ford Model T, when one cheap and fine product of P&G was produced, it would reach national consumers through national advertising and national placing, and consumers did not need other choices. In a sense, companies like P&G and Ford played a historic role in the progress of human society, as they allocated social resources with the highest efficiency and served the society to the maximum.

P&G, however, cannot take control of the situation in the Internet era. According to the U.S. MarketWatch report, the 2015 Q4 financial statement issued by P&G showed that the company achieved net profits of USD $521 million during the report period, largely down by nearly 80%; the quarterly revenue was USD $17.79 billion, down by 9.2% year on year, which was lower than the USD 18.06 billion expected by the Wall Street.

According to the 2016 Q2 performance, the sales of P&G declined sharply in the Chinese market. According to the performance of the latest quarter (2016 Q3) ending March 31, 2016, its sales only grew by 1% in the Chinese market, not considering impacts of factors like exchange rate. The net sales of this company declined to USD $15.8 billion in the three quarters, with profits of USD $2.7 billion.

A giant company like P&G must restructure its products in the Internet era where everything is starting to become out of control. According to report, P&G suffered performance decline in the global and Chinese markets; P&G has been trying to turn this situation around since 2014, focusing on less and fast-growing brands. P&G had sold 50 brands by 2015, including the well-known VS, so as to simplify its investment portfolio and place emphasis on product lines that grow faster. However, P&G's performance has still not improved. P&G opened its cross-border e-commerce in the Chinese market in 2015 in the hope of taking back its eroded share through cross-border e-commerce.

Source: Qdaily

Story Thinking

I. What is a product story?

A product story is a "brand story". In short, it is the cultural connotation given to a product in addition to its functions so as to enrich the inside information of the brand. a product story arouses sympathies from consumers in vivid, funny and touching expressions.

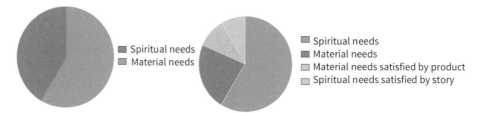

The Proportion of User Needs

> *Emotional experiences: psychological experiences driven by emotion. People feel the happiness as well as the hurt of romantic love. Love can be so sweet that you feel like soaking in the honey pot; love can be so bitter that it breaks your heart.*

The industrial age carries functions while the Internet age carries fun and emotion. As Steve Jobs said, "Apple has always tried to be at the intersection of technology and liberal arts". Functional attributes are necessary for a product, but emotional attributes have become the standard configuration for an excellent product. We are perfectly happy to pay a high price for an iPhone not because it has more functions than other cellphones. We are paying for the aesthetic feeling from the excellent design and experience. Now let's move on to Huawei and MI. Huawei pursues functionality and technology. Ren Zhengfei once said that communication, image and operation system are the most important functions of a cellphone, which is obviously the logic of the industrial age. MI, as an Internet enterprise, makes cellphones exceeding the users' expectations not only in terms of functionality, but also the emotional attributes such as "exclusive for fanciers", "self-improvement", "cool", etc. Such products bring strong emotional experiences which are far beyond the commercial value of the products.[①] That is the victory of emotional experience over functional experience.

Emotional products are personalized and become a "charming person". An Internet brand is the conspiracy among the founder, the products and the fans. The company CEO acts as a spokesperson and fans act as the bees that immediately spread the products around as long as they are the best. Another exceedance occurs once marketing is integrated with products. "I've been learning from Microsoft in the past two decades. It emphasized marketing, but I think there is no marketing at all for a successful company. Good products are the best marketing", said Lei Jun.

II. Why tell product stories?

Here is a Jewish teaching story: Truth, naked and cold, had been turned away from every door in the village. Her nakedness frightened the people. When Parable found her she was huddled in a corner, shivering and hungry. Taking pity on her, Parable gathered her up and took her home. There, she dressed Truth in story, warmed her and sent her out again. Clothed in story, Truth knocked again at the doors and was readily welcomed into the villagers' houses. They invited her to eat at their tables and warm herself by their fires.

The story exists in real life, too. A common featured British woman, divorced, lived on subsistence with her child. Suddenly, ideas came and she started writing. Today, the payments for books written by her have exceeded USD one billion, more than the assets of the British Queen. She has earned incomparable copy fees and her books have been printed in 450 million volumes, only second to the Bible and Selected Works of Mao Zedong.

Warner Bros made her stories into movies. This movie series soon became the highest-grossing series in the global movie history, with a total box office reaching USD 7.8 billion. This is J.K. Rowling and her *Harry Potter* books (see Figure 4-3).

People are born to love stories and to voluntarily spread stories. When racking our brains to preach our brands to consumers, we might as well tell them a story. As a matter of fact, a successful brand knows how to tell stories. For a brand planner, telling stories is essentially a wise strategy of communication. It combines creation, EQ, consumer psychology, ability of expression, neuroscience and a lot of other fields. A good story helps the brand to convey information more efficiently and is convincing. Enterprises need to tell good stories not only to sell products, but also to allow their consumers to accept their concepts.

Enterprises become humanized, more multi-dimensional and vivid when telling stories, attracting consumers to communicate with you emotionally and thus to take actions and want to know more about your enterprise. When learning about the entrepreneurial story of a company, the changes brought along to customers' life by a company or the special experiences of an employee or partner, you will feel the same way: you will feel as if emotionally tied to the company in the story. Story is a form of organization information that is the easiest for human brains to accept. A heart-winning leader not only has excellent insights and objectives, but also tells good stories to touch and persuade others to accept his insights.

Figure 4-3   An illustration of J.K. Rowling and her *Harry Potter* series.

"If you want build a boat, do not hire people to collect wood or assign them any tasks. What you need to do is to inspire their longings for the sea. To inspire their longings for the sea, you need to tell them a story about the sea."

Psychological research shows that vivid and emotion-inducing stimulations enter into the mind more easily and are better processed by the brain when coding. A good story arouses intensive emotions of people, be it affection, sadness, wild joy, anger or fear. As long as it is strong, such emotion can easily generate memory.

💡 **Case Study**   **King of Glory**

King of Glory is very hot, with daily active users exceeding 50 million.

On the bus which took me home during the Spring Festival, I took out my cellphone and opened King of Glory, ready to play some rounds. Interestingly, there was the familiar "Timi" sound of this Tencent game, here and there, now and again around me. Then I noticed that there were several people playing the game.

Thus, I began the topic with "You are also playing King of Glory" and added each other as friend to start to play the game.

King of Glory has gradually become a new way to socialize and the common choice of 200 million young people who have something in common to talk about so long as they love this mobile game.

For half a year, I have been discussing this mobile game on Microblog and WeChat moments, showing that its popularity is not transient. King of Glory is more than hot, as can be seen from Baidu Index and App Store data.

So here comes the question: how did King of Glory come to be so hot? The highlights discussed below can also serve as reference for the operation method of other games.

To put it simply, in my opinion, there are three main reasons for why King of Glory became hot: good timing, good product, and good promotion.

I. Right time window

With the development of the mobile Internet and intelligent hardware, the mobile game industry in China experienced insane growth in 2014 through to rationality and maturity in 2016, the market gradually changed from incremental market to stock market, the "entrance dividend" almost disappeared, and the competition in the mobile game industry became more intensified, with product differentiation being not big.

It is difficult to reproduce the phenomenon of a game, after being roughly made, rapidly going live to make a quick buck. Instead, the high quality and blockbuster mobile games will be loved by players, behind which, the deeper reason is players' changing demand and increasingly higher requirements for product quality.

The MOBA mobile game: King of Glory happens to have the attributes of a blockbuster and high quality, with multiplayer online battle as the core, and emphasizing both sociability and competitiveness.

II. Ultimate game experience

1. Four points of the core MOBA game

The first is the playing method: the pace of the game is fast, and it is highly competitive. A game takes about 15-20 minutes and tests the team command, leading pace, and team battle cooperation. Those player behaviors are based on the desire for victory, and have players deeply experience the tension and stimulation of e-sports.

In addition, the playing method is diverse. There are different playing methods for different heroes. Every game is a fresh battle, making it relatively difficult to grow bored. The maker irregularly provides updates with new heroes or skins so players always sense its novelty.

The second is balance: MOBA players are very concerned about whether the game is green and whether they would be crashed because other players spend heavily on the game.

Meanwhile, it is crucial as to whether the matching mechanism is appropriate to match comparable teammates and opponents so all players compete fairly and impartially.

The Third is honing in: the team of the maker constantly hones the game with the spirit of craftsman, including regulating the basic attributes of each character, and has the game graphics, role design, and dubbing reach the ultimate level so players feel their heart.

Four is sociability: As a multiplayer online battle arena (MOBA) game, the game trend is determined by whether there are friends to team up with. No Friends equals No Fun.

And the friend relation chain has been the point which Tencent is best at.

Not only can you play with WeChat friends and QQ friends, but also you can invite nearby players based on LBS.

2. Introduction of spread motivation design

For the spread of the game, besides strong support from the marketing department, it is very important to think about how to have players recommend and share, and to introduce the spread motivation design in the game in order to depend on good reputation and players' mutual recommendation and sharing.

One core point of spread motivation is to give users the opportunity to show off, to have a sense of achievement.

Many people have never played a MOBA game before; their achievements, therefore, are not good and it is easy to lose them. How to also get them to have a sense of achievement?

King of Glory is very good in that regard. There will be cool and shining screenshots if a player is the best player, has a winning streak or levels up in the game to make them feel very good!

There will also be different achievement tags like best player, fashionista, winner in life, team elite, and complete victory obtained during the game. These will be displayed in the information about players to bring the sense of achievement and fun to them.

3. Easy playing starting and low barriers of participation

Initially, King of Glory was not the only MOBA game in China: there were also games such as We MOBA, Fight for Freedom, and Glory. Most of the MOBA games in China learn from LOL; however, mobile games are not as complex as client games, and it is difficult to simplify and improve them for the mobile terminal.

The advantage of King of Glory lies in the ease of getting started compared to other MOBA mobile games. Even if you had never played a MOBA game before, you would feel that this game is easy when you first start to play it and you will wonder if your opponent is merely a primary school student.

The case source quoted from: Jianshu
http://www.zuixu.com/gl/a/5939.html

III. How to tell product stories

Of all time, a story is widely the oldest form of organizing information. In the era of mobile Internet, a story is also the most popular form of organizing information on social media that attracts users to experience and interact.

As mentioned before, a marketing story is essentially a wise strategy of communication. Marketing talents must realize it so that they will not mix brand stories with other fields similarly highlighting the skill of telling stories, e.g., fictions, screenplays, news writing, etc. You need not to conceive a long story. A 10-character copy or a 2-minute short video can tell a story as well.

1. The KISS principle

The KISS principle originates in David Mamet's movie theories, meaning "Keeping it Simple and Stupid", being the highest realm for user experience.

To understand it in a simpler manner, a product shall be made so simple that even an idiot can use it. Thus it is called the "lazy principle". In other words, "less is more". This theory has been widely applied in product designing as well as storytelling.

Psychological researches reveal that human minds are selective for information processing and will get tired of complex information and shield them out of habit. Human minds prefer simple information.

The Distillation Principle

2.   The distillation principle

Most advices for storytelling are about building stories from the exterior to the interior. There are many examples in literatures or screenplays, such as the "Eight Elements Method": context, trigger, exploration, accident, choice, climax, reversal and solution. It is a misconception that you think you can make up a good story just based on these elements.

Sometimes, saying too much will weaken the influence of a story. A good story comes from a "distillation" process and your task is to extract complex information into a wonderful and attractive story.

3.   Archetypal psychology

Carl Gustav Jung, a Swiss psychologist believes that "Archetype" is sort of motif, a common symbol of human culture under collective unconsciousness. There are always some characters or types of characters repeatedly appearing in different stories. Psychologists have developed six archetypal concepts from the evolution of archetypal psychology: orphan, vagrant, warrior, altruist, innocent and magician. If we observe closely enough, we'll find that many famous stories grow out of these concepts.

Human emotions are varied and changeable, but most of them can be hit by these concepts, as they originate in the psychological experiences deposited and inherited by our ancestors since the ancient times.

Let scholars do the research on plot types and perfect story lines. We, the market players, shall focus on transmitting emotions through stories. Emotions make thoughts and expressive information alive. Just as colors and shapes, emotions are critical components of experiences of our audiences, adding details into their memories and imagination.

4.   The sense principle

Mark Twain, a famous American writer, once proposed a rule for writing: "Don't say the old lady screamed. Bring her on and let her scream." Psychological researches show that stories are coded in human brain areas responsible for social and emotional activities—cerebral limbic system[1], amygdala and those areas trusting senses in brain, not those working to remember symbols, numbers and letters. In this regard, numbers and languages are far less representative of the fact than memories and images.

In marketing, we need to know how to motivate the senses for human beings to understand the world—smell, taste, hearing, touch and vision—so as to simulate influential experiences. If, for the first time, you hear the story that "one woke up in a bath tub full of ice blocks in Las Vegas, finding his kidneys gone", you can almost feel the cold of the ice blocks in the bath tub and the click of ice blocks when he stood up, as if you can see the hand-written note left by the criminal, asking him to call the hospital as soon as possible. Such a story, full of sensational details, makes people feel immersive even before they begin to doubt its credibility.

①

Cerebral limbic system: a key component of the brain and playing a vital role. Current researches show that it is related to several neurological and psychological disorders including AD, epilepsy, schizophrenia, depression, etc. The proper understanding of the system facilitates us to better identify brain functions and relevant disorders.

IV. What kind of product stories to tell

What kind of stories are we telling? In brand stories, the brand concepts are implanted so as to express and spread the brand highly effectively. Never underestimate the energy and role of a good story. A good story disseminates the core appeal or reputation of a brand so that people can spread the story in multiple channels and with multiple means, feel about the brand value implanted in the story and voluntarily spread it. So, how to tell a good brand story?

1.   Stories of leaders

Most brand stories are related to legendary brand founders. Some brand stories are even the chronicle of entrepreneurial events. Although there are numerous brand stories, those having only one sentence often concentrate the cultural

Source: Ma Yun's interview, compiled from information released by Hangzhou West Lake Mingzhu TV

①

Positive energy: a kind of motivation and emotion that leads one to be healthy, optimistic and active. Today, Chinese people label "positive energy" to all people and things that are positive, healthy, inspiring, encouraging and full of hope. This term has sublimed to an emblematical symbol, tied to our emotions and expressing our deepest longings and expectations.

deposition of the brand, stimulate the resonation of the consumers and lead to word-of-mouth spreading.

Many enterprise leaders have notable stories. Enterprises shall learn to explore their stories. Such stories may not be so magnificent. Some of them may be details in work and a nearly eccentric pursuit, which are of great value to the brand.

In September 2014, on the occasion of the listing of Alibaba, a piece of news was widely spreading, which later produced profound influences, on the Internet: Ma Yun shouted at those stealing a manhole cover and asked them to put it back. In a speech, Ma Yun said, "It was back in 1995. I went to work on bike, seeing some guys stealing a manhole cover on Wener Street. I could not play kungfu and they were much stronger than me. I could never fight them. Then I rode on my bike, looking for help or the police. About five minutes later, I didn't find the police. I thought of the manhole cover. Some days ago, a kid fell into the manhole and drowned. I didn't think it a minor matter. I returned to the scene, on my bike, shouting at them and asked them to put it back. They stared at me. I might have run away if they came at me. Anyhow, I boosted my courage and, again, asked them to put it back. At this moment, someone came. I told them that someone was stealing the manhole cover. We must stop them and put it back. I got excited before I noticed the camera aside. It was a test by them (the TV station). Someone told me that I was the only one who passed the test that night. It is pretty interesting, I think. Sometimes change happens in the world. If you don't act, such change will not be yours. If you act, you may be the beneficiary of the change" (words of

Jack Ma in an interview with Hangzhou Xi Hu Ming Zhu TV station in 1995).

The old interview video of Ma Yun became popular on Microblog. People greatly praised the "positive energy①" and never forgot to ridicule Ma Yun: Look at what he had achieved today. It must be promising to be a loser with a feeling for justice. This video tickled many people on Microblog. Someone teased that Ma Yun's first appearance in the public eye "was to maintain the justice for human beings". Others said that Ma Yun's act was "adorkable". Many others commented that "this was the spirit" and "success was not by chance".

Since then, Ma Yun became a person with a feeling for justice, brave to stop and disclose people and things causing damages to the society or enterprises. Alibaba has developed exactly under the influence of Ma Yun's personal characteristics and Ma Yun himself became a moving billboard of Alibaba. Another example. Chucheng Orange told a story about the old but vigorous Chu Shijian, bettering other numerous orange suppliers; Wang Shi told a story about hill climbing and thus saved 300 million's advertisement for Vanke...You can imagine the impact. Enterpreneurs' stories are unique and non-copyable. Touching and inspiring stories can easily move the consumers, deeply impress them and arouse a heart of admiration.

As a result, telling stories of people, of founders and operators, can create unique genes of a brand and characteristic brand personality.

2. How to tell product stories

Telling product stories shall highlight product quality. Many people may have not noticed that Google has changed its logo in low profile. The change is so subtle that most people cannot discern: the "G" and "L" are slightly displaced (see Figure 4-4).

But the title "A change not discerned by 99.9% users" inspired people's interest to find the change. Everybody wants to be the 0.1%. Thus, a change becomes a story, and a story becomes a kind of propaganda. Google tells the story also intending to present its meticulous and excellent image. In the past, it cost a lot for enterprises to tell stories: layout on paper, time schedule in TV commercial, etc. It is not so available as it is now. In the Internet times, media is everywhere. If you want to, your enterprise can develop a "private plot"—We

Media. We can tell stories on Microblog, WeChat, Taobao pages, APP... So what are you waiting for?

Product problems are inevitable for all enterprises and brands. One of the typical cases in China is the refrigerator crisis of Haier[①], a well-established Chinese brand for home appliances. Haier destroyed all defective refrigerators, no matter what the defect was. It was unimaginable for Chinese consumers who had been used to industry and economy and the idea of "not too bad". Zhang Ruimin told the story loudly, and the effect was visible. Consumers believe that Haier will learn lessons and become more confident in its products.

Google
Google

Figure 4-4   The Google logo change.
Source: information publicized on
Google's official website

Thus, to tell a good brand story, enterprises need to focus on products themselves, considering both quality and innovation.

V. No blind imitation in product stories

For the moment, many enterprises begin their "story marketing", making a great whoop and a holler. Others rush their heads into action, asking "masters" for advice and find stories to match up with their businesses. As a matter of fact, the marketing stories of many enterprises are nothing but blind imitations and ugly performances.

Case Study   The Story of Zhang Xiaolong and His Products

The Founder of Wechat-Zhang Xiaolong. Source: Reorganized based on Business magazine

In this age, the one that can best represent the extremism of product managers is "the father of WeChat", Zhang Xiaolong. The great success of WeChat makes Zhang's product development process seem like a Hollywood thriller.

At the initial stage, Zhang implemented a rigorous "1,000/100/10" rule, requiring every product manager to check 1,000 user feedbacks on forums, reply to and follow 100 user blogs, and survey, analyze and study 10 users every month.

Zhang has an interesting summary that a hundred-million-user-level product manager does not have to make thorough consideration of all aspects of humanity and the product, but must strike a balance between Zhang's aesthetic principle of seeking balance in extreme opposition is just a prominent feature of the mobile Internet product managers.

According to him, the age of the mobile Internet is changing so fast that the old product analysis mode has been outdated. Product managers should rely on their intuition and sensibility, rather than diagrams

---

1,000/100/10

Rule

Every product manager must check 1,000 user feedbacks on forums, reply to and follow 100 user blogs, and survey, analyze and study 10 users every month.

1000/100/10 Rule from Zhang Xiaolong. Source: Reorganized based on Business magazine

Haier's refrigerator crisis: in 1985, Zhang Ruimin was a new arrival of Haier (then Qingdao Refrigerator Works). One day, a friend wanted to buy a refrigerator. He chose among many refrigerators and lots of them were defective. Finally, he was able to pick one. When the friend left, Zhang Ruimin ordered a thorough inspection on over 400 refrigerators in the warehouse. 76 were found with varied defects. Zhang Ruimin convened the workers at the workshop and asked what they planned to do. "If I permit the sale of these refrigerators, that means I permit you to produce another 760 defective refrigerators in the future." He announced that all these refrigerators should be destroyed by whoever made them. He personally took a hammer and started the process. Many workers were in tears. Zhang Ruimin told them that defective products are nothing but wastes. Three years later, Haier was awarded the first golden prize for quality by the state for the industry of refrigerators.

and analyses, to grasp the user demands. Product managers should always be literary and artistic, but not rational.

It is indeed so. The "free texting" of WeChat 1.0 did not touch the pain spot of the users at all. Chinese people cannot exhaust the monthly message package provided by their operators. WeChat 1.2 turned to "picture sharing", with little market response, failing its expectation of "mobile social contact dominated by pictures". Usually, product managers would give up by this time.

It was not until WeChat enabled free calls through the "voice communication" in Version 2.0, that the market was ignited and the number of users saw explosive growth.

The WeChat with voice function undoubtedly took a share from the operators. It is said that Chinese operators expressed their complaints of extreme realism and extreme idealism. Simple beauty should be the focus of a product, satisfying the "desire, hatred and ignorance" of the users. Beauty is greed.

Even though this kind of balance has contradictions, if you must connect arts with utility, you must rebalance the aesthetics and benefits. According to Zhang, if the relativity therein is removed, contradictions will no longer be seen.

Through the senior management of Tencent, many people tried to persuade him to quit, but Zhang chose to ignore their request. Maybe history is indeed created by madmen. We say that the mobile Internet product managers must be mad, because the principles on product creation are widely divergent. The product creation in traditional marketing should satisfy the user demands and the feelings of the suppliers, banks and operators; in a word, you should create "a commodity that satisfies everybody".

Zhang likes the song "A Million Tons of Faith" by Wang Feng. "Don't believe in TV ads. Don't believe in rankings...Don't wait for the good people's help. The good people are digging the coal... You can believe the worst things. They happen around us every day. You need at least a million tons of faith, so that you may manage to live on..."

We can appropriately guess that Zhang stuck to his will and hope while listening to that song and overcame all the difficulties. With the resolute passion, he blended the humanity, art, and philosophy in his opinion on WeChat.

When the competitor of WeChat, MiTalk, "naively" thought WeChat was going to plagiarize its successful doodling function, WeChat 3.0 unexpectedly provided "People Nearby" and "Shake". Now MiTalk has already disappeared.

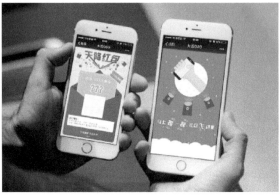

Shake a Red Packet In 2015 Spring Festival.
Source: Reorganized based on materials published on the WeChat official website

"People Nearby" provides WeChat with access to the data of QQ and mail users. This powerful promotion with direct purpose brought the number of WeChat users above 20 million, establishing the leading position.

"Shake" is another practice and copy of Zhang's lonely experience. The act of shake, the rifle sound from CS, and the picture of naked David upon the split of the page are all designs after repeated tries of Zhang's team. Details blended in design aesthetics, their combination must meet the feelings required by Zhang, paying respects to Freud and arousing "sexual impulse" or "ecstasy".

During the 2015 Spring Festival, "Shake a Red Packet" of WeChat became an overnight sensation. From 9:00 a.m. the day before the Lunar New Year's Day, WeChat began to encourage the users to shake a few of random red packets, blessings, and interactive pages through the CCTV News Channel, preparing for the Spring Festival Gala in the evening. At 22:30, with the advertising of the mascot "Yangyang", the users ushered in the climax of "Shake a Red Packet". According to the official data of WeChat, between 20:00 and 20:42, the total number of shakes exceeded 7.2 billion; between 22:32 and 22:42, 120 million red packets were sent out; the shake times reached the peak at 22:34, i.e. 810 million times a minute. Red packet reception and dispatch on that day reached 1.01 billion times in total; between 20:00 and 0:48, the interactive times of Shake reached 11 billion. The sudden popularity of WeChat red packet expanded the market share of WeChat mobile payment overnight.

Zhang gave the definition in the tone of Jobs: Only minimalism cannot be surpassed. In 2016, he was even worried that WeChat might stick to the users, and ridiculously proposed the "use-and-leave" product logic.

That is a typical "God's perspective". WeChat has entered non-human consideration. The ambition of WeChat can no longer be defined by an app; it is aimed at the entire world, to be a place where the social contact, emotions, and self-realization of the users can be satisfied, a world of philosophy.

Zhang is ready to go against the world again. The aircraft battle added to WeChat 5.0 by Zhang is simple, straightforward, and fun, testing the players' endurance and skills when it gets along, which is similar to his unique life filled with twists and turns, dangers and opportunities. Indeed, there are few people who can stand fast in solitude and freely express themselves via their own products.

If the moments, official accounts, micropayment, and service accounts realize the entrepreneurship of others, "Mini Programs" belongs to Zhang himself. So he was very "nervous" and prepared for it for over a year.

"Mini Programs" is a de-centered self-redemption in the first place.

Zhang might have already realized that WeChat may finally become a "boring platform" like Baidu Search and Taobao. He would rather renovate the product himself than be eliminated later by others.

He allows the merchants to obtain data flow through his product by means of the "Mini Programs", to connect everything that can be connected.

Different from the URL relied on by the current Internet world, the Internet portals relied on by "Mini Programs" are QR codes. It has even got rid of such traditional Internet forms as browsers and pages, able to connect existing Internet application scenarios as well as the real world without screens. It realizes the connection of everything. What you see is what you get; what is connected is what is generated.

Zhang once described a scene at his WeChat open class that people scan the QR code of the coach station to buy tickets with no need for queuing, registration, and so on, and they leave after using it. McDonald's has now brought that scene into reality at its cashiers of underground parking garages, hospitals, etc.

On May 23, 2012, Zhang wrote in his moments that the portal of PC Internet is at the search bar, while that of the mobile Internet is the QR code. WeChat is not only a product, but also the demarcation point between the old world and the new world.

WeChat has been updated several times, but you can always see a little figure standing alone looking at the big blue earth in the distance. Some suggested that another figure be added, but Zhang said, "No. People are lonely and need communication." You might not know that the little figure is just Zhang Xiaolong himself.

Source: Adapted from *Business* magazine

Chapter 5

Service Marketing Mode

Topics:

1. Studio Service Mode
2. Personalized Service Mode
3. User Participation Service Mode
4. 3D Printing Service Mode
5. Integrated Service Mode
6. Industrial Service Mode

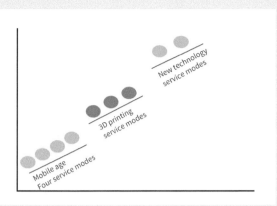

With the popularization of smart phones, the mobile Internet is rapidly penetrating into various fields of society, facilitating people's life and work and propelling social innovation and economic growth. The goods production mode has changed accordingly from the traditional product mode to: the four service modes based on the mobile age, the three service modes based on 3D printing, and the two service modes based on new technology, as shown in Figure 5-1.

Figure 5-1   Service Modes

We should choose those service modes that can meet the customers' demands and bring benefits and profits for the enterprise, maintaining the competitive edge of the enterprise in the market. The following elements should be taken into account during service mode selection:

(1) Market potential.

(2) Profitability.

(3) Market competitiveness. In comprehensive consideration of the market capacity, will the service to be designed and developed be competitive? Choose the service mode that can help give play to the core technology advantage of the enterprise for design and development while considering the competitive weaknesses of the market.

(4) Available resources. Consider the convenience, economic efficiency, and environmental effect of the service mode to be developed.

(5) Existing technology level and production capacity. Fully consider whether the service to be designed can be executed and shown by existing production capacity.

(6) Distribution ability, distribution channels, and market service ability.

(7) National policies, laws and regulations, etc.

Studio Service Mode

A studio is a place of creative production and work. It is not only an office, but also a place where several like-minded entrepreneurs work together.

As the studio has a small structure and a few members, with few requirements and rules, it enjoys better flexibility and higher efficiency. It is usually established by members with the same hobbies who have better professional spirit than the relevant departments of other companies.

The service provided by studios is simple, sometimes unable to serve customers with all-round requirements. Sometimes it is hard for the studios to bear commercial risks due to their low-cost operation mode. It is a common phenomenon that studios of different industries have irregular service levels.

In this "talent-first" age, contemporary undergraduates must prepare themselves in advance so as to earn a living in

 Case Study   3D Studio of Harbin Undergraduates

On March 30, 2016, in the Pioneer Park of Harbin Engineering University, a 3D printing studio established by some undergraduates was opened for business, promoting relevant technology at the same time. This studio's 3D printer was also assembled by the students, with an accuracy of 100 microns, and it can print mechanical arms, model airplanes, robots, and vases, etc. as programmed.

This studio has over 20 employees who are still university students. They have great passion for entrepreneurship and hope to fight for their own careers.

The case source quoted from: 3D Studio of Undergraduates; Harbin Undergraduates Establish Their Own 3D Printing Studio

http://www.guangyuanol.cn/news/shehui/2016/0331/551994.html

the future full of challenges. Of course, there are many ways they can train themselves, such as taking an internship and doing part-time jobs. But in this rigorous age, we must strive to be innovative and develop a school of our own. We do not have to be the trendsetter but should have our own style and own way.

In current society, entrepreneurship has become a trend of self-development and experience increasing among undergraduates. It not only can strengthen their will and accumulate their experience, but also can relieve the burden of their parents. So, there are many students exploring in this direction, gaining more and better practical experience to face the future challenges while sticking to their principles.

In recent years, studios, thanks to their features like low threshold, small investment and easy operation, have won extensive attention from the undergraduates, becoming a new carrier and new mode in the early stage of entrepreneurship.

Venture studios are constituted by one or several individuals who have the same ideal and dare to innovate, bonded by interest, working as a team relying on their skills to undertake and complete relevant business independently and to gain relevant remuneration. They are a newly emerging group, new-type "micro" enterprises.①

Impacted by the international financial crisis, plus the imperfect employment market of China, the talent market has high requirements for talents, while most professionals are unrecognized in the fierce domestic market. Therefore, studios described above have come into being.

The Studio Mode Becomes the Mainstream of Undergraduate Entrepreneurship

(1) The studio has become a new hotspot choice for the undergraduates.

Currently, there are more than 1,000 venture studios established by undergraduates within five years after graduation, and there are over 100,000 students willing to establish venture studios. The studio mode has been a hotspot among the undergraduates, a new choice for the "grassroots" civilians.

(2) Studios have a small initial scale and are often of the "partnership" mode. Popular with undergraduate teams or fresh graduate teams, this combination is known as "partner"-type studio venture mode. It is reported that the first three sources of studio members are: university classmates (50.45%); members of the same student organization (45.88%), and friends (37.56%). This kind of staff mode ensures less initial investment, strong motive, and clear nature of the studio, which is helpful to the long-term development of the studio.

(3) New media have become the new favorite marketing publicity means of studios. Taking Chen Anni, a graduate of Guangdong University of Foreign Studies in China, the representative of "post-90s" undergraduate venture studios, as an example: her comic "Sorry, I only Live 1% of My Life" received over 400,000 reposts and over 300,000 likes within three days. The "Kuaikan Comics" app she promoted received 300,000 daily downloads. She organized the M2 Art Studio in university and, after graduating, went to Beijing where she registered the "Dream for Granted" Studio. "The Great Anni", who has over eight million fans, posts online comics and sells related products via the cartoon figures of Nima and Wang Xiaoming. It is obvious that we cannot ignore the contributions of new media to the marketing publicity of venture studios.

①
Micro: Refers to those much smaller than similar things in volume or length, e.g., micro-car, micro-fiction, and micro-television.

Case Study Super Curriculum of Yu Jiawen Studio

In August 2011, Yu Jiawen and his university classmates established a studio together and promoted the first version of "Friday Super Curriculum". Although this "crude" product developed within a week could only display the course name, site, and lecturer name and could only be used by the students of South China Institute of Software Engineering, GU, it still won the support of many students. Yu saw the potential of this product and then promoted it to other nearby universities rapidly.

Just as its name implies, the "Friday Super Curriculum" mainly focuses on the curriculum. It is the first domestic campus social app connected with the educational administration system that supports one-click automatic entering of the curriculum into cellphones.

It supports real-time downloading of the latest course information and the manual adding of audited courses. Clicking the free periods in the curriculum will display all the courses of those periods, including

Super Curriculum App. Source: 360 Encyclopedia

public optional courses and specialized courses of each college, with student ratings for your reference.

In this way, students can attend classes as needed and readily make their Straight-A plans. For individual students without an educational administration system, the team communicated with the university authority and obtained the curriculum of the whole university which has been entered into the background, so as to prevent the trouble of manual entering. You do not have to input all the information of a course and can enter the curriculum into your cellphone with several simple steps. Courses that are not entered in time can also be shared when a student enters the information. In addition, the students can also add off-campus courses such as TOEFL and IELTS, which can be shared with other students after background approval. To ensure the course quality, "disguised courses" such as group purchase information are strictly filtered out. It is said that the next step of "Fri-

day" is to share the curriculum information of various universities, enabling the students to attend classes of different universities.

Since November 2014, the "Super Auditor Month—Collection of Excellent Courses in China" has been carried out by "Friday", the 10-million user level app, in 3,000 universities nationwide. The students are excited that they can finally attend the classes of "other people's teachers".

The "Auditor Month" program covers tens of millions of students in 3,000 universities nationwide. Students have the chance to win a bonus of CNY 1,000 or a Polaroid by sending "university + recommended course + periods + lecturer name + reason for recommendation + (course pictures)" to the "Friday" team via microblog, the chat community in the app, or e-mail.

As a campus social app, "Friday" has its unique way of recovering the classroom atmosphere. There's a "flooding notebook" module in the current version, where the students can chat freely and still keep the classroom absolutely silent. However, in order to ensure the class quality and focus on the basic function of curriculum, the team plans to cancel that module. The "Pass Notes" function is still reserved. "Man-show boys" can still quietly send a "note" to the lovely girl sitting in front.

The Super Curriculum has been going astray in transformation. The slogan "Cut Boring Classes and Chase Your Crush" popping out when you open the app has deviated from its original intention (to be the best curriculum software in China), revealing the impure motive behind.

The case source quoted from: 360 Encyclopedia 2014/11/24
https://baike.so.com/doc/7917754-8191871.html

Personalized Service Mode

Personalized customization means that the user gets involved in the production process to make designated patterns and characters printed on the product, and then gets a commodity with strong personal attributes.

"Customization" has become a simple and fashionable lifestyle. Now when consumers buy a luxury product, they not only require the product function, but also focus on the expression of their emotions.

We can say that customization itself is an expression of the lifestyle of certain consumer groups. The consumption of modern society is filled with passion and personalization. Especially, the "post-

80s" main-force consumers do not like traditional ordinary products, but prefer limited, DIY, and customized products, enjoying the unique consumption experience brought by personalized and creative products. "M-ZONE" once made use of this consumer psychology of the young generation and promoted the slogan of "My zone, my rules"; the "Only for you" personal customization concept of KASO also advocates the flaunty values of the new-generation consumers, which is well received by young consumers.

The unique attributes of customized products can satisfy the consumers in spirit and individuality. As the first domestic

① KASO: Guangzhou KASO Commerce and Trade Co., Ltd. Headquartered in Guangzhou, the frontier city leading the economy and popular culture in China, it is an enterprise specializing in providing high-end wine customization service for individuals, enterprises and institutions, and private groups.

enterprise providing professional customized service in China, KASO really understands the demand of the consumers. It integrates more artistic imagination, fresh design elements and innovative concepts in the red wine package design by means of various skilled creative techniques, making the product show the life of art and render brand-new mental feelings and visual experience.

IN KASO①, consumers can participate in design and experience the joy of DIY. It will be precious when you make it yourself. The personal experience and individual aesthetic taste of "customiza-tion" renders a kind of beauty full of affection, and the connotation of the product is also fully embodied.

Customization represents a lifestyle of "Understanding and satisfying oneself". It can have nothing to do with luxury, but must represent the aesthetic taste and the unique lifestyle of the customer. It also enables more consumers to enjoy the honorable lifestyle brought by personalized consumption. It can be predicted that "customization" is drawing closer and closer to us. To understand and choose customization will enable us to keep up with the age.

Case Study — Customization on the Red Collar Production Line

RCOLLAR Suit Production

Every suit on the production line of Red Collar Group is customized for the customer. Each suit has an electronic tag on it that contains all the customization information.

The upgrade of consumption level and ideas has let more and more consumers get unsatisfied with the stereotyped ready-made clothes. "People-oriented" custom-made clothes have become popular again. But the fascinating texture, handicrafts, and exclusive designer of high-end customization often mean daunting prices.

Walking into the Internet factory of Red Collar Group, you'll be overwhelmed by the hot wave of a labor-intensive workshop filled with roaring machines and workers.

But when you take a close look, you'll find that it is different from traditional suit production lines in many ways: six cutting beds are arranged in a line, cutting each piece of cloth according to the tips given by the computer; every suit on the production line has its own colors, styles and textures; every worker sits in front of a computer recognition terminal, and when a suit comes, he or she first scans the electronic card on it and then processes according to the tips...

This factory is an important part of the C2M mode of Red Collar Group.

C2M (Customer to Manufacturer) means to establish a direct interaction platform between the consumers and the manufacturer and remove such intermediate links as shopping malls and distributors, where the whole process from product customization, design, production to logistics and after-sales service relies on data driving and network operation. How does this platform combine personalized customization and flow line production?

The suit customization system independently developed by Red Collar has established a database of suit formats and sizes corresponding to the sizes of human bodies. The system can conduct data modeling for the body shape and size of the customer and make an exclusive data format through 3D printing. When the data are delivered to the material preparation department, the automatic cutting bed will do the cutting work. All pieces of cloth for the suit will be hanged on a hook with an electronic card containing the customer requirements for the lapel, pockets, sleeve edges, buttons, and embroidery. The computer recognition terminal on the production line will read such information and give tips for operation, completing the customization on the production line.

The dressing adviser, Hai Na, who was taking the measurements of a customer, showed the Red Collar customization system to the journalist, "The system provides diversified formats, crafts, styles, and sizes for the customers. There are currently over 1,000 trillion of design combinations and 100 trillion of style combinations to choose from."

In the process of traditional suit customization, all the procedures of measuring, patterning, cutting, tailoring and ironing need manual fabrication, which can satisfy the personal demand of the customer to the maximum but has low efficiency, long production cycle, and high labor cost. The industrial production line, while largely increasing the efficiency and reducing costs, can hardly satisfy the personal demand of the customer with stereotyped ready-made clothes and also reduces the added value of the product.

The pure hand-made high-end suit has a production cycle of three to six months and a minimum price of about CNY 10,000; while the Red Collar customized suit requires seven days at most from order receiving to delivery, and the price can be as low as CNY 2,000 according to different textures.

In 2014, Red Collar Group enjoyed a growth over 150% in customization business, sales revenue and profits while achieving zero inventories.

The C2M mode removes the cost of intermediate links like shopping malls and reduces the cost of the enterprise. It realizes one-piece flow and mass production of personalized products on the production line through data driving, helping increase the added value of the clothes and bring higher profits for the enterprise.

When the cost of intermediate and production links is reduced, consumers will also benefit. Now suit customization is also affordable for ordinary people.

The case source quoted from: Fu Zhongming, China Economic Net 2015/07/07
http://www.ce.cn/xwzx/gnsz/gdxw/201507/07/t20150707_5856343.shtml

User Participation Service Mode

User participation R&D means that the user comes into contact with the product before, during and after sales and participates in innovation, and the enterprise adopts the innovation idea proposed by the user and improves the product.

With the dynamic changes of the market and the ever-diversified demands of the consumer, product innovation, as the lifeline of the enterprise, is significant for the enterprise to establish and keep its competitive edge. In the age of the mobile Internet, user's thinking has been emphasized and received by more and more enterprises. The limited internal resources are obviously not enough for product innovation; the function of users should be given full play in product innovation.

The enterprise must cultivate its ability of integrating external knowledge and resources in order to keep the impetus and capacity of product innovation. The core of the Internet age is knowledge sharing, resource sharing and interest sharing. One important feature is de-centering. The internal resources of the enterprise are not enough; users are the most important external resources of the enterprise, and their role in product innovation has been more and more significant.

The sense of participation is the most important reflection of user's thinking. Lei Jun, founder of MIUI, believes that what MIUI sells is the sense of participation, and that this is the real secret of MIUI's success. This C2B (Customer to Business) mode is the direction of travel for the future development of e-commerce. Many famous enterprises have adapted themselves to this appeal of the users and won a place in the fierce market by effectively using such network social tools as microblogs, WeChat, and communities.

The common process of traditional innovation is as follows: the enterprise discovers consumer demand through market surveys and then designs brand-new products and services according to the demand. However, can the market survey result accurately reflect the market demand? When the new product and service enter the

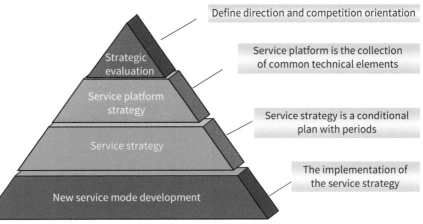

User Participation Service Mode. Source: Baidu Encyclopedia

market, has the market demand changed already? These uncontrollable elements lead to the failure of more than half of the traditional innovation cases. Then how can we reduce the failures? To attract the customers for direct participation in innovation might be a good choice.

Toyota once held an event of "Buy your ideas", which was open to everybody, from housewives to insiders. In that event, Toyota paid JPY 380 million for over 380,000 ideas about R&D, design, production, and selling. Toyota adopted 85% of the ideas, which unexpectedly generated JPY 16 billion of income.

You are the one who understands yourself the best. Similarly, the consumers understand themselves best. The passion and ability of innovation of the consumers can be turned into an important resource of the enterprise. Usually the contact with the consumers before, during and after sales provides excellent opportunities for the consumers to participate in innovation.

Case Study — Haier Collects Users' Opinions on Site

The second largest consumer electronics show in the world in 2012, SINOCES, was a good stage for enterprises to display their high-tech and new products. Numerous enterprises promoted their products to the buyers through this platform. But a journalist saw a different scene at Haier's stand: buyers and users from all over the world were telling their actual needs and gave suggestions after using the product, while the Haier personnel made careful records.

This "abnormal" phenomenon is nothing new to the Haier personnel. It is an innovation mode where Haier lets the users participate: the consumers propose their demands and ideas, and Haier turns them into products with first-class resources, and the products can only be released in the market after comprehensive experience and strict supervision by the consumers. That's why the scene mentioned above appeared during the show.

Only the products that are developed based on user demand and that pass the examination of the consumers can be accepted by the consumers. So, receiving an order is not the end of our work, but the start.

Our purpose is to collect the real demands of global users and identify the real problems. Besides SINOCES, every global exposition, online interactive community, offline store, and even the homes of the users are all the interactive platforms for Haier and its consumers.

The Haier stand has become a special area for communication with global users. It is the terminal experience area of Haier, and the products will only be released after the whole-process experience and final approval of the buyers; it is the customer communication area where the buyers can tell us their new demands and feedbacks; it is also a creative area where we'll record all your good ideas. Not only on the site of the show, we've also established creative factories, experience areas and feedback platforms online where the consumers can propose their ideas, demands and suggestions.

The people communicating with the buyers here are not the sales or service personnel of Haier, but our R&D personnel.

All the products displayed here are made according to the consumer demands and consumer surveys. The idea of this crystal series washing machine just came from the consumer. It is produced after surveying over 20,000 people by household surveys, forums, and network surveys, etc. There are over 700 buyers at this show, which are great user resources for Haier. We can understand the demands of global consumers and propel the upgrading of our products according to their feedbacks, so as to ensure our products can truly satisfy consumer demands.

Under the background of global economic slowdown and sluggish demand, home appliance enterprises around the world are facing difficulties, but Haier keeps its growth against the trend. In the first quarter of this year, Haier realized a year-on-year growth of 45% in the American market, 26% in the Australian market, and 60% in the Japanese market, achieving steady and rapid development.

The rapid development of Haier benefits from the practice of the win-win mode of "employee and order as one". We've turned from the original command receivers to CEOs making our own decisions, so we must develop products centering on the user demand. Our value will be embodied only when consumer demand is satisfied. That requires us to walk out of the lab and communicate with the users on the Internet and at expositions in person.

Continuing to be the No. 1 brand of white goods in the world, becoming the focus of the world, independently developing the first space refrigerator in China...The "abnormal behavior" may just be the reason for Haier to have created all those "miracles". But when you really understand that abnormal behavior, you'll find the so-called "miracles" are just inevitable.

The case source quoted from: Wang Tengjiao, ZOL.COM.CN 2012/07/09
http://jd.zol.com.cn/305/3058043.html

The enterprise must stay alert to the consumer information and take the chance of discovering business opportunities through them.

In order to provide profound experience for users, MIUI lets them participate in product R&D from the beginning, including market operation. We gradually find that the age of "participation consumption" has come and has satisfied the new consumption psychology of the users. Allowing user participation can satisfy the "on-site intervention" psychological need of young people and help express their passion of "influencing the world". Previously, it was commonly seen in substance-type UGC (user-generated substance) mode products. The famous "B Station" (bilibili.tv) in the anime circle is a typical example. Young people that love anime and creation contribute to the site by teasing, reposting, and parodic re-creation, etc. to create a unique subcultural discourse system[1].

To establish the sense of participation is to open the process of production, service providing, brand building, and selling to the users and to build a touchable and accessible brand that grows with the users. I've summarized three strategies and three tactics, internally called "the three-three rule of sense of participation".

Three strategies: hot goods, fans, and We Media.

Three tactics: open the participation nodes, design interactions, and spread reputation events.

"Hot goods" is the product strategy. You should have the courage to operate one product at a time and to make it the No. 1 product in the market. Unfocused product lines can hardly result in scale effect; scattered resources may impede the development of the sense of participation.

"Fans" is the user strategy. The sense of participation can only spread with "trust support", by which the weak users turn into strong users of greater trust. The fan culture should first make the employees fans of the product, and then benefit the users. Function and information sharing are the initial benefit incentives, so we often say that "Teasing is also a kind of participation". Then come honor and benefit. Only the sense of participation that benefits both the enterprise and the user can last.

Internet Thought

"We Media[2]" is the substance strategy. The de-centering of the Internet has wiped out authorities and information asymmetry. To carry out We Media is to make the enterprise itself an information node of the Internet, ensuring faster information flow-rate, flattened information dissemination structure as well as flattened internal organizational structure, and encouraging every employee and every user to be "the spokesman of the product". It is suggested that the thought of "useful, emotional and interactive" be followed in content operation, sending useful information only and preventing information overload; each piece of information should express emotions to guide the user for further participation and sharing.

To "open the participation nodes" is to open the process of production, service providing, brand building and selling, and select the nodes that benefit both the enterprise and the users. Only the participation that benefits both parties can last. The nodes to be opened should be based on function demand; there will be more participants in rigid demand.

To "design interactions" is to carry out relevant design on the opened nodes. It is suggested that the design thought of "simple, beneficial, interesting, and real" be followed in interaction and that the interaction mode be constantly improved like the product. The "WeChat Red Packet" program during the 2014 Spring Festival is a good example of interaction design, where people can snatch the red packets, which is fun and simple.

To "spread reputation events" is to firstly select the first batch of identifiers of the product, develop the sense of participation in a small scope, and turn the content generated from the interactions into topics and events for propaganda to spread the reputation and attract millions of people to participate. It will enhance the sense of participation of the existing participants, bringing a fast-spreading storm effect.

The sense of participation means a critical leap of consumer demand. Consumer demand has transcended the prod-

① *System generally refers to the entirety composed of things within a certain scope or similar things according to a certain order and internal relations.*

② *We Media: also known as "citizen media" or "personal media", refers to the general independent personal civilian disseminators who deliver normative and non-normative information to un-specific majorities or specific individuals by modern and electronic means.*

uct, not limited to the material attribute of the product, but extending to its social attribute: nowadays the users buy a prod-uct not only for what it can do, but also for what they can do with the product and what experience they can be involved in.

3D Printing Service Mode

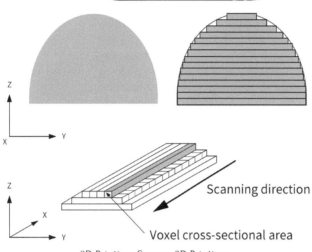

3D Printing. Source: 3D Printing

3D printing (3DP) is a kind of rapid prototyping technology, constructing objects by layered printing with such adhesive materials as powdered metal or plastic based on digital model files.

3D printing is usually carried out with a digital technology material printer. It is often used for model fabrication in the fields of mold making and industrial design and has gradually been used for the direct manufacturing of some products. Some spare parts have already fabricated by this means. It is widely applied in the fields of jewelry, footwear, industrial design, architecture, engineering and construction (AEC), automobile, aerospace, dentistry and medical industry, education, GIS, civil engineering, and guns.

The ordinary printer of our daily lives can print planar objects designed by the computer, and the so-called 3D printer has similar working principles to the ordinary printers, but with different printing materials. The printing materials of ordinary printers are ink and papers, while the 3D printer has different materials such as metal, ceramic, plastic, and sand, which are genuine raw materials. When the printer is connected to the computer, under the control of the computer, the printer can stack the "printing materials" layer by layer and finally turn the blueprint into a real object. Informally, the 3D printer is a kind of equipment that can "print" real 3D objects, e.g., a robot, a toy car, various molds, and even food.

The reason it is still called "printer" is because the technical principle of layered processing is very similar to the ink-jet printing of ordinary printers. This printing technique is called 3D printing technique.

3D printing has many different techniques. Their difference lies in creating the parts with available materials and different layer structures. Commonly used materials for 3D printing include nylon glass fiber, polylactic acid, ABS resin, durable nylon material, plaster material, aluminum, titanium alloy, stainless steel, silver plating, gold plating, and rubber-like material.

The design process of partitioned 3D printing of 3D model[1] is: carry out modeling with CAD or computer animation modeling software, and partition the 3D model into layered cross-sections, so as to direct the printer for layered printing.

The most outstanding advantage of 3D printing is that it can generate the parts of any shape directly from the computer graphic data without machining or any mold, which drastically shortens the development cycle of the product and improves the productivity and production cost.

Let's look at the advantages of 3D printing:

1: No cost added for fabricating complex objects;

2: No cost added for production diversification;

3: No need for assembly;

4: Instant delivery;

5: Unlimited design space;

6: No need for skill;

7: Space-saving and portable;

8: Less waste by-products;

9: Unlimited combination of materials;

10: Accurate replication of the entity.

① *3D model: the polygon presentation of an object, usually displayed by the computer or other video equipment. The object displayed can be an entity of the real world or an imaginary object. Any object existing in the physical nature can be presented by 3D model.*

Cloud Manufacturing

Cloud manufacturing is a new concept developed based on the idea of "Manufacturing is service", with reference to the thought of cloud computing. Cloud manufacturing is the product of the combination of advanced information technology, manufacturing technology and emerging technology of the Internet of Things, reflecting the idea of "Manufacturing is service". With the cutting-edge IT concepts including cloud computing, it supports the manufacturing industry to provide service of high added value, low cost and global manufacturing for the products under the background of extensive network resources.

1. Background

The service orientation of manufacturing, knowledge-based innovation ability, the aggregating and collaborative capacity for various manufacturing resources, and environmental friendliness have become the key elements of current enterprise competition and the trend of informational development of the manufacturing industry. The manufacturing industry of China is in a critical historical period, turning from production to service, from the low end to the middle and high end of the value chain, from a large manufacturer to a strong manufacturer, and from made-in-China to created-in-China. It is a crucial problem to be solved in the next five to ten years of China to cultivate new manufacturing service modes that can meet the TQCSEK requirement of the shortest time to market (Time), the best quality (Quality), the lowest cost (Cost), the best service (Service), the cleanest environment (Environment), and knowledge-based innovation (Knowledge), so as to support green and low-carbon manufacturing, realize created-in-China, and propel the change in the pattern of economic growth.

Meanwhile, advanced technology represented by cloud computing, the Internet of Things, cyber-physical systems (CPS), virtualization technology, service-oriented technology (e.g., knowledge service and service technology), and high-performance computing is enjoying rapid development and applied in various industries.

2. Structure

(1) Physical Resource Layer (P-Layer): P-Layer is the physical manufacturing resource layer that connects various physical resources into the network via embedded cloud terminal, RFID, and the Internet of Things, etc. to achieve the overall interconnection of the physical resources, so as to create virtual resources of cloud manufacturing, thus providing interface support for virtual resource encapsulation and resource transfer of the cloud manufacturing.

(2) Resource Layer (R-Layer): R-Layer is the virtual resource layer that converts the various manufacturing resources connected to the network into virtual manufacturing resources and encapsulates such virtual manufacturing resources into cloud service via cloud service definition tools, and virtualization tools, etc. and releases them to the cloud manufacturing service center. The main functions provided by this layer include cloud access, cloud service definition, virtualization, cloud service release management, resource quality management, resource provider pricing and settlement management, and resource partitioning management.

(3) Cloud Manufacturing Service Layer (C-Layer): C-Layer is the cloud manufacturing service center layer that collects the various resource services released by R-Layer and creates various cloud manufacturing service data centers.

(4) Core Service Layer (S-Layer): S-Layer is the core service layer that provides various core services and functions of the comprehensive management of manufacturing cloud service for the three

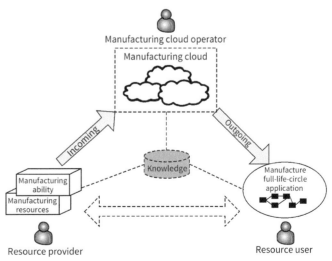

Figure 5-2　Cloud Manufacturing. Source: 3D Printing

①

CSP is the latest achievement of world steel in the end of the 20th century, one of the most important technical progresses of the steel industry. SMS designed a new-type thin-slab conticaster, which formed the compact casting and rolling production line when connected with the tandem mill. It is called the CSP technology.

categories of users (CSP①, CSD, and cloud service operator), including: cloud service standardization and testing management, and interface management, etc. for CSP; user management, system management, cloud service management, data management, and cloud service release management for cloud service operators; and cloud task management, high performance search and dispatching management service, etc. for CSD.

(5) Application Interface Layer (P-Layer): P-Layer is the application interface layer that provides different professional application interfaces and general management interfaces such as user registration and verification for specific manufacturing application fields.

(6) User Layer (U-Layer): U-Layer is the application layer of cloud manufacturing, oriented to various fields and industries of manufacturing. Users of different industries can utilize the cloud service in the cloud manufacturing service center via the cloud service web portals and various user interfaces (including mobile terminal, PC terminal, and special-purpose terminal).

3. Operating Principle

According to Figure 5-2, there are three kinds of users in the cloud manufacturing system, i.e., resource provider, manufacturing cloud operator, and resource user. The resource provider perceives and conducts virtualized access for the manufacturing resources and manufacturing ability during the full life cycle of the product, and then provides them to the third-party operation platform (the manufacturing cloud operator) as service; the manufacturing cloud operator conducts efficient management and operation of the cloud service, providing service for the resource user in a dynamic and flexible way as requested by the resource user; the resource user can utilize the various application services (outgoing) dynamically according to needs with the support of the manufacturing cloud operation platform, and can realize the collaboration and interaction between multiple subjects. In the process of manufacturing cloud operation, knowledge plays the core role, supporting the virtualized access and encapsulation of manufacturing resources and manufacturing ability as well as such functions as efficient management and intelligent search based on cloud service.

4. Features

(1) Service-oriented and demand-oriented manufacturing. Cloud manufacturing has abandoned the usual manufacturing orientation to equipment, resources, orders, and production, and has transformed to real service- and demand-oriented manufacturing. In cloud manufacturing, anything that can be encapsulated and virtualized is manufacturing cloud service (including manufacturing resources, manufacturing ability, and manufacturing knowledge). This big change is the basis of realizing the transformation from manufacturing-type enterprise to service-type enterprise, and Manufacturing as a Service.

(2) Uncertain manufacturing. In cloud manufacturing, there is no "one and only" optimum solution to the satisfaction of cloud service to manufacturing demand, but only the satisfactory solution or non-inferior solution that can be obtained with current technology and methods. That is the uncertain manufacturing ability of cloud manufacturing, which covers cloud manufacturing task description, mapping of task and cloud service, cloud service selection and binding, cloud service combination selection, and manufacturing result evaluation.

(3) User-participated manufacturing. Cloud manufacturing emphasizes embedding the computing resources, ability, and knowledge into the network and environment, so as to shift or bring back the focus of the manufacturer to user demand. Cloud manufacturing is devoted to building a public manufacturing environment where the manufacturer, the customer, and the intermediary, etc. can adequately communicate. Under the cloud manufacturing mode, user participation is not limited to traditional user demand proposal and user evaluation but penetrates into every link of the full life cycle of manufacturing. Under this mode, the identity of customer or user is not unique, that is, a user is both the consumer of cloud service and the provider or developer of cloud service. It reflects a kind of user-participated manufacturing, including human-computer interaction, computer-human interaction, computer-computer interaction, and human-human interaction.

(4) Transparent and integrated manufacturing. Cloud manufacturing abstracts

and virtualizes all the manufacturing resources, ability and knowledge into a "power strip" visible and available to the users, i.e., the manufacturing cloud service, while other things are transparent to the users. When the user carries out various manufacturing activities via the cloud service, the invocation of such service is transparent, i.e., all the manufacturing operation details can be "hidden" to the user so that the user will regard the cloud manufacturing system as a seamless integrated system. The transparency of cloud manufacturing can be reflected in the aspects of location, registration, and use.

(5) Active manufacturing. In the current manufacturing mode, if the enterprise does not have any order or if its equipment, etc. is left unused, the enterprise cannot carry out manufacturing or enjoy benefits from the resources, which is a passive manufacturing mode. However, in cloud manufacturing, manufacturing activities and cloud service are active, that is, through the cloud manufacturing service platform built by the third party, orders can actively seek manufacturers and the cloud service can actively seek renting with the technical support of knowledge, semanteme, data mining, machine learning, and statistical reasoning. That is a kind of intelligent active manufacturing mode.

(6) Multi-user supportive manufacturing. The traditional network-based manufacturing mode (e.g., ASP[①] and manufacturing grid) focuses on connecting the scattered manufacturing resources via the network to form virtual centralized resources, and on decomposing a complex manufacturing task into several simple tasks which concurrently operate on different manufacturing resource nodes via the scheduling mechanism and then collecting the execution results. It reflects the thought of "centralized utilization of scattered resources". However, cloud manufacturing not only reflects that thought, but also effectively realizes the thought of "centralized resources for scattered service", i.e., to centralize the manufacturing resources scattered in different places via a large server to form a physical service center and then provide service invocation, and resource renting, etc. for multiple users at different places.

(7) Use-as-needed and payment supportive manufacturing. Cloud manufacturing is a new service-oriented pay-as-needed manufacturing mode driven by demand. In this mode, the user utilizes the cloud service in the manufacturing cloud service center in a demand-driven, user-led, and pay-as-needed way. The user invokes one or several existing cloud services as needed and pays accordingly. The user does not have to pay much attention to the information of the manufacturing resource service provider; the two of them are in a "bound-as-needed", "pay-as-you-go", and "dissolve-as-ended" relation.

(8) Low-threshold and crowdsourcing manufacturing. Traditional manufacturers must have their own factories, equipment, materials, information facilities, and technical personnel, etc. as well as corresponding design, manufacturing, management, and selling abilities. In cloud manufacturing, meanwhile, the enterprise does not have to own those conditions and abilities. The manufacturing resources or abilities which the enterprise does not have can be achieved through "outsourcing", i.e., to invoke or rent the resources, abilities and cloud services in the cloud manufacturing system to complete the enterprise's production task. That has reduced access threshold of enterprises and made the production and enterprise organization mode more flexible and diversified.

(9) Agile manufacturing. In the cloud manufacturing mode, the enterprise needs to focus only on its core service; other relevant business or services can be completed by invoking the cloud service in the cloud manufacturing. This kind of production mode is very flexible and reflects the idea of agile manufacturing.

(10) Specialized manufacturing. The cloud manufacturing virtualizes all the manufacturing resources, abilities and knowledge into cloud droplets (i.e., manufacturing cloud services) via the platform established by the third party, and then aggregates them into specialized manufacturing clouds of different types (e.g., design cloud, simulation cloud, management cloud, and experiment cloud). It reflects the features of large scale, intensification[②] and specialization.

(11) Manufacturing based on capacity sharing and transactions. Compared with traditional network-based manufacturing, cloud manufacturing shares not only the manufacturing resources, but also manufacturing abilities. With the support of corresponding knowledge base, database, and model base, it realizes virtualized encapsulation, description, release and invocation of manufacturing resources and abilities

①

ASP: the abbreviation of Active Server Page, an application developed by Microsoft to replace the CGI script program. It is a simple and convenient programming tool which can interact with databases and other programs.

②

Intensification: relative to the extensive form. Intensive operation is to reorganize the various operation elements based on benefits (social benefits and economic benefits), so as to achieve the maximum ROI with the lowest cost.

based on knowledge, thus really achieving the comprehensive sharing and transaction of manufacturing resources and abilities and improving the utilization ratio.

(12) Knowledge-based manufacturing. The application of knowledge is inseparable in the full life cycle of cloud manufacturing, including:

① virtualized encapsulation and access of manufacturing resources and abilities based on knowledge;

② cloud service description and manufacturing cloud construction;

③ cloud service searching, matching, aggregating and combining;

④ efficient intelligent cloud service invocation and optimal configuration;

⑤ fault tolerance management and task immigration;

⑥ business process management of the cloud manufacturing enterprises.

(13) Group-innovation-based manufacturing. In the cloud manufacturing mode, any individual, unit or enterprise can contribute their manufacturing resources, abilities and knowledge to the cloud manufacturing platform. And any enterprise can carry out its manufacturing activities based on such resources, abilities and knowledge. Cloud manufacturing reflects a Wikipedia-type manufacturing mode based on group innovation.

(14) Green and low carbon manufacturing. One of the goals of cloud manufacturing is to realize the overall sharing and collaboration of manufacturing resources, abilities and knowledge while centering on the TQCSEFK target, so as to increase the utilization rate of the resources. Achieving cloud manufacturing is to achieve green and low carbon manufacturing to some extent.

5. Application

The first is the R&D design ability service platform for large group enterprises. Cloud manufacturing can integrate the existing computing resources, software resources and data resources in the large group enterprises by means of advanced information technology such as network technology, establish the R&D design ability service platform for complex products, provide technical ability, software application and data service for the subordinate enterprises, and support such product development activities as multi-disciplinary optimization, performance analysis, and virtual verification, thus greatly improving the product innovation and design ability. Such service platforms are mainly for the subordinate enterprises of the groups.

The second important direction is that as China has become the country with the richest manufacturing resources in the world, for the problem of scattered resources and low utilization rate, cloud manufacturing can establish region-oriented processing resources sharing and service platforms by means of such advanced technology as information technology, virtualization, the Internet of Things, and RFID, so as to achieve efficient sharing and optimal configuration of processing resources within the region and propel the regional manufacturing development.

In addition, the manufacturing service support platform is also an important development direction of cloud manufacturing. As service has become the main source of value of manufacturers, we can establish manufacturing service support platforms to support manufacturers to transform from mere product providers to total solution providers and system integrators. The platform can provide such services as online monitoring, remote diagnosis, and overhaul to propel the manufacturers toward the high end of the industrial value chain. This platform is mainly for enterprises utilizing large equipment.

Besides the service platform for large enterprises, cloud manufacturing can also serve the massive medium-sized and small-sized enterprises. For the situation of shortage of capital and talents for information construction of the middle- and small-sized enterprises, we can establish public service platforms for them, providing services like product design, craft, manufacturing, purchase, and marketing and resources like informational knowledge, product, solution, and application case, so as to propel their development.

We are at the dawn of the age of a huge scattered mobile Internet system, where big data, large enterprises, and huge financial networks cover the world. However, as the basis of mass production is scale economy, the mass production is a centralized process centered on specialized activities.

3D printing is the catalyst of cloud manufacturing. Cloud manufacturing will become a super-large network distributed system composed of small manufacturers. Wikipedia defines cloud manufacturing as having various manufacturing resources and abilities, able to intelligently detect and connect to a wider mobile Internet, with automatic management and control.

Chris Andersen described this centralized mode as "an ant carrying a loudspeaker" in his works *The Long Tail*. The voice of individuals could never be heard until the Internet provided a global platform.

What if you want to customize a bike today? You can rely on the manufacturing cloud, too. Cloud manufacturing will automatically match several companies according to the printing task of customized parts. The company completing the task will also deliver the bike to you. You will find a bike customized with 100 parts, large or small and metal or plastic ones, outside your door the next day.

Each cloud manufacturer may be small. But just like the cellphone worth a billion or the anthill, they will have an overall efficiency greater than the sum of each part after integration.

Integrated Service Mode

In 2012, the trend of combination of software and hardware industries and vertical integration of industrial chains was more and more obvious. Apple is a typical case. It independently designs chips for iPhone and iPad and develops operation systems and other functions for these products. This kind of vertical integration is an important reason for the success of Apple mobile equipment.[1] After Google and Amazon followed the example of Apple, Microsoft also released the Surface tablet PC of its own brand out of the same thought. There were few "large and comprehensive" enterprises, but when we entered the age of the mobile Internet, many enterprises have begun to expand their upstream and downstream businesses and vertically integrate the industrial chain under the leadership of Apple. That has become the most obvious feature of the sci-tech industry development in 2012.

On February 10, 2017, the milk powder giant Mead Johnson reached an agreement with the global consumer products leader Reckitt Benckiser that Reckitt Benckiser would purchase Mead Johnson at the total price of about USD $17.9 billion, or USD $90 per share. This may be the largest purchase ever by Reckitt Benckiser.

Kasper Jakobsen, CEO of Mead Johnson, said that this merger could help both parties to expand the scale and realize diversified operation. And Rakesh Kapoor, CEO of Reckitt Benckiser, expressed that the global layout of Mead Johnson could significantly strengthen the layout of Reckitt Benckiser in developing markets, and that China would become its second largest "supermarket" after the merger.

It is inevitable that Reckitt Benckiser has not been doing very well in China. Although it entered the Chinese market as early as 1995, it has always been troubled by localization. After several years of development, it only has a few brands known to the Chinese people, such as Durex, Dosia, and Dettol. In its more than 20 years in the Chinese market, Reckitt Benckiser has been suffering losses in all its businesses except for the condom. In the first half of 2016, it had a net profit of GBP 528 million, with a year-on-year decrease of 26%.

When Durex was struggling alone, Reckitt Benckiser might have discovered the milk powder opportunities behind the two-child policy of China.

As the growth of home and personal care products has slowed down, currently, 40% of the sales of Reckitt Benckiser comes from hygiene and cleaning products, and 33% from health products; but the enterprise has not seen any significant growth in the sales in emerging markets. And it has always been unable to accomplish its wish of sharing the daily chemical market of China.

There are two differing opinions on whether Reckitt Benckiser can restore its glory after the joining of Mead Johnson. One is that the cooperation between two strong parties can help Mead Johnson build a more specialized platform of healthy food for babies, mothers, the middle-aged, and the elderly. And Mead Johnson may be able to compete with Nestlé and Danone in relevant fields.

The other is that whether Reckitt Benckiser will succeed after its purchase of Mead Johnson still depends on the advantages of independent operation after purchase or on whether greater investment can bring soaring performance. It is hard to draw a conclusion now, however, because Mead Johnson has to climb down from its high horse if it wants to develop in the Chinese market.

①
Mobile equipment: also known as a mobile device and handheld device. A pocket-sized computing device with which you can access all kinds of information anytime anywhere. It usually has a small display screen for touch input or a small keyboard.

The mobile Internet has been changing the entire sci-tech industry and entrepreneurial environment since its emergence, and has created some brand-new business modes. For example, the smart watch released by Neusoft has many benefits for the user's exercise and personal health management; the Pebble watch, when connected with iPhone or Android cellphones via Bluetooth, can measure speed and time when the user is jogging or cycling, control music play, and measure the distance in a golf game; SQUARE conducts mobile payment by a tiny card reader inserted in iPhone, and the annual transaction amount has reached USD $8 billion; the well-sold home electronic product of the US, the smart room thermometer Nest Learning Thermostat, has integrated sensor, machine perception, and network technology so as to perceive the air temperature and automatically adjust the indoor temperature; Taiwan's Adonit has an integrated stylus, and an editing and drawing app, breathing new life into this ordinary product.

💡 Case Study   Vertical Integration of Acer Products

With the rapid development of mobile networks and smart equipment, it is an indisputable fact that the global PC market has been shrinking in recent years. According to the latest report of the market research company Canalys, in the first quarter of 2016, the sales volume of PCs experienced a year-on-year decrease of 13%. That put PC manufacturers under pressure. Acer, former No. 2 manufacturer in the global PC market, has found it very difficult to rise to Top 3 in the market. In this situation, how Acer will face the future has been a focus of the industry.

As pointed out in the open letter titled "After Three Revolutions, Acer Has Been Walking on the Right Road and Seen the Morning Light in Front" to the shareholders written by Shi Zhenrong, the founder and Honorary Chairman of Acer, after the transformation over two and a half years, Acer has indeed seen the sign of recovery and is now walking in the right direction toward the new vision of "Hardware + Software + Service".

In the first half of 2016, the new technology of Acer was rapidly applied in the global market, including the liquid ring-type fan-free cooling system for Acer Switch Alpha 12 and the ultra-thin metal fan cooling equipment for the new Predator products. Besides, in terms of developing emerging markets, Acer released its sub-brand Predator for the rising e-sports field in 2015 and established official strategic partnership with the world-first-class LOL team, EDG, participating in large e-sports events like NEST,

holding e-sports parties gathering the fans, and rigorously promoting the e-sports industry guide. In this way, Acer has been gradually walking out of the hard time.

In fact, the recent gradual recovery of Acer has drawn much attention. In 2016, in addition to continuously enhancing the "Hardware + Software + Service" strategic mode transformation, Acer also built a new vertical business mode integrating intelligent connection equipment, BeingWare. By combining hardware, service, and BYOC (Build Your Own Cloud), Acer is practicing the original brand intention of "Breaking the barriers between people and technology" in the age of the mobile Internet, Internet of Things, cloud computing and AI technology.

In terms of current market share, Acer's game computers rank No. 3 worldwide, and the two-in-one detachable laptop ranks No. 2, only next to Microsoft's Surface. When the traditional IT field is facing unprecedented challenges, Acer, an enterprise with 40 years of experience in the PC industry, is also actively seeking the direction of change.

From the desktop and laptop PCs familiar to common users, to projectors, displays, and full-range commercial products and solutions, and to AI, cloud computing, and the latest research and cooperative development results in the field of cloud integration, Acer can still produce excellent PC products, but is no longer merely a PC hardware manufacturer. Diversified development is a crucial element for Acer to keep its brand vitality in the post-PC age.

The case source quoted from: Technews2016/06/25
http://www.diankeji.com/news/26865.html

Industrial Service Mode

I. Micro-manufacturing

Micro-manufacturing is a new highly efficient, green, and high-accuracy technology used for processing various 3D micro-parts.

One of the enterprises' core competences in modern industry is large scale. Big enterprises often have more advantages than smaller ones. However, the third industrial revolution has changed the organizational form of the manufacturing industry—enterprises are smaller and smaller, and the process of product design and manufacturing is getting more creative. The traditional concept of consumers has been broken; consumers can also participate in production and has turned into prosumers.

One of the key basic techniques of this revolution is 3D printing. With the maturing and wide application of this technique, the distributed industrial structure is taking shape, which will drastically change the organizational form of the industry. However, 3D printing has not seen any qualitative change, and the future development path of the industry remains somewhat uncertain.

The Age of "Micro-manufacturing" is Taking Shape

What will future manufacturing be like? There may be fewer and fewer industrial goods made through mass production, which will be replaced by personally customized products. It will evolve along with the development of the Internet, digital technology[1] and 3D printing.

In the past, larger enterprises were more competitive, but in the future, the competitive enterprises will be the smaller ones. Some people think that this remark from Jack Ma is ridiculous, and that it is too early to make that conclusion. But he might really have predicted a trend. There may be a day when everyone can provide a design scheme in online communities, for jewelry, clothes, watches or even vehicles. And to turn such highly personalized products into reality requires technical support. 3D printing is an important technical means.

For example, a lover of bracelets wants to design a bracelet he likes and turn it into a wearable product. He can initiate the idea on the mobile Internet and upload his design drawings. The drawings may still have defects, but it may be perfected by other people who see it online. Or they can also adjust his design into the way they like.

There may be more people who want to own that bracelet, perhaps a few doz-

① *Digital technology emerged together with electronic computers. It transforms various information including pictures, texts, sound and images into the binary digits "0" and "1" recognizable by the computer via certain equipment, and then carries out computing, processing, storing, transferring, spreading, and restoring.*

💡 **Case Study** | The Micro Factory of Mebotics LLC

Mebotics LLC in Massachusetts, USA, has released a micro factory, claiming that it is not only a 3D printer, but also a "mechanical processing factory in the box".

The micro factory comprises a networked desktop device and additive manufacturing and cutting equipment. It can print four colors or multiple materials, and has the functional parts for computer etching and computer-controlled milling. It contains the print head and the milling head; thus, it is not limited to being a 3D printer. It can be used to print, cut, and etch plastic, wood and some light metal materials.

Product features:

Quiet and clean milling available indoors.

One machine for both 3D printing and cutting.

Access to the Internet, supporting panel operation.

Able to print two materials or four colors at a time.

You can send your own design into the machine or download the desired design online with the machine. Jeremy Fryer-Biggs, one of the four co-founders of Mebotics, said, "If you have a database of Hummer parts, you can connect the device to a Wi-Fi hotspot and download the part you need from the contents; you can then give the order of printing anytime anywhere." You can also insert a code segment into the design document to tell the machine when to use the milling head and when to shift to the print head. You can remotely start up the machine and monitor the whole process.

In addition, the micro factory is equipped with a vacuum port where you can install a dust collector to clean up the wood and metal filings.

Source: News information

ens or even hundreds. And the 3D printer can satisfy their demand of having that bracelet in a short time, and if the product is not satisfactory, it can still be constantly improved.

In fact, the future will not be dominated by large-scale standardized production. The design process in which many people participate can be realized on the mobile Internet. The two stages of manufacturing, therefore, have both changed. Designing is no longer mysterious; anyone can design on the mobile Internet, or people can cooperate to design a product online. And the production mode will not be large-scale factory production anymore; production can be carried out in the community. The user can "package" designs into software. This manufacturing process is called "micro-manufacturing". Every household can be deemed a producer. The previous centralized production mode will be replaced by this organizational structure of distributed production.

Many years ago, Kevin Kelly expressed in his Out of Control, What Technology Wants and other writings that such community production process would make social production highly fragmentized; small- and micro-sized enterprises based on the unit of household would be connected via the Internet and would realize highly innovative designs; everybody could take part in innovation. Now that mode is drawing closer and closer to us. The age of "micro-manufacturing" is taking shape, which is a trend worth much attention.

II. Agile Manufacturing

Scale economy refers to the phenomenon of increasing the economic benefit by expanding the production scale. Scale economy reflects the relationship between the production elements as well as the concentration degree and the economic benefit. The advantage of scale economy is that as the output increases, the long-term average total cost decreases.

Agile manufacturing means that the manufacturer effectively and collaboratively responds to user demand by rapidly allocating various resources (including technology, management, and people) via modern communication means to realize the agility of manufacturing. Agility is the core. It is the enterprise's ability to respond to a constantly changing and unpredictable operation environment; it is also the comprehensive presentation of the enterprise's survival ability and leading ability in the market. It is mainly reflected in the demand, design, and manufacturing of the product.

Agile manufacturing is implemented with the support of three pillar resources, i.e., innovative organization and management structure, advanced manufacturing technology (oriented to information technology and flexible intelligent technology), and management personnel with technology and knowledge. It is to centralize the flexible production technology, the laborers with technology and knowledge, and the flexible management that can propel intra-enterprise and inter-enterprise cooperation, and then to rapidly respond to the fast-changing market demand and market progress through the established common basic structure. Agile manufacturing has more sensitive and more rapid reaction capacity than other manufacturing modes.

The dilemma exists that we want to rapidly produce quality products while at the same time reducing manufacturing costs. The core lies in the basic economic law called "scale economy".[1] Scale economy is an invisible power supporting the modern industrial economy, and is the economic law that makes large-scale production profitable.

💡 Case Study — Agile Manufacturing Contributes to Material Performance Tests

The rapidly rising 3D printing is redefining manufacturing in key industries such as aerospace and transportation, and the military. To accelerate this process, scientists at Lawrence Livermore National Laboratory (LLNL), USA, are exploring manufacturing to targets as needed and using them for testing the material performance under extreme conditions by making use of the unparalleled flexibility of 3D printing.

Via an additive manufacturing process called two-photon polymerization direct laser writing (2PPDLW), the LLNL-led research team has prepared the first millimeter-size low-density foam reservoir target. This object has nanoscale features and can be used for material testing on the OMEGA laser of Rochester in New York. They are the first research team that uses this process to manufacture precision macro components. The main purpose of this Omega-targeted research is to apply the same process to the National Ignition Facility Project (NIF) of the US. Similar components need to be prepared to improve the performance of the future target.

Thanks to 3D printing, James Oakdale, a post-doctor at LLNL, has been able to manufacture these polymer foam target components in a few hours instead of the traditional several weeks. The improvement of manufacturing control also means the researchers can change the attributes of these materials more easily, such as density, elasticity, and fragility.

"In the past, when we made a mistake in target preparation, it would take two months to replace it," said Biener, "but now we can do it the next day or overnight. The advantage of this method is largely reducing the time needed from a concept to delivery for developing a target component. It also opens the gate to the objects that cannot be realized via traditional manufacturing techniques."

It is reported that such material strength testing via high power laser system (e.g., OMEGA or NIF) is usually applied to computer models that verify the material performance under strong pressure. According to Biener, this 2PPDLW 3D printing technique can also be used to develop the material depots for high-throughput "shotgun experiment". Usually, each of these material depots contains hundreds of materials which are slightly different from others in feature size and other attributes.

According to Michael Stadermann, the principal of LLNL target S&T team, the manufacturing-on-demand ability of 3D printing is very attractive to NIF and can shorten the cycle of future experiments.

"It can easily control the object you're testing, and you do not need any mechanical processing after 3D printing," said Stadermann. "It is really helpful to print out things in the shape you want, especially for those materials that cannot be processed."

The case source quoted from: emat, gkzhan.com 2016/10/31
http://info.machine.hc360.com/2016/10/311805614272.shtml

Chapter 6

Service Value Marketing

Topics:

1. Value Goal Orientation
2. Price Strategy Operation
3. A Good Product Spreads Itself
4. Tipping Point-Hot Sale Model-Hot Sale Item
5. Tool Kit - 16 Methods for Service Upgrade

Value Goal Orientation

There are five value orientations of enterprises' value marketing under mobile Internet conditions: user value, service value, product value, brand value and enterprise value.

User value is the starting point for the measurement of every value. It refers to the quantitative identity expressed by users in the manner of monetary measurement that is greater than the product or service value, because the product (or service) attributive characters and core claims effectively fit the consumption values of users.

For example, the IWC watches produced in Switzerland have errors every day and are not as accurate as electronic watches; however, users consider them to be worth the high price, and even form a law of value in their perception of Swiss watches: the fancier a watch is, the more likely it is to have errors, and a watch without error is not a good one.

User satisfaction and user value have distinct meanings.

Indicator	Customer satisfaction	Customer value
Paradigmatic connotation	The customer's reaction to or feeling about what he or she has received; namely, a comparison of the actual performance of the product against a standard	The customer desires more from the product or service
Object of evaluation	A particular product/service or supplier	Independent of any particular product/service or supplier
Subject of evaluation	Customers of enterprises	Customers of enterprises and competitors or third parties
Content of evaluation	A comparison of enterprise performance	A comparison of enterprise performance or competitor performance
Basis of evaluation	Empirical, such as "Am I satisfied?", emphasizing "looking back"	Perception of differences, such as "Which supplier will I choose?", emphasizing the present and "looking ahead", or "what if I do not choose one"
Content of action	Customer service	Exclusive marketing strategy
Type of action	Tactical, focusing on continuous improvement, customer service, and deficiency and mistake correction	Strategic, focusing on proposing and performing customer value propositions, and creating differentiated value that surpasses value of competitors
Changes of data	Static, mainly reflecting past endeavors	Dynamic, mainly reflecting endeavors of competitors
Orientation of data	Tends to exhibit a historical orientation; is a judgment formed during or after product (service) use or consumption	Exhibits a future orientation; is independent of the timing of the product use/consumption
Application of data	Provides a report for the enterprises: how they are doing (or how they have done) with their value creation efforts	Provides direction for the enterprises: what they should do to create value, belonging to the strategic level

Comparison between customer satisfaction and customer value

Customer satisfaction shows an enterprise how it is doing (namely, providing a report), while customer value shows an enterprise what it should do (namely, providing a direction). Such differences explain why customer value is highly thought of.

However, in operational practice, many satisfied customers select competitors, showing that customer satisfaction cannot be used to predict customers' future consumption behaviors, and high satisfaction cannot ensure profitability. This does not mean that there is no relation between customer satisfaction and market performance; in fact, customer satisfaction always influences customer loyalty, to thus directly influence enterprise profits. While customer value directly influences the enterprise's market performance, which is proved by many recent empirical studies. According to the study results, the position of an enterprise's customer value relative to its competitors dynamically influences the market shares obtained by the enterprise as well as the profitability.

Customer value is neither isolated with customer satisfaction, nor mutually exclusive. Customer value directly drives customer satisfaction, or to be more precise, customer satisfaction should serve as the indicator and medium of customers' perception of customer value. The published research results have proved the dependency and complementarity of customer satisfaction and customer value and hold that only by constantly providing cus-tomers with high value can an enterprise obtain reliable and continued customer satisfaction, and only the continued customer satisfaction can guarantee high customer loyalty and then the higher market shares.

The orientation goal of enterprise marketing is the total user value which is composed of product value, service value, brand value, and enterprise value. The change of any value thereof will influence the total value. Product value is composed of product function, technical substance, cost, and appearance, and service value refers to the various additional product services, which are satisfactory or more than satisfactory, provided to customers by an enterprise before, in, and after sale of product entities; service value has an increasing proportion in the total user value in the era of the mobile Internet.

In the eighty years since marketing was conceived, the "center of power" in the marketing world has been shifting: stage one was the age of advertising orientation in which advertising agencies created advertisements; stage two, the age of 4P marketing strategy mix in which enterprises built their own marketing teams; stage three, the age of terminal first in which retailers rose to the fore; stage four, the age of e-commerce driven by PC Internet; stage five, the age of "prosumerism" with the marketing power shifting from sellers to buyers and user engagement increased, in which co-creations lead to enjoying together.

PARSS Rule:
Strategy Mix for Implementing Value Orientation

P – Players

We need to know who the "founding members" are and what the solutions for the contradictory demands of players are, before establishing the entire value chain of an enterprise.

Marketers should at least ask themselves the following questions:

Can we spot all the players influencing the enterprise value chain? They include our company, competitors, and potential cross-industry ravagers outside the industry, as well as suppliers, complementary parties, users, and critics.

Which users should we investigate and interview to have them participate in product R&D and service upgrade?

Are there any opportunities for us to cooperate with competitors?

Can we cooperate with the cross-industry ravager? If yes, how will the cooperation be in order to complement both parties?

Can we cooperate with those with emerging technology, such as consumer finance and big data companies, and new material laboratories? If yes, which section of our value chain will be improved from it?

A – Added Value

The added value of an enterprise is the addition to its existing value. Besides the above players, the accounting department of the enterprise should also participate, as cost is also a player.

A marketer should raise at least the following questions:

What methods are available to the enterprise to improve the added value without adding cost?

What ways are available to the enterprise to improve the added value by adding a small amount of cost?

If it requires increasing costs to largely increase the added value, what channels are available to the enterprise for digesting or passing on costs?

Ask every marketer to list the demand directions of the added value as many as possible, only considering the user demand.

Please combine like terms in the list of added value listed by the marketer, classify them into lists of product-added value and service-added value, and ask the technology R&D engineers and customer service department to answer.

R – Rules

An essential part during the establishment of the value goal orientation is to make systematic game rules: what rules can maximize the strengths of players? How to sort out respective rights and obligations?

A marketer should raise at least the following questions:

Which one of our current operation rules can continue to be applied?

What rules have hindered our development?

What new rules do we need to make to create new value?

What contracts are needed to guarantee the execution of those new rules?

Who is to supervise the new rules?

Do the rule executors execute the plan every time?

S – Share

Value is meaningless without spread. Product value and service value will convert into user value only after they are spread. However, in the era of the mobile Internet, analysts replace spreaders, and super users play an increasingly apparent role in the sharing. Furthermore, mobile marketing is better in terms of reducing spread costs.

A marketer should raise at least the following questions:

Who are our fans? How many loyal super users are among our fans? How many among those super users are glad to share our substance marketing relating to products and services?

What sharing content and tools can we provide to the sharers?

What concrete incentive plans can we provide to the sharers?

Can we hold the meeting of sharers? If yes, how often?

How do we deal with the complaints or criticism of sharers?

S – Service

The idea of everything as service runs throughout mobile marketing. Services to users, employees, partners and even competitors are truly the value pattern of service creation.

A marketer should ask at least the following questions:

If an employee reaches standards in terms of the performance or number of years of serving the company, what value-added services should we offer him/her?

Before serving, does every one of us learn to listen to user complaints and list user complaints as a ladder for our growth?

What services of competitors are better than ours? What are the most advanced service metrics in the industry?

Do we begin with service slogan, assignment and execution plan?

What services of ours can be outsourced?

"You don't have to blow out the other fellow's light to let your own shine," said the American financier Bernard Baruch. The best method to win is to make ourselves stronger.

 ## Price Strategy Operation

Top management can first think about the following key questions when conducting market research based on demand and elasticity:

(1) How low will a price lead to the question about the quality?

(2) How high should a price be set so that it will not be deemed as artificially high?

(3) What price will make customers start to feel expensive?

(4) What price will make customers

How TO Price it Riyht?!

① *Price skimming: also known as high-pricing or skimming price, namely, setting a relatively high price for a product when it is first marketed (even the price will stop some people from buying), so as to recover investment and obtain considerable profits ASAP before competitors develop similar products.*

② *Penetration pricing is a marketing strategy where the price of a product is set low initially when it enters the market, to attract as many consumers as possible.*

feel that it is too expensive to buy?

After establishing the pricing goals, the marketing management should estimate the total revenue at different prices.

Select a price strategy.

The most basic, long-term pricing framework for a product or service should be laid down after the pricing objectives are defined. The price strategy a marketing manager needs is to define the initial price and point out the trends of the price movements over the product life cycle.

The enterprise needs to determine a competitive price range on the special market segment according to the product positioning. Changes of the price level from general gain to high gain are according to the changes of the product itself, target customers served, promotion strategy, or distribution channel, and they are faster on the Internet. Therefore, the change of a price strategy requires the dramatic changes of the marketing mix.

Enterprises serious about the pricing strategy may select from the following four basic pricing strategies: price skimming, penetration pricing, moderate pricing, and competitive pricing.

1. Price Skimming

Price skimming① is sometimes referred to as a "market-plus" approach because the price is higher relative to prices of competitive products. The price skimming gets its name from "skimming the cream off the top", which is often used by enterprises for their new products. For example, the U.S. pharmaceutical company Genzyme was the first in launching the Ceredase tablets for hypofunction, which allow patients to avoid the pain of physiological function degeneration and lead normal lives, and the company charged more than USD $300,000 for a one-year treatment.

Some companies frequently use the price skimming at the initial stage of their products and then lower prices over time because their technologies are in the unique monopoly position at the beginning. Such pricing type is called riding down the demand curve. Callaway Golf Company will immediately lower the price of the old model once launching new club products. Benz often lowers the price of the old model when launching the new

model. According to a manager at a manufacturing enterprise of Chanel purses (with the retail price of more than USD $2,000/piece), they will take back and destroy the unsold inventory instead of selling it at a discount.

Enterprises like Tiffany & Co., and Neiman Marcus, a U.S. boutique department store, have executed price skimming, which is always their basic price strategy, despite the occasional discount sale. The luxury goods market has been so made, even in the Internet age.

The price skimming strategy will work best if the price of a product is higher than the average market price but consumers are still willing to buy it. Enterprises can use the price skimming effectively if their products can be legally protected or contain technological innovation or restrict the entry of competitors in certain aspect. The price skimming is an executable strategy so long as the demand exceeds supply, and demands can always be created.

A successful price skimming strategy enables the management department to rapidly recover its costs of product development or "user education". Companies generally believe that the best method is to test the market with a high price, and then lower it if the sales volume is low, implying, "If there are any premium-price buyers on the market, we approach them first to maximize our revenue per unit". A successful price skimming strategy is not only applicable to products.

2. Penetration Pricing

Penetration pricing② strategy is the very opposite of the price skimming strategy, which refers to a strategy where the price of a product is set relatively low in order for it to reach the huge market. The low price is set to capture a large share of the market, thus to lower the production costs. Penetration pricing will be a wise choice if a marketing manager sets the company's pricing objective as obtaining a large market share.

Penetration pricing means lowering the sales profit per commodity unit: it, therefore, requires a higher sales volume than price skimming does so as to reach the break-even point. If it takes a long time to obtain high sales volume, the recovery of product development costs will also be slow. The apparent objective of penetration pricing is to keep out competition.

Penetration pricing is quite effective on price-sensitive markets. If the demand is elastic, the price should decline rapidly, because the market can be rapidly expanded with a lower price. Likewise, if consumers are sensitive to prices and the market competition is fierce, the product's initial price should be set low, and then slightly lowered or maintained at a low level.

The success of Walmart lies with its penetration pricing, and other chain enterprises have also used this strategy well. For example, one-dollar stores have now become quite popular in the U.S., and have become another choice for more and more people to shop because they consider prices of at Walmart to be slightly high and the shopping there to be cumbersome: Walmart generally opens its megastores on the edge of cities, while the small one-dollar stores can be opened at downtown communities to get close to residents; and parking is cumbersome at Walmart where people have to pass a huge parking lot, while they can quickly go in and out of a one-dollar store.

If an enterprise implements the fixed cost pricing model with each sale helping recover the fixed cost, the penetration pricing can promote sales and largely increase profits, provided that, certainly, its market size increases or competitors take no part in the competition. Low prices can attract more buyers into the market, and the increased sales will help expand production scale or develop new technology, which will help reduce costs.

Penetration pricing will be quite effective if an experience curve can lead to significant decline of fixed costs per unit. The so-called experience curve means that as a company's production experience increases, the per-unit costs will go down, showing the role the law of marginal cost decline plays.

The biggest advantage of the penetration pricing is that it discourages the market entry of competitors, while the disadvantage thereof is that the penetration means mass production and selling a large quantity of products at a low price, and if the produced products fail to be completely sold, the enterprise will lose a huge amount of manufacturing cost and even cause factories to close due to unmarketable products.

Another issue with the penetration pricing is that when a famous brand is to gain market shares through penetration pricing, the action will eventually lead to a failure.

For example, Omega was a brand more prestigious than Rolex; it used the penetration pricing strategy in order to improve its market shares, but this led to the flooding of low-priced products onto the market, which destroyed its brand image. Omega never won sufficient market shares in the competition of "low price— low brand image", thus it failed to prove the strategy of lowering its brand image and canceling high-price positioning for strong buyers to be correct (Lacoste clothing experienced the same).

3. Moderate Pricing

The third pricing strategy available to enterprises is the moderate pricing: pricing according to the competition realities, namely, charging a price that is the same or very close to the competitor's price.

Moderate pricing has the advantage of simplicity, while its disadvantage is that this strategy easily ignores demand or cost; however, if a company is relatively small, meeting the competition may be the safest way.

4. Considering the Competitive Market to Fine-tune the Basic Price

Marketing managers should set a basic price, namely, the general price level for enterprises to sell commodities or services, after understanding the influences of price strategies on enterprise production and marketing. The general price level correlates with pricing policy: it may be higher than market price (price skimming), flat with market price (moderate pricing), or lower than market price (penetration pricing). And the final step of pricing is to fine-tune the basic price.

Fine-tuning refers to the short-term adjustment that does not change the general price level. This pricing method allows enterprises to adjust prices to cope with competition on certain markets, to adapt to changing government regulation behaviors, to make the most of the extraordinary demand situations, or to meet promotion and market positioning goals. Various measures can be used to fine-tune the basic price, such as discount, geographic pricing, or special pricing strategies.

The basic price can be adjusted downward using discount and discount-related allowance, rebate, point, value-based pricing, and so on. Managers can encourage customers to do things normally they will not do through different forms of discount. The most common methods are as follows:

(1) Quantity discount. Buyers receive a quantity discount when they get a low price for buying a large quantity of commodities or above a certain amount. The cumulative quantity discount is a discount on catalog prices offered to a buyer for all commodities purchased over a specific period, to improve customer loyalty. The noncumulative quantity discount is not a discount for the cumulative consumption

Figure 6-1   Audi Advertisements. Source: Organized from data published on Autohome.com.cn

over a specific period, but a discount on catalog prices offered to a single order, to encourage big orders. For example, luxury clothing stores often have users apply for membership cards through the quantity discount method and offer discounts only when the one-time purchase or total purchase amount within a year reaches a certain limit. Cash discount refers to a price discount offered to consumers, industrial users, or marketing middlemen, in return for prompt payment of a bill, which is frequently used as the mobile payment technology matures because prompt payment saves sellers' cost of carry and cost of demanding payment and allows sellers to avoid bad debts.

(2) Functional discount. Placing middlemen (like wholesalers or retailers) should be compensated if they provide services or play the placing role for manufacturers, which compensation is generally achieved by a certain discount on the basic price and called functional discount or trade discount. The functional discounts differ greatly, depending on placing characteristics and roles of middlemen.

(3) Seasonal discount. Also called trade discount, seasonal discount is compensation offered to distributors for their promotion of manufacturers' products and is both a pricing tool and a promotion means. As a pricing tool, it is similar to the functional discount. For example, a manufacturer needs to pay one-third of the costs in exchange for a retailer advertising product of the manufacturer; if the retailer holds a special product exhibition, the manufacturer needs to include a certain quantity of free goods in the next order of the retailer.

(4) Cash back. Cash back is a cash refund given for the buyer of a product during a specific period, and it may be in the form of discount or cash refund on purchase amount, to stimulate demand.

(5) Interest-free financing. Sales of new cars declined in the middle to late 20th century, and makers provided an inter-est-free financing service, i.e., car buyers could borrow money interest-free, to attract people to car showrooms, as shown in Figure 6-1.

5. Geographic Pricing

Many manufacturers transport their goods all over China and even markets around the world; therefore, the transportation costs greatly influence the total product costs. The following are the most common geographic pricing methods:

(1) FOB origin pricing. Also known as FOB factory or FOB shipping point, FOB origin pricing is a price strategy that requires the buyer to pay the shipping cost from the shipping point ("free on board"). The farther the buyer is from the seller, the more the buyer pays, because shipping cost normally increases as shipping distances increase. It is also called "freight collect" pricing method.

(2) Unified delivery pricing. Companies will adopt the unified delivery pricing (also called "postage stamp" pricing) if the marketing managers hope to charge the same prices (including transportation costs) to people who buy the same items. According to the unified delivery pricing, the sellers pay the actual freight, and issue bills with the same freight to each buyer. This pricing is also called "freight included" pricing method.

(3) Interval pricing. A marketing manager may modify the basic price with the interval pricing strategy, if he wants to balance the total expenses of buyers by zone within a large geographical range (but not necessarily all markets of the seller). Interval pricing (also known as zone pricing) is a modification of unified delivery pricing: enterprises do not specify a same freight rate, but divide it into several parts or intervals, and charge the same freight rate for all customers within a designated interval.

(4) Freight subsidy pricing. In the event of the freight subsidy pricing strategy, sellers pay all or part of the actual

freight, instead of passing on freight to buyers. Managers will adopt such strategy on an intensively competitive market, or to rapidly break into a new market.

(5) Basic pricing. In the event of basic pricing, sellers designate a place as a base point, to charge all buyers for freight from that point, regardless of the place from which the goods are shipped.

6. Special Pricing Strategies

Unlike geographic pricing, special pricing strategies are unique and without clear categories; they are used by managers for a variety of reasons, such as stimulating demands for certain products under fierce competition conditions, increasing store patronage, and providing more varieties at a certain price. Special pricing strategies include single price strategy, flexible pricing[①], trade-in, professional service pricing, price line, leader pricing, bait pricing, odd-even pricing, price bundling, and two-part pricing.

(1) Single price strategy. The single price strategy refers to providing all commodities and services at the single price (or two or three prices).

Retailers using such pricing strategy include One Price Clothing Stores, Dre$$ to the Nine$, and Your $10 Store.

The single price saves buyers from price comparisons in the decision process, and consumers only need to look for the suitable and high-quality commodities.

(2) Flexible pricing. Flexible pricing, also known as variable pricing, refers to a price strategy where different customers pay different prices for the same quantity of products of the same nature, which is often used in sale of commodities purchased by choice, commodities under exclusive rights, and most commodities for enterprises (excluding consumables), and commonly adopted by car suppliers, household appliance retailers, and manufacturers of industrial units and spare parts.

(3) Trade-in. Flexible pricing is usually introduced with trade-in. Consumers must reach two price agreements: one for the new commodity, and one for the existing commodity, when merchants launch the trade-in.

Customers to trade in care more about prices of the old commodities for discount-sale, instead of prices of new commodities to buy.

(4) Professional service pricing. This strategy is used by people who are experienced, specially trained, and often licensed by relevant institutions, like lawyers, doctors, and family financial advisors.

(5) Price line. A price line will form when a seller establishes a series of prices for a category of commodities and refers to pricing for several commodities of a product line at a certain price.

7. Leader Pricing

Leader pricing, also known as loss-leader pricing, is an attempt by the marketing manager to attract customers by selling a product near or even below cost in the hope that they will buy other items once they are in the store. Such pricing type appears weekly in the advertisements of supermarkets, special sale stores, and department stores. Leader pricing is normally used on well-known items that consumers can easily recognize as bargains at the special price. The goal is not necessarily to sell large quantities of leader items, but to try to appeal to customers to buy other items.

For example, a health club attracts customers by giving a one-month free trial; a lawyer gives a free initial consultation; a restaurant distributes two-for-one coupon and free meal coupon to the chain restaurant: all of those belong to such pricing model.

Bait pricing is deceptive in contrast to leader pricing that is a genuine attempt to give consumers a low price. Bait pricing tries to attract consumers to a store with false or misleading price advertising and then persuades consumers to buy more expensive products through hard selling.

8. Odd-even Pricing

Odd-even pricing, also known as psychological pricing, means pricing at an odd-numbered price to indicate the cheapness and at even-numbered price to imply the quality. Many retailers have priced their products in odd numbers (such as USD $99.95 or USD $49.95) over the years using such strategy, to make consumers feel that they are paying less to buy a product.

9. Price Bundling

Price bundling sells two or more products in a bundle at a special price. For example, Microsoft launched software "suites" to bundle spreadsheets, word processing system, graphics, e-mail, Internet access, and microcomputer components for sale.

① *Flexible pricing refers to the principle or technique of determining price adjustment direction according to price elasticity.*

10. Two-part Pricing

Two-part pricing refers to charging two separate prices when selling a single commodity or service. Tennis clubs and health clubs charge a membership fee and a flat fee each time a customer uses certain equipment; in other cases, they charge a base fee for a certain level of usage, such as 10 table tennis activities per month, and an additional fee for the activities exceeding that number.

Two-part pricing may attract the consumers who would not pay a high fee even if the service is available for unlimited times. For example, a health club may only sell 100 membership cards at USD $700 annual fee and such members can use the equipment for unlimited times. The total revenue will be USD $70,000.

11. Competitive Pricing

The nascent mobile commerce companies sometimes will carry out mobile marketing using free or subsidized policy and special price campaigns, to create hot sale commodities, increase user stickiness[①], and increase user retention.

Zhubajie app is a creative online transaction platform with powerful functions, where users can find all the creative design they desire. This app obtains commission income from the creative assignments on the platform where 10 million registered users provide creativity, development, design and promotion services, etc. Zhubajie specially launched the "Qixi Festival" services on the Qixi Festival (Chinese Valentine's Day) in 2014: charging CNY 10 to put together keywords into a heart shape, CNY 77 to customize romantic videos, and CNY 99 to make couple avatars, ghostwrite love letters, and record couples meetings. Those prices were far lower than cost. The best way to have an explosive number of users is the pricing strategy regardless of cost.

The well-known Uber and Didi Chuxing implemented a price strategy that subsidized both drivers and passengers.

Enterprise background: Uber (Uber Technologies, Inc.) is a tech company co-founded by Travis Kalanik, a UCLA dropout, and his friend Garrett Campo in 2009 in Silicon Valley in the U.S. The car-hailing app Uber was formally operated in Shanghai, Shenzhen, and Guangzhou in February 2014, and in Beijing in July 2014, to mainly cover Sanlitun and China World Trade Center areas at first.

The well-known Didi Express and UBER.
Source: Ahwang.cn

Established on June 6, 2012, Didi Chuxing belongs to Beijing Xiaoju Technology Co., Ltd., and formally went live in Beijing on September 9 after three months of preparations and driver end promotion. Its users exceeded 100 million and drivers exceeded one million by March 2014, with average daily orders reaching 5,218,300, becoming the transaction platform with the largest number of average daily orders on the mobile Internet.

After Didi Express went live in February 2015, the contest on China's travel market did not end; instead, it ushered in the more brutal "second half" that started the lengthy and costly competition between Didi Express and People's Uber.

Nine days after Didi Express went live, Didi announced the launch of "free express for all the people" in 12 cities including Beijing, Tianjin, Hangzhou, Guangzhou, Shenzhen, Chengdu, Wuhan, Chongqing, Nanjing, Changsha, Dalian, and Xi'an where all passengers might take free Didi Express on every money in the following month, for which Didi invested CNY one billion.

Didi Express's fierce money throwing was quite effective. According to the data released by Didi, the user coverage of Didi Premier (Express) reached 88.4% in 2015, and the average daily orders accounted for 84.1% in the express (premier) related mobile travel service industry of China.

In the official announcement on August 2, 2016, Didi Chuxing officially announced the strategic agreement with Uber Global under which Didi Chuxing would acquire all assets such as the brand, business, and data of Uber China, both parties would mutually hold shares[②] to become the minority stockholder of each other: Uber would hold 5.89% equity of Didi, equal to a 17.7% economic interest, and other Chinese shareholders of Uber China would receive a total of 2.3% economic interest, and Cheng Wei, the Founder and Chairman of Didi Chuxing, would join the board of Uber, and Travis Kalanik, the Founder of Uber, would join the board of Didi Chuxing. The most vocal doubt before and after the two online car-hailing platforms announced the merger was: "Will there still be subsidies?".

① *User stickiness refers to increasing the mutual usage of users and enterprises, like with the mutual relationships in our daily life.*

② *Shareholding refers to holding certain shares. A shareholder holding 30% shares can be called controlling, and if he is the biggest shareholder, he can also be called relative controlling; a shareholder holding more than 50% shares can be called absolute controlling.*

A Good Product Spreads Itself

Word-of-mouth communication of a product is essentially the results produced by the media attribute of the product or service. To give play to the media attribute hidden in the product itself, one must proceed with supreme product and emotional experience.

Only by becoming supreme will a product become popular in the age of Internet economy. A supreme product has strong brand effect, and will catch the eyes of innumerable consumers when launched, even without the spending on advertising.

Products that are not extremely well made generally need to be advertised and publicized widely until bought by consumers with the demand, however, products that are extremely well made sell themselves, and have the best word-of-mouth: users would tell each other and actively order them, which is the manifestation of the media attribute supreme products have.

Enterprises do not have to master the most advanced technology to make supreme products. Revolutionary products are always in the minority, and the pursuit of the ultimate is not equal to starting all over again. Enterprises should proceed with improvement of user experience, rather than pursue the higher, faster, stronger, or newer.

Nowadays, consumers are overwhelmed by the enormously rich daily necessities and the various commodities with different functions; however, the more functions a commodity has, the more complex its operation will be, which becomes a burden to many users. A supreme product that offers the ultimate experience to users has strong media attributes. Products are not only a function carrier, but also a natural medium with high communication value.

The media attribute of a product is also reflected in the emotional experience offered to users. A product will be possible to spread itself when it gains the emotional acceptance of consumers. If it is functions that decide the practical value of a product, then it is the emotional experience that decides the humanistic connotation thereof. Another means to give play to the media attribute of a product is to have it stimulate the emotional resonance of users.

Online services are growing in the age of Internet economy. The design of Alipay bill highly values strengthening the satisfaction of user experience and leads

Case Study   The Beast Flower Shop

Without a physical store or even a Taobao store, but only with several photos of a flower gift box and 140 characters of text description on Microblog (a Chinese microblog), the Beast Flower Shop has attracted hundreds of thousands of followers since opening a Microblog at the end of December 2011, with regular customers even including many stars in show business.

The Beast is different from Roseonly in terms of the user emotional appeals they satisfy, and its flowers have stories. An enterprise with a story easily receives the attention of investors and consumers, and a product with a story is more easily remembered by people, especially when you are the main character in the story.

In this regard, the representative work of the Beast, the story of "Monet Garden" has been widely spread, which was tailored for a certain customer wishing to show the artistic conception of Monet's masterwork, Agapanthus Triptych, with the creation lasting for several months.

The Beast's flower ordering model, in which customers only need to tell their intentions, is completely different from the traditional ordering model. There is a story and a complex behind each bouquet of flowers.

For example, a certain customer would require "putting dolls in the shapes of her two daughters, one aged four, and the other aged one, into the bouquet for their father"; a certain customer would require "sending flowers to his girlfriend in the hope that the bouquet could reproduce the scene where they met two years ago: a certain mall in Wujiaochang, rain, movie, and dinner at Fumao Crayfish", etc.

Such business model of the Beast makes flowers no longer a product but an expression of user emotion. The moment when a customer receives a flower, what she receives is not only the flower, but also a story and an emotion, and she herself is the main character of that story and that emotion. Such experiences are beyond what traditional flower shops can offer. The Beast offers opportunities to customers that the traditional flower shops fail to offer, which is the key to the success of the Beast.

The case source quoted from: Huxiu.com 2013/10/18
https://www.huxiu.com/article/21660/1.html

to the emotional resonance of many users. Unlike the traditional bank statements with simple and dull day-to-day account, Alipay bill has vivid and interesting interface design, and titles that are close to people. In the bill columns, Alipay also provides the user's ranking among the consumer group in his area with the help of the strong data statistical function, with the expression: "My annual spending exceeds x% people in x city", making users take pleasure in posting their bills.

On the other hand, enterprises can learn details and information through the Annual Report, for example, Alipay declared men in Tumxuk City, Xinjiang as "most dearly loving women" on the Report because men in the city bought the largest number of commodities for women. The interesting consumption details changed the dull image of the traditional bills. However, such creativity depended on strong data statistics and classification functions and could never be achieved at a time without computers and the Internet.

In fact, banks understand users' consumption data as well as Alipay does; however, banks will not design products and services using the Internet thinking habits closest to people like Alipay does, due to the functional factor.

In this age of increasingly developed networks and growing consumers who prefer to stay at home, only the easy, convenient, simple, and interesting packaging forms will stimulate the emotional resonance of users; otherwise, users will not be attracted, let alone engaging in word-of-mouth communication about a product.

In a word, enterprises should possess the Internet thinking, and deeply mine the media attribute of products to reduce publicity costs, increase promotional efficiency, and enable the product brands to gain better popularity and reputation. This is the meaning of "a good product speaks for itself".

Tipping Point–Hot Sale Model–Hot Sale Item

Product pricing relates to user demand and demand thirst. In the age of the mobile Internet where users' right of speech is growing, the difficulty of marketing lies in how to make users "thirsty". Users are apparently not thirsty in the age of surplus of products; the demand thirst is a market phenomenon created by the mobile marketers. The bigger user demand is, the higher the demand thirst, and the less the supply of a product, the higher the price, and vice versa. Creating high-priced hot sale items and hot sale models is the highest level of marketers. The Law of THH must be followed to reach such level (see Figure 6-2).

This law may be described by such marketing logic: firstly, focus the marketing on 1,000 geeks as a trial, who can be intermediaries, public relations firms, opinion leaders, and celebrities, and serve as the tipping point, publicity station, and engine; secondly, focus the marketing on a very few users among the expected 1,000,000 to sell to, namely, 1% super users, who are sharers, critics, and connectors; finally, turn the hot sale model that will possibly be briefly in vogue into a hot sale item that will continue to be popular, namely, turning popularity into a trend.

As shown in Figure 6-2, why is the number of geeks which form the tipping point 1,000? What if it were 100? According to the brilliant work Tipping Point by maverick thinker Malcolm Gladwell of *The New Yorker*, there are three rules for the phenomena that trigger the trends: the Law of the Few, the Stickiness Factor, and the Power of Context, wherein, the Law of the Few constituted by connectors, mavens, and salesmen is very close to the concept of geek in this book. People with excellent socializing gifts have the ability to keep a "weak tie", a casual social connection, with many people. More than that, they are happy with the weak tie, and they involve in many fields and then connect all of them.

It is worth noting that such a weak tie should never be belittled. The weak tie always plays a bigger role than the fixed tie when you want to learn new information or new idea, because, after all, your friends understand almost the same situation as you. With enormous social connections, long lists of weak ties, and a place in each field, connectors must be able to quickly and efficiently spread information and achieve the "tipping" role.

Besides, connectors also have a characteristic: their emotions are contagious. Emotions are shown from the inside out; however, the contagious effect of emotions shows that they can also influence from the outside in. Some people are better at expressing emotions and feelings, and they are called "senders of emotion" by psychologists.

In short, connectors (connecting personality) as the information collector and publisher, mavens (knowledge-based personality), and salesmen (contagious personality) can efficiently spread information and produce "tipping" effect as activists of social circles. Those three types are very good at socializing and spreading, and are able to transmit "original viruses" to many people, i.e., influencing many people. Such people also exist in the business trends: merchants like to invite stars and Microblog opinion leaders to help them begin the initial publicity because the latter have characteristics of the Law of the Few and can spread information to many people in an instant, not to mention the promotion effect of mavens who speak with more authority.

However, according to the Tipping Point, the effective number of people to trigger a small trend does not exceed 150, and 150 is a magic number.

However, 150 is not a magic number but a wrong number in China, because the US population is less than 300 million while the Chinese population is more than 1.4 billion in China. Therefore, according to this proportion, the 150 geeks in the U.S. should amount to 1,000 in China. From this perspective, we should not blindly follow Western business school textbooks because they are written based on the na-

1,000	10,000	10 million
Tipping point	Hot sale model	Hot sale item

Law of THH

1,000 geeks ignite the wildfire, causing 10,000 super users to create the catfish effect which triggers 1,000,000 users to use the product and form the trend when conditions are ripe.

Figure 6.2 Law of THH.

tional conditions of the U.S. A trend will not be triggered if the number of geeks is too small. The starting scale decides the extent of popularity. The task of marketers is to put their thoughts into others' minds to take money from their pockets into the marketers' own, which is quite hard; they are in fact initiating a large-scale ideological reform campaign when trying to have others accept their own thoughts, ideas, or products, which certainly requires 1,000 tipping points to change the tide, not less (because of the liability to being prevailed over by competitors) nor more.

The instance in which Allen Zhang invited 1,000 users to serve as the 1,000 tipping points of WeChat before the launch of WeChat in 2011 proved that a hot sale item starts from 1,000 tipping points.

💡 Case Study How did Adidas Make Hot Sale Models?

Adidas is a well-known German sports brand, and holds a place in merchandise for basketball, cricket, football, baseball, handball, athletics, tennis, boxing, swimming and the latest extreme sports.

This sportswear giant enjoyed good sales trends in 2016 and it is expected to create a record high. It was gradually taking back the lost market shares from Nike and Under Armour. Adidas has performed marketing magic tricks one after another over the last two years by continuously making hot sale models, to attract the total attention of consumers.

There are always some better background stories behind magnificent stage performances.

Adidas Air Yeezy. Source: Adidas Official Website

The rapper Kanye West launched his first fashion series products in collaboration with Adidas - the Yeezy collection of sneakers in an evening of the New York Fashion Week in February 2015, which is endearingly called Yezi (Mandarin for coconut, with the pronunciation similar to Yeezy) sneakers by more Chinese consumers. 9,000 pairs of Yeezy sneakers priced at USD $350 were snapped up in the U.S. within a few minutes after the launch, while the average price offered by resellers was USD $1,500, and some scalpers even priced them at five times the original price.

However, the real intention of Adidas was concealed by those glaring sales results: Kanye who stayed at Nike for four years with his own Air Yeezy product line told angrily about his original intention of leaving Nike for Adidas: Nike was shackling his creative freedom; they were not giving him the opportunity to grow; Adidas lets him live his dreams out.

In fact, his words show the difference between Nike and Adidas in terms of orientation: the former pays more attention to technological content, while the latter is gradually moving towards the fashion world.

At least for the Yeezy sneakers that are suede high-top sneakers complete with side zips and patented springy soles made from spaceship-grade foam, what receives attention is not the technological content therein, but the sleek appearance.

This was only a small show where sports brand Adidas, the perennial runner-up in the sneaker area, mounted a challenge against Nike, the U.S. giant, not by taking the full product line to charge, but came from a smaller perspective: through the single product + hot sale model it bypassed Nike's heavily fortified "Maginot Line", and pried up new market vitality directly from edges of the map with fashion concept.

Adidas made at least three hot sale models of shoes in over two years from Stan Smith to the newly launched Adidas Originals NMD; however, it appeared to the outside world that Adidas was always playing the hunger marketing through a small quantity of supply and then stock-out.

Adidas released the sales strategy for NMD in China on the special node - March 15, 2015 World Consumer Rights Day: "first come, first served" limited sale in some stores. There were already people queuing on Nanjing West Road, Shanghai by noon of the following day, and in the afternoon, as there were too many people, Adidas canceled the sale of Nanjing West Road Store, and subsequently canceled the sales plan of Beijing Sanlitun Store. Prices of the 15 models of NMD sold on March 17 rose to CNY 2,500-CNY 4,000 on non-official purchasing channels, while the original prices were between CNY 1,099 and CNY 1,499.

Apparently, only the limited sale was not enough to cause a boom NMD's popularity, and if Adidas always used such a trick for new sneakers, it would easily bore consumers, especially while the frequency was as high as four models in two years. How, then, did Adidas make it?

Pay attention to preparation. It is not difficult to find throughout Adidas' making of hot sale models that Adidas was a super preparation master and brought different surprises to consumers every time.

Battle one: Adidas tested by returning an old product.

The return of Stan Smith could stir different memories of innumerable people and tell a large number of good stories, which is the tipping point the social marketing values most. And in fact, Stan Smith met the expectations. From the outside, the going viral of this shoe model was because of the good story, a brand story as all-matching as the shoe model.

But in fact, the process was not that simple: besides continuing to increase the fashion elements in the remaking, Adidas also made many efforts behind the scenes. Jon Wexle, Adidas' Director of Marketing,

said in a media report that it took five steps to make Stan Smith sneakers popular: ① Stop launching new products and "clear up" the market; ② Subtly reintroduce them through a single fashion show; ③ Get celebrities wearing them; ④ Release a limited batch to consumers; ⑤ Let people go crazy for them.

While the five steps of preparation seemed to be quite simple, they were in fact not. The event control is the key to preparation, and this marketing by Adidas could not be called hunger marketing but despair marketing.

At the end of the battle of Stan Smith, Adidas pushed the personalized fashion demands to an extreme: it offered three different colors in its "Stan Yourself" campaign to shoe fans, and buyers could replace the original Smith avatar on the tongue with their own avatar; Stan Smith continued to stay as a hot topic on the social network via the word-of-mouth communication of ordinary people, and truly made itself different, and resurrected classical models with "full HP".

In the subsequent marketing of Yeezy and NMD, tactics like same models with celebrities, hunger marketing, and personalized customization were conducted in turn. For example, simultaneously with the sale of NMD in Europe in December of 2015, stars like Kris Wu, Shawn Yue, Fan Bingbing, Andy Lau, Deng Chao and Charlene Choi appeared on catwalks wearing NMD shoes, as encouraged by Eason Chan, Adidas' spokesperson in China. Also during the sale, Adidas announced that only around 10,000 pairs, 25 models in total, would be sold on the Chinese market in 20 major cities in Mainland China including Beijing, Shanghai, Guangzhou and Chengdu; and Adidas "predicted" that the sale would be hot; therefore, it stipulated that

Adidas Originals NMD.
Source: Adidas Official Website

ID card registration should be required for the purchase of NMD, and everyone could only buy one pair in stores.

What else? The similar preparation was insufficient by itself to constantly stimulate the market demands, but it might cause consumers to have aesthetic fatigue due to too frequent hunger marketing, instead.

Apparently, if the magic trick for hot sale model is repeatedly re-performed, the effect will become weaker and weaker; however, this problem did not happen to NMD. The key was that the additional value given to NMD by Adidas this time was in fact not feelings, but colors.

Adidas shoes had long impressed consumers with the black and white colors, while it was the "color revolution" that served as the trump card for Adidas to enter the fashion world from the sports world this time.

For users, it was not the black and white, but the colorful Adidas shoes that gave them a different sense of presence, sportive and fashionable, which was the additional value different from Stan Smith shoes that stress feelings and Yeezy sneakers that stress style.

Regarding Adidas as a preparation master who constantly teases might be what Adidas expected. Only by hiding their own true changes in the mesmerizing preparation could it better beat its competitors.

This was the best camouflage of a magician, and Adidas was doing something secretly behind the scenes.

Firstly, quietly using trials and errors in the design. The color revolution on NMD that received much attention was in fact operated on Adidas very early. Adidas' Senior Director Kathryn O'Brien said, "We wanted to dig into this whole idea that color is an emotion". O'Brien mainly promoted a model of purple sneakers: Ultra Boost in 2015, and she said jokingly, "I almost got thrown out of the window." However, the model turned out to be hot. According to a study, 85% of shoppers choose a product based on its color. This result promoted Adidas to shift from black and white to chromatic colors.

Secondly, continuing to increase technological content. Unlike the high-tech shoes of Nike, the technological content of Adidas does not only show in the wearing comfort of users, but also in the attempt to integrate into fashion. For example, the patented Boost cushioning technology of Adidas that is deemed to fight Nike's Flyknit technology proved a resounding success in 2015, not through the technology itself, but through fashion, especially the Ultra Boost worn by Kanye West almost put Nike in the shade overnight that the trend website Highsnobiety jokingly said in the report that there were more people wearing Ultra Boost to the Fashion Week than those in the NYC Marathon.

Sometimes technology is not shown through parameters. Often its effect will be better when it is felt by people themselves and experienced by users themselves.

Thirdly, making personalization the ultimate experience of users. There is a very interesting gimmick in Adidas' plan, namely applying 3D printing technology in shoe making with the ultimate goal of letting everyone get shoes suitable for them. This assumption that sounds quite "techy" still shows Adidas' changes from competition in technology to competition in fashion.

Adidas wanted not only to have users buy the hot sale models, but also to eventually turn hot sale models into shoes commonly seen on the street.

The hot sale model of Adidas may be a specific model; however, more diverse personalized elements are added to the model to facilitate users' selection, resulting in that under the hot sale model, each color matching, fabric selection, and pattern vertically find a way into a small consumer circle. All this was in fact gradually competed through the collaboration between various fashion designers and Adidas's technology elements.

The ultimate secret to this magic show which Adidas performed through preparation such as rhythm, feelings, and hunger was allowing the hot sale model to be not just a popular commodity among the people, but individual favorites that meet demands of different customers, and change from simple functional sneakers into personalized fashion makers.

The case source quoted from: Organized from data published on Adidas Official Website2016/07/25
http://news.zol.com.cn/595/5952575.html

Tool Kit – 16 Methods for Service Upgrade

Service is the most important method for enterprises to win customers. The competition of enterprises nowadays is in some sense service competition. "Service marketing" is a marketing means that focuses on customers and then provides services to eventually achieve beneficial exchanges. According to calculations, the cost required to develop a new customer is five times the cost required to maintain an old customer. With such reality, the timeliness, thoughtfulness and extremeness of enterprise services are the key to victory.

1. Establishing a database

Homelink. Source: Lianjia.com

Homelink, China's largest property agency, has about 8,000 stores and 150,000 brokers in 32 cities in China, and an Internet team composed of about 1,000 people. Data have been the important asset that Homelink is proud of, which include house data, user data and transaction data. For instance, when a user searches for house sources via its app or website, the system will present characteristics and preferences of user transaction behaviors by analyzing the high-frequency interactive data during users' looking for a house, to help the user concretize his demand, establish the user's relationship map with house sources, achieve precise matching, remove and reconstruct redundant and complex processes in the transaction scenario, and improve both user experience and operation efficiency. According to Homelink's data, behind each transaction are 12,000 page views, and this figure for the Beijing Homelink is 17,000, which means that Homelink has not only fostered or gathered the first online important real estate users, but also consumers are moving online, and their means of acting are undergoing quite large changes after moving home.

2. Building trust

Mobile marketing's distribution system is based on the "trust agents" theory, and the so-called fission and replication are the passing on of such trust. When your user is satisfied with your service, he will pass on such trust to his friends who trust you via your user and it is possible for the trust to be passed on continuously, so your service is the source of trust. Such kind of trust is in your product itself also in your service. In essence, however, the service is more important than the product, because we do not lack good products or the purchase places today. Why should people buy your products sold in WeChat Moments only upon your sharing, when you cannot issue receipt vouchers as the basis for after-sales rights and have no third-party guarantees? The key is the trust from the service.

3. Exceeding customers' expectations

A service aim determined by Walmart's founder, Sam Walton, is "exceed your customers' expectations", which attracts followers across the world; however, only Haidilao Hotpot from Jianyang, Sichuan has learned the essence of this. Strictly speaking, what Haidilao provides cannot be called service but spoiling, always a scarce resource. Service exceeding expectations is essentially attentive service that relies heavily on the human factor, as the format can be copied but not the human.

4. Exploring users' demands to the full

Uber adopts different marketing strategies in different markets in the world. Uber competed with Didi in China in terms of cash burning and preference offering, while in India, it tried the method that suits the taste of local people. For example, Indians are in love with movies and music, so Uber provided them with movies and music in cars, which was well received by the local population.

5. Cooperating with strong resources

In 2017, China Railway showed its will to collaborate with Alibaba, in the hope of strategically expanding a broader cooperation platform and deepening cooperation in fields of CRII express, international logistics, electronic payment and mixed-ownership reform, based on consolidating cooperation in the Alipay application, real-name information verification service and station navigation. Jack Ma stated that Alibaba would look at the integration of high-speed rail network and Internet, and research and promote the pilot work of high-speed rail e-commerce service, to jointly create convenience for the high-speed rail mobile life. Such cooperation was a result of both parties innovating the cooperation mode and giving full play to respective advantages, and it would help effectively increase the resource utilization efficiency and effectiveness, promote the supply-side structural reform, achieve integration of high-speed rail network and Internet, build smarter rail with all strength, make high-speed rail an integrated service carrier for the enjoyment of travel, tourism, shopping and leisure, make high-speed rail life a new lifestyle, and enable the people to better enjoy the high-speed rail outcomes and have more sense of gain.

6. Internet application

SAIC Motor Corporation Limited (SAIC) has realized that its future revenue can depend not only on the traditional automobile manufacturing industry, but also car-related services, which can be seen from its RX 5 implementation. The world's first mass-produced Internet-based SUV, Roewe RX5, was jointly built by SAIC and Alibaba and launched in mid-2016; the monthly sales of RX 5 had reached nearly 25,000 by the end of 2016. The in-car OS: YunOS for Car is the key for the SUV to achieve multiple Internet services, and it is updated once every three months. The service substance of Internet-based cars with this OS has currently covered finance, insurance, parking, maintenance, traffic safety, navigation, music, charging and car sharing fields, etc. The manufacturer's suggested retail price (MSRP) for the most expensive non-Internet-based RX 5 is CNY 138,800, and the MSRP for the cheapest Internet-based RX 5 is CNY 148,800, with a difference of only CNY 10,000; however, behind this price difference are performance and customer experience improvement that far exceed expectations, including the significant improvement in safety, intelligent interconnection and comfort configuration, etc. Such practice seems to be like the way of thinking of Internet enterprises: they sell hardware for free and earn money by services, and it was such strategy that partly promoted the hot sale of RX 5. According to data, the Internet-based RX 5 accounted for 70% of the total sales. SAIC, via Internet-based cars with YunOS such as RX 5, could complete the data exchange on the cloud, and publicize the car data originally in the black box. More importantly, use of YunOS will generate a persona of each user, and those high-quality personae are the important basis for SAIC to provide services to users. Only in this way can SAIC turn cars from a tool to a platform.

7. Reward model

Consumption in China is now on the rise in which commodity consumption is changing towards service consumption; residents' spending on service consumption largely increases, while the commodity consumption grows relatively slowly, meaning that consumers have increasingly high requirements for service level, and the traditional service standards will be constantly challenged. The breakthrough for service improvement lies in the initiative of service providers, and the reward model is without doubt a model worth trying.

The reward model similar to tipping in the west has quietly emerged in some chain restaurants in the past two years, for example, waiters/waitresses in Haidilao and Xibei wear a QR code on their chest which you can scan with your phone to reward a waiter/waitress if you consider him/her to be attentive. Coincidentally, the reward model has also emerged in the express industry: Jingdong users can reward couriers who deliver packages to them with own Jingdou (consumers have the chance to get different amounts of Jingdou after purchase): to reward couriers with Jingdou by giving a "virtual gift"; Hanting Express has also launched the "cleaner point reward function": customers can comment on and reward cleaners via its Huazhu app, awarding 200 points for five-star cleaners, with the points deducted from customer accounts and instantly added to the cleaner's accounts.

For the service personnel, rewards are income in addition to regular salaries, which end up being happy surprises; while for consumers, it makes sense that they are willing to pay additional expenses for satisfactory services after enjoying a high-quality service. On the premise of active service and voluntary payment, the beneficiaries of rewards are not only the service personnel, and behind rewards is improvement of consumers' satisfaction towards the service quality.

The reward economy has expedited the artisan spirit and driven the service upgrade in the west. A reward can show workers society's respect and encouragement, to give them the motivation and patience to keep improving. Such atmosphere, once formed, will drive the service upgrade of the entire industry.

8. Membership system

Mao Zedong pointed out in the On Coalition Government in 1945, "The people, and the people alone, are the motive force in the making of world history"! This argument was re-verified 50 years later by a U.S. retail company: "The members, and the members alone, are the motive force in the making of retail history"!

Warren Buffett and Charlie Munger are both fans of Costco, the second largest retailer in the U.S. and the seventh largest one in the world, which opened a store in Shanghai, China by the end of 2017. The rise of e-commerce has had a massive impact on the traditional retail industry in the past decade (2006-2016). However, there are still some traditional retailers like Costco, ROSS and TJX which have withstood this impact and have bucked the trend. Costco is the most representative of these: its market value grew by 1.7 times in the past decade; such data might be nothing to be proud of; however, the results were praiseworthy in the context where the traditional retailers closed or transformed one after another as impacted by e-commerce. Like a tortoise, Costco walked not too hastily nor too slowly with an annual revenue growth of 4%-6%. We can see from analysis of its business mode, operation efficiency and performance, etc. on a micro-level, and its market competition and strategy, etc. on a macro-level that the membership system was an important reason for Costco's success.

Members are not the most important, but the only thing that matters to Costco.

Costco's revenue is divided into sales revenue and membership fees. Costco charges fixed membership fees in advance, and the profitability only relates to the number of members and does not directly relate to the commodities sold and gross margin level. According to the analysis on the financial data of the company in the past 10 years, we can find that membership fees are the main source of profits of the company, accounting for about 3/4 of the net profits. The membership system is the main difference between Costco and general supermarkets in terms of the form, which requires users to prepay fixed membership fees to become members and allows only members or families and friends accompanied by members to enter Costco stores for consumption.

This threshold of Costco makes it focus more on member customers: the most extensive middle class in the U.S., and focus more on the services provided, on the one hand; the prepayment mechanism can form the "buffet effect" in psychology to effectively improve users' activity in purchase, besides providing the sustainable and stable cash flow for the business activities, on the other hand. Its member renewal rate reached 90% and annual growth rate reached 7%. The core of member retention lies in the maximization of the consumer surplus[①]: members will be retained when the consumer surplus is far higher than the membership fee. By word-of-mouth marketing alone, its members steadily increase by 7%-8% every year.

① *Consumer surplus is the amount a buyer is willing to pay minus the amount the buyer actually pays.*

9. Targeting market segments

Targeting market segments will achieve the ultimate service. As the world's largest hotel group with the most diverse business lines, Wyndham Hotel Group excels at providing corresponding products and services according to tourists' characteristics, preferences and demands. Wyndham Hotel has carved its path to vigorously develop female business travelers and create the Women On Their Way website in 1990s when other hotel groups were immersed in serving conventional male business travelers. On its website, women business travelers can share travel plans, look for travel tips, and make travel arrangements, while the hotel plays the role of travel service adviser. In addition, Wyndham Hotel provides a series of characteristic services tailored for women business travelers (such as woman vacation tips, honeymoon travel service, and special rooms and floors for women) by analyzing users' travel demands on the website and social media with big data. The hotel has successfully pulled away from other hotel groups by focusing on women business travelers.

10. Improving the hardware level

The service experience felt by consumers is generally affected by the service facilities. For example, the core value of hotels is sleep; hotels cannot control the sleep quality of customers themselves; however, the room layout, mattress, bed sheet, pillow and even lighting in hotels will directly affect the sleep experience. Therefore, the devices and facilities used in the service industry should be called the certainties among the uncertainties. Airbnb is the world's largest bed & breakfast (B&B) sharing website. B&Bs have more obvious individual differences in terms of facilities than branded chain hotels, and consumers will feel more uncertainty before check-in, so Airbnb pays attention to concrete elements like B&B decoration, furniture, utensils and surroundings. Airbnb features a vacation home located in the luxuriant and green Bromma forest at the outskirts of Stockholm, the capital of Sweden, which is converted from an out-of-service bus, and complete with various modern living facilities, such as stylish sofa, HDTV, wooden bookcase and a single bed, which interplay with the fantastic scenery outside the vacation home. The towering trees and foraging small animals everywhere outside the window make a person feel as if he time-traveled to the agrarian age when people work after sunrise and rest after sunset.

11. Improving the professional quality of employees

United Airlines Perfect Attendance Award of the Year.
Source: United Airlines

Services themselves are inseparable from employees. How does the meal delivery service by a flight attendant who pulls a long face compare to that by a flight attendant with a sincere smile? The food itself is the same, but the perception of the service quality is quite different. Therefore, in the substance marketing of the service industry, careful cultivation of the professional and affable image of employees can subconsciously affect customers' perception of employees and can thus affect their perception of the services themselves.

United Airlines is one of the world's top-ranking large airlines. The aviation industry is a service industry with quite high requirements for the professional quality of its employees, where employees' professional dedication and dependability will directly influence passengers' view of the airlines. In what aspects is the dependability of employees represented? It is not easy for flight attendants who have intensive workloads, long working hours, and often work in three shifts to be present at work throughout the year. Therefore, a perfect attendance largely represents the dedication of employees, and United Airlines feels the same way.

12. Focusing on the process

The service process greatly influences users. Customers can try the devices as much as they like in the bright and spacious Apple Stores and the staff will patiently answer any questions customers may have. The whole process from entering store to leaving is relaxing and pleasant. The cost of this quality trial process is relatively low to Apple. For the service industry where the production and consumption proceed at the same time (such as a barber doing a haircut), companies should focus more on the service process because they will incur costs to have customers "try" services. The Progressive Corporation in Ohio, in the U.S., is the fourth largest provider of car insurance in the U.S. As its name suggests, Progressive is an innovative force in the car insurance industry of the U.S. and has continued to launch new

insurance types of products in the industry that are highly mature and fiercely competitive. Due to the complexity of the new insurance service products, the company makes great efforts to introduce the details and process of its insurance products. Progressive specially introduced its funny spokeswoman, Flo, in 2008, who vividly introduces the different insurance types of Progressive through humorous language and performance. Such light comedy style has successfully attracted a large audience of potential insurance buyers. Generally, it is not convenient to experience and try the service process and details in the manner of a "trial"; however, with the appropriate tools to clearly and vividly describe the complex process, will buyers have so many doubts?

13. Strengthening the technical foundation

In general, the service effect and perception have considerable uncertainties, especially for highly professional services such as healthcare. Customers may struggle with the choices when to buy such a kind of service, because they may not sufficiently know about the professionalism of or fully trust the medical institutions. Then how to dispel such doubts about the service professionalism? The companies must show the solid service foundation (i.e., the expertise and professional literacy); however, the public's trust in the service foundation cannot be easily built through advertising slogans; this requires long-term, sustained and effective efforts for the foundation to take root. This is the important role substance marketing can play in the service industry, especially in the professional service industry. The U.S. Cleveland Clinic built

in 1921 is a large integrated hospital that ranks among the top ten in the U.S., with not only leading medical professionals, but also the extensive publicity of the professional levels of the hospital and doctors through long-term, sustained, and effective content construction. In patients' opinions, Cleveland Clinic has a deep professional foundation and it is trustworthy. The hospital has started the enterprise blog on Facebook early in 2012, which is operated and managed by a manager with five marketing professionals, with the contributions to content coming from a writing team composed of 40 doctors and nurses. Furthermore, there are three to five posts every day on its Facebook page, with the content being mainly about health tips etc., with monthly page views of more than three million from patients from all over the world.

14. Intellectualization

Intellectualization is a trend. Let's take the car-sharing under the action of car intellectualization + interconnection as an example. The parking problem of shared cars is a bottleneck problem

car-sharing; however, parking services will increasingly be connected to the platforms with the popularization of Internet-based cars, and the following scene is likely to become a reality with the development of intellectualization: when you reserve a car, an unmanned vehicle will automatically drive to you, and after you finish the use, you just need to walk out the vehicle, and it will automatically drive to the nearest charging pile for charging. Also, some hotels have put intelligent robots in their lobbies to increase the service highlights.

15. Standardization

Enterprises should achieve service standardization, technology standardization, product standardization and process standardization as much as possible. The service standardization is the process in which the service standards are formulated and implemented, and the standardized principles and methods are utilized to effectuate the quality objectives of services, achieve the standardization of service methods, and form the procedures of service processes so as to obtain quality services. Standardization can effectively promote enterprises to improve service quality, and it is an important way for enterprises to build brand images. For example, the time and motion study experts, Frank and Lillian Gilbreth, after they analyzed and studied the bricklaying movement, invented a method to reduce the number of movements required to lay one brick from 18 to only 5, and even 2 under special circumstances. The management authorities of UPS (an American express company) used the time and motion study in Frederick Winslow Taylor's *Principles of Scientific Management* to conduct time study for the delivery routes and motions of the delivery drivers, and designed precise working procedures, including opening the vehicle door, delivering packages to consignees, and recording. Those motions seemed to be stereotyped, but they produced good effects, enabling UPS to deliver 130 packages per person per day, while the Federal Transit Inc. only picked up and delivered 80 packages per person per day. Those motions greatly increased the work efficiency of UPS.

16. Building a system

More and more enterprises are maintaining their glory by transforming themselves from industry to service. They devote themselves to providing customers with package solutions, with the hardware setup being only a carrier to support the solutions, and meeting customers' comprehensive demands through comprehensive, systematic and targeted solutions, to achieve good win-win cooperation. For example, the Fortune 500 enterprise Lexmark has developed from a professional manufacturer of printers into an enterprise providing customers with total solutions like document capture, secure transmission, improved workflow, and increased work efficiency with printers as the terminal equipment, to grow as customers grow. Such enterprises have achieved the highest level of service marketing.

Part 3

Substance

Chapter 7

Redefining Substance Marketing

Topics:

1. The Three Directions of Mobile Substance Marketing
2. Redefining Substance Marketing
3. Presentation Forms of "Content Prevails"

The word "sell" constantly appears in all our lives. In the age of the mobile Internet, people are selling their appearance, experience, performance, original intention, feelings, passion, resources, physical power, eloquence, creativity, offline promotion, and idleness. In any case, everybody is selling something in this age. Moreover, selling is actually buying on behalf of the users and thinking on behalf the users.

The scarcity of the 20th century left us many drawbacks which will need a long time before they can be eradicated; however, we have already taken the first steps.

In 2001, China's first generation of "digital citizens" grew up, and the "post-2000" ones were itching for a try. Those teenagers using the Internet for the first time at 12 years old in 1996 are now all more than 20 years old. Among them, boys are going away from TVs. One choice is the rich and colorful mobile Internet world without annoying advertisements, and another is the traditional computer network TV. Faced with these options, they are turning toward the former. The sign of an age transition is the shift of attention of young people.

While this shift may not be on a large scale, it is indeed happening: this group is abandoning broadcast television and computers and turning to the mobile Internet which follows the economics of the niche market. When there is more choice, they pay more attention to the things they like. Facts have proved that their favorite things are not those stereotyped contents and rigid dogmas filled with commercial advertisements. They are taking back their attention, or at least starting to cherish their attention.

The lesson for the entertainment industry is obvious: give people what they want, which is such a mess. If they want non-mainstream stuff, they will have it. Irrational movies draw large audiences. As we are reconsidering the special status of hot topics and super stars, we have also recognized that in this brand-new market, the nature of products has changed, and the nature and motive of the participants have also changed.

Due to the instinct of human beings, we are used to regarding things in an absolute and extreme way, like two sides of a coin. An object should be either black or white, and either a hot topic or a failure.

Of course this world is not orderly, and is multilayered and consistent with the laws of statistics. We must remind you that a coin not only has an obverse side and reverse side: it has a lateral side too. Mobile marketing is a kind of three-dimensional marketing with all the three sides. If the product and the user are the obverse and reverse sides of marketing, then content sharing is the lateral side. We have forgotten that most products are not well sold: the products we see on the goods shelves are generally the well-sold ones, at least better than those that are not on the shelves. However, the popularity of the majority of products is at most ordinary in any industry from music to clothing. Most products are filtered out by the word "hot", but they survive by some means. This is because the "hot" economics is not the only feasible economics. Hot products are exceptions and not the rule; however, we can clearly see the whole industry through their aureole.

Science and technology does not have a class nature, not to mention any application option. Since the first year of virtual reality in 2016, there have been questions such as: will the content generated by stronger technology be taken over by "villains"? When the VR mobile marketing becomes the "nuclear weapon" of substance marketing, will it be utilized by the "commercial terrorism"? Will "too many choices of content" make people dizzy?

In the age of the mobile Internet, people often say that the only constant is "change". The mode, marketing, users, substance, and content consumption are all changing. So how should we grab the opportunities this age brings? In this chapter, we have redefined substance marketing, representing the new mode of substance marketing in the age of mobile Internet. We have transformed and upgraded the traditional substance marketing mode and matched innovative presentation forms with new carriers, helping you to be accepted by more users.

During the interaction between innovative culture and traditional culture, we have constantly seen new sparks which we call "substance of content" collectively: this includes new words, new catchwords, and new ideas. When the cultural spirit of an age is exchanged or replaced to achieve reasonable integration with the cultural industry, considerations on the content development of the cultural industry are required.

The Three Directions of Mobile Substance Marketing

Marketers often say that "everything is cost except marketing". As for mobile Internet marketing, this can be changed to "everything is cost except content".

The fundamental purpose of entrepreneurial marketing is to realize revenues and profits, and content marketing is the revenues. To sell the stock equity of an enterprise in external financing requires content marketing. To sell a product or service, one should focus on the product, i.e., the product content. The most direct way is to sell the content.

Selling the enterprise

Selling the product

Substance of Content as marketing

The Three Directions of Mobile Substance Marketing

I. Selling the Enterprise

These days, there are few founders with venture stories. There are fewer still who have fascinating venture stories. Before 2017, the substance marketing of the mobile Internet was like the wind; over 50% enterprises in the emerging industries were blown over by the wind and withered like flowers. In the first half of 2016, the venture stories of many "post-1990" ones were very crazy, overstating their first fortune as an entrepreneur in most cases. The plot of winning the venture capital with one's originality or an exquisite PPT no longer exists in substance marketing.

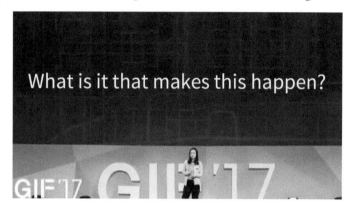

The Founder of Mobike-Hu Weiwei. Source: The official account of Wharton Business

A female journalist, however, has succeeded in becoming the head of a company worth 10 billion: she is Hu Weiwei, founder of the popular Mobike.

Although implemented without advertising, Mobike has a surprising self-propagation as substance marketing. It has no WeChat social transmission platform, but can realize self-propagation of the content. This is a very wise strategy: making the venture plot into the brand story.

In her speech, Get Inspired, Hu Weiwei said 10 years ago, she was just an ordinary automobile journalist, like any other white-collar worker. Helpful people may often appear at an entrepreneur's turning point to success. One day in 2014, a friend working in the Mercedes-Benz China Design Center told Hu that in the future there might be an innovation trend for travel tools. The chairman of NIO, Li Bin, asked her whether she would like to do a sharing travel project. She later discussed it again with Zhang Peng, founder of GeekPark.

In her plain speech, Hu's venture story touched us and won our trust, and we could see that her story was the best substance marketing for her enterprise.

1. Mobike Is not a Solution to Survival Problems, but a Feeling

Hu Weiwei said that cycling in the morning or evening is romantic. For a girl, there may be a romantic love story with the one she loves. It can be seen from her big data analysis on the springing up of the "shared bicycles" that she is the only person who can make big data appear so beautiful. In the big data analysis, there is an impressive city: Shenzhen. Someone says Shenzhen is a sleepless city. When Hu was in Shenzhen, she joked that she did not know why there could be so many people in Shenzhen cycling 24 hours a day. Later a user replied to her that there were people like the cleaners who got off work at 2:00 a.m. when there were no public vehicles. Hu was touched by that reply, and the user was touched by her affection.

Hu said something in the speech that can be the best slogan of Mobike: Light up a city with bicycles! From the scattered sparks in the beginning to the later starry space, users can also feel Hu's excitement when her dream is lit up.

This proves that if you want to move others, you must first move yourself.

2. Good at Borrowing from Others' Strengths

Through the story of Hu Weiwei, many users have seen her resources behind Sinovation Ventures, Tencent, and Meituan, the founders of which are all very influential in their industries. When any of them mentions Mobike in his WeChat moments, the users recognize it immediately. Hu's story, therefore, lets everybody see the strength and resources which lie behind her.

The effect of this substance marketing where the founder tells her story is that by December 2016, "online car booking" in China had a user scale of 168 million, an increase by 46.16 million (37.9%) compared with the first half of 2016. The potential user scale of shared bicycles, meanwhile, will certainly be no less than that number.

II. Selling the Substance of Content

This is an age of "substance as marketing" and "substance of content as consumption". This means that the age of the mobile Internet has ushered in the paying mode.

When the Internet was at its most epidemic time, large platforms competed to promote free modes; in the end, however, the free ones proved to be the most expensive ones. Users, then, have gradually accepted the paying mode and lost interest in free things.

Luogic Show, a Chinese talk show, complied with this trend and became typical of "substance as marketing" in the age of the mobile Internet.

The founder of Luogic Show, Luo Zhenyu (Luo Pang), is a We Media worker. In ancient times, he would have been called a storyteller, but in the age of the mobile Internet, he is a fashionable We Media worker. Luogic Show is a very popular talk show at present. His fans are mostly those born after 1980 and after 1990. His independent and rational thinking advocated in the slogan, "Have guts, have substance, be interesting" is in line with the liberalism and Internet thinking which those users pursue.

What makes the Luogic Show so fascinating to users?

1. Content Propagated in Fragmented Time: The Golden 60 Seconds

The Luogic Show follows the habit of users (or audience) in its content form. People often listened to the radio in the past, and that habit has turned into learning everything "with a smartphone and earphones" in the age of the mobile Internet.

The content of each section of the Luogic Show is kept within about 60 seconds, which is neither prolix nor time-consuming. Users can use their phones on the way to work and spend some seconds finishing listening to the content. They can both kill boring traveling time and get to know interesting things.

Luo said, "How can we touch these users? In China, there are too many young people living in a system or an organization. They want to enjoy the free connection rendered by the Internet, which enables them to be equal, free, to share and to create something. We help them to open such a window, establishing real connections with them."

Luogic Show-A Chinese Talk Show. Source: Luogic Show

2. Pay-to-read

The true core of pay-to-read is not the payment, but ensuring the continuous and stable high-quality experience of the users and to keep improving the user experience. That's what the Luogic Show is doing. The membership system promoted by Luo is 5,000 regular members and 500 die-hard members, paying CNY 200 and CNY 1,200, respectively, for two years. Although it is a mission impossible in the eyes of traditional media workers, that membership system earned CNY 1.6 million within half a day. That is indeed "substance as marketing".

3. Gather Communities with Personality and Thoughts

In the age of the mobile Internet, the cost of connection is rapidly decreasing. Everyone can be a node with high connectivity, and the value will return to individuals increasingly rapidly. In many fields of innovation, a charming personality will conquer large traditional organizations. In industrial society, people are connected by "things" but in the Internet society they are connected by "people". To innovate, consideration must be given to the aspect of the human,

The Founder of Luogic Show, -Luo Zhenyu, His Microblog has 1,233,358 fans. Source: Luo Zhenyu's Microblog

rather than the material and exterior things. The Luogic Show constantly emphasizes the "USB-flash-disk-type living", i.e., "Carrying information, without a system, pluggable anytime, and free collaboration". In the future, people can create value for themselves with their personality and gifts.

The biggest difference between Luogic Show and other We Media is that the former has a paying member group of tens of thousands of people besides the millions of users. This group has been the core power of the Luogic Show for expanding its business scope. It recruits only once a year, clearly declaring an upper limit of 100,000 members. During the recruitment, it does not promise any material rewards for the members; the members pay the membership fees for "community supporting" and "value identification". The member group of Luogic Show is a venture and knowledge community based on values.

III. Selling the Product

Every age has a hot product which has not only perfect quality but also content packaging. The most attractive part is the product story. Such enterprises as Haidilao, Huangtaiji, Diaoye Sirloin, and Majiajia have enjoyed great achievements in micro-marketing. Their prime time was jointly created by traditions and the Internet. These popular "Internet Plus" enterprises have some things in common in their hot products: "post-1980" and "post-1990" founders, attractive product stories, and youthful product packaging. Huangtaiji was once the hot topic of entrepreneurs, the subverter of the industry. In fact, many people advertised themselves through Huangtaiji. Huangtaiji has always been making its brand heard by people, from "the boss is a technical nerd of Baidu", "the boss drives a Benz to deliver pancakes", "the boss's wife is a beauty", "the alien store design", to the controversial theory that "the taste doesn't matter, what matters is to do the things people have never done" and to complement the part that "should be completed at first", such as the brand and user experience; but Huangtaiji does not pay attention to the R&D of product quality, which is why it keeps declining.

 Redefining Substance Marketing

Mobile substance marketing: if you come to understand the mobile Internet in a more profound way, you will discover its three basic attributes: it is human-oriented, evolving, and opening. Human-oriented is the foundation of the mobile philosophy, evolving is the gene, and opening is the keynote. Therefore, when the content with the tags of the age is edified by innovative modes and goes through the technology, platform, application, and practical activities of the mobile Internet, we call it mobile substance marketing.

Mobile substance marketing means conveying the enterprise-related content via such media as mobile pictures, mobile characters, and H5 animation, so as to give confidence to the users and propel the enterprise marketing. Their carriers can be the brand logo, the brand slogan, the enterprise album, the official website, the official account, advertisements, or even T-shirts, paper cups, and handbags. Different carriers have different media, but the core content conveyed must be consistent.

In the age of the mobile Internet, one thing which is often ignored is enterprise brand. The upgrading of the brand is often derived from different tactical ideas in content interpretation. People often say that the mobile Internet is just a tool of this age; contrarily, in this book, the mobile Internet is regarded as the best product of the age. The essential attribute of the mobile substance marketing is to return to the original source of the enterprise, carry out substance marketing centering on the enterprise brand, and build a propagating system in line with the trend of the times to build the enterprise brand into a truly timeless brand. It includes all methods of substance marketing and involves the established or shared content, in the purpose of contacting and influencing existing and potential consumers, understanding their needs and establishing certain relationships with them by such information transmission, i.e., "to set up relationships with the users". It is easier to set up such relationships via mobile substance marketing.

We can utilize several tactical ideas for content packaging in order to set up relationships with users via mobile substance marketing:

For many traditional entrepreneurs, the marketing of brand content is nothing else but a time-consuming battle where they must prevent cross-boundary looting and face the fierce competition between similar products at the same time. It is not a one-man or short-lived battle but a battle of a group lasting a lifetime. Once you are distracted, you will face not only the complaints from the users but also the clean sweep of the market by your competitors. In this battle, more and more enterprises choose content products as their weapon and break through the psychological defense of the audience by entertaining propagation modes, drawing closer to them, thus creating unique and exclusive brand experience.

How, then, should we handle the relationship between the brand and the content? How to maximize the brand propagation effect? How to match with the overall brand strategy? Let's explore the tactical ideas in the battle of brand substance marketing together.

I. The Ambush—the One Who Can Blend Wins

In the age of the mobile Internet, substance marketing with feelings is very important. During this process, the biggest value of substance marketing is the concealment of propagation: to strategically blend the brand logo,[1] brand image,[2] and brand concept into the content product, so as to subconsciously deliver the brand information to the target consumers during contact with the audience. The ambush is the key tactic that determines the result of the battle. That is to say you should elaborately select the content product and plan the way of placement, integrating the brand and content as one inalienable part of the content delivered to the audience. In this way, you can touch the heart of the consumers without noticing.

Whether the brand and the content can be highly integrated depends on the matching degree of four aspects.

The first is the matching degree between the content product target and the audience brand target consumers. Only when the two coincide can the brand information be accurately delivered to the target audience, achieving effective propagation.

The second is the matching degree between the placement environment and the brand image. The placement environment includes the atmosphere, the keynote, the plot, and the users. The discrepancy between brand image and the placement environment will deliver incorrect brand information and even conflict with the existing brand knowledge of the audience, leading to cognitive confusion and going against the enhancement of the brand image.

The third is the matching degree between the information that can be carried by the content product and the information that needs to be delivered according to the overall brand strategy. Whether the content can convey the information required by the brand and can coincide with the information conveyed in other links of the overall brand strategy will directly influence the effect of brand communication.

The fourth is the matching degree between other brands to be placed into the content product and the enterprise's own brand. On the one hand, in terms of the same category, you should check whether your brand has the exclusive resource, i.e., whether all the similar products appearing in the content product are of your brand. For example, if a TV drama features cellphones from both Huawei and MIUI, the effect of placement will be less than ideal. On the other hand, you should also know the brands placed in other categories. Brand substance marketing often influences

① Brand logo: this refers to the part of the brand that is recognizable and easy to remember but cannot be addressed by languages, including symbols, patterns, or obvious colors or typefaces. The brand logo and brand name are both elements constituting a complete brand. The brand logo can create brand recognition, brand association, and brand preference of the consumers, thus influencing the quality reflected by the brand and the brand loyalty of the customers.

② Brand image: this refers to the characteristics reflected by the enterprise or its brand in the market and among the public; it reflects the evaluation and cognition of the public, especially the consumers, about the brand. Brand image is inseparable from the brand; the image is the feature presented by the brand and reflects the strength and nature of the brand.

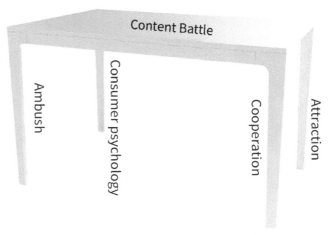

There are four kinds of Content Battle-Ambush, Consumer Psychology, Cooperation, Attraction.

the consumers by showing a lifestyle yearned for or praised by most people, and that specific lifestyle is built by the combination of various brands. Whether to appear together with the other brands has great influence on the result of the substance marketing. Matching with high-end brands can improve the image and status of the brand. For example, Omega successfully leaped from being the third-rate market in Switzerland to the top market by matching with BMW placed in the "007" movie series. Cooperating with brands that are similar to the status of your own brand can establish a relation with a corresponding lifestyle.

①

Sense of participation: to open the process of production, service providing, brand building, and selling to the users and to build a touchable and accessible brand that grows with the users.

II. Consumer Psychology—the One Focusing on the Sense of Participation① Wins

To fight the battle of brand content marketing, both the enterprise and the content provider face big challenges on the "degree": they should naturally and reasonably show the brand information in the content product to ensure adequate perception of the consumers, and should, at the same time, ensure the quality of the content product, preventing too strong a commercial atmosphere that may annoy the consumers. Therefore, besides the matching of the brand and the content product, you should pay more attention to the presentation mode of the brand in the content product.

Generally, there are three levels of placement of a brand in the content product:

The first level is to separately show the brand logo in the content product, and the brand features have nothing to do with the content, such as product prop placement, title sponsorship, and logo board. The brand placed in this way is highly replaceable, without strong stimulation to the audience, and has difficulties in in-

---

Case Study | Reunion of the "Nation's Family" after 12 Years Leaves Only Feelings for the Pepsi Micro Film

2017 Pepsi. Source: Pepsi

Pepsi makes "Happy" its marketing core every year and "Take the Happy Home" as its core content marketing. In 2017, Pepsi chose the "Home with Kids" crew reunited after 12 years, which is a crew carrying the memories of the post-1970, post-1980, and post-1990 generations.

In terms of sensation, the actors and actresses selected by Pepsi this time have satisfied the needs of various netizens. For the old fans who yell every day that "I can watch them for a day as long as they come out together again", their dream has been realized. Although the Xia kids have all grown up, the kinship delivered by the nation's family has lasted for 12 years.

The long-awaited reunion is much more than "Time kills beauty". In this micro film, Pepsi presented family affection and warm feelings which are extremely expected by the netizens.

The micro film "Take the Happy Home together for 2017" is not a mere sequel of "Home with Kids". It tells a New Year story of "Take the Happy Home" after 12 years.

The scene was not deliberately recreated, the classic lines of the kids did not reappear at the table, and a mysterious new role was added to the old cast. The grown-up Liu Xing has become a policeman and Xiaoxue a business elite. When Liu Mei entered the door, took off her shoes and put her bag aside, the fans exclaimed that "The nation's family of 12 years ago has come back".

The plot was frank. Although there were some cliffhangers in the beginning, people could still easily guess the ending. An unsolved birth secret of an unexpected son, an emotional appeal for family reunion, a group of good actors/actresses carrying the memories of the audience, and a slightly disappointing playscript, at last, only the old feelings can make people repost this film.

We have to admit that Pepsi has been very smart in choosing the material for its "Take the Happy Home" series micro films in recent years. They can always target good intellectual properties (IPs) that can arouse collective memories, harvesting applause and empathy. And the film "The Monkey King" at the beginning of this year greatly benefited the brand. While the plot was flat for the nation's family, it still triggered the tender feelings of many people thanks to its IP which aroused cross-generation empathy.

The case source quoted from: Huang Yao, NetEase Entertainment 2017/01/10
http://news.21food.cn/13/2774258.html

creasing the brand association and brand preference.

The second level is to consciously choose the content product highly matched with the brand for placement after considering the similarities between the consumers of the brand and the audience of the content product. For example, the brand can appear in a proper scene, conversation or activity. This way it is tenderer and better matched with the brand but may possibly fail to arouse the empathy of the audience due to the simplicity of the brand information delivered.

The third level is to show the brand appeal by means of the content and even make the audience profoundly perceive the connotation and value of the brand.

To engage in psychological warfare with consumers, "experiential" placement is one of the effective ways of realizing the third level of placement. "Experience" overturns the past blind infusion of brand information to the audience; it lets the brand appear at a proper time as an important tool for developing the plot and makes the consumers agree with a lifestyle, unconsciously influencing their attitude toward the brand. This method carries richer and more profound brand information which is perfectly matched with the content product, so that the brand is irreplaceable. It can often achieve the effect of being greater than the sum of its parts, i.e., 1+1>2.

 Case Study

The Best Red Packet Snatching Guide 2017: Snatch Them All in Alipay and QQ

During the Spring Festival of 2017, the two platforms Alipay and QQ made great efforts in their red packet activities.

Alipay Red Packets

This year Alipay promoted the red packet snatching with five "Fu" characters, but what is different is that the red packets were randomly distributed instead of equally, through which the maximum price can be CNY 666.66.

Alipay also promoted the AR Red Packet which is more interesting and could be played with friends. You could ask for personal red packets and group red packets.

QQ Red Packets

1. This year QQ promoted an activity of searching for red packets in a map. It regularly gave out red packets every day, at different times for different areas. When clicking on a red packet, a small camouflaged game would appear where you would have to guess which red packet among the three was the real one. It was fun and you could get red packets while playing.

2. You may be used to the Alipay red packets and WeChat red packets but you may not be very familiar with QQ red packets. Upon the New Year, you can greet your QQ friends and ask for a red packet, and you can also ask for red packets from the group owners.

3. You could also give out red packets, the amount of which can be modified to a minimum price of CNY 0.01.

Source: Reorganized according to the materials on Huxiu.com

2017 Alipay Red Packet

2017 Alipay Red Packet

2017 Alipay Red Packet

2017 Alipay Red Packet-QQ (short for Tencent QQ) is an instant messaging (IM) software from Tencent.

2017 QQ Red Packet

III. Cooperation—the One Who Understands Resources Integration Wins

Brand substance marketing is not a battle to be fought by you alone. It requires the integration of various resources and cooperation from both within and outside.

"Cooperation from within" usually refers to the operation of substance marketing activities for a single brand. This promotion mode involves many aspects, including the brand enterprise, the production company, media, the game developer, the entertainment company or other content product providers, as well as the professional advertising agency company. The enterprise needs to closely cooperate with other parties during operation, become deeply involved in the content industry chain, and participate in the whole process of the planning, production, and release of the content product. In addition to integrating the various resources in the industry chain, the enterprise still needs to utilize multiple marketing means, such as advertising (pre-movie advertisements, outdoor advertisements, etc.), terminal promotion, database mails, PR activities, media coverage, movie premiere (or music and book signing sessions), and sidelights of the content product, laying comprehensive entertainment siege to the target consumers. For example, you can promote some online activities or small games via the official account to attract the users and expand the influence of brand placement.

"Cooperation from outside" emphasizes including the brand substance marketing activities into the overall brand promotion system and considering the placed role and value under the overall marketing planning framework. Due to the limitation of the content product carrier, brand substance marketing can only deliver limited information, just reminding the audience

💡 Case Study — Maybelline and Baofeng Mojing cooperated in VR advertisement

Virtual Reality (VR) technology is seen in almost every sector of our daily life, even in the fashion industry. Maybelline launched a special fashion show in Shanghai. "National goddess" Angelababy attended and announced that she became the new endorser of Maybelline. This show was special because it amazed the public with another highlight, an incredible mixture of science and beauty – the VR panorama commercial created for Maybelline by the technical team from Baofeng Mojing. The video was displayed for the first time on the show.

Maybelline and Baofeng Mojing cooperated in VR Advertisement. Source: Sohu.com

Maybelline and Baofeng Mojing cooperated in VR Advertisement. Source: Sohu.com

Audacious as always, Maybelline brought in the VR to the show. Reporters and journalists could soak in the trendy atmosphere of New York just by wearing the VR headset developed by Baofeng Mojing.

As we found out, it was the first time a cosmetics brand tried a VR commercial, which also marked the success of Baofeng Technology in exploring new ways of marketing through fashion industry. While giving a touch of science to the high-street cosmetics brand, this innovative mixture also reflected "unique beauty" and other stylish elements of both parties.

It is well known that cosmetics brands tend to present a more visualized experience for their consumers. Blended with VR, they are drawn closer to consumers with the help of technology as consumers have a chance to feel the products via "immersive" and "interactive" experience. Guided by the idea of "creating new marketing modes" in 2016, Baofeng Technology has put more weights on the "VR+" cross-cutting partnership and has speeded up its pace to implement it. The cooperation with Maybelline was a breakthrough in "VR + fashion".

The case source quoted from: boluo @hiavr.com 2016/07/13
https://www.hiavr.com/news/industry/8030.html

of the brand in most cases. When the audience becomes interested in the brand because of the substance marketing, the enterprise needs to let the audience understand the brand in a more comprehensive and more profound way by means of other communication tools. The enterprise should fully include other activities into its substance marketing so as to extend the placed value by integrated marketing communication and pursue the effect beyond the content product. Only by highly conforming to the overall brand strategy of the enterprise can substance marketing strengthen the trust of the consumers and establish lasting brand relationships, such as the content bundling marketing between stars, and between the stars and the enterprise brand.

IV. Attraction—Perseverance Means Victory

One of the biggest differences between brand substance marketing and traditional advertising is that the medium attached by the brand information is substance marketing. The existence of substance marketing is time-sensitive. Although some classical works may still be popular after several years, in the age of the mobile Internet, the time of large-scale release and popularity is limited, like the blink of an eye. Brand, however, is created by continuous propagation without which a brand will not be influential. Given this, a protracted war must be fought for brand substance marketing. Do not let the brand information disappear after all the efforts in substance marketing.

Firstly, focus on the continuity of substance marketing. For example, continuously place the brand in a certain category of content products and plan for periodical substance dissemination. In this way, you can deliver the brand information to uniform audience groups and create scale effects at the same time, letting the audience think of your brand when they see relevant content products.

Secondly, focus on the time sensitivity of substance marketing. For example, take the prime time after the release of the content product and make reviews by various kinds of publicity means to keep the content fresh, letting the users receive the latest information and deepening their impression of the brand. You can take full advantage of the resources of the content product based on the time sensitivity of the event and invite the hottest star of the moment to shoot a commercial as the brand spokesperson or to take part in the promotion activities of the brand.

Presentation Forms of "Content Prevails"[①]

If the brand substance is marketed through entertainment, will the brand still be the same brand? How to place the brand into substance marketing? These are questions many entrepreneurs ask.

Brand substance marketing means that the brand carries out brand communication via the content as the carrier. The fundamental principle of substance marketing is that since the entertainment nature of the content product can attract the attention of the audience, the brand is then placed into the content platform, so that the audience will receive the brand information and experience the brand characteristics while enjoying the entertainment content. Seen from the perspective of development of substance marketing, the consumers receive the brand-related information through the presentation of the content product, and whether the brand communication is accurate or not, to a large extent, depends on the quality of the content carrier. Despite the quality of the content product, the combination degree of the brand and the content product will directly decide the effect of brand communication. With the subtle changes in the relationship between the entertainment nature of the content platform and the commercial nature of the brand placement, the relation between the brand and the carrier is remote in some cases, and close in others. According to the degree of the brand's involvement in the content product, we divide the content products and brand communication into several types for the moment to help the enterprises to distinguish the various effects brought by different combination degrees of the substance and the brand.

① *"Content prevails": means that the way of survival of websites lies in their content quality. Providing quality network resources for the users is the foundation of a website. With the rapid development of the Internet, all kinds of websites emerge. Repetition, sameness, and even cheating about the content have become a hidden trouble. Improving the user experience has become the key to the construction and existence of websites at present. Letting users find what they want and obtain valuable materials from the site is the basis for the existence of a website.*

I. As Vague as a Touch on the Surface

Such content platforms as TV dramas, movies, programs, and even sports events can all help deliver brand information; however, based on the product type and connotation of the brand, not all content platforms can be fully utilized. The brand cannot be fully embedded into the content carrier and is vaguely placed on the margins.

Simple placement, like the universal soft advertisement at present, is to separately show the brand logo in the program while the brand or the product feature almost has nothing to do with the program content, e.g., title sponsorship, sponsorship, and logo board. In this substance marketing mode, the brand does not have to exist in the program content; the brand symbol is shown at the edge by the forms of sound, characters, or pictures. The absence of the brand in the content product will not impact the delivery of the content information.

In this situation, the communication effect is only an incidental increase of the brand awareness because of the popularity of the carrier. The characteristics of the placed brand should match that of the carrier as much as possible. The placement methods may be slightly different, but adequate considerations should be given to the commonness between the target consumers and the audience of the content carrier, i.e., to consider delivering proper brand information to proper people via proper content platforms.

II. Obviously Placed both Inside and Outside

In recent years, we can frequently see in movies and TV dramas that previously concealed brand logos have been displayed again, such as the whole box of Mengniu milk in the skits in the Spring Festival Gala and the Nokia cellphones in the movie "A World without Thieves". This is the most common way of brand substance marketing to directly place the brand into the content carrier as real products.

Placing the products can, firstly, prevent consumers' repulsion against the brand, unconsciously delivering the brand information to the audience through the scenario of the content carrier; and, secondly, it can combine the figures in the TV drama or movie with the brand to create a celebrity effect.

These brands are placed into TV dramas and movies and appear in front of the audience as props. The audience cannot avoid the brand during the TV drama or movie. Here the brand is further placed. It is outside the content carrier; there must be some props in the content carrier, but these props may not be limited to a certain brand. Though props are necessary, the brand can be replaced or removed. The content can still be conveyed without the brand, so this mode is still a free status with limited effect.

Brand placement must be natural in

Case Study | Fashion Week

Fashion Week is a dynamic exhibition highlighting the latest collections of fashion designers and brands. As an event gathering tycoons of fashion and culture industry, it is organized generally in metropolises of advanced fashion culture and design industry.

Out of the world's Fashion Week venues, those held in Paris, Milan, London, New York and Tokyo are regarded as having the most influence. In China, the most famous one is China Fashion Week in Beijing, followed by Shanghai Fashion Week and Hong Kong Fashion Week China's Beijing Fashion Week has enjoyed rapid development and become one of the top-ranked fashion week events across the globe. Local Fashion Week events such as those organized in Shanghai, Guangzhou, Qingdao, Dalian, Harbin, and Shenyang also gained considerable growth. Over the recent years, China's Fashion Week events have introduced more international elements, and seen remarkable improvement in management and quality of designs blending with unique oriental qualities.

Fashion Week events are organized in February or March (Spring/Summer) and September or October (Autumn/Winter). During the event, models, designers, celebrities, photographers, makeup artists, show directors, and modeling agents, as well as members of the media, art colleges and other related institutions gather to celebrate the grand annual festival.

The case source quoted from: Baidu Baike 2017/04/28
https://baike.baidu.com/item/%E6%97%B6%E8%A3%85%E5%91%A8/2904747

the first place, without too many commercial traces that may impact the entertainment of the content and go against the original purpose. Besides, the plot should be taken into full consideration. BMW paid its advertising fees to appear in "A World without Thieves", but this had negative results due to the line in the movie, "Those who drive in good cars may not always be good people".

III. Penetration into Content with Seamless Integration

To place the brand completely into the content carrier as an indispensable part of the content is the desired effect of many product placements. As the brand and the content are integrated as one, the brand information can be "implicitly" delivered to the audience when they focus on the content, and the audience will subconsciously receive relatively complete and accurate brand experience which they cannot deny, thus achieving a seamless combination of the entertainment nature of the content and the commercial nature of the brand.

In this situation, the brand delivers not only simple surface information, but also multi-level and multi-aspect information via auditory and visual senses. In operation, placements in dialogues, the plot and images can all serve the delivery of the brand information. During the presentation of the content, the protagonist's use of and feelings about the brand can make the audience experience the brand indirectly.

This degree of placement is more effective for the brand and more acceptable to the audience. But it requires preparation in advance of the formation of the content, with long operation cycle and complicated process.

IV. Good Brands Tell Good Stories

There has been a trend for brand substance marketing in recent years. This mode of substance marketing has broken the methods where an adman makes the advertisement or a content maker places the advertisements; in this mode, the adman customizes the content product for the brand from a commercial perspective of brand publicity. And the content product has a wide scope, including mass communication carriers such as printed materials (books, newspapers, and magazines), electronic publications (databases, electronic audiovisual products, optical discs, and game software), and audiovisual communication (movies and TV dramas, videos, and broadcasting). In addition, the entertainment and news events sponsored by some brands are also a kind of content platforms.

Substance serving the brand means to arrange entertaining and eye-catching plots or events from the standpoint of the brand and to make them into content products, thus releasing the commercial value of the brand while reducing the defense of the audience.

To make the brand substance entertaining and to let the audience naturally receive the brand in a relaxed state can achieve more accurate communication with the target consumer groups as well as better brand communication effect. Now in the US, the admen wandering on Madison Square Garden have been aiming at the commercial opportunities of Hollywood, hoping to recapture the consumers' attention via this new type of substance marketing.

In recent years, there have been endless micro films and small videos customized for brands, from eight minutes to one

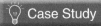 Case Study   **The Once Popular Motorola**

Years ago, a movie called "Cellphone" took Motorola as its clue. In the movie, all actors and actresses used Motorola cellphones. Besides the various models of Motorola cellphones, the symbolic ringtone of Motorola also appeared frequently in the movie. Most importantly, the entire plot developed around cellphones. The different cellphone models chosen by different roles also provided examples for the audience, giving the audience a profound understanding of the product features and the spiritual connotation of the brand, which at that time achieved a communication effect in which the sum was greater than its parts.

The case source quoted from: Guo Peng, Head of Marketing 2008/02/13
http://info.ceo.hc360.com/2008/02/13070555045-2.shtml

hour, funny clips or industry feature films, all aimed at building the brands. BMW began to make short films that show its extraordinary drivability years ago. With attractive plots and excellent actors/actresses, such films are widely spread online. The entertaining content plus the commercial atmosphere of the brand makes the boundaries between advertisements, substance marketing, and entertainment marketing increasingly blurred.

 Case Study   2D "Trendy Business"

The 2D World of Old Luxury Brands

The Prada 2018 Spring and Autumn Show won extreme attention with its 2D elements. The site was decorated by eight visual artists with cartoon heroines, which reflected the power of the woman. In this season, Prada applied cartoon elements to women's oversize coats, which is a new style in the fashion world and a new mark of Prada. With the collision between 2D elements and oversize designs, the new products release of Prada can be rated as perfect.

Last time when the "2D" trend was confronted with an old luxury brand was the spring-summer advertisement by Louis Vuitton 2016. At that time, LV invited Lightning, the virtual female role in the Japanese movie game "Final Fantasy XIII", to be its brand spokesperson, seeming to have taken the lead to "break the dimensional wall". Lightning in fact has a closer connection with Prada, however. Five years ago, Lightning and other roles were already wearing Prada's menswear in the game, and clothes jointly designed by the brand and cartoons and games, as well as 2D images printed on the clothes, came into being very early, too.

The "2D" in Japanese refers to the "planar space" in a narrow sense, i.e., Japanese animations, cartoons, games and peripheral products. Although its narrow sense ACG is a Japanese concept, loosely speaking, things slightly related to it can be included in the scope of "pan-2D", e.g., Marvel and DC, and even Disney that hits the edge. Even if you think most 2D figures have the so-called "eighth-grade-disease", you still have to admit that they never make mistakes in clothing and they are actually very fashion-forward. Moreover, the so-called "dimensional wall" has been unconsciously broken many times.

The famous One Piece is the first 2D opportunity targeted by the fashion world. Monkey D. Luffy, the figure wearing a red waistcoat, jean shorts, flip flops, and a big straw hat with a typical sailing style, became the cover person of the Japanese men's fashion magazine Men's Non-No Vol. 1, 2010; he was the first 2D cover person in 24 years since the founding of the magazine.

As every person shooting cover photos will have deliberately designed styles, Luffy also took off his casual clothes and put on formal wear. The Diet Butcher business suit and Sophnet mountaineering jacket restrained his casual feeling. Nevertheless, he did not routinely wear the three-piece suit. The rolled trouser legs and the stitched colorful coat showed his leisure and freedom, with that symbolic straw hat. Everything showed that he was still that positive and ambitious man who "will be the king of pirates" in spite of his suit.

Luffy appeared on the cover of Men's Non-No again in 2010, wearing his "classical clothes" and standing together with Kimura Takuya. Later, in the theatrical version of One Piece in 2015, the new styles of the straw pirate hats were contracted by Armani.

When Cartoon Characters Meet the Fashion World

The fashion world has adequate reasons to choose cartoon characters for entering the 2D world. *Taking One Piece* as an example, by November 2013, it had a global circulation of 345 million, the largest circulation of any cartoon around the world. You can often see little boys carefully reading it in the subway of Paris. From 8-year-old French boys to the 44-year-old Kimura Takuya, the cartoon almost covers the potential consumer groups of all the luxury brands.

Even though encouraged by the big brands, the old diehards still find there is a wall between the created "2D" world and their real life. But for the keen fashion world, it is more like a dimension door between the two worlds. We have to admit that those 2D characters that do not make mistakes in clothing can inspire the designers in our real life.

The hot Japanese embroidered coats last year perfectly reflected the westerners' simple and rough understanding of the oriental beauty. In the DSquared2 2016 Autumn-Winter men's wear, there were monkeys picking peaches, circling dragons and phoenixes, cranes and pines, and even tigers going down the mountain embroidered on glossy satins. The "unfamiliar" oriental embroidery that fascinates the westerners and the Japanese robes worn by them like nightgowns has come out of the shows and hit the streets.

Post—1990 Are the Main Consumers of 2D Fashion

From Japan to the world, the "2D" fashion has different social backgrounds but also proper forms. In recent years, "2D" elements have been influencing the mainstream culture in a more and more profound way; this is due to its own development path—by deep integration with movies, music and fashion the content, values, users and business forms with the tag of

"2D" have come into the mainstream.

Data show that on the basis of increasingly obvious IP operation of cartoons, 2D users have seen stable growth. By 2017, the pan-2D users in China had exceeded 300 million; on average, two out of three young people are 2D users, where post-1990 generations account for more than 95%. This consumer group and the potential consumers of fashion brands are largely overlapped.

"If we like it, we buy it. 2D users are very simple," said the famous game voice actress, Xiaonie. She has been fond of 2D culture since childhood. Her favorite cartoon images are Supersonico and Umaru-chan; she once played Supersonico in an anime expo. When she came into contact with 2D for the first time, she thought that those cartoon characters were almighty and their images and poems were charming. Xiaonie chose animation as her university major. She became the hottest Chinajoy model in 2014 and dubbed for Shuang'er in the game The Duke of Mount Deer.

Data show that there are about 174 million post-1990 ones in China, and about 92.8 million of them are 2D fans, which renders a market scale of over CNY 200 billion. Surveys reveal that the 2D users are willing to pay for cartoons, photos, peripheral products, voice actors/actresses, virtual idols, and so on. According to statistics, the 2D users spend over CNY 1,700 on peripheral 2D products on average every year. It is not difficult for the fashion industry to take a share of this huge market.

The case source quoted from: ifeng.com 2017/10/31
https://www.xzbu.com/1/view-10936327.htm

💡 Case Study　Substance Marketing Report Analysis

In 2014, Internet thinking, MIUI mode, We Media, and other concepts and news about substance marketing kept upgrading the industry's understanding of dissemination. Recently, iiMedia Research has done a rough analysis on the trend of the current mobile advertisement market. Multiple data have shown that mobile advertisements are more and more popular with advertisers. And with the greater demand for mobile advertisements, the users have higher requirements for the content; it is extremely urgent for the advertisers to reform the content.

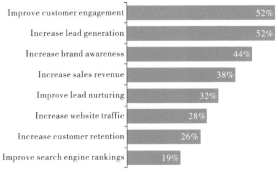

What are the MOST IMPORTANT OBJECTIVES of a content marketing strategy?

Source: iresearch.cn

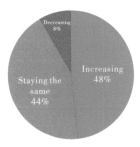

How is your content marketing BUDGET CHANGING?

Source: iresearch.cn

However, some enterprises have not given sufficient attention to the great effect of current substance marketing. According to the survey data of Ascend2, a foreign organization, marketers need capital support to overcome obstacles and achieve the goal of substance marketing, while less than half (48%) of the enterprises plan to increase the substance marketing budget. Though substance marketing has a high success rate, there are still 8% of enterprises planning to reduce relevant budget.

With the overall trend for mobile advertising, how should these enterprises make their marketing strategies in 2015? And with what strategies can the marketers including We Media obtain the maximum marketing effect at the minimum cost?

At present, the most important objective of substance marketing for the enterprises lies in improving consumer participation and expanding the market, which is the opinion of more than half (52%) of the interviewed enterprises. To achieve that objective, the

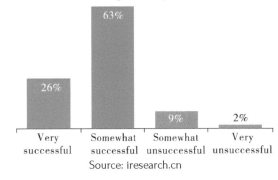

How do you RATE THE SUCCESS of content marketing to achieve important objectives?

Source: iresearch.cn

What are the MOST EFFECTIVE types of content used?

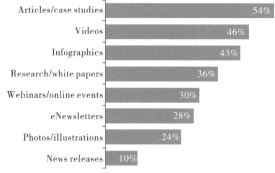

Articles/case studies — 54%
Videos — 46%
Infographics — 43%
Research/white papers — 36%
Webinars/online events — 30%
eNewsletters — 28%
Photos/illustrations — 24%
News releases — 10%

Source: iresearch.cn

marketers must keep creating relevant and attractive contents.

As to the evaluation about substance marketing, although most enterprises are still unable to directly relate substance marketing to their performance, nearly 90% of enterprises think that the substance marketing has successfully realized their objectives, 26% of which deem the effect outstand-

What are the MOST DIFFICULT types of cntent to create?

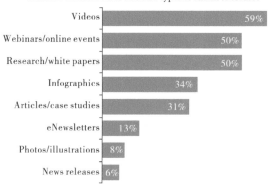

Videos — 59%
Webinars/online events — 50%
Research/white papers — 50%
Infographics — 34%
Articles/case studies — 31%
eNewsletters — 13%
Photos/illustrations — 8%
News releases — 6%

Source: iresearch.cn

ing. Those figures have increased compared with some relevant surveys last year, which has reflected the change in substance marketing ideas of many enterprises. However, the content is a time-consum-

What are the MOST EFFECTIVE RESOURCES for creating content?

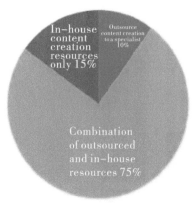

In-house content creation resources only 15%

Outsource content creation to a specialist 10%

Combination of outsourced and in-house resources 75%

Source: iresearch.cn

ing strategy which needs the support from leaders and teams.

As to the current industry challenges, the survey indicates that the lack of content innovation resources is the leading factor that impedes the success of substance marketing, accounting for 53%. 42% of the marketers said that the lack of effective strategies to

Comps most effective types of content with most difficult to create

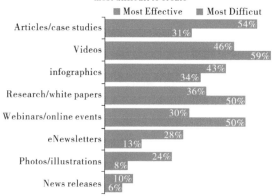

■ Most Effective ■ Most Difficut

Articles/case studies — 54% / 31%
Videos — 46% / 59%
infographics — 43% / 34%
Research/white papers — 36% / 50%
Webinars/online events — 30% / 50%
eNewsletters — 28% / 13%
Photos/illustrations — 24% / 8%
News releases — 10% / 6%

Source: iresearch.cn

realize content innovation and release is the biggest obstacle. In addition, budget and lack of support from management are also great difficulties for the success of substance marketing.

In 2014, the communication mode of information patterns seemed to be welcomed by users. But infor-

What are the MOST USEFUL METRICS for measuring content morketing performance?

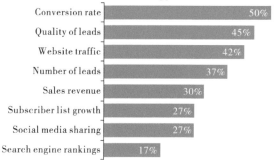

Conversion rate — 50%
Quality of leads — 45%
Website traffic — 42%
Number of leads — 37%
Sales revenue — 30%
Subscriber list growth — 27%
Social media sharing — 27%
Search engine rankings — 17%

Source: iresearch.cn

mation presentation in pictures is not favored by conversion rate in terms of substance marketing related to enterprise performance. According to the survey data, articles are regarded as the most effective method for substance marketing, which accounts for 54%, followed by videos and pictures which account for 46% and 43%, respectively.

As to content creation, the most difficult types of content are videos, research reports, and so on. 59% of marketers think videos are the most difficult content. These diversified forms with rich contents often require resources outside the enterprise, which is relatively hard when the enterprise has not attached adequate importance to substance marketing.

Of course, enterprises with adequate expenditure for substance marketing often engage outsourcing companies instead of their own employees for content creation.

85% of enterprises said they had outsourced all or part of content creation, which also gave them the expertise and ability which cannot be realized within the enterprise. But as the communication effect of substance marketing is more and more emphasized by enterprises, the budget still has large space of growth in the future, which renders higher requirements for the outsourcing companies or the internal substance marketers.

In the survey, the lack of content creation resources is the reality for most marketing departments. But the lack of effective strategies is also an obstacle. To design an effective substance marketing strategy requires the marketers to strike a balance between "what is the most effective" and "what can be created in reality".

As mentioned above, to improve consumer participation and create potential customers are the main objectives of substance marketing. So as for evaluating substance marketing, over half of the enterprises believe that to measure the consumer response and the quality of the potential customers created is the most effective indicator of measuring the performance of substance marketing.

The case source quoted from: iresearch.cn 2015/3/25

http://www.useit.com.cn/thread-8618-1-1.html

Chapter 8

Substance Management: Mobile Brand Management

Topics:

1. What Is Brand?
2. Mobile Brand Building
3. Mobile Brand Identity System
4. Substance Dissemination of Mobile Brand

2016 was the turning point for the brand Internet campaign at which point brand interconnection has entered the second half. The first half was the world of traditional brand marketing, while the second half is turning from traditional consulting and information branding to the "Internet Plus" vertical application fields of various industries and to the deep service fields. Content entrepreneurship and content development will be the evolving direction of brand interconnection. We used to think that the brand, culture, and communication were three independent subsystems or subdisciplines, and the cross section between the three was called content. This chapter will start from the basic principle of brand.

What Is Brand?

Product homogeneity leads to numerous choices in a fierce market. Enterprises are seeking a method to establish an emotional connection, and further irreplaceable relationships, with customers. The brand is the users' impression of the enterprise. A strong and powerful brand can stand out in the crowded market, making people love it, trust it, and believe in its superiority. No matter for a start-up brand, an NPO, or a product, people's cognition and feelings about the brand determines whether it will succeed. A brand has three elements: popularity, reputation, and designation①.

Brand History

The word "brand"② came from the ancient Scandinavian word "brands" which means to "ignite". The word "branding" was originally a mark for property ownership or place of origin for thousands of years. You may not know that about 4,000 years ago, marks were put on rented domestic animals or slaves to show ownership. In the U.S., up until the beginning of the 19th century, brands were still stamped on escaped prisoners, slaves, vagrants, thieves, or fanatical pagans as a sign of humiliation. In the famous American novel *Uncle Tom's Cabin*, all the negro slaves wore a mark or stigma. It has been common for various tribes and alliances around the world to show their sources with marks.

The three ancestor enterprises that first applied brands are P&G, Philips, and Ford. P&G, founded in 1837, was at first a manufacturer of soaps and candles, which was comprehensively upgraded thanks to branding and won a good reputation in the local market. Philips was founded in 1891, and Ford began its operation in 1903. Gradually, people became accustomed to the brand-oriented lifestyle. Now these three brands have lasted for over a century. That's the sustainable development brought by the brand.

The Brand Evolution of Ford

Ford not only contributed production and management experience to the world, but also began brand building upon its founding. Ford's brand evolution is shown in Figure 8-1.

When Ford was established in 1903, there were 88 automobile manufacturers in the U.S. In 1908, Ford released Model T whose sales volume took up 60% of the market share. By 1927, Ford had sold 1.5 million Model T vehicles.

In the 1930s, Ford promoted its classical car series, including the Lincoln, and entered the luxury high-end consumer market; in the 1950s, it promoted the Thunder Bird. Now Ford has such sub-

Figure 8-1   The Brand Evolution of Ford Series.
Source: Hongbing Hua, Top-level Design

① Designation: the sequence according to which a brand is associated among similar brands of the same category. For example, KFC and McDonald's are known to all, but when it comes to hamburgers, people may first think of McDonald's and then KFC. Compared by the keyword of hamburger, McDonald's is more famous than KFC. When it comes to fried drumsticks, meanwhile, the first brand which comes to our mind will be KFC, and then McDonald's. Compared by this keyword, KFC is more famous.

② Brand: the intuitive feelings of a person about a product, a service or a company.

1887	1969
1893	1985
1907	1986
1915	2010
	2011

Brand Evolution of Coca Cola.

It can be seen from the overall trademark design and the brand design of Coca Cola that it is selling a temptation, a smooth feeling. Its trademark looks smooth and makes people believe that it drinks smooth, too.

One has to say Coca Cola found a very smart Chinese translation for its name; many enterprises have difficulty in thinking of a good name.

Why is this? Good names were all taken in the 1980s, e.g., Gree and Haier. And as Robust ("Lebaishi" in Chinese), can you register a name of "Lewanshi"? No! Even "Lewanshi" is under protection! Good names like Wahaha have all been taken. But this does not matter. We have something better. Top-level design is about reverse thinking, thinking of what has not yet been thought of and doing what has not yet been done.

The case source quoted from: Hongbing Hua, Top-level Design 2013 年出版

Figure 8-2   The 39 contact points of the brand.
Source: 2011, ALINA WHEELER, brand marketing expert
The Success Secrets of Outstanding Brands

ordinate vehicle brands such as Ford, Lincoln, Mazda, Jaguar, Land Rover, and Aston Martin. After 100 years, Ford has seen some changes in its brand image, but has enjoyed a higher brand value.

1.   Three Major Functions of the Brand

David Haigh, CEO of the British Brand Finance consultant company, proposed that the brand is a choice.

Function 1: Navigation

The brand can help consumers to make a choice among a great pile of dazzling and confusing products.

Function 2: Warranty

The brand means the quality of the product or service, assuring the consumers that they have made the correct choice.

Function 3: Connection

The brand uses special images, characters and association to propel the consumers to identify it. In the age of the Internet, a good brand propels the users to advertise it automatically.

2.   The 39 Contact Points of the Brand

Each contact point is an opportunity of increasing the awareness, reputation, and consumer loyalty of the brand. See Figure 8-2.

3.   What Is Brand Identity?

The brand identity is a tangible mnemonic symbol available for sensory perception; you can look at it, touch it, feel it, grab it, and listen to it. Brand identity can let the consumers know the brand, its concept and meaning, and expand its differences from other brands. Various different elements of the brand identity should be integrated into the entire identity system. In the age of

Steve Jobs and iPhone.

VR mobile marketing, the brand identity should be reproduced in 360 degrees without any blind angles.

When Steve Jobs was poaching the president of Pepsi, John Sculley, in 1985, he asked this question, "Do you want to spend the rest of your life selling sugar water or changing the world?" Pepsi, Apple and jeans, these unrelated brands created consumer association relying on brand identity. Brand innovation has changed the world.

In the age of the Internet, brands are buried by massive information. It is extremely important for a brand to build the brand identity system if it wants to stand out. Can you identify the following vehicle brands in Figures 8-3 and 8-4?

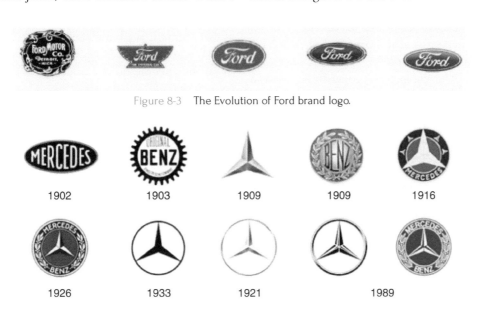

Figure 8-3   The Evolution of Ford brand logo.

Figure 8-4   The Evolution of Mercedes-Benz brand logo. Source: Autohome

Mobile Brand Building

Brand building is a firm code of conduct for establishing the continuous cognition of the customers and strengthening the consumer loyalty. It requires the investment from the senior management and the intention of continuous investment in the future. Brand building[①] means seizing every opportunity to convince people why they should choose the brand among so many choices. Brand building helps the enterprise to be a leading brand and provides the best link between the employees and the customers.

I. Victory Belongs to the Most Indomitable

Figure below shows the seven procedures of brand building:

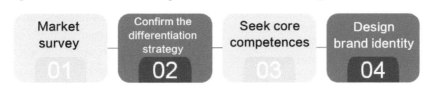

The seven procedures of brand building.

> ①
>
> *We keep investing resources in our core competences. The first is to understand our customers, which is never too much. The second is innovation. And the third is brand building. We keep delivering more information to the consumers.*
> *--A.G. Lafley, Business Week, 2009*

II. Choose the Opportunity for Brand Building

Emotional brand building is like mixing a cocktail, integrating anthropology, imagination, sensory experience, and the foresight for responses to the future.
--Marco Ghobbe, Emotional Branding

A New Company, a New Product, and a New Opportunity

We are creating a new horizon. We need a business card and a website.

We have developed a new product, and we should give it a name and a trademark.

We need to raise a large amount of money, and the proposal should have brand characteristics.

Our company is going to be listed in the spring.

We need venture capital, even though we do not have a customer right now.

Change of the Company Name and Address

Our brand name is no longer suitable for us and our competition environment.

We need to change a name as our trademark has been rejected.

We need to change our brand name because it has negative meanings in the local language where we want to expand the new market.

Our name will mislead the customers.

Our brand is being upgraded to Internet Plus.

Our brand website has been written off.

Reinvigorate the Brand

We want a new orientation and to reinvigorate our aging brand.

Our current products and service are not within the original industry at the founding of our company; our main business has changed.

We need to present our brand in a clearer way. Our brand is not differentiated enough.

We want to be a global brand. And we need new strength to enter the market.

No one knows us.

Our stock has fallen in value.

We want to attract better new markets.

We need to wake up the investors.

Brand Aging

Our products are great, but our brand feels obsolete.

Is our brand identity suitable for the Internet?

Our brand identity falls behind other competitors due to the lack of modern temperament.

We have 60 departments with different names, which is very confusing.

Everybody knows our brand, but all of them think it needs a make-over.

We love our trademark; it is known to all. But people do not understand the connotation of its characters.

Establish an Integrated Communication System

We have not shown consistent brand appearances to the customers.

We are lacking in visual consistency. We should upgrade our brand structure for business combination of the company.

Our packaging is not special. Our competitor has better packaging and sales volume than ours. We need competitive edges.

Our marketing plans look like they are from different companies, with different styles.

We should look like an international enterprise.

Our brand does not have much attraction to the "post-1990" generation in front of the Internet.

Upon Merger and Acquisition

We need to deliver clear information to the shareholders that this is a reasonable acquisition for the purpose of making us stronger.

We need to deliver the message of one plus one being greater than two.

We need to integrate the brand equity of the company acquired.

We will tell the world that we are the leader after the merger.

We need a new name and a new image.

The two industry giants have merged. How should we manage our brand identity?

We should retain the old customers after the acquisition.

III. Key Stakeholders (Consumer Business)

Research of the brand stakeholders will provide extensive information for brand positioning, brand information setting, and brand strategizing as the brand building develops.

To seize opportunities to build a first-class brand, the key is to find the stakeholders who affect the success. Word-of-mouth and reputation affect far beyond the target customers. Modern enterprises call their own employees "internal customers" because the latter have great influence. It often brings an exceptionally high return by understanding characteristics, behavior patterns, demands, and perceptions of the stakeholders.

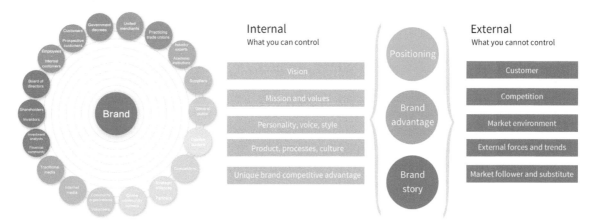

Key Stakeholders of Brand. Source: Alina Wheeler, Designing Brand Identity: An Essential Guide for the Whole Branding Team

IV. Brand Positioning

The cornerstone for every successful brand is the brand positioning strategy that drives the overall planning, marketing, and sales activities. The rapidly changing market is saturated with products and information that dazzle consumers, and the brand positioning exists to create a new situation in such market. Brand posi-

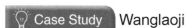
Case Study   Wanglaoji

In Guangdong before 2002, the traditional herbal teas (such as tea granules, home-made tea, and tea made by herbal tea houses) were generally taken by consumers as "drugs" because of their significant efficacy in reducing internal heat, and they were not required to and should not be drunk frequently. The brand "Wanglaoji" with a history of more than a century is the alternative name of herbal tea. People think of Wanglaoji when speaking of herbal tea, and vice versa. As a result, Wanglaoji, burdened with the brand name, was unable to make the Cantonese accept it as a kind of beverage that can be drunk frequently, and its sales were greatly restricted. Wanglaoji repositioned itself as a beverage that can prevent internal heat in 2002, which enabled it to immediately open up the market in China and largely increase the sales.

1. Differences between sales and marketing

Sales and marketing use similar approaches. The focus of a sales activity is the product, while the focus of a market-oriented enterprise is the customers. The product is defined and is finite to the enterprise, but the product means infinite possibilities in the minds of customers. Marketing penetrates the minds of consumers. An enterprise that knows marketing feels pulse for customers and prescribes the corresponding "medicine".

2. The unique statement

What: The only (category)
How: that (differentiation characteristic)
Who: for (customer)
Where: in (market area)
Why: because (purpose and demand)
We: who (conformity consumer psychology)
Case: Harley-Davidson Motor is——
What: The only motorcycle manufacturer
How: that makes imposing and loud motorcycles
Who: for macho guys (or macho wannabees)
Where: mostly in the U.S.
Why: because they want to become cowboys who lead unrestrained lives
When: in an era of decreasing personal freedom
We: motorcycle fans

tioning finds new ways in the gaps of the market to attract users by taking advantage of changes in population, technology, market cycles, and consumer trends. Brand positioning can help a brand establish its competitive advantages.

V. Brand Naming

A perfect brand name is easy to say and can stand the test of time; it stands for something, and helps the brand extend; it sounds rhythmic, and it looks great in the text of an e-mail or in the brand trademark. A well-chosen brand name is an essential asset that represents the well-known brand 24/7. Therefore, a brand name should be protected for its Chinese name, English name, network domain name, logo, registered patent of interpretative text, and copyright.

A brand name is mentioned day in and day out, in conversations, e-mails, voicemails, websites, on products, on business cards, and in presentations.

A name that is miscommunicated, is hard to pronounce, or is not memorable will hurt the marketing efforts of the enterprise. It can subject an enterprise to legal risks for no reason or alienation from a market due to offending prospective customers. It is a highly challenging task to find a perfect name that is not registered. Brand naming requires proceeding in a creative, directional, and strategic manner.

There are various reasons for a company to change its brand name: to make itself sound friendlier and more approachable; to make itself not sound outdated; or to indicate the customers that the brand has been changed.

Name changes are often accompanied with the enhancement of brand value and belief. The future direction of a brand must be considered, therefore, during the process of brand naming and brand identification. The name is generally created by a top designer, the trademark is designed by a graphic designer, and the brand naming and brand strategy making is a task that should be completed through the collaboration of professionals from different fields under the guidance of the top designer.

1. Naming of Chinese Brands

Among the well-known Internet enterprises in China, a particularly large number of them use animals as enterprise trademarks, mascots, product names, or trade names; for example, there are eight trademarks or names containing animals among the top 10 tourism websites of China, such as Ctrip's dolphin, Qunar's camel, Tuniu's bull, eLong's dragon, Lvmama's donkey (see Figure 8-5).

Likewise, animals account for at least half among the top ten live streaming and audio platforms of China, such as Douyu (fish), Huya (tiger), Maotouying (owl), and Huomao (cat), as shown in Figure 8-6. In the e-commerce field of China, Tmall has a cat, Jingdong has a metal dog, Suning has a lion, and Gome has a tiger (see Figure 8-7).

Next, let's see names relating to plants that are selected by the Chinese Internet companies, such as Douban, Tudou, Xiaomi, Mogujie, Wandoujia, Jianguoyun, Mgtv, Huajiao, Lizhi, and Guokr, as shown in Figure 8-8. Those plant names are not much used in the traditional industries because traditionally they do not have too many special meanings. Internet companies, meanwhile, are increasingly using names with reduplicated words, such as DingTalk, QQ, and Momo, as shown in Figure 8-9.

Figure 8-5   There are 8 trademarks or names containing Animals among the top 10 tourism websites of China. Source: Sohu.com

Figure 8-6　Animals account for at least half among the top 10 live streaming and audio platforms of China. Source: Sohu.com

Figure 8-7　In the e-commerce field of China, Tmall has a cat, Jingdong has a metal dog, Suning has a lion, and Gome has a tiger. Source: Sohu.com

Figure 8-8　Names relating to plants that are selected by the Chinese Internet companies. Source: Sohu.com

Figure 8-9　Internet companies are increasingly using names with reduplicated words. Source: Sohu.com

The Chinese time-honored brands prefer characters with good meanings, and mostly contain three characters, such as Neiliansheng, Refosian, Rongbaozhai, Quanjude, Tongrentang, Yueshengzhai, Laozhengxing, and Caizhizhai. Compared to the century-old shops that favor Rui (auspicious), Heng (permanent), Tong (connected), Da (extended), De (virtue), Ren (benevolence), Long (prosperous), Yu (abundant), Fu (blessing), Sheng (flourishing), Tong (great harmony), Guang (light), Kang (well-being), and Bao (treasure), etc., modern Chinese enterprises prefer Rui (farsighted), Zun (respected), Xiang (enjoyment), Shang (esteemed), Xin (credit), Rong (honor), Hua (magnificent), Ya (elegant), You (excellent), Jia (good), Hao (heroic), and Jue (noble), etc. Which names are more memorable? Let's say three competitive brands, one named Youchengtong (excellent,

honest, connected), one named Meibaozhuo (beautiful, treasure, outstanding), and one named Black Bat. Which one will you be most likely to remember five minutes later?

Apparently, the noun is easier to remember, namely, "Black Bat".

The Chinese Internet's becoming a "zoo" reflects that the art of competition for attention has risen to a certain level. The Chinese Internet entrepreneurs are far better than the contemporary entrepreneurs in other industries of China in terms of self-knowledge iteration, idea refreshing, and vision broadness, and are first-rate even in today's world.

2.　Six Criteria for Naming a Brand

(1) Memorability. User cognition is the first driving force of user consumption.

(2) Ease of spreading. A name using a concrete concept that people are quite

familiar with in their daily life, such as an animal or plant, is easier to spread in the mobile context.

(3) Good implication. An auspicious name is always good.

(4) Good association. A good name must be associated with the industry or product positioning of the enterprise, to remind users of the basic attributes of the product.

(5) Attention attracting. A name that attracts attention can avoid being submerged by information and lower the spread costs in the age of attention economy.

(6) Ease of registration. The name should meet requirements for trademark registration, logo registration, and domain name registration. It is better that the applied and registered trademark and logo have graphic-text interpretations, and such interpretations are then applied for and registered as intellectual property of the enterprise in the form of "works registration certificate", to constitute another form of protection.

Case Study | Name and Trademark

Lenovo started to use the name "Lenovo" for its laptops in order to go out of China into Asia and the rest of the world. By saying that Lenovo made a mistake in using "Lenovo", the outside world mainly meant that it had "wasted" the ThinkPad brand it had acquired. There were certainly some who said that as long as Lenovo did not conflict with the cultural ideology, such as consumer culture, geographical culture, ethnic culture, and linguistic culture, of the target market in terms of brand name, the brand would not cause ambiguity to or be misunderstood by the market, and could still become bigger, even if the market acceptance was slow. For instance, Xiuzheng Pharmaceutical's Sidashu Brand does not contain much culture content in itself. The enterprise considers Sidashu to contain the meaning of "quick and comfortable", but this is quite strange to the market. Just as the saying goes, "If names be not correct, language is not in accordance with the truth of things. If language be not in accordance with the truth of things, affairs are difficult to be carried on to success", such difficulty, in my opinion, means the increase of brand communication costs, such as strengthening the memory for the character of "Sidashu" by using homophone (similar to fourth uncle in Chinese). However, such type of brand names that originally seem to lack culture content has an advantage, i.e., the strong differentiation, making competitors difficult to imitate and cling to. Competitors are too far to catch up with such brands once they are formed.

1. 8 points for a good name

(1) Meaningful

A brand name should communicate the essence of the brand and must conform to the brand image and connotation the enterprise wants to convey.

(2) Distinctive

A brand name should be unique, easy to remember, pronounce, and spell, and different from competitors.

(3) Forward-looking

A brand name should accompany the company's growth, change, and success, etc., must have sustainability and preserve elasticity, and should last long.

(4) Modular

A brand name should enable the company to easily build brand extensions.

(5) Registerable

A brand name should be registered as a trademark and domain name of the company.

(6) Positive

A brand name should have a positive meaning for the target market of the brand and should not lead to negative associations.

(7) Visual

A brand name should look proper in the brand trademark/logo, business letters, and brand architecture.

(8) Harmonious

If possible, after a brand is named, how harmonious the name is with the company's main founder and his industry should be checked on the principles of the I Ching ("Book of Changes"), a book of ancient Chinese philosophy.

2.   Types of brand names

(1) Founder

Many enterprises are named after their founders, such as Ben & Jerry's Ice Cream, Chanel Perfume, Armani, Martha Stewart, Ralph Lauren, and Mrs. Fields. Those names might be easier to register.

(2) Descriptive names

Those names describe the nature of the enterprises, such as Toys "R" Us, Find Great People, E-Trade, and RoyalFlush. The benefit of a descriptive name is that it directly describes the nature of the company, but a potential disadvantage is that the name may become limiting as a company grows and diversifies. Furthermore, some descriptive names are difficult to register and protect because they are too generic.

(3) Fictitious names

A made-up name, such as Kodak, Xerox, Sony, or TiVo, is unique and easy to register trademark; however, an enterprise needs to invest heavily to foster its target market, to have customers know the service, product, or what the enterprise does. Haagen-Dazs is a fictitious foreign name and they are doing quite well in the consumer market. This is a good example of fictitious brand naming.

(4) Metaphor

Things, places, people, animals, processes, mythological figures, or foreign words can be used in this type of name to allude to a characteristic of an enterprise. For example, names like Benz are interesting to visualize and they tell stories.

(5) Acronym

Such names are not easy to remember or register and protect. The acronyms IBM and GE became well known after the enterprises were famous with their full names. There are so many new names that dazzle consumers that are acronyms, and the enterprises need to advertise the acronyms with substantial spending. Acronyms should not be used at the beginning of the founding.

(6) Wordplay

Some names alter the spelling of a word to create a unique name, such as Cingular and Netflix.

(7) Combinations of the above

Many best names combine the above naming types, such as Cingular Wireless, Citibank, and Hope's Cookies. Customers and investors like nice names that they can understand.

(8) Traditional culture

Names like Zhubajie (zbj.com), Alibaba, and Baidu are derived from the traditional culture.

The case source quoted from: Hongbing Hua,
Top-level Design, Published in 2013

VI. Brand Taglines

Brand taglines can evoke emotional responses in consumers and consequently influence their buying behaviors. A brand tagline is a short phrase that captures brand personality and essence, stands for the brand positioning, and distinguishes the company from its competitors.

According to the brand creativity practice of the author, the following brand taglines have driven the hot sales of products:

Eliminate toxins, and feel refreshed and relaxed
    --Paidu Yangyan (Detox & Beautifying) Capsules
Nongfu Spring, slightly sweet
    --Nongfu Spring Co., Ltd.
Eighteen years of waiting has been for this day
    --Shaoxing Nv'erhong Brewing Co., Ltd.
Family health protected by 3Trees
    --SKSHU Paint Co., Ltd.
Dried bean curd sticks made with the heart
    --Henan Anyang Shuangqiang Bean Products Co., Ltd. (dried bean curd sticks)
Protect your sleep
    --Beijing Guoxin Kechuang Biotech. Co., Ltd.
The truest sound reproduced
    -- Guangzhou Leeyin Building Material Co., Ltd.
Huasheng Flour sublimates the flour
    --Jiangsu Yanhu Huasheng Flour Co., Ltd.
Love is like a tidal wave, you can never resist the temptation
    --Jiangxi Kangyi Food Co., Ltd. (ice cream series)
Ceramics that think
    -- Guangdong KITO Ceramics Co., Ltd.
Sleep with whoever you want
    --Guangxi Hisleep Mattress Group Co., Ltd.
Chinese ink for every household
    --Zhongshan Dongpeng Chemical Co., Ltd. (printing ink)
Less friction, more harmony
    --Shandong Meipaili Grease Co., Ltd.
Where there are Chinese, there is Wallace
    --Wallace Restaurant Management Co., Ltd.

Deep breath with breathing paint
    --Jinan Cuibao Coating Co., Ltd.
Zhang Xiaoquan scissors cut everything but lingering affection
    --Hangzhou Zhang Xiaoquan Scissors Co., Ltd.
Not all light fixtures are for appreciation
    --Zhongshan Kinglong Lighting Co., Ltd.
Harmonize with and benefit the people
    --Zhejiang Howell Illuminating Technology Co., Ltd. (LED lighting products)
Light the future
    --Cnlight Co., Ltd.

1. Essential characteristics

Concise
Different from competitors
Unique
Grasping brand essence and positioning
Easy to remember and say
No negative meaning
Displayed in several words
Can be registered to obtain trademark right and be protected by law
Can evoke an emotional response
Inspiring users to relate
Stimulating users to purchase

2. A summary of taglines

(1) Imperative: to command actions and usually start with a verb

YouTube	Broadcast yourself
Nike	Just do it
Mini Cooper	Let's motor
HP	Invent
Apple	Think different
Toshiba	Don't copy. Lead
Mutual of Omaha	Begin today
Virgin Mobile	Live without a plan
Outward Bound	Live bigger
NBA	I love this game

(2) Descriptive: to describe briefly the service, product, or brand promise

Philips	Sense and sensibility
PNC	The thinking behind the money
Target	Expect more. Pay less.
Concentrics	People. Process. Results.
MSNBC	The whole picture
Ernst & Young	From thought to finish
Allstate	You're in good hands
GE	Imagination at work
Gree	Made in China. Loved by the world.

(3) Superlative: to position the brand as a market leader

DeBeers	A diamond is forever

BMW	The ultimate driving machine
Lufthansa	There's no better way to fly
National Guard	American at their best
Hoechst	Future in life sciences
Alibaba	To make it easy to do business anywhere
Letv	Breaking Boundaries with Ecosystem Synergy

(4) Provocative: to provoke thought; frequently a question

Sears	Where else?
Microsoft	Where are you going today?
Benz	What makes a symbol endure?
Dairy Council	Got milk?
Robust	Did you drink it today?

(5) Specific: to show the industry field of the enterprise

HSBC	The world's local bank
The New York Times	All the news that's fit to print
Olay	Love the skin you're in
Volkswagen	Drivers wanted
eBay	Happy hunting
Minolta	The essentials of imaging
Letv	Letv ecosystem, beyond your imagination

 Mobile Brand Identity System

I. Vision

It takes courage to build a vision. Great ideas, enterprises, products, or services are built by dreamers who have the ability to see what others cannot see and the tenacity to put their dreams into practice.

Brand identity begins with a conversation about the future. Face-to-face communication and hearing the vision in person are keys to the brand identity creating process. Leaders who have the courage to take time to share their wild dreams and challenges deeply understand how to build culture and brands with the power of symbols and stories. All good brands tell good stories.

II. Meaning

The best brands are built on some big ideas, and have a defined set of values, strategic positioning, and an expression that makes them different. Symbols are blood vessels for brand meanings and will become very powerful when they are frequently used and understood what behind them. Symbols are the fastest way for communication among people. Interestingly, a user will love a brand more after he knows the meaning behind the brand symbol.

III. Ecologicalization

In the age of Internet with full, open access to information, the humanization of brand, authenticity of marketing, and ecological chain of production will be tested by the netizens.

IV. Flexibility

An efficient brand identity should be able to respond to the future change and growth of a company and support the changing and evolving marketing strategies. A brand should support the Internet-enabled evolution of the enterprise.

Mobile Brand Identity System. Source: Alina Wheeler,
Designing Brand Identity: An Essential Guide for the Whole Branding Team

V. Entertainment

Brands place more emphasis on entertainment in the age of the mobile Internet. Entertainment is the main feature of the Internet in the age of "here comes everybody".

VI. Value

Building brand awareness, increasing brand recognition, communicating our characteristics and quality to customers, and expressing that we can provide a value different from competitors can all create considerable benefits. Good brands have a premium.

 Case Study | **Brand Recognition**

1. Named after the Greek goddess of victory, Nike has a logo that is a tick symbolizing a wing, designed by Carolyn Davidson in 1971, which is meaningful to a company that markets sport shoes. In 1988, Nike's "Just do it" tagline became a battle cry for an entire generation of athletes. When consumers see the symbol, they will relate it to "Just do it" and be inspired by the big idea.

2. Apple's customers quickly become brand zealots. They think innovation and fun when they see the Apple logo. The logo, an apple with a bite out of it, is a friendly symbol of knowledge designed by Rob Janoff in 1976. And as widely spread by the brand fans, this logo is a symbol of anarchy from the PC world. The original logo was chromatic and filled with rainbow stripes, but now it is a simple monochromatic icon.

3. When the Benz logo was designed by Gottlieb Daimler in 1909, it was a three-pointed star that represented the company's "domination of the land, the sea, and the air". Now this trademark stands for the fastest cars on the road and stands for extreme luxury. The logo has been dramatically simplified in the 20th century but remains highly recognizable.

4. The "O", created by Sol Sender and his Sender LLC, symbolized the dawn of a new day, and was designed for Barack Obama's U.S. presidential campaign in 2008. This symbol was charged with a deeper level of meaning and resonated with all walks of life, after Obama proposed the messages of hope and change. It became part of the largest social media campaign in history.

5. The Russian flag. Russia is a vast country stretching across the frigid zone, subfrigid zone, and temperate zone. On its flag, the tricolor three horizontal rectangles are connected to represent this geographic location characteristic of Russia: the white represents the natural landscape snow throughout the year; the blue represents subfrigid zone and the rich natural resources such as underground mineral resources, forest, and waterpower of Russia; the red represents the temperate zone and Russia's long history and contributions to human civilization. There is another saying that the white stands for freedom, the blue stands for the goddess who protects Russia, and the red stands for power and strength.

6. The U.S. flag, which is a rectangle with the proportions of 19:10, is called the Star-Spangled Banner. The upper-left corner is a blue field of stars of which represents the number of states of the U.S.; outside the field of stars are 13 red and white stripes, standing for the original 13 colonies of North America. According to Washington, the red stripes stood for England, and the white stripes stood for the freedom obtained after separating from England. A more common saying is that the red stands for strength and courage, the white stands for purity and innocence, and blue stands for vigilance, perseverance and justice. An act was passed by the U.S. Congress in 1818 that the red and white stripes should be fixed to 13, and the number of five-pointed stars should be consistent with the number of states of the U.S. One new star should be added to the flag for one new state added, which should generally be implemented on July 4 of the year following addition of the new state. So far, there have been 50 stars on the flag, representing the 50 states of the U.S. June 14 every year is Flag Day, and commemorative activities are held throughout the U.S. to show respect to the flag and love to the United States.

7. Meaning drives creativity

Designers can convert meanings into unique visual forms of expression; therefore, it is critical that meanings are clearly explained so that they can be

Brand Recognition

understood, communicated, and approved. All elements of the brand identity system should be under a creative logic framework.

8. Meaning builds consensus

Like a campfire, meaning is a rallying point used to build consensus between decision makers and investors. Consensus on brand essence and attributes can build synthetical effect and guide all subsequent visual expression solutions, naming, and key messages design.

9. Meaning evolves over time

A company's business model may change greatly as the company grows. Similarly, the meaning designed to a trademark may evolve as the company grows.

10. Meaning stimulates repeated purchase

A brand meaning deeply rooted among the users will strengthen the user consumption stickiness and stimulate repeated purchase.

The case source quoted from: Hongbing Hua, Top-level Design, Published in 2013

VII. Certainty

In psychology, certainty is authenticity, and refers to self-knowledge and making choices based on self-knowledge. Organizations that clearly know themselves and their purpose already have a solid foundation at the beginning of building brand identity. They will create brands that are sustainable and genuine. Brand expression must fit the organization's unique mission, vision, history, culture, values, and personality.

An average 120 million people around the world drink Coca-Cola products every day. The brand design company Turner Duckworth revitalized the iconic brand presence and conducted a series of integrated visual designs, from cups to trucks all showing the relaxation and pleasure of drinking the coke beverage.

After research revealed that there was a cultural longing for Coca-Cola to again become a trendsetter, this branding process gave Coca-Cola the confidence to express the biggest emotional appeal through the simplest visual design.

VIII. Differentiation

Innumerable brands compete for the attention of users. The noisy market is filled with countless choices. Why should consumers choose one brand over others?

It is not enough to be just different. Brands need to demonstrate their uniqueness and make it easy for customers to understand their characteristics.

IX. Durability

Brands are messengers of trust. We are living in a society in which social systems, technology, lifestyles, and languages constantly change. Brands that are recognizable and familiar will reassure consumers. Durability depends on an enterprise's long-term commitment to core ideas and capacity to be flexible.

Coca Cola

Source: Alina Wheeler, Designing
Brand Identity: An Essential Guide for the Whole Branding Team

Trademarks' and enterprises' date of origination:

Trademarks and enterprises	date of origination	Trademarks and enterprises	date of origination	Trademarks and enterprises	date of origination
Löwenbräu Brewery	1383	Guinness	1862	Olympics	1865
Mitsubishi	1870	Nestlé	1875	Bass Brewery	1875
John Deere	1876	Johnson & Johnson	1886	Coca-Cola	1887
General Electric	1892	Prudential	1896	Michelin	1896
Shell Oil	1900	Ford Motor	1903	Nabisco	1900
Rolls-Royce	1905	Chanel	1910	Mercedes-Benz	1911
Prada	1913	IBM	1924	Greyhound	1926
London Underground	1933	Lancome	1935	Volkswagen	1938
IKEA	1943	CBS	1951	NBC	1956
Chase Manhattan	1960	International Paper	1960	Motorola	1960
Westinghouse	1960	UPS	1961	Weyerhaeuser	1961
McDonald's	1962	General Foods Corporation	1962	Wool Bureau	1964
Rohm and Haas Company	1964	Mobil	1965	Diners Club	1966
Exxon	1966	Metropolitan Life	1967	L'eggs	1971
Eastman Kodak	1971	Nike	1971	Quaker Oats	1972
Infogrames	1973	Merrill Lynch	1973	United Way	1974
I Love NY	1975	Dunkin' Donuts	1974	Citicorp	1976
PBS	1976	United	1976	Apple	1977
Transamerica	1979	AT&T	1984	Google	1998

In Nike Swoosh, "swoosh" is the onomato-poeia of motion and speed.

This famous Nike Swoosh was designed by graphic design student Carolyn Davidson in 1971 for Phil Knight, the owner of Nike. Nike was feeble at that time, Davidson had just graduated from design school and was in need of a job, and Knight needed someone to design a logo for the shoes he produced. Therefore, he hired Davidson and asked her to design a stripe logo that had something to do with movement.

Nike swoosh is one of the most well-known and most counterfeited logos in the world. Nike started to use the "Just do it" slogan in their commercial in 1988.

"A successful branding process is the maximum use of creativity to express the business purpose. It is about understanding operation. It is about creating the brand story."

Evolution of the Nike Logo

Evolution of the Nike Logo. The case source quoted from: Hongbing Hua, Top-level Design, Published in 2013

X. Brand Evolution

Evolution of the brand "The Shell Pecten": The brand spirit continues no matter how the visual symbol changes. The core of brands is consumers who are not only people buying products and services, but also "beneficiaries" within the larger scope, including consumers, enterprise employees, and external agents. Each type of beneficiary has a different perspective of brand experience, but there should be consistency in brand behavior.

Communications: In brand science, communication refers to communicating information to the internal employees and external audience of an enterprise in the brand promotion process.

1. Ecologicalization

Whether a customer uses a product, talks to a service person, or purchases an iPhone, the brand should look familiar with the customer and achieve the desired brand benefit. Coherence is an indicator that measures whether all the pieces of brand identity are held together. It is the base for the product to build trust, foster loyalty, and delight the customers. It should be constant and the brand ecology should be maintained. In the age of the Internet, applying the Internet ecological spirit of "concentration, perfection" in the enterprise brand building reflects the consistent coherence.

2. How to achieve coherence?

Consistent expectations and sticking to core concept

The enterprise should know its brand positioning and the image it wants customers to perceive. They should use a consistent voice developed from a core concept in all communication media to express the concentration spirit.

3. Unified company strategy

As a company diversifies, a consistent company strategy is needed by each business division to promote their awareness and acceptance; however, the external publicity should be unified.

Every touchpoint is a brand experience. Coherence starts with understanding

Evolution of the Shell Pecten

"A product brand becomes more and more important over time as it is the guarantee of quality and price"

Evolution of the brand "The Shell Pecten".
Source: Hongbing Hua, Top-Level Design

161

the needs and preferences of the target customers and then designing a brand experience that meets the expected goal.

4. Look and feel

A brand identity system should be unified visually and structurally. It is built on overall brand architecture and designed with special colors, typefaces, and formats. The identity system should facilitate consumers' recognition of the enterprise and support brand attributes across different media.

5. Uniform quality

Uniform quality means that the enterprise must pay considerable attention to all its brands and services. If the quality of any brand under it is not superior enough, this will reduce the valuation of assets of the enterprise in realities and in intangible feelings.

6. Simplicity and plainness

Communicating product and service information in clear and consistent language can help customers make choices. A brand name that complies with the brand architecture logic and coherence also makes it easier for consumers to make choices.

7. Flexibility

A brand needs to be flexible to achieve innovation. A brand identity system should leave space for the enterprise to innovate. No one can predict accurately what new products or services an enterprise will launch in five years, or what new devices we will use to communicate and how our purchasing pattern will change. Brands that embrace changes are bound to be flexible brands that can quickly seize new opportunities in the market. In the age of the Internet in which everything changes quickly, the flexibility kept by a brand identity system is the flexibility of integrating into the Internet.

Family Branding

Root plan, brand tree

Figure 8-10   Family branding. Source: Hongbing Hua, Top-Level Design

8. Embracing changes

(1) Marketing flexibility. An efficient brand identity positions a company for constant change and growth in the future. It must effectively operate in a wide range of customer touchpoints. A good system can embrace the evolution of marketing strategies and business models.

(2) Brand architecture. Brand identity systems must be able to extend, namely, the marketing of any new product or service can predict the future by using the enterprises' flexible and durable brand architecture logic.

(3) Long-lasting and recognizable. Tools in the brand identity Tool Kit should be used with creativity, to keep the brand easily recognizable. The balance between control and creativity should be carefully designed, to make it possible to adhere to some standards and achieve specific marketing objectives.

9. Parent brand

Most parent brands are low-profile, and mainly face institutional investors, investors in shares, and the press. The role of parent brands today is quietly changing, not only responsible for investors, but also facing a bigger customer chain, including employees, consumers, government, banks, insurers, security providers, and other interested intermediaries. Some parent brands are creating their own identities, particularly in relation to the legal issues.

10. Brand tree

Many parent brands can be structured into an "umbrella brand" owning a number of sub-brands. Relations of those sub-brands are as shown in Figure 8-10.

The sub-brands can be the products of a company, and the parent brand is the manufacturer and owner of the products. The behavior and reputation of the two often correlate with and affect each other. This structure is also applicable to countries: the European Union (EU) is a parent brand, and its member states are sub-brands; the behavior of the sub-brand directly affects the reputation and fame of the parent brand, for example, the European debt crisis caused by Greece affected the brand image of the EU.

The sub-brands may be a combination of many brands which are closely tied by characteristics of the parent brand that

As a parent company, Apple has the mission to propagate belief. It ingeniously names all products by beginning with "i", to complete the product serialization while infinitely extending the brand belief.

One day, there may be "iTV", "iElevator", "iCooker", "iGame", "iFilm" or "iAnime". Apple will continue the "i" in the world as long as its "root of belief" exists.

Source: Baidu Wenku

holds high the banner of the founder. The characteristics of the parent brand are fundamental to the success. The parent brand plays a decisive role and forms the value system of sub-brands.

If sub-brands are branches and leaves of a tree, the parent brand is the root deep in the soil. DNA of the root decides attributes of branches and leaves. Therefore, the concept and cultural construction of the parent brand is quite important. We should not make light of the invisible things, because what obscure our eyes may be the thriving branches and leaves.

Sub-brands may be more famous than the parent brand. It is not necessary for a sub-brand to stay consistent with the parent brand or other sub-brands. A new sub-brand is more likely to break away from the parent brand, to attract different customers. A sub-brand can be set at a different price range for products and services than that of the parent brand.

11. Commitment

A brand is an asset that needs to be well protected and nurtured. A top down mandate and a bottom up understanding of brand importance are required for the active and effective management of the brand asset. The best companies provide their employees with tools that promote brand champions. Proposing, protecting, and enhancing the brand requires ambition and rigorous approach to ensure its integrity. Always keeping the commitment is the brand bottom line in the information age.

12. Managing the assets

The most important thing in sustaining a brand identity is to actively take the responsibility to manage the brand asset. A common mistake is that everyone thinks they have finished the hardest part after completing a new brand identity. In fact, the whole process is just beginning, and the hard work still lies ahead.

13. Building the brand

Not only do large multinational enterprises need to manage the brand identity system, small and medium-sized enterprises and non-profit organizations also need an individual to supervise and manage the brand assets and report to the executor. The functional perspective is to keep moving, conducting management, and monitoring standards and tools that help preserve the brand, and stick to the core principles, and know when to become flexible.

Apple series. Source: Hongbing Hua, Top-Level Design

14. Value

Creating value is undoubtedly the goal of almost all organizations. Enterprises have started to expand the value conversation with customers, to pursue sustainability. It has become a new business model for all brands to create value and profits while taking corporate social responsibility and environmental sustainability responsibility. A brand is an intangible asset, and the brand identity covers all concrete expression from packaging to website and supports the brand's intangible asset value.

(1) Brand is an asset. Brand identity is regarded as a strategic tool and an asset which can seize every opportunity to build brand awareness and brand recognition, show the brand uniqueness and quality, and express the brand differences. It is a priority for enterprises to adhere to the brand identity uniform standards and resolutely pursue quality excellence.

(2) Value is protected by law. Trademarks and trade dress must be protected by law in both local and global markets. Enterprises must educate employees and partners to comply with legal provisions.

15. Value creating the asset

The essence of enterprise strategy is to answer the question: where are the future customers? This is a tradeoff process and a question of logical sequence in the management science: where are the future customers? Where is the future of the enterprise? Solving this problem will figure out where the starting point of the management science research is.

The fast-growing enterprises during global economic recovery before 2008 were amazing and conformed to Newtonian mechanics in a way. The mechanics of Isaac Newton tells us:

F	M×A
Force	Mass × Acceleration
Enterprise Competitiveness	Asset × Asset Acceleration
Enterprise Operating Income	Capital × (Brand + Product)

When studying the law of universal gravitation, Newton was infatuated with the marvelous law of the Earth moving around the sun along a fixed orbit, but he could not understand "when did the Earth begin" and "why it moves around the sun"; therefore, he conceived of God as the first mover to move the Earth around the sun.

Newton described such a universe: planets trace an elliptical motion around the sun, and the centripetal force for them to maintain the circular motion is from the sun's gravity; however, a key problem here is that the planets must first be set in motion, but the sun's gravity only attracts planets towards the sun and is impossible to make planets follow a circular motion. What puzzled Newton was how the initial tangential motion of planets happened. Therefore, Newton had to explain that it was God who made the first move, and with the initial tangential velocity, planets could completely run according to his law of universal gravitation. He said, "...without the divine power it could never put them into a circulating motion." This was the origin of Newton's thought of God as the first mover, which is criticized by the later generations. A later historian of science commented, "Newton drove God out of the solar system, and had God push the solar system from outside, and then God had nothing to do with the solar system."

The later generations criticize Newton's thought of God as the first mover mainly because they think that this thought showed the science's return to the religious theology after the Copernican Revolution. This thought hindered Newton's scientific research and led him to accomplish nothing in his later life.

From the modern cosmology, the "first mover" could be completely solved within the physical framework, without the need for "divine power". If Newton lived till now, he would certainly not ask about the "first mover" of the solar system; however, according to his personality, he would ask what the "cosmic singularity" is, where time or space did not exist in the Big Bang theory, and he might say that is the "first blow" of God. Is this not a process of infinite approximation to the scientific truth?

Albert Einstein proposed a new formula on the mass-energy relation to prove how energy happened:

E	mc^2
Energy	Mass × Speed of light squared

If Newton's formula is the most appropriate to explain how to achieve the scale of an enterprise, then what is the source of energy to promote the enterprise to constantly speed up? Apparently, it is Einstein's formula of the theory of relativity.

| Enterprise Energy | Enterprise Scale × Premium Profit Margin |
| Enterprise Profit | Operating Income × Premium Profit Margin |

Overview of Research of Western Scholars on the Concept of Customer Value	
Definition of Value	Defined by
Economic value to the customer (EVC) refers to the maximum amount a customer firm would be willing to pay, given comprehensive knowledge of a focal product offering and the other available competitive product offerings.	Forbis and Mehta (1981)

Definition of Value	Defined by
Value is the price a customer is willing to pay, which is driven by the perceived benefits of the product to the customer.	Christopher (1982)
In the market, value is generally defined as "quality at a reasonable price" and is considered to be more important to consumers than quality, as price is the quality affordable to consumers.	Progressive Grocer (1984)
Use value represents the relevant value displayed by the product during the customer's use, especially in industrial products, the value analyst is primary concerned with use value--the performance and reliability of the product--rather than its existing value (based on prestige or aesthetics, cost value, or exchange value)	Reuter (1988)
In the value model of Zeithaml, value is: 1. Low price 2. Whatever I want in a product 3. The quality I get for the price I pay 4. What I get for what I give. Customer perceived value is customer's overall assessment of the utility of a product/service, based on perceptions of what is received and what is given.	Zeithaml (1988)
Customer's overall assessment of the utility of a product based on perceptions of what is received and what is given	Zeithaml, Parasuraman and Berry (1990)
Ratio between perceived benefits and perceived sacrifice	Monroe (1991)
Buyers' perceptions of value represent a tradeoff between the quality or benefits they perceive in the product relative to the sacrifice they perceive by paying the price	Monroe (1991)
The perceived worth in monetary units of the set of economic, technical, service, and social benefits received by a customer firm in exchange for the price paid for a product offering, taking into consideration the available alternative suppliers' offerings and prices	Anderson, Jain and Chintagunta (1993)
Customer value is market-perceived quality adjusted for the relative price of your product	Gale (1994)
Trade-off between desirable attributes compared with sacrifice attributes	Woodruff and Gardial (1996)
Customer value is the emotional bond established between a customer and a producer after the customer has used a salient product or service produced by the supplier and found the product to provide an added value	Butz and Goodstein (1996)
Customer value is an interactive relativistic preference experience	Holbrook (1996)
The customer's assessment of the value that has been created for them by a supplier, given the trade-offs between all relevant benefits and sacrifices in a specific use situation	Flint, Woodruff and Gardial (1997)
Value is a trade-off between benefits and costs	Woodruff and Gardial (1997)
Customer value is a customer's perceived preference for and evaluation of those product attributes, attribute performances, and consequences arising from use that facilitate (or block) achieving the customer's goals and purposes in use situations	Woodruff (1997)
Value is defined as the centrally held, enduring core beliefs, desired end-states, or higher order goals of the individual customer or customer organization that guide behavior	Flint, Woodruff and Gardial (1997)

Definition of Value	Defined by
Value is the desire of a customer to obtain a specific product for a certain purpose	Richard L. Oliver (1998)
The value process is the beginning and ending of relationship marketing. A relationship marketing strategy must create more value for the customer or for some other party, such as a distributor, than the value of the mere transactions of goods or services in single episodes. Customer perceived value (CPV) in a relationship context can be described with the following two equations: CPV = (Core Solution + Additional Services) / 　　　(Price + Relationship Costs) CPV = Core Value ± Added Value	Gronroos (2000)
Customer delivered value is the difference between total customer value and total customer cost	Kotler (2001)
Value is the perceived trade-off between multiple benefits and sacrifices gained	Achim Walter, Thomas Ritter, Hans Georg Gemunden (2001)

16. Trademark

You can literally select all shapes and characters and apply them in the trademark design. The territory of trademark expands on a daily basis, from text description to image connotation, focusing on either the script or the image.

Classification of these designs, however, is not highly distinguished and a lot of trademark designs are a mix of types of elements.

So, does it make any practical sense to classify all the designs? Although companies require different types of visual designs and there is not a clear rule to follow, designers tend to concentrate on a series of options that give directions and drive physical inspirations and pick one that best suits the customer's requirements. As such, classification of designs has merit.

17. Identification of brand logo

Brand identification logo represents structural relation among logotype, symbol and slogan. In some special cases, logotype and symbol are allowed to be separated in a brand identification logo. There are also horizontal and vertical variations of a logo for use in different applications.

The logo of "Lenovo 联想" change to "Lenovo".
Source: Hongbing Hua, Top-level Design

18. Categories of brand marks

Word marks

Word marks are a company name, acronym, or product name that has been designed to convey a brand attribute and positioning. Some examples of this are IKEA, ebay, Google, and Nokia.

Letterforms

Letterform logos use one or more letters of the alphabet. These letterforms act as a mnemonic device for the company name. Examples of this are Univision, IBM, Unilever, and UPS.

Emblems

Company name and a pictorial element, two elements of emblem logos, are never separated. Examples of this include TiVo, OXO (brand of household products), and LEED (Leadership in Energy & Environmental Design, a green building rating system).

Pictorial marks

Pictorial marks are an immediately recognizable literal image that has been simplified and stylized. Examples include: Apple, NBC, CBS, POLP, and Lacoste.

Abstract or symbolic marks

Abstract or symbolic marks are symbols that convey a big idea. These logos often embody a company's strategic ambiguity. Examples of this are Target, Sprint, Nike, and HSBC.

19. Brand books

Brand books, spirit books, and thought books can all serve to educate, inspire and build brand awareness. A brand strategy would never influence anyone if it stayed in the conference room, on Page 3 of a marketing plan or in someone's mind.

A company's visions and the meaning of a brand need a communication vehicle that is accessible, portable, and personal. Online brand sites often contain "Who we are" and "What our brand stands for", in addition to standards, templates, and guidelines.

Timing is everything. A company undergoing organizational change must clearly convey "where is the car headed for". Generally speaking, the brand identity process sparks a new clarity about the brand. It is a smart move for a company to building the awareness about how each employee can assist in building the brand.

Foreword	Typography	Formatting	Signage	Image library
Message from CEO	Font size	Formatting elements	External signage	Photography
Our missions and values	Supporting typefaces	Horizontal or vertical	Internal signage	Book gallery
Our brand	Special-purpose font	Grid	Color	Culture wall
Our propositions	Fonts used for instrument processing	Purchase order	Typography	Reproduction files
Role of brand identity	US business partner	Receipt	Materials and finishes	Brand mark only
How to use the guidelines	Corporate letterhead	Shipping manifest	Polished baking finish	Brand logo variations
Brand identity elements	Typing template	Reimbursement sheet	Fabrication guidelines	Full color
Brand mark	Division letterhead	Marketing materials	Company flag	One color
Logotype	Personalized letterhead	Voice	Vehicle identification	Black
Signature	Second sheet	Video	Vans	White
Tagline	#10 envelope	Signature placement	Cars	PC platform
Name in text	Monarch letterhead	Folder	Buses	MAC platform
Incorrect usage of elements	Monarch envelope	Covers	Planes	App platform
Domain name	Memo template	Recommended grids	Trucks	Miscellaneous
Nomenclature	Business cards for corporate	Brochure system, size, variations	Packaging	Whom to contact with questions
Colloquial vs. legal names	Business cards for sales force	Mastheads	Legal considerations	FAQ
Corporate	Notepads	Product sheets	Package sizes	Design inquiries
Division	News release	Direct mails	Package grids	Clearance process
Business unit	Mailing labels	Newsletters	Product signatures	Legal information
Product and service	Window envelope	Posters	Labeling system	Ordering information
Trademarks	Large mailing envelope	Postcards	Boxes	Preparation samples
Acronym	Announcements	Advertising	Bags	Color Swatches on Coated Stock
Color	Invitations	Advertising signatures	Cartons	Color Swatches on Coated Stock
Brand color system	CD labels	Tagline usage	Uniforms	Color Swatches on uncoated Stock
Default color system	International business partner	Signature placement	Spring	Color Swatches on uncoated Stock
Supporting color system	A-4 letterhead	Typography	Summer	
Signature color options	A-4 personalized letterhead	Television ad grids	Fall	

Foreword	Typography	Formatting	Signage	Image library
Incorrect use of color	A-4 business envelope	Presentations and proposals	Winter	
Signatures	Business cards	Vertical covers	Rain gear	
Corporate signature	Digital media	Horizontal covers	Ephemera	
Signature variations	Website	Covers with windows	Golf shirts	
Incorrect signature usage	Intranet	Interior grids	Baseball caps	
Subsidiary signatures	Extranet	PowerPoint templates	Ties	
Product signatures	Blogs	PowerPoint imagery	Portfolios	
Signature with tagline	Architecture	Exhibits	Pens	
Incorrect tagline treatment	Style guides	Trade show booth	Umbrellas	
Clear space around signature	Interface	Banners	Mugs	
Signature sizes	Contents	Point of purchase	Pins	
	Color	Name tags	Scarves	
	Typefaces		Golf balls	
	Imagery		Memo cubes	
	Sound		Mouse pads	

Brand Books. Source: Designing Brand Identity: An Essential Guide for the Whole Branding Team, Alina Wheeler

20. Brand families

A great number of leading brands around us are in fact owned by a few companies. By owning several brands, a company sells its products successfully to different target consumer groups without damaging its reputation with those groups. For instance, a company may sell chocolate at a high price to its up-end consumers and sell the same product in cheaper-looking packages to a completely different group. The company, without doing so, would only sell to limited consumers, leaving the other potential consumer groups as fair game to its rivals.

Arcaadia is one of the UK's most successful fashion retailers, but it only trades on the stock market under the name of Arcaadia. This brand will not split its sales channels by levels in its marketing operation and management.

Kraft Foods is wellknown in numerous countries. Among its other products, Philadephia cream cheese is the most popular one. It would be so hard for a brand to extend into other sectors if it has built a reputation in a specific area. For example, would you give your credit to Heinz coffee or Nissan crisps? For this reason, Kraft Foods also owns some other brands, such as those listed in the following figure. These are, however, only a small part of its hundreds of brands.

Arcaadia	
High street brand	Differentials
Topshop	Trading on its newly regained "cool" image, it features in popular fashion magazines as "the place for shopping" and promotes well-known and new designs.
Topman	The male equivalent of Topshop and often found in the same store. It targets young males and delivers a younger feel than Burtons, its stable-mate.
Evans	Targeting larger women (16+ UK dress size) between ages of 25–55. Evans is known for ensuring that women in this group – often ignored by other chains, including Arcaadia's own – are not condemned to wearing unstylish clothes.
Dorothy Perkins	With a wide customer base of 20 to 50-year-old women, the average Dorothy Perkins customer is in their mid-30s. It is known as being affordable and up-to-the-minute in terms of fashion and boasts stores in most UK towns.
Burtons	Over a century old, Burtons targets 25 to 34-year-old men, selling everything from leisurewear to suits.

High street brand	Differentials
Miss Selfridge	Established in 1966, this brand updates itself completely once every couple of years. It now has stores worldwide and is particularly strong in the young female customer base.
Wallis	A boutique brand established in 1923, it boasts an in-house team of five designers who produce ten looks each year. The brand is seen as a fashion leader.
Ourfit	This is a comparatively new store that is found in out-of-town retail parks and acts as an outlet for big-name branded clothes left over from Arcaadia's other stores at the end of the season. Customers are attracted by bargains.

Brand Family-Arcaadia. Source: Designing Brand Identity: An Essential Guide for the Whole Branding Team, Alina Wheeler

Kraft		
Product	Brand	International reach
Coffee	Maxwell House	Instant coffee popular in USA, China mainland, France, Germany, Hong Kong Special Administrative Region (HKSAR), Ireland, Poland, Russia, South Korea and UK.
	Carte Noir	One of the fastest growing brands in the UK basing its product on a long tradition of coffee-making. Popular in Ireland and the UK.
	Kenco	Super premium coffee brand in Belgium, France, Ireland and UK.
	Kaffee HAG	The world's first decaffeinated brand of coffee and popular in Austria, Germany and Italy.
Drinks	Capri-sun	Sold in the USA.
	KoolAid	Sold in the USA.
Cheese	Philadelphia	More than USD $100 million in sales around the world including North America, Australia, Austria, Belgium, Germany, Holland, HKSAR, Ireland, Italy, Japan, Philippines, Saudi Arabia, Scandinavia, Singapore, UK and Venezuela.
	Dairylea	Processed cheese slices aimed at children in Ireland and the UK.
	Dairylea lunchables	Convenience snacks aimed at the kids' lunchbox market.
	Kraft Singles	Processed cheese slices aimed at the sandwich market in Australia, HKSAR, Indonesia, Malaysia, Singapore, South Korea, Spain, Philippines and UK.
	El Caserio	The number one processed cheese slice in Spain.
	Cheez Whiz	Spreadable, real-cheese brand created for children in Philippines and Venezuela.
Chocolate and confectionery	Lifesavers	Sold in the USA.
	Toblerone	Launched in Switzerland in 1908, popular in over 100 countries.
	Marabou	Sold in Denmark, Finland and Sweden.
	Freia	Sold in Norway.
	Suchard	Popular in Austria, France, Germany, Spain, Switzerland and the UK.
	Daim	Popular in Austria, France, Germany, Spain, Switzerland and the UK.
	Bis	Sold in Argentina and Brazil.
	Terry's	Sold in the UK.
Biscuits	Ritz cheese crackers	Sold in Central America, China, Ecuador, Indonesia, Peru, Thailand, Venezuela and the UK.
Desserts	Bird's Custard	Powdered custard popular in Ireland and the UK.
	Bird's Angel Delight	Powdered dessert popular in Ireland and the UK.
Food	Vegemite	Sold in Australia and New Zealand and also exported globally.
	Taco Bell food kits	Sold in the USA and Europe.
	Oscar Mayer bacon	Sold in the USA.
	Shake 'n' bake	Sold in the USA.
	Oven Fry	Sold in the USA, Thailand, Venezuela and the UK.
	Nabisco	Sold globally.
	Jello	Sold in the USA.

Brand Family-Kraft. Source: Designing Brand Identity: An Essential Guide for the Whole Branding Team, Alina Wheeler

21. More than simple

Finally, let's talk about simplicity, one of the attributes of the "spirit of Internet" and its crucial influence on brand innovation. In this age of information explosion, it is increasingly hard to make a brand known to the customer. This forces companies to embody simplicity into their brands. We have picked an interesting sample from extensive cases addressing the simplicity principle. Although developed for years, this brand framework generates amazing power in the Internet era for it follows the principle of simplicity.

At any moment, consumers remain loyal to themselves instead of the brand. However, when we look at humanity, we gain the insight that loyalty is there for reasons, which may be need, satisfaction, accomplishment or achievement. Given this fact, how should we change our mind and operate more rationally?

(1) Shifting focus from "our brand" to "consumers"

Traditional brand loyalty, by looking from the outside, emphasizes a customer-centered idea where requirements of customers should be prioritized. In fact, a self-oriented core is identified deep inside. We say what we, but not consumers, like; we have a strong desire to become an eye-candy to consumers; and we even try to influence, educate, move, and control consumers. However, capricious consumers have made the whole brand communication and advertising process exhausting. In the times of the mobile Internet, when we are operating in an environment of open-

ness and sharing, the right thing to do is to keep a low profile and become a certain label of consumers while truly put customers at the center, listening to the voice from the bottom of their hearts, communicating with them with care, and offering services with a hundred percent dedication.

(2) Shifting focus from "static consumers" to "dynamic consumers"

Companies tend to draw a portrait of their target consumer, based on which they build up all brand operation strategies. As consumers ourselves, we all know that consumers are the most erratic group on this planet, with their ages, living conditions, social status, buying power, even buying habits and preferences being dynamic. While marketing our brand in this era of the mobile Internet, therefore, we should admit and accept this dynamism and develop a dynamic mind to identify, care, and satisfy consumers' needs.

(3) Shifting the concept from "I'm here" to "I'm here for you"

Facing tons of information in today's world, it's far less than enough to interest our potential customers merely by saying "Hey, I'm here". What we really should figure out in brand communication is how to make customers feel that they are closely related to our brand! Good examples in this regard are Taobao, JD and some other e-commerce platforms, who have tried to understand customers' needs and preferences by studying items in their carts, and proactively screen and recommend products of customers' interest. By making this solid shift from "Taobao for all" to "Taobao for me", they have gained their

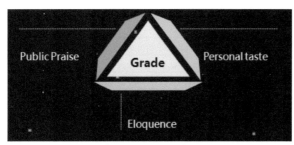
Three explanations of grade

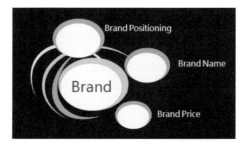
Three explanations of brand

What is a brand?

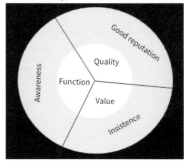
The Three "Inner Elements" and "Outer Elements"

success in achieving the goal of "I'm here for customers".

22. Brand and grade explanation

The three inner elements of brand refer to function, quality and value, which determine the customer value of a brand; while its three outer elements are awareness, good reputation, and insistence, which determine the market value of a brand.

 ## Substance Dissemination of Mobile Brand

I. What is good content?

Substance and dissemination never separate. Effectiveness of content is often curbed without dissemination. For example, if an article is read by 10,000 readers initially, and it is shared by 1,000 of them to another 100 readers, respectively, it is read by 100,000 readers, 10 times of the initial readers. What will happen if the 100,000 readers keep sharing? On the other hand, not all content captures attention quickly and enjoys the viral effect. The question is why some brand substance goes viral and is shared by a large number of people, while other content is just a one-hit wonder which does not make any ripples? What types of content have the potential to go viral?

1. Professional content with insights

Professional content, once you put it right, will appeal to everyone. Look at Baidu Baike, a Chinese-language, collaborative, web-based encyclopedia. No matter how deeply fragmented the Internet may be, people need content of that type to build up their knowledge.

Professional communication is necessary for development of the Internet, on any level and in any direction. Insightful content itself is gold and valued by all, who will be more than happy to share it.

Let us take the hot WeChat marketing[①] as an example. You will probably not want to share a dull and plain article about earning money on WeChat. However, if the content just cuts to the chase with delicate wording, practical first-hand experiences and unique opinions, readers will definitely share it even though they do not fully understand it, just broadcasting to their friends that they are intelligent enough to read articles of this excellence.

2. Useful and helpful content

Natural, is it not? Users will not read to the end of a useless article, not to mention sharing it. Useful content is helpful for us or others, such as everyday tips and tourism guides, which provide pragmatic information not only needed by the readers but also their friends, coworkers, and family members. This drives sharing.

In most cases, substance marketers put identification of customer needs and points of interest at the top of their to-do list. The reason is that content aiming at customers' interest is useful and helpful for them. For example, the blogs and posts offering information for healthcare in winter will be useful in late fall, and therefore most shared at that time.

3. Emotion–evoking content

Emotion contributes to sharing and forwarding behaviors. Readers tend to share content that they have resonance with and they just cannot help to release their emotions regardless of the excitement, anger, sympathy, or surprise. Sharing is then made possible.

While resonant content is way more popular than those emotion insulators, content bringing up joy has better performance than sadness igniters. However, content whipping up strong emotions, such as extreme rage and panic, has a greater potential to be shared. This rule is manipulated proficiently on Microblog, is it not?

4. Unique and novel content

Customers are more than happy to share unique and novel information.

It is obvious that novelty is important. The public is attracted to news and hot topics, particularly on the Internet. Sources releasing masses of first-hand information and news easily earn a flock of followers. Tens of thousands of eyes are drawn every time there is something bizarre in this era when a minor thing sparks up a big debate. So, your content will enjoy fairly ideal dissemination if you post it early enough.

Uniqueness, on the other hand, sticks out for content on the Internet overload-

① *One of the marketing modes used by companies or individuals in the era of Internet economy, WeChat marketing emerges along with this popular app, which breaks the limitations of physical distance. By registering on WeChat, users are linked with their friends on this platform, and able to subscribe to information as needed. Businesses achieve P2P marketing by providing information and promoting their products.*

ed with similar information. Like news, people are more interested in fresh and different things in terms of theories, methods and skills. Taking Qzone marketing as an example: comparing with fans earning guides, customers may be fond of an article introducing a new skill which may not be practicable. The reason is simple: it is novel and I have learned something.

In fact, another factor hiding behind uniqueness and novelty also drives sharing. In most cases, customers share specific content to tell other people "I know this", "I'm well informed", "I pay attention to the underlying truth", or "I rock!" In other words, they share content to raise their profile, often subconsciously.

5. Content that drives social communication

There is a term that defines the content driving social communication: social currency.

Advocates of social currency believe that what customers discussed on Microblog and WeChat is a reflection that defines them. That is why they tend to share content that makes them look really good; in other words, people like talking about something that enables great self-admiration. Your brand, therefore, should create such content for customers to toss around and offer an opportunity for them to feel great, proud and insightful. They will in turn tell others about you, spontaneously.

6. Content that helps expression

In the real world, people bury deep in their mind things that they dare not or do not know how to say out loud. You may find on Microblogs a number of popular accounts who write posts with guaranteed sharing. Why? They make the voice from the bottom of many people's hearts heard in a precise and smart way. Inarticulate readers feel extremely satisfied by reading their cutting remarks.

Those accounts speak for their readers with shrewd language by making astute analogies, so that readers need no more words to say but simply to share and forward. This is why some people could have their content extensively shared by making public criticism of some big names.

7. Contentious content

Contentious content gains attention of a large number of readers. This is because people hold various opinions and that brings up a need for discussion, in which readers want more people to be involved and are therefore willing to be an active distributor and promulgator in order to find more support.

Contentious content or ambiguous issues are natural topic makers. Some smart

---

💡 Case Study **A great move – Buy a lifetime supply of liquor**

Jiangxiaobai Liquor recently offered people a chance to buy the lifetime supply of booze for a single payment of CNY 99,999. This offer, though lasted shortly, helped the well-known online liquor brand draw the attention of a large number of consumers.

What has made this brand widely known is the unique charm delivered by the combination of delicate bottle design and simple but heart-touching slogans. However, as you dig deeper, you may notice that Jiangxiaobai gained its success not only by virtue of the "expression bottle" but also with every drop of creativity over decades. Browsing under the #simple life# hashtag topic, customers will find it a brand having deep love for life. It is no more than suitable to summarize its strategy as "conveying emotions through details".

Jiangxiaobai Liquor offered people a chance to buy the lifetime supply of booze for a single payment of CNY 99,999. This offer helped the well-known online liquor brand draw the attention of a large number of consumers. Source: Official website of Jiangxiaobai

What Jiangxiaobai printed on its package is not slogans, but emotions and stories that remind customers of their beloved ones.

The case source quoted from: Sina Blog 2017/11/12
http://blog.sina.com.cn/s/blog_16aa4974a0102xbdq.html

guys would have a couple of disputable topics included in the content to induce share and spread.

8. Valuable stories

We all prefer story-based content. The greater the story, the more reader interest, and the more likely it is to be shared. The reason here is, compared with theory lecturing, storytelling is more life-like and touching, and is likely to trigger emotional waves or curiosity.

II. How to disseminate good content

In this era of the mobile Internet, a common challenge for almost all content platforms is how to deliver good content to customers and improve affinity and loyalty. As the last crucial step of brand operation, brand substance dissemination is directed to two outlets: 1) intra-product dissemination, in which the content is published in the content modules of the product; and 2) exterior dissemination, which refers to promulgating the content to social media and other platforms in order to generate the Domino effect.

1. Intra–product dissemination

This includes four operation modes: free-flow, special recommendation, push notification, and ranking by weight. Each requires support to product distribution mechanism.

(1) Free-flow

In this mode, content is published in content module of the product without intended artificial intervention, and customers are expected to discover and read it by themselves. Dissemination is mainly influenced by preset product mechanism. For example, posts in Baidu Tieba are listed by time sequence and those with latest replies are moved to the top. On Zhihu, answers are listed according to a like-based mechanism. When a user likes an answer, it will appear on the timeline of this user's fans. Common free-flow mechanisms include time sequence, latest reply and liking of fans.

(2) Special recommendation

Special recommendation is regularly applied by substance marketers, who manually pick some content and recommend it at operation positions. In general, recommended content gains more attention. On the first day following the new year holiday, Apple launched "Post-holiday Schedule Adjustment" and "Hug Your Work" zones in its App Store. This collective recommendation of popular apps related to time management and work efficiency corresponded exactly with office workers. Operation measures of this mode mainly include setting recommendation positions at large traffic inlets, pin-on-top, and special labels.

(3) Push notification

One of the widely applied operation measures in the era of the mobile Internet, this mode is referred to as Push or floating popup in case of apps, or internal message or desktop popup window back to the times of PC Internet. The reason why push notification became one of the most powerful operation measures is that information can be displayed preferentially in an enforced manner to maximize attention of customers. Good results have been seen. However, consumers now give less response to this method since it has been abused.

APP Store Special recommendation.
Source: Huxiu.com

(4) Ranking by weight

By applying this mode, content is subject to multi-dimensional value assessment and the sequence of content is regulated according to certain logic. Examples are ranks of most downloaded apps, rising-star apps and fantastic new apps in Xiaomi market. These ranks recommend apps in terms of total download, specific download per unit time and freshness, offering a chance of collective exposure for apps listed out. A merit of weight-based ranking is it explores new content with great potential and value, and highlight long-tail content, so that users know outstanding apps other than WeChat, QQ, and Alipay.

Other similar examples are ranks for new content, daily report, 7-day hot topics, and 30-day hot topics on Jianshu.com. As the volume of content on the home page expands and information flows more rapidly, this weight-based ranking mechanism will help extend exposure of good content and keep it long enough in fast information flood.

2. Exterior dissemination

At the end of the day, intra-product dissemination is restricted by the number of users, whereas exterior channels, and social media in particular, enable a much greater dissemination given the diversity and scale of their user base. Exterior dissemination is achieved on social media and content aggregation platforms.

APP Store Ranking by weight.
Source: Huxiu.com

(1) Social media platforms

At present, most if not all apps are designed with share-to-social-media function. Everyone is expecting to inject more power to their content with the positive effect of social-network dividend and attracts a tremendous number of readers.

Content can be disseminated on social media by means of original content distribution and content synchronization. In the former mode, users share links from inside the product. This mode is advantageous since it drives increase of download volume by embedding download entrance on the content page.

The other mode, substance synchronization, requires publication of content in the content ecology of social media such as official accounts of WeChat and microblogs of Microblog. This mode is advantageous since it facilitates dissemination as social media grant relatively high weight to content published in its own content ecology. On the contrary, WeChat, for example, would curb the exhibition of articles shared from external links once the number of their readers reached a certain level.

Features of social media should be contemplated when disseminating substance on their platforms. Efforts are required to study headings planning and content layout patterns in order to make full use of the potential of platforms.

(2) Content aggregation platform

In addition to social media, there are platforms which do not generate content. Instead, they aggregate content from other platforms as a container to enable users to read diversified content.

Examples of this type include Toutiao and Yidian Zixun, which allow authors of we-media and source sites, such as Huxiu.com, TMT, 36Kr, and some other science and technology-oriented media, to synchronize authorized content to their platforms. These sci-tech media then release the restriction on size of their own user bases by putting their content to aggregation platforms and disseminating it to more target groups.

III. Substance trend of mobile brand

Figure 8-11   Mobile marketing rises to the leading place.
Source: QB Institute

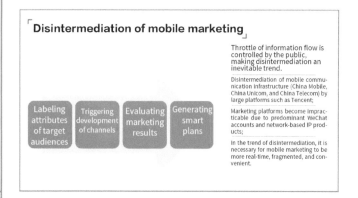

Figure 8-12   Disintermediation of mobile marketing. Source: QB Institute

In the future, marketing in China will focus on mobile marketing and smart end device will be the major battlefield of digital marketing. This can be proved by the rapid development of China's mobile AD market to the second largest in the world, way faster than the UK and Japan. Let's have a look at the new trends of mobile marketing as shown in Figure 8-11.

Over its first five years from 2012 to 2017, mobile marketing has finished disintermediation. The year 2018 will be a start for mobile marketing to take off. See Figure 8-12.

In times of traditional marketing, Integrated Marketing Communication, a study of instrumental integration based on mass communication media, was applied to facilitate brand communication in the age of integration.

In times of mobile marketing, broadcasting, TV, newspaper and magazine, the four major tools for mass communication are undergoing the process of disintermediation, giving place to new media, AI, short video, and live streaming. See Figures 8-13 and 8-14.

For traditional media in both China and other countries, roads are getting rougher under the impact from Internet and new media. *Newsweek*, a decades-old US magazine, has stopped printing paper *NY Times* and undersold *The Boston Globe*, one of its affiliates, at USD $70 million. In China, *Good Luck MONEY+* ceased publication after the last issue in August 2013; *HisLife* and the once-famous game magazine *Play!* stopped publication; even *Evening News* launched in 1999 was shut down on the first day of 2014. It is the first paper that ever ceased since the founding of Shanghai United Media Group.

We can see that traditional tools lost their users during disintermediation. They were not defeated by competitors but abandoned by users.

Contrary to the fall of traditional media, it becomes a trend to start businesses focusing on content. See Figure 8-15. All marketing and public relation efforts of a company and a brand are presented eventually by content.

Many companies have transformed into content generators, such as Coca-Cola and Durex. They keep creating content based on their products for the purpose of promotion.

According to State of We-media Industry: Now and Future by NetEase Inc.'s Artificial Intelligence Division (NetEase AI), more than 65% we-media operators say that material collection is the most time-consuming task in the work cycle; 75% of them need more than two hours to collect materials and 17% need more than six hours.

The collection, processing, and presentation of real materials stand as key factors for dissemination of we-media. In the meantime, staying alert against the absence of truth due to content inundation remains a more noteworthy issue for we-media groups which generally lack public credibility. First, we-media content is being generated in an environment with an underdeveloped system of rules. Absence of necessary external regulation and "gatekeepers" in a professional sense makes it easier to output obscene content, rumors, and false information. Moreover, a considerable part of we-media marketing data should be questioned due to rampant fans and click trading. Searching "buy fans", "buy clicks" and keywords like these in Baidu, you can see a lot of information concerning "buy xxx number of WeChat followers in a day", "super-fans buying combo, CNY 10 only" and so on. It is actually an open secret that major Microblog, WeChat and other we-media accounts are buying a great number of "Zombie fans" to achieve remarkable data of views and followers, so as to attract

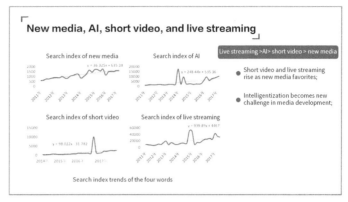

Figure 8-13   New media, AI, short video, and live streaming.
Source: QB Institute

Figure 8-14   Waterloo of newspapers.
Source: QB Institute

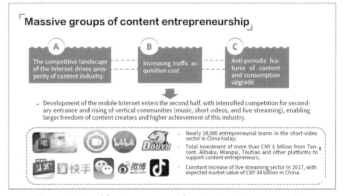

Figure 8-15   Massive groups of content entrepreneurship.
Source: QB Institute

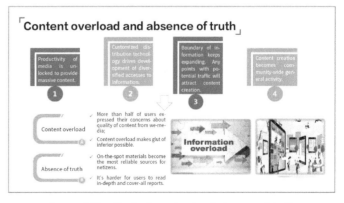

Figure 8-16   Content overload and absence of truth.
Source: QB Institute

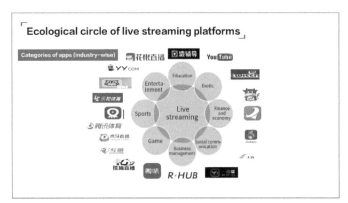

Figure 8-17   Ecological circle of short video platforms.
Source: QB Institute

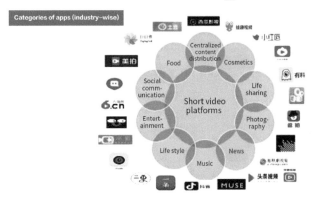

Figure 8-18   Ecological circle of short video platforms.
Source: QB Institute

Without a sound demonstration system in place, credibility of we-media remains in big doubt. See Figure 8-16.

As shown in Figures 8-17 and 8-18, in the development trend of substance distribution platforms, live streaming and short video formed two major forces, which gained fabulous growth in 2016 and became the latest social communication methods, marking 2016 as an important milestone in the history of China's live streaming platforms.

This year, China saw an unprecedented boom of live streaming platforms: users broke the 300 million line, investment giants poured in huge capital, related companies transformed operation mode successively, and hundreds of startup platforms flocked into this sector. At its peak time, there were more than 200 platforms competing in a "nation-wide" live streaming battle. However, this sector has developed along with porn, money-laundering, violence and other negatives. The unrestrained rampant development in China was only curbed by the Provisions on the Administration of Internet Live-Streaming Services issued by the State Internet Information Office on November 4, 2016. On the contrary, the growth of short video apps never stopped its momentum. Early in 2017, Faceu jumped to the top in Cheetah Global Lab's biggest-rise rank for its 32x rank rise in February. Although the explosion of short video apps was discharged by live streaming apps in the middle of the year, the former went back on track in the end of the year.

Mobile marketing features not only rapidness, but also shortness. From Xiaokaxiu founded in 2015, Meipai in 2016, Kuaishou in early 2017 to Douyin in mid-2017, the success of short videos on these platforms, regardless of whether it was because of help form KOLs, or the strategy of making "upgrade" from vulgarity to intellectuality, proved that shortness is essential to the fragmented content of mobile marketing.

In fact, the world itself was originally full of short things, such as Classic of Poetry of ancient China and Homeric Hymns of ancient Rome. However, industrial revolutions extended not only the production chains of all industries, but also our concise languages. The thriving of the mobile Internet represents another "renaissance" in a different form.

People's enthusiasm for short videos lies in humanity, one of the fundamental

advertisement and gain commercial profit. However, media operation based on such made-up data is not sustainable and may harm the sound development of the entire we-media ecology.

Besides, we-media can be founded easily and operated by people of different levels of competency, knowledge, and skill. There is not a commonly accepted standard to evaluate them and no industry-wide specifications are developed.

Major problems of we-media content include false information, clickbait, exaggeration, advertorial, and mixture of opinions and news. Credibility plays a crucial role when we-media creators seek recognition but as some insider said: "public credibility is a vulnerable spot of we-media."

Lacking dedicated material collection force, information sources, and a professional "gatekeeper" system, the selection of content and decision-making processes are controlled by individuals or small teams. To pursue commercial benefits or simply catch more eyes, some we-media operators even deliberately created untrue content.

features of the mobile Internet. As indicated in Mobile Internet Panoramic Cogitation, the underlying idea about the mobile Internet is that it should be human-centric, evolutionary and open. It is the three essential attributes of humanism (humanity, "times of everybody" idea, and "emotion reigns" concept) that enables the mobile Internet to enlighten the people. To its core, we-media is nothing but the product of equal dissemination in the light of humanism.

According to the latest statistics of app traffic published in October 2017, social communication apps rank at the top. It is noteworthy that iQiyi, a major content creator, jumps to the third place. This is a manifest evidence that the era of content is about to come. See Figure 8-19.

Figure 8-19   Traffic of mobile apps. Source: QB Institute

💡 Case Study   How Durex generate product-centered we-media content

Durex always creates brand dissemination substance of high quality praised as textbook examples. It won big success again on Thanksgiving in 2017. Every one hour from 10:00 am to 22:00 pm that day, its official account published a typical poster, concise layout and suggestive language as always, flirting with various brands including chewing gum, auto, chocolate, jeans, and even something seemingly unrelated like aged vinegar.

The case source quoted from: Official Microblog account of Durex 2017/11/24
https://www.sohu.com/a/206379204_99907325

How Durex generate product-centered we-media content?

Globalwise, the way for people to communicate information is changing from news links to content links. Content intelligentization is an advanced form of all other intelligent forms. We are witnessing the invasion of new species. See Figure 8-20.

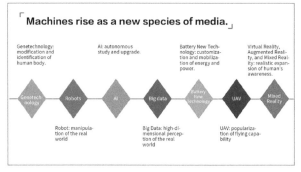

Figure 8-20   Machines rise as a new species of media.
Source: QB Institute

More new species have cut across their boundaries and participated in content intelligentization. This has speeded up content update and iteration. Content represents business opportunities. We should grasp them to trigger new business opportunities by using the underlying data technologies vertically in a sector. See Figure 8-21.

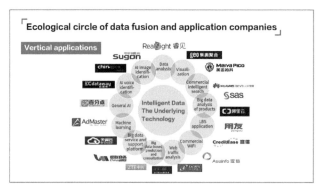

Figure 8-21   Ecological circle of data fusion and application companies.
Source: QB Institute

While we can say that the civilizations along the coastline of the Atlantic represent the fruits of industrial revolutions a century ago, their counterparts along the Pacific coastline, particularly China and the US, have made a great advance in intellectual content generation. See Figure 8-22.

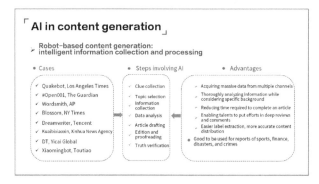

Figure 8-22   AI in content generation.
Source: QB Institute

Case Study — Commercialization of Douyin

A product which activated the young generation's eagerness to express themselves, Douyin was about to embark on its journey of commercialization.

Frankly, Douyin did not gain the pioneer advantage as there were already relatively good products such as Kuaishou, Meipai, Miaopai and Xiaokaxiu when it entered the short video sector. Zhang Yiming, investor of Douyin, asserted that short video would be the next whirlwind. Holding the same perspective as Zhang, Tencent, Alibaba, Microblog and Meitu enhanced According to latest data from Douyin, average daily VV (video views) in August hits the line of one billion; while data of QuestMobile, a thirty-party research agency, indicates that Douyin boasts the number of DAU (daily active users) of over 10 million. In early May, it just made its VV to a bit more that 100 million and maintained DAU at millions.

Unlike Kuaishou, who left a public impression of revealing the harsh life endured by the poor, Douyin has played its own tone, unique and a bit ridiculous, deployment in their short video businesses. In the meantime, Tencent poured investment to Kuaishou, the sector-leader. Bearing pressure from powerful competitors, Douyin successfully maintained its fast growth speed as a dark horse in this sector. Today, it is often compared with Kuaishou and rooted in the life and perception of young Chinese living in first- and second-tier cities. A profile of Douyin users is that more than 85% of them are younger than 24. It's obvious from those data that Douyin has landed a fairly good first punch. In August of this year, Toutiao claimed investment of some hundreds of millions to push Douyin into the international market, promoting Douyin's growth to a higher level.

Lately, Douyin has officially launched its commercialization by making three brand advertisement videos in cooperation with Airbnb, Harbin Beer, and Chevrolet. In fact, business models of short video sector have lacked variety, merely focusing on advertisements, e-commerce, live shows and MCN, with numerous problems requiring solutions.

Wang Xiaowei, Product Manager of Douyin, said that Douyin has reached a significant size with pretty good data and community atmosphere. By making use of proven brand advertising models, we have seen great results of advertisement of quality content. By starting its commercialization process, Douyin can also do a meaningful job in helping popular accounts monetize or become famous. The most appealing aspect now is that many brands have recognized its growth and quality, and they are becoming interested. What's new for Douyin in making the three advertise-ments for Airbnb, Harbin Beer, and Chevrolet, is that it made its first attempt at in-feed advertising. This is also the first time to trail advertisers presenting their native in-feed advertisements on vertical screens. As Wang put it, "this is something no one has ever done before" and it is where Douyin concentrates its power. By far, the three advertisements are among the most liked, commented on, and shared videos. User feed-back is generally positive. One user comment below the Chevrolet Malibu XL advertisement was that "I have watched this over 20 times".

In addition to native video in-feed advertisements, Douyin has launched another commercial cooperation model – customized internal challenge. As for the business possibilities in the future, Wang said that no limit is set but models more suitable for the product are preferred.

In addition to trials on the platform end, Wang also disclosed that Douyin would launch more mechanisms to help monetize popular accounts. In its cooperation with Mobike, JD, Didi and Pizza Hut, Douyin reaped satisfactory results in terms of cooperation models, user feedback and VV data. An example is the short video for Mobike by VAVA, which received great response. More than 250,000 users liked this video. It is definitely a hot video. However, before admitting it is an advertisement, it is above all a piece of high quality content. Partners also responded positively. They believe that vertical-screen advertisements will be a trend and they are pretty fond of the young and passionate atmosphere of Douyin community.

Currently, monetization models in short video sector lack variety, merely by platform-based commerce or driving traffic to live streaming. In its plans on native brand advertisements, Douyin considers the involvement of popular accounts by making customized videos for them so as to achieve an intra-product positive cycle and thus monetize the value of popular accounts. For example, Zhang Xinyao, Boogie93, Damiaoge and some other accounts participated in the short video of Mobike, which gained great response. More than 200,000 users interacted with Zhang Xinyao over the video. Unique tone, massive traffic and super distribution capability have made Douyin an incomparable product in the short video sector. In the meantime, content created by popular accounts can be distributed in a customized way by using our algorithm. The truth is, many of our popular accounts also registered on Microblog. However, their content on Microblog was less shared. Popular accounts and regular users recognize each other, and they both agree with this young and cool quality.

The case source quoted from: Gao Xiaoqian, With Billion-level Daily View, How Can Douyin Open the Door of Commercialization? 2017/09/29
http://36kr.com/p/5095703.html

南通冠洲国际贸易有限公司
Capglobal international Co.,Ltd.

Capglobal International Co., Ltd.
Source: Woosii Research

Woshi-The China brand (In English is "crouching Lion"), It conveys the meaning of "being static but ready for action". The icon is a vivid image of a lion.
One out of three customers wears our hat

Nantong Capglobal International Co., Ltd. was founded in 2004 as a cap exporter. In 2006, Capglobal established its own knit cap workshops and received orders from the National Football League (NFL). It established fabric cap workshops in 2008, started production of knit caps for New Era worldwide in 2009, acquired certification by New Era, BSCL, adidas, and New Balance in 2010. It created a value of more than 100 million CNY and organized its own design and development teams in 2013. It became the Best Global Supplier of New Era in 2014, built up design force in Europe and sales force in the US in 2015, and grew to the world's largest knit cap manufacturer in 2016. It now supplies woven caps to New Era throughout the world.

During 13 years of hard work, Capglobal has obtained five international invention patents and ten Chinese patents. This represents not only quality improvement of its products and leading innovations, but also increases the strength of Chinese companies. Capglobal now has more than 800 employees, floor area of 48000 sqm, and annual value of 170 million CNY. It has established partnerships with more than 80 international brands. Key accounts include New Era, New Balance, PUMA, Fila, Champion, Ellesse, Arc'teryx, and Salewa. In light of a culture encouraging friendship, team work and innovation, the company is investing great efforts to build a young and assertive team. Capglobal is determined to grow not necessarily into the biggest, but the best headwear designer and producer. Its target in 2018 is to elevate the revenue to above 200 million CNY and build the first smart pattern-making factory in the industry. To achieve this target, innovation is the first step. A company can only survive by renovating its mind and injecting innovative ideas into its brand.

Considering the necessity of innovation, Mr. Ji Jun, founder of Capglobal, invited Mr. Hongbing Hua, a highly prestigious marketing expert, for in-depth consulting. Under the tutelage of Mr. Hua, Capglobal will be implementing new innovation in the company's domestic and international brands.

The domestic brand, Woshi (meaning "crouching Lion" in English) conveys the meaning of "being static but ready for action". The icon is a vivid image of a lion. Six ranges of caps were quickly determined to be the flagship products for the market in China, specifically: Qin, Tang, Song, Ming, Qing and Chinese Dream (known as the "six caps" for short). The six caps are unique products; they respectively inherit and innovate in the ornamental articles in the six dynasties, and they represent the inheritance and innovation of Chinese culture, with incomparable national emotions and fashionable styles.

The sports brand is Guanjie ("Capglobal" in English). In addition to maintaining its original marketing line, great operation models of foreign sports companies are learned and integrated to facilitate development of the sports industry in China.

Capglobal's innovation is not limited to brand and culture. Manufacturing and business models are also part of the plan. "We believe every product essentially comes down to SERVICE, we decided to break the old sales mode and promote a customer- and client-oriented brand value. Our target is to apply mobile internet technology and enable our customers to design their own caps. We will complete their orders within 72 hours. We are now building a customized application, improving current cap construction and providing more options for our customers. We are also constructing a cap brand for Chinese people that is designed and built to provide style and comfort, with a perfect fit for our culture."

Qin

Tang

Song

Ming

Qing

Chinese dream

The six caps are unique products-They respectively inherit and innovate in the ornamental articles in the six dynasties. The six cap designs feature Chinese history

Deep Substance of Management

Chapter 9

Topics:

1. Three Renaissance Movements
2. IP-based Substance Marketing

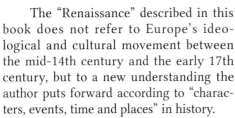

Three Renaissance Movements

The "Renaissance" described in this book does not refer to Europe's ideological and cultural movement between the mid-14th century and the early 17th century, but to a new understanding the author puts forward according to "characters, events, time and places" in history.

Undoubtedly, the Renaissance is the mother of the word "content" and now we are experiencing the third Renaissance. As European Renaissance urban culture and castle culture have been a calling card for Europe-bound tourism, it dawns on emerging economies such as the "BRIC" countries (Brazil, Russia, India and China) that marketing the time-honored traditional culture of nations all over the world through urban content is an infant industry. Therefore, marketing urban content has become one of the marketing trends since 2017.

At this moment, we are on the eve of the climax of the third Renaissance. The first Renaissance built steadily toward a climax in the ancient civilization period about 2,000 years ago, and for the second Renaissance about 500 years ago in Europe. Now, as the fourth Industrial Revolution and the third Renaissance are simultaneously dawning upon the world, science, art and the Internet will together embark on a great epic journey with the aid of the mobile Internet.

I. The First Renaissance (more than 2,000 years ago)

At the mention of the Renaissance, Europe's Renaissance movement in the Middle Ages springs to mind perhaps because it has exerted such a huge impact on modern society. Yet, this perception is just a narrow understanding. In the book, the author has adopted a new historical outlook of self-writing to reproduce the first Renaissance of humankind. From the perspective of the author's conception of history, every worldwide Renaissance that goes down in history as a major turning point possesses three conditions: it takes hundreds of years to complete; it consists of origin and climax; and its widespread influence is felt in science, industry and commerce.

According to the second edition of *The Encyclopedia of China*, there are four ancient civilizations including Babylon, Egypt, India and China. However, this view is not recognized by the mainstream global history field, for example, ancient Babylon is a stage rather than a hub of civilization. A more mainstream view advocates that the first civilization bloom originated from ancient Greece and China in the 6th century BC. In the wake of it, two figures rose to fame in the Orient and Occident: Pythagoras and Confucius.

Born in Samos, Greece, between 580 BC and 590 BC, Pythagoras lived to the age of 75. While in the same period, a sage called Confucius on par with him came to prominence in the Orient. Coincidentally, the two of them not only shared a similarity in age but also in profession as both were educators.

For Pythagoras, this occidental sage explored the laws of nature his entire life. His oriental counterpart, Confucius, focused mainly on human relationships and trained three thousand disciples, eventually forming the core of traditional Chinese culture, Confucianism. In addition, Confucius compiled the ultimate in literature, the *Classic of Poetry*, China's earliest of its kind. Meanwhile, the era of Confucius fostered a galaxy of masters, such as Laozi prior to him, who founded the Taoist school, and Sunzi who followed at his heels, and who was hailed as the "Ultimate Master of War". In nearly same time and space, Confucius spearheaded the way for China to join in the first Renaissance of mankind.

Moreover, the Pythagorean school established the scientific system of geometry which had a big impact on Plato who cultivated Aristotle. Before Newton's classical mechanics, Aristotle's theory of physics reigned supreme in the whole western world.

The first Renaissance laid the foundations for Confucius who shaped China as a center of ethics, and for Pythagoras who shaped the western world as a hub of physics, mathematics and other science. Both have enjoyed dominance which has endured through the ages. However, as the mutual fusion by the Internet between the oriental and occidental world is in progress, these two worlds have come to know well their respective strengths. Specifically, the Orient which values ethics has to fill the gap in science, democracy and laws, which is affirmed by Xi Jinping's consistent emphasis on the dignity of the constitution. This is also true of the occidental world. While focusing on science and rule of law, it also begins to absorb the ethics typical of the oriental world, leading to the popularity of Confucius institutes in European and American countries.

Both in the Orient and Occident, the first Renaissance began brilliantly yet ended in a totally different way.

At the back of the spring and autumn and the Warring States periods, the Qin dynasty conquered the other six of the Seven Warring States and this feudal system ended China's first Renaissance with "burning of books and burying of scholars", giving rise to a unified China. And for the occidental world, in the 1st century AD, Jesus was born and Christianity united Europe. However, in tandem with the arrival of God, the first Renaissance came to a halt. From then on, Europe sank into the long period of the Middle Ages under the reign of the church, and China into the endless night that was feudal society.

II. The Second Renaissance (1436–1616)

In 1436, Basilica di Santa Maria del Fiore was completed, signifying the beginning of the second Renaissance and in 1616, William Shakespeare's life drew to a close, representing the end of this movement. This 200-year Renaissance bears a relation with a city and a family, but it has no relation to China.

The Medicis, the prestigious plutocratic Florentine family, were at the very heart of the Renaissance and one of its family members, Cosimo di Giovanni de' Medici, was the first to support the building Basilica di Santa Maria del Fiore. After completion of the Basilica, it was Cosimo who used the word "renaissance" to describe it, formally lifting the curtain of Europe's second Renaissance.

He not only provided financial support in reviving culture and art, but also took pains to collect ancient books. The Medici family owned the largest library in Europe. Moreover, in the dark Middle Ages, a galaxy of artists of the early Renaissance were given shelter by Cosimo, including as Fra Angelico, Fra Filippo Lippi, sculptor Donatello and modern guru of western architecture Filippo Brunelleschi. Cosimo once recalled, "what I do is not only in the honor of God, but also leaves me with fond memories. I feel greatly fulfilled and enriched. Over the past 50 years, all I've done is to make and spend money. Of course, spending money (sponsoring others) is more joyful than making money." It was a known fact to him that his wealth would disappear into thin air one day, but the art works he protected would echo

down the centuries. The real climax of the European Renaissance was just around the corner. His grandson, Lorenzo de' Medici (1449—1492), the Magnificent, would later succeed him. Lorenzo followed the family tradition, not procuring art works to keep for appreciation, but discovering artists, and protecting and supporting them. Two of the three Renaissance masters were created by him, namely Leonardo di ser Piero da Vinci and Michelangelo di Lodovico Buonarroti Simoni. In 1488, Lorenzo opened the world's first art school that fostered the third Renaissance master Raffaello Sanzio da Urbino.

How great was the impact of the Renaissance on Europe and the world? It was earth-shaking! For more than 1,000 years under the reign of the church, European art only served God and lacked humanism. However, the Renaissance broke the ice and breathed humanism into it. Take Michelangelo's famous sculpture, David,

Santa Maria della Salute in Venice.
Source: http://www.youkecn.com

as an example. Although it was inspired by the story of King David in the Bible, it projected a handsome and healthy masculine charm which bore no relation to the religious theme typical of the Bible. However, at that time, what he had done was considered "outrageous" in Europe.

Hailed as the "godfather" of the second Renaissance, Lorenzo was buried at San Lorenzo Church when he died at the age of 43 in 1492. Many years later, at the request of the Pope, Michelangelo personally designed and carved the statue for Lorenzo's tombstone, namely the well-known figures of Day, Night, Dusk and Dawn. They perhaps implied that the curtain of great era was to fall, dawn dying into darkness.

In the same year of Lorenzo's death, Christopher Columbus discovered the new continent, giving rise to globalization. At this moment, far-flung China in the Orient was in its fifth year under the reign of Emperor Xiaozong of the Ming Dynasty. In the following two centuries, Europe initiated the Industrial Revolution while China inaugurated the "Kangqian Period of Harmony".

It is necessary to shed light on the fact that the first to lift the curtain of this movement in the second Renaissance, was the first poet of the new era, Dante Alighieri, and the last to draw the curtain is William Shakespeare. In 1616, Shakespeare, the last master of the second Renaissance, took his last breath.

III. The Third Renaissance (1919 – today)

At the beginning of the 20th century, the third Renaissance formally stepped onto the historical stage. This time, it was spearheaded by China with India at its back and found an echo in United States, representing the shift of the new starting point of the whole world to the Pacific Ocean from the Atlantic.

The third Renaissance revolved around the topic of the glory of populism. Now, cast your mind back to the first and second Renaissance when the birth of God and glory of humanism respectively embodied the two previous movements. And

it is easy to sketch the trajectory of the human thought: from God to the people.

In 1856, American poet Walt Whitman published the second edition of the *Leaves of Grass* where he repeatedly referred to the grass leaf, a symbol of all ordinary and common nature.

In 1913, Indian poet Rabindranath Tagore won the Nobel Prize in Literature with *Stray Birds, The Crescent Moon and Gitanjaei* as his representative works. The laureate's lines are brim with sympathy and mercy towards all tiny things.

Well–turned Lines in the *Stray Birds*:

(1)
Stray birds of summer come to my window to sing and fly away.
and yellow leaves of autumn, Which have no songs, Flutter and fall there with a sign.

(2)
O troupe of little vagrants of the world, Leave your footprints in my words.

Well–turned Lines in the *Saying Goodbye to Cambridge Again*:

Quietly I take my leave
Just as quietly I came,
Waving gently farewell
To the western clouds aflame.
The golden riverside willow
Is the bride at twilight;
Her reflection in waves
Ripples in my heart bright.
The green weeds on the sludge
Sway freely underwater;
In the soft waves of Cam Rill
To be a weed I'm eager.

In 1928, Chinese poet Xu Zhimo published the Saying Goodbye to Cambridge Again.

Over a couple of decades before and after this period, the three literary gurus inaugurated the third Renaissance, a "micro-era" that sings the praises of populist consciousness, on the theme of trivial things like "grass", "bird", "bridge" and more.

Despite that, still, we define the May Fourth Movement in 1919 as the prelude to the third Renaissance.

In the three decades around 1919, China had seen numerous great artists, which seems hard to reappear in history. To set the stage for the arrival of superstars, Mr. Hu Shih took pains to phase out the three-thousand-year Classical Chinese and phase in the Written Vernacular Chinese, thus bringing into being the superstars.

In 1918, Lu Xun published *A Madman's Diary* which zeroed in on ordinary people and things, and even his Baicao Garden to Sanwei Bookstore bore a relation to ordinariness; in 1921, Guo Moruo published *The Goddesses*, the ultimate of romanticism of the commons; in 1927, Zhu Ziqing published *Moonlight over the Lotus Pond*, rendering the breathtaking landscapes of the lotus pond in the Tsinghua Garden he passed by "every day"; in 1928, Dai Wangshu published *A Lane in the Rain*, projecting the worldly rain and omnipresent streets as heaven; in 1938, Ba Jin wrote *Spring*; in 1941, out of admiration of a tree, Mao Dun wrote *Tribute to the White Poplar*; in 1957, Lao She wrote his famous *Teahouse* against the backdrop of Beijingers' hang-out... Qi Baishi (a famous Chinese painter) was keen on the shrimp, Xu Beihong the horse, Li Keran the ox, Huang Zhou the donkey and Li Taiping the dog. Moreover, Mei Lanfang's Beijing Opera was dubbed "one of the three world performing systems" ...

The author describes the three Renaissance movements in human history as "heaven, heaven in the world of man, and the world of man". What does the world of man have? The world of man is where grass, trees, flowers and huts are strewn and where 99% of the population is the populace and 1% of the population the nobility. Therefore, the ultimate goal of the Renaissance is to shine the light of humanism on the populace who account for 99% of the population.

Just like an expanse of grassland bathed in the light of dawn, the mobile Internet sets high value on all of tiny nature, absorbing dribs and drabs of morning dew and shedding the rays in all directions.

IP–based Substance Marketing

For the first time, the Report on the Work of the Government of 2016 referred to the proposal of "boosting the digital creative economy", and soon incorporated it into the "13th Five-Year Plan" as one of the five pillars of strategic emerging industry. As the core of the digital creative economy is no more than the production and distribution of content, China's infinitely raising the status of "content" means that the supercapitalists are attaching great importance to content. Due to the closed industrial market and the open cyberspace, there must be huge binary opportunities for profit. For that reason, there is a big possibility that the digital creative economy will become an important prop for the directional over-issue currency by China.

With two social apps as its ace in the hole, Tencent has held firmly in hand the production and distribution of content and Alibaba cannot be on par with it just by virtue of e-commerce custom. Faced with this, Alibaba has to constantly purchase many big-name content platforms such as Microblog, YouTube and a variety of media and use its own platforms to produce a plenty of UGC[①] content (Taobao) and PGC[②] content (Tmall). For that reason, if a seller possesses original high-quality IP content, it can convert it into an incredible number of resources.

I. What Is IP?

In recent years, IP has been a buzz word. Well, then, just what is IP?

In the past, at the mention of IP, IP address or Intellectual Property would spring to mind. However, now, what the two letters mean has already gone beyond the two categories and is becoming a phenomenal marketing concept. In nature,

---

① UGC (User Generated Content) : this term refers to the user-generated original content that springs from the concept of Web 2.0 characterized by the promotion of personalization. Instead of a specific business, it marks a new way for users to use the Internet that focuses on both download and upload rather than previously sole download.

② PGC (Professional Generated Content): this is an Internet term and refers to professionally generated content (video website) and professionally produced content (Microblog). It is used to refer to individualized content that is created from diverse perspectives to popularize democracy and virtual social relationships.

it is to make the connection between brands and consumers back to the connection between people so as to rebuild trust and foster closer human relationships, thereby making the products more heartwarming and charming. In the context of "IP marketing", the "IP" has a much broader semantic coverage. Specifically, it more refers to the content or the individual that is able to get rid of a single platform and gain popularity and be distributed at multiple platforms by virtue of their own appeal. So, it is indeed a kind of "potential asset". If it is in the case of currently popular content forms, it can be a word, a concept, a person, an official account, a name, an emoji or an online celebrity like Papi Jiang and Mi Meng.

1. The Business Logic of IP Marketing

The business logic of IP marketing can be condensed into one sentence: brands continue to produce high-quality content using the character of spokespersons to output values so as to gather fans. If fans accept the values, namely achieving the recognition of identity and character, they will trust the products. This process contains three layers of logic:

(1) It is easier for individuals to develop trust and emotional connections with users. In the past, the marketing that focused on brands has created aloof brand images, striking people as a distant thing. Yet, IP marketing that centers on personal connection infuses warmth into brands through the charm of the personalities of spokespersons. Take Chen Ou who creates the buzzing phrase that "I'm Chen Ou, I speak for myself" and Dong Mingzhu as an example. Both of them have exerted a positive impact on bridging the gap between brands and consumers and out of trust in their characters, consumers have a good impression of their products.

(2) In nature, the migration of traffic from platforms to individuals to achieve low-cost and cross-platform communication underlies the great popularity of IP marketing. As we all know, in tandem with the depletion in all kinds of Internet profitability, there is a constant jump on marketing costs. Consequently, the traffic has been monopolized by the big-name platforms and e-commerce traders are regressing to be stuck in the differential rent trap of the physical e-commerce. According to relevant data, at present, the customer acquisition cost of common e-commerce traders stands over CNY 100 and even higher for some traders in niche products who have to pay traffic fees to platforms. Against the backdrop, brands are in bad need of cheaper and more accurate distribution ways and IP marketing exactly comes up to people's expectations, which can be seen from the rise of the online celebrity economy. The cost the individual online celebrity takes to distribute the traffic is much lower than that of the platform. Meanwhile, it is more accurate and more likely to produce brand viscosity.

(3) In addition to taking advantage of online celebrities, many brands have begun to cultivate their own IP and attract fans with the aid of self-media and content productivity so as to obtain their own popular traffic and potential energy. In this way, they cannot only slash distribution costs, but also get rid of the restriction of the single platform so as to achieve cross-platform traffic distribution. For example, Luo Zhenyu and Luo Yonghao seem to be born with great traffic. Undoubtedly, this means of traffic distribution is more economical, accurate and efficient.

Consumer demands shift from the functional level to the spiritual level. The consumption behavior itself possesses two kinds of attributes: one is the economic attribute, that is to exchange the functions of products; the other is the social attribute, that is to exchange the social meaning of products. Take buying clothes as an example. Our consumption behavior is to cover the body on the one hand and to satisfy individual aesthetic needs on the other. Through social media, the social attributes of this consumer behavior are further known to all and to express consumers' own identity, taste, values and other spiritual demands through consumption has become the main buying motive. So, what strikes a chord with consumers is no longer the product itself, but the spiritual value behind it. Nowadays, we do not lack materials, but the warmth. Therefore, infusing warmth into products is becoming a new consumer demand and is also the value of IP marketing.

2. Criteria for IP Evaluation

IP popularization will inevitably lead to the perception that the IP concept seems to contain all things with seemingly powerful essence and wide extension. However, no matter how wide extension the IP contains in the context of IP marketing, in nature, it still implies the "intellectual brainchildren" and can never get rid of the essential element of the "content". Therefore, this book points out that it is necessary to follow the two standards about how to treat IP marketing: ①whether it has the source of original content with diversified development ability; and ②whether it has an impact on a particular population.

The two standards have set a limit to IP marketing at the macro and essential level and highlight the original content with diversified development ability - whether the IP can adapt to multiple platforms and presentation forms. The more easily it can be changed, the greater the business value is. Needless to say, the originality which is the essence of intellectual property is also essential.

Of course, though not all original content will be a hit with customers, the marketing-worthy IP certainly stands to be paid for by even vertical minority if it is not the majority, which fundamentally underlies whether the original content has the IP development value.

II. How to identify high–value IP

1. Content value

There are three dimensions to content value: three-value index, cross-medium index, and compatibility index. The broader and deeper the dimension, the higher the value of IP.

Three-value index: degree to which the value, cultural and philosophical systems of the work accord with current ideology.

Cross-medium index: adaptability of IP into multiple material types, such as games, videos, and so on which are distributed on multi-media platforms to influence diverse audiences. "Medium " here refers to "a way of communicating information and news to people, such as newspapers, television, etc."

Compatibility index: autonomy in and scope for content adaptation.

2. Personification

Why is personification so important?
(1) it promotes intimacy;
(2) it is recognizable;
(3) it is conducive to interaction;
(4) personifed IP evolves constantly.

The most important thing for personification is that it embodies the noema of the general public and that it bursts with sufficient vitality in the memory zone of the general public. Four factors determine the influence of personification: iconic style, iconic slogan, and iconic media platform and iconic stem.

3. Influence

(1) Popularity
How to assess popularity?
- Network coverage during a certain period, including reading and media platforms;
- Audience feature extraction;
- Work dissemination on channels including Baidu search index, post bar, microblog, forum, etc.;
- Serialization of work, approach to brand management and others;
- Data such as the number of hits, favorites, subscriptions, recommendations, rewards, etc. on the website platform.
(2) Following
Two criteria apply to the assessment of following: size and bill-paying habits.
(3) Own traffic
Ability to gain a footing outside itself with its own attractiveness and distribute works on multiple platforms to generate traffic; ability to trigger post-view public praise, which generates traffic.
(4) Author popularity and participation

4. Subculture

This book assesses the level of subculture activity from two perspectives:
(1) Community size
(2) Derivatization potential
Subculture helps to obtain immediate economic benefits and has a significant role to play in further shaping IP.

Dimensions	Specific parameters
Content value	Three-view index
	Cross-medium index
	Compatibility index

Dimensions	Specific parameters
Personification	Style
	Slogans and attitudes
	Personality image
	Popular stems
	Audience quality
Influence	Following
	Traffic
	Topic popularity
Subculture	Community size
	Derivatization potential

How to identify high-value IP? Source: Everyone is A Product Manager

III. Why IP substance marketing

New changes in the market environment are necessarily behind the rise of new marketing technologies and trends. Brand substance marketing currently faces five major macro-market challenges:

1. Increasing decentralization and fragmentation in the media environment

The "prime time" that went viral through the TV broadcast mechanism led by China Central Television (CCTV) is long gone. More and more platforms which integrate social networking and content distribution, such as Microblog, WeChat, Toutiao, and Yidian Zixun, have emerged in an increasingly competitive market, each grabbing a market share. This means brands have many platforms on which they can make a sound. It is both an opportunity and a crisis. It is an opportunity because these platforms offer new growth; it is also a crisis because efforts go in all directions and the cost of trial and error increases.

2. More obvious consumption upgrading in a diversified consumption scenario

Moguls such as online Tmall and J.D. and offline Wanda Plaza have the lion's share in the consumption market, harvesting most of the traffic thanks to their first-mover advantage and brand strength. In this age of personalization and consumption upgrading, however, there are always subdivided niche markets and consumer demands, whether online or offline, neglected by moguls. Yitiao, Mogujie, Xiaohongshu and other online retailers represent subdivisions of the consumption scenario that users can choose from.

3. Independent brand marketing often lacks in strategy and content continuity

Independent, fragmented marketing consumes enormous marketing resources on its 0-to-1 journeys. This is the day-to-day growth of most Chinese brands, which can be attributed to: ① Lack of awareness to cultivate content. ② Cost constraints. Many brands aspire to the operating philosophy of "minimum investment with maximum output." Operators with this profiteering attitude are capricious and naturally fail to accumulate and cultivate premium content. ③ Following the trend blindly. "Following" translates to an absence of careful planning and being divorced from the actual market.

4. Poor content dissemination and cross-platform penetration due to insufficient creativity

The rise of new media has equipped most brands with ideas and departments for new media marketing. However, oper-

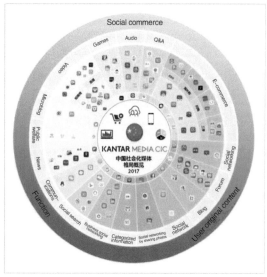

Why IP substance marketing? Source: Everyone is A Product Manager

ator creativity is a problem when WeChat public accounts have reached 20 million in number.

5. Brand image is not based on fragmented content

In fact, the root cause of 5 lies in 3 and 4 above. As the "source of original content with the potential for diversified development," the "diversity" and "originality" of IP (especially premium IP) marketing can only rely on continuous content output to break through platform barriers, thereby connecting to users in a diversified consumer scenario, in the face of the above market challenges.

IV. How to create IP substance marketing

According to incomplete statistics, the credibility of advertisements among consumers has shown a downward trend. 86% of consumers skip pre-movie advertising when surfing the web and 44% of them ignore junk mail, but 61% show willingness to read the contents that enterprises push because these contents are more likely to rouse purchasing behavior. The survey shows that 60% of users will search for related products after reading interesting contents, 70% will feel closer to the company after being exposed to "substance marketing", and 78% believe that companies providing content to users are more trustworthy.

It is thus clear from the above that users prefer "substance marketing" over traditional advertising. It's an idea worthy of contemplation to develop virtual personalities and write documents that are highly likely to convert dormant purchases into actual purchases in the present-day marketing environment where straightforward advertising and advertorials are being disregarded. "Convert dormant purchases into actual purchases" is used here to mean "how many orders your content is converted into". David Ogilvy said: "Advertorials improve sales". Of course, we must note that David Ogilvy lived in a different age. What he says is only partially true. Abandoning traditional thinking on advertising and incorporating ideas such as e-commerce, content and conversion into present-day advertising is the only key to the era of Marketing 3.0. Then, how to create the IP-based marketing contents?

1. Affinity

In general, a master tasked with content operation has numerous "loyal fans" who watch his advertisements simply because they are fans. Some fans find fun in telling precisely when a document will be converted into an advertisement and what kind of advertisement. Some even say they would give a negative comment if they see no advertisement. However, most enterprises do not have men of such affinity or online celebrities. And even if they do, conversion into sales may not necessarily come. If you do not have men of affinity, you do not have high-quality IP. The first thing therefore is to have a person of affinity, someone with a "virtual personality". To have self-owned IP and a "corporate personality" that resembles that of a human, the following steps are necessary:

The first step begins with the disseminator. For example, when the image of XYZ Co., Ltd. is being promoted, the logo can be designed in such a way as to weaken the identity of the company and highlight that it features people as the central force.

The second step is to build modules. A shopping module is indispensable, and shopping must be a smooth and complete process. But this module should not

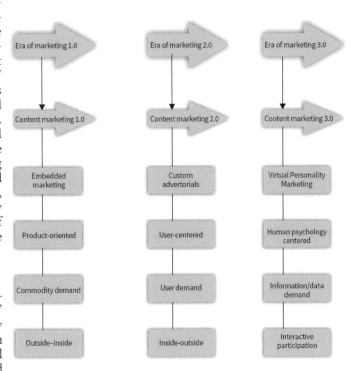

Era of virtual personality marketing

Era of Virtual Personality Marketing. Source: Everyone is A Product Manager appear unsightly. It should highlight the content directly related to the life of the personality to be shaped—almost the same as the creation of a net celebrity: weakened "corporate status" and highlighted "personality."

The third step is the choice of topics. "Content comes first" and the personality created speaks the loudest. More attention should be given to life and its inspirations. At the same time, information regarding the "dry goods" of the industry that the personality corresponds to should be shared, thus turning a lifeless business into a true-to-life "man" with hobbies, curiosity, and troubles.

Substance marketing through a "virtual personality" adds a human dimension to brand image and wins the heart of the consumer. It eventually transforms their good impression of the brand into orders.

2. A "person" with an interesting virtual personality that is competent in promoting sales

Content that is interesting but does not promote sales will not make progress at all; content that promotes sales but is boring will be disgusting. Documents are carefully crafted papers of creativity and practical value, or illustrated texts containing brilliant cross-talk appealing to readers.

3. Built-in substance of content marketing

Substance marketing occurs in the "flesh" of articles. Readers read advertisements whilst reading articles. This is more effective than post-article advertisements, the advertisement section of newspapers, or the advertisement periods between TV programs. The huge difference between

---

💡 Case Study　Funny bone is not a guarantee of sales

A famous blogger has created ad slogans for Nanfu, a leading battery brand of China. Although he is well known for creating quality slogans, Nanfu has gained limited benefit from these excellent words.

The truth is, while the slogans were good per se, they did not encourage buying, i.e., they did not solve problems for the company. A 10-piece package sold at CNY 19.9 only gained 15,141 comments (by July 26, 2016); on the contrary, a rival product sold at CNY 25.9 attracted 58,757 comments. The slogans were read by more than 100,000 people, but resulted in negative conversion (compared with competitors). This reason is that, instead of being a personalized character of Nanfu, the blogger is merely a slogan creator, not a booster of conversion rate.

These slogans were funny but not practical, as shown in figure, therefore lacked "marketing strength". In creating these slogans, the blogger has made several mistakes:

1. He did not dig deep into scenarios of "battery use". In other words, he failed to identify customer's needs and pain points. Discovery of customer's potential needs is a must-have ability for product managers and marketers.

2. He let go of the characteristics of secondary dissemination. Simple image ads, which need mastery of slogan, are extremely hard to be spread through daily conversations among real customers.

3. Online retailers do organize campaigns to stimulate needs. The truth is, while there are solid needs

Ad slogans of Nanfu Battery.

for batteries, the blogger has forgotten to remind customers of the awkwardness when they don't have batteries prepared. Only by this way of thinking can the slogan be successful in driving needs, just like telling women that they always need one more dress. We should not repeat these mistakes in facilitating slogan-based marketing and brand personalization.

virtual personality content operation and traditional copywriting is the need to create different IPs on one product and establish correlations from scratch. Simple, staged dissemination of documents is thus turned into continuous multi-IP virtual personality content operation.

4. Incubation of the virtual personality platform using multiple means

When the self-development of corporate virtual personality is complete, the transition from PGC to UGC begins. The self-development of corporate virtual personality is limited in terms of manpower, finance, and resources. The development of media, consulting, and e-commerce is social; therefore, the direction of content is social.

Note the following when assisting UGC in shaping virtual personality content:

(1) Confidence: It is necessary to understand UGC quality and user operation experience when e-commerce is made to reach every corner of society. Specific incentive mechanisms should be added so user trust and engagement are enhanced. For example, categorized "consumer recommendation lists" encourage users to generate high-quality content and effectively enhance user recognition of the platform.

(2) Interaction: A core of marketing activities is to establish and develop a good enterprise-consumer relationship, that is, the interaction between content and users.

This is the sense of participation Xiaomi which always accentuates. For example, voice messages and self-produced videos can be distributed so the "personality" of content is more graphically reflected; relationships are established in "chat" between businesses and users who feel businesses are like friends who value and care about them.

(3) Online and offline activities: Users are invited to participate in the lucky draw at a discount. Welfare with a built-in personality is different from ordinary "price reduction". "The milk of human kindness" is the top priority of a virtual personality platform, where businesses conduct intimate interactions like real-life friends with users in the hope that a closer long-term relationship with the user is established.

Internet thinking urges content operation to ultimately convert advertising into orders. In an era when content is first and foremost, core competitiveness is embodied by the virtual personality built into user psychology as well as user interaction, topics that users are genuinely interested in, and a true-to-life "virtual personality". "People-oriented and emotionally moving" interactive activities are carried out in various ways so that users are impressed by the enterprise in their first interaction and say it is a good product rather than a good document. Just like drizzle which "gives moisture without producing any sound," these efforts will enable users to trust this "personality," determine their ranking of the products and eventually convince them to buy.

V. How to create super IPs

1. Content can brew itself

This may be the most important basis for super IPs. Content that cannot be brewed, that which does not motivate user curiosity, engagement and dissemination, has only a limited life. Whether it is Supercell's CoC (Clash of Clans), which has just been acquired by Tencent, long-lasting Doraemon, or Brown Bear and Keni Rabbit that became popular on mobile social networking app Line, premium content has always played a part.

2. Original but adaptable and replicable

Super IPs must be quite adaptable to be popular; they should be able to be interpreted, cited, and continuously adapted. If content can brew itself, it gets a score of 1; if content that can brew itself can be adapted, it gets a score of 10.

Star Wars 7 delivered only CNY 700 million while Mermaid garnered up to CNY 3.4 billion in the box office in China. In terms of IP value, Star Wars is at least 100 times that of Mermaid. The reason is that sequels of Star Wars continue to be produced, and novels, games, and peripheral products are simultaneously released. Its derivative potential far exceeds that of Mermaid.

3. A sufficiently differentiated personality

Differentiation may become more and more important in the future. In theory of orientation, differentiation is used to describe the phenomenon that subdivisions of categories occupy the mind of users. The first such domestic sci-fi work that comes to mind is Three Bodies, the most likely U.S. cartoons are Batman and Iron Man, the Chinese cartoon that comes to mind is Cribug, and the domestic web-based talk show is Let's Talk, and so on. Each IP is unique, because the personality it highlights appeals to fans. Just like the fans of old Luo said, "You only need to concentrate. We will help you win."

4. A subscription mechanism worthy of waiting is in the making

Detective Conan is still being updated, and Dragon Ball is still going. The plot may seem outdated, but consumers who grew up with Arnold Schwarzenegger and Bruce Willis in video halls first think of the cinema when Die Hard 5 and Terminator 5 are screened. They have been watching these movies for so long that they have grown attached to them.

5. Social currency represented by credit value

This means IP is a node on the social chain that reshapes trust and plays a leadership role in the new credit system. When brand IP becomes someone else's topic of conversation, brand comes out of the user's mind and becomes a topic in his chat with others or is shared on social media. IP is now an important tag for users to express their feelings and show their personal preferences. Compared to concepts such as "super single product" or "trending item", "super IP" thinks more about brand scalability and durability, and it sounds less speculative than "super single product" or "trending item".

💡 Case Study   Gugongtaobao

The Forbidden City recently launched Hip-Hop Style H5 to follow the hip-hop marketing trend that came with TV series "China Hip-Hop".

This unbelievable H5 titled "I received a WeChat message from your mother" is up to the highest hip-hop standards. It is a perfect example of Gugongtaobao's longstanding commitment to IP.

Forbidden City IP came from the National Palace Museum in Taipei. Five years ago, the "I got it" sealing tape revolutionized people's perceptions with a prideful tone, and at the same time awakened the operating team in the Beijing Imperial Palace.

They began to subvert the pretentious, lofty royal attitude and communicate with young users in an original, funny yet serious manner.

Embracing young people with subcultures is the secret of success of Gugongtaobao.

Posters of Gugongtaobao

Using cultural elements such as modern network terminology, Duanzi, Meng, and 2D, the emperors, concubines, and officials of the Ming and Qing dynasties reinterpret the colorful culture of the Imperial Palace

Notepad series of Gugongtaobao

in a young and faddish way. Gugongtaobao suddenly became a cute and interesting little partner who happily chats with fans and users.

Personification activated Gugongtaobao. As fans engage in more interactions, Gugongtaobao opens its arms to embrace the newest and hottest trends. The wider it reaches out for people, the larger the number of the fans who come.

When it comes to influence, Gugongtaobao generated enormous traffic. This hot online store sustained by emperors and empresses is a generator of traffic in its own right. In addition, Microblog and WeChat, where content is spread, have a lot of loyal "subjects". Nearly one million Microblog users follow with interest all year round, and more than one hundred thousand WeChat tweets on this have come out.

We do not need to say much about content quality. Every once in a while, photos and words of a "hot cake" would flood the screen. Gugongtaobao is also rolling out court-bead headset, the emperor's folding fans, baggage tag titled "trip arranged by the emperor" and other hot online products that make trendsetters busy with grass growing.

The case source quoted from: Sina Microblog 2017/10/16
http://www.woshipm.com/operate/812167.html

Big Data Substance Marketing

Chapter 10

Topics:

1. Knowing About Big Data
2. Big Data Marketing
3. Tool Kit - 22 Methods for Substance of Content
   Marketing

Knowing About Big Data

I. Definition of big data

In the era of Internet today, big data has become an indispensable tool in marketing activities. Anyone who controls the data will grasp the lifeline of market and use precision marketing tactics to meet customer's specific needs.

As data volume undergoes explosive growth due to rapid development of mobile Internet, cloud computing, IoT, machine-type communication and other emerging communication technologies, data structures and types are increasingly complicated. The marketing industry also enters the times of Internet-based big data.

Big data is defined as a set of data of a gigantic size that is beyond the capability of traditional database software tools in acquisition, storage, management and analysis. Big data is featured by massive volume, high circulation velocity, a variety of data types, and low value density. The "4V" is further explained in Figure 10-1.

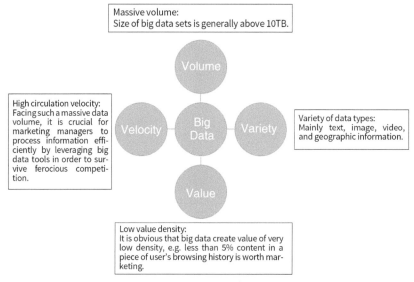

Figure 10-1   Features of big data.

II. Application value of mobile big data marketing

Since it analyzes user's behavior by using the extensive Internet, big data will continue to be a popular technology. More industries have recognized the importance of big data for marketing. The age of Information Technology (IT), marked by development of the Internet, will soon evolve to the age of Data Technology (DT).

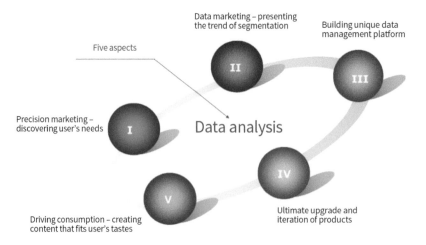

Figure 10-2   Five aspects of data analysis.

As a representation of technologies at data level, DT is applied in data collection, analysis, and mining to facilitate deeper study of a certain industry and segment target consumer groups at a more accurate level. This reflects the strength of big data in raising marketing precision and it is the secret of big data marketing.

Application value of mobile big data marketing mainly rests on the depth of data analysis. For an app generating hundreds of millions data flows every day, how can we deal with this huge traffic? As indicated in Figure 10-2, we can analyze the data from five aspects:

1. Precision marketing–discovering user's needs

Big data has brought about a new advertising mode – precision advertising based on identification of user's needs. In the precision marketing based on big data, advertisers are offered with such data services as market forecast and analysis of competitors, user preference, and dynamic consumer trend, which help them discover the best matching user groups with the highest consumption potential, so that they may manage to allocate their ad budget more reasonably. From this point of view, marketing against the backdrop of big data is doing "subtraction operation".

2. Data marketing–presenting the trend of segmentation

As the data marketing industry becomes more mature, advertisers have put forward higher requirements on precision marketing, driving the development of big data marketing from the stage of concept structuring to practical application in more market segments.

Since the end of 2016, companies engaged in big data analysis and data-based industrial consulting have steered their development to focus on specific industries as the application of big data varies in different sectors, such as automotive, FMCG, beauty products, bulk products, and finance. In the future, they tend to extract more detailed sector-specific data to provide precision marketing services.

3. Building unique data management platform

The importance of big data has been recognized by an increasing number of professional agencies, who have developed enormous databases over years of accumulation. The question is how they can leverage these data effectively.

Along with development of big data technology, a large number of data analytics consulting companies have emerged, focusing their business on bid data marketing. Today, any one enterprise can build a similar big data platform, and use it to provide competitor analysis, channel exploration marketing strategies, and other consulting services.

4. Ultimate upgrade and iteration of products

User's needs determine the direction of ultimate product upgrade. For marketing managers, there is no sluggish market but weak product. Concealed in big data, user's needs should be scooped out. A marketing manager should also play the role of a product manager in this "user-first" age.

5. Driving consumption–creating content that fits user's tastes

It's the content you have shared that users don't like, not the product. In the logic of mobile marketing, content goes before the product. How can a company create useful content? Big data has the answer.

III. Definition of cloud computing: from cloud computing to IoT

1. Definition of cloud computing

Cloud computing is a new supplement, consumption, and delivery model for IT services based on Internet protocols, and it typically involves provisioning of dynamically scalable and often virtualized resources. Based on a narrow definition, cloud computing refers to delivery and consumption model of IT infrastructure, meaning that resources are obtained from the Internet in an on-demand and scalable way; while based on a broader definition, cloud computing refers to delivery and consumption model of services, meaning that services are obtained from the Internet in an on-demand and scalable way. Services can be related to IT, software, and Internet, or any other things. This denotes that computing power could be a commodity circulating through the Internet.

Development of Internet presents two trends: Internet of Things (IoT) and Cyber Physical Systems (CPS). Both revolutionary trends stress the spread of expansion of Internet to everyday objects, pointing out the direction for mobile marketing in the next decade.

While traditional Internet connects machines and web pages, mobile Internet features people to people, and people to information connection. If PC-based Internet stars the first half in the game of the Internet, the leading role of the second half will be mobile Internet, IoT and CPS. This is because mobile Internet has sparked the rapid growth of Internet apps in all industries worldwide, and that is why IoT and CPS become the tangible technical trend. The idea of IoT was first introduced at MIT in 1999, meaning the networked connection among everyday objects, tools, devices or computers. We can view the IoT as a network of wireless sensors that has connected all objects of our daily life, which can be big or small, and change with location and time. In this idea, every object is identified with RFID, sensors, or electronic technology (e.g., GPS).

Since the introduction of IPv6, any one object on the earth can be distinguished by two IP addresses, including computers and special devices. As Internet researchers have estimated that every one of us is surrounded by 1,000-5,000 objects, the IoT should be designed to track hundreds of trillions of static or moving objects, and build connection with them. To this end, all objects in the IoT need to be coded. In order to simplify the process of identification, searching and storage, minor objects can be filtered by setting some thresholds. It is obvious that IoT has broadened the boundary of Internet, and gained more ground in Asia and Europe. Particularly, it shows the way for development of the Industrial Revolution 4.0.

In the era of mobile Internet to come, all objects and devices are instrumented, interconnected, and interacted with each other intelligently. This communication can be made between people and things or among the things themselves. Three communication patterns co-exist: namely H2H (human-to-human), H2T (human-to-thing), and T2T (thing-to-thing). Here things include machines such as PCs and cell phones. The idea here is to connect things (including human and machine objects) at any time and any place intelligently with low cost. Any place connections include at the PC, indoor (away from PC), outdoors, and on the move. Any time connections include daytime, night, outdoors and indoors, and on the move as well.

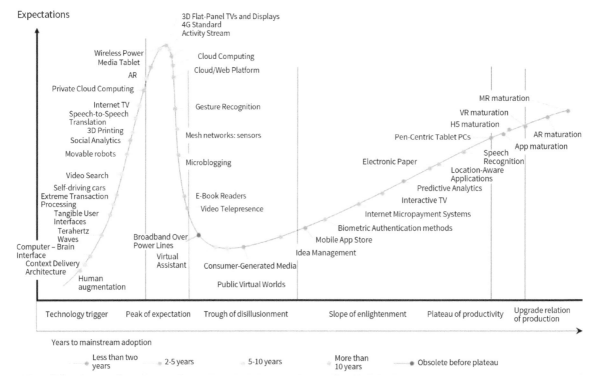

Hype Cycle for Emerging Technologies (2017)

The dynamic connections will grow exponentially into a new dynamic network of networks, called the Internet of Things (IoT). The IoT is still in its infancy stage of development. Today, many prototypes of IoT with restricted areas of coverage are under experimentation. Cloud computing researchers expect to use the cloud and future Internet technologies to support fast, efficient, and intelligent interactions among humans, machines, and any objects on Earth. A smart Earth should have intelligent cities, clean water, efficient power, convenient transportation, good food supplies, responsible banks, fast telecommunications, green IT, better schools, good health care, abundant resources, and so on. This dream living environment may take some time to reach fruition at different parts of the world.

A CPS is the result of interaction between computational processes and the physical world. A CPS integrates "cyber" (heterogeneous, asynchronous) with "physical" (concurrent and information-dense) objects. A CPS merges the "3C" technologies of computation, communication, and control into an intelligent closed feedback system between the physical world and the information world, a concept which is actively explored in the United States, China and some other countries. The IoT emphasizes various networking connections among physical objects, while the CPS emphasizes exploration of virtual reality (VR) applications in the physical world. We may transform how we interact with the physical world just like the Internet transformed how we interact with the virtual world. On the arena of international Internet technol-

ogies, China has two technologies that outpaced the West: mobile Internet and VR. In 2016, the year deemed as the start of China's VR industry, a strong power of technical application was developed and guided VR industry from technical application to deep research, and to application upgrade. While iPhone updates once every year, VR devices are developed on a track of monthly upgrade, adding more interesting facts that support the revolutionary evolution of marketing theories. At the beginning of 2017, almost overnight, people found that objects, tools and methods of marketing research were changed. Wide application of technology has changed the ground of marketing research, and is therefore the very reason that motivated the author to publish the book of Mobile Marketing Management.

2. Application of cloud computing: Google App Engine

Google has the world's largest search engine facilities. The company has extensive experience in massive data processing that has led to new insights into data-center design and novel programming models that scale to incredible sizes. The Google platform is based on its search engine expertise, but this infrastructure is applicable to many other areas. Google has hundreds of data centers and has installed more than 460,000 servers worldwide. For example, 200 Google data centers are used at one time for a number of cloud applications. Google's App Engine (GAE) offers a PaaS platform supporting various cloud and web applications. Google has pioneered cloud development by leveraging the large number of data centers it operates. For

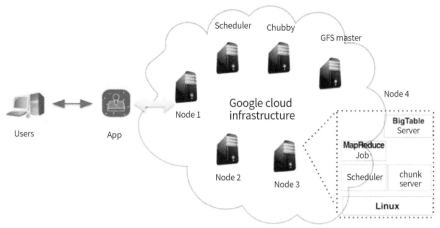

Figure 10-3   Google cloud platform and major building blocks, the blocks shown are large clusters of low-cost servers.

example, Google pioneered cloud services in Gmail, Google Docs, and Google Earth, among other applications. These applications can support a large number of users simultaneously with high availability (HA). Notable technology achievements include the Google File System (GFS), MapReduce, BigTable, and Chubby. In 2008, Google announced the GAE web application platform which is becoming a common platform for many small cloud service providers. This platform specializes in supporting scalable (elastic) web applications. GAE enables users to run their applications on a large number of data centers associated with Google's search engine operations. In addition, Google responds quickly to applications.

Figure 10-3 shows the major building blocks of the Google cloud platform which has been used to deliver the cloud services based on big data. GFS is used for storing large amounts of data. MapReduce is for use in application program development. Chubby is used for distributed application lock services. BigTable offers a storage service for accessing structured data. Users can interact with Google applications via the web interface provided by each application. Third-party application providers can use GAE to build cloud applications for providing services. The applications all run in data centers under tight management by Google engineers. Inside each data center, there are thousands of servers forming different clusters.

GAE runs the user program on Google's infrastructure. As it is a platform running third-party programs, application developers now do not need to worry about the maintenance of servers. GAE can be thought of as the combination of several software components. The front-end is an application framework which is similar to other web application frameworks such as ASP, J2EE, and JSP. At present, GAE supports Python and Java programming environments. The applications can run similar to web application containers. The front-end can be used as the dynamic web serving infrastructure which can provide the full support of common technologies and bolster big data operation for cloud computing.

3. Influence of Internet, cloud computing and VR on marketing

In 2005, the concept of the Internet entered the limelight. It could connect the world's objects in a sensory manner. The approach is to tag things through RFID, feel things through sensors and wireless networks, and think things by building embedded systems that interact with human activities. A road map for IoT development is shown in Figure 10-4 to anticipate the desired technology advances to make the IoT a reality in 25 years. In 2002, the U.S. National Science Foundation (NSF) called for the convergence of cutting-edge technologies including ubiquitous computing and nanotechnology.

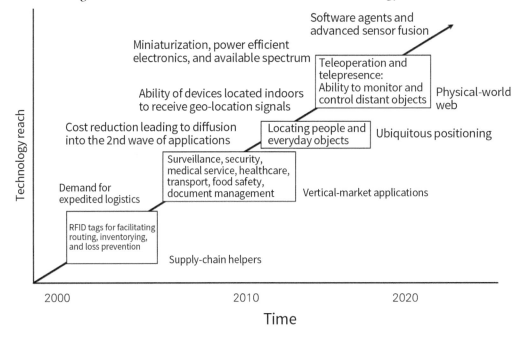

Figure 10-4   Technology development of IoT.

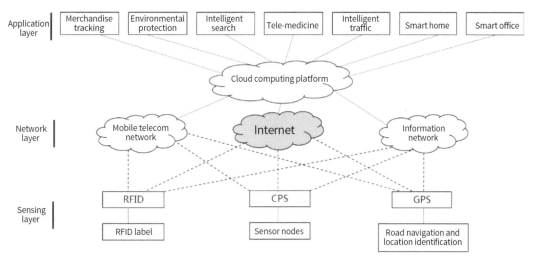

Figure 10-5   The architecture of an IoT: consisting of sensing devices that are connected to various applications via mobile networks, the Internet, and processing clouds.

In April 2008, the U.S. National Intelligence Council published a report titled "Disruptive Civil Technologies," which also identified the IoT as a critical technology on U.S. interests out to 2025. Quantitatively speaking, the IoT should be designed to encode 50 trillion to 100 trillion objects. Moreover, mobile technologies should be applied to follow the movement of those objects. With today's population of more than 6 billion worldwide, that means every person is surrounded by thousands of objects on a daily basis.

The IoT system is likely to have an event-driven tower-shaped architecture. As shown in Figure 10-5, it has interactive three-layer architecture. The top layer is formed by driven applications. Such as the world in the future, which is not a world preliminary Internet consisting of online and offline parts, but only virtual and physical. The bottom layers represent various types of sensing devices: namely RFID tags, ZigBee or other types of sensors, and road-mapping GPS navigators. The sensing devices are locally or wide-

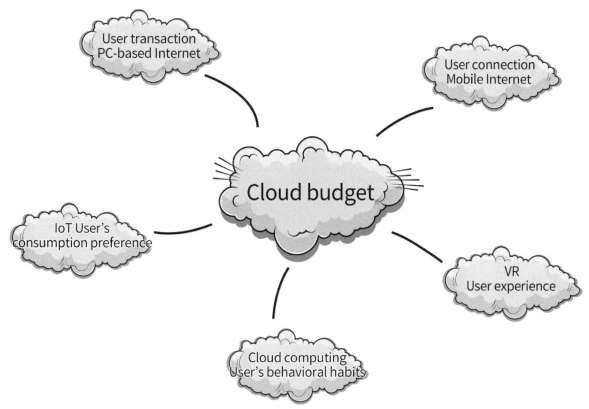

Logic Talkshow of China depicted five clouds of the Information Age.

area-connected in the form of RFID networks, sensor networks, and GPSs. In this way, they are not only connected, but also support the virtual reality in the physical world. Signals or information collected at these sensing devices are linked to the applications through the cloud computing platforms at the middle layer.

When viewing the influence of Internet evolution on marketing from a user's standpoint, we may draw the following conclusions: PC-based Internet has changed the way of transaction – product marketing is made possible in virtual cyber space; mobile Internet has changed how users communicate with each other – user

experience (positive or negative feedback) previously isolated by vertical management systems of traditional marketing is now accessible to other users, and the balance of interest has tilted to consumers; IoT has changed user's consumption preference and impacted production procedures directly related to marketing; cloud computing has changed behavioral habits of users, who are able to live in a better world of intelligent Internet; VR has changed user experience, which was an after-sales term but is made possible before the purchase. All these changes, though user-centered, have driven revolutionary and disruptive transformation of marketing research.

Big Data Marketing

I. Definition of big data marketing

Big data marketing refers to the process in which massive behavioral data is collected through the Internet to help advertisers identify target audience, and predict content, serving time, modes of ads, followed by ad serving. Along with popularization of digital living space, the size of global information is growing exponentially. It is based on this trend that

the big data, cloud computing and other new ideas and modes have emerged to undoubtedly cause another round of big data marketing. Leveraging the massive data collected from multiple platforms, big data marketing studies user preference, ad serving, product upgrade, content consumption and channel transformation.

II. Characteristics of results of big data marketing

Along with the development of the Internet, the size of stored data sees drastic

1	Structured	Including data of defined type, format or structure, such as transaction data and OLAP.
2	Semi-structured	Including textual data files with a discernable pattern, enabling parsing, such as XML data files that are self-describing and defined by an xml schema.
3	Quasi-structured	Including textual data with erratic data formats, which can be formatted with tools, such as web clickstream data that may contain some inconsistencies in data values and formats.
4	Unstructured	Data that has no inherent structure and is usually stored as different types of files, such as text documents, PDFs, images and videos.
5	Structured reversal	Logic concealed in data is extracted by brain-thinking based on experience with the help of computers and semi-AI, in order to acquire credible data.

Figure 10-6 Data increase tends to be unstructured.

expansion over time. The tremendous size of data is one of the major features of big data marketing. There has been 800,000 petabytes (PB) of data stored worldwide as of the year 2000, and this number is expected to reach 35 zettabytes (ZB) by 2020. Twitter alone generates more than 7 terabytes (TB) of data every single day; Facebook produces 10 TB daily – and some enterprises are compiling terabytes of data hourly.

Due to the complexity of data itself, the first choice for processing large amount of data is massively parallel processing in a parallel computing environment, a bit like collecting like terms in mathematics. This makes it possible to extract, transform, load and analyze data concurrently. The big data used in big data marketing is unstructured or semi-structured, and different techniques and tools are required for processing and analysis. At present, intelligent analytics of big data has been well developed.

The most prominent characteristics of big data marketing are represented in its structure. The increase trend of differently structured data is shown in Figure 10-6.

Specifically:

(1) Structured data: including data of defined type, format or structure, such as transaction data and OLAP.

(2) Semi-structured data: including textual data files with a discernable pattern, enabling parsing, such as XML data files that are self-describing and defined by an XML schema.

(3) Quasi-structured data: including textual data with erratic data formats, which can be formatted with tools.

(4) Unstructured data: including data that has no inherent structure and is usually stored as different types of files, such as text documents, PDFs, images and videos.

(5) Structured reversal: logic concealed in data is extracted by brain-thinking based on experience with the help of computers and semi-AI, in order to acquire credible data.

III. The 5–W model of big data marketing

The 5-W model of big data marketing reveals the five fundamental steps in the marketing process (see Figure 10-7).

Who: who is the target?

For example, find 99% of ordinary users and 1% of key users (super users) to identify the target of big data marketing.

What: what is to be pushed?

Screen out categorization information of users from big data management files and identify the content that exactly slakes user's thirst of content on the basis of user preference for information.

Where: where to push?

Analyze on the basis of user information acquired from orders and, depending on different information categories, select the information media for message push.

Why: why should users purchase?

Before studying why should users purchase, we should figure out first that under what circumstances users will not purchase or will hesitate, crack their concerns one by one, and then serve positive feedback to them.

Worth: is it worth buying?

Generally, positive feedback of existing customers acts as a catalyst for purchase by new users. If "flash sale" and similar deal-facilitating information is added, users will consider that it is worth buying.

Figure 10-7   The 5-W model of big data marketing.

Xiao Guan Tea

Master's Works

Premium products by eight tea masters

Placards of Xiao Guan Tea. Source: Baidu Baike

Respected as China's national drink, tea is not only an indispensable part of life for most Chinese, but a symbol of this country's history and culture originated thousands of years ago. However, as the widely circulated saying goes: 70,000 equal one Lipton! This assertion, while startling, is true. Currently, less than 10 out of China's 70,000 more tea companies, large or small, have enjoyed an annual turnover of above CNY 1 billion. Lack of accurate market positioning, absence of universally accepted criteria, disregard for consumer's needs, brandless development mode, and regionalized operation have all put sand in the wheels of China's tea industry on its way to upgrade and even globalization. Facing these conditions, it is imperative to make a change. At this moment, Xiao Guan Tea (XGT) has made itself seen as a manufacturer of modernistic tea products. Pledged to offer creative tea experience, it is promoting a revolution of China's tea industry with the combination of innovative ideas and traditional tea culture.

Breaking traditional restrictions to build a trendy and tasty modern brand

In the fast-paced modern world, it is extravagant for people to sip a cup of good tea for a break in their busy life. XGT's "grand goal", to make a stylish and modern tea product, was inspired by coffee culture, which benefited from development and spread of instant coffee. The inherent exotic traits of instant coffee also helped a lot in facilitating its marketing among urban trendies.

"Unlike coffee, it's inconvenient to buy and drink tea for many urban residents who, particularly the young generations, consider tea-drinking an outdated

activity. We have to bring in new ideas into our products, as well as the package, brewing experience, and marketing mode," said Mei Jiang, CMO of XGT. Positioning user experience at the center was the disruptive move that XGT had taken to crack traditional ideas on package design.

While benchmarking its product to "modernistic tea", XGT had pushed the design of product and experience to the utmost, and tried to deliver qualities of vogue and reverence from the perspectives of urban population, particularly high-end group demanding excellent taste. To this end, XGT invited Hideo Kambara, a great master of industrial design from Japan, who invested nearly two years to eventually complete the design of handy aluminum can after dozens of revisions. In addition to stylish look, the handy can also makes preservation and brewing easy.

Redefine tea-drinking experience in cooperation with Apple Store designer

XGT also gave full play to the popular concept "experience economy". "We are determined to build XGT into the Apple of tea industry," said Yu Jinjiang, Vice President of XGT. This frank statement was proven not a jest. Last month, XGT opened its first Tea Store on Floor 3 of Henglong Plaza, Ji'nan. The Tea Store was designed by Tim Kobe, designer of the Apple Store, who redefined experience of IT devices with his innovative design together with Steve Jobs.

Roadside tea stores seem old and rustic; luxurious club-type tea houses keep most people far away. We should bring down the wall between tea and consumers. "Tea Store is not merely a tea retailer store, or product exhibition center, we are making effort to build a space where people would like to stay," introduced Mr Yu. XGT hold a branding concept that is so similar to that of Apple: positioning consumers at the center, and delivering a sense of freedom, vogue and quality with well-designed space.

It was the first time that Tim Kobe blended his international perspectives and user experience elements into the design of traditional Chinese tea. Interaction between human and tea, human and space, was successfully activated. Immersing in the space of Tea Store, consumers are enabled to experience everything about tea with their eyes, ears, nose, tongue, body and mind.

In addition to remarkable innovations in decoration and space, XGT also introduced service ideas of Apple Store and cooperated with TANG UX Consulting, a leading user experience designer in China to bring these ideas into reality. Abandoning cashier counters in the store, XGT released customers from the pressure of purchase. It also provided convenient electronic payment system to avoid queues. Moreover, some humanistic technical details were intended to surprise customers. For example, lightly pushing the partition board of display cabinet, you can play a video of tea-making by a master.

Criteria of good tea established by eight tea-making masters

Some people may argue that tea is charming for there is not a standard to restrict it. However, this also makes it hard to provide consumers with consistent and clear information about the product and price due to the opaque operation and subjective pricing methods. Unified standard conveys an impression of credibility to consumers.

XGT invited eight most eminent representatives of the top eight Famous Chinese Teas, including Qi Guo-wei, master of West Lake Longjing, Xie Sishi, the 49th successor of Huangshan Maofeng, and Zou Bingliang, master of Puer, to each deliver a tea product that embodies their supreme mastery up to specific standards: places of origin, harvest time points, plunking methods were clearly specified to guarantee quality and value of every leaf.

Clear market positioning, standardized products, ultimate user experience, and innovative ideas have activated the great potential of XGT to start making international influences.

Chicago Business Journal, The Arizona Republic, Boston Business Journal, Austin Business Journal, Los Angeles Business, and Yahoo, among hundreds of other media, gave wide coverage to XGT, speaking highly of this dark horse of China's tea industry. XGT is going global as a successful example of China's high-end tea brands.

Dedicated Chinese tea manufacturers have long been pained by the heartbreaking reality that "there are famous teas in China but no famous brands". When TWG, Lipton, and other international brand swept through the planet, and Starbucks was intended to introduce its Teavana to China, the appearance of XGT was absolutely a fillip to this country's tea industry. As Mr Mei put it, "Applying clear product positioning and cutting-edge marketing strategies, XGT has created the innovative idea of 'experience consumption' which distinguished it from other traditional industries. I believe that more and more Chinese tea brand will follow our steps and rise in the world again in a brand new image." He revealed that XGT would open 200 stores in high-end malls across China, spreading its iconic experience service and standard products in a vaster market space.

The case source quoted from: Qilu Evening News 2016/11/14
http://www.chawenyi.com/news/7572

Tool Kit – 22 Methods for Substance of Content Marketing

I. Selling concepts

Being different is far more important than being better! It is particularly hard to do better because being a little better would be often ignored, unless it is so much better that the marketing becomes unnecessary. At this time, you need a unique concept to help the brand stand out.

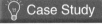 **Case Study**   A Flying Chicken

In Jifei Town, Changning County, Yunnan Province, Wang Jiaohu, a college-educated village official, developed a friendship with "chickens" during poverty alleviation when he tried to raise "flying chickens" on Jifei Mountain. During the period of poverty alleviation in 2015, Wang Jiaohu was transferred to do the related work. At one time when he was in Jifei Village, he was shocked but also inspired by a chicken flying out of the woods on the roadside: now that people were pursuing ecological health, there should be a market for this flying chicken. As a result, he set up a specialized cooperative and obtained more than 200 mu of forest from farmers to take the lead in raising chickens. Through the cooperative, he dynamically integrated the "Six Unifications" (namely unified baby chick supply, unified construction standards, unified epidemic prevention, unified adult chicken recovery, unified branding and unified technical services) with household breeding, carving out a path of integration of "production, supply and marketing".

After the establishment of the cooperative, he always strived for quality and stuck to the way of ecological and standardized development. In terms of quality assurance for chickens, he persisted in feeding chickens without any feedstuff, putting chickens in a purely ecological place to breed and selling chickens aged over 10 months only. And he always highlighted the concept of "flying chickens" in external promotion and marketing contents, which won the favor of those who paid more attention to ecologically healthy foods and resulted in a favorable sales volume.

The case source quoted from: CCTV.COM 2017/03/24
http://travel.sina.com.cn/domestic/news/2017-03-24/detail-ifycstww1027927.shtml

II. Selling pain points

Selling pain points means that an enterprise sells products by digging out the user's pain points.

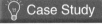 **Case Study**   VIVO: SELFIE WITH SOFT LIGHT BRIGHTENS YOUR BEAUTY

As young people were complaining about imperfect self-timers, VIVO launched its soft-light self-timer which could take the most beautiful photos of you with soft light instead of emphasizing clarity and reality. Beautiful selfies completely met the needs of consumers, and this concept was so strengthened that this type of cellphone sold like hot cakes.

The case source quoted from: Sina Microblog 2016-11-16
https://weibo.com/vivomobile?is_search=0&visible=0&is_hot=1&is_tag=0&profile_ftype=1&page=3#feedtop

Placards of VIVO X9. Source: Sina Microblog

III. Selling new consumptions

New consumption is a form of upgraded consumption, which refers to feelings and benefits above the product.

💡 Case Study   Six Walnuts

Six Walnuts are sugar-free and low-sugar walnut plant protein beverages. They make a feature of brain breathing and meet the customers' demands for effective alleviation of mental fatigue, suitable for students, white-collar workers and other workers. In recent years, it has stood out and emerged from tens of thousands of beverages with its new consumption concept of brain breathing, and has become an influential brand in the plant protein beverage industry.

Placards of Six Walnuts. Source: NetEase News

IV. Highlighting individuality

Differentiation is achieved by highlighting individuality, brand image building is promoted by brand characters, and specific groups are attracted by brand characters to personalize the brand so that a deep differentiated impression can be given to the public. For example, Chengdu: a city you never say goodbye to; Yichun: a city called Spring; Netherlands: the country of tulips; Denmark: kingdom of fairy tales; Finland: the only Santa Claus Village in the world recognized by the United Nations.

V. Selling imagination

Estee Lauder invited a famous singer and a "post-1995" supermodel to shoot an imaginative lipstick advertisement in which everyone could be empowered by the lipstick to conquer the world with a singing voice. "A lipstick that could sing" awakened consumers' curiosity and ignited consumers' desire to buy.

VI. Creating scenes

Scenes are created and related with brand awareness, brand emotions and brand associations to make consumers remember the brand and buy its products.

💡 Case Study   ZHOUHEIYA Opens Stores at High-speed Rail Stations

As an emerging mode of transportation in recent years, the high-speed rail has attracted a large number of businesses with the large passenger flow and the high brand exposure at its stations. A store built at the high-speed rail station is not only a sales outlet but also a communication window. In addition, ZHOUHEIYA has named the high-speed rail train G512 from Hankou to Beijing West after it. As this high-speed train features a high attendance rate and high commercial values for tourists, ZHOUHEIYA has increased its popularity through high-speed rail stations and the train named after it, and has built up the consumer group's awareness of and trust in its brand in the setting of the high-speed rail station or train.

ZHOUHEIYA store. Source: Sohu.com

💡 Case Study   Xiaomi Mattress: the Best-selling Non-electronic Product in Xiaomi's Eco-chain Companies

"Mom, I wish you an extra 15 minutes of sleep every day!" This is a mattress that reflects the filial piety of children who do not live with their parents. It is four-layered so that the hardness can be easily adjusted at any time. Just a few simple words - embrace your parents by your filial piety - make Xiaomi sell more than six million mattresses a day. This is a successful case where the scene is related with brand emotions.

Source: Sina Microblog

Evian Natural Mineral Water and NongFu Spring

Figure 10-8   A bottle of Evian natural mineral water.

The Evian natural mineral water (see Figure 10-8) is sourced from a small town of France, Evian, which is backed by the Alps and facing Lake Leman, far away from pollution and human contact. With 15 years of natural filtration and mineralization in glacial sands, the Evian natural mineral water has been filled with natural, balanced and pure mineral components in the long process of natural filtration.

In France, Evian has become a trusted choice for pregnant and lactating mothers. Since Evian water source was discovered in 1789, the Evian Natural Mineral Water has been exported to 140 countries and regions around the world.

In the same way, the Chinese mineral water brand NongFu Spring expresses the natural and healthy nature of its water as well as the advantages of its pure source by boasting, "We are the porters of nature", to arouse consumers' brand associations.

The case source quoted from: Baidu Baike 2015/6/19
https://baike.baidu.com/item/%E4%BE%9D%E4%BA%91/4619925?fr=aladdin

VII. Telling stories

1.   Tell startup stories to accurate users, and use stories to impress consumers, attract fans and build brands

💡 Case Study   Ma Yun's Story of "Eighteen Arhats"

Ma Yun and his Alibaba are business legends, and the startup story of his team is glorious and full of positive energy that moves and motivates consumers.

It is said that on the fifth day of the Chinese lunar year, namely February 20, 1999, 18 men gathered to hold a mobilization meeting at 3F, Building No.16, Lakeside Garden. In this humble house with only one shabby sofa, most of them sat on the ground (see Figure 10-9), and Ma Yun stood in their midst for two hours to mobilize them to start the business with him. This is Ma Yun's story of "Eighteen Arhats". Having gone through ups and downs, this seemingly inconspicuous team becomes the hero to create the age of

Figure 10-9   Ma Yun's Story of "Eighteen Arhats"

Alibaba. "We are ordinary people and do something extraordinary together," Ma Yun said.

The case source quoted from: NetEase News 2014/09/20
http://tech.163.com/14/0920/09/A6IULT2000094ODU_all.html

2.   Make a beginning and let others tell stories

💡 Case Study   Everyone Who Yearns for Freedom has a dream of Harley

Shakespeare said, "There are a thousand Hamlets in a thousand people's eyes." This shows that the subjectivity of art acceptance stems from the different expectations of the recipients. And everyone who yearns for freedom has a dream of riding a Harley! The Harley motorcycle is also labeled freedom, independence, taste, initiative, rebellion and unruliness. Compared with the car, the motorcycle is more challenging. The motorcycle rider is brave and fearless like a medieval European knight. With the hoof beats similar to Harley, the rider rides towards us as if he were a knight riding a tall horse, which is the most attractive point of the Harley motorcycle. Although the Chinese people have not experienced the Westward Movement when cowboys carved out in the western region or the Hippie Movement in the 1960s and 1970s, the desire for freedom and independence was beyond borders. There are only a few things that can completely relax a man, and motorcycling is one of them. You cannot realize this unless you ride a motorcycle freely on the road along with the boom of the engine. Harley is grasping and magnifying the dream of yearn- ing for freedom in everyone's inner heart. Only in this way can this brand become more deeply rooted.

3. Keep a firm grasp on the most vulnerable part of the user's heart to move the user

 Case Study | 999 GANMAOLING

999 GANMAOLING released an advertising clip which was considered the "Best Ad of the Year" in 2017 and which moved the audience to tears. In this advertising clip, every scene was based on a real life experience, and every character was just like the ordinary people around you, and even like you and me. It was so real that the audience was moved so much and the most vulnerable parts of our hearts were touched. This clip showed you the coldness and helplessness of the real world first, and then gave you and the world a warm and wonderful relief. Consequently, we knew the ordinary little warmth in life, and bore in mind this advertising clip discovering and spreading the warmth together with the advertiser's brand.

VIII. Taking advantage of herd mentality in marketing

One of Ma Yun's greatest achievements is to use a "bad review" to solve the honesty problem that had existed amongst small vendors in China for thousands of years. Most of us now often refer to dianping.com before choosing a restaurant. The Internet has memories, and we should have good designs to make all customers say nice things about us.

Based on people's herd mentality, Ma Yun invented the "bad review" with which the customer could eliminate bad sellers and could effectively avoid consumption risks. Didi also adopts the mode of "good review" on its platform to effectively improve the overall service level of drivers.

IX. Selling experiences

The best way to expand in this age is the user experience for which the following points should be noticed.

1. Get customers involved

 Case Study | Customers Make Sachets by Themselves

On the ancient street of Wuzhen, a shop selling perfumes discarded its old way to spread out various perfumes for sale, and put perfumes in different small boxes named "Eternal Love", "Good Health", etc. for customers to make sachets by themselves. Such experiential interaction greatly enhanced the sense of ceremony for customers. And the price of each sachet increased from CNY 5 to CNY 30 for this experience.

2. Change from product-centered to experience-centered

Case Study | An Experience of Street Stall-style Decoration at Wangjing Xiaoyao

The decoration of Wangjing Xiaoyao tells everyone that this is a street stall without any improvement. We hope that everyone can re-experience the old style and features of Beijing. Therefore, we always say that the welcome dinner for good brothers must be given at Wangjing Xiaoyao. This is the collective memory for the generation after 1970s or 1980s. It is a process of downgraded consumption, in which the past experiences are brought back to the present but people's experiences with food and products become particularly important.

Case Study | Baby's Kitchen Sees the World with the Eyes of Kids

In the design and decoration of Baby's Kitchen, all the employees involved in decoration, design, layout and preparation were required to bend down to see things from the angle of view of a 3-, 4- or 5-year-old kid: what should it look like here? Did it look good from this angle? Was it necessary for children?

X. Smart exposure

In some cases, a powerful event exposure allows the product to spread quickly. Wang Baoqiang, a Chinese grassroots star, won sympathy of the public and made his movie "Buddies in India" a blockbuster when the extramarital affair of his wife was exposed in 2016.

XI. IPs (Intellectual Properties)

Everything that makes someone else associate with you is an intellectual property (IP), including visual sense (e.g., Hermes yellow), auditory sense (e.g., Intel's classic sound effects), sense of smell (e.g., special aroma in Shangri-La Hotel's lobby) and even brand identity (e.g., Crystal Orange Hotel's social responsibilities). IP is a brand memory and an original, sustainable and recognizable collection of value contents with unique values. Any product, service, people, space, spirit, content, slogan, logo, identity, mascot, anniversary, trade name or so on can be an IP.

XII. Good names

In China, brand names have undergone three stages of evolution. Good names of the Age 1.0 were mostly born in 1960s and 1970s, such as Huaqiang Square, China CITIC Bank and Evergrande Group; those of the Age 2.0 gradually became more fashionable, such as Rejoice and GreenTree Inn; and those of the Age 3.0 were friendly, conveying a strong sense of relevance to their categories and characterized by the form of "noun + category", such as Xiaomi, Guazi Used Cars and Three Squirrels. You may review and put into practice the six standards for brand naming as set out in Chapter 8.

XIII. Making the founder an IP

To look: it is to introduce who I am and what I can bring to the user.

To listen: it is to figure out how to spread and what to spread.

To ask: it is to interact with super users.

To feel: it is to transform the cult of personality into the loyalty to enterprises and brands.

Based on these four principles (to look, to listen, to ask and to feel), everyone should have his/her own big IP! The most typical big IP founder is Steve Jobs whose innovation, vision and ingenuity fascinate consumers. And these consumers have developed an affinity for the Apple brand represented by him and have bought the products of this brand because they like Steve Jobs. Other similar big IPs include Gabrielle Chanel and Giorgio Armani.

Case Study | Yoga Gurus Endorsed Themselves with Startup Shops all over India

In India, you can see the pictures of some extraordinary long-haired people with red dots between eyebrows and in orange or white robes on the signboards of some shops in the street. These people are the Indian yoga gurus and these shops are their startup shops. In addition to their spiritual centers throughout the world, Indian yoga gurus are associating their names with toothpaste, honey, rice and flour. They are not only cultivating followers, but also expanding their wallets.

Guru brands become IPs and need no advertising

Centering on daily cosmetic, skin care and food industries, Yoga gurus' own brands are marching towards clothes and textile trades.

Yoga Gurus Endorsed Themselves
with Startup Shops all over India.

They rely on the traditional concept of advocating nature, calling upon people to stay away from chemical products and to return to a pure and natural lifestyle. With the strong appeal of the gurus, these products have rapidly swept into the Indian market.

The low price is at play in making these products quickly take over the market: a facial cleanser for CNY 5, a lipstick for CNY 2, 250ml of honey for CNY 7, a bag of biscuits for CNY 1, a bag of instant noodles for CNY 1, 200ml of shampoo for no more than CNY 10, a bottle of tableware detergent for CNY 1, etc. These prices are favored by the low-income population in India.

Despite the fact that a large amount of promotional funds must be invested in all new brands before they enter the market, guru brands basically rely on gurus introducing the products to their followers by word-of-mouth instead of advertisements. Indian yoga gurus are so high-profile that various occasions can be their promotion meetings. Their personal websites and Facebook pages are the best free advertising spaces.

Although yoga has become a body-building movement in foreign countries, it was originally a practice of Hinduism with strong religious ideas. Therefore in India, yoga gurus are not instructors who teach people to perform some difficult twisting actions but religiously spiritual leaders. We can say that everyone relates to yoga in India.

Guru brands sell anything

Baba Ramdev is the most successful IP among several "entrepreneurial" yoga gurus. He established his own yoga institution in 1995, and appeared in a morning yoga program at a TV station in 2003. Since then, he has gained fame and won a large number of followers with his influence covering India and even the world. In 2006, he was invited by the former UN Secretary General Kofi A. Annan to deliver a speech at the United Nations. His daily necessities brand Patanjal already has more than 500 products. Since his brand was established in 2012, the turnover has increased tenfold. In the financial year of 2016-2017, the turnover exceeded INR 100 billion (CNY 1 equivalent to INR 10). According to the *Times of India*, Ramdev invested INR 400 billion in setting up an independent security company in July 2017, and employed a large number of ex-servicemen and police officers as trainers.

India's *Business Today* reported that Ramdev would launch his clothing brand in April 2018 with an expectation of INR 50 billion of sales in the first year.

The Ayurveda-based traditional herbal health brand created by another spiritual leader, Sri SriTattva, who is also known as the founder of the Art of Living Foundation, is in full swing and is expected to have 1,000 stores throughout India in the next two years. At a spiritual center of the Art of Living Foundation in Bangalore, the reporter saw a large number of customers flooding into the supermarket here as soon as it opened for business. There were a variety of products in this supermarket, ranging from Sri SriTattva's CDs and books to clothes, foods, cleaning supplies, skin care products, health care products and so on. And most of these products, e.g., shampoos and shower gels, were labeled natural and free of additives, and health care products were also made from pure plant extracts with a great diversity of categories covering eye drops and crack prevention creams. More importantly, their prices were very low. The reporter found that a blouse made of pure cotton cost CNY 40-50 only, and that foods and beverages were cheaper than those in ordinary supermarkets. No wonder this supermarket attracted so many people as soon as it opened for business. In addition, a lot of people bought products as gifts for their friends and family members.

Return to an Indian lifestyle

There are many gurus now and again, especially in this age. As the saying goes, the times produce their heroes. The deep reason behind the success of Indian yoga gurus' brands is that they have followed the policies made by Modi's government. Modi practices yoga, wears khurta and promotes "Made in India". He set up the "International Day of Yoga" and the "National Day of Ayurveda" in hopes that Indians would be free from Western influence and return to an Indian lifestyle. As analyzed by Reuters, Modi's support for India's commercial development has received wide acclaim while delivering to Hindu nationalists a message that India should be a country ruled by Hinduism and serving Hinduism.

The common grounds of these yoga gurus' brands are that they work in concert with Modi's concept, that they emphasize their products are rooted

Protein Shampoo

in the ancient Indian tradition, and that they appeal to consumers for their patriotism and consider Unilever, Colgate, Nestle and other multinationals imaginary enemies. They call upon everyone to leave his/her money in India and serve India. As Ramdev wrote in an advertisement, "These multinationals are selling harmful and hazardous chemical products to our country after East India Company had plundered our country for 200 years." As a result, these Indian guru brands cater for the consumers' desire for nature with the banner of "Green, Free of Additives and Healthy".

Yoga gurus endorse their own stores, which makes the founder an IP.

The case source quoted from: Pictures and texts from the Global Times 2018/1/8
https://baijiahao.baidu.com/s?id=1588975495253841187&wfr=spider&for=pc

XIV. Guided spread

A good spread shall have at least the following nine targets:

TO C: to make customers see, including product quality, service concept, creative innovation, public support, etc.

TO B: to make partners and distributors see and let them know our confidence and future benefits.

TO M: to make manufacturers see and try to make ourselves a leader in a particular segment.

TO T: to make talents see and let them understand our capabilities and future development.

TO A: to make the academic community see, and win some authoritative awards to drive the academic community to continuously study and spread.

TO VC: to make venture capitals see and let them believe in our performance and potential.

TO CO: to make competitors see, and continue to consolidate our position.

TO DE: to make derivative industries see and help our brand march towards a derivative field.

TO L: to make leaders see our opinions so as to facilitate the spread of our brand.

Case Study Dmallovo's True Love Studio

In the new trend of substance marketing, Dmallovo created a super IP for diamonds studio, and formed a commercial chain to spread the brand philosophy to "let love be more romantic". Based on the brand culture of spreading love, sharing love and gaining love, Dmallovo embraced the diamonds with emotions, and set up nine proposal scenes in the form of reality shows and with the scene-based service experience as an entry point, whereby consumers were placed in the nine scenes of classified characters and then network dramas that consumers loved were used to interpret the proposal culture of the nine characters. The wonderful love concept has led a good many celebrities and stars to Dmallovo's studio.

As opinion leaders, a lot of A-listers, such as Song Hye Kyo, Song Joong Ki, Chen Xiao and Michelle Chen, have invariably become the advocates of the relationship to "let love be more romantic". E-commerce-based programs, entertainment-based e-commerce and interactive entertainment connect the design to the market, fueling a new business value and an ecosystem for new retail.

XV. Consumer business

Super users establish connections with companies and brands through consumption, cultivate trust and dependence on them, and ultimately form partnerships with them in the form of benefit sharing. This is the process of turning consumers into agents.

Case Study WeChat Marketing

WeChat marketing is a marketing model developed with the lowest cost and the highest efficiency. High loyalty, strong social relation and credibility are the core elements of it. In the context that users and fans are now everything, a well-known e-commerce platform has launched a campaign called "I Endorse New Year Goods for My Hometown", encouraging users to share and display the New Year goods of their hometowns through this social platform and to transform these shared contents into stores. This campaign makes each ordinary consumer a consumer business, which is a big step towards the Internet marketing.

XVI. Free of charge

Free of charge is the most efficient way of spread and marketing.

WeChat allows everyone to use its services for free, sweeping the entire Chinese community and gaining tremendous commercial value. And similarly by offering free contents, Baidu, Douban, etc. have accumulated a huge user base and have gained huge market value.

XVII. Financial mode

Maotai is the most successful brand which is operated with financial ideas and methods. As the price increases year after year, its product has become a hard currency that can maintain and even add value.

XVIII. Speaking with data

The audience will never see any brand or product on the market in the same manner as they read theses, but enterprises should be good at communicating with the outside world with comparative data to enhance credibility.

XIX. Theme culture

It refers to the method to promote a unique culture and give brand distinctive features, such as calligraphy and painting art hotels, music hotels, lover art hotels, cat bookstores and other theme cultures.

XX. Hunger marketing

Hunger marketing refers to the marketing strategy that a supplier intentionally reduces its output in order to readjust the relation between supply and demand and creates a false impression that supply exceeds demand so as to protect the product image and maintain a higher sales price and profitability of the product. For example, people had to queue up to pre-order a Tesla, and Apple fans also queued up overnight for the release of a new Apple product.

Why is there still a long queue or a shortage of supply in today's material abundance?

The answer given by fans of these brands is "rigid demand".

We have observed that in the process of hunger marketing, vendors arouse the customers' desire to buy through a large number of advertising promotions, and then make them wait for a long time with the limited supply. Effectively stimulating and enhancing the user's desire to buy can allow vendors to increase the selling price of the product or to lay a customer base for future mass sales.

XXI. Virus–like spread

As the We Media is highly developing now, everyone may be We Media, and every topic may spread like virus. How to make good use of the We Media, and what and how to say on the We Media are concerns of each enterprise. Take advantage of the influence of higher-ups and celebrities in the industry; leverage punsters and industrial or regional influential people or contents; allow users to create and spread the public praise; and let potential customers bring traffic.

XXII. Positive energy: encouraging users in a positive way

Users need positive information and guidance. The authoritative position of a brand should be continuously consolidated in the industry to give positive encouragement and guidance to users.

Part 4

Super User

Chapter 11

Vital Few

Topics:

1. Focusing on 1%
2. Value of 1%
3. From 1% to 99%

In the traditional marketing age, users are oriented as "high/middle/low income earners", thus leading to the brand orientation of "high/middle/low end". In the mobile age, the discriminative concept about the users' income is abandoned; the users are identified by consumption participation degree according to non-economic indicators such as social achievement, education level, and occupational direction. Users in the mobile age are classified into four types: the public, the elites, the rulers, and the special group. The former three are easy to understand, while the special group refers to the consumer group with special demands: firstly, people with special need, e.g., diabetic patients and hypertensive patients; secondly, people with special circles and hobbies, e.g., the art circle and outdoor adventure circle; thirdly, buyers that are related to the consumers but are not the consumers, e.g., children buying gifts for parents and parents buying daily use articles for children. The super users in this chapter are the elites, the rulers, and the special group, through whom the consumption and concept of the public are guided. The transfer of Apple from its former niche market to the mass market owes to the guiding of the super users, the elites, the rulers, and the special group.

The difference between the four types of people lies in their cognitive gap. Several bricks on the floor will be deemed as just a heap of stones by the public, while the elites will see their composition and function, the rulers will see the skyscraper that can be built with them, and the special group their unique edges and corners and aesthetic sense. If the world is totally different in the eyes of people with different cognitions, then people with different thoughts will show different behaviors. And there are certain rules in those behaviors.

The cognitive gap between the public, the elites, the rulers, and the special group lies in the following aspects:

The people gradually live in groups. They have weak independent thinking ability and are deeply affected by education and the surroundings. Usually they trust the people around them, emphasize relationships, and take pride in privileges. They always follow the various fragmented news online which is inconsistent and filled with emotional nonsenses. They'd rather spend money on game equipment and anchorwomen than learning, thus they don't have independent thinking ability and are easily incited and utilized.

The elites are individuals. They want real benefits. Usually they trust systems and regulations more. They'd like to obey various rules and utilize their abilities on that basis. They are more rational, willing to buy books, attend lectures and trainings, and pay for knowledge. Most paid knowledge is targeted at this group. They are good at modeling and then copy and spread the model rapidly.

The rulers pursue harmony and completeness. They are good at helping others to fulfill themselves. They have macroscopic ideological patterns, fond of maximizing the benefit of a team instead of an individual. As the helmsman, they must keep the ship balanced, which is the great foundation of all innovations and changes. They will hold up the sinking society and give people positive hope no matter what happens.

The special group pursue their own demand. They usually spend the least time on consumption among all the four types, because they know their need exactly. Once they develop a sense of trust in a certain brand or product, they may rely on it for many years. So this group has the highest loyalty, including patients with chronic diseases, maverick artists, and hard-working parents. They are the representatives of tenacity and loyalty.

Focusing on 1%

Now many enterprises say that 80% of their annual advertising expenses are wasted. That indicates that more than half of the communication in their marketing work is invalid. When we focus on the 80% target customers and the 20% potential customers, shall we pay more attention to the 1% "opinion leaders"? This "minority" affects and changes the opinions and behaviors of the public.

And we also find in practice that the extraordinary influence of the 1% "opinion leaders" penetrates into the popularization and promotion process of all new products and technology.

I. Principles for Dissemination

The dissemination of some things (usually known as the "viral dissemination"①) has three common features: It is infectious; it is with small changes and obvious consequences; and, it is sudden but not gradual. Based on the analysis of the above, the three elements of setting the fashion are proposed: the law of few, the stickness factor, and the power of context.

> ①
>
> *Viral dissemination: refers to the virus-like dissemination and spreading of marketing information to thousands and millions of audience via the activeness and social network of the public.*

1. Law of Few

This law studies people's behaviors of information dissemination. There are three kinds of people who play vital roles in dissemination: mavens, connectors, and salesmen. They initiate and drive the whole process of dissemination: mavens are the database providing information for people; connectors are the adhesive spreading the information to different places; salesmen are responsible for "the last kilometer", i.e., to persuade people to receive the information.

Mavens refer to those people with rich knowledge in a certain field. As to websites, many successful website founders are mavens of this field or are able to summon the mavens. DoNews, oriented as an IT media platform, has the IT media mavens like Liu Ren and Keso; Douban couldn't be founded without Abei's accumulation of "a wall of CDs, two walls of books, and tickets of three continents"; the restaurant comments on dianping.com are closely related to Zhang Tao's interest in food... And in a comprehensive view, these websites all served mavens in the initial stage (the talents on DoNews, the bookworms on Douban, and the foodies on dianping.com), who gathered at the sites and provided the most important information for the sites, forming the databases. Maybe that can tell, to some extent, whether the site is successful or not in the initial stage.

Connectors are those people good at social relationships, who may be involved in several fields at the same time. We all know the "six degrees of separation" theory that says the average interval between any two persons in the world is six persons. But in fact, not everyone has only a distance of six persons from others; it actually means some people are less than six degrees away from other people, and most people in the world are connected through these people. For example, in the circle of IT Blogger, Keso, Laobai, Wang Jianshuo, Tongos, Che Dong, Webleon, and Hopesome are typical connectors. "When an idea or a product is closer to a connector, it's more likely to be promoted." If you want your website to be promoted among the target audience more rapidly, you should go communicate with the connectors in the field.

Salesmen are the people who can convince you. They may not be learned mavens or sociable connectors, but they can solve the problem of "the last kilometer", i.e., to persuade people to receive the

information. The viral dissemination of the information largely depends on the efforts of eloquent salesmen. Making every user your salesman may be the dream of every website.

2. Stickness Factor

The law of few reveals people's behaviors of information dissemination, while the stickness factor explains the feature of the disseminated information. Under the same conditions, the information with higher stickness factor is more likely to set the fashion. What is stickness? It's whether the people who have received the information have any impression of such information, or take any corresponding actions, and the degree of such actions.

However, the vast amount of information produced in the information age has made the stickness of the information a problem. Now let's look at some simple examples of website operation to understand the stickness.

The first degree of stickness is the impression of the audience. The simplest example is the name of the information. A good name can greatly increase the stickness of the information, e.g., PodLook, Taobao, and 265 which all doubled the effect of website development. Similarly, the communication capacity of Weblog and Podcast is definitely less than that of "Blogs" and "Boke" (the Chinese of Podcast). In this respect, dianping.com really made a detour. Its current domain name "dianping.com" is not perfect, but is much better than the initial "zsurvey.com". There are certainly many other ways to increase the stickness of information besides the name, as well as many theoretical researches in this field. The well-known Positioning[1] theory is just of this kind.

Information with high stickness not only can leave a deep impression on people, but, more importantly, can affect people's behaviors.

We all know that interactivity is a basic feature of Web 2.0. So how to increase the interaction initiative of the users by the stickness of the website is a topic worth studying. Douban has done a good job in this respect. Two of its tips are quoted below:

·Please click "Useful" or "Useless" to decide the order of these comments.

·Your Recommendations are automatically generated according to your

① *Positioning: proposed "the concept that is the most influential on American marketing"—positioning, which changed the old marketing understanding of "satisfying the need" and developed the marketing method of "winning competition".*

favorites and comments. Everyone has a different list. When you have more favorites and comments, Douban will make more accurate and diversified recommendations for you...

These kinds of tips may seem cumbrous for people fond of terse styles, but they are not. These warm and timely tips as well as the reasonable layout of information have produced the strong stickness of Douban. The users unconsciously participate in the website and then take a fancy to it. Further attracted by the stickness, they become the "salesmen" of the website, propelling the epidemic dissemination of the website.

The key of leaving a deep impression on people is the internal quality of the information. But the stickness factor tells us that good internal quality is not enough to make the information spread rapidly. Maybe a slight improvement at some negligible places can make your information irresistible.

3. Power of Context

In the smart ancient description of "Favorable climatic, geographical and human conditions", we know that we've never ignored the power of context.

The "Broken Windows Theory" explains the influence of specific situations on people, and then on information dissemination. Its core lies in "Crimes are the inevitable results of disorder". People are used to explaining things with their internal features, ignoring the role of the specific situation, e.g., "The cut-in angle of this website is more beneficial to communication" and "The service of this website can better motivate interaction than that website". But human behaviors are the results of the social environment. The external environment, instead of the nature of the things, determines our mentality.

II. Taking the 1% "Few"

The microblog economy has been transferring from the "few" to the "public".

Microblogs have long been the latest carrier of comments and opinions of some high-end people, and the opinions of such people with certain "right of speech" are having increasing influence. Such influence has come to the attention of some clever manufacturers who have turned to microblog marketing.

It is reported that some wine company cooperated with a professional microblog communication platform to have organized a large-scale free trial of new wine products among the red wine lovers on microblogs. The company sent its wine to the bloggers who posted their feelings and evaluations about the product after tasting it, which rapidly boomed the evaluation on that kind of wine in the microblog circle.

According to the responsible person of the company, that incident has brought them the following benefits:

The relevant items of the company at Google search increased from 500 to more than 20,000 within two months. In these two months, "there might be about 300,000 people getting to know the company through microblogs". The company has been publicized and promoted, which has created invisible incomes.

Their sales volume of wine has doubled, which is a great real income. The reason for the above effect is not simple. According to an online "advertising credibility" survey from the China Consumers Association, 70% of netizens don't trust commercial ads. That doubt about the advertising credibility directly led to the prosperity of various experience exchange platforms. Young people tend to exchange experience with many users online before buying some commodity. The relatively high-end orientation, word-of-mouth dissemination, and individual experience, feelings and evaluations about the relevant product, service or hot spot all satisfy people's demand—the "emptiness" resulted from the misleading commercial ads has just been utilized by microblog marketing. Microblog marketing emphasizes accurate interaction, intention, and identification. And by means of microblog marketing, the manufacturers aim to bring marketing back to its word-of-mouth nature. They emphasize interactive communication, influencing the public by the few, and transferring the numerical success of the dissemination to the quality. When the effect of mass communication keeps reducing, seizing the 1% "few" will achieve unexpected communication effect.

1. The Mobile Internet Is Redefining the "Few"

Speaking of the few, the mobile Internet has brought great changes to "people".

The diversified scenes of consumption, communication, and life directly lead to diversified personalities. We can say that everyone living in the mobile Internet age has real fragmented personalities and plays fragmented social roles.

And these personalities and roles can realize seamless connection in time and space, which leads to the fragmentation of the emotional and consumption demands of people. Everyone will have more and more vertical behaviors (personalities) within limited time—such hobbies as jogging, mountain climbing, travelling, writing, public welfare, and lecturing may all take place in "me" and "I" may get more and more involved, professional and strict to myself in every aspect.

In a jogging team, if everyone else wears NIKE, "I" would want a pair of NB; if everyone else uses Codoon, I would use KEEP. Then the personalized behavior of taking part in a jogging team will be re-personalized again and again for infinite times, finally realizing the purpose of "I am what I am". Now, I'm not sure whether you have realized that when talking about the "few" today, you need to no longer satisfy "the demands of a few people", but to satisfy "a few demands of people". Maybe you'll ask, "Is there any difference? Isn't it just a game of words?"

Of course not. There's not only a difference, but also a big difference. For example, the demands of a few people may easily lead to products like "Fixed Gear"[1] bicycles, while a few demands of people may make every bicycle be equipped with the experience of "Fixed Gear". The former is vertical, and the latter is transverse. The former may shrink, but the latter may produce popularized niche products.

It gives us the enlightenment that the niche products in the future should never pursue the "few" of the audience, but the "few" of scenes, because the users are getting flatter and everyone has thousands of "niche" demands waiting to be expressed in a greater style.

2. "Few" Has Become the Core Product Power of This Age

In recent years, more and more niche products have been popularized, and more and more public products have begun to pursue the "few".

NB is one of the former. You'll find that its sneakers chased after by a few upper-class people in the past have become the "sneakers on the street" now. Why? Because everyone desires an extreme and personalized expression of himself. So the best product can satisfy the personalized demand of every user. Each user can find himself and a "niche" sense of honor when perceiving, consuming, and experiencing the product.

In this sense, the "few" has become the new core competence of every product. The core substance of the so-called tiny times is also the "few".

Steve Jobs endowed Apple with the culture of "few". Though Apple is so popular, he still makes every user feel "honored" and "personalized".

Coca Cola is one of the latter. The innovation of Coca Cola that is the easiest to be ignored in recent years is its packaging. From the buzzwords last year to the popular lyrics used this year, Coca Cola provides the users with the possibility of being the "few" to the maximum while keeping its maximum large-scale productivity.

When a girl walks out of the convenience store with a Coca Cola bottle written with "Sad people shouldn't listen to slow songs" of Mayday, I can more or less see her stories. That's why she chooses that package—to let you see "my" heart, feel "my" difference, and even have some sympathy for "me" by some means.

And by doing this, Coca Cola delivers another important message, i.e., the so-called "few" and "style", mainly in front of the acquaintances of the user, such as colleagues, beauties, leaders, friends, and customers, instead of a stranger. On that premise, any "few" can be copied for numerous times on one person, which provides the possibility of the popularization and commercialization of the niche product.

In the mobile Internet age, this kind of "few" is what the current products should aim for.

III. "Immeasurable" Value of the Super User

The "Beauty Talk" community of Sephora[2] is an online exchange forum for users. A netizen called "katie1724" is almost a member of the "Hall of Fame" here. She has given over 4,000 "hearts" (equivalent to the "likes" of Facebook), and posts and replies to messages for 5-10 times every day.

She gives her opinions on everything about the brand, from the shade of blusher to the benefits of seasonal creams.

① *Fixed Gear: also known as "Fixie Bike" or fixed-gear bicycle, is a kind of bicycle without one-way free wheels, whose wheels and pedals are always linked. That is to say, the rear flywheel is fixed on the hub, unable to rotate, and is connected to the crankset by the chain; the force on the pedals will be exerted on the rear wheel after magnification via the gear ratio, making the pedals unable to keep motionless during sliding.*

② *Sephora joined the global luxury brand company LVMH in 1997, owning 1,665 stores in 21 countries around the world. It provides comprehensive product choices in the stores: skin care, beauty products, and perfumes; it has selected prestigious cosmetic brands and the latest products, such as the microbubble technique, as well as the exclusive Sephora Chinese brands.*

The real name of "katie1724" is Katie Magilskiy, a 32-year-old legislative assistant in Pittsburgh who loves all the products of Sephora. She began to use the Sephora products when living in France (Sephora was founded in 1970 in France), and then she began to use the online community of Sephora as a creative social tool. She spends approximately USD $100 buying Sephora products every month. But those "super users" like Katie come to the attention of their favorite brands not because of their money.

Quite a few enterprises are using their die-hard users to create value for them. Some most active consumers can bring extraordinary reputation influence and brand communication for the enterprises, which cannot be achieved even by the enterprise employees. These super users answer product-related questions, post insightful blogs, and even provide valuable market and product feedbacks for enterprises—without charge. Brigitte Dolan, Executive Vice President of Interactive Media of Sephora, said, "We used to have a section called 'unsolved mysteries'. But we had to change that section, because our super users take answering the questions there as a personal challenge, and they give answers really fast."

The senior management of LEGO is also collecting creative ideas for their products by their online community. There's also another LEGO community exclusively for younger users. In that community, a user called "JayZX535" stays online for 3.5 hours on average every day. From last November to this April, he read over 68,000 posts online. More importantly, he has posted and replied to over 1,200 messages, providing fresh contents for the community every day. According to Mark Fordkil, the responsible person of the LEGO children community, this website has 10,000 to 12,000 active members every month, about 1% of which meet the definition of "super user".

Sony hadn't opened its online user community until November 2015, but it had already been communicating with the users via Facebook in the previous years. In 2009, a group of disgruntled customers opened a Facebook page titled "There's Something Wrong with My Sony TV", and the senior management of Sony responded promptly. The person who opened that page is Bill Giedretis, 53 years old. He opened that page in a rage when his TV broke down. He said, "At first I thought I would receive a lawyer's letter from Sony, but then I got their call saying that their new president wanted to talk with me. I was startled." That conversation with the senior management turned Bill from an angry customer to a super user. Now he logs in the Facebook page for several times every day to answer other consumers' questions and calm them down. When the page got popular, there might have been more than 10,000 members complaining about Sony on it every day, and the "fireman" of Sony has almost been the second job of Bill. But the difference is, just like he said, "I don't take money from Sony for that".

Rob Tarkoff, CEO of Lithium Technologies, pointed out that the super users like Katie and Bill not only can provide loyal service for their favorite brands, but also have the credibility incomparable by the enterprise employees. He said, "Traditional CEOs or managers may say, 'We can hire those people directly.' But once they are hired by you, their relations with other people in the community will change. They'll become marketers." According to the research of Forrester in 2012, 46% of people trust the evaluation articles written by consumers more, and only 15% believe in the social media articles directly published by the brands. Although that may not be a strong power in the business world, it still grants remarkable rights to the super users. Peter Szijjarto said that the value of super users is "immeasurable".

 **Case Study** Century-old Harley: How to Make All Generations Super Users

As the global top-class leisure motorcycle brand, Harley-Davidson Motor is the epitome of the American brand development history since 1903. For a century, Harley-Davidson has always been the representative for the freeway, the original motive, and the good time. The image of Harley-Davidson motorcycles has taken root in the heart of every motorcycle fan in the world. The fans are crazily loyal to the V-type double-cylinder-driven motorcycle and its manufacturer.

In 1983, the company set up the Harley Owners Group (HOG) as its brand community which gathered the fans. Today, HOG has expanded to 115 countries, with over 800,000 members, as well as thousands of

Harley-Davidson Motor. Source: the official website of Harley-Davidson Motor

loyal fans in China. The loyal users of HOG are mostly young and middle-aged men with high consumption power. For them, HOG is a way of existence.

The first Harley-Davidson motorcycle was born in 1903. According to records, it was assembled by William Harley and Arthur Davidson with farraginous parts in a work shed in Milwaukee, Wisconsin. When these young men were sweating in the shed, they might have dreamed about being millionaires, but never could they bind Harley-Davidson with the American spirit.

But things changed during WWII. The heroes of the American people were Macarthur, Eisenhower, Barton, as well as a group of pilots in the movie, who were desperados riding around on motorcycles. At the other end of their road were air duels, death, and medals.

American pilots laid the foundation for the motorcycle culture. Besides the deafening motor, Harley riders also need the black leather jackets which are exclusive to the pilots. The profound influence can also be seen from the motorcycle clubs emerging after the war. "Hell's Angels" is a typical case of them.

Olson recalled that the words "Hell's Angels" gave him a great inspiration for his MC (short for the "motorcycle club"). He inherited the name and even plagiarized the "Hell's Angels" symbol of SDU (red letters on the white background) as his own club logo which must be sewn on the back of the black leather jacket. With the rise of MCs, there has been an extremely American scene: in the sunset, with engine roars, dense smoke, and a scorched smell of tires, a group of strong men in black leather jackets are riding up rapidly on Harley-Davidson motorcycles from the horizon, expressionless and somehow proud. The leading macho character is called Marlon Brando.

The Wild One is a movie based on an actual event in 1947 called "Hollister Riot". During the National Day activity in a small town of California, the annual "Gypsy Parade" sponsored by American Motorcyclist Association (AMA) was held. 4,000 motorcyclists swarmed in across the nation, turning the scene into an uncontrollable riot of beating, smashing and looting.

Afterwards, AMA claimed that "99% of the motorcyclists are law-abiding citizens; only 1% of them are rioters". That directly led to the new term in English—"the one percent", referring to those antisocial motorcyclists and motorcycle clubs. It is strange that *The Wild One* was imitating the pilots and many of those imitators were demobilized soldiers, but why would those battle heroes harm the country they just protected with their life? We can only say that the crueler and more exciting the war is, the more boring the peace will be. The psychological gap made it hard for those heroes to fit in the normal life and brought them to the bottom of society. Just like one of them said, "We just love showing off, so we make a big noise and everybody would look at us."

The case source quoted from: China Marketing 2013/10/17
http://www.cmmo.cn/article-166110-1.html

Value of 1%

I. What Is Value?

According to the One Degree Theory, for the enterprise, value is a kind of profitability expressed by the premium[①] way, as well as the social responsibility and obligation borne by the enterprise. For the consumers, value is their assessed value in monetary form of the product of the enterprise, and their satisfaction degree of cultural and psychological demands besides the functional demand for the product. For the channel distributors of the enterprise, value is a kind of competitiveness of the market terminal, the guarantee for the profit margin and rate of return of a single store, a single counter, and a single product. For the suppliers, partners, or other industry-related third parties, value is the best way of jointly increasing the profitability or reducing the cost by mutual value creating.

①

Premium: the actually paid amount exceeds the nominal value or face value of the securities or shares.

By comparing the wealth addition, reduction and multiplication principles, you'll find that both addition and reduction take the price as their basic market competition mode, but the competition theory of multiplication is based on value. Value is different from price. The price is set by the factory and passively accepted by the consumers. In a competitive industry, enterprises are often forced to reduce the price to attract the consumers. So the price war is inevitable.

But value is confirmed by the consumers. What the enterprises should do is to innovate in various operation elements to satisfy the customers' value. In the same competitive industry, the enterprises and the customers form a value union sticking to the same value law; both parties take what they need, and the enterprises can maintain a higher growth rate of profitability.

The success of the luxury marketing theory in the world is based on the adherence to the value law. The marketing modes of luxury goods across the world have the following common features.

1.　Targeting the 99% Profit at the 1% People

Let the 1% people believe that they are the few elites in society, so that they can enjoy those luxury goods. And in order to show their value, they need to pay the high price that is denied by the 99% people. Those 1% social elites will believe the ad of CK underpants that says, "Confidence from inside out". They think wearing the CK underpants is the reason for their confidence in work and in life.

2.　Profitability of the Single Product and the Single Store as the Priority

The distribution channels of luxury goods pursue not the quantity, but the profitability; the product design of luxury

goods also doesn't pursue the innovation in styles, colors or packaging; instead, luxury goods have only a few product types. There are two benefits about that: firstly, the R&D expenditure and the inventory pressure of the channel distributors and agents are saved; secondly, a hint can be given to the consumers by raising the price year by year: the luxury good you buy will never reduce in value. For example, the No. 1 watch in the world, Patek Philippe, suggests to its customers, "Patek Philippe is not for you. It's for your next generation."

What is Value?

3.　Allying with the Third Party for Common Appreciation of the Brand Value

Why are the luxury goods always in five-star hotels or deluxe shopping malls? Don't they know that there are more people in the wholesale markets or supermarkets? Because these brands are helping each other to stick to the premium ability together (See above figure). Why do the luxury goods seldom give discounts? Why don't they provide gifts or promotions? Why would you still believe the famous Swiss watch is worth its price when the salesperson tells you that "It's normal for a famous watch to have 3-minute deviation every day"? The author doesn't mean to encourage all the middle- and small-sized Chinese enterprises to sell luxury goods, but wants to summarize some ways and rules from the operation theories of the luxury goods to get rid of the price war.

Wealth multiplication = (customer + product + brand + channel) x value

II. Effectively Distinguishing Product Value and Customer Value

Marketing professor Zhang Mingli of the College of Economics and Management of Beijing University of Aeronautics and Astronautics has distinguished the product value and customer value. The customer value is converted from the product value. Despite the customer cost, even if the measuring unit is the same, the product value is not necessarily equal to the customer value, or not all the product value can definitely be converted to the customer value. There is a difference between the two. Similarly, the product price is not necessarily equal to the customer cost, or not all the customer cost can definitely be converted to the product price. There is a difference in between, too.

1. The reason for the difference between customer value and product value

The amount of the customer value[1] depends on the satisfaction degree of the customer demand, relying on the subjective feeling of the customer. But the product value is not so; it is determined by the objective attributes of the product, i.e., the actual product and augmented product produced centering on the core product, including the quality, features, design, brand, packaging, and additional services. For example, the product value of a TV set is mainly to receive television signals and transform them into image and acoustical signals, which is determined by the circuit structure of the TV set. But the customer value is determined neither by the circuit structure nor the television signals; it is the satisfaction degree of the customer demand, the degree of satisfying the customer demand by using the TV set, e.g., making the customer relaxed and pleased with entertainment programs and enabling the customer to learn with educational programs. The same TV set has the same product value, but different people may get different customer values when using the TV set. Let's look at an extreme example. Let's say there are two areas, A and B; A doesn't have any TV signal while B has diversified TV programs; when a TV set is used in A, the customer value would be zero, for the customer's demand of watching TV can't be satisfied without TV sig-

nals; but when the TV set is moved to B, the customer can get relatively high customer value, because there are diversified programs. It is the same TV set, with the same objective attributes, so the product value will not change; but the customer values differ drastically for customers of different areas.

2. The product value conversion rate

The acquisition of customer value still relies on the product value, but it is not equal to the product value. The value the customer acquires from the product and the value the product can provide may be consistent or inconsistent. Let's presume that the customer cost is zero. In most cases, the product value is higher than the customer value. Now the customer's demand is satisfied by consuming the product, but he doesn't give full play to the product. The product doesn't satisfy the other demands of the customer yet, but the customer doesn't know it. For example, the customer has bought a computer, but is only using the powerful computer as a typewriter or a game machine due to his lack of computer knowledge; now the product value is higher than the customer value. Sometimes the product value may be equal to the customer value; at that time, the product value is all given play to and satisfies the customer demand. For example, when the customer has bought a proper amount of drink, the product value will all convert to the customer value. The customer value equals the product of product value multiplied by product value conversion rate minus customer cost.

The product value conversion rate means the amount of product value converted to customer value, the value of which is between 0 and 1. It can be seen that when the product value is the same, the higher the product value conversion rate, the higher the customer value; the lower the product value conversion rate, the lower the customer value.

Customer value = product value x product value conversion rate – customer cost

---

3. The reason for the difference between customer cost and product price

The customer cost refers to the money, time, and energy, etc. paid for the

product that satisfies his demand. It has many aspects and is continuous. Its aspects include not only the monetary cost, but also time cost, and energy cost, etc. Its continuity means that the customer cost is

---

[1] Customer value: the benefits the supplier can provide for its customer by taking part in the production and operation activities in some way, i.e., the balance between the benefits the customer receives through buying the commodity and the cost paid by the customer (purchase cost and post-purchase cost). The enterprise can investigate the customer value from the aspects of potential customer value, perceived value, and actually realized customer value.

throughout the whole consumption cycle of the product; the customer may pay the cost in every stage of the consumption cycle. The product price is included in the customer cost. The customer cost can never be less than the product price, because the product price is only the monetary amount the customer pays at the purchase stage, but he will still pay other costs like time and energy in other stages of the consumption cycle. Even the monetary cost may include other aspects than just the product price. For example, the customer is going to buy a car; then besides the price of the car, he will also pay 17% value-added tax, 3%-8% consumption tax, additional tax, urban construction tax, insurance tax, the license fee, and sanitation fees, etc., totaling tens of thousands yuan, upon the purchase. In most cases, the product price is the biggest part of the customer cost. Sometimes, in the whole consumption cycle, the customer only needs to pay the product price, without any other cost; then the product price is the customer cost.

4. Product price share

The formula in Figure 11-1 shows the relation between the customer cost and product price. The customer cost equals the ratio of product price to product price share. Let's assume that all the costs paid by the customer in the whole product consumption cycle can be converted in a monetary form; then the proportion of the product price in the total monetary amount is the product price share, which is between 0 and 1. A higher product price share means that the customer has paid less cost in addition to the product price. When the product price share is 1, it means that the customer has paid the maximum cost in addition to the product price; when the share is 0, it means that the product price is not included in the customer cost, and now the product price is 0, e.g., some trial products for feedback.

Customer cost = product price + product price share

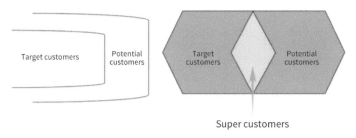

Super customers

Figure 11-1   Comparison of traditional customers and modern customers.

5. The attributes or core propositions of the product (or service)

When the attributes or core propositions of the product (or service) conform to the core values of the customer, he will express his approval in a way measured by money beyond the product or service value. Several key words need to be made clear here.

Why isn't it the attributes or core propositions of the brand, but the product (or service)? In the optional new theoretical customer value models of the new period, the brand of the enterprise is not the total elements that stimulate or conform to the core values of the customer, or we cannot explain the existence of the customization manual workshops in such big cities as Beijing and Shanghai for hundreds of years. Some enterprises don't have any brand logo and can't have chains or franchises, but they have strong premium ability and never lack long-term users.

More importantly, you can never create a large enterprise with premium ability without brand building. In order to give a more comprehensive and accurate definition to customer value, a method suitable for all enterprises is adopted in this book—to begin with the attributes or core propositions of the product (or service).

6. Customer value is not equal to product (or service) value, but is more than product value

That's because the product (or service) value is based on the product functions and service convenience, but the customer value is not like that. For example, if analyzed by the value provided by product functions, a more expensive watch should be more accurate, but the famous mechanical Swiss watch has deviations every day. A man bought an IWC watch which has a deviation of over three minutes every day, but he has forgiven that deviation and has developed a value law that the more expensive the watch, the greater the deviation, and that a watch without deviation is not a good watch.

Moreover, the convenience is the basic value of product service, but the service of world-class luxury goods is seldom convenient. They have only a few distribution channels and exclusive stores; this is not convenient at all, but people just go after them. The product value and service standard of Mercedes-Benz are first-class in the world, but its value in the eyes of most Chinese people is the symbol of "upstarts". It's obvious that it should rebuild its brand value in the heart of the customers.

The openness of the information age and the diversity of consumption choices have made polarization possible between the customers and the product or service. On the one hand, the customers have higher randomness and diversity in purchase; in most cases, they emphasize experiencing changes instead of consumption loyalty, though they may pay higher costs for that.

On the other hand, more and more customers have joined the group of brand worshippers. They not only are loyal to a certain product, service, or brand, but also enthusiastically encourage and even pay for others to buy their favorite product. The difference between brand worshippers and brand loyalists is the long-term irrational consumption of the former. The marketing principle of year-by-year price rise of luxury goods is just based on that they believe their super worshippers are not sensitive to the price, but to whether they are sticking to their value law.

As shown in the following figure, the space of loyal purchase is shrinking between random purchase and worshipful purchase; the polarization is more and more serious.

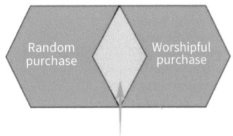

Loyal purchase of super users

The loyal purchase of customers.

	Customer Satisfaction	Customer Value
Paradigmatic connotation	The customer's reactions or feelings, i.e., the comparison between the actual performance and the standard of the product	The customer wants more things from the product or service
Object of evaluation	The evaluation on specific product, service, or supplier	The evaluation independent of any specific product, service or supplier
Subject of evaluation	The customers of the enterprise	The customers of the enterprise, the competitors, or the third parties
Content of evaluation	Comparison of enterprise performance	The comparison of enterprise performance or competitors' performance
Basis of evaluation	Empirical, e.g., "Am I satisfied?", focusing on "looking backward"	Perception of differences, e.g., "Which supplier will I choose?", focusing on "looking forward", or "What if I don't choose?"
Content of action	Customer service	Exclusive marketing theories
Type of action	Strategic, focusing on continuously improving customer service and correcting deficiencies and mistakes	Theoretical, focusing on proposing and performing the customer value propositions and creating differentiated value that excels the competitors
Change of data	Static, reflecting the past efforts	Dynamic, reflecting the efforts of the competitors
Orientation of data	Prone to past-oriented: the judgment developed during or after the product (service) consumption	Shown as future-oriented, independent of the time of use and consumption of the product
Application of data	Provide a report for the enterprises: about their performance during value creating	Guide the enterprises: what should they do to create value, from the theoretical perspective

Customer value is not equal to product (or service) value, but is more than product value. Source: Woosii Research

Arranging the Aircraft Cabin according to the Super User Principle

Nowadays, the cabins of most airlines are divided into the first class, business class, and economy class. Though the economy class seats account for the largest proportion, the airlines are not earning incomes by the economy tickets. Traditional airlines make money via the business class.

Let's take Boeing 777 of British Airways as an example. This aircraft has 224 seats and flies the London-Washington line every day. If all the tickets are sold out, the total sale of all the 122 economy seats is USD $106,872. Meanwhile, the total sale of the super economy class is USD $105,320. We can see that the sale of the 40 super economy seats is almost the same as that of the 122 economy seats.

Again, the business class has 48 seats, with a sale of USD $322,704, and the 14 first-class seats have a sale of USD $122,010. In comparison, the 14 first-class seats in the front of the aircraft bring the revenue of over USD $120,000 for the company, more than the total sale of the 122 economy seats.

According to the analysis, the total sale of the super economy class, business class, and first class of this Boeing 777 is USD $550,034. In the total revenue of the flight, the 45% passengers have paid the 84% revenue.

Except for non-stop flights across the Atlantic, most airlines adopt transfers for flights over six hours.

For example, the passengers can depart from Stockholm, Sweden, transfer in London, and then fly to Washington. In this flight, although the tickets are cheaper than those of non-stop flights, the percentage of the total revenue is similar to that of non-stop flights, i.e., most of the revenue comes from the few super users.

In fact, there were no classes in earlier business aviation; all the seats were business type, and the only difference was whether the passenger would sit in the front or in the back. And in those years, planes represented a luxury experience and high cost, just like space travel today. In 1950, the air ticket from Washington to London cost USD $675, about USD $6,800 of today, which is equivalent to a first-class ticket.

Airlines have always been reducing the cost to let more people be able to afford air travel. In 1952, some airlines executed the market strategy of differential fare. The ticket from New York to London cost USD $395 for business super users and USD $270 for travelling users. The same route, the same plane, but different ticket prices. The travel ticket must be bought in advance, without any flexibility, while the full price ticket could be bought at any time and was available for flight change.

The principle is obvious. Travelling users have relatively fixed plans and few temporary cancellations, so cheap tickets are more attractive to them. But the super users of the business class don't care about the ticket price; they favor the flexibility of time arrangement, for they may go to the airport to buy a ticket one hour before departure. Through this system, the airlines can orient different passenger groups to different markets according to their demands.

Afterwards, three events taking place between 1969 and 1978 thoroughly changed the development of modern aviation industry. Boeing 747 was put into operation, the Concorde took its maiden flight, the American Aviation Authority revoked the air traffic control and the government stopped intervening in air traffic services. Boeing 747 and Concorde provided a more comfortable flying experience, and the change of rights and liabilities of the American Aviation Authority gave greater independence to the airlines.

At first, the cabins were simply divided into the first class and economy class. The full-price-ticket passengers sat in the front rows, and the discount-ticket passengers sat in the back. Afterwards, the airlines redesigned the first-class cabin and added comfortable and capacious seats, providing differentiated services for the full-price-ticket users.

It must be mentioned that in the 1970s and 1980s, in order to avoid competition with the Concorde, most of the traditional airlines reduced their first-class seats and arranged more economy seats and business seats.

Though the Concorde has retired and some airlines have added their first-class seats, the influence of Concorde still exists to some extent. Among the numerous transoceanic airlines, only six have first-class cabins. We can see that the first-class cabin has quit the stage.

We know that, compared with the economy class, the business class provides more capacious seat space and better service, but the differences between the business class and the first-class of some airlines are only the slightly expanded space and food of different flavors. If there aren't essential differences in the flying experience, there will be few users buying the expensive first-class tickets. Meanwhile, the management cost for the first class cabin is huge. That's why more and more airlines have canceled their first class and arranged more business seats. After all, in most air routes around the world, first class cannot be completely full every time. And the economy class is only meant for filling the plane.

The case source quoted from: hangkwd 2017/11/15
http://www.360doc.com/content/17/1115/17/30525389_704105161.shtml

1 / 9 / 90

(Super users) (Associated users) (Ordinary users)

The 1990 Rule

The 1990 rule means that the emergence of a fashionable thing must be firstly led by the 1% super users; once the fashion is set, it will drive the surrounding 9% associated people to join the group, and the rest 90% public will gradually pay attention to it. The crucial part of the 1990 Rule is the 1% that can set the trend, who will influence the 9%, and then the 90%.

The vertical field follows the 1990 Operating Rule.

In the age of the mobile Internet, both enterprises and individuals need the ability of understanding and empathy, as the saying goes, "Know the enemy and know yourself, and you can fight a hundred battles without defeat."

In the Internet culture, the 1% rule is the No. 1 rule of Internet community participation. It says that only 1% of the users actively create new contents for the website, while the rest 99% are all lurkers.

One of its variants is the "90:9:1 rule" (sometimes shown as 89:10:1). It describes that in a cooperative website like Wiki, 90% of the community participants just browse the contents, 9% edit the contents, and only 1% actively create new contents.

These two rules can be compared with similar rules in the known information science, such as the 80/20 rule which is also called Pareto Theory meaning that 20% of people in an organization will produce 80% of the vitality, but the vitality can be defined.

I. Features of Super Users

The super user refers to the general values, behavior patterns, and corresponding cultural phenomena shown by the user groups. It takes the abnormal consuming behaviors of the super users as the basis, and the communities as the carrier. It's a subculture different from the mainstream or official culture of society.

According to the research of scholars, the super user culture has at least the following three features.

1. Participation

Deep participation is an important manifestation of the consuming behaviors of fans, so participation is the primary feature of fan culture. Jenkins analyzed the participation culture of TV fans in the book Text Plagiarism. He pointed out that the users of cultural products don't just read or watch; they'd also like to adapt or recreate the original text as they like, thus "producing" their own cultural products which are communicated on the Internet. According to Kozinets's research on the fan community of The X-Files, super users are not watching the play passively; they interact with the play by deep participation—they spontaneously develop professional appreciation standards for the play, including whether the story is reasonable, the pictures are aesthetic, and the perform-

ers are suitable or not. In this way, they develop the unique taste of a group. The super users also bring the elements in the play (including pictures, signs, and classical lines) into their daily life to show their identity of a user. In a word, the deep participation of super users not only brings them closer to their favorite products, but also lets them create their own special meanings.

2. Worship

Worship is users' extreme expression of their love for something, and the worship culture has permeated into the quasi-religious features of the super user communities, including the worship to cultural products, brands of consumer goods, sports clubs, and celebrities. The fans hereof can be called super users. For example, Barbas pointed out through his study on the Hollywood fans that Hollywood is the dream factory of its fans, and the worship culture of the fans is an important part of the Hollywood culture. These super users strongly worship the personalities of the movie stars. They actively imitate the way of dressing, dietary mode, and articles of daily use of their idols, and hope to get as close as possible to the "ideal self" in this way. Another example is the overnight queuing of Apple fans to buy the newly released products. This crazy pursuit of new products is also a reflection of the worship culture.

3. Sociality

Many studies have shown that super users have close contact with each other in the communities. They support and help each other as loyal partners. As they are relatively influential, their communities would be important reference groups for individual lives. Geraghty has found that the super users have a relation network for mutual support. They communicate with each other via e-mails, etc. and share their life experiences. They even turn to the other users, instead of their friends, family members or doctors, for consultation and relevant suggestions.

Furthermore, Baym has studied the communication practice of soap opera fans in the network communities: they often post the soap-opera-related information, speculate the story line, criticize, and even rewrite the story. Baym has found that this kind of free communication and discussion actually immensely increases the sense of joy and the meaning of watching the soap opera; community communication has become an important way for the super users to express themselves, show their talents and gain the recognition from others.

II. Types of Super Users

In the first place, we need to understand that the so-called KOLs (Key Opinion Leaders) are divided into three types.

1. Highly Related Real Users

These opinion leaders can't be bought with money. Since they are real users, they may not advertise your product for money. On the contrary, if they really like your brand or product, they may speak for you when you sponsor them. And that would be the most real and the most reliable voice. Strategically, we should know how to match the key words of the brand with the atlases of these real users, so that we will know whether they identify with the product and like the brand.

2. Big Grassroots Accounts

These are not opinion leaders at all; they are big marketing accounts that claim to have large numbers of fans (many of which are fake), and their dissemination ability and fan clubs are not "big". But if you pay or even write your own articles, they would be very happy to earn the money by a simple repost. That will also solve your problem of the "repost" key performance indicator (KPI), which is a win-win situation. But if they are only slick talkers, the effect would be limited. And the brands that rely on these accounts for their KPI will only be cheating themselves. You'll find that in the execution of the opinion leader strategy, to look for, contact, and communicate with these accounts is not the hardest part; the most difficult part is to help them write natural ads, to manage the release time, repost time, and propagation paths of these ads so that the life cycle of the information can continue, and then to follow and report the results for later improvement. The second part of the work is the most valuable and, at the same time, easy to be ignored.

However, people of the marketing industry in other countries don't call them "opinion leaders", and they don't have the concept of "big marketing account". These people are collectively called "social influencers"; and what they do is seriously and professionally called "influence marketing" in the academic field. It's not the simple "repost upon payment" as we deem it. Since 2015, there even have been companies specialized in influence marketing, which charge more than community management.

Enterprises often can't "see" the communication effects in media. Marketing will only see obvious results when it is stuck to. These "opinion leaders" are more professional and more rational than ordinary people; it is harder for us to change their "opinions", but once their opinions are changed, they will bring great fortune for the enterprise.

3. 1,000 "Super Users"

Simply speaking, the key point of "1,000 super users" is a creator, such as the artists, musicians, photographers, craftsmen, performers, animators, designers, video makers, and writers, i.e., anyone that creates artistic works, can make a living as long as he has 1,000 super users.

The "super user" here refers to those people who are willing to buy all of your works no matter what they are. They are willing to drive 200 miles to listen to you singing; they would buy your deluxe HD package even if they already have an LD version; they'll add your name to Google Alerts and follow your relevant information; they'll collect the eBay page that sells your OP works into their favorites; they'll attend your debut; they'll buy your works and ask you to sign them; they buy those T-shirts, mugs and caps related to you; they can't wait to appreciate your next work. They are the super users. According to a conservative assumption, the super users annually spend their daily salary to support you. The "daily salary" here is an average value, for the die-hard fans will surely pay much more than that. Let's also assume that each super user spends USD $100 on you every year; then if you have 1,000 super users, you will earn USD $100,000 every year, which, net of proper expenditures, is enough living for most people.

1,000 is a possible number. If you have one more fan every day, it will only take three years to go from 0 to 1,000. The super user method is feasible. Trying to please the super users is also pleasant and exciting, which can keep the artists real to themselves by receiving material rewards

and can let them focus on the uniqueness of their work which is appreciated by the super users.

The key problem is you must keep in direct touch with the 1,000 super users. And they'll support you directly. They may attend your home concert, buy your DVD online, or buy your photos on Pictopia.

You should maintain all your fans' economic support as much as possible. And you can benefit from that direct feedback and love.

The network connection technology and the small-scale manufacturing technology have made such circle possible. Blogs and RSS are spreading the news and upcoming events or new works of the creators. Your past works, résumé and relevant catalogues are demonstrated online. Diskmakers, Blurb, rapid prototyping stores, MySpace, Facebook, and the whole digital world have enabled us to easily and rapidly carry out small-batch copying and dissemination at a small cost. Now you don't have to own one million fans to create new works; 1,000 are enough.

This small group of super users is enough to support your living. On their periphery are ordinary users who may not buy all your works or pursue direct contact with you, but will buy most of your works. You can develop ordinary users while cultivating super users. Owning a new batch of super users means you've harvested more ordinary users. If it goes on like that, you may possibly have millions of super users and achieve great success.

III. Winning the Trust of Super Users with Soft Power

Soft power is making people feel comfortable. That's the top-notch soft power. A gentleman is like jade; a man who makes others comfortable is like a piece of gentle and beautiful jade. Their charisma comes from the abundance, restraint, tenderness, and goodness, showing a sense of nobility from the inside out.

Soft power can be divided into five levels: appearance, ability, temperament, character, and mentality, which are corresponding to five levels of quality: appearance, talent, personality, moral quality,

and mercy. Starting from the appearance, respecting the talent, agreeing with the personality, lasting for the moral quality, and ending with the mercy is the complete path of soft power.

For those high-level people, the purpose of work is solving problems. So no matter what the users may say, they can give a gentle response that makes people feel comfortable. This kind of people won't care who solved the problem or whether someone has acted beyond his authority, and they won't think about whether the situation has embarrassed someone or not. People of lower levels are more likely to be self-contemptuous and unconfident. Their deeply rooted inferiority will produce the compensation psychology which is a kind of "displacement".

The former earns tens of millions a year, for he's worth it. Maybe the degree of making people comfortable can be a measuring indicator. People of higher levels are more likely to respect others and understand the meaning of equality, value, human dignity, and self-cultivation contained in respect.

The feast of Li Ka-shing is a good example of making people feel comfortable. There are over 30 classmates in the CEO class of Cheung Kong Graduate School of Business (CKGSB), including famous people like Feng Lun, Jack Ma, Guo Guangchang, and Niu Gensheng. Once CKGSB took the CEO classmates to visit

well-know business magnate Li Ka-shing in Hong Kong.

When the elevator door opened, Li shook hands with every student. That was a special beginning. Then, Li gave out his business cards, and everyone grabbed a number from a plate. That number decided the table they'd be eating at and where they'd stand during photographing, which prevented misunderstanding and embarrassment.

Then the dinner began. There were four tables, each of which had an extra set of tableware. Li sat at every table each for about 15 minutes during the 1-hour dinner time. All the students were touched by his considerate and careful arrangement.

In the end, Li didn't leave. He shook hands with everybody, one by one. He even went to the waiter at the corner to shake hands with him. The whole process made everyone feel comfortable.

 **Reading Link**   How to Deal with Super Users—the Example of Pony Ma

Everybody is talking about entrepreneurship. The entrepreneurship is not imaginary; it is formed by the attitude of the entrepreneur toward everything and every person. Some people say the current achievement of Tencent is attributed to the high IQ of Pony Ma, but in fact, Ma has a higher EQ. He's a talent in dealing with people, and that's the main reason for Tencent's stable competence and continuous rapid development.

How Pony Ma Treats His Partners

There was a time when Tencent had an important strategy conference. Ma attached great importance to that conference and he invited Richard Liu, Michael Yao, and Wang Xing. The conference was to begin at 10:00 a.m. Ma arrived at the VIP room at 9:30 a.m. As a rule, the guests should arrive early to communicate with the host first. But at 9:40, Liu and Wang were still not there, except for Yao.

Then all the staff got worried, but Ma didn't show any anxiety. Liu and Wang didn't appear at 9:50. The Tencent staff were so worried that they kept contacting the assistants of the two guests. Ma still didn't have any anxious expression, and even didn't ask where they were.

The two guests still didn't arrive at 9:55 when they must enter the venue. The assistant told Ma that

Liu and Wang said they would directly go to the venue, instead of the VIP room. Ma slightly nodded upon that message and still didn't have any unhappy expression.

An important release event of an enterprise is like a family feast; if the guests don't come or come late, the host will feel disgraced. So many of such hosts will get nervous, anxious and even angry like ants on a hot pan. But Ma didn't.

There is a book titled *Detail Is the Key of Success* that talks about how Chinese people sometimes pay too much attention to details, but we should have a broader mental pattern when dealing with people.

Crystal clear water feeds no fish; extremely strict people have no friend. If you have too high a requirement for your partners, you'll lose them. This teaches us to grasp the principal contradiction of things instead of focusing on the secondary contradiction. For Pony Ma, as long as Liu and Wang come and clearly express their opinions, nothing else matters.

Ma is clear about what he wants and doesn't want with the partners. That's one of the major reasons why so many enterprises want to be linked with Tencent.

How Pony Ma Pays the Senior Management

If Tencent is not a listed company, we may never know how generous Ma is to his senior management.

The annual report shows that a senior executive may probably get HKD 274 million a year. It's not a million, ten millions, or a hundred millions. It's nearly three hundred millions! Is there any other chairman of Chinese enterprises doing like that? More unexpectedly, Ma's annual salary is only CNY 32,828,000, which is one ninth of that of the senior executive.

Why would people like to be the head of an enterprise? Because in most enterprises, the head has the highest salary, which decreases from top to bottom progressively. But Pony Ma overturns that rule, and that's his broad mental pattern. There won't be any senior executive who's not willing to die for such a generous chairman!

As the saying goes, "People follow the example of their superiors." With such a superior, how would the senior management pay their employees? Ma and his team are never mean in terms of paying their excellent employees. The employees of Tencent have the strongest sense of gain. That's why they are extremely loyal, with the lowest talent outflow. As the employee of Tencent, the only thing you should do is accomplishing your own work; you don't have to think about your benefits, for they will flow to you like running water.

The competitiveness of such an enterprise is dreadful!

What is money? Money is a tool that helps you fulfill your dream.

Pony Ma's dream is to make Tencent a respectable company, and money is only his tool.

Why have some enterprises stopped developing or even declined when they came to a certain stage? Because the head of the enterprise didn't upgrade his perception about money and still regards money as his target like he did in the initial stage of his enterprise. Many bosses are always thinking about employing the best workers with the least money and taking advantage of their employees. In fact, a clever boss must let the employees feel like they are taking advantage of the company.

Some people like to take their money with them, while others spend their money on themselves or others. There's a difference of cognitive pattern in between. An entrepreneur that can't retain his employees with money or buy wisdom or management ideas with money will never build a great company.

Produce Wisdom with Brain and Create Culture with Heart

The first workday after a long vacation, the employees of many enterprises are not willing to go to work, i.e., the post-holiday syndrome. But the employees of Tencent all come very early, because they know they will see Pony Ma today who will greet everyone he meets and give large red packets.

The scene of Tencent employees queuing for red packets can be called spectacular. There are people queuing at dawn, and the queue reaches thousands of people at 9:00 a.m.

When Tencent was founded in 1998, Ma set the rule of kick-off red packets, and he would hand them out them all by himself. Though the amount is not big, it shows the boss's respect and good wishes to the employees. And WeChat red packet was just inspired by the corporate culture of Ma's kick-off red packets. That persistence has not only turned the post-holiday workday into a company celebration, but also helped Ma to equally share the market with Alipay.

What the employees can remember are those things that can move them to tears. Sophisticated theories come from the brain, but warm stories go to the heart. After a time, you may forget the wisdom from the brain, but you'll never forget the affection in the heart.

How Pony Ma Treats Resigning Employees

Some bosses may regard the leaving employees as disloyal and may suppress them by many means. But Ma won't do that; he'll support them. Some people find it strange that Mobike can appear in the Sudoku of WeChat. Why would Pony Ma help Hu Weiwei like that? Some say that's because Tencent has invested in Mobike. But why didn't it invest in ofo? There's a secret to many people here. Hu Weiwei was once the subordinate of Pony Ma. She worked for two years for auto.qq.com and then left.

Tencent can be deemed as the Whampoa Military Academy in the Internet venture circle, which cultivates great generals of the circle. With his current mental pattern, Ma even would like to see a great Internet company to be established by a former employee of Tencent.

The case source quoted from: Chi Zhongbo, Pattern Is Everything 2017/11/27
http://finance.sina.com.cn/manage/mroll/2017-11-27/doc-ifypceiq4049493.shtml

Behavioral Characteristics of Super Users

Chapter 12

Topics:

1. The Rise of Communities
2. Brand Communities
3. Community Leaders

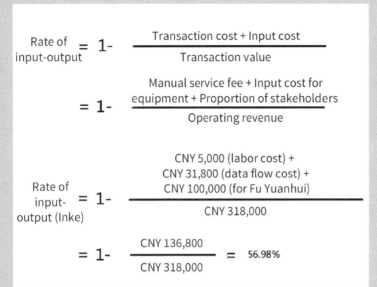

$$\text{Rate of input-output} = 1 - \frac{\text{Transaction cost} + \text{Input cost}}{\text{Transaction value}}$$

$$= 1 - \frac{\text{Manual service fee} + \text{Input cost for equipment} + \text{Proportion of stakeholders}}{\text{Operating revenue}}$$

$$\text{Rate of input-output (Inke)} = 1 - \frac{\begin{array}{c}\text{CNY 5,000 (labor cost)} + \\ \text{CNY 31,800 (data flow cost)} + \\ \text{CNY 100,000 (for Fu Yuanhui)}\end{array}}{\text{CNY 318,000}}$$

$$= 1 - \frac{\text{CNY 136,800}}{\text{CNY 318,000}} = 56.98\%$$

Figure 12-1   The Financial Accounting Method

In the traditional business mode, enterprises believe in the "2:8 Rule", i.e., 80% of the profits are produced by 20% of the customers; but contrarily, the fact is 80% of the enterprises' energy is spent on the few troublesome customers among the 80% customers, which is a big headache of the managers. The managers try to put 80% of their energy on the 20% high-quality customers who can create profits, but the results are seldom ideal. The mobile Internet has brought a new situation that solves the problem of the traditional management. Now the enterprises can finally put their major efforts and money on the key high-quality customers, as the Internet enterprises follow the "1:99" rule instead of the "2:8" rule, i.e., the profits of Internet enterprises are created by the 1% "super users".

Let's take the popular Inke Live as an example. Inke claims to have over 100 million users. According to the "5:1" ratio of "zombie fans" to daily users, it may have about 20 million active users. On August 10, 2016, the live show of the Olympic celebrity Fu Yuanhui had 10,540,000 online audiences, and the rebroadcast the next day had only 300,000 audiences. The more impressive is that Fu received 3,185,000 "diamonds" from the fans during the 1-hour live show, which are worth CNY 318,000 as one diamond costs CNY 0.1.

According to the rules of Inke, the proportion between the platform and the anchor is 68:32, so the platform will get CNY 216,000 at least. No wonder Fu kept saying "You don't need to send me gifts" during the show. The reason is simple: the live platform earns money by the online celebrities and earns much more than the celebrities themselves. According to Inke, it only has 180,000 anchors on the platform, accounting for less than 1% compared with its 20 million fans. What does that indicate? It indicates that Internet platform companies make money with their 1% super users from the 99% ordinary fans. The 1% super user rule of Inke has shown that the Internet enterprises have a lower cost; they only need to serve the 1% super users well, and can leave the 99% users to the network technology. According to financial accounting, the cost of serving the users by technology or equipment is much lower than that of serving the users by people.

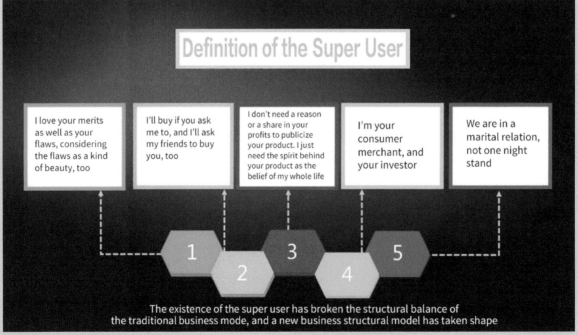

Figure 12-2   The Definition of Behavioral Characteristics of Super Users

The financial accounting method provided by management accounting is shown in Figure 12-1.

Obviously, Internet companies have better efficiency and benefits than entity economy. So Inke dares to claim to be the Internet company with the highest profit and the lowest cost among the large Chinese live platforms.

The above behaviors have broken the bottom line of traditional consumer psychology and behavior researchers. They would not figure out why the super users would think and act like that with all their data models. Only the Internet companies can trade "emotions" like products, and that's the secret of their high efficiency.

The existence of the super user has broken the structural balance of the traditional business mode, and a new business model structure has taken shape.

The definition of the behavioral characteristics of super users (as shown in Figure 12-2):

(1) I love your merits as well as your flaws, considering the flaws as a kind of beauty, too.

(2) I'll buy if you ask me to, and I'll ask my friends to buy you, too.

(3) I don't need a reason or a share in your profits to publicize your product. I just need the spirit behind your product as the belief of my whole life.

(4) I'm your consumer merchant, and your investor.

(5) We are in a marital relationship, not a one-night stand.

The Rise of Communities

Before the industrial revolution, the daily life of the agrarian age was centered on the three traditional frameworks: the core family, the kinship family, and the close community established between the same clan or cognation. Most people were born, raised and died in the same place, and few left their consanguineous community. If they leave the protection of their consanguineous community and their family, they would surely die—without a job, education, or support during illness. In those regularly operating primitive communities, the clan leaders were the makers and executors of the laws; their words were the orders, and to maintain the operation of the consanguineous community mainly depended on inheriting the ancestral system or wisdom.

The outbreak of the industrial revolution totally destroyed the consanguineous communities. People walked out of the consanguineous communities to build new cities. In the city, policemen appeared and began to replace family lynches with court judgments; people began to do the jobs they liked, marry the people they loved, and live in the places they desired, without worrying about the punishment from the clan leader; they could even have only one meal a week with their family. The country and the market have replaced the clan leaders to be the backbone of people's living. Social contact got livelier, for the weakened consanguineous communities must be replaced by a new mode, i.e., the social communities.

As long as the emotional function of the community is not totally replaced, it will not disappear from the world; the difference is that the material function of the community has been taken over by social organizations. In the mobile Internet age, the functions of the community have experienced a qualitative change again; now it not only contains emotional and social functions, but also will be the summation of all relations in the future.

People caring about environmental protection make up a relationship community; homosexuals make up a relationship community; and single mothers, lover losers, insomniacs, people against light pollution... Communities are turning from emotion-oriented and value-oriented to relationship-oriented. People become a group, and the future community scholars, because of relationships.

Compared with the cold technology of PC Internet, the relationship community proposition of the mobile Internet is more honorable. The respect for humanity is the nature of mobile Internet, starting from careful observation, understanding, tolerance, and awe. It begins with the establishment of community relationships and ends with the respect for human creativity. The UGC function, sharing economy, and results sharing, etc. are all the fruits of relationship communities' respect for humanity.

The brilliance of humanity is the fundamental power for the mobile Internet to take root. Among the sci-tech inventions over the years, the smartphone is the one closest to us. We often hear that "Internet Plus" means connecting everything. What on earth is going to be connected? And by what? Through the smartphone, humanity is the smallest unit, the best protocol, and the last logic for the connection. Humanization is the final destination of the connection, the starting point of all trans-boundary integrations, and the reason for the existence of commercialization. No matter whether it is an interaction or a platform, it should be considered, developed, designed, operated, upgraded, and improved based on humanity. Humanity is the core of all relationships.

People define the community as: a residential community can be interpreted as a regional existence, showing a correlated connection; the community can be a special social relation which contains the community spirit or community emotion. When it comes to the community, we have to mention the fans. The mode of fans is consumer-oriented, consumer-initiated, and consumer-driven self-organizing communities with the support or platform provided by the brands. It is much different from the traditional customer relation management and membership mode, for the brands can't control the fans, but actually, the brands can possibly be infinitely close to controlling those fans having strong relations with them. Fans cultivation is accumulated by repeated brand-fan interactions, fan-fan interactions, online-offline interactions, and inside-outside interactions. Through fans cultivation, the brand can finally capture the demand and lifestyle upgraded or posted by the fans themselves.

The brand needs to provide a platform for circles and communities, as well as reward mechanisms or resources to increase the activeness of the fans, e.g., fan meeting, special event, customized products for fans, and purchase limitation for fans, while cultivating the trust of fans during the interactions and events. One of the six influence elements mentioned in the book *Influence* of Robert B. Cialdini is "social identity", that is, a saying, a thing, or a product, once identified by people, will exert a great influence. And identification comes from the same hobby. The niche brands have gained brand influence and the market by catering to the hobbies and winning the identification of some people.

In the Internet society, the social methods of people are more and more Internet-based. As long as they can use such social tools as microblog, WeChat, and QQ, they can get to know more people having the same hobbies with them. Social tools are a big magnetic field attracting numerous people who form a large community due to their same interest in the social tools. And in that large community, each person is a small magnetic field around which people with the same interest will gather to form a small community. For example, Facebook was designed to facilitate the communication and interaction between the college students, but because of its convenience, it rapidly developed beyond the campus as propelled by the Internet. According to the report of a market research enterprise in San Francisco, the US, Facebook has a market value of USD $220 billion, totally deserving the title of "giant". Currently, among the registered users of Facebook, there are only less than one-third student users. In October 2012, Facebook declared that its users had reached one billion, which equaled half of the population with the access to the Internet in the world or 15% of the world population.

The reason for the rapid development of social platforms mainly lies in their interactivity. The users can timely interact, share and communicate through these platforms. These users gather on the social platforms and gradually form large communities.

By the end of 2017, the market size of the network community economy of China will exceed CNY 400 billion, the number of network communities will exceed five million, and network community users will exceed 390 million. The number of network community users of China is close to 46% of Chinese cellphone netizens. The network communities are still in the initial expansion stage. The business mode of leading network communities is not mature yet, and the large number of middle and rear communities still has large space in operation quality optimization and commercial value increasing.

The Top 5 platforms of active network communities are: WeChat groups, QQ groups, WeChat official accounts, self-built website apps, and microblogs. Chat tools and real-time information platforms are the most popular, and self-built apps are also winning more and more attention from the network communities. In the current network community operation in China, 53.6% operators think the most serious problem is the "Poor activeness of the users"; 43.5% think the "Low loyalty of the users" is hindering the further development of the communities; besides, obvious problems still include the lack of external cooperation resources and inadequate operation systematization. Increasing the user stickness and seeking for quality resources is the key to community operation. 18.3% of the Chinese network community users have ever participated in the offline activities organized by the network communities. The online-to-offline (O2O) transfer channel has been opened already, with vast development space. The interaction in the network communities usually can overcome the limitation of geographic space, but is also unstable and unconfined, leading to the difficulty in maintaining the activeness of the communities; offline activities initiated with the network com-

munities as the media can help strengthen the relations, deepen the interactions, and maintain the vitality of the communities.

In the Internet field, MIUI, Luogic Show, and "Papi Girl", etc. from China are all regarded as the representatives of fan economy effect. MIUI has given full play to fan economy, keeping increasing gathering platforms for its fans by building communities and online forums. Luogic Show was only a video We Media in the beginning, which has gradually developed into popular community e-commerce with the increase of clicks and fans. Its founder Luo Zhenyu expressed that his We Media platform was an Internet-based community in essence. In 2013, Luogic Show initiated the Internet charging mode; without promising any membership service, it collected CNY 1.6 million of membership fees within six hours at its first member recruitment.

Many people think that Luogic Show is a media platform guiding the fans with

Member	Duties
Founder	Having personal charisma, convincing in a certain field, able to call upon certain groups of people; having certain prestige, able to attract a group of people to join the community, with long-term and correct considerations on the orientation, expansion, sustainability, and future layout, etc. of the community
Manager	Having good self-management ability, taking the lead to observe the community rules; responsible and patient, strictly abiding by the duties; cohesive and friendly, decisive and composed, considering the interests of the whole; fair in meting out rewards and punishments, able to evaluate the member behaviors and execute rewards and punishments accordingly with the platform tools
Participant	Can be diversified, but should take part in the community activities or discussions as much as possible; the activeness determines the participation degree, and if you want high activeness, you should introduce some "geniuses", "cute girls" and "funny people" into the community to stimulate the overall activeness of the community
Pioneer	Understand the connection, good at negotiating and communicating; the core and resource of communities are people; only when the resource in the community is fully utilized can the potential of the community be given full play to; so the pioneer should be able to dig out the potential of the community, publicize and spread the community on various platforms, and complete various kinds of cooperation after joining in different communities.
Differentiator	With strong learning capacity and deep understanding of the community culture, having participated in the community building and familiar with all the details; the differentiator is the super seeded user during the future large-scale community replication, the basis of community replication
Cooperator	Identifying the community, with matched resources; one log cannot prop up a tottering building, so the best way is to exploit some cooperators for resource exchange, like sharing with other communities to mutually increase the influence, or carrying out cross-boundary cooperation for mutual benefits
Payer	The operation and maintenance of the community requires a cost, and both time and materials can be deemed as money; so the community must have a payer providing the financial sources; the reason for the payment can be buying relevant products or the output of the community, sponsorship based on a certain reason, etc.

Community organizers and duties. Source: Woosii Research.

contents and earning cash with ads. But Luo doesn't mean to make money with video ads; the highly active WeChat and microblog users are what he values the most. By establishing communities, creating connections between the people, grafting resources, and producing commercial opportunities, Luo means to make everybody create assets with his authority and credibility in a small field in his friends circle, so that a great number of people will rebuild the commercial civilization.

Luogic Show firstly targets the "post-1985" white-collar intellectuals who have the same values and desire to have a spiritual superiority in a community.

Luogic Show provides the enlightenment and shortcut for these users' independent thinking, evoking their independent thinking ability to the maximum, arousing their motives, and developing the habit of sharing.

Videos are the entrance and business card for Luo to establish the community.

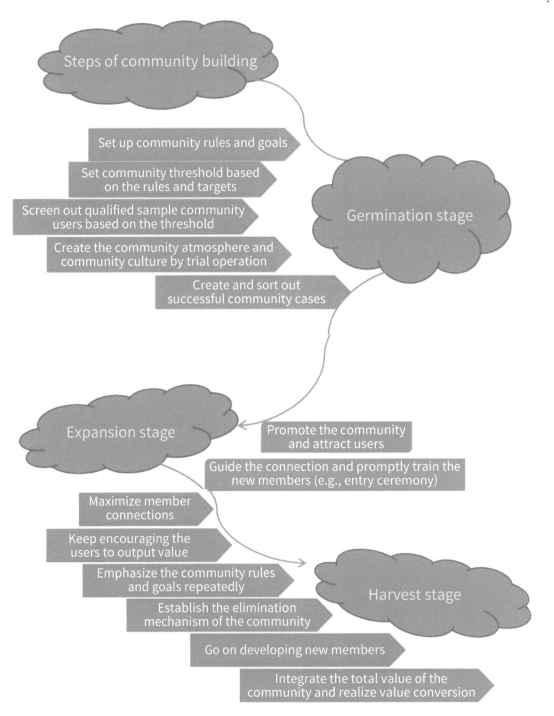

Steps of community building

Set up community rules and goals

Set community threshold based on the rules and targets

Screen out qualified sample community users based on the threshold

Create the community atmosphere and community culture by trial operation

Create and sort out successful community cases

Germination stage

Expansion stage

Promote the community and attract users

Guide the connection and promptly train the new members (e.g., entry ceremony)

Maximize member connections

Keep encouraging the users to output value

Emphasize the community rules and goals repeatedly

Establish the elimination mechanism of the community

Harvest stage

Go on developing new members

Integrate the total value of the community and realize value conversion

Luogic Show

Through the extensive spreading of the videos, people having the same values with him can gather at WeChat and take part in various interactions.

Meanwhile, he tried two ways of spreading: firstly, connect the internal member relations, e.g., the "Dine and Dash" activity where he asked the members to persuade various restaurant owners over the country to provide a meal for the members for free, thus spreading the show. Secondly, spread outward. Examples are Luo's book selling, crowd funding moon cake selling, and the promotion of Liu's Kiwi. Through these projects, people in the community can sell commodities and gain rewards, and more importantly, those talented people can show themselves in front of the three million users of Luogic Show, winning support with their own gifts and creating a new node.

Luogic Show has content interaction, value output, and even has cultivated the paying mode of the users. It is prospering in the field of communities, providing a good direction of transformation for many substance platforms.

But the platform is too dependent on the personal influence of Luo, which will be a bottleneck of its development. According to the famous "Dunbar's number", the human intelligence allows a man to have about 150 stable social contacts. The rapid development of the Internet has broken the limit of the human brain, and the interpersonal connections have shown the feature of "externalization" storage. With the accumulation of interpersonal resources within the community, there will be an outward momentum attracting more new members.

Brand Communities

The brand community is defined as "a specialized non-geographical community built upon the whole set of social relations between the consumers of a certain brand". The connection link of the brand community is the consumers' emotional benefit toward the brand. In the brand community, the consumers, based on their special affection for the brand, believe that the experience value and image value advocated by the brand agree with their own view of life and values so that they will have an empathy with the brand. In terms of manifestation, in order to enhance the sense of belonging to the brand, the consumers in the community will show their worship and loyalty to the brand logo through internally approved ceremonies, which is an extension of the consumption community.

The brand community has broken the geographical boundary of traditional communities, with the consumers' emotional benefit toward the brand as the connection link. The concept contains the following three aspects: firstly, the brand community is established upon a specific brand, so the community is specific, too; secondly, the brand community has surpassed the geographical limitation; lastly, the brand community is built on the basis of the whole set of social relations between the brand users, so it is a kind of community.

The brand community has three basic features similar to the "traditional communities", i.e., common consciousness, common rites and traditions, and sense of responsibility.

Those features reflect the nature of a community, and are the necessary conditions for a brand community. A brand community will never exist in absence of any of those features.

Western communitarianists generally define the community as "an entity with common value, norms, and goals where every member regards the common goals as their own goals". Therefore, the brand community has its own values and responsibilities. Meanwhile, the community norms need to be established, distinguishing the fans by systems, levels and roles; and the community should have different distribution methods of rights and interests, incentive intervention, and punitive measures, etc. to influence and control the collective actions of the community and increase the identification. By community identification which enhances the trust between the fans in the community and their trust in the brand and strengthens the affection and common consciousness of the community, the community behaviors will

①

Customer loyalty means the customer's affection of attachment or admiration of the product or service of the enterprise, mainly embodied by the emotional loyalty, behavioral loyalty, and conscious loyalty of the customer. Emotional loyalty means the customer's total identification and satisfaction on the philosophy, behaviors, and visual image of the enterprise. Behavioral loyalty means the customer's repeated purchase behavior toward the product and service of the enterprise; and conscious loyalty means the customer's future consumption intention toward the product and service of the enterprise.

be more effective and there will be more benefits and mutual effects for the community. During the network building of the brand community, relationship maintenance and resource mobilization are very crucial; also, brand stories and brand culture need to be created to provide the fans with the demands for communication and gathering, to be the commonly identified brand elements. The authority relations, trust relations, and norms, etc. involved in the brand community are all specific forms of social capital. That means the brand needs to re-understand and attach importance to the social capital.

In the brand community scenario, the members' higher level of identification of the brand and the community will develop into the common sense of community of all the members. The sense of community is a sense of belonging, i.e., the members believe that they are connected with each other and with the whole community and that their demands can be satisfied through such connections. According to McMillian and Chavis, when an individual joins a community, gains the membership and influence, satisfies his demands, and establishes the emotional connections shared with other members, he will have the sense of community toward this group. "Gaining the membership" hereby means the consumer puts some efforts into the activities of the brand community in order to be a member, and thus occupy a certain social position in the community and generate the senses of belonging and safety. "Influence" means the community member feels the influence of the community on himself and is able to influence other members and the whole community in turn.

"Satisfying his demands" means the community member gains the desired rewards by participating in the brand community activities, including the status in the community and the improvement of ability. "Emotional connections shared with other members" refers to the emotional connections produced between the members and between the member and the community when the community member is building and showing himself with the brand and enterprise image or history. Rosenbaum et al. creatively combine the sense of community with the loyalty program of the enterprises, and

divide the consumer loyalty programs of enterprises into the following two types: (1) Sense-of-community loyalty program, i.e., the enterprise cultivates the consumers' sense of community to win their loyalty; (2) Non-sense-of-community loyalty program, i.e., the enterprise gives material benefits to the consumers to win their loyalty. Meanwhile, according to the data they collected, based on empirical tests, they found that the sense-of-community loyalty program can explain 80% of the customer loyalty①. That fully shows the significant role of the sense-of-community loyalty program in cultivating customer loyalty, and also verifies the validity of that division method.

In a community, the power of both individuals and the collective can never be underestimated. There are numerous cases where the Internet celebrity microblogs affect the direction of public opinions. When a celebrity with tens of millions of microblog fans reposts a comment, he will create huge influence in a minute and then guide the public opinions. When a celebrity calls for something on his microblog, countless fans will respond immediately. With the support of the fans, a microblog celebrity can hold an event or launch a topic by doing half the work with double results. Thus we can see the influence of a social platform opinion leader. Such power of the community is a kind of manifestation of the brand community.

The microblog social platform has influenced the mode of information dissemination. Everyone on the platform can make live reports on an issue via the microblog, different from the previous situation that only professional news agencies could make such reports. On the microblog, everyone can express and show himself, post messages anytime anywhere, and promptly interact with other users.

As the microblog has no limit or requirement for the post status of the user, it can better complete the expression of the user. So the post status of microblog users has obvious personalized characteristics. Its features of flexibility, timeliness, and rapidness have made it not only a social platform, but also a media platform. The propagation speed and power of microblogs for the emergencies in recent years can't be ignored. And people are used to learning the latest news about emergencies via microblogs. In the age of mobile Internet, all the microblog users have become the fastest information dissemination tools and the members of a large correspondent team; they are the witnesses and the fastest disseminators of the news events. And the microblog has been called "the fastest and the most grassroots news conference hall".

The later rising WeChat has continued the influence of the microblog. WeChat has divided different communities more accurately with strong relationships, and such strong relationships have also been utilized by many merchants so that micro-commerce has been developing rapidly. You may have heard of the Six Degrees of Separation[1], i.e., one can get to know all the people in the world via six or fewer people. So we can see how a man can influence a group, and how the group can rapidly influence the whole interpersonal network in turn with the mutual relations. The community has weakened the individuality and reinforced the collectivity.

①

Six Degrees of Separation: it doesn't mean that any two persons can only be connected by six persons; it presents the important concept that any two persons who don't know each other at all can always be inevitably connected by some means.

 Case Study MIUI Cellphones

On September 28, 2012, MIUI declared via the microblog that its sales volume had reached four million cellphones. During the third-round purchase on September 20th, 300,000 MIUI 1S cellphones were sold out within four minutes and 12 seconds, which was a new record and dumbfounded the industry. The 2nd-generation MIUI engineering cellphone was also released with a limited amount on September 22, and the official edition will be released in the second half of October. Compared with the difficult situation of other cellphone manufacturers, MIUI is almost developing at the "satellite" speed.

MIUI created a legend within three years. In the summer of 2012, it broke the financing record of Chinese enterprises of that year with the financing estimated at USD $4 billion. Then it declared it had sold out 7,190,000 cellphones in 2012, with the sales income (incl. tax) of CNY 12.6 billion. A venture company with a history of less than three years that only began to sell products over a year ago has ascended to the ten-billion club; such performance should be the one and only among the venture companies around the world.

There were once many people interpreting the success of MIUI as the result of hunger marketing. And some directly call it a disguised mode of futures, i.e., to lock the users' advance payment and postpone the delivery of goods, while the ultrahigh cost performance upon the product release has gradually achieved the ultrahigh profits of the product sales. MIUI is only earning the actual profit several months later with a relatively low price at present.

But in fact, only the low price and the high configuration still can't make MIUI a legend. What is more legendary than the sales performance of over seven million cellphones is the more than five million loyal fans—MIUI fans. Now most We Media are belittling the microblog, like no one is using it and it is doomed. Actually, according to the latest data, the rank of microblog is still rising, indicating that its users are still increasing. Many users now spend more time on WeChat, who previously were checking their friends'

Lei Jun's Microblog has over eight million fans.
Source: microblog

posts on the microblog. People now use the microblog mainly to follow the Internet celebrities, to hear their voices, as the microblog is the only way to get in contact with those celebrities, which is irreplaceable by other social tools. And when a hot issue takes place, people will at first check the microblog. So the microblog actually has become a social medium where the celebrities speak while the ordinary users watch – it has become a social medium that reports hot news. Back to the subject at hand, let's look at the data of Lei Jun and MIUI on the microblog. Lei Jun's microblog has over eight million fans, which was only four million in February 2013 and doubled in one year.

He updates at least one post every day, 90% of which are centered on MIUI. Yeah, that is what he is, a model worker. Li Wanqiang, another founder of MIUI, who has nearly five million microblog fans, has relatively varied updates, nearly half of which are related to MIUI. The official microblog of MIUI has over eight million fans, which was also about four million in February 2013 and doubled later. Meanwhile, Lei Jun and MIUI also have a lot of fans on Tencent Microblog, only slightly fewer than those on Sina Microblog. All those fans amount to nearly 30 million, at least above the ten-million level even if net of the zombie fans and repeated fans. So Lei has been using the microblog as his main battlefield to promptly deliver the products and brand of MIUI to the fans and continuously bring in new fans. With so many fans, as long as your products are not bad, what can't you sell? Besides, the MIUI cellphones are nice products, with their own advantages and selling points. QQ Space is an interesting social tool; most large websites and manufacturers don't pay much attention to it, but MIUI has gathered a great number of fans on it.

The QQ Space of MIUI has 1.9 million fans. It updates the posts every day, and basically each post will be reposted for thousands of times, and even tens of thousands, which is far more than the reposts on the microblog. Each log will have tens of thousands of visits, and even hundreds of thousands. People who have ever operated the websites would know that tens of thousands of visits on a single article is good enough. And the QQ Space is available for customization. The users can find many of the same functions as on the MIUI website; of course it finally will skip to the MIUI website. According to the analysis of ALEXA, the QQ Space contributes 5% to the flow of MIUI's website, which is very considerable. Most domestic websites and large brands don't pay much attention to QQ Space, but it should be a valuable social tool, for most people aged between 20 and 40 have been using QQ for over 10 years, with great stickness. If the QQ Space can be well utilized, it will be a great social tool for the fans of vertical websites or vertical e-commerce

Product launch of MIUI 2012. Source: digi.163.com

circles. The ALEXA rank of MIUI community is No. 5612, according to which the daily IP is estimated to be 150,000 and the PV is about 800,000. 80% of the flow is contributed by the MIUI forum where there are numerous enthusiastic cellphone fans and any post can have hundreds of replies and tens of thousands of visits. It may be one of the hottest cellphone forums in China. Many people think the forums have declined, but vertical forums are still valuable social tools, as they support texts and pictures as well as continuous replies and can answer many users' questions promptly. For the moment, there haven't been any social tools good enough to replace the vertical forums, or WeChat would not overturn the forums.

The case source quoted from: huxiu.com 2014/03/27
http://www.woshipm.com/operate/75694.html

Content + Community + Business

The power of community cannot be underestimated, nor can the commercial potential of community.

The development of the mobile Internet has changed the way information is disseminated, while the development of the digital community has changed the marketing methods for enterprises and highlighted the importance of the community business. The community business is a business form that those who have the same hobbies and interests gather together with the aid of a social media tool or carrier, and the enterprise offers a product or service to this community by virtue of the same carrier. In the age of mobile Internet, the community carriers are greatly diversified. WeChat, QQ Group and various social service-based apps can be the carriers of community business marketing.

Content is a media attribute that serves as a traffic inlet; community is a relation attribute that is used to deposit traffic; and business is a transaction attribute that is used to realize the value of traffic.

Users gather for good products, contents and tools, then deposit and stay to form a community with interactive participation methods, common values and interests, and finally set up a deep connection and meet their demands with customized C2B transactions.

1. Content: all industries are media

The advent of the mobile Internet has greatly enhanced the efficiency of collaboration among people, and has significantly improved the efficiency of information production and dissemination. In a social network where everyone is We Media, the content is advertising. A good content can easily generate the effect of communication.

All industries are media - there will be money wherever we see. All business operations of an enterprise are symbols and media, and all links, from product R&D and design to production, packaging, logistics and transportation, and even to display and sales at channel terminals, establish contact with consumers and potential consumers and disseminate brand information. In addition to the product itself, all of them are traffic inlets.

For Xiaomi, all of its products are media; and for Coca-Cola, the packaging of each bottle is also a media (well known as the bottle case). As enterprise media has become an inevitable trend, each enterprise should cultivate its own media attributes. A lot of enterprises have begun to set foot in various fragmented social media channels, and their managers have started to run We Media. This is a good thing, but many people have misunderstood the cultivation of media attributes and have used the media as a simple channel for information distribution. In addition, they've never thought deeply about media productization - unfriendly advertising and self-flattery are no longer effective. Media is product. Treating media communication itself as a product that requires patience, stimulating a sense of participation and building a community are crucial to form good public impression.

The fundamental difference between the new media landscape and the traditional media lies in recognition. In the new media landscape, only recognition can create value. Without recognition, traditional media methods will try in vain to bombard the audience with advertising campaigns.

2. Community: all relations are channels

Before the advent of the Internet, brand manufacturers or retailers needed to reach out to target consumers as much as possible by constantly opening new stores. The advent of the Internet has broken the space constraints and has enabled people to buy a wide variety of goods without leaving their homes. This business phenomenon implies a change in business logic - from preemption of space resources to that of time resources, namely the user's attention. When users migrate to the mobile Internet and social networks on a large scale, brand owners and retailers must gradually shift their positions. According to data from the catering industry, 56% of the surveyed restaurants have offered coupons, and 68% have been available for group purchases. Nowadays, mature O2O cooperation modes, such as coupons and group purchases, are highly recognized and widely accepted by restaurants.

In addition, the comprehensive recognition of O2O service modes, such as free discovery, user interaction and event marketing, also reaches more than 50%. This reflects that restaurant owners have the need for promotion of their own brands, and that they want users to know more about their own brands and services through interactions and events so as to form the good public impression or drive the brand spread. The traditional physical channels have become ineffective gradually and have been replaced by online relation networks that are mainly manifested as Microblog, WeChat, forums and other social networks that can be multilaterally influential.

Restaurants have taken a shot at this in a small scale, which shows that most restaurants do not pay enough attention to new media marketing or even do not understand how to operate. However, it is undeniable that Internet thinking will give a new life to the catering industry and will make gourmet restaurants shine. Through MI Community and online and offline events, a large number of cellphone enthusiasts have gathered for Xiaomi cellphones. Also through this social network, these MI fans have continuously given advices for the iteration of Xiaomi cellphones and have constantly helped Xiaomi intensify the good public impression. This group of people forms the fan community of Xiaomi. The community here refers in particular to the Internet community, which is a fixed group formed by those consumers who are satisfied with the same commercial products and have the same interests and values. It is composed of the consumers congenial to each other, and is characterized by decentralization, interest base, fixed center and scattered edges.

3. Business: all links are experiences

In addition to followers and interests, the community is carrying a very complex business ecosystem. The fundamental reason behind it is the inevitability of human socialization. In other words, the community ecosystem that we are focusing on now is based on business and products, and it spreads across time and regions with the Internet as its carrier. The fundamental value of business community ecosystem is to achieve different levels of consumer satisfaction in the community. Here is a

①

Smart Community: it refers to the new community form for the future, which makes full use of the Internet and the IoT, involves various fields including smart building, smart home, road network monitoring, smart hospital, urban lifeline management, food and drug management, ticket management, home care, personal health and digital life, etc. It seizes the great opportunities in the new round of technological innovation revolution and in the wave of the information industry, brings into full play the developed information communication technology (ICT) industry, the advanced RFID-related technologies, the excellent telecommunication and information infrastructure as well as other advantages, expedites the breakthrough in key industrial technologies through the construction of ICT infrastructure, certification and security platforms and demonstration projects, establishes a smart environment for urban (community) development, and forms new modes for life, industrial development and social management based on massive information and intelligent filtering and processing.

relatively simple example. It used to be enough for us to have a house in which to live. But now as the competitions become fiercer and fiercer, the developers have to put forward a series of coups, including free parking space, various shops and clubs nearby for your leisure and entertainment, etc.

These supporting facilities are used to increase the added value of housing and living. Therefore, the community will slowly set up an ecosystem and form a closed loop of life and business.

This ecological model will get developed and improved gradually, and will provide consumers with multi-dimensional services so as to generate a complete business system. It is such business logic that the current hot topic, "Smart Community"①, is based on. Real estate developers and property management companies like Vanke, Longfor and Sino-Ocean are transforming traditional properties and establishing a business ecosystem centering on residents with the aid of the Internet and with the view of subverting the traditional business model to manage properties. This is also a community business model in nature. Community business is a "micro-eco-system" with incremental thinking, which is natural and win-win. In the community business model, the content is like a sharp blade. Here we take the relatively mature catering industry as an example. No matter how O2O and Internet thinking are aggressive, catering companies must return to the essence of catering, focus on products and Service, offer good user dining experiences, center on taste, environment and service, and then drive and intensify the spread of restaurant reputation with the Internet.

Ddcoupon, which had ever maximized the impact of coupons, and a large number of high-profile group-buying websites were closed down. However, the 58.com is working so hard that it has been listed officially and has left its rivals behind. JD has formed the good public impression with its fast logistics and delivery. Frankly speaking, the Internet is just a value-added service for traditional enterprises, and only the core product & service experience can attract users, meet their basic needs and carve out an inlet. But it fails to effectively deposit fan users, so the community has become a necessary condition to deposit users, and the commer-

cial liquidity has been an effective way to derive profit points. These three elements appear to be separated from one another, but the business logics within them are integrated. In the future, business will be based on people rather than products, and on communities rather than manufacturers. All in all, the community business is a user-led and data-driven Customer to Business (C2B) model in nature.

A community always needs a manager to formulate the game rules. This is still a network idea based on the self-interest. However, the most important social attribute of the mobile Internet is the "round table" mode, which has the following characteristics:

● There is no manager but moderator only;

● Game rules are enforced by the moderators after they have been approved by the majority;

● There is neither lowliness nor nobleness on the round table, and quality is the basis for everything;

● Equal opportunity and going Dutch for all;

● Speak with contents, and follow whoever is right;

● Automatic ad block function;

● User's creed: I run if you chase me;

● Follower's creed: I love you if you have no advertisement; and

● Product R&D: we create together.

Community business can meet the enterprise's needs for individualized services by offering individualized physical products or services, etc. These individualized products and services are available for specific target groups to some extent. For example, after registering an account with Kuaiyue, you can "sell" your skills, and a company or person in need of such skills can find you through Kuaiyue.

In the age of the community, enterprises should change their marketing concepts. In the past, people thought that marketing was only related to consumers. Now people are slowly realizing that marketing is not only related to consumers but also to the community. Today in the process of marketing, the enterprise should first set up a community that can positively interact with consumers, and then should run it well. If this community runs well, the enterprise will develop rapidly. The development of the mobile Internet has changed the marketing method of 4Ps widely used by traditional enterprises. In the past, a TV ad might create a sales miracle. But now, this effect is declining because there are fewer and fewer people watching TV. Today, if an enterprise wants to make a success of advertising and marketing programs, it should express itself in an individualized way more on the Internet than TVs.

The development of the community puts forward higher requirements for the enterprise's publicity methods. In the publicity process, the enterprise should learn to interact with consumers, create influence and make its information transparent. Only the interaction can make consumers really like you, follow you and stay with you in a community. The enterprise not only should have a community but also should have the ability to influence the community. Only if the enterprise influences the community, consumers will recognize its services and products. When the enterprise is attracting and influencing consumers, its information must be transparent because the authenticity determines everything. If a community member finds out any asymmetric information, he or she will immediately challenge the enterprise together with other members.

The most important thing for the community is to have an opinion leader, under whose leadership a trust relationship can be established with community members and the value can be delivered to them quickly in community marketing. The age of Internet emphasizes the ultimate thinking, and so does the community. In addition to an opinion leader, the community should have good products

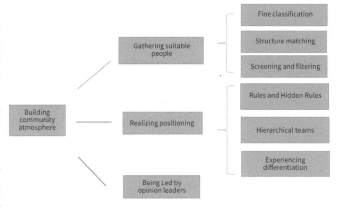

The Development of the Community

and services, should communicate with members in real time, and should listen to the opinions and suggestions given by members to make them a part of it. Community marketing is more concerned with the public impression. With the public impression, whether good or bad, one can influence all. For example, the social e-commerce is mainly engaged in business in the circle of friends where the good public impression of a product or service is spread among acquaintances. This spread mode has a strong sense of trust and is more easily accepted with the influence reaching strangers through acquaintances to form a large market. In this process, if one thinks a product or service good, he or she will tell his or her friends in the social community, and the product or service will soon establish a good public impression.

With the rise of the mobile Internet, the community business will be equally important for the development of the enterprise. Therefore, whoever knows how to spread will seize the opportunity and occupy the market.

 ## Community Leaders

"Opinion leader" is traditionally defined as: those intermediary roles with certain influence in the process of delivering the media information to the social groups. In 1940, Paul Lazarsfeld et al. carried out a voter survey for the local election of Erie County, in Ohio, the US. While analyzing the relevance between the media and the voting behaviors, they unexpectedly found that the information from the media had first influenced the opinion leaders in the groups, who then "interpreted" the information along with their own explanations to the other people. That is to say, ideas often

flow from the broadcast and print media to the opinion leaders, and then from the opinion leaders to the inactive groups. That is the so-called "two-step flow of communication" which opened up a new field of group relationships in communication process research. In the later Decatur study, the four decisive influences of opinion leaders on the daily life of other people were mainly investigated: purchasing behaviors, fashion, public events, and choosing a movie. Its research strategy is aimed to distinguish the opinion leaders with comprehensive influences and those with single influence.

In the scope of marketing, the influence modes of the opinion leaders have been discovered: ① in terms of deciding to change the using habit or to adopt new products, the personal influence of opinion leaders is more obvious than the official media; ② the consumption influence is horizontal, and people tend to look for opinion leaders in their own hierarchy; ③ the range of influence of the opinion leader is related to his position in the life cycle, corresponding to his own consumption experience; ④ people above the average social status are more likely to be opinion leaders. Later, in the researches of consuming behaviors, the opinion leader has been further defined as "a person who provides more information or more frequently for other people than other consumers, thus influencing the purchase decision of other people to a larger extent". On the Internet, a person who's fond of a certain brand is called "fan", and a person who can speak for a certain brand and has supporters is called "opinion leader", i.e., the super user. Such opinion leaders are a group, through which the brand connects the fans and the fans get to know the brand.

The relations between the parties can be explained in a sentence: if a product can bring many benefits for the user, the user will like and accept it and recommend it to other people who haven't used it; if a product can bring extreme benefits for the user, the user will become a super user who will refute those people who speak ill of the product.

A person who likes a brand is a fan; a person who likes a brand and publicizes it on the social media is an opinion leader. The latter publicizes and maintains the product with facts and cases, so he has both opinions and the influence of a leader.

Large brands don't just bribe the opinion leaders as imagined by other people. That may probably harm them in the

Case Study   Big V Store (Davdian)

As an emerging maternal and infant e-commerce platform, Big V Store is an outstanding player among the successful community e-commerce cases. The accurate breakthrough point of parent-child reading, the systematic management and operation of the community, and the mode of helping the moms to open stores and gain brokerages have almost developed to a self-cycling community eco-platform. Within two years, Big V Store obtained the Aplus Angel Round of Yu Minhong, the GSR Ventures Round A, and the Lightspeed China Partners Round B investments, and received the tens of millions of dollars from the Round B+ investments led by Steamboat Ventures under Disney in March 2016. It currently has 5 million registered users, nearly 700,000 mom store owners, and a monthly sales volume of over CNY 150 million.

In the face of the double-oligarchy pattern of Alibaba and JD.com in the e-commerce field, it seems that the traditional B2C e-commerce can hardly find any new opportunities. But the founder Wu Fanghua

believed that the e-commerce based on "recommendation" was still hopeful.

In the maternal and infant field, mothers naturally like to share the daily affairs of their children, and would like to accept the products recommended by other moms. They are naturally advantaged in terms of population-based recommendations. Besides, many stay-at-home mothers have the need to relieve the economic pressure of the family, so Big V Store encourages them to open their own stores.

In terms of community management, in addition to gradually realizing productization via tools and app, Big V Store has also established regional "V Clubs" covering all the provinces of China. It discovers the opinion leaders in the V Clubs through content activities and trains them into "class leaders" responsible for the daily management of the V Clubs. In 2016, it launched the "Mom Gas Station", selecting influential moms to be the station leaders to organize offline activities. Those "Big V" moms have shared part of the operation work while satisfying their social need and realizing their self-value. Besides, Big V Store has signed contracts with nearly 900 organizations for providing the offline activity venues for the moms.

As a powerful black horse, the Big V Store community has solved the operation pressure brought by the sharply increasing users with its self-operating system, enhanced the emotional connection with vigorous interactions, and promoted the sales increase with frequent high-quality content dissemination.

Advertising slogans of Big V Store (Davdian).

Source: pgpop.com

The case source quoted from: Jianshu.com 2016/12/28

http://www.chinaz.com/news/2016/1228/634848.shtml

end. Emotional connection has become a general rule of the game. Many world brands discover such opinion leaders on the blogs, and microblogs, etc. and invite them to visit their places of origin (France, the US, and Japan, etc.) and attend their annual meetings, fashion shows, parties, and press conferences, to enhance their relations without asking them to write articles.

The emergence of the opinion leader group is a necessary trend of brand building on the Internet, an inevitable result of social media marketing. Many brands treat the opinion leader group as their own employees, but this group stands in a third-party position to maintain the brand. The brands need such roles and teams.

Currently, there are several methods to organize this group, on the QQ groups, microblog groups, or some classification in the e-mail. Keeping in touch is the priority of the brands, and the emotional stickness is the magic key of the enterprises. This group has been getting larger and more active; they can be seen on all kinds of social media. They are the people who say "No" for the brands, and they have loyal fans.

Virtual communities are "collectives organized on the basis of shared benefits or purposes to conduct common activities in the online virtual world". As a kind of surreal interpersonal communication, online virtual communities have many forms, e.g., forums, chat rooms, and BBS. And the communication contents involve all aspects of social life. Among them, the virtual community activities with the topic of consumption information not only are the community contents of the cyberspace, but also have developed into a new business mode of the website communities, indicating the future trend of e-commerce.

The virtual communities, relying on the advantage of Internet technology, have transcended the space-time boundaries, broken the narrow information influence chain in traditional communities, and essentially realized the equal right to receive information. Of course, it doesn't thoroughly resolve the influence of some participants as opinion leaders; they are still the "interpreters" of the information and the advisers for decision-making. In terms of the advantage of the right of speech, there are two kinds of people who are most likely to be the opinion leaders: the presupposed technical superiors, e.g., the forum moderators or administrators with higher authorities; the community members produced by the competitive mechanism during the communication, e.g., the prestigious high-level netizens who show new characteristics of their role different from the traditional real communities.

The communication role of the opinion leaders in real communities has the following features: having a specialty or being able to provide incisive judgments; with higher media contact degree or interest; with greater advantages in social resource utilization.

I. Role–related characteristics of opinion leaders in virtual communities

When we identify the role-related characteristics of an opinion leader in a virtual community, the first problem is about the technologies to discover the opinion leader. In fact, people have always been committed to finding opinion leaders in consumer groups so that they can exert targeted influence and improve the effectiveness of marketing spread. But actually, the identification of opinion leaders in a group is very difficult. On the one hand, there are very few general-minded opinion leaders who can exert comprehensive influence. On the other hand, opinion leaders are not the official authority of the group, but are identified subjectively by group members. In a virtual community, the identities of its participants and their hidden social characteristics make it easier for us to focus on the technical presentation of this virtual community only and ignore the existence of opinion leaders in the "Internet network". In contrast to opinion leaders in the real community, we may start with the following aspects.

1. Identity form

The opinion leaders in the virtual community are absent in the narrowly defined chain of spread influence because the presentation of the sunk intermediate level is caused by the equalization used by the Internet media. Everyone can participate in spread, accept information and express opinions with equal technical capabilities, and it seems that there be no need for filtration or translation by others. But this is just a technical possibility that the Internet offers to the general public. In essence, the forms of identity presentation have never disappeared for traditional opinion leaders. The traditional intermediate level "sinks" into the general audience, but the information source elements (gatherers, editors, gatekeepers and invited organizers) within the media "emerge" for the same reason and become the "quasi-audience" vaguely equivalent to the audience, which essentially makes them possible to mutate into a broadly defined spread level. In a manner of speaking, the opinion leaders in the virtual community may also have the value function of the intermediary influence. And in terms of identity presentation, they may be the organizers and technical managers of the virtual community, or the superiors in interactions or competitions. Behind the information symmetry of the virtual community still stand the differences in right of using and in degree of trust. Although all the social positions and resources possessed in reality have been hidden, the absence of symbols has not weakened the presence of their influence.

2. Knowledge advantages

The so-called equalization of online communication means that everyone has equal rights to express their opinions with the support of search technology. However, it only achieves the formal equality. When it goes deep into the content of the message, each participant will reveal his or her knowledge and experience possessed in the real world to make his or her opinions differently influential, especially in the spread of consumption information.

The exchange of consumption information in the virtual community corresponds to the actual consumer demand. Online services provided by the network tend to be positioned by product categories or target consumers. The information exchanged by the participants must center on consumption knowledge and experience. Therefore, their professional images are continued just like in the real world. The opinions expressed by those high-ranking and highly respected netizens are more likely to be sought and recognized by the public.

3. Virtual context expression

In the surreal context of virtual communities, does the flow of identity mean the freeness of value? In other words, how many responsibilities are there in the real world when people spread the consumption information? Opinion leaders' motivations for information spread are related to their credibility. According to those interactive communications in chat rooms and online games, people's understanding of the online interpersonal form seems to be far away from reality - virtual identities, virtual interactions and virtual emotions which are viewed as compensations for the reality rather than equivalents to the real ones. But most people exchange the consumption information in order to meet their actual demands for consumption.

As a source of information for consumption decision-making, the virtual community attracts people to be a part of it. In such a common physical space, people derive a kind of "plausibility" that constitutes the opinion leaders' motivations for value expression and that becomes a measure of value for the followers to select the information. The exchange of consumption information in the virtual context is based on the actual consumption of products. If an opinion leader wants to gain influence on web pages, he or she must express the authenticity of product knowledge and consumption experience, otherwise it will be difficult to exert the corresponding influence.

II. Roles of opinion leaders in information spread in virtual communities

The roles of opinion leaders in information spread in virtual communities are closely related with the existence value of virtual communities, and are mainly manifested in the following aspects.

1. Opinion leaders are the information reference for consumption decision-making

The reason why a community is attractive to its members is because they think communication in the community is meaningful and important. As sources of information for consumption decision-making, opinion leaders in both real and virtual communities reflect their influence in a mutually overlapping manner. In these two kinds of community contexts, opinion leaders have the same authority of opinions. But the opinion leaders in the real community are attached with definite social identity characteristics that are often closely related to followers, such as professionals, leaders, relatives and friends. Therefore, they have high credibility and even make alternative decisions. In the virtual community, opinion leaders can be identified only with information contents and cannot be reliably guaranteed by interpersonal relations. Therefore, their opinions are often expressed as information references. People enrich their consumption knowledge, verify their judgments, supplement their consumption information, and avoid the commercial propaganda from other media with the aid of opinion leaders. Of course, we cannot expect virtual communities to replace other sources of consumption information. It is enough that opinion leaders have such a reference role.

2. Opinion leaders are the necessary condition for online operation branding

Internet operations are rapidly moving from population websites to community services, and websites and vendors have chosen virtual communities as platforms for marketing spread (a virtual community in this sense is an arena). The audience enjoys the freedom of spread media, have free access to communities, transform and organize the information in a flexible way, and use the media fully based on their own needs. This creates a more mobile audience than other media. And online operators, in order to realize commercial operations, must pursue the market segmentation of virtual communities or the nature of spread focus, and must establish firm attractions for members. Therefore, the development of the virtual community is bound to be affected by the strategies for online operation branding. Although the conditions for branding are manifold, opinion leaders are indispensable to online interpersonal attraction.

The appeal of opinion leaders is the driving force for people to participate in virtual community exchanges. If a website wants to be definitely recognized by the audience, it must furnish authentic and reliable consumption information, and must have the advices of its opinion leaders justified by the actual consumption behaviors. Therefore, website administrators can act as opinion leaders in person to select the information for posting. At the same time, they can technically control the spread

process, filter out the bad information, and designedly cultivate prestigious opinion leaders from the participants. This is the strategy for website branding.

3. Opinion leaders are the driving force to maintain the existence of virtual communities

The virtual community is an open collection of people in cyberspace. Its existence and development are based on the participation of its members in addition to the technical platforms provided by the website. There are two conditions for high participation of virtual community members in consumption information: the information needs of general community members and the activeness of opinion leaders. "When ordinary people encounter situations where they need to decide whether to believe, buy, join, escape, support, like or dislike, they will seek guidance from opinion leaders." This is also the driving force for consumption information exchange activities in the virtual community. On the Internet, official websites and thematic forums for specific products have brought together hypertext-based consumption information to meet people's three-dimensional information needs quickly and easily. These needs that are inherently and evidently of the utilitarian nature of consumer behaviors will intensify the behaviors of the participants in case they are satisfied in the virtual community.

Opinion leaders may not be motivated to participate in community activities by acting as advisors or mentors for others. They have formed interests in and habits of using web media because of the confidence in their own knowledge and the skillful use of technologies. Showing their abilities in a virtual community and providing guidance to others can give them a sense of accomplishment. In turn, their participation will make the virtual community so active and prestigious that it can develop and grow stronger.

4. Opinion Leaders reject transformation into commercial roles

Compared with the commercial propaganda of the formal media, opinion leaders of virtual communities have more credible motivations for information spread because they are in the similar mental state to that of consumers.

Therefore, the roles of opinion leaders are naturally valued by propagandists. For marketing purposes, manufacturers and vendors may use virtual communities to hide their business identities as propagandists and act as opinion leaders in such communities. But it is precisely because of the virtual nature of the online community that the general audience stay alert to the identity and standpoint of the information publisher. Once opinion leaders have been found to be spokespersons for commercial interests, their influence in information spread will decline accordingly. Therefore, vendors should be cautious about attempts to transform opinion leaders into commercial roles. Meanwhile, impartial opinion leaders should remain neutral and may adopt the two-sided information arrangement, that is, provide both positive and negative information. The information should be compared and judged by the audience themselves, otherwise it'll be doubted by the audience.

As the online media are increasingly involved in our lives, the roles of opinion leaders in information spread should have richer connotations and values and deserve deeper thought.

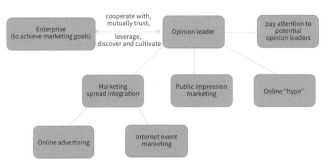

The value of opinion leaders.

Case Study — Little Red Book

Little Red Book is an app designed for discovering the good things around the world. It is oriented as a UGC information platform, where the users can discover the good things around the world, put the offline shopping scenes online, and add the endorsement of real buyers. The users upload the content, and other users shopping overseas can obtain the detailed product "guide" on Little Red Book.

Since its release in March 2014, Little Red Book has been a pure UGC community. In the beginning, its usage scenario was: having no idea what to buy overseas, and how to find the overseas commodities with better reputation? With the improving life quality and rising consumption level of young people, more and more people have the demand of buying overseas commodities and like to share the things they buy with others. Little Red Book is just developed on the basis of that core demand. Relying on its efficient promotion and product upgrading, it has seen rapid development within two years and now has over 20 million users. The overseas shopping sharing community has become the stronghold of Little Red Book, quietly making it an outstanding player among the numerous cross-border e-commerce platforms.

Little Red Book has found that the notes in the community are largely published by female users shopping overseas, or are some results searched from Baidu and some officially issued announcements. The core users of the Little Red Book community are young and middle-aged females fond of overseas shopping and high quality. They are mostly the "post-1985" and "post-1990" students and white collars in the first-tier cities. They are the new-generation main force of consumption, representing the consumer groups of the coming mass market. They hope to find some commodities that can better match their lifestyle and their cognition about life. The domestic commodity categories are limited, and platforms such as Taobao are more likely to have mixed kinds of sellers, while the consumers want global commodities.

So we summarize the demands of the core users of Little Red Book as follows:

1. I like travelling overseas, and shopping is inevitable during the travel. But I don't know what is worth buying. I hope someone can give me some suggestions.

2. With the improving life quality, I buy things not only for basic use; I hope they can bring me more spiritual satisfaction and show my uniqueness in front of other people.

3. I bought a nice limited-edition bag overseas at a good price yesterday, and I want to show it off.

4. I like surfing the Internet. When I see something good shared by other people, I would want it, too, and I would buy it.

Little Red Book built a UGC community centering on the above pain spots. The community is featured by the activeness of the users; the attraction comes from the likes, comments, follows and favorites between the uses, which can rapidly increase user clicks and user stickness. It doesn't have to worry about the transactions as long as there is a large flow. That also has paved the way for the later introduction of the e-commerce mode.

The early stage was for verifying and exploring the product goal and direction. As there were not many users, the operation was mainly focused on the updates and content quality of the UGC community. As a UGC community is produced by the original contents of the users, the contents and the atmosphere of the community should be the focus of operation. Later, these users will be the core opinion leaders of the Little Red Book products, i.e., the seeded users, who will continuously produce high-quality contents for Little Red Book and maintain the high activeness of the community.

It can be seen from Baidu search that the operation of Little Red Book in that stage was mainly focused on the opinion leaders who produced high-quality contents to increase the daily active users in the

Little Red Book Community

community. So it is very important to find and maintain a group of high-quality core users (opinion leaders) of overseas shopping. In this stage, the product strategy was dominated by operation.

The opinion leaders have played a key role in the development of the community, deciding the future of Little Red Book. So the operation strategy is focused on Little Red Book celebrities, including signing contracts with a few celebrities, supporting the celebrities, and making stars in the community. Therefore, the community tends to centralize, and the celebrities become the weights of the community.

The case source quoted from: Su Jie, Everyone Is a Product Manager 2017/02/21
http://www.woshipm.com/evaluating/587399.html

III. Community leaders and community influence

1. Precise contact

As interest-based platforms are springing up on the Internet, super users have begun to share their experience with those interested in the same field and naturally attracted them. In this way, the interest-based platform has become a natural funnel to naturally filter out those who are not interested in the platform-related field, and filter in those who are really interested in such field. For example, those who often gather on beauty makeup platforms are usually the population interested in beauty makeup. Therefore, the platforms of this kind usually focus on women, and there are few people not interested in beauty makeup. The Internet reduces to zero the distance between people from all parts of the world.

2. Interaction with opinion leaders without geographical restrictions

In the age of old media, physical distance barriers did exist because followers had to arrive at the site to interact with super users. For instance, the interactions between super users and their followers could be made only through onsite signing events or speeches. As a result, many followers lost the chance to interact with super users for geographic reasons. But since super users started to build their homes on the Internet, their followers around the world have been able to leave messages to them at any time, and they have been also able to interact with their followers at their own convenience. Therefore, super users can establish long-term relations with a large number of followers.

3. Influence and marketing benefits of data assessors

The biggest change brought about by the Internet is that many of the information that could not be tracked in the past can take the form of data. For instance, it was difficult to know in the past how many people paid attention to a super user and how many people responded to a message sent by the super user. Today's Internet technology counts visitors by tracking IPs and by recording each visitor through his or her web account, so all of this has become the traceable information on the Internet. In Taiwan, China, the blogging platform PIXNET commonly used by super users and the Facebook follower club can record the number of visits to them on a daily basis and the number of followers, and even can estimate how often super users interact with their followers and how much influence super users have on their followers.

4. Information consolidation capability

If a super user has a large number of followers and interacts well with them, what he or she says will have a great influence on his or her followers. The value of super users comes from their experience accumulated in a certain field and their deep understanding of such field, so super users have more reliable views on the information related to such field. Sharing with super users may greatly reduce the time and the experienced cost spent by netizens in searching everywhere for information. Therefore, super users have built reliable images in the hearts of netizens, and netizens may directly refer to the super user in a certain field for information about such field. We once met with several highly influential technical opinion leaders, one of which allowed us to personally experience the power of the opinion leader. There were around 20,000 people visiting the blog space of this opinion leader and viewing the information he had shared on a daily basis. When we casually asked him what the digital watch he was wearing could do, this webmaster, called "Just Wanna Learn" on the Internet, spontaneously began to introduce the features of this watch, such as smooth interface and convenient message receipt. His introduction aroused our interests in digital watches. And when we asked about the digital watch of another brand, he also spontaneously introduced the features of that watch together with the differences between these two brands. At that time, we deeply thought that he was indeed an opinion leader. He really had a lot of experience and was able to make "rookies" like us know the features of the digital watch and the differences between different brands in a short time. By sharing with him for five minutes, we already knew the information that would have taken a few hours to understand. It is the deep understanding of a certain field that has made opinion leaders reliable sources of information in the minds of netizens and exert an influence on netizens.

The talented should carefully treat the followers they've accumulated, and thereby develop a sense of responsibility to their followers. They shall think about what contents the netizens are interested in or what contents are valuable. Therefore, they need to spend a large part of their time each day in browsing websites and finding out the appropriate content to share with netizens. For the talented, continuously finding out the information that meets the needs of their followers is much more difficult than sharing what they already know. They should not only digest a lot of new knowledge on the Internet, but also identify from numerous messages the very one that can arouse everyone's interest, and then subtly find out hot topics and quickly share them with everyone.

5. Community influence

Online communities are characterized by high crowding level and rapid dissemination of information, that is, the rate of influence of the community, also called "community influence rate" for short. This concept is like how we drive at a certain speed in km/h. The stronger the engine, the faster the speed, and the more kilometers the car can run per hour. Applied to the community influence, this concept is about how many people the influence of key opinion leaders can reach at each minute and how many likes these people can give.

 Case Study   Real Estate or Canada Goose

In early 2017, Canada Goose, a brand of clothing which is very popular in the Chinese community, announced that its IPO would be made in February 2017. In the initial public offering plan, Canada Goose expected to sell 10% to 15% of its shares with the financing amount of USD $200 to $300 million, which would make the value of this previously unrecognized "goose" reach USD two billion in the capital market.

The study found that it was the super users in the Chinese world that made this "goose" soar. In 2016, the down apparel brand, Canada Goose developed from three exclusive shops into a street icon in China's first- and second-tier cities within just one year. For a

Advertisements of CANADA GOOSE.
Source: finance.ifeng.com

time, white-collar workers in high-end office buildings did not dare go out without this "goose". Promoted by Chinese goose fans, Canada Goose has caught up with and nearly surpassed Monder, an old down apparel brand in France.

Canada Goose is most recognized by users for its strong warmth, and its target users are Arctic explorers and outdoor workers in alpine regions. Founded in 1957 by a Canadian-born Polish immigrant, Sam Tick, this "goose" had annual sales of around USD $10 million before 2013.

At the time that the third generation of his family took over the business (in 1997), the sales amounted to less than USD $3 million.

What kind of power has made this "goose" soar? Initially, people found that Hollywood began to favor the brand with long shots of its rough logo frequently

The President of Russia, Vladimir Putin has endorsed this "goose" for a long time. Source: finance.ifeng.com

appearing in many blockbusters like the 007 Series, Maggie's plan and X-Men 2 to seduce their fans. Then, Chinese big stars were also found to like the brand. Through WeChat, fans were surprised to find that Chinese stars such as Fan Bingbing, Zhang Ziyi and other A-listers were wearing the apparel during exterior shooting. And it is the most intriguing that the President of Russia, Vladimir Putin, has endorsed this "goose" for a long time. All endorsements by these stars were voluntary. Supposedly only in the age of mobile Internet could this miracle happen. The influence of super users attracted followers for branding marketing. For instance, the launch of Canada Goose's e-commerce platform in 2015 has rapidly spawned the

The launch of Canada Goose's e-commerce platform in 2015 has rapidly spawned the agent purchasing market. Source: Global Purchase

agent purchasing market, leading to Canada's short supply of clothes in Chinese people's favorite size, M.

To show off, the marketing director of Canada Goose stated that Canada Goose had never deliberately placed product advertisements, and it was usually the producer or stylist that wanted and invited them. No matter how far this "goose" can fly, it at least justifies such a mobile marketing principle: whoever has super users will be wooed by their followers.

Chapter 13

Application Principle of Super User: Sharing Economy

Topics:

1. Principle of Sharing
2. Consumer Business

Principle of Sharing

Can a bed be shared? A sofa? An office? An idea? Or an employee? These impossible things in the age of traditional economy have been made miraculously possible today.

Airbnb, a travel house rent community, provides people with accommodation during their vacation. WeWork, with an estimate value of USD $24 billion, has overset the traditional office rental pattern and made office sharing possible, which has let us see the power of sharing economy. ZBJ.com hadn't made any breakthrough since its establishment several years ago, till it added the sharing mode; since then its estimate value has soared to CNY 10 billion.

"When I was travelling in Hawaii, I couldn't get used to the western food of the local hotel. And the cost of washing a shirt equals that of buying one. But the American friends traveling with us chose to live in a local apartment. Their housing expense was only USD $10 per person per day." That's the recounting of a real experience of a Chinese tourist. Living in other people's home during travel may sound a little unimaginable, but this short-term

Types of Sharing Economy

vacation rental mode has been flourishing in foreign countries. The most famous practitioners of this business mode are the American short-term rental websites, HomeAway and Airbnb. They put the houses online for transactions with the users, and make profits by charging ad-rate or commissions. HomeAway charges the landlords or land agents who provide the housing resources, while Airbnb collects commissions of different proportions from the landlords and the tenants, respectively. No matter in which mode, HomeAway and

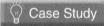 **Case Study** Making Orders (Yuedan)

Making Orders is a platform for time selling and skill transaction, devoted to helping more people with time or skills earn cash rapidly. There are over one million skillful talents in the app; you can buy the time or skills shared by them at will and make an appointment with them promptly. If you have spare time or skills, there are tens of thousands of demands from the over 10 million users on the platform waiting for you every day.

The essence of sharing economy is to create more value with idle resources. Currently, most of the mature sharing economy modes have material objects as the subject of sharing. But when it is applauded in the industry, people have ignored the important concept of "labor value of human" in the transactions.

Within half a year since its release, Making Orders has overturned the mode of sharing economy with its mode of "time transaction platform", becoming a black horse among the sharing economy platforms. It has seen surprising hundredfold growth in the sharing

accommodation market within four years.

Data have shown that the Chinese online short-term rental market began to accelerate in 2012. The market scale of that year was CNY 140 million, CNY 800 million in 2013, CNY 3.8 billion in 2014, and CNY 10.5 billion in 2015.

The peer-to-peer (P2P) online loan market of China had a scale of CNY 2.7 billion in 2013, which soared to CNY 975 billion in 2015. The P2P online loan and crowd funding in the field of capital sharing has developed to a large scale and is still developing rapidly. According to the data, the scale of the Chinese online crowd funding market was about CNY 15 billion in 2015, and the total market scale of P2P loan and online crowd funding was CNY 990 billion.

Sharing has become a New Normal of current society, obscuring the boundary between work and life. Sharing everywhere means opportunities everywhere. Sharing economy has become the door to future fortune.

The case source quoted from: Baidu Baike 2017/06/16
Case address: https://baike.baidu.com/item/%E7%BA%A6%E5%8D%95/18776599

Airbnb have established an online information release and transaction platform, like Taobao in China. Simply speaking, they are like intermediary resource integration agents, putting idle houses of the landlords online for the option of people who are going to travel.

During the explosion of HomeAway and Airbnb, Chinese entrepreneurs quickly copied them into the Chinese market: Airizu, Mayi Short-term Rental, Tujia, Xiaozhu Short-term Rental, and Aizuke, etc., among which Tujia is the most highly regarded as the Chinese edition of HomeAway and Airbnb. Tujia puts all accommodation types except traditional hotels online, including the inns, apartments, resorts, homestay houses, and villas, to provide short-term rental service, some housekeeper service and trusteeship for customers. Compared with HomeAway and Airbnb, due to the immature "trust system" in China, Tujia added many Chinese features to its business mode. On the one hand, it promises to the owners that they will take care of the houses and share the revenue accordingly; on the other hand, it transacts with the tenants directly as the house provider. The biggest problem of hotels is the housing resource; the hotel operators need to firstly contract for the houses before operation. Contracting requires expenses, and so does the maintenance for years; they will suffer losses if there are not enough guests. Tujia has changed that traditional business mode of house contracting into revenue sharing, different from the operation mode and logic of traditional hotels. When there are guests, it shares the revenue with the owners; when there are no guests, it doesn't have to pay to the owners.

With that brand-new housing resource acquisition and use mode, many owners, especially owners of idle tourism real estate, are willing to hand over their houses to Tujia. Now there are about 37% American and European travelers living in vacation rental houses instead of hotels during their trips, while the percentage of Chinese travelers is less than 10%. The Chinese tourist market is experiencing explosive development, with a large scale of tourist consumption and great demands for vacation hotels. So Tujia really has a promising prospect.

If you are still waving at taxis on the street, you won't get a taxi generally, because of the emergence of DiDi and Kuaidadi. Since the emergence of such applications, taxi drivers have been busy receiving orders, and the speeding taxis you see on the streets are mostly aiming at their order guests. So you'll find it hard to get a taxi if you still can't use a taxiing app. Also, the emergence of such apps has led to decreasing rate of audience of broadcasting stations, because the drivers, an important audience group of broadcastings, are now listening to the order broadcasts. The competitor of broadcastings is not TV or cellphone, but the taxiing app. So now there's "a way of death" which is dying without seeing your enemy. That is cross-boundary robbery.

DiDi has changed the traditional taxiing market pattern and cultivated the modern traveling mode of the mobile Internet age. Besides, DiDi has also promoted a new high-end business brand—DiDi Tailored Taxi, similar to yongche.com. DiDi Tailored Taxi provides quality service for high-end businessmen: instant response, professional service, high-end vehicles, and professional driving companions. DiDi Tailored Taxi and yongche.com mobilize the idle resources by effectively scheduling their vehicles, legalize the traditional carpooling mode, and integrate the market resources by creating the new traveling service mode to maximize the utilization of social resources. The emergence of WeChat Exercise and WeChat Reading marks the further completion of the WeChat loop as well as a higher level of business development of the sharing economy. Such personal things as reading and exercise have also been a part of the sharing economy.

If someone asked you to give your car key or door key to a stranger several years ago, you must have looked at him in doubt. We wouldn't give a bike or a chair to a stranger for custody, not to mention our house or cars. But today, many people are reassured to do that with strangers.

Airbnb and Uber have opened the windows of sharing economy in homestay accommodation and transportation, respectively, bringing a new start of the sharing economy. Any free asset, skill, virtual thing, time and talent can be shared within the legal range, from pet care to yacht rental, and you can even rent out your bathroom to someone in urgent need via Airbnb. Since many of these vast resources are idle, their prices are lower than the market prices; and thanks to the convenience brought by the mobile Internet, the sharing economy mode has permeated into various fields including clothing, food, accommodation, and transportation.

Of course, the development of sharing economy has not been smooth sailing. In June 2013, the first malignant accident of Airbnb took place—"the looting scandal". A landlord called EJ found his apartment in San Francisco robbed of everything by the tenants brought by Airbnb.

He wrote in his letter to Airbnb, "They dug a hole in my cabinet and took away my passport, cash, credit cards and the jewelry of my grandma. They also took my camera, iPod, the old computer and the external hard drive which contained all my photos and logs. They looted everything of mine." That might be the concern of everyone about sharing economy. Without an intermediary company or brand

endorsement, how can we guarantee the safety between people?

But after that scandal, Airbnb started more comprehensive safety countermeasures, including doubling the service personnel, setting up a department for safety and trust, establishing the landlord safety education center, designing enhancement tools to verify the user information, facilitating the communication between landlords and tenants before subscription, and providing insurance service for the landlords. Meanwhile, the data of each reservation—booking, payment, landlord-tenant communication, and evaluation—are all on the Airbnb platform, so that the company can fully trace every deal.

Main fields of the sharing economy market

Consumer Business

In the age of agricultural economy, the core of economic activities was the land, and the landowners possessed a great amount of wealth; in the age of industrial economy, the core of economic activities was the product, and the entrepreneurs were the ones everybody envied; in the post-industrial economy age, the core of economic activities was the channel, where the distributors① were the most glamorous figures. Then, in the current age of mobile Internet, what is the core of economic activities? And who are the ones most favored by the age? In the age of sharing economy, the consumer businesses will be those ones of the age!

Nowadays, legal businessmen all find it harder and harder to do business. In spite of the quality, there are too many products in the market now which have been inundant. It is really hard to sell the good products, for the intermediate link from the manufacturers to the consumers is full of unimaginable competitions, too. Once a product gets popular, there'll be fake products, and the final victims will be the manufacturer and the consumers. When the economic activities come to the terminal, those who own the consumers will earn the money! Now every businessman is thinking about how to own and

target the consumers.

In the past, all the product profits were created by the consumers but taken by the manufacturers and distributors, and the consumers had nothing but the product whose price was much higher than its value. We could only buy things blindly, passively and reluctantly due to the asymmetric information, and we only had a few choices.

Today, as the market is opened, there have been more and more good products. And we have adequate power of decision about where to buy and what to buy.

Therefore, the consumers have been the core of economic activities for the manufacturers and distributors, where there is great fortune and numerous opportunities!

The economic competition of the sharing economy age is centered on the consumers, so an insightful and capable consumer should organize surrounding consumers to share the wealth with the manufacturers. Organizing and managing the consumers, as it is a kind of labor, will have earnings. That's a commercial activity. So such a consumer is also a business, i.e., the consumer business. In fact, the behavior of the consumer business has existed for a long time, but this concept

① *Distributors: the units or individuals owning only sales or services in a certain area or field. Distributors have independent operating agencies and the ownership of the commodities (buy out the products/services of the manufacturers); they operate multiple types of commodities and gain the operating profits. Their operating activities are not or are rarely limited by the suppliers; the two parties take responsibilities according to their rights, respectively.*

has been ignored by us. For example, you bought a beautiful and cheap garment and told your colleagues and friends, but they didn't know where to buy it, so you took them there. That is to say, you've led the consumption. But the store owner didn't give any benefit; it was just a favor you did for your friends. What you did is already the behavior of a consumer business, only you were doing it without earnings.

The process of competing for consumers or owning and targeting consumers is just the process of gathering individual consumers into a group, which, in the competition of the new age, can only be completed by consumers instead of the manufacturers or the distributors, because consumers have the consistent standpoint and are easy to have uniform ideas and cooperative actions. Why? Because there have been numerous manufacturers and distributors jointly taking our money away, leaving us with unworthy or even fake products, which has harmed our purchase desire and confidence in happy consumption. Since individual consumers will inevitably form consumer groups, if you, as a consumer, have not united others as a consumer business today, others will unite you as consumer businesses tomorrow! We don't have to talk much about the economic interest relationships therein. Maybe in a short time, when you meet your friend, he will tell you proudly that he's a consumer business!

Li Keqiang mentioned at Davos that the global sharing economy had been rapidly developing currently, establishing a reasonable wealth distribution pattern with low cost, fast speed, and joint fortune creating. In this age of revolutionary changes, the consumers will also change from their previous roles in production and consumption into the consumer businesses.

What kind of group is the group of Consumer Business? It depends on the structure of the platform and the scale of the platform organization. It can be a large company or a small company, a large team or an individual. Consumer Business is a business subject in the first place, with unique features as a brand-new business subject, e.g.:

(1) Consumer Business is a brand-new opportunity marketer giving others not only products but also opportunities.

(2) Consumer Business advocates "Spend what should be spent and earn what shouldn't be earned", bringing a brand-new profit distribution rule.

(3) Consumer Business doesn't have to invest and there are a number of employees and scientists working for him. It's a business subject with no risk.

(4) Consumer Business is only spreading an opportunity of saving and making money, not responsible for specific operation. He's the best operator enjoying financial freedom.

(5) Consumer Business is a business mode with the lightest asset.

(6) Consumer Business could be the primary occupation or the secondary occupation.

(7) Consumer Business brings a consumption revolution, where the consumers participate in profit distribution, more people have become consumers, and the distribution is more reasonable.

(8) Consumer Business will be the key subject of sales, superior to the original stores, as the best complementation of the new age.

It can be seen that in the current sharing economy age, the core of economic activities will be the consumers, and the consumer businesses will be the favorite group of the age! And the platform is of significant meaning to the ones favored by the age. The existence of the platform is meant to release the value hidden in excess capacity by uniting with others: capital, time, expertise, and creativity, etc. To utilize the value of excess capacity is just sharing economy.

🔍 Case Study Ecological Consumption Theory of Shiyi Culture

Shandong Shiyi Culture is a comprehensive industrial group integrating culture, public welfare, sports, health, entertainment, funds, films and television, and insurance. With culture + Internet as the portal, the new financial trend as the guide, by means of the operation philosophy integrating online consumption, exchange operation, and offline service, the group substantially improves the supply side efficiency and urges the suppliers to complete their service for the customers, guiding the second consumption revolution of China and establishing a brand-new culture and health industry consumption platform of "New Culture, New Mode, New Retail, and Comprehensive Health".

Group photo of Shiyi Culture 2017

Focusing on the platform construction of multi-industrial integration and collaborative revitalization, the group provides professional services such as value-added consumption, assets management, healthy life, sports, leisure and entertainment, and public welfare relying on the diversified resource advantages in various industries and the global member channels.

Now Shiyi Culture has set up branches in multiple Chinese cities, and made large-scale equity investments in Wynn Group, Qijiu Sports, Yiran Jewelry, and Manulife Insurance successively, owning the core IPs of various correlative industries, and gradually developing the unique business mode and capital accumulation with core competitiveness. The core culture of Shiyi is "kind"; integrity, friendliness, responsibility, and passion are the codes of conduct of all the employees of Shiyi; and to help more people live their ideal life is the mission of Shiyi.

Shiyi provides cultured products and services for customers relying on its copyrighted 4C operation model and 4C product model. The users can enjoy benefits in the discount class, have a good time in the class upgrade promotion lucky draw, appreciate and invest in artworks in the first class, and experience the new technology in the smart class. It's the first domestic C2B+F2C new retail e-commerce platform in the current environment of new age and new culture.

The ecological environment of closed-loop consumption:

The super users establish a relationship with Shiyi Culture by consumption, and then Shiyi Culture returns bonus points to the super users, by which the super users can make the second-time consumption.

Bonus points are value-added rewards given to the super users. It is a closed-loop consumption scene from the super users to Shiyi Culture, the basis of which is the ecological consumption theory in the loop.

The four conditions of the ecological consumption theory are as follows:

Ecological need: the customer demand

Ecological environment: the operation mode

Ecological industry: the industry conditions

Ecological culture: the brand concept

By the design of this closed-loop consumption ecological environment, Shiyi has rapidly gathered high-quality customers, i.e., the super users, and has fully operated the user resources in a relatively closed scene, benefiting the users to the maximum, improving the users' trust in and reliance on the products and services of Shiyi, and accumulating a large batch of high-quality users for the enterprise.

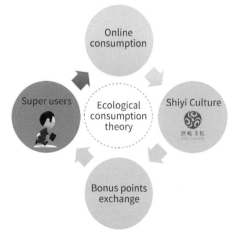

Ecological Consumption Theory

Chapter 14

The Marketing Law of Super Users

Topics:

1. Psychological Cognition Rules of Common Users
2. Psychological Cognition Rules of Super Users

To experience the entrepreneurship in China, you can go sit a while in the Start-up Cafes. "Order a cup of coffee and enjoy the free open office environment for a day." From the 3W® Coffee, Garage Café, and Binggo Café on the Zhongguancun Street of Beijing to places in Hangzhou, Shenzhen, Wuhan, Chengdu, and Urumchi, innovative start-up incubators named as cafes are blooming everywhere in China. Groups of young people fight against time for their dreams regardless of day or night in such places. That's the real scene of grassroots and public entrepreneurship in China.

With the rapid advancing of the Internet, mobile platforms, and big data, etc., there have been endless new business forms and modes, which has triggered a new round of entrepreneurship. In this sense, entrepreneurship not only refers to that of undergraduates or poor people, but also may involve every industry, especially those unbreakable industries in your eyes, which are more likely to be permeated by the mobile Internet.

Such industries as banking and communications have already been impacted; so what other industries can't be impacted?

We've noticed that there has been a trend since 2014: firstly, outsiders defeat insiders; secondly, some small- and micro-sized enterprises have thoroughly changed the whole industry by fragmented development and the passionate participation of the public.

The wealth will be restructured in the mobile Internet age, and the transformation and upgrading of the service mode, manufacturing mode, transaction mode, and payment mode will surely force those non-transforming enterprises in turn. The wealth in the past 30 years since the reform and opening up has certain laws. But the wealth in the coming 30 years is uncertain. But one thing is for sure, that is, it must have something to do with the mobile Internet's application of the marketing law of super users.

3W is the contacts circle constituted by the leading entrepreneurs and investors of the Chinese Internet industry. 3W is an organization of corporate operation, including the businesses of angel investment, clubs, enterprise public relations, conference organization, and cafes. 3W Coffee is a café operational entity owned by 3W.

Psychological Cognition Rules of Common Users

The starting point of understanding the consumer behaviors is the stimulus-response model shown in Figure 14-1. The stimulus of marketing and environment enters the consciousness of the consumer, and then a set of psychological processes reflecting the consumer features leads to the decision-making process and purchase decision. The task of the marketer is to figure out what has happened in the consumer's consciousness between the external marketing stimulus and the final purchase decision.

The four key psychological processes, i.e., cognition, emotion, memory, and association, influence the response of the consumer fundamentally.

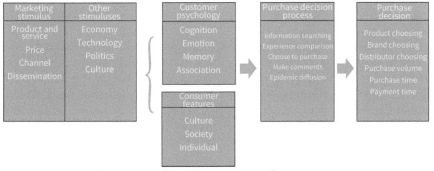

Figure 14-1   The behavior pattern of consumers.

I. Motives: Freud, Maslow, and Herzberg

We have many needs at any time. Some are biogenic needs caused by physiological stress, such as hunger, thirst, or illness; while some are psychogenic needs caused by psychological stress, such as the desire for acknowledgment, respect, and the sense of belonging. When the need is strong enough to drive us to take actions, the need turns into the motive. The motive has the directivity—we'll choose a target instead of another, and the intensity—we'll pursue the target with more or less energy.

There are three most famous human motivation theories, i.e., the theories of Sigmund Freud, Abraham H. Maslow, and Frederick Herzberg, which have provided different directions for consumer analysis and marketing strategy.

The Theory of Freud Freud held that most of the psychological factors constituting human behaviors are unconscious and that no one can completely understand his own motives. When someone is investigating a certain brand, he or she responds not only to the clearly expressed brand performance, but also to those factors that are not clearly realized by him/her, such as the shape, size, weight, texture, color and brand of the product. A technique called "laddering" can help us track from the instrumental motivation to the final internal motivation of a person. Then the marketer can decide the degree of information and appeal to be developed.

Many motivation researchers are still using the traditional explanations of Freud today. Jan Cállebaut defined that a product can satisfy different motives of a customer. For example, whisky can satisfy people's needs for social contact and entertainment, social status or recreation. Different whisky brands need to be oriented to one of the three appeals in the perspective of motives. Another motivation researcher, Clotaire Rapaille, is devoted to solving the "code" behind the product behaviors.

Sina Microblog Before the emergence of WeChat, the development of Sina Microblog was actually propelled by celebrities and their circles of acquaintances. Promotion via celebrities was well used by Sina when it operated the blogs in the earlier years. But different from the blogs, it is easier for the microblogs, featured by the limit of 140 words and the sharing of texts and pictures anytime anywhere, to blend into our life, allowing the users to fully utilize their fragmented time to post more trivial and daily things more frequently. If the once popular celebrity blogs are long serials expected by the fans every day, then the fragmented microblogs are little windows to the daily life and emotions of the celebrities. We can follow the life and inner feelings of other people more easily and more frequently through the microblogs, which better satisfies our desire of prying. Freud held that prying into others'

privacy is the natural instinct of people which derives from their childhood curiosity about their own life experience and is also required by their personal growth.

The Theory of Maslow Maslow tried to explain why people are driven by specific needs at specific time. He held that human needs can be listed in the ascending order of urgency as physiological need, safety need, social need, esteem, and self-actualization. And people will try to satisfy the most important need first, and then the secondary need. For example, a man suffering hunger and cold (the primary need) won't care about the news of the art circle (the fifth need), other people's opinions about him (the third or the fourth need), or whether the air he's breathing is clean or not (the second need); but when he's got enough water and food, the secondary need will stand out.

The Theory of Herzberg Herzberg proposed the Two-factor Theory which distinguished the dissatisfiers (factors causing dissatisfaction) and the satisfiers (factors causing satisfaction). The purchase behavior cannot be motivated by just removing the dissatisfiers; a product must have satisfiers. For example, a computer without warranty might be a dissatisfier. However, the warranty still may not serve as a satisfier or arouse the purchase motive, because the warranty is not the real satisfier of a computer, while simple operation might be.

The theory of Herzberg has two levels of meanings. Firstly, the seller should eliminate the dissatisfiers as much as possible (e.g., unqualified training manual or incomplete service policies). Although those factors can't ensure the selling of the commodity, they can destroy the deal easily. Secondly, the seller must recognize the major factors of product satisfaction and purchase motives in the market and provide appropriate products accordingly.

Cognition A person with motives is ready to act anytime, while his way of act is influenced by his environmental perception. In marketing, the cognition is more important than the fact, because the cognition will influence the actual behaviors of the consumers. Cognition means the process where a person chooses, organizes, and explains the information he receives to generate a meaningful description of the external world. It depends on not only the physical stimulus, but also the relationship between the stimulus and the surrounding environment as well as the personal status quo. A man may think that a fast-speaking salesperson is overbearing and insincere, but another man may find that salesperson smart and helpful. Everyone may have different responses to that salesperson.

People may have different cognitions about the same stimulus because of three cognitive processes: selective attention, selective distortion, and selective retention.

Selective Attention Attention means the processing capacity distributed for some stimuli. Intentional attention is purposeful attention; unintentional attention is the attention caused by someone or something. It is estimated that an ordinary man comes into contact with over 1,500 ads or brand messages every day. As we can't pay attention to all these messages, we screen out most of the stimuli, and that process is called selective attention. Selective attention means the marketer must try to draw the attention of the consumers, and the real challenge is to know the kinds of stimuli that can win people's attention.

Some research results are shown below:

(1) People are more likely to pay attention to the stimuli relevant to their current need. A man with the purchase motive for a computer may pay attention to a computer ad, instead of a DVD ad.

(2) People are more likely to pay attention to the stimuli they expect. In a computer store, you are more likely to pay attention to the computer products instead of radios, because you don't expect any radio to be in that store.

(3) People are more likely to pay attention to the stimuli that are much different from ordinary stimuli. On a computer advertisement, you are more likely to see the computer ad of USD $100 reduction instead of the 5-dollar one.

Although we screen out many stimuli, we'll still be influenced by a number of unexpected stimuli, e.g., unexpected offers from e-mails, phone calls or the salespersons. In order to prevent their products being screened out, the marketers should try everything to draw the attention of the consumers during the promotion.

Selective Distortion Even if the stimulus can be noticed, the way of notice might not always be what the communicator wants. Selective distortion means the tendency of interpreting the information

according to the preconception. Consumers often distort the information to make it conform to their previous belief and expectation about the product and the brand.

A "blind test" on the product flavor has shown the power of the consumers' brand belief. In the test, two groups of consumers tasted a product; one group didn't know the brand, while the other knew it. Although they tasted the same product, the two groups always gave different opinions!

The reason why the consumers give different opinions about the same product (with and without the brand logo) must be that their brand and product belief (formed by past experience or brand marketing activities) has somehow changed their product perception. Such cases can be found in every product. When the consumers distort neutral or obscure brand information into positive information, the selective distortion is beneficial to the marketers of powerful brands. In other words, the coffee of that brand tastes better, the car of that brand drives smoother, and the waiting time in that bank seems shorter... All of those are determined by the brand.

Selective Retention Most of us don't remember much of the information we see, but we will retain the information that supports our attitude and belief. Due to selective retention, we may remember the advantages of our favorite product but forget the advantages of other competitive brands. The selective retention is also beneficial to the power brands. That's also why marketers must keep sending messages again and again, so as to ensure their messages are not ignored.

Subliminal[①] Perception The selective cognition mechanism requires the active participation and thinking of consumers. The marketers selling armchairs to the elderly for years are always interested in the concept of subliminal perception. They hold that the marketers should place the concealed and subliminal messages into the ads or packages. The consumers won't recognize these messages, but their behaviors will be influenced by them. Although the psychological process contains many subtle subliminal impacts, there's no proof that the marketers can systematically control the subconscious of the consumers, especially their significant or deep-rooted brand beliefs.

Emotion The responses of the consumers are not always cognitive and

① Subliminal: a psychological term referring to the part of human mental activities that can't be cognized or is not cognized, "the process of human mental activities that has happened but is not in a conscious state yet". Freud divided the subconscious into preconsciousness and unconsciousness, or preconsciousness and subconsciousness.

① Dibaofu: a formula independently developed by P&G, used for the Safeguard products. Its major chemical composition is called "triclocarban", effective in removing and restraining viruses. Generally, washing hands is a kind of mechanical virus elimination, and you may still get in contact with lots of bacteria after washing your hands. A bacteriostatic environment can be created by using "Dibaofu".

rational; most of them are sensitive and can arouse various emotions. A brand or a product may make the consumers proud, happy, or confident. An ad may bring pleasure, disgust, or doubt.

The two examples below can explain the function of emotions on the consumers' decision-making.

Haagen-Dazs is reputed by *The New York Times* as "the Rolls-Royce of ice creams". It is a world-famous ice cream brand of 60 years of history, developing from a family manual workshop to the current global No. 1 ice cream brand. Haagen-Dazs always claims itself as an eternal affection, and never worries about marketing. For those loyal fans, Haagen-Dazs is all about love, just like roses. Haagen-Dazs relates its products with the sweetness of love, attracting frequent couples as customers. The tender and romantic atmosphere in and outside its stores strengthens its brand image. All of its product manuals and posters show the romantic scenes of hugging couples, fully expressing the brand appeal of "enjoyable experience". The decoration, lighting, lines of tables and chairs, and colors of its exclusive stores are all emphasizing that theme. The slogan most familiar to the Chinese consumers is, "If you love her, take her to Haagen-Dazs."

An ad of Safeguard of P&G must be known to many people, which is played on various big TV stations and can be called the best case of the excellent marketing strategy of P&G. It's like this: in the classroom, the children sneeze one by one (it's obvious that they've got a cold); then a young mother appears and says earnestly, "Children are easy to catch a cold, because they are impacted by the viruses. Want to eliminate the viruses? Please use Safeguard!" Then Safeguard appears with a series of function descriptions; then comes the voice-over, "Keep the viruses away from you—Safeguard!" As the No. 1 brand in the fancy soap market of China, Safeguard occupies 41.95% of the market, which is far beyond the competitors. That's a result of its constant advertisement placement, but its adherence to the appeal of "virus elimination" for ten years is the root cause for its success.

Right upon its release to the market, Safeguard focused its appeal on "virus elimination", arguing that the human body is very easy to be infected by bacteria during football playing, bus taking, and games by means of the recommendation of Chinese Medical Association and experiments. Obviously, Safeguard was educating the consumers, so as to expand its market. Then it timely claimed that the active Dibaofu① contained in its product not only could remove the microorganisms on the skin, but also could restrain the regen-

Memory Cognition

eration of the bacteria effectively. By the didactic ad expression and the induction of the approachable advertising characters, Safeguard has successfully established the brand image of "virus elimination expert" in the heart of the consumers.

Memory Cognition Psychologists divide the memory into short-term memory (temporarily stored information with limited capacity) and long-term memory (persistently stored information with basically unlimited capacity). All the information and experience accumulated in our life can grow into long-term memory.

As to the long-term memory structure, the most commonly held idea is that we will form a certain association model. For example, the associative network memory model regards the long-term memory as composed of a series of nodes and links. The information storing nodes are connected by links of different intensity degrees. Any form of information can be stored in this memory network, including literal, visual, abstract, and contextual information. The process of extension and activation from one node to another determines the amount of the information we can search and what information can be truly recalled in a specific situation. When we encode the external information (e.g., when we read or hear a word or phrase) or retrieve the internal information from our long-term memory (e.g., when we think of a certain concept), a node in our memory will be activated; and if that activated node is strongly related to other nodes, the other relevant nodes will be activated, too.

In this model, we can regard the consumers' brand knowledge as a node with multiple correlations in the memory. The intensity and structure of these correlations will decide the information we can recall about the brand. Brand association includes all the thoughts, feelings, perceptions, impressions, experiences, beliefs, and attitudes relevant to the brand node.

We can regard marketing as a method ensuring that the consumers can experience the product and service so as to form a proper brand knowledge structure and store it in their memory. P&G likes to create the mental map that can describe the specific brand knowledge of the consumers. The map shows the important relations between the consumers and the brand, as well as the intensity, the consumers' preference degree, and uniqueness of such relations, which are all caused by the marketing scheme.

Memory Process The memory is a constructive process, for we can't completely and accurately remember information and events. Usually we only remember some fragments and replenish the missing parts with other known information. "How to Win People's Heart" in the following marketing insights section has provided some practical tips to help the marketers to ensure the internal or external ideas of their companies to be remembered and to exert an influence.

Memory encoding explains how and where the information enters the memory. The relation intensity in the memory depends on the processed amount of information (e.g., how much do we consider about the information) and the way of processing during encoding. Generally, when we focus more on the meaning of the information, we'll have a stronger relation in our memory. An on-site advertising research shows that compared with repeatedly played ads with low involvement and persuasion, the ads with high involvement and persuasion that are not often played have a greater influence on the sales.

Memory retrieval means how the information is retrieved from the memory.

Association Psychologically, association is a reflection process between reproductive imagination and creative imagination, reintegrated from a certain presentation to another presentation. In marketing, it is the transition of the thought from one object to another object: the former object is often concrete, simple, or of the natural world, while the latter is usually more universal, complicated, uncertain, and social. It's a special method of imagery thinking, for the two don't have such inevitable and logical relation between a premise and its conclusion. However, the latter doesn't emerge out of the void, and the former does not transit to the latter randomly. During that transition, the former must have thought-provoking features, and the latter must apply such features to the maximum, reintegrating them; thus the new object will be born naturally, which must better embody the essence of the features of the original object and deepen, expand, and enhance the meanings of those features.

As shown by numerous consumer psychology and marketing surveys as well as empirical researches, the selling of the product and service is significantly related to the product's association in the consumers' mind. When the enterprise is building its brand image, the product image will jointly form some relations with the existing relevant images, behaviors, experiences, and perceptions of the consumers, thus forming the brand association.

That is the psychological basis of brand association. Once it takes shape, the brand association will seriously influence the purchase decision-making of the consumers.

According to Keller, brand association can be divided into the following three types: attributes, benefits, and attitudes. We can measure and establish positive and healthy brand images by those three association types.

II. Marketing Insights: How to Win People's Heart

①

The tipping point: a concept put forward by the British writer Malcolm Gladwell in his book The Tipping Point, which explains the reasons of many unintelligible fashion trends and discovers the factors therein. He explains that a fashion trend can be easily promoted by mastering such factors.

With reference to the concept firstly proposed by Malcolm Gladwell in his book *The Tipping Point*①, brothers Chip Heath and Dan Heath began to explore what on earth makes a conception take root in the heart of the audience. After investigating a number of conceptions of various sources (including urban legend, conspiracy theory, public policy authorization, and product design), they've found that all the great conceptions have six features which can be summarized as the acronym of "SUCCES":

(1) Simple: seize the core and hit the bull's eye. Adopt and refine an idea, and remove all the immaterial things, e.g., "The tickets of Southwest Airlines are cheap".

(2) Unexpected: make surprise moves and attract the attention. The customer service of Nordstrom is world-renowned, for it surprisingly exceeds the existing high expectation of the customers. They not only assist with purchase, but also care about the personal status of the customers: ironing the customer's shirt before a meeting, warming up the customer's car when he/she is about to finish the purchase, or providing gift packing even if the commodity is bought at Macy's, a retail competitor.

(3) Concrete: ensure that any conception can be easily comprehended and remembered. Boeing Co. successfully designed the 727 aircraft because the thousands of engineers of the company confirmed a concrete target—the aircraft must be able to carry 131 people, fly directly from New York to Miami, and land on the runway of LaGuardia Airport (which is not available for large aircrafts).

(4) Credibility: the conception must be credible. The Indian overnight express service company Safexpress successfully overcame the doubt of a Bollywood film studio about its express ability: it sent 69,000 "Harry Potter" books to the bookstores over the nation before 8:00 a.m. of the release day of the latest fiction.

(5) Emotion: help people comprehend the essence of the conception. Research on anti-smoke ads has shown that emotional ads are more convincing and more impressive than fact-based ads.

(6) Stories: let people use a conception by storytelling. Research also shows that narration can cause psychological stimulation, and visual events can make later memory and learning easier.

The Heath brothers think great conceptions are created relying on the above features instead of coming out of nothing. The advertisement of Subway is an example. The protagonist of the ad is a man called Jared who eats two Subway sandwiches every day. After three months, he loses 100 pounds. That ad increased the sales volume of Subway by 18% after one year. According to the Heath brothers, that conception got high scores in all the above six aspects.

(1) Simple: lose weight.

(2) Unexpected: lose weight by eating fast food.

(3) Concrete: lose weight by eating two Subway sandwiches every day.

(4) Credible: 100 pounds as the proof.

(5) Emotion: overcome the troublesome weight problem.

(6) Stories: personally telling how incredible it is to lose weight by eating two Subway sandwiches every day.

Psychological Cognition Rules of Super Users

The basic psychological process mentioned above is crucial to the actual purchase decision-making of the consumers. The following are the major questions the

marketers should ask about the consumer behaviors, i.e., who, what, when, where, how, why, and we.

Who will buy our product and service?
Who will make the product purchase decision?
Who will influence the product purchase decision?
How is the purchase decision made?
Who will act what roles?
What will the customer buy? What needs must be satisfied?
Why would the customer buy a certain product?
Where do they buy the product or service?
When will they buy it? Are there seasonal changes?
How does the customer think about our product?
What's the customer's attitude toward our product?
What social factors are determining the purchase decision?
Do the lifestyles of the customers influence their decision?
How do the personal factors or demographic factors influence the purchase decision?

Wise companies try to comprehensively understand the purchase decision-making process of the customers, including all their experiences of learning, choosing, using, and handling the product. Marketing scholars have developed a "stage model" of the purchase decision-making process. The consumers will go through five stages: information searching, experience comparison, choosing to purchase, make comments, and epidemic diffusion. Obviously, the purchase process starts before the actual purchase and still lasts a long time after the purchase.

The purchase of the consumers may not always go through all the five stages successively, and may get over or reverse some stages. When you buy a toothpaste brand frequently used by you, you'll skip information searching and evaluation and directly enter the stage of choosing to purchase. That frame takes all possible factors into consideration when the consumers face new high-involvement purchase. The decision-making rule of super users is very different from that of common users, mainly shown in the five stages.

I. Information Searching

Surveys have shown that for durable goods, half of the consumers only go to one store. For home appliances, only 30% consumers pay attention to more than one brand. We can divide the participation levels of searching into two kinds: the medium searching status is called heightened attention, under which a person is more likely to receive the product information; under the high searching level, the person may begin active information search, where he will search for data, call his friends, and get familiar with the product online or in the store.

The major information sources of the consumers include four types:

Personal source: family, friends, neighbors, and acquaintances;

Commercial source: ads, network, salespersons, distributors, packaging, and demonstrations;

Public source: the mass media, and the consumer rating agency;

Experience source: handling, checking and using the product.

The relative amount and influence of the above information sources vary with

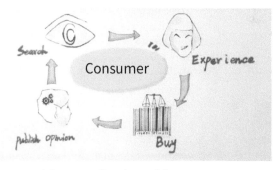

Information Searching of Consumer

the product type and the features of the buyer. Usually, the largest product information amount for the consumers comes from the commercial source which is controlled by the marketers. However, the most effective information usually comes from the personal or experience sources, as well as the public source which is an independent authority.

Each information source has different influences on the purchase decision. The commercial source is generally for informing, and the personal source for judging or evaluating. For example, physicians often get to know new drugs via the commercial source, but will give evaluations by consulting other doctors.

Another portal is the vertical niche app. In the age of mobile Internet, BAT[①] is still very strong, but is also passing by. In some industries with online and offline transactions and some professional vertical fields, BAT has lost its dominance in terms of flow advantage, and has to enhance itself by investments and incorporation.

DiDi and Eleme are sensational venture projects emerging in 2014. DiDi has been subordinated by Tencent, and Eleme also chose to ally with dianping.com. The key to success of these two cases is targeting the offline market which is the blind zone of BAT. To persuade the taxi drivers to install a taxiing app is not what Tencent would like to do, nor is looking for small restaurants for cooperation with big business in the eyes of Baidu and Alibaba.

As apps are becoming mobile portals that bring massive users, they'll certainly be a trend. Of course, the first targets must be those apps that will never be uninstalled. The diversification and professionalization of apps has led to the result that people don't want to download apps and uninstall those that are not opened in a while. The apps tend to be simplified; the users won't easily download a new app to occupy their cellphone space and flow. So we can solve this problem in two ways. Firstly, keep digging the apps that will never be uninstalled by the users, e.g., the social media (WeChat, Microblog, and QQ), videos, and music. Or secondly, create your own light app. The light app is a fashionable trend at present. It doesn't require the users to click for download and occupy the internal storage, but the users can obtain rich information just in a moment, such as videos, music, and interaction. The "lightness" of mini programs is relatively in line with people's Internet life habits at present.

Nowadays, information searching relies not only on Baidu alone, but also on various apps of the vertical industries, e.g., dianping.com for restaurant searching, ctrip.com and Qunar.com for hotel and air ticket searching, etc.

II. Experience Comparison

Shifting from the "product" to "experience" is the second stage feature of the super users.

Experience consumption is a new consumption mode, where the consumers will try out and feel the commodity by direct experience, thus guiding the consumption of the new commodity. This consumption mode is a marketing innovation, and is well-received by the consumers.

Experience consumption allows the consumers to directly feel the new commodity, helpful for getting familiar with the commodity performance, understanding the functions, and learning the usage, thus rapidly arousing the purchase desire of the consumers. Meanwhile, by experience consumption, the manufacturer can directly get to know the appeal and dig out the demand of the consumers and improve the commodity design and quality during interaction with the consumers, creating new value for them, which will be one stroke serving multiple purposes.

There are diversified methods for experience comparison, three of which are relatively successful, including giving away, free use, and trial use.

1. Giving away

Directly giving away the commodity to the consumer is the simplest experience consumption. Generally speaking, household goods and food are suitable to be directly given away. When a new drink needs to be promoted, the manufacturer puts a basketball stand in the store and asks the customers to throw the ball in turn. Those who score a goal will get a bottle of the new drink for free, and they need to fill in a feedback form after drinking. This method is interesting and attracts many customers. If they think it tastes good, they'll pass on the news from mouth to mouth, thus rapidly achieving the effect of marketing.

2. Free Use

The essence of freely used commodities is free service, letting the consumers experience the service function, which is very effective for new commodities that only produce results upon firsthand experience. There's a kind of new physiotherapy equipment that can prevent and treat various chronic diseases, helpful for improving the physical quality. Generally, the consumers won't trust such equipment at their first contact with it; therefore, the manufacturer arranged a hall with multiple pieces of such equipment for free use of the customers. Thanks to the favorable effect, people queued to use them every day. The market was rapidly opened by the free use experience, and many customers provided feedbacks, which formed a virtuous cycle of promotion.

3. Trial Use

Trial use has been widely carried out, very effective for the marketing of bulk merchandises, especially durable consumer goods. Two big Japanese companies, Toyota and Panasonic, both have large demonstration squares where they show their latest cars, home appliances and digital electronic products to the customers. They encourage the customers for trial use during the demonstration and teach them the usage on site. They are afraid to break the goods during the trial use, and they listen to the customers' opinions and propose improvement schemes. The active participation of the consumers plays an irreplaceable role in satisfying the consumers with new commodities, which really shows the great power of experience consumption.

Experts think that when the economy is developed to a certain degree, the key point of consumption will shift from "products" and "services" to "experience". That's a natural state of human development.

However, the basis and carrier of "experience comparison" are still traditional commodities and services. The difference is that there has been the "experience value" condensed in those commodities and services, such as entertainment factors and cultural factors.

III. Choosing to Purchase

The complexity of the purchase decision-making process of different consumers varies due to many factors, the major factors of which are the participation degree and the brand difference. Super users have a much higher participation degree than common users. The greater the difference between the different brands of the same product category, the higher the product price. The consumers will feel greater risks when they are lacking in product knowledge and purchase experience, and the purchase process will be more complex, too. For example, the purchase complexities of toothpaste and matches and of computers and vehicles are obviously different.

There are four types of purchasing behaviors based on the participation degree of the buyer and the brand difference degree.

1. Complex Purchasing Behaviors

If the consumer is highly involved and knows that there are significant differences between the existing brands, types, and specifications, the complex purchasing behavior will be generated. The complex purchase behavior means the consumer will go through the stages of massive information collecting, comprehensive product evaluating, prudent purchase decision-making, and careful post-purchase evaluating. For example, the home computer is expensive, with great differences between different brands. If someone wants to buy a home computer but doesn't know anything about hard disk, internal storage, mainboard, CPU, resolution, and Windows, so that he can't judge the performance, quality and price of different brands, hasty purchase would be very risky. Therefore, he needs to collect massive data, make clear lots of questions, and gradually build a belief for the product which will turn into an attitude, and then he can make a prudent purchase decision.

For complex purchasing behaviors, the marketers should make strategies to help the buyers master the product knowledge, publicize the advantages of the brand by print media, broadcast media, and salespersons, and mobilize the shop assistants and family and friends of the buyers to influence their final purchase decision, thus simplifying the purchase process.

2. Habitual Purchasing Behaviors

The consumers' purchasing behavior for cheap and frequently bought commodities is the simplest. This kind of commodities has little differences in brands, and the consumers are very familiar with them. They don't spend time in choosing and just buy them on site right away. Oil and salt are such commodities. This simple purchasing behavior doesn't go through information searching, product feature evaluating, and final decision-making, etc.

The major marketing strategies for habitual purchasing behaviors are:

(1) Propel trial use by means of price and selling. As the product has little unique advantages compared with other similar brands to make the customers interested, we can only adopt the reasonable price, benefits, sales exhibition, demonstration, giving away, and prize-giving sales to attract them for trial use. Once they get to know and get used to some product, they may frequently buy it and develop that into a purchasing habit.

(2) Strengthen the consumers' impression by large amounts of repeated ads. In the situation of low involvement and little brand difference, the consumers don't actively collect brand information or evaluate the brands; they just passively receive the information from various dissemination modes including the ads, and choose according to their familiarity degree toward the brands. They choose a certain brand not necessarily because they are touched by the ad or loyal to that brand, but because they are familiar with it. They don't even evaluate it after purchasing, for they don't really care. The purchase process is: forming the brand belief by passive learning, purchasing behavior, and then the evaluating process (if any). So enterprises must make the customers receive the ad information passively and get familiar with the brand.

For better effects, the ad information should be short and powerful, emphasizing a few key points and highlighting the visual symbol and visual image. According to the classical control theory, when a product symbol is continuously repeated, the buyer will recognize the product among the numerous similar products.

(3) Increase the purchase involvement and brand difference. In habitual purchasing behaviors, the consumers only buy their familiar brands and seldom consider about changing the brand. If the competitor transforms the low-participation product to high-participation product by technical progress and product upgrading and enlarge the difference with similar products, it will propel the consumers to change their original habitual purchasing behavior and seek for the new brand. The main way of increasing the involvement is to add important functions to unimportant products, and to widen the gap with similar products in price and level.

For example, if a shampoo only has the function of cleaning, it is a low-participation product and has no difference from other similar products, and can only compete through a low price; if the anti-dandruff function is added, the involvement is increased, and the sales can be expanded even if the price is raised; and if the nutritious function is added, too, both the involvement and brand difference will be further increased.

3. Diversity-seeking Purchasing Behaviors

Some commodities have obvious differences between brands, but the consumers don't want to waste time on it and just keep buying different brands. For example, when buying desserts, the consumers won't spend time in choosing and evaluating; they'll just buy another brand next time. They do that not because they are not satisfied with the product, but because they are seeking for diversity. They may buy chocolate sandwich biscuits this time, and cream sandwich biscuits next time. They are not unsatisfied with the chocolate ones, but they just want to have a change.

The market leaders and challengers have different marketing strategies for the diversity-seeking purchasing behaviors. The market leaders try to occupy the shelves, prevent stock-out, and release reminding ads, to encourage the consumers to develop the habitual purchasing behavior, while the challengers try to encourage the consumers to change their original habitual purchasing behavior by lower price, discounts, coupons, free samples, and ads emphasizing the trial use of the new brand.

4. Incongruity-solving Purchasing Behaviors

Some commodities have little differences between brands and are not frequently bought by the consumers; buying such commodities may be risky. The consumers may usually go to several stores to compare their products, and then spend a short time buying one, as there's no obvious difference between the various brands. Generally, when the product has a reasonable price and is convenient to be bought, the consumer will decide to buy it, such as a sofa, though the consumer will choose the style and color, the differences are slight, so he will buy one right away if it is suitable.

After the purchase, the consumer may find something incongruent or unsatisfactory, or hear someone else praising another similar commodity. Then he will search for more information and reasons during usage to relieve such incongruity and to prove that his purchase decision is right.

For such purchasing behaviors, the marketers should provide complete after-sales service and information beneficial to the enterprise and the product by various means, so as to make the customer believe that his choice is correct.

IV. Making Comments

Good products are always participated by the users. Super users have participated in the creation process of the products.

We'll take Microsoft as an example in the hope of providing you with some inspiration.

After the great success in the PC age, Microsoft met quite a few setbacks in the Internet age. At that time, its managers were distressed and didn't know why such newly established small companies like Google and Facebook could develop so fast under the competition of Microsoft, and even exceeded Microsoft in some aspects. What's the problem?

Microsoft has always been pursuing the "perfect" developing mode which doesn't allow any mistake, strict about every period. To execute that plan, no one is allowed to make mistakes. And that's a problem itself. You can see that the engineers are working behind closed doors in the whole process, making the best product in their opinion, but the users haven't participated in it. When the users haven't experienced your product yet, how can you ensure the product is good, suitable for them, or perfect? So products related to the end users must involve the users. Listen to their comments about your product and timely make corrections and improvements accordingly. In a word, it is good when the users think it good!

There are two modes based on the involvement degree of the users, i.e. the heavy mode and the light mode.

The first is the heavy mode. In this mode, the users participate in and use the product in an in-depth manner. Usually they would show high activeness and gradually develop trust and dependence on the product; sometimes they can even have a sense of belonging and pride during the product use and participation. What kind of products belongs to the heavy mode? There are two kinds: 1) the users deeply participate in the R&D of the product; 2) the product itself requires the in-depth

participation of the users; the product substance is produced and output by the users on the platform.

MIUI is a typical case of the heavy mode. It lets the users participate in the R&D process of the products. The engineers of MIUI must stay on the forums every week to listen to people's opinions about their products and the "floating" user demands; when they get to know the pain spots of the users, they can develop new functions or improve the original product to solve the users' problems. MIUI always keeps upgrading its products weekly. The product bugs proposed by the users this week may be restored in the new MIUI system next week. The users are really a part of the R&D of its products.

The second is the light mode. The product itself requires the in-depth participation of the users; in other words, the users are the producers. There are many such products at present, with high user activeness. For instance, Wikipedia is a product of such user mode. The creators of Wikipedia are not a group of selected experts, but thousands of various amateurs, enthusiastic fans, and spectators who indeed have created a great product.

In this mode, the users not only use the product, but also own the product. The sense of ownership makes the users complain about the problems they meet, and, more importantly, participate in improving the product, which leads to the result that "Everybody is the product manager". The products such as Inke, microblogs, Douban, Zhihu, and Baidu Zhidao all belong to this mode.

There's another type of products that belongs to the light mode, i.e. the users are lightly involved in the products. This type of products usually has an obvious major function, and the users only use them out of specific purposes and demands. For example, many e-commerce products nowadays have added a community or the live function to the product to increase the participation and activeness of the users.

The app of jumei.com has a community where the users can watch the live show of makeup talents, and post their moments, etc.; the app of Mogu Street also has a community where the users can share beautiful clothes, watch the live show of dressing talents, and discuss the hottest topics; the app of JD.com also has stories that popularize some life tips or common knowledge. The forms are diversified, but there's only one final purpose: retain the users, making them spend more time using the product and more interested in the product and finally pay for the product. However, in this mode, the users are still not very active in participating, because they haven't developed a habit yet. How to increase the users' passion for participation and help them develop the habit is still a problem to consider.

How to fully embody this concept in website operation is a topic worth studying. Psychologists pointed out that people tend to come to entirely different conclusions when they are in a group compared with the conclusions made when they are alone. That's because when people become a part of a group, they are more likely to feel the pressure from people around and the influence of social norms, etc. Any emerging and ideological dissemination should resort to this power of groups, of course, including the concept of website operation.

Then, how to apply that influence in website operation? The BBS community is obviously a method. It's not hard to find that the unique cultures of many great websites are developed by the users in community systems like BBS, e.g. "the dianping.com syndrome" and the Douban fans culture. But certainly, water can both carry a boat and overturn it. Quite a few large community websites have experienced the collective escape of netizens.

As a segmented social network site, Douban lets the users edit the contents by themselves, forming the unique personal center and the content-rich sharing center, which is the most outstanding and central technical application of Douban. Douban has gathered all the important technical applications of the age of Web 2.0, including SNS, WIKI, RSS, TAG, and BLOG, making such functions as "Like-minded", "Personal image", and comment orientation possible.

"Guess you like it", "Where to buy this book", and "Grade and comment" of Douban are the most typical. Let's take "Guess you like it" as an example. User A writes a piece of reading notes by the BLOG technology, which is tagged manually or automatically with the TAG technology, and then the tagged notes are processed with the function of RSS. Then here comes B (seeking for the like-minded A) who has found A's blog with some tag and then the things and people like A with the TAG and RSS functions of Douban, i.e. "Guess you like it". That's the first kind of "Guess you like it". Then thousands of As and Bs form the interest circle on Douban. You may have marked the things you've read, want to read, or like, and those techniques of Douban will automatically find the things you may be interested in, i.e. deducing your hobbies according to your behaviors. That's the second kind of "Guess you like it".

In fact, these techniques are very common now, but the key of Douban's success is to perfectly combine them to meet the demands like searching for like-minded people. And Douban began to do it very early. It can rapidly find new things that the user hasn't watched but likes, and gather people with the same interest. That is dramatically helpful for Douban to cultivate deep-diving users and attract more new users.

We've found some methods according to the above descriptions of the psychological process of common users:

(1) Contrast: common users compare the goods of various stores and buy the brand with the highest cost performance;

(2) Exclusion: to choose the product that they are most likely to buy according to their cognition;

(3) Priority: to buy the most needed thing first based on the time sequence;

(4) Quantity orientation: to choose the optimal brand according to the quantity of the things to buy;

(5) Location choice: the age, income, habits, and purchasing category will all influence the purchasing channel o the consumer.

V. Epidemic Diffusion

The purchasing behavior rule of common users is "cognition—purchase--evaluation", because they are only the buyers of the product or service, while the purchasing behavior rule of super users is "cognition—purchase--diffusion".

The reason why super users act as "free spokespersons" or "free agents" is the epidemic diffusion effect of their behaviors, which is caused by the following three situations.

(1) Cultural identity. As the marketers adopt the substance marketing strategy of the 4S theory, the culture contained in the product arouses the empathy of the users, making them believe that they are not promoting the product, but the culture behind it.

(2) The sense of participation. As the marketers adopt the method of letting the users participate in product creating of the 4S theory, they make the users believe that they are not promoting other people's product, but their own product. The product contains their efforts, creativity or inspiration. So the super users think they are not promoting some universal mass-produced product, but something they created with their wisdom.

(3) Emotions. As the marketers adopt the site dissemination strategy of the 4S theory and touch the softest part of the users' heart with pictures, texts or videos, making the super users spread out their emotions without hesitation. They believe they are not spreading a product with emotions, but the emotional empathy in the product.

Besides the three common diffusion effects above, when the super user becomes the consumer business of the product or the minority shareholder of the enterprise, he will also have epidemic diffusion behaviors driven by the benefits.

Part 5

Space

Chapter 15

Introduction of Marketing Space

Topics:

1. The Evolution of Marketing Channels
2. Age of Market Space 3.0
3. Operational Tools

We have always considered marketing experience and trading space either real (offline physical stores) or virtual (online cellphone stores). However, with the advancement of mobile technologies in the age of screens, it has become possible to fuse online and offline spaces into a unified virtual reality one. This is the theory of "screen is space".

(1) The screen itself is a space-time interface.

(2) The space-time interface itself is a closed loop (experience, transaction and service).

(3) The closed loop itself is to invite marketing.

Marketing innovation is driven by the desire for marketing efficiency, that is, whether we can accomplish all marketing links in one space and form a closed loop for efficient marketing.

Marketing is a science about both "Market" and "Field", a methodology to study how to complete transactions in a "Field", and an advanced form whereby senior marketers study how to create a larger market and to use new technological tools to complete transactions with lower cost and higher efficiency. Fortunately, the mobile Internet's virtual reality device presents a "New Field" that has never appeared in world marketing history and the mobile technology of virtual reality resolves the difficulty in marketing efficiency. This part begins with four revolutions in the history of marketing space, elaborating on the new marketing genes that are brought about by the humanity liberation caused by mobile marketing humanization - "human beings are all small universes", and finally revealing the ultimate mission of marketing innovation that mobile marketing has accomplished: the virtual reality technology builds up a brand new mobile marketing space centering on marketing efficiency and cost.

The Evolution of Marketing Channels

I. Marketing Channels

Most producers do not sell their products directly to end consumers. There is a range of marketing intermediaries to perform different functions between producers and end consumers. These intermediaries form marketing channels (also known as trade channels or distribution channels). In general, marketing channels are streamlined processes that facilitate the smooth use or consumption of products or services. They are a series of pathways along which a product or service must go ahead to be consumed by end consumers after its production.

Those intermediaries who buy in products, acquire their ownership and then sell them out to exploit the difference in pricing are called middlemen[1]. Those who look for consumers and may negotiate with consumers on behalf of producers or manufacturers but do not acquire any product ownership are called agents[2]. And those who support distribution activities but neither acquire any product ownership nor participate in any trading negotiation are called ancillary agencies[3].

All types of channels will be very important for a company to achieve success and will affect all other marketing decisions. Marketers should evaluate different types of marketing channels from the perspective of the whole process (production - distribution - sales - service).

II. Importance of Marketing Channels

Marketing Channel System is a special element of the company's distribution channel, and its decision-making is one of the most important issues that must be faced by the company's managers. In the United States, distributors usually earn a gross profit of 30% to 50% of the final sale price. By contrast, advertising costs account for only 5% to 7% of the final price. The marketing channel is also an important opportunity cost, which focuses on turning potentiality into profitability (that is, converting potential consumers into those who bring profits). The purpose of marketing channels is not only to serve the market, but also to create a market.

Channel selection will affect all other marketing decisions. A company fixes its price depending on whether it uses an exclusive shop or a high-end boutique.

The company's decisions on sales staff and advertisements also depend on how much training and incentives the distributor needs from the company. In addition, channel decisions include relatively long-term cooperation with other companies, as well as a series of policies and procedures. If a car manufacturer authorizes an independent dealer to sell its cars, the manufacturer cannot buy back its dealership on the next day to sell its cars in its own shops. Meanwhile, channel selection itself relies on the marketing strategy that the company has established based on market segmentation, target market selection and positioning considerations. All-round marketers will ensure that all these decisions from different fields can be combined to create the greatest value.

In the management of middlemen, the company must decide how much energy it will use for Advance Strategy and Pull Strategy, respectively. Advance Strategy uses the manufacturer's sales teams, promotional funds or other means to urge middlemen to buy, and promote and sell the products to end-users. The scenarios in which Advance Strategy applies include: the product has lower brand loyalty in the category, the consumer selects the brand in the shop, the consumer buys a product on impulse, or the advantages of the product are well known. In light of the Pull Strategy, manufacturers use advertisements, promotional activities and other means of communication to attract consumers to buy products from middlemen so as to encourage middlemen to place more orders. The scenarios in which the Pull Strategy applies include high brand loyalty and high product involvement. It means that people can recognize the difference among brands and can know which brand to buy before entering the shop.

 Case Study   NIKE

Nike logo.

On June 29, 2016 (Beijing time), Nike reported its fourth quarter financial results. As of May 31, 2016, Nike's net profit was USD $846 million, which was lower than the USD $865 million reported in the same period of last year, and its revenue was USD $8.24 billion, a year-on-year increase of 6%. Throughout the 2016 fiscal year, Nike's total revenue increased to USD $32.4 billion by 6% on a year-on-year basis and its annual net profit reached USD $3.76 billion. According to Townsend, Nike's fourth-quarter revenue of USD $8.24 billion was lower than the average analyst forecast – USD $8.28 billion, while the EPS (earnings per share) was unchanged at USD $0.49, USD $0.01 higher than the analyst forecast. Nike's share price dropped sharply by 6.7% to USD $49.51 in after-hour trading. Nike's global futures orders from June to November totaled USD $14.9 billion, an increase of 11% from the same period of last year, which was lower than 13% expected by analysts. The lower-than-expected futures orders again triggered investors' concern that the world's largest sports brand might have entered a period of slower growth. In the Greater China region, Nike's sales growth was 30% and 28%, respectively, in the first and second fiscal quarters of 2016, 27% in the third quarter, and 23% (calculated at constant exchange rates) in the fourth quarter. Its growth reached 27% in the whole 2016 fiscal year.

In addition, its sales revenues in Western Europe, Japan and emerging markets also featured a double-digit growth.

Then look at Nike's most important North American market. In the fourth fiscal quarter, its sales in North America increased slightly by 0.1% from the third quarter to USD $3.72 billion, which might be thanks to the Cavaliers' championship. According to CNBC expert Jim Cramer, Nike's basketball shoes sales increased by 2% on the second day of the Cavaliers' championship. Nike's revenue in the fourth quarter of 2016 mainly came from two brands as usual by category: Nike and Converse. Of this revenue of USD $8.24 billion, USD $7.7 billion came from Nike brand, which experienced a growth of 8% on a year-on-year basis. This growth might be a result of such events as the global celebration of Nike's Air Max series during this quarter, the retirement of Nike's NBA star Kobe Bryant, the NBA playoffs, the Champions League, the Copa America and the eve of the Euro Cup.

From the perspective of marketing channels, online retailing and offline direct-sale stores are Nike's most important sales channels. Nike continues to increase investment in the basic operations of these two direct selling platforms. The latest financial report shows that Nike.com's online business features a year-on-year growth of 51% which enables its direct selling revenue to grow by 25% to USD $7.9 billion and get far ahead of the wholesale growth of 9%. As of May 31 2018, the number of Nike's global direct-sale stores increased to 919, compared with 832 in the same period last year.

The case source quoted from: Nike's Profits Exceeds Expectations! Nike Gives Thanks to the Cavaliers' Championship and to the Greater China Region, but Still Needs to Guard Against UA and Adidas 2016/06/29
https://www.huxiu.com/article/154329.html

III. Hybrid Channel and Multi–Channel Marketing

Companies often adopt hybrid channel or multi-channel marketing with an eye to increase the number of channels in any market segment. Hybrid channel or multi-channel marketing means that a company uses two or more marketing channels to reach the customer base. HP sells its products to large customers through its sales staff, to medium-sized customers by telemarketing, to small customers via direct mails, and to smaller customers through retailers while selling exclusive products on the Internet.

In the multi-channel marketing, each channel targets the consumers in different market segments, or the different consumption needs of the same consumer, and sells the right products to them in the right way and in the right place at a relatively low price. If it fails to do so, problems like channel conflicts, excessive costs or insufficient demands may arise.

Additionally, if a retailer that sells products mainly through mailing lists and the Internet invests heavily in setting up physical stores, different consequences may occur. Those customers who are close to physical stores buy less through mailing lists but with their online purchases unchanged. Facts have proved that for those customers who like to spend time browsing, purchases both through mailing lists and from physical stores are very pleasant because these channels are interchangeable. But those customers who prefer purchases through the Internet pay more attention to the transaction itself and the efficiency, so they will not be affected by the introduction of physical stores. Although the convenience and the barrier-free experience have increased returns in physical stores, the additional purchases made by the customers asking for returns make up for the loss in revenue.

Companies that are operating hybrid channels must ensure that these channels be well-integrated and match the preferred trading style of each target customer group. Customers expect channel integration to make the following envisions come true:

(1) Based on the principle of proximity, they could take from a chain store the products on which they've placed orders online.

(2) Based on the principle of proximity, they could return to a nearby retail store the products on which they've placed orders online.

(3) They could get discounts and promotional offers based on all online and offline purchases.

(4) They could receive the door-to-door service from nearby stores.

 Case Study　REI

Recreational Equipment Inc. (REI).

The outdoor goods supplier REI (Recreational Equipment Inc.) has seamlessly integrated its retail stores, websites, Internet shopping areas, mail order catalogs, value-priced sales points and free order numbers, which is widely acclaimed by industry researchers. When a product runs out of stock in a physical store, what the customer should do is just visit the retailer's website to make place the order. Those customers who are unfamiliar with the Internet may go to the front desk to ask shop staff to place orders for them. REI has not only promoted the flow of customers from the physical store to the Internet, but also brought online buyers to its physical stores. If a customer browses REI's webpages and stops to read an article on hiking and camping titled 'Learning & Sharing', the website will pop up an in-store promotion advertisement for hiking shoes.

Like many retailers, REI has found that the consumers who shop through two channels spend much more than those who shop through a single channel and that those who shop through three channels spend the most.

Source: Why REI, the Largest Outdoor Goods Retailer in the United States, has Been Successful

IV. Level of Channel

Producers and end customers are integral parts of each channel. The length of a channel can be represented by the number of intermediary levels. Here are examples of several different lengths of consumer product marketing channels.

Zero-Level Channel[①] is also known as Direct Marketing Channel, which covers door-to-door sales, home shows, mail order, telemarketing, TV shopping, Internet marketing and factory outlet stores.

One-Level Channel involves only one middleman such as a retailer. Two-Level Channel consists of two middlemen, which are usually a wholesaler and a retailer in the consumer market. Three-Level Channel features three middlemen. For example, in the meat packaging industry, a wholesaler sells products to a turnover who then sells the same to a retailer. However, from a producer's perspective, the more channels there are, the more difficult it is to obtain the end-user information or take control. Figure 15-1 shows the common marketing channels for the organizational market. An Industrial product manufacturer may sell its products directly to industrial customers through its sales personnel, or to industrial distributors who then sell the same to industrial customers, or directly to industrial customers through its representatives or sales branches.

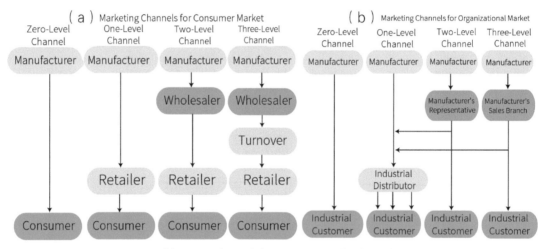

Figure 15-1   Marketing channels for consumer and industrial products.

The channel generally refers to the positive movement of a product from its source to its user. But the so-called reverse flow channel has been proposed, playing an important role in the following circumstances:

(1) Reused products or containers (e.g., barrels filled with drinking water repeatedly);

(2) Products that can be refurbished for resale (e.g., circuit boards or engines);

(3) Recycled products (e.g., discarded paper or tires);

(4) Discarded products and packages;

(5) Trade-in products.

There are several types of middlemen that work in various reverse-flow channels, including: manufacturers' recycling centers, community groups, waste collection personnel, recycling centers, waste recycling brokers and central processing warehouses. In recent years, there have been many creative solutions companies in these fields, such as Greenopolis.

iPhone Trade-in

On March 26, 2015, Apple planned to launch an iPhone trade-in program in China after it had already launched a similar plan in the United States to boost sales.

It was reported that in China's trade-in program, Apple's employees would be responsible for assessing the depreciation of the old iPhones purchased from Greater China and then determining their values. Foxconn would buy these old iPhones directly from Apple.

Foxconn would refurbish these iPhones that could not work well, and then sell them through its EFEIHU.COM and FLNET.COM as well as Alibaba's TAOBAO.COM.

Foxconn also planned to sell refurbished iPhones in physical stores in the future, and might also allow users to trade in used iPhones online.

IDC analysts said that in 2014, Apple sold 46.30 million iPhones in China with the sales increasing 42% year-on-year and accounting for 24% of Apple's global sales in the same period.

The case source quoted from: Have You Cut a Kidney for the IPhone? Apple Says That It is not Enough and Plans to Launch IPhone Trade-in in China, Bloomberg.com© 2015/03/26

https://www.huxiu.com/article/111214/1.html

V. Identification and Test of the Main Channel Plan

All channel plans - from sales personnel to agents, distributors, resellers, direct mail, telemarketing and Internet - have their own advantages and disadvantages. Sales personnel are able to handle complicated commodities and transactions, but the costs for doing so are expensive. The cost of using Internet is very low, but it hardly handles complicated commodity transaction. Distributors are able to create sales volumes, but the companies lose the opportunity to contact customers directly. Distributor's multiple customers may share the cost of its sales representatives, but their marketing efforts also are weaker than the marketing efforts of the manufacturer's own sales representatives.

Four elements are intrinsic to the channel plan: type of middlemen, number of middlemen, channel member's conditions and responsibilities, and middlemen's operating capability.

1. Type of middlemen

By taking an electronic product manufacturer producing satellite radio for example, with respect to its selection of channel, it may sell its radio as an automobile component directly to automobile manufacturers, automobile distributors or automobile lease companies, or sell its radio to satellite radio franchised dealers through direct marketers or distributors, or sell its radio through company stores, online retailers and catalog sales, or sell its radio in large-scale shopping malls. Sometimes, due to great difficulties or high cost, or lack of effectiveness for the main channel, companies may choose a new or unconventional channel. The advantage of unconventional channel is that the competition is low during the initial period when a company's product enters into this unconventional channel.

2. Number of middlemen

There are three kinds of channel strategies depending on the number of middlemen: exclusive distribution, selective distribution and intensive distribution

(1) Exclusive Distribution refers to the targeted sales of one or several varieties of commodities bearing the same brand conducted by distributors, meaning that the number of middlemen is strictly restricted. It is suitable for manufacturers to control and maintain the balance between middlemen's service level and production output, in addition, an exclusive distribution usually contains exclusive transaction arrangement, i.e., distributors shall sell products to consumers based on manufacturer's instructions. As required by exclusive distribution, distributors are required to have adequate understanding on their distributed products together with more enthusiasm in marketing. Exclusive distribution requires that companies and middlemen shall establish close partner relationship, which is mainly applied in selling new automobiles and some commonly used household electric appliances as well as female garment brands. In the nowadays increasingly price-driven commercial field, the exclusive transactions between suppliers and retailers are becoming the main field where specialized enterprises are seeking advantages.

(2) Selective Distribution refers to the sales of specific products by selecting certain middlemen at one's own discretion. As to existing and newly established enterprises, the advantage of selective distribution lies in that there is no worry about the competition brought about by too many distribution agencies while sufficient coverage is achieved, and it has more control power and lower cost compared with intensive distribution.

(3) In Intensive Distribution[①], manufacturers will try their best to sell their products or services in more stores. This strategy is usually applied to snack food, soft drink, newspaper, candy, chewing gum and other products that consumers buy in high frequency or the places of purchase are diversified.

Manufacturers have been trying to shift from exclusive distribution and selective distribution to more intensive distribution in order to increase their product coverage and sales volume. This strategy may be effective in a short run, but it may produce damage to long-term business performance if it is not done properly. The reason is that it encourages the fierce competition among retainers. Price war may erode profit, weaken the interest of retailers in supporting product and damage brand assets.

Some companies dislike selling their products everywhere. After Sears Department Store acquired Kmart Chain Discount Store, Nike Corporation withdrew all its products from Sears for ensuring that no Nike product is sold in Kmart.

3. Conditions and responsibilities of channel members

Channel members must be respected and have the opportunity to make a profit. The main elements in a "Trade Relationship Portfolio" include: price policy, sales conditions, distributor regional rights and both parties' service and responsibility.

(1) **Price policy.** Manufacturers stipulate a series of price list and subsidy list to make middlemen believe the balance of its profit distribution.

(2) **Sales conditions.** By providing distributors with the guarantees relating to product quality or price difference, as well as certain cash discounts for those distributors who make earlier payment, distributors are encouraged to purchase more commodities.

(3) **Distributor regional rights.** This refers to the determination of a distributor's marketing territory and the stipulation of the conditions for other distributors to be allowed to enter this marketing territory by manufacturers. A distributor usually likes to treat all sales performances in its authorized marketing territory as its own sales performance, regardless of whether or not these sales are achieved by such distributor.

(4) **Service and responsibility of both parties.** The service and responsibility of both parties must be defined with great care, particularly when franchising, exclusive agent or the like channels are adopted.

McDonald's provides franchised dealers with house, marketing support, book-keeping system, personnel training, general administration and technical assistance. In return, franchised dealers are required to comply with McDonald's corporate standards in facilities and equipment, give due cooperation to McDonald's new marketing plans, provide McDonald's with necessary information and purchase supplies from designated suppliers.

www.guazi.com, a second-hand car direct selling network, was officially launched in September 27, 2015, and now it has been developed as China's biggest second-hand car directly selling platform. www.guazi.com helps buyers trade with sellers face to face. Through direct selling mode, www.guazi.com removes middlemen from the transaction, thus it offers the price difference charged by middlemen to buyers and sellers and realizes a win-win transaction featured with "sellers sell more, while buyers save more".

4. Operating ability of middlemen

This means middlemen's fund scale, fund-raising capability, number of teams, radius of business coverage, construction of VIP client files and other situations which are intrinsic to their channel plans.

 **Case Study** | McDonald's

China-based Hejun Vanguard Group once contributed its assistance to win the antitrust campaign against Coca-Cola and Apple, and now it is targeting US fast food giant: McDonald's. Hejun Vanguard Group lodged a complaint with China's regulatory authorities, arguing that McDonald's attempt to sell its business in China may cause harm to employees and consumers.

McDonald's has agreed to sell its business entity in China Mainland and Hong Kong to sell CITIC Limited and US private equity firm Carlyle Group at the price of USD $2.1 billion, and this consortium will be a 20-year principal franchisor.

Hejun Vanguard Group, headquartered in Beijing, always acts for and on behalf of Chinese companies to combat foreign companies, and as disclosed to Reuters' reporter, it has lodged a complaint with the Antitrust Division of Ministry of Commerce of PRC and other governmental agencies in charge of franchising.

Hejun Vanguard Group didn't request that the Ministry of Commerce of PRC hold back this transaction;

instead, it strongly advocated to apply strict review and examination and take necessary measures to prevent McDonald's from "abusing" its leading position in China's fast-food hamburger market. In addition, it also called on the Ministry of Commerce of PRC to investigate McDonald's alleged violations of China's franchise laws and regulations, saying that it has not properly registered all of its stores in China.

Regardless of how the situation will develop with regard to McDonald's and Hejun Vanguard Group, it is not difficult to see the quite developed marketing channels of McDonald's as well as its extensive business coverage.

The case source quoted from: Netease News 2017/02/19
http://news.163.com/17/0219/00/CDJM3F1700018AOQ_all.html

VI. Test the Main Channel Plan

Every channel plan is required to be tested in economic efficiency, controllability and adaptability.

1. Economic efficiency standard

Every channel will generate different sales volumes and costs. According to the added value generated from each marketing unit and the cost incurred from each transaction, 11 channels are put into order as follows: Internet, partner, telemarketing, retailer, distributor, agent, value-added sales partner, company sales representative, AR (augmented reality), VR (virtual reality) and MR (mixed reality) (as shown in Figure 15-2).

2. Controllability and adaptability standard

The issue of control shall be considered when using agents. Agents will focused on those customers who purchased commodities the most, rather than those customers who purchased the products of the company. In addition, agents' salespersons may not master the technical details of company's products, or, they are unable to use marketing materials effectively and

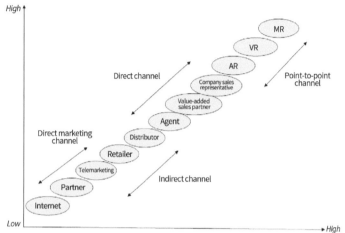

Figure 15-2   Eleven channels leading to economic efficiency.

efficiently. The future channels will be point-to-point channels, i.e., a brand new channel space consisting of AR, VR and MR. In order for channel development, channel members are required to make a commitment to each other during a specific period of time. However, as a matter of fact, these commitments degenerate manufacturers' ability to respond to the market and market uncertainty. Manufacturers need to seek highly adaptable channel structure and policy.

VII. Features of Marketing Communication Mix

Advertisements can be communicated to geographically scattered purchasers, build up long-term image for products (such as Coca-Cola ads) or trigger quick selling (Macy's ads relating to ads marketing). Since ads have diversified forms and usages, it is difficult to summarize them all. However, some features are noteworthy:

(1) Comparability. Ads allow sellers to repeat a same piece of information, also allow purchasers to receive and compare multiple pieces of information from multiple competitors.

(2) Brand reinforcement. The artistic use of printing patterns, sounds and colors provides enterprises and their brands/products with an opportunity for imprinting their brands or product features vividly into the minds of customers.

(3) Control. This refers to the selection of advertisers of which brand and product features shall be addressed when communicating such brand and product features.

Marketing promotion companies may use discount coupon, contest, bonus and other marketing promotion tools to win stronger and quicker customer response, including product addressing, gloomy sales rectification and other marketing measures with short-term effect. The marketing promotion tools are able to result in three unique advantages:

(1) **Attractiveness.** They are able to attract consumers' attention and guide them towards advertised products.

(2) **Incentive.** They contain concession, induction or contribution of certain degree, which bring about values to consumers.

(3) **Participation.** They contain a unique invitation to consumers for them to be involved in the transaction immediately.

PR and marketers usually show inadequacy in utilizing public relations. However, a well-defined PR plan and other communication mix elements contained therein will be very effective, particularly when a company is ready to challenge consumers' wrong concepts. The attractiveness of PR and publicity is based on the following unique features:

(1) **High credibility.** For readers, a news story and feature article are more realistic and credible than ads, because, in the mind of consumers, ads include exaggeration and are not real.

(2) **High communication.** PR is able to communicate information to targeted potential customers rather than mass media targeted customers, thus it increases potential customer base.

(3) **Dramatic.** PR is able to tell stories behind enterprise, brand or product.

(4) **Event and experience.** As long as event and experience have the following features, they have many advantages:

● Correlation. Since consumers are able to be placed into event and experience, a suitable event or experience is highly correlated.

● Participation. The liveliness and real-time of event and experience generate higher participation of consumers, because nowadays consumers are more focused on how they are experienced.

● Connotation. Event usually is an indirect "soft selling".

(5) **Direct selling and interactive marketing.** Direct selling and interactive marketing may be carried out through multiple means: telephone, Internet or personnel. They have three common features:

● Customization of hierarchy: It is possible to prepare information according to target customer individuals.

● Upgraded telling: A piece of information can be prepared promptly.

● Humanization: It is possible to change information according to the reaction of individuals.

(6) **Word-of-mouth marketing.** Word-of-mouth include online and offline multiple forms. Three noteworthy features of word-of-mouth marketing are

● Influence. Since people always trust the person whom they know and respect, word-of-mouth has high influence, such as celebrity endorsement.

● Privacy. Word-of-mouth may be a very private dialogue, and these dialogues can reflect personal fact, opinion and experience.

● Timely. Word-of-mouth always takes place at the time when people need it and are interested in it.

(7) **Personal selling.** In the later stage of a purchase process, personal selling is the most effective tool, particularly after a built-up or meaningful event or experience. With respect to purchaser preference, belief and action, personal selling has three important features:

● Interpersonal interaction. Personal selling creates direct interaction between two and more persons, in which everyone is able to observe the reaction of others.

● Cultivation. Personal selling can develop private friendship and other relationships, i.e. to market yourself and to make others trust in you.

● Reaction. The purchaser can make his/her personal choice and is encouraged to give direct reactions.

VIII. Point-to-Point Marketing

The ultimate business goal of mobile Internet is to wipe out all middlemen thus to realize point-to-point connection between manufacturers and consumers. The development of science and technology changed marketing channels, and future market channels will be point-to-point channels. Further discussion on VR, AR and MR will be presented to you in subsequent sections.

1. Management of integrated marketing communication process

Many companies only rely on one or two communication tools. This practice has been always there, though mass market has been segmented into multiple small markets, but each small market shall have its own suitable ways; new media is emerging in large numbers; and consumers become more and more smart and clever. The existence of a large number of communication tools, information and audiences makes integrated marketing communication imperative. Companies are required to adopt a "360-degree angle of view" of consumers to fully understand all different ways of communication to influence daily customer behaviors.

2. Integrated marketing communication

Integrated marketing communication (IMC) means a plan-making process for ensuring that all brand contacts received by the customers or potential customers of products, service or organization are correlated and consistent with such customers. This planning process will assess the strategic function of all kinds of communication ways including common ads, direct reaction, marketing promotion and PR, and will combine these ways skillfully, and produce clear, consistent and maximized influence through seamless information integration.

Media companies and ad agent companies are now exploring their abilities and providing marketing personnel with multiple transaction platforms, and this expanded ability enables marketing personnel more easily to integrate multiple media attributes and related marketing services into one communication plan.

Media collaboration may go beyond media category, or may take place within the same media; however, marketing personnel shall combine interpersonal communication with non-interpersonal communication through multi-media and multi-stage movement to realize maximized influence and improve information arrival rate and influence. For example, when marketing combines with ads, the effect is stronger. The popularity and attitude created by ads marketing activity is able to improve directly the sales success possibility. Ads are able to communicate brand positioning, and ads presented with the assistance of Internet and research engines have stronger request for consumers for immediate action.

Many enterprises will coordinate well their own online and offline communication activities. Ads (particularly, print ads) on website can make people have better understanding of company products, find store location and access more product or service information. Even if consumers fail to place a purchase order online, marketing personnel may use a website to attract consumers to purchase in a physical store.

IMC has been replaced gradually by "Field Communication". This will be discussed in detail in Chapter 18.

3. Execution of integrated marketing communication

Large advertising agency companies improved their integrated services. These agency companies acquired marketing promotion agency companies, PR companies, packaging design consulting institutions, website developers and direct mail agencies, which accelerated the birth of one-stop service. They provide strategic and practical suggestions for multiple forms of communication in order to assist their customers in improving the overall communication effect, thus making themselves no longer an agency firm but a new type of communication firm.

IBM (Ogilvy advertising company), Colgate (Young & Rubicam advertising company), GE (BBDO Worldwide advertising company) and many other international customers have chosen to assign most of their communication tasks to all-service agency companies; of course, this resulted in more integrated and effective communication as well as lower marketing communication total cost.

IMC may make information more consistent, and helps in building up brand assets for creating a better sales performance. It forces the management to think about several issues such as every method for contact between consumers and companies, how a company communicates its market positioning, the relative importance and time effect of every media. It assigns the duties which did not exist before to some persons to allow them to unify the brand images and information generated from thousands of company activities. IMC improves companies' ability in communicating suitable information to consumers at the right time, the right place and through the right communication methods.

4. Mobile marketing

Mobile Marketing refers to a marketing method in which product or service information is communicated to customers by direct contact with a customer without a middleman, and its purchase decision-making process is completed basically on mobile terminals.

5. Micro distribution

Micro distribution is acting as the supplier for millions of micro stores rather than opening a micro store; without the need to develop an app, it is a handheld department store for millions of consumers. Micro distribution is the third-tier distribution shopping mall established in WeChat public platform. This third-tier distribution shall achieve an endless loop model; in WeChat marketing network economy era, it is an innovation of corporate marketing model as well as a network marketing method generated along with the rapid rise of WeChat marketing. WeChat distribution is an enterprise data marketing method in the age of big data. It is a three-level distribution WeChat store system developed on the basis of WeChat public platform to provide chain stores and distribution channels on WeChat for brand companies and merchants. WeChat distribution helps the merchants to rapidly turn the We Media into their own distributors with high viscosity (as shown in Figure 15-3). In China, micro distribution is now flourishing.

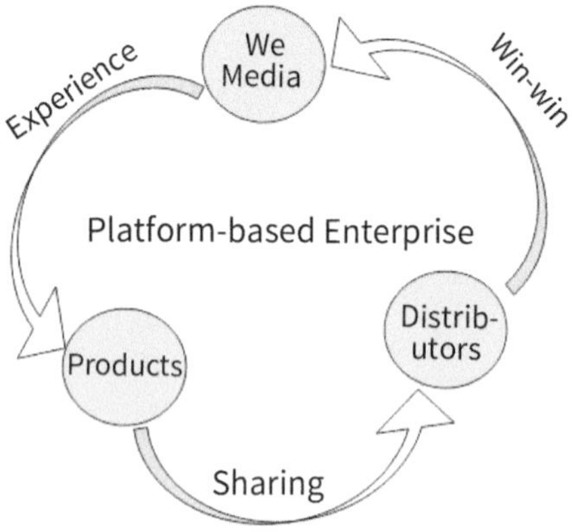

Figure 15-3　Micro distribution.

Third Screen: It refers to cellphone screen. First Screen refers to television and Second Screen refers to computer.

Along with the popularity of cellphones as well as marketers' ability to customize personal information according to demographic information and other consumer behavior characteristics, mobile marketing naturally becomes a communication tool.

According to eMarketer's estimate, global cellphone users as of 2016 reached 4.3 billion, accounting for 58.7% of the total global population. Cellphones provide an important opportunity for advertisers to make contact with consumers through a "Third Screen"①. Some companies accelerated their steps towards a multidimensional marketing world. Bank of America is a pioneer in banking industry in terms of using cellphone marketing.

Bank of America used a cellphone as its communication channel, also its tool providing bank financial solutions to its customers of different lifestyles. Among 59 million customers of Bank of America, there are two million customers who are using a cellphone banking app. Bank of America treated these customers as its live ads for attracting more customers, because 8%–10% of mobile users are new users. Mobile banking service initially was targeted to users between of the ages of 18 to 30 – particularly, college students. But now, banks began to pay more attention to other groups, such as older and wealthier customers. Compared with a traditional browser, bank's smartphone app has advantages of simple navigation, ease of use, and convenient login, so it was highly welcomed by users. Among 8 mobile customers, only one customer may use bank outlets or ATM, and all other customers will handle their banking transactions through cellphone banking service. Through the bank's marketing efforts, mobile marketing integrated all the following elements:

Website provided mobile service trial version; TV ads addressed the advantages of mobile banking service; and just by clicking the banner ads in cellphones, smartphone users are able to download the Bank of America app, or know more information about mobile banking services.

IX. Major Customer Management

Marketers usually will pick out their major customers, including critical customers, nationwide customers, global customers and corporate customers. These customers have vital importance; all of them have their own different divisions that are located in different areas and adopt unified procurement price, and their services are carried out in a coordinated way. Major account managers (MAM) usually report their work directly to national sales manager, also MAMs are required to supervise their sales representatives to visit major customers within their own areas.

Major customers usually are managed by a strategic customer management team. The members of this team come from different functional departments which integrated new product development, technical support, supply chain, marketing activity and multi-channel communication so as to cover all customer relationship aspects. P&G specially set up a strategic customer management team in Bentonville Arkansas where Wal-Mart is headquartered, and 300 workers in this team are working together with the Wal-Mart team promoting both parties' business operation performance. This kind of cooperation exists everywhere in the world where Wal-Mart is headquartered, such as Europe, Asia and Latin America. P&G praised highly this cooperation between of both parties, because this cooperation saved billions of USD expenditure for P&G.

Major customer management is now on the way to sustainable development and growth. Along with the increase in buyer concentration brought about by company mergers and acquisitions, it is a common phenomenon that very few buyers will account for the highest sales volume of a company. Many companies began concentrated procurement, which gave them more bargaining power. As products become more and more complicated, more and more buyer company teams participated in the procurement process. Therefore, a traditional salesman may not have the ability, authority or coverage necessary for effectively marketing to major customers.

When selecting major customers, companies will usually focus on those customers who have large and concentrated purchase, require receiving high-level service in different areas, are sensitive to price and hope to establish long-term cooperation ties. The duties of MAMs include single-point contact with customers, customer business volume development and upgrading, understanding of customer decision-making process, determination of added value upgrading chance, provision of competitor's information, sales negotiation and customer service arrangement.

Many major customers hope to receive more added value rather than preferential price. They are more fond of this fully devoted and exclusive "one-to-one" contact; separated bill and special guarantee; electronic data exchange and sharing; priority in delivery; customized products; as well as high-efficient maintenance, repair and upgrading service. These are companies' commercial value. Establish personal relationship with the person who assesses major customer transaction, and let this person see the success possibility and vested interest of the transaction; these are essential conditions for maintaining customer loyalty.

Age of Market Space 3.0

I. Definition

The marketing space means a transaction process in which the marketed product is brought to the user. It must be completed in a closed space. The traditional marketing space refers to a country fair, an exclusive shop or an online store. And the modern marketing space may be a virtual reality space, an online store, or a closed trade space like an exclusive shop.

The marketing space has experienced the evolution from Country Fair (1.0), Exclusive Shop (2.0), and Online Store (3.0) to Virtual Reality Space (4.0).

The development of marketing is inseparable from the market because marketing is actually a science about both "Market" and "Field", and a methodology to study how to complete transactions in a "Field". "Market" and "Field" are exactly the combination of "Transaction" and "Space". With the passage of time and the application of new technological tools, the concept of "Field" has been continuously changing and upgrading, and is more and more human-oriented.

II. Age of the Country Fair (1.0)

The Country Fair refers to a form of commodity trading activity that is held on a regular basis by gathering a large crowd, especially a form of trade organization that prevails in the times when and the regions where the commodity economy is underdeveloped. The country fair, which originated from people's gatherings in the prehistoric period, often appears in religious festivals and memorial rallies and comes with folk entertainment. Jiang Yikui, a poet and writer in the Ming Dynasty, described the country fair in his book, A Visit to Chang'an - Di Liu's Memorial Temple, "People gathered all the goods in the Capital here for trading, taking mats as stores and setting boundaries to form a fair which lasted four days and nights; and it was commonly known as the Diliang Gathering." It is easy to see from this that the "field" of the country fair is embodied in "taking mats as stores and setting boundaries to form a fair", and characterized by high mobility, convenience and tax exemption. But these characteristics are also limitations! High mobility means that there is no fixed place. Therefore, your mobility will lead to a loss of a lot of consumers if the returned customers cannot find you. Strong convenience means that your products are not diversified, and undiversified products will limit your consumer base. And tax exemption means that your transaction amount is so small that you do not meet the taxation standard.

The Temple Fair, also known as "temple market" or "festival fair", is a folk religion and yearly festive custom of the Han nationality. It is usually held during the Spring Festival, the Lantern Festival and other Chinese festivals. As one of the forms of Chinese country fair trading, the temple fair has its formation and development closely related to the religious activities in temples. For example, temple fairs are held during temple festivals or prescribed dates, and are set up mostly inside and around temples for activities such as worship, entertainment and shopping. The temple fair prevails in vast areas of China. It is a traditional folk activity that has been popular in China. Folk custom is a life culture created, enjoyed and passed down by a large number of people in a country or a nation. The temple fair is an organic part of this life culture with its birth, existence, and evolution closely related to the lives of ordinary people.

III. Age of the Exclusive Shop (2.0)

The Exclusive Shop is a retail business form that specializes in or authorizes the operation of a major brand of products. It is also known as the franchised store. An exclusive shop is not necessarily a store with a well-known brand. The exclusive shop refers to a franchised store that specializes in certain types of industry-related products. With the refinement of the social division of labor, each industry has its own exclusive shops which are more and more refined. The exclusive shops in various industries not only meet social needs but also promote their own brands. What's more, the exclusive shop can make the latest product developed by a company known to customers in the first time. With the one-stop service from product sales to after-sales service, people are more and more accustomed to shopping in exclusive shops.

Exclusive shops are famous for their strong immobility, product diversification and service awareness. And it is well known that the after-sales service did rise in exclusive shops. The presence of exclusive shops brings a lot of conveniences to the daily life of consumers, helping them with discrimination, selection and preferential treatment during shopping. Exclusive shops also take advantage of consumers' greed for special offers to stimulate their desires to buy with some cost-effective promotions. One of the benefits that come with it should belong to the brand. In other words, consumers may choose your brand based on a deep and good impression when they have demands, because your brand makes consumers believe that they are preferentially treated. But are these consumers indeed preferentially treated? In actuality, they are not. This is only because that the consumers have deeply interiorized the brands of these exclusive shops and consequently developed confidence in them. An exclusive shop will be undoubtedly successful if it can do this.

Case Study | Convenience Store

The Convenience Store may be a physical store near a residential area, or a virtual store providing online shopping. It refers to the small retail store or online store which mainly offers instant goods or services in the manner of self-selection shopping for the utmost purpose of meeting the customer's need for convenience. It is a retail business form that meets the customer's urgent need or need for convenience. Originating in the United States, this business form has been divided into two branches, namely, traditional convenience store and petroleum-based convenience store. The rise of convenience stores is due to the large sizes of and the suburban locations of supermarkets. Changes in supermarkets are reflected in many aspects such as distance, time, commodities and monthly services. The locations of supermarkets which are usually far away from residential areas force shoppers to drive, the large shopping area and the high variety of goods cause shoppers to spend more time and energy, and shoppers have to stand in a long queue, waiting for checkout, all of which make those who only want to buy several products or to meet their immediate needs feel very inconvenient. So people need a small supermarket that can meet their needs for convenient shopping to fill this gap.

Different from supermarkets or boutiques, convenience stores are distributed over corners of a community or a street, and are the places which are the closest to us.

Supermarkets brought the first wave of revolution in consumption concept, and convenience stores existing everywhere brought the second. To "get what you forget" has become the marketing core of convenience stores in the United States. Although convenience stores appeared at different time and have been developing under different backgrounds in the United States, Japan and other countries, they, on the whole, are a retail business form that is split off from supermarkets after the supermarkets have developed to a relatively mature stage. On the one hand, the development of supermarkets has its own insurmountable obstacles, namely "inconvenience of shopping"; but on the other hand, it provides advanced sales methods and management techniques for convenience stores. Specifically, convenience stores have four "convenient" business characteristics that distinguish them from supermarkets: ①convenient distance; ②convenient shopping; ③convenient time; and ④convenient service.

The case source quoted from: Baidu Baike 2017/07/11
https://baike.baidu.com/item/%E4%BE%BF%E5%88%A9%E5%BA%97/3237606?fr=aladdin

IV. Impacts of Brands on the Age 2.0

When you buy sportswear, you think of Nike, Adidas, or Li Ning, Anta, and 361°, etc.; when you buy clothes you think of Belle, Baleno, Metersbonwe, and Jeanswest, etc.; when you buy electrical appliances you will choose Gree, TCL, Skyworth, and Haier, etc. No matter what items you buy, the brands you know will appear in your mind at first. A brand's good publicity will be implanted in consumers' hearts, urging consumers to buy it at exclusive shops.

Excellent brands will directly affect consumers' choices. The slogan that Nong-Fu Spring is a bit sweet has profoundly affected consumers, virtually causing them to choose NongFu Spring rather than other mineral water brands. Of course, it also has competitors like Ganten and C'estbon. The brand will create more sales space to exclusive shops. In recent years, there have been more and more advertisements for cars, which are due to the decline of the auto market. The outside world said, "Selling cars is no longer profitable", but car brands have been investing heavily in advertising and exhibiting because the brand publicity can increase consumers' desires to buy and directly affect the sales of exclusive shops.

V. Age of the Online Store (3.0)

As a form of e-commerce, the online store is a website that enables people to make actual purchases while browsing and to complete the entire process of transaction by paying with various online payment methods. The advantages of an online shop are mainly reflected in: convenience and efficiency, fast transaction, overstock prevention, easy handling, diversification, security, wide application and convenient distribution.

Operational Tools

I. Mobile Operation

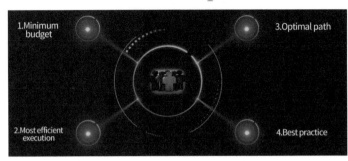

Dimensions of product operation in the Mobile Age.

The traditional business defines mobile operation as follows: the mobile operation refers to the planning, organization, programming, implementation and control of the product operation process, which is also a general term for various management tasks closely related to product production and service creation. For a product, the work scope of operational staff spans from the plan to the official launch, from the preparation of a variety of operation plans and proposals to the organization and implementation of operation programs at the time of product launch as well as the effective monitoring and evaluation of various promotional effects.

The operation covers search engine operation (SEO), publication of advertorials, editing and review of contents, acquisition of potential users, operation of super users, planning of activities, and even some public relations and media work. In short, all the trivial matters that contribute to the increase of user data, corporate income growth and the increase in activeness are related to operations, and higher-level operations also include the economization of corporate expenses in a category of operation.

II. Positions in Mobile Operation

1. Content Operation

The main function of content operations is to continuously create high-quality contents for product sharing.

2. Promotion Operation

If the product is still in development and relies mainly on free promotion channels, SEO specialists must be deployed at first. The reason is that only high-quality contents are not enough and that it is also necessary to turn these contents into the search engine-approved ones so as to obtain higher weights and improve the performance of these contents in search engines. In addition to SEO specialists, other specialists may be deployed for advertorial marketing, community promotion, video

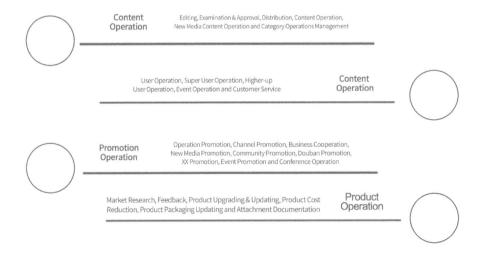

Positions in mobile operation.

marketing, e-book marketing, EDM promotion, QQ group promotion and so on.

Since the birth of Microblog and WeChat, operators have turned their attention to new media operations, namely, Microblog operation, WeChat operation and community operation, and have introduced traffic from Microblog and WeChat to increase the traffic of the entire website by means of content and event planning.

The Mini Program launched by Tencent is also one of the platforms for promotion.

3. User Operation

User operations are also common positions in operation teams. How to increase the user loyalty and make users more active is a major concern for the user operation personnel.

4. Product Operation

In the Mobile Age, product iterations and follow-ups are speeding up, and product operations must be conducted from four dimensions, namely, product, user, cost and core advantage.

III. Product Operation

All methods that are used to connect users with products to generate product value and business value are called product operations. If a product fails to reach the user after production, it cannot reflect the product value or realize the commercial value. Operations are used to connect users with products. Now that the user needs are constantly changing, products need to be continuously iteratively improved

to meet these user needs. Without operations, changes in these user needs cannot be always understood.

In this process, it is necessary to plan the product operation route in advance, to write an operational copy, to set up the framework for operational knowledge system, and to make different capability requirements for operation supervisors and operation managers.

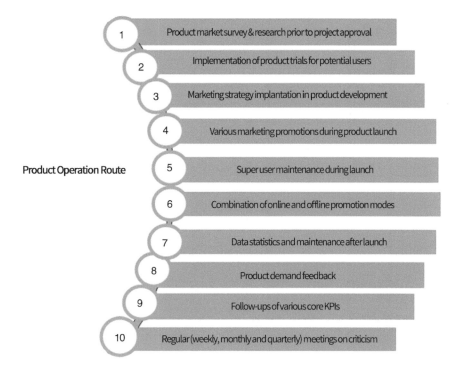

Product operation route.

IV. Framework for Operational Copywriting

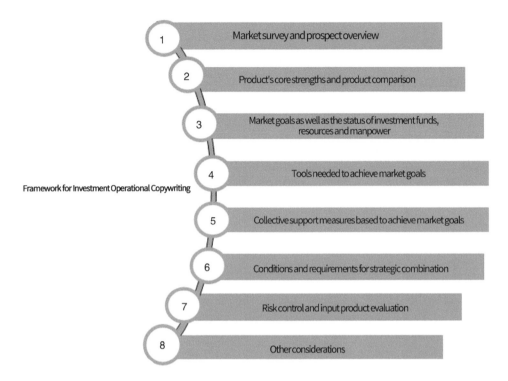

1	Market survey and prospect overview
2	Product's core strengths and product comparison
3	Market goals as well as the status of investment funds, resources and manpower
4	Tools needed to achieve market goals
5	Collective support measures based to achieve market goals
6	Conditions and requirements for strategic combination
7	Risk control and input product evaluation
8	Other considerations

Framework for Investment Operational Copywriting

Framework for investment operational copywriting.

V. Capability Standards for Primary Operation

Capability Item		S/N	Assessment Factor	Beginner P1
Quality Requirements	Basic Quality	1	Knowledge management	3
		2	Time management	2
		3	Office skills	3
		4	Capability to collect information	3
		5	Executive force	2
		6	Creativity	3
		7	Contingency ability	3
		8	Communication skills	2
	Key Quality	9	Mentality and emotional quotient (EQ)	1
		10	Logic capability	1
		11	Industry knowledge	1
		12	Knowledge of contract laws	0
		13	Competitive product analysis	0
		14	Speech ability	0
		15	Talent training	0
		16	Understanding	1
Professional Skills	Operational Capabilities and Product Capabilities	17	Super user management	0
		18	Big data analysis	0
		19	Data analysis	0
		20	Operation direction	0
		21	Content management	0
		22	User management	1
		23	Communication management	0

Capability Item		S/N	Assessment Factor	Beginner P1
Professional Skills	Operational Capabilities and Product Capabilities	24	Hotspot research	0
		25	Space operation capabilities	0
		26	Marketing promotion rules	0
		27	Brand management	0
		28	Media management	0
		29	Product innovation capabilities	0
		30	Market analysis	0
		31	User analysis	0
		32	Product planning	0
		33	Leadership	0
Total score				26

Capability survey for primary operation

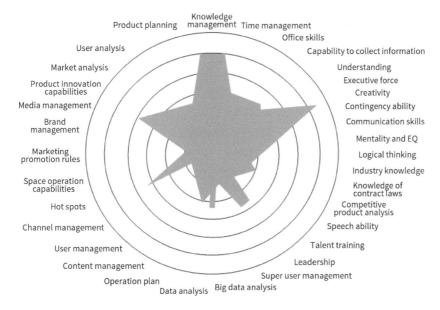

Capability distribution for primary operation.

VI. Capability Standards for Operation Supervisors

Capability Item		S/N	Assessment Factor	Beginner P1	The Skilled P2
Quality Requirements	Basic Quality	1	Knowledge management	3	3
		2	Time management	2	2
		3	Office skills	3	3
		4	Capability to collect information	3	3
		5	Executive force	2	2
		6	Creativity	3	2
		7	Contingency ability	3	3
		8	Communication skills	2	2
	Key Quality	9	Mentality and EQ	1	3
		10	Logic capability	1	2
		11	Industry knowledge	1	2
		12	Knowledge of contract laws	0	1
		13	Competitive product analysis	0	1
		14	Speech ability	0	1
		15	Talent training	0	0
		16	Understanding	1	3

Capability Item		S/N	Assessment Factor	Beginner P1	The Skilled P2
Professional Skills	Operational Capabilities and Product Capabilities	17	Super user management	0	3
		18	Big data analysis	0	2
		19	Data analysis	0	3
		20	Operation direction	0	2
		21	Content management	0	2
		22	User management	1	2
		23	Communication management	0	2
		24	Hotspot research	0	2
		25	Space operation capabilities	0	1
		26	Marketing promotion rules	0	1
		27	Brand management	0	2
		28	Media management	0	2
		29	Product innovation capabilities	0	1
		30	Market analysis	0	1
		31	User analysis	0	1
		32	Product planning	0	1
		33	Leadership	0	1
Total score				26	61

Capability survey for operation supervisors.

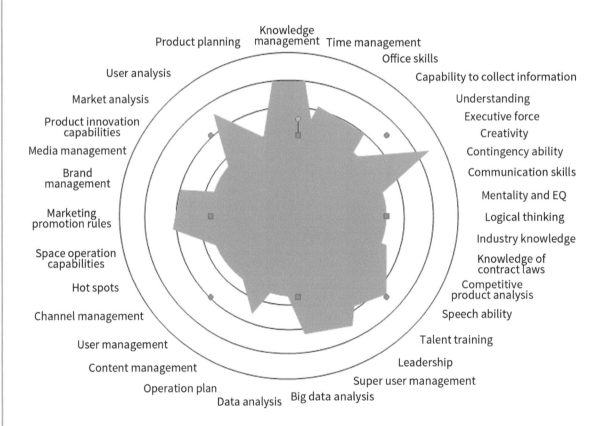

Capability distribution for operation supervisors.

VII. Capability Standards for Operation Managers

Capability Item		S/N	Assessment Factor	Beginner P1	The Skilled P2	Backbone P3
Quality Requirements	Basic Quality	1	Knowledge management	3	3	4
		2	Time management	2	2	4
		3	Office skills	3	3	3
		4	Capability to collect information	3	3	4
		5	Executive force	2	2	4
		6	Creativity	3	2	4
		7	Contingency ability	3	3	4
		8	Communication skills	2	2	3
	Key Quality	9	Mentality and EQ	1	3	3
		10	Logic capability	1	2	4
		11	Industry knowledge	1	2	3
		12	Knowledge of contract laws	0	1	2
		13	Competitive product analysis	0	1	1
		14	Speech ability	0	1	1
		15	Talent training	0	0	2
		16	Understanding	1	3	2
Professional Skills	Operational Capabilities and Product Capabilities	17	Super user management	0	3	3
		18	Big data analysis	0	2	3
		19	Data analysis	0	3	4
		20	Operation direction	0	2	3
		21	Content management	0	2	3
		22	User management	1	2	3
		23	Communication management	0	2	3
		24	Hotspot research	0	2	2
		25	Space operation capabilities	0	1	3
		26	Marketing promotion rules	0	1	3
		27	Brand management	0	2	2
		28	Media management	0	2	2
		29	Product innovation capabilities	0	1	2
		30	Market analysis	0	1	2
		31	User analysis	0	1	2
		32	Product planning	0	1	2
		33	Leadership	0	1	3
Total score				26	61	

Capability survey for operation managers.

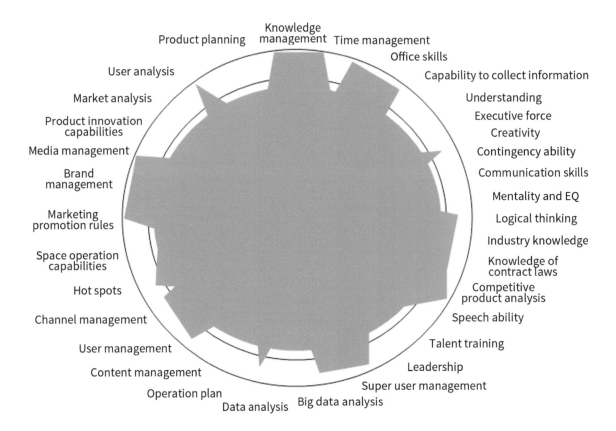

Capability distribution for operation manager.

VIII. Capability Test for General Manager of Marketing

Rule: these questions listed below are choice questions with one point for "Yes" and 0 points for "No". There is one point for each question.

Quality

1. Have you learned history? .... Yes ( ) No ( )
2. Do you know the history of the four industrial revolutions? .... Yes ( ) No ( )
3. Have you learned Chinese? .... Yes ( ) No ( )
4. Have you learned economic geography? .... Yes ( ) No ( )
5. Is China's first monograph on literary theory the *Literary Mind and the Carving of Dragons*?
   .... Yes ( ) No ( )
6. Have you learned philosophy? And have you read more than 10 philosophy monographs?
   .... Yes ( ) No ( )
7. Have you learned economics? .... Yes ( ) No ( )
8. Is the horizontal demand curve completely inelastic? .... Yes ( ) No ( )
9. Have you learned math? Do you know calculus? .... Yes ( ) No ( )
10. Did you drive through a red light after drinking? .... Yes ( ) No ( )
11. Do you berate them when your subordinates make a mistake during work? .... Yes ( ) No ( )
12. Do you feel you are fair? .... Yes ( ) No ( )
13. Will you choose your company in spite of benefits? .... Yes ( ) No ( )
14. Will you consider your subordinates' suggestions for you? .... Yes ( ) No ( )
15. Do you think everyone is really equal? .... Yes ( ) No ( )
16. Can you tolerate your subordinates' criticism of you? .... Yes ( ) No ( )
17. Have you ever told a lie? .... Yes ( ) No ( )
18. Do you think the result is more important than explanation? .... Yes ( ) No ( )
19. Do you often think of a problem from someone else's position? .... Yes ( ) No ( )
20. Can you write a new product marketing program? .... Yes ( ) No ( )

Experience

21. Do you have more than 5 years of management experience?.................................... Yes ( ) No ( )
22. Do you have more than 3 years of work experience in marketing and sales? .... Yes ( ) No ( )
23. Did you participate in starting a business? .... Yes ( ) No ( )
24. Did you lead a marketing team with more than 30 members? .... Yes ( ) No ( )
25. Were you defrauded by improperly signing an economic contract? .... Yes ( ) No ( )
26. Did your personal sales reach over CNY 100,000? .... Yes ( ) No ( )
27. Do you have team spirit? .... Yes ( ) No ( )
28. Have you ever experienced three rejections when selling the same product? .... Yes ( ) No ( )
29. Do you have a strong sense of responsibility for customers, enterprises and society? Yes ( ) No ( )
30. Do you think that all major customers are obtained with service? .... Yes ( ) No ( )
31. Do you have a keen market insight? .... Yes ( ) No ( )
32. Have you been engaged in post-sale management and after-sales service? .... Yes ( ) No ( )
33. Are you familiar with the use of the latest web chat tools?................................... Yes ( ) No ( )
34. Do you have market analysis skills and are proficient in market analysis tools?......... Yes ( ) No ( )
35. Did you do a complete new product market research? .... Yes ( ) No ( )
36. Did you successfully promote a brand and make it a success in the market?.............. Yes ( ) No ( )
37. Are you good at developing marketing strategies based on changes in market demands?
.... Yes ( ) No ( )
38. Do you know the Marketing Theory of 4Ps and did you ever successfully put it into practice?
.... Yes ( ) No ( )
39. Do you have strong negotiation and communication skills? .... Yes ( ) No ( )
40. Will you continue to contact the other party to follow up if a transaction fails? .... Yes ( ) No ( )

Psychology

41. Do you think you know how to be grateful? .... Yes ( ) No ( )
42. Will you go across the bottom line under special circumstances? .... Yes ( ) No ( )
43. Have you ever imagined that you were Ma Yun's CEO? .... Yes ( ) No ( )
44. Do you have strong adaptability?.. Yes ( ) No ( )
45. Will you choose to be tolerant and understanding of the company's first unfair treatment?
.... Yes ( ) No ( )
46. Can you give your subordinates a sense of security? .... Yes ( ) No ( )
47. Are you trustworthy? .... Yes ( ) No ( )
48. Will choose to follow the crowd and be a softhead? .... Yes ( ) No ( )
49. Have you learned to listen instead of talking a lot?.. Yes ( ) No ( )
50. Do you think you can resolve very acute conflicts? .... Yes ( ) No ( )
51. Can you control your emotions? .... Yes ( ) No ( )
52. Do you think that sense is more important than sensibility in the judgment of results?
.... Yes ( ) No ( )
53. Will you give rewards to those who make contributions or comforts to those who work hard?
.... Yes ( ) No ( )
54. Do you always believe that tomorrow will be better?.. Yes ( ) No ( )
55. Will you first reflect on the problems of yourself when a goal fails? .... Yes ( ) No ( )
56. Do you trust your subordinates and give them independent conditions as appropriate?
.... Yes ( ) No ( )
57. Will you inspire your subordinates to find a way out when they have difficulties in working?
.... Yes ( ) No ( )
58. Can you often reflect on yourself? .... Yes ( ) No ( )
59. Will you play the psychiatrist role for employees? .... Yes ( ) No ( )
60. Do you now think that your inner heart is full of sunshine every day and that you can bring positive energy to others? .... Yes ( ) No ( )

Expertise

61. Do you know the theories of 4Ps, 4Cs, 4Rs or 4Vs, and can you discuss them? .... Yes ( ) No ( )
62. Do you know the principles and methods of micromarketing? .... Yes ( ) No ( )
63. Do you know the Internet marketing theory? .... Yes ( ) No ( )
64. Do you know the principles of big data marketing? .... Yes ( ) No ( )
65. Can you make an Internet marketing plan? .... Yes ( ) No ( )
66. Do you know the mobile marketing and the Theory of 4Ss thoroughly? .... Yes ( ) No ( )
67. Do you think the market needs to be segmented? .... Yes ( ) No ( )
68. Do you think a product needs to be positioned? And do you know how to position a product?
.... Yes ( ) No ( )
69. Do you think users need to be sorted? .... Yes ( ) No ( )
70. Do you know various marketing channels and their selection methods?.................... Yes ( ) No ( )
71. Do you know the SWOT analysis? .... Yes ( ) No ( )
72. Can you develop a performance assessment system?... Yes ( ) No ( )
73. Do you know about e-commerce? And are you familiar with the process of opening an online store?
.... Yes ( ) No ( )
74. Can you work out the performance ratio of marketing input to output? .... Yes ( ) No ( )
75. Do you know what content marketing is? And, can you judge whether the content is good or bad?
.... Yes ( ) No ( )
76. Have you learned cost accounting and been aware of several ways to reduce costs?   Yes ( ) No ( )
77. Do you have the ability to report marketing results to the board with simple numbers?
.... Yes ( ) No ( )
78. Do you know more about direct marketing? .... Yes ( ) No ( )
79. Do you have the ability to read financial statements? .... Yes ( ) No ( )
80. Can you prepare weekly, monthly, quarterly or yearly work plans? .... Yes ( ) No ( )

Skills

81. Can you make a H5 page? .... Yes ( ) No ( )
82. Can you make a PPT slide? .... Yes ( ) No ( )
83. Can you make a webpage? .... Yes ( ) No ( )
84. Can you collect and organize network data? .... Yes ( ) No ( )
85. Do you know any of ERP, CRM or SCM? .... Yes ( ) No ( )
86. Do you know the differences among service account, official account and mini program?
.... Yes ( ) No ( )
87. Do you know the agency system and the distribution system? .... Yes ( ) No ( )
88. Do you know the auxiliary analysis software DW/DM? .... Yes ( ) No ( )
89. Can you make full use of office software? .... Yes ( ) No ( )
90. Do you know the basic logic and principles of software programming? .... Yes ( ) No ( )
91. Do you know the concept that everyone is a consumer? .... Yes ( ) No ( )
92. Do you know what new media is? .... Yes ( ) No ( )
93. Do you know what it takes to develop software? .... Yes ( ) No ( )
94. Do you know the difference between hardware and software?................................... Yes ( ) No ( )
95. Do you know the importance of corporate information security? .... Yes ( ) No ( )
96. Do you know the importance of building a corporate customer database?................. Yes ( ) No ( )
97. Do you know how to apply virtual reality technology to corporate business? .... Yes ( ) No ( )
98. Do you often pay attention to scientific trends? .... Yes ( ) No ( )
99. Will you convince the board to approve your plan? .... Yes ( ) No ( )
100. If the board does not approve your plan, will you choose to modify your plan and respect the board's resolution? .... Yes ( ) No ( )

Total Score(   )

Network Marketing Space

Chapter 16

Topics:

1. E-commerce Marketing
2. Cross-border E-commerce

E-commerce Marketing

E-commerce generally refers to a new commerce operation model that buyers and sellers do various business activities without meeting each other, but on a basis of browser/server applications in the open Internet environment to consummate online shopping on the part of consumers, online transactions among merchants, online electronic payments as well as various business activities, trading activities, financial activities and related integrated service activities among a wide range of commercial trade activities around the world. It is a business activity which is performed by means of the microcomputer technology and the network communication technology. And governments, scholars and businessmen in various countries have defined it differently based on their own positions and participations in e-commerce. E-commerce includes ABC, B2B, B2C, C2C, B2M, M2C, B2A (i.e., B2G), C2A (i.e., C2G), O2O and other business models.

I. E-Commerce features

E-Commerce has the following basic features:

(1) Universality. As a new type of transaction, E-commerce brings manufacturers, distribution companies, consumers and governments into a network economy and digital-based new space.

(2) Convenience. In an E-commerce environment, people are no longer restricted by geographic regions, where customers are able to complete complicated commercial activities in the past through very simple and convenient ways, such as, they are able to deposit and withdraw account funds or inquire about account information 24h through online banking service, while the quality of banking services to

Online retail sales have seen an explosive growth in recent years. Obviously, the reason is that online retailers can predictably provide a convenient, content-rich and personalized shopping experience for a wide range of customers and vendors. Since there is no cost related to physical shops, personnel or stock in trade, online retailers can offer small batches of products to the market and make profits. Online retailers compete in the following three areas: interaction between customers and websites, delivery, and ability to solve problems (if any).

We should distinguish between pure-clicking companies, which start on websites but have never existed in any corporate forms before, and brick-and-click companies, which come from existing traditional companies with online websites established to provide information or implement e-commerce.

companies and customers has been improved significantly.

(3) Integrity. E-commerce is able to standardize transaction processing workflow by integrating manual operation and electronic information processing into an integral process, thus it not only improves human and material resources utilization rate, but also improves system operation accuracy.

(4) Security. In e-commerce, security is a core issue with vital importance, which requires networks to provide an end-to-end security solution, such as an encryption mechanism, signature mechanism, security management, access control, and firewall and anti-virus protection,

① *Search engine: refers to a system that automatically collects information from the Internet and conducts certain sorting and then provides the information to users.*

② *Internet service provider: also known as Internet service supplier, refers to those companies engaged in providing Internet services. Usually, large-scale telecommunication companies have the business acting as Internet service providers.*

Case Study — Pure-clicking Companies

There are various types of pure-clicking companies: search engines①, Internet service providers (ISPs) ②, e-commerce websites, trading websites, content websites and driving websites. E-commerce websites offer a variety of products and services for sale, including bestsellers, music, toys, insurance, stocks, apparels and financial services. They adopt different competitive strategies, for instance, AutoNation leads in automobile purchase and related services; Hotels.com is an industry leader in hotel booking information; Buy.com is leading in terms of price; and Winespectator is a sales expert specialized in a single category of products.

Source: Baidu Baike

quite different from traditional commercial activities.

(5) **Coordination.** Commercial activity itself is a process of coordination, which requires coordination among customers and company internal departments, manufacturers, wholesaler and retailers; in e-commerce environment, it requires great collaboration among banks, distribution centers, communication departments and technical services departments. The whole process of e-commerce is usually integrated as one integral process.

(6) **Integration.** E-commerce was built on computer network and applied high integration to all functionalities of e-commerce activities also to all parties involved in commercial activities. High integration makes e-commerce have further improved efficiency.

II. Classification of e-commerce

E-commerce is classified into nine commercial models namely ABC, B2B, B2C, C2C, B2M, M2C, B2A (i.e., B2G), C2A (i.e., C2G) and O2O.

ABC model (Agents to Business to Consumer)

ABC model is a new type of e-commerce model and known as the fourth major model following Alibaba B2B model, Jingdong Mall B2C model, and Taobao C2C model, which is a production, business operation and consumption integrated e-commerce platform jointly constructed by agents, business entities and consumers. These three players in this model may switch their roles. All players offer service and support each other, thus they form a genuine community of interests.

Currently, the relatively famous ABC based website is www.taozfu.com.

A distributor has three roles acting as an agent, business entity and consumer, who can switch among these three roles. Everyone is the master of this platform, where manufacturers, consumers, business operators, partners and management providers offer services and support each other and form a genuine community of interests; they share the resources and grow together in production and marketing and eventually realize the concept advocated by www.taozfu.com, which is joint production, joint marketing and joint happiness.

B2B model (Business to Business)

In general, this refers to enterprises to merchants e-commerce, i.e., the product, service and information exchange among enterprises through Internet. Colloquially, B2B means that supply/purchase both parties in an e-commerce transaction are all business entities (enterprises or companies), in which all of them complete a commercial transaction process by using Internet technologies or various commercial network platforms (as shown in Figure 16-1). This process includes: release of supply/demand information, placement and confirmation of purchase order, payment process, issue/transmission/ receipt of notes, and determination of distribution plan and supervision of distribution process. B2B sometimes is written as BtoB, but is often called B2B (2=to). For example, Tmall is a giant in B2B field.

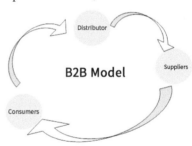

Figure 16-1 B2B model.

 **Case Study** Taozfu

Taozfu is a new e-commerce platform that makes an effective connection of agents, consumers and vendors as well as an integration of production and marketing operations with commission agents as the main body. It adopts the mixed marketing model of "online store + service shop + marketing service system + consumer alliance", making the integration of network marketing, chain operations, traditional channels, services and consumption chains, and guiding the customers' needs to the information-centered management. In terms of value, it reflects the values of two or more parties in the process of offering services from one party to another party in order to achieve a win-win situation and establish an interactive, three-dimensional and all around unlimited circulation.

The case source quoted from: Baidu Baike 2011/09/25
https://wenku.baidu.com/view/73620c966bec0975f465e221.html

Alibaba Group submitted its application to the State Trademark Bureau for the registration of "Double 11" trademark on November 1, 2011, and acquired the exclusive right for this trademark on December 28, 2012; at the end of October 2014, Alibaba Group issued a letter of notice advocating its ownership of the "Double 11" trademark. On November 12, 2015, the closing day of the seventh Tmall "Double 11" global shopping carnival, the transaction volume for whole day reached CNY 91.217 billion, in which wireless transaction volume amounted to CNY 62.642 billion, accounting for 68.67% of the total.

On November 11, 2016, according to Alibaba platform data which was not audited, as of 00:06:58, the gross merchandise volume (GMV) in Tmall Taobao Platform exceeded CNY 10 billion. At 15:19, November 11, the GMV record of CNY 91.2 billion in 2015 was broken. At 24:00, November 11, the whole-day transaction volume exceeded CNY 120.7 billion (as shown in Figure 16-2).

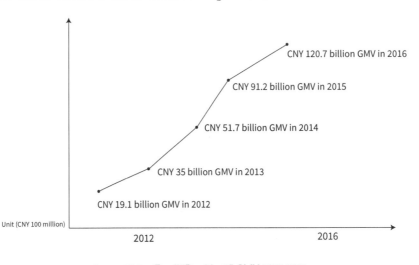

Figure 16-2 Tmall "Double 11" GMV 2012-2016.

1. Main features of B2B model

Vertical model - B2B is a vertical model faced to manufacturing industry and business industry. Vertical B2B can be divided into two directions, i.e., upstream and downstream. Manufacturers and retailers may establish goods supply relationship with upstream suppliers; for example, Dell Computer Company cooperates with upstream chip and main board manufacturers through this business model. Manufacturers may establish merchandise sales relationship with downstream distributors, such as, the transactions between Cisco and its distributors. Simply speaking, B2B websites under this model are similar to online stores, and as a matter of fact, these websites are corporate websites, i.e., enterprises open virtual stores in their websites, through which they are able to vigorously publicize their products for more customers to know their products promoting transaction through more convenient and faster means. Or, these websites may be maintained by business entities for them to publicize their operated commodities aiming also at marketing and transaction expansion by using intuitive and more convenient methods.

Comprehensive model - B2B is a business model faced to intermediate market. This transaction model is a horizontal B2B, which concentrates the similar transaction processes of every trade into one space, thus providing purchasers and suppliers a chance of transaction.

Self-built model - B2B is a business model that is self-built by industrial leading enterprise. Based on the degree of their own information system constructions, the large-scale leading enterprises built industrial-oriented e-commerce platform centered on their own product supply chain. Industrial leading enterprise connected the entire industrial chain together through their own e-commerce platforms, thus upstream/downstream enterprises in the supply chain realized information sharing, communication and transaction through this platform. However, these e-commerce platforms are too closed and lack industrial chain deep integration.

Association model - Associated industries B2B model is a multi-industry e-commerce platform built up by associated industries through the integration of comprehensive B2B model and vertical B2B model in order to improve the popularity and accuracy of current e-commerce transaction platform information.

2. B2B flow

(1) Commercial customer issues a "Purchase Order" to distributor, which shall include a series of product related information such as product name and quantity.

(2) When distributor receives a "Purchase Order", it inquires about the product according to the requirement under "Purchase Order", then issues "Purchase Order Inquiry".

(3) When supplier receives and reviews "Purchase Order Inquiry", it feeds back the result to distributor, telling whether the product is available and other related information.

(4) As long as distributor confirms that supplier is able to meet the requirement under "Purchase Order" of commercial customer, it issues "Transportation Inquiry" to transporter.

(5) When transporter receives "Transportation Inquiry", it feeds back the inquiry result to distributor, such as whether it has capability for the transportation as well as the transport date, and path and method.

(6) As long as it is confirmed that the transportation is possible, distributor promptly gives a yes answer to business customer's "Purchase Order", while it issues "Shipment Notice" to supplier and notifies transporter to get ready for transportation.

(7) When transporter receives "Transportation Notice", it starts the transportation. Then, business customer issues "Payment Notice" to payment gateway. Payment gateway and bank settle payment documents, etc.

(8) Payment gateway issues transaction success "Transfer Notice" to distributor.

3. Business operation model

Currently, not all B2B websites with a relatively successful performance adopted the online transaction model; in particular, many industry websites have no online transaction operations, instead, they are focusing on network marketing and brand building for transaction purposes. According to the analysis and study on current relatively successful B2B industry websites, we summarized seven kinds of B2B industry website business operation models as well as their corresponding combination schemes.

(1) Information service model.

These websites are required to establish a product database containing a wide range of product classifications and product varieties, complete product parameters and detailed product descriptions; particularly, they have to pay great attention to the quality of product information, and need more of the latest, true and accurate product information for comprehensive improvement of procurement experience, so as to attract more procurers and suppliers access to websites for information release, information browsing and query. The profit-making model of these websites mainly comes from the membership fee, advertising fee and pay-per-click fee, and network marketing basic service fee charged to small and medium suppliers and enterprises; the representative websites include china.chemnet.com (listed in 2006), wjw.cn, texnet.com.cn, tnc.com.cn, plantb2b.com, bmlink.com and dzsc.com.

(2) Alliance agency service model.

Enterprises whose products are directly sold to consumers usually will engage franchisees and agents to sell their products, and generally, the business operation model of these enterprises is the type of design + production + marketing. All these websites functionalities and web pages have been designed to be centered on the demands of branded companies and distributors; for example, a garment website shall have good industry information contents including dynamic, gallery and fashion trend, and is required to collect all garment brands information and create extensive and accurate franchisees and agents database. The profit-making model of these websites comes from the advertising fee and membership fee charged to branded companies, in which advertising fees may account for the majority of their total income. The representative websites include efu.com.cn, hometexnet.com, qgyyzs.net, zghzp.com, spzs.com and tjkx.com.

(3) Original equipment manufacturer (OEM) information service model.

These websites are targeted to outsourced production and service industries; the profit-making model of these B2B websites is to charge a fee to factories for looking for better purchase orders, and to provide site visit to factories, photos and guarantee for charge collecting, and to focus on the authenticity, richness and accuracy of the content of factory production capacity information.

Representative foreign-trade comprehensive websites include 1688.com, globalsources.com and made-in-china.com.

(4) Small online wholesale transaction service model.

These websites are required to have very good understanding of retailers' demands, build up a perfect online credit system and payment system, have rich varieties of products and detailed information; and now, comprehensive and large industry websites more easily achieve success. Representative domestic trade websites include 1688.com and eelly.com., while representative foreign trade websites include dhgate.com and aliexpress.com. Currently, this trade has relatively high entry threshold; domestic trade website 1688.com has an outstanding advantage, since it is supported by Alipay and Taobao store keepers; due to extreme scattering of retailers, a broader network is required for promotion, for which Alibaba has strong monetary fund support.

(5) Corporate competition intelligence service model.

The core management of the team must have an industrial background; otherwise, it is impossible to access information sources, and large-scale enterprises hardly will pay the bill. These websites may be operated preferably by analysts resigned from these websites or individuals with a certain industry background from trade association, chamber of commerce and trade business entities; the market demands are relatively huge and many industries allow the survival of several websites. The profit-making models include membership fees, sales reporting, consulting, journal release, meeting and advertising fees. The most representative websites include mysteel.com (listed in 2011), chem99.com, oilgas.com.cn, cctd.com.cn, ap-ec.cn, cngrain.com and webtex.cn.

(6) Business opportunity + technical service model.

The profit-making models of technical communities include the income from job recruitment service, technical meeting service, training school advertising, software advertising service and equipment advertising. More importantly, when adding customer loyalty operation to business, these websites are required to offer good services to both technical beginner-hands and master-hands, and enable master-hands to show their abilities and products for them to get mental satisfaction, while beginner-hands have the opportunity to learn new things, ask master-hands questions, such that the technical community has its inner driving force for achieving long-term and sustainable development. Generally, the website shall have Q&A, blogs, gallery, job recruitment, downloading, personal space, microblog and conference columns. Currently, the representative websites include gkong.com, chinakong.com, luosi.com, ccement.com and zhue.com.cn.

(7) B2B + domain name + construction + optimization service model.

For operating these websites well, the website teams are required to have experience in corporate website construction and operation, industry website operation and corporate website search engine optimization ranking. Some companies with corporate construction or corporate network marketing service background selected this model to construct their B2B industry websites, and the profit-making model is also relatively mature, except that, due to lack of B2B industry website operation background, many companies' B2B industry websites just became white elephants rather than playing their substantial role for marketing. Those companies that made success in running B2B industry website may have greater success, if they choose this business operation model. The representative websites include chem17.com, ybzhan.cn, china.chemnet.com and texnet.com.cn; chem17.com and ybzhan.cn are the websites under Zhejiang Mtnets Co., Ltd., and there are other 24 websites adopting the same service model.

B2C (Business to Customer) model

B2C model is the earliest e-commerce model that existed in China, and B2C e-commerce payment combines pay-on-delivery and pay online; and most enterprises select outsourced logistics service for goods delivery to save their operating cost. Along with the change of user consumption behavior and excellent enterprise demonstration effect, the number of online purchasers keeps growing. In addition, some large-scale examinations such as civil service examination also began to adopt B2C model.

1.   Basic demands of B2C model

B2C model's basic demands include user management demand, customer demand and distributor demand.

User management demand: user registration and user information management.

Customer demand: provide customers with electronic directories, and help users search and identify their demanded commodities; conduct comparison study of similar products, and help users in making purchase decision; commodity evaluation; shopping cart; place purchase order for purchased products; cancel and modify purchase order; make payment online; and track purchase order status.

Distributor demand: inspect customer registration information; handle customer purchase order; complete settlement for customer's purchased product, and handle customer payment; conduct e-auction; conduct commodity information release; issue and manage network ads; manage commodity inventory; track product selling process; establish interface with logistics system; establish interface with bank;

execute customer relationship management; and provide after-service.

For B2C online e-commerce platform, enterprises usually adopt multi-channel distribution and other like methods in their selling process, thus their HR cost and investment are huge. Huiya e-commerce system is committed to build up an online distribution channel for enterprises that is integrated with CRM management[①], procurement management, purchase-sales-inventory management and membership management, and this system differs from a simple e-commerce system. E-commerce system will provide enterprises with end-to-end e-commerce consulting service and platform construction.

2.   Product functionalities

Foreground functional modules include: commodity display, site search, user management, online ordering, bulk purchase, merchants joining, website announcement, help center and friendly links.

Background functional modules include: customer management, purchase order management, commodity management, selling management, customer service management, procurement management inventory management, outbound management, return management, finance management, statistical statement, rights management and operation log (as shown in Figure 16-3).

① *CRM management: i.e., customer relationship management, which is a process for enterprises to provide their customers with innovative and personalized interactions and services by using appropriate information technologies and Internet techniques in order to improve their core competitive power, coordinate with customers in the phases of selling, marketing and service rendering and upgrade their management methods.*

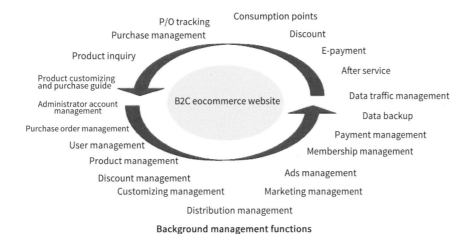

Foreground user functions

Consumption points

P/O tracking
Purchase management

Discount

Product inquiry

E-payment

Product customizing and purchase guide

After service

Administrator account management

B2C eocommerce website

Data traffic management

Purchase order management

Data backup

User management

Payment management

Product management

Membership management

Discount management

Ads management

Customizing management

Marketing management

Distribution management

Background management functions

Figure 16-3   B2C E-commerce model.

3.   Platform design principles

(1) **Easy to use:** the techniques used for software design and development shall impose no special requirements to user

browser, and the software operation interface shall be simple and concise and easy to use by all operators.

(2) **High efficiency:** the software page design shall be magnificent, artistic and

simple, which can reflect the corporate culture, the browsing speed shall be fast and main information shall be addressed. The software navigation shall have clear hierarchies that are convenient for viewers to browse their wanted information.

(3) **Reasonable structure:** columns are arranged so that they are reasonably complying with human browsing habits. Reasonable software hierarchical design with very few clicks will enable operators to find their wanted information.

(4) **Extensible and accessible:** in consideration of the future development demands and the stages of software application, software design shall be as concise as possible. The coupling degree between all functional modules should be low for easy extension of the software and smooth automatic connection with other applications.

(5) **Security and stability:** while software accessibility is fully considered, software security and stability are also the most important issues. Software uses SQL injection protection, uploaded file check and key data encryption to ensure secure and reliable software.

(6) **Strong concurrency:** considering that multiple users may operate the software simultaneously, the software shall support operation by multiple users by establishing high-speed buffer mechanism and improving user access speed.

(7) **Portability and sustainability:** the adopted development techniques not only meet app demands, but also shall be suitable for future development trends and convenient for future upgrading and transplanting. Users' secondary development cost shall be reduced and users' investment benefit shall be protected.

(8) **Personalized:** provide more personalized services to customers by using registered users information or COOKI and the like techniques.

(9) **Interactivity:** the software has feedback mechanism for realizing automatic response mechanism and high interaction.

(10) **Creative:** based on the industry status quo and trade features, the features shall have unique and attractive style that can fully present the management flow of a marketing company.

(11) **Good maintainability:** software maintenance shall be simple and easy to operate, such that internal website admin-istrators are able to maintain software column contents by themselves.

4. Marketing strategy

(1) Deletion

In a B2C e-commerce model, the majority of us may believe that "inventory and logistics" are essential elements, which cause high cost. Why should we eliminate these two elements since they cause high cost? Most of us believe that absolutely these two elements cannot be eliminated. Nothing is impossible, and there are always more solutions than problems. So far, some e-commerce websites have eliminated these two elements. There are two methods to eliminate these two elements: firstly, when selling information products, do not sell physical products. Secondly, when selling physical products, related resources must be integrated.

(2) Decrease and increase

All B2C websites are supported by a large amount of advertising fees. The biggest advantage of network is that it is a low-cost marketing platform. For achieving fast development, B2C websites have to decrease hard advertising and operating costs, then spend more efforts in making marketing innovations.

Payment mode: most B2C websites only select two or three simple payment modes; as a matter of fact, whether or not a payment mode is easy and convenient is directly linked to customer purchase desire. Most consumers belong to impulsive-type buyers who will be transformed into intellectual-type buyers, if they encounter certain troubles in their process of purchase. Therefore, the more convenient the payment mode is, the more benefits B2C sales will receive. And, this rule is especially important. The main reason for China's SP industry's crazy market is that its payment mode is very convenient. If all SP services are paid through post mail payment, it is impossible that today's crazy market would exist. If you want to be engaged in B2C trade, you have to maintain a payment mode that is superior over industrial standards, and the most convenient payment mode will help you achieve success in marketing.

(3) Creation

Purchase guide information: most B2C websites only present and sell products, their website content is dull, which hardly retains returned customers. Many consumers may feel blind and aimless when they are choosing so many similar products. If consumers are able to have better understanding of the products they want to buy and make comparison among similar products by reading very reasonable purchase guide information, then they will buy a satisfactory product. Make customers satisfied and, in return, they may buy products on your website in the future. The purchase of products by customers is not the purchase of the products, instead, the purchase of benefits brought about by the products. Humanized purchase guide information can help customers access all product information quickly.

Shopping culture: most of shopping websites lack shopping culture. What is shopping culture? Shopping culture requires your shopping website to have a kind of atmosphere where customers feel comfortable when purchasing your products.

(4) Warehousing and logistic service

Along with the increasing development of e-commerce, logistics and distribution business also is on the way to increasing expansion, even with supply falling short of demand. Therefore, warehousing and logistics businesses are flourishing in recent years. In addition to warehousing, drop-shipping and goods distribution, these primary businesses also provide distribution tacking, end consumer goods return and complaint handling and like services. Also, many comprehensive warehousing and logistics companies provide suppliers with specific logistics solutions, such as high-efficient goods distribution plans and low-cost goods distribution options. These enterprises are concentrated mainly in resource-intensive cities such as Shanghai, Beijing and Guangzhou; Shanghai based Swork Warehousing and logistics Company spent just three years to be developed as a nationally famous logistics and distribution base, and launched Taobao, Tmall, Jingdong and yhd.com e-commerce cooperation platforms. In addition to serving small and medium store sellers, Swork has paid more efforts to cooperate with brand dealers, such as Sanzhuliang, Converse Flagship Store, Shanghai Household Chemicals and tianmeijianyd.tmall.com. In selecting these enterprises, main considerations include shipment speed, logistics and distribution cost, commodity safety and p/o handling volume.

C2C (Consumer to Consumer) model

Similarly with B2B and B2C, C2C is one of several e-commerce models, and differently, C2C is customer to customer model. C2C e-commerce platform is to provide an online transaction platform for both buyers and sellers. Sellers are able to provide commodities to the platform for online auction, while buyers are free to select and bid for commodities.

C2C actually is a proper term of e-commerce, which is an e-commerce among individuals. C2C is consumer to consumer, the English word "to" sounds like "two", so CtoC is simply written as C2C. C refers to consumer or customer, C2C means consumer (customer) to consumer (customer). C2C refers to e-commerce among individuals. For example, Consumer A has a computer he or she wishes to sell it to another consumer through an online transaction, and this type of transaction is called C2C e-commerce. The representative websites include taobao.com and paipai.com.

B2M (Business to Manager) model

B2M refers to marketing-oriented e-commerce enterprises (e-commerce companies or companies for which e-commerce is their most important marketing channel). A B2M e-commerce company is a marketing-oriented station established based on customer demands; such company promotes this station and conduct standardized purchase guide management through online/offline multiple channels so as to enable such station to function as an enterprise important marketing channel.

B2M network marketing hosting service providers use network marketing accurately and efficiently for improving enterprise sales volume based on their analysis and study of enterprise product and service features and through hosting of corporate network marketing.

Scope of B2M network marketing hosting services: website operation hosting, search engine ads hosting, B2B marketing hosting, B2C online store sales agent, blog marketing, community marketing, blind advertising, SEO optimization, video marketing, cluster marketing, email marketing, network activity planning and network marketing training, etc. It provides comprehensive hosting service for enterprises to integrate their network marketing.

A B2M network marketing hosting service provider is not a network marketing advertiser, nor a simple Internet window of a company, nor a simple product publicizing and service organ of a company. Instead, it is a marketing-oriented service institution by taking customer demand as its core, carrying out product and service integration and guiding customer demands. With B2M marketing service, customers are able to find their demands; at the same time, customers are guided to generate more new demands, such that customer demands

are satisfied and customer values are further explored.

In enterprise marketing channels, B2M marketing service is one of the important channels for an enterprise to explore the market; through integration of enterprise products or services, it transforms enterprise traditional business models to have better products or services marketing and to provide customers with better, convenient and timely services with the application of B2M marketing channel. By making full use of Internet advantages, B2M further expands enterprise business scope and becomes enterprise's important marketing channel as well as an important source of growth.

 Case Study   Taobao.com

Taobao.com is the biggest network retail website in Asia committing to become the world's biggest personal business transaction website. Taobao.com was invested and founded by Alibaba Group on May 10, 2003. Since the existence of Taobao.com, it successively launched personal online shop, Alipay, Alisoftware, Yahoo Express and Alimama and other products and value-added services. The current business scope of Taobao.com contains C2C (customer to customer) and B2C (business to customer). According to the disclosure of Mr. Zhang Yong, CFO of Taobao.com and President of Tmall, in Beijing China B2C E-commerce Summit on April 28, 2010, the daily independent access IPs of Taobao.com exceeded 40 million, meaning that over 40 million consumers are shopping in Taobao.com, which is more than Amazon. In addition, so far Taobao has 190 million registered members, accounting for half of the Chinese netizen population, and covering the majority of Chinese online buyers; the transaction volume in 2008 amounted to CNY 99.96 billion, according for 80% of online shopping market. At present, Taobao.com has developed an integrated network transaction platform covering C2C as its primary business and B2C as its complementary business.

Taobao.com advocates an honest, active and fast network transaction culture and says "shopping may not happen, but credit may never be lost". While providing Taobao members with secure and efficient network transaction platform, Taobao commits to provide a large population of netizens with opportunities in opening an online store, entrepreneurship by Internet and meeting friends while doing business.

1. Profit—making model

(1) Transaction commission. Transaction commission is the primary source of C2C website revenue at

any time. The reason is that C2C platform is only a transaction platform, which provides both parties in a transaction with a business opportunity, like an exchange space or a supermarket in real life, and taking a certain percentage from transaction is the nature of such market. Taobao currently charges nothing to all merchants, as Jack Ma said: "Taobao will charge nothing for three years. China's C2C market is now on the stage of market cultivation, and the free-of-charge mode will be good for gaining more space for future development." Today's free-of-charge model of Taobao is a duplication of Alibaba's model. Prior to collecting fees, Alibaba also experienced a 3-year free-of-charge period.

(2) Income from advertising. The position of Taobao.com on the Internet is just like the position of a large-scale supermarket in real life, it is a place frequently visited by netizens, has high popularity, frequent rate of clicking and a large number of membership base; and all enterprises never want to lose the potential business opportunities there. So, the advertising income brought by its position on the Internet is also one of the major revenue sources for the website.

(3) "Home Page Gold Space" recommendation fee. Except for those netizens with special purposes, 70% of them usually feel enough just viewing the home page of a website. Therefore, the ads and exhibition spaces in the website's home page have an expensive commercial value. For the "Gold Space" in a website home page, the website may sell them at a fixed price, or, through auction, allowing the purchasers or awarded bidders to exhibit their commodities in such spaces within a specified time.

(4) Website provides value-added services. Taobao.com provides a transaction platform to both buy-

ers and sellers; it also provides them with transaction related services. It tries its best to satisfy all kinds of customer demands for realizing seller/buyer transactions. Now there are a large number of commodity varieties at Taobao.com, it is not easy for buyers to find their wanted commodities; for this, a website may launch a search service for improving efficiency. Sellers are allowed to purchase key words for promoting their product ranking in the search result in order to realize more transactions.

2. C2C credit model

(1) Registration authentication. The execution of registration authentication has two purposes: (i) prevent illegal users from attempting to practice fraud in the transaction platform; and (ii) confirm user identity, by supervising user's transaction, and putting user transaction records into archives for limiting their business operation behaviors.

(2) Transaction real name authentication. User registration only allows a user to log in an account number in Taobao platform, which is just a user code. When doing transaction, the real identities of the seller and buyer shall be verified, i.e., adopting transaction real name system, in order to confirm the seller and the buyer in the transaction are real persons. In this way, even if a user's account is stolen, the thief is unable to use a false identity for doing a transaction without true data of the real user.

(3) Archiving of transaction records and establishment of credibility index. All buyer/seller transactions shall be recorded, and the transaction results shall go through certain credibility index authentication standards. In this way, buyers and sellers are able to check the confidence level of the other party through a credibility index in future transactions, and decide whether or not the transaction shall proceed, thereby reducing the practice of fraud.

(4) Establishment of punishment/warning system. Taobao.com shall establish stringent punishment/warning system for punishing and warning those illegal transactions. For example, dealing with a person who conducted an illegal transaction, his/her credibility index may be reduced, or his/her account number may be deleted, or legal means may be triggered, if the case is serious enough. In addition, departments in charge of website supervision also severely crack down on illegal traders for maintaining the normal conduct of online transactions.

(5) Adopt online payment. Taobao.com online payment techniques are quite mature. Alipay (China) Network Technology Co., Ltd. is a domestic leading third-party independent payment platform founded by Alibaba Group.

Alipay is committed to providing China e-commerce with "simple, secure and fast" online payment solutions.

(6) Online communication community. Taobao.com constructed online communities for providing users with experience exchange platforms. By exchanging experience among all netizens, this helps in applying effective supervision of fraud practices. Also, netizens may learn lessons from others to prevent repeated practice of fraud from re-occurrence. In addition its role in the construction of a credit model, the online community may help a website know the voice of users, so that the website is able to make sustainable improvement and maturity.

3. Payment mode

Users have worries about payment security, because the transaction online is not a face-to-face transaction and too many unknowns exist. The existence of third-party payment platforms undoubtedly presents Taobao.com as the best payment mode. Alipay ensures the security of online payment by users, in addition, it establishes mutual trust for users in network space, thus Alipay moves one step forward to constructing a clean Internet environment. Alipay's innovative product techniques, unique ideas and mass user base attract more and more Internet merchants, who actively select Alipay as their online payment system. Alipay transaction is an innovation in Internet development, also a milestone in e-commerce development.

4. Distribution model

Based on China's current logistics status quo, Taobao.com invited logistics companies to provide special services and preferential prices for users, and stipulated the rules for use of recommended logistics services; whether such rules are executed depends on whether the delivery is completed. Sellers may select recommended logistics companies at their own discretion or upon the request of buyers.

The case source quoted from: mbalib.com2016/11/13 http://doc.mbalib.com/view/df52058a720b8f82288fc9f2fc11d312.html

M2C (Manager to Consumer) model

M2C, an e-commerce model firstly proposed by Tang Junhua, CEO of baike.eelly.com in 2012, is a business model based on the complementary advantages of Internet and ground channels and through sharing of terminal marketing channels and after-service outlets to deliver products from manufacturers directly to consumers together with M2C distribution service and M2C after service, in order to make terminals active and reduce commodity circulation links.

M2C model achieved new development in the Internet decoration industry. In 2015, the Internet decoration industry was on the rise and seems to have flourished overnight bringing in hundreds of millions of dollars

Traditional decoration industry began to have a hard time and face decline. A large number of the Internet decoration companies moved into the market with great power. Vertical Internet decoration e-commerce platform lyh8.cn proposed a new M2C concept - Manufacturers & Managers to Consumers, thus it proposed free-of-charge Internet decoration construction supervision, i.e., it added a management function.

1. Specific applications of M2C commercial model

(1) In relation to manufacturers: M2C e-commerce marketing platform provides users with secure commodity transaction and exhibition platform service, in addition, it provides marketing channel platform and business operation management platform service. It provides users with market development, channel management, product distribution and brand promotion solutions. It helps users optimize, explore and stabilize commodity circulation channels and business operation management platform systems for achieving resource integration, channel stability, cost saving and improvement of efficiency. It is aimed at saving sales costs, eliminating unfair competition and forged/fake commodities, and bringing the business ecosystem back to an orderly environment where market share is won by quality and service. Mainly including:

● Activate baike.eelly.com M2C e-commerce marketing platform service.

● Provide M2C shop (eliminating profit-sharing wholesale tiers, saving channel construction cost and publicizing expense, decreasing terminal selling price).

● Stipulate reasonable product M2C member price and entrepreneurial commission (saving the fixed salary expenditure and promotion/publicizing expense of invalid salesmen).

● Provide M2C distribution service (distributed by manufacturer, eliminating forged and fake products and market price chaos).

● Provide M2C after-service (manufacturer offered service, professional and reliable).

● Easy to operate, convenient to manage, powerful function, saved human, financial and material resources.

(2) In relation to entrepreneurship: obtain free-of-charge M2C shop through baike.eelly.com M2C e-commerce marketing platform, and receive the entrepreneurial commission specified by manufacturer after successful selling, thus independent entrepreneurs are able to do global business easily without relocation, capital investment, procurement and shipment.

● Activate M2C shop without pay (real name system and threshold free).

● Carry out shop management (doing business without capital investment, easy to learn).

● Receive M2C distribution service support (zero inventories, zero risk and zero investment).

● Receive entrepreneurial commission (distributed by manufacturer through the platform).

● Third-party settlement is reasonable and secure.

● Freedom and equality, fair, easy and relaxed, full-time/part-time possible.

(3) In relation to consumers: register M2C VIP member, shopping at M2C member price, distribution service and after-service via M2C, such that M2C VIP members receive tangible benefits, shopping at ease and after-service guaranteed.

● Log in baike.eelly.com M2C online shopping platform (shopping mall) (shopping at ease).

● Search commodities, shopping in M2C shop (convenient and fast).

● Receive M2C distribution service (at preferential price).

● Receive M2C after-service (professional and secure after-service).

● System payment platform, third-party consumption supervision, and payment at delivery.

● Clear source of product, reasonable price, convenient and fast, secured after-service.

2. Advantages of M2C

The biggest advantage of M2C is its price. By taking garments for example,

M2C refers to factory to consumer such that, all price increases are eliminated, and consumers are provided with the most reasonable price while enjoying first-class garments.

It is known to all businessmen engaged in marketing branded garments that selling garments in shopping malls generally adopts a sales commission model, 25%-30% of branded garment sales volume will be paid as the shopping mall rental, plus the regional agent fee, outlet decoration fee, shop sales personnel and other expenses. The total accounts for about 70%-90% of the sales volume, and these sums will be paid by consumers at the end, which absolutely is unfair to consumers. By adopting M2C model, AMURS*ACTIVE reduced the product purchase price significantly. Moreover, based on the current market situation, M2C model adopted by AMURS*ACTIVE certainly will be the trend of future garment consumption in China firstly for ensuring product quality, secondly for meeting the most important feature of the Internet which is "fast", and thirdly for bringing product value to where it is.

It can be concluded that the assurance of fast product delivery time, quality and lowest price can only be achieved by constructing factories in China, such that, middlemen can be bypassed, advantage in price can be guaranteed, and genuine high-quality and inexpensive garments can be purchased by netizens.

III. Platform construction

As the ancient Chinese proverb goes: "A handy tool makes a handy man." In order to achieve the long-term development of your company, here is a good faith advice: if you desire to use the Internet to help your business, you are advised to choose carefully a trustworthy, reputable and capable website design company. Then, how to choose the right website design company? There are many website construction providers. Since this industry is a quickly established industry, there are many non-professional companies doing business. Therefore, all users shall do their due diligence in choosing their website design companies. The following pointers are provided herein for your reference.

1. Fixed office space

You may have encountered this: when you request to pay a site visit to the office of your website design company, this company may refuse your request by giving you various reasons, while committing to offer you various services at a price very much lower than regular market price. It can be imagined that those website design companies unwilling to tell their office address to customers and refusing the site visit are all companies that are more or less fraudulent; and their commitments are unpractical and void because they have no office environment and technical capacity.

2. Website design experience

We suggest choosing those website design companies with extensive website design experience because (i) experienced website design companies will have wide consideration during website design, and have better understanding of customer demands; and (ii) experienced website design companies have a large number of customers, which makes bankruptcy an implausible scenario.

3. How about their own websites?

As professional website design companies, if their own company websites are a complete mess, do you believe that such companies have genuine design capabilities? Do you expect that they will take responsibility for your website design and construction?

4. Consult website design experts

As the Internet has evolved, whether or not a website is good is no longer decided by animation coverage, color, sound or video and other superficial things. The backend management, information real-time update, traffic statistic and analysis and online communication techniques supporting website normal operation are crucial considerations. Of course, website designers may boast that they have such techniques, but you will need to ask if: these techniques are indeed theirs. Also, you need to find out if updating or upgrading is possible and if such techniques are advanced, reliable and practical in technology.

5. HR balance principle

If all the employees of a website construction company are salesmen, you should be weary; because salesmen receive kickbacks, therefore, a reasonable percentage of technical personnel and salesmen is necessary to ensure that customer funds can be genuinely used for website construction. This is the HR balance principle addressed in mobile marketing management.

6. Do not only check their own websites

There are some website design companies whose own websites are even designed and constructed by others, so you have to be careful when checking their websites. Small screen-shot images in a website can't represent everytihng. The website should have the linkages to the websites of the company's customers. Make sure to check them out, because, when a website page is zoomed out, it will look nice, but you can't see the details, so you should visit the original websites for details; in that way, you can also feel the access speed of those websites, which is important for you to see whether the company is careful in its service, as a good website concerns not only the design, but also the fact that the images have the best effect while they are kept the smallest in size for having a faster website access speed.

7. You shall have an alert mind

Some website design companies want to win your business rather than consider how to serve you, so they will make promises they do not intend to keep. Therefore, you need to have an alert mind when choosing which company you will hire based on their real qualifications, not their empty promises.

8. Cost performance

For a medium-sized website, a price quote is not enough; a comprehensive website-making planning program shall be submitted. Quality website design is expensive. An extremely low quote is impossible to provide you with a high-website design. Also, there is no way to guarantee the website project quality and service level. There are many people engaged in or alleged to be engaged in website construction, including self-study students; however, website developer's experience is rather important. In addition, team work and a project management execution process are crucial in fulfilling and launching the construction of a website; as such, the quality of websites will differ greatly. When comparing expenses in choosing a website development company, what you should compare is "cost performance", i.e., when you compare the same expense, whether you will receive the best result.

IV. O2O Marketing

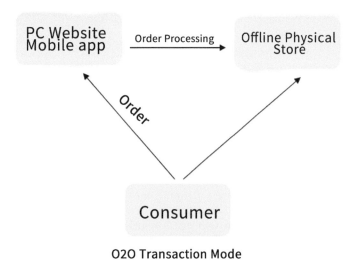

O2O Transaction Mode

Figure 16-4   O2O transaction mode.

We don't know when people have become accustomed to looking for various "local services" with their computers or phones and have started intimate relationships with the network. Internet and reality are increasingly associated with consumer behaviors. Everything begins to touch the Internet from PC terminals to mobile terminals. In the O2O business model, apps can accomplish the profound combination with the mobile Internet, realize the deep integration between the O2O platform and the mobile terminal by being downloaded and applied to the mobile terminal, achieve direct trading by combining the information of both buyer and seller to make direct communication between mobile terminals, and consummate transactions at any time without any terminal or geographical limitations (as shown in Figure 16-4).

1. O2O Marketing Method

(1) Experiential marketing

In O2O marketing, experiential marketing is the most common method. Experiential marketing is a marketing method to redefine and redesign a way of thinking by stimulating and mobilizing a consumer's perceptual and rational factors like Sense, Feel, Think, Act and Relate mainly by means of seeing, hearing, using and participating.

People will pursue a higher level of spiritual experience after their basic material needs are met. At this time, the level of prices becomes less important, and what people value more is whether they have the spiritual experience they really want. As a result, experiential marketing naturally becomes a new trend in industry development. And this experience can be completely move to apps to allow users to achieve the virtual experience in a certain form on apps, which can stimulate consumers' desire to buy and accordingly boost the offline direct purchasing behaviors.

The game of Pokémon Go. Source: Sohu.com

For example, Pokémon is a Japanese anime with which a lot of people have spent watching during their childhood. When its fans were very young, they often

Case Study   Etsy's Emotional Marketing

Etsy is an online store platform featuring the sale of handmade items. It was compared by the New York Times with eBay, Amazon and Grandma's Basement. Although it is less famous than major e-commerce websites such as Taobao and eBay, the Etsy website offers an unusual network service for everyone with its unique business model and diversified profit models.

Compared to transactions, Etsy cares more about the interpersonal communication, including communication between Etsy and sellers, between sellers and sellers, and between sellers and consumers. And this centers on "socializing operations and taking emotional measures for users."

Just as MySpace's initial development was based on the large number of offline bands and their fan bases that had existed already, Etsy had no ability to create a handwork enthusiast community out of thin air. In fact, Robert Kalin, one of Etsy's founders, was totally obsessed with handmade items and fully familiar with the large-sized professional and amateur handwork enthusiast groups in major cities like New York and Los Angeles. These enthusiasts often organized communication activities and sold their own works therein.

Therefore, at the beginning of establishing Etsy, Kalin adopted a comprehensive word-of-mouth marketing strategy and focused on spreading the Etsy brand through a variety of offline events. These events included to hold sewing competitions, to fund traditional handicraft fairs, and to set up various street interest groups. By means of such grassroots marketing, Etsy obtained the effect of publicity which was far better than millions of dollars of ad campaigns on traditional media.

Etsy's business model is designed to access quality sources.

Etsy's crowd-sourced brand marketing has expanded the brand influence in specific user groups at a very low cost with the skillful use of the enthusiasm of handicraft makers to communicate with each other.

And to support this, Etsy has designed a variety of website features to create an excellent online community atmosphere.

One of the howling successes achieved by Etsy is the exposure through the Internet of the offline handwork enthusiast community that has existed already. Today, the socialized function design of the Etsy website has become an example that various DIY websites want to copy.

And there are six interactive components playing crucial roles in the formation of Etsy's online community: Forum, Virtual Lab (Etsy's online classroom for users), Public Chat, Web Group Setting, Widget and Storque.

The case source quoted from: Baidu Baike 2016/02/27
https://baike.baidu.com/item/etsy/3794335?fr=aladdin

fantasized about when they could have their own Pokémons. Since the launch, the game Pokémon Go has spread around the whole world. Incorporating the advanced AR technology, it enables players to capture, fight and exchange in the real world. Additionally featuring a large number of social elements, this game has numerous real scenes as well as rich contents and playing methods. As the latest work of Nintendo's Pokémon Series which is based on the classic anime the Pokémon, the Pokémon Go embodies a variety of Poms and allows players to train Poms to complete the collection and obtain more glory values.

(2) Direct marketing

Originating in the United States, direct marketing is also known as direct selling and is divided into several categories including direct mail marketing, catalog marketing, telemarketing and computer network marketing. With the vigorous development of e-commerce, the mobile marketing method represented by apps has become a new direct marketing channel. For direct marketing, the key point is the accurate audience. On the basis of location based services (LBSs), "anywhere" is no longer anywhere, but becomes a targeted location in the age of mobile Internet. Vendors can push purchase invitations to consumers at a specified location through the apps in consumers' cellphones.

In the age of O2O, the direct marketing experience is also changing. Direct marketing and its database focus on the behaviors of each consumer and potential consumer, predicting the consumers' future behaviors based on their past ones. This kind of information is processed on an individual basis, and even if there are tens of thousands of consumers, it can still be used to analyze personal behaviors and make decisions.

(3) Emotional marketing

The emotional marketing is to take the consumers' personal emotional differences and needs as the emotional marketing core of brand marketing strategies, and take advantage of emotional packaging, emotional promotion, emotional advertising, emotional word-of-mouth, emotional design and other strategies to achieve a company's business goals.

Emotional branding is the process of shaping a brand personality, allowing a brand to have its own unique emotions, highlighting the personalization of the brand, and thinking about the emotional brand from the sensory perspective of the consumers so as to obtain the sensory element model of the emotional brand.

When the enterprise marketing satisfies a customer's emotional factors, it will lead up to the customer's positive inner experience - satisfaction, pleasure, passion and other positive emotions - so that the customer can have his/her emotional conflicts eliminated and can reach a harmonious inner state to directly affect his/her subsequent purchase behaviors.

(4) Database marketing

Database marketing is a marketing mode in which a company collects and accumulates the user's information, and then carries out in-depth customer mining and relation maintenance in a targeted manner with the aid of e-mails, SMSs, telephones and mails after analysis and selection of this information. Its core work is data mining.

With newspapers, magazines, the Internet and TVs as its carriers, the traditional advertising only faces a vague population, and it is impossible to count up the number of target audience among it. Therefore, its effectiveness and response rate are always disappointing. The retailer giant Wanamaker said, "I know half the money I spend on advertising is wasted, but I can never find out which half." Database marketing is the only measurable advertising form by which advertisers can accurately know how to get customer responses and where these responses come from, and this kind of information will be used to continue, expand or redefine/readjust marketing plans.

The database marketing is also known as a brand-new sales method that aims to establish a one-to-one interactive communication relation with customers and relies on a large customer information base to carry out long-term promotion activities. It is a dynamic database management system that has the content covering existing and potential customers and that can be updated at any time.

O2O is an industry based on the user base. The mobile Internet is no longer a world for Internet elites only after 2-3 years of development. As the mobile Internet is entering into the lives of ordinary people, O2O has increased to a certain size, namely Big User or Big Data, which means more vendors and more offline information is moved online. This also embodies the business value and future of O2O. Users' consumption and usage habits, etc. will generate great commercial values for the future O2O.

2. Four Crucial Elements of O2O Marketing

With the rise of mobile networks and Internet finance, the living consumption is also moving towards them. O2O will directly change everyone's consumer behavior mode for life service products so as to change the concept from "consumption for products" to "consumption for life".

(1) Who does it

Marketing is imperative for every enterprise, and most entrepreneurs have the idea of "entrusting someone with marketing" or "entrusting media with marketing".

"Professional" marketing companies or personnel may have a much stronger knowledge of marketing than the enterprise itself, but they know less about the corporate culture and the product operated by the enterprise. As a result, they need to learn more. Additionally in terms of the knowledge difficulty, the O2O marketing knowledge is relatively easier to learn while the enterprise's exclusive substance is so extensive that it is more difficult to grasp or understand. Therefore, marketing companies or personnel are "professionals" relatively.

(2) Where to do it

After deciding to do O2O marketing by itself, the first question will be where to do it. And the answer is that we will always be where users are. More specifically, on the mobile Internet, apps are your influencing tools which are the spread channels too.

According to statistics, in 2013, the online shopping population of China reached 302 million and the utilization rate reached 48.9%, increasing by 6% over 2012. At the same time, the mobile commerce market showed a huge market potential. Cellphone shopping boomed in the mobile commerce market with the number of users reaching 144 million. In addition, upon a "shuffle following the wild growth", group buying has entered a period of rational development with a user population of 141 million and a utilization rate of 22.8%, featuring an increase of 8.0% and a yearly user growth of 68.9% over 2012. It is the business application with the fastest growth.

(3) How to do it

Nowadays, O2O is a marketing system which conducts promotions through the combination of service and substance marketing to make an enterprise truly powerful. In other words, the termination of service is not the end, and the most valuable closed loop of O2O is not built for the platform interests but for the marketing. In the combination of online and offline, the offline is absolutely not the end of influence but the next start. If we regard the termination of service as an end, we can neither increase our return on investment (ROI) nor realize the difference between online marketing and traditional marketing.

(4) Conversion rate

What is the purpose of O2O marketing? There may be various answers: to sell products, to promote products, to attract investment, to make money online, and to cultivate loyal users, etc.

In general, people just know the purpose of O2O marketing but often ignore the "conversion rate". Therefore, people should become aware that it is necessary to take conversion into consideration whenever the marketing is needed, and should understand the nature of conversion. The essence of Internet marketing lies in interaction, which has two objectives: to build trust and to improve conversion rate. Interactive communication is to enhance the customer trust with professional services and to narrow the distance between enterprises and customers with customer-friendly performances. Online marketing is interactive.

Showing the details of a product or service to a buyer by means of visual marketing falls within the category of promotional information and never affects the conversion rate of orders. On this account, vendors should highlight the values of a product or service in its description.

And the product or service should have two characteristics: discoverability and accessibility.

Every marketer engaged in O2O should realize the importance of marketing conversion rate. To improve the marketing conversion rate, the marketer must stand at the user's point of view to improve his/her own O2O marketing ideas, optimize marketing platforms and processes, attach importance to the user experience, be good at guiding users to interaction, actively maintain the relations with potential customers, and pursue sustainable O2O marketing strategies.

For mobile marketing, the traffic entrance is not considered as online or offline but as virtual or real. The QR code, which now remains only one function, i.e., "scanning code to entry", has become the only entrance for mobile marketing O2O (as shown in Figures 16-5 and 16-6).

(1) QR code for real category. It means that offline vendors provide QR codes to consumers for scanning to conclude the transaction.

(2) QR code for virtual category. It means that online Internet vendors and QR code vendors receive commissions on the transactions that they have helped enterprises consummate. It commonly takes the forms of electronic VIP, points redemption, electronic ticketing, electronic gift voucher and so on.

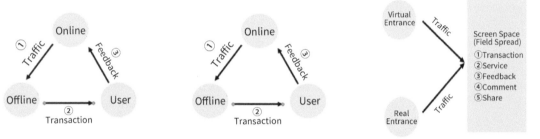

Figure 16-5　O2O prototypes in the age of separation of online from offline.

Figure 16-6　O2O prototype for mobile marketing.

Common applications of QR codes		
Industry Sector	Application	Example
Online shopping	To buy a product by scanning the QR code wall in the metro passageway	YHD.COM and various supermarkets
QR code payment	To scan the QR code with a cellphone to effect the payment	Alipay and Starbucks
Information reading	To scan the QR code on the newspaper to read more	Outdoor advertisement and single-page advertisement
Quality control	To use QR codes to store information in the manufacturing process	DPM QR code technology
Food traceability	To track food sources and logistics with QR codes	Meat and vegetable labels
E-ticketing	To electronize various tickets with QR codes	QR code e-tickets for the Humble Administrator's Garden of Suzhou
Traffic management	To use QR codes to manage vehicle information	QR code vehicle license
Meeting sign-in	To scan the QR code for authentication to sign in a meeting	Meeting sign-in
Anti-counterfeiting cryptic QR code	It cannot be easily copied because it needs to be scanned by infrared laser for authentication	Important information encryption
High-end interactive marketing	To interact with high-end brands to accurately identify the genuineness	Wine, watches, etc.
Bus QR code	To scan the QR code to obtain the information on bus routes and transfer, etc.	Baidu map
Recruitment QR code	To get the details of employers and jobs quickly and easily and deliver resumés	Resumé delivery and talent search

Common Applications of QR Codes

Cross-border E-commerce

I. What is cross-border e-commerce?

Originating from "small foreign trade"[①], cross-border e-commerce began in 2005 when individual buyers purchased products from foreign countries through Internet platforms and made payments through third-party payment methods, and sellers delivered such products by courier service. With years of development, the cross-border e-commerce now has the following two meanings:

In a narrow sense, it refers to the transaction process in which trading parties in different countries conclude a transaction and make the corresponding payment through the Internet, and deliver the product to the consumer by means of courier service or parcel post through cross-border logistics. This process is basically equivalent to cross-border retail[②].

The narrowly defined cross-border e-commerce is the sale of small parcels on the Internet basically to end consumers (namely B2C or C2C). However, with the development of cross-border e-commerce, some Class-B vendors engaged in fragmented or small wholesales have become a part of consumer groups (i.e., B2B). Since it is very difficult to distinguish between such Class-B vendors and Class-C indi-

vidual consumers in the real world, the narrowly defined cross-border e-commerce has also included this part in the cross-border retail.

And in a broad sense, the cross-border e-commerce is an international commercial activity that trading parties in different countries electronize such traditional import and export trading links as display, negotiation and transaction by means of e-commerce, and then deliver products through cross-border logistics to consummate the transaction. This process is basically equivalent to foreign trade e-commerce. The broadly defined cross-border e-commerce statistically relies on its commodity transactions (excluding services). It includes both cross-border retail (narrowly defined) and B2B transactions in the cross-border e-commerce. Such B2B transactions not only include the online transactions concluded through cross-border trading platforms, but also include the offline transactions consummated through negotiations on the Internet. It differs greatly from the transaction process for traditional foreign trade. The B2B in the cross-border e-commerce is the major substance of this book.

II. Transaction Process for Cross-border E-commerce

In principle, the export process for cross-border e-commerce is as follows: an exporter/manufacturer displays its products online through a cross-border e-commerce enterprise (platform-based/self-supporting[③]) which entrusts a domestic logistics enterprise with the delivery of products after the products have been ordered and fully paid, and after customs clearance and inspection in both exporting and importing countries, such products are finally delivered by an overseas logistics enterprise to the consumer or enterprise. In practice, some cross-border e-commerce enterprises directly cooperate with third-party integrated service platforms, allowing these platforms to handle logistics, customs clearance and inspection as well as other links for them. And some simplify the operation of cross-border e-commerce by setting up overseas ware-

houses. In any case, the process remains within the above framework.

The import process for cross-border e-commerce is basically the same except that the direction is opposite to the export process. It can be seen that the cross-border e-commerce has the characteristics of both general e-commerce and traditional international trade. Its trade flow is much more complicated than that of the general e-commerce because it involves international transportation, import/export clearance, international payment and settlement as well as other related links. Furthermore, it needs to pay more attention to the e-commerce features of international display and operations than traditional international trade. Cross-border e-commerce also plays an increasingly important role in international trade.

① *Small foreign trade: it is an innovative model that meets the interests of all the three parties: seller, individual buyer and e-commerce platform.*

② *Cross-border retail: Opposite to the cross-border wholesale, it refers to the trading activity that a product dealer or maker sells the product to individual consumers or social group consumers.*

③ *Self-supporting: it means that manufacturers directly run their own products.*

III. Future Trends of Cross-border E-commerce

1. Product categories and sales markets will be diversified

(1) Product categories will be diversified. Product categories for cross-border e-commerce are becoming more and more comprehensive, extending from the digital products without logistics, e.g., online music and video, to the easily carried products, e.g., apparel, computers and accessories, jewelry, cosmetics and consumer electronics, and even to the products with higher logistic requirements, e.g., fresh food, furniture and automobiles. With the continuous appearance of diversified cross-border logistic solutions, product categories will continue to expand and complement each other.

(2) Sales markets will be diversified. The future growth of cross-border e-commerce will mainly come from the diversified growth of sales markets. The emerging markets such as Brazil and East Asia will rise rapidly, while the developed sales markets like Europe and the United States maintain sustained growth. In these emerging markets, the unreasonable domestic industrial structures, especially the underdevelopment of the consumer product industry, result in a large number of consumer demands, but these demands stay unsatisfied because the offline retail channels are less mature and the local markets are smaller. If the local cross-border transactions become more convenient and the mobile Internet is widely popularized, the cross-border consumption in these markets will boom.

2. Information service orientation will be converted into comprehensive service orientation

The information service oriented cross-border e-commerce platform surviving on membership fees and PPC (Pay-Per-Click) fees is now facing a development bottleneck, while the comprehensive service oriented platform increases the satisfaction of both parties to a transaction by offering one-stop service and receives online trading commissions with the liquidity rate significantly higher than the former. It is crystal clear that the latter represents the general trend.

3. Mobile terminals will become the major transaction channels

With the continuous development of mobile technology and the rapid spread of smart phones and tablet computers, the future cross-border e-commerce will be "dominated by mobile terminals". Mobile e-commerce allows consumers to shop anywhere and anytime so that suppliers can do business without limitations of time and space. And those emerging countries that directly enter the mobile e-commerce cross-border market will present a huge incremental market.

In China, mobile terminals are developing at a faster rate, and mobile netizens are increasingly penetrating the nation's population. According to statistics, the number of Chinese mobile netizens was 620 million in 2015, accounting for about 45% of the Chinese population. An analysis report showed that mobile shopping user coverage was as high as 51.9% in the second quarter of 2016.

4. Industrial ecology will be better

China's cross-border e-commerce will change from a traditional chain model to a platform-based ecosystem model, radiating from the ecosystems with one ring linked with another and one circle around another, such as both parties to a cross-border transaction, cross-border finance, cross-border logistics, comprehensive foreign trade services, derivative services (including third partner, search keyword optimization, personnel training and consulting), big data and cloud computing. Everyone in these ecosystems will benefit from and serve the entire ecosphere.

5. Consumption and corporate operation will be globalized

The development of cross-border e-commerce has led to a clear trend of consumption globalization, interaction with consumers without borders and customization. Flexible production and data sharing will be popular. Consumers and enterprises communicate with each other through the e-commerce platform to understand each other; and vendors collect fragmented data through omnichannel and accurately identify and collect consumer needs by means of data mining to accomplish precision marketing. Interactions between buyers and sellers will lay a more realistic foundation for the customization of C2B and C2M and will enhance the flexibility of production and facilitate market-based supply chain organization.

The development of cross-border e-commerce also fuels the globalization of corporate operations. According to the statistics of Analysys, Alibaba, Tencent, Amazon, and Facebook's overseas revenues have increased year by year in recent years. E-commerce enterprises paying more attention to the global market will be uniquely positioned in the market, and the development of cross-border e-commerce will also allow enterprises to quickly globalize business processes and to make assets lighter, sensitivity greater and decisions more accurate.

6. New trade rules and orders will come into being

In August 2016, Alibaba proposed the eWTP initiative to set up a world e-commerce platform. This platform will serve as a private sector to lead a market-driven, open, transparent and multi-stakeholder-involved international communication platform, performing the functions of focusing on the global Internet economy and e-commerce development, exploring development trends and difficulties, generalizing commercial practices and best practices, incubating trade rules and industry standards as well as promoting communications, cooperation and capacity building. Its purpose and goal are to promote the development of inclusive trading, to facilitate the development of small businesses, to expedite the globalization of consumption, and to drive the development of young people. This initiative reveals a strong message that with the rapid development of cross-border e-commerce and its enhanced position in global international trade, more and more leading enterprises in the cross-border e-commerce will pay close attention to and plan to participate in the formulation of standards for the international trade rules in the Age of Internet. As a result, new rules and orders for international trade will come into being.

IV. Development of B2B cross-border e-commerce export platform

In traditional international trade, nearly all transactions are completed among enterprises. In the Internet era, more and more enterprises are doing their business by adopting information technologies and linking to various B2B e-commerce platforms.

The development of B2B cross-border e-commerce can be divided into the following two periods:

(1) B2B platform is an information open platform. During this period, openness is the bond of foreign trade companies; through interface to B2B platform, business directory and commodities are presented in websites for information exchange.

(2) B2B platform is a transaction platform. Along with technology development, maturity of payment system and logistic service, security and credit are guaranteed, business model gradually became mature, so more and more foreign trade companies have used B2B platforms to realize their entire transaction process. At present, enterprises are able to release and browse trade information through different network service platforms, which lead them to realize trade negotiation, contract signing until payment for purchased goods. Network platforms also provide them with up/middle/downstream trade paths, effectively connecting suppliers, service providers, middleman and procurers, thus improving the trading cost and efficiency.

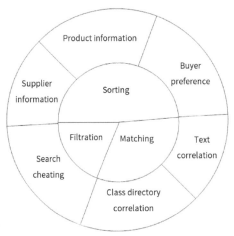

Figure 16-7   Cross-border B2B platform search sorting mechanism.

V. Cross-border B2B platform search sorting definition and principle

1. Definition and purpose of cross-border B2B platform search sorting function

Definition: the fundamental function of websites is search, enabling users to express their demands and receive answers quickly and clearly; and sorting is the search result.

Purpose: cross-border B2B platform search sorting function is designed to provide users quickly and efficiently the matched most suitable products, suppliers or other related information.

2. Category of cross-border B2B platform search sorting

Class directory browsing sorting (categories), products search sorting (products), suppliers search sorting (suppliers) and supplier in-shop search sorting are all the sorting methods of cross-border B2B platform search sorting. These four sorting methods are largely identical but with minor differences.

3. Cross-border B2B platform search sorting principle

(1) Buyer-oriented. Most users are buyers; a search platform will selectively search suppliers' products to meet buyers' preference.

(2) Punish cheating severely. Cheating may hurt buyer's experience and undermine market fairness greatly. Starting from supplier ports, a search platform persists that it will "punish cheating severely" as its crucial principle, and those suppliers violating this principle will be punished severely by the search platform.

4. Cross-border B2B platform search sorting mechanism

Cross-border e-commerce integrates with mobility. A cellphone has already been considered another human living organ and existed in people's daily life, thus more and more things have been integrated with cellphones, which is no exception to cross-border e-commerce. Cross-border e-commerce has been integrated with mobile end gradually (as shown in Figure 16-7).

Mobile end Amazon.

 **Online celebrity marketing: everyone is a universe in the age of online celebrities**

Online celebrity effectively triggers the individual power of fans and gathers a group of fans with the same interest together. At the same time, through frequent and deep interaction, affection and trust will be established with fans, thus fans are led to consumption for gaining a fat profit; and eventually a "grassroot" becomes a "celebrity", and online celebrity economy flourishes. All these shall be owed to the development of time and technologies as well as those technical entrepreneurs who are brave enough to make innovation happen.

In order to realize "online celebrity economy" from "online celebrity", the entire system is required to have high-quality social assets and suitable business model. So-called "online celebrity" bypassed traditional celebrity-making pattern by taking Internet advantages, promptly broke traditional celebrity-making and money-making machines, and eventually changed the ecological chain of many industries. In late August 2015, Taobao gave the definition of "online celebrity economy" for the first time in history.

1.   What is online celebrity economy?

Online celebrity economy always goes like this: carrying out marketing and visual promotion represented by fashion talents and oriented by online celebrity taste, together with targeted marketing by relying on mass fans, and eventually transforming fans to power of purchase. As a matter of fact, online celebrities are civilian stars who lead customers to receive their recommended consumptions through personalized publicizing and packaging. Online celebrity economy has the following three characteristics:

1. Shaper. Shaper refers to product and personal brand shaping; shaping of personalized brand is to shop product brand.

Therefore, as to the products recommended by an online celebrity, consumers usually will not have too much concern regarding the brand of the recommended product; instead, they care about the recommendation of the online celebrity. In such a way, it well illustrates the characteristics of social e-commerce.

2. Civilian nature. Online celebrities are civilians in general cases rather than so-called big stars, who may feel easy to resonate with consumers and are easily imitated by consumers.

3. Interaction. Online celebrity economy has strong interaction. Consumers hardly can communicate and interact with traditional TV stars; conversely, consumers are allowed to chat with online celebrity economy stars, know what they are doing every day, interact, exchange views and ask questions, during which, a sense of credibility can be easily developed.

Because of these three major characteristics, all consumption stimulations by online celebrity economy will produce an immediate effect which to enterprises has a magnificent demonstration effect; and as the result, the traditional pure buying and selling relationship will slowly enter into social e-commerce. Social e-commerce is based on interpersonal relationships, rather than buying/selling of products.

2.   What is the real nature of online celebrity economy?

In essence, online celebrity is a personalized network content shaping featured with strong transmissibility and influence. The bottom-layer logic behind its a brand new operation model of network platform based content production, communication and consumption. Therefore, online celebrity economy in essence is a content industry, and user attraction relies on content.

All cashable forms of online celebrity economy actually are the extension of "content + community + e-commerce"; in which, content is the most important, which is personalized, directly faced to users and able to attract remarkable flow of fans; and cashability can be realized only through e-commerce deployment by fans.

Online celebrity economy is not an IT industry, nor is it high-tech and Internet industries; instead, it is a content industry; therefore, what attracts customers is content. In the mobile Internet and video era, personal brand is crucial to attract users' attention, also it is the source attracting their attention. Consumers in the video era likely believe more personal brands, personal recommendation and individual brands as well as their role linking between consumers and consumer products. Therefore, what attracts flow is not a platform or app, it is the content industry.

In an online celebrity economy chain, an online celebrity may share 10%-20% of sales volume, or 30%-40%, if the profit is considerably acceptable.

This means that e-commerce companies such as garment companies will no longer flow from Taobao; 40-50 online celebrity signings will bring their flow and fans. Therefore, e-commerce companies are allowed to offer services without purchase of flow, such as warehousing, logistic, distribution, plate-making and O&M services for interaction with fans.

Why does an online celebrity have a desire to interact with fans more than stars? Because, each interaction will make money. Stars cannot sell commodities to fans which may make them feel degraded; conversely, online celebrities are more like living style guiders who are able to interact directly with fans, directly sell commodities to fans, and also online celebrities have a stronger aspiration to interact with fans.

Chapter 17

Marketing Space 4.0 – Mobile End-to-end Marketing

Topics:

1. Mobile Space for Virtual Reality
2. Artificial Intelligence - A New Scene for Holistic Marketing
3. Blockchain - Creating a New Space for Trust
4. Augmented Reality (AR) Space

Mobile Space for Virtual Reality

Five Methods For VR Marketing

To experience a product or a scene without direct body contact is what lots of people dream about. With virtual reality (VR), this is no longer a dream. There is no doubt that the combination of VR and marketing must lead to a big market. VR overturns traditional channels and allows product contents to be spread in a point-to-point manner within a virtual reality space.

5 poppies coming up from the ground.

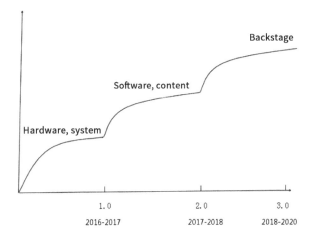

Five Methods For VR Marketing

Age 1.0: hardware and systems have become mature with hardware iterating rapidly in such a manner as specified by Moore's Law

Age 2.0: basic functions of the software have been realized and their contents will increase rapidly in the next one or two years

Age 3.0: the whole technological niche has been improved with competitions centering on backstage big data

The in-depth application of VR in the industry requires the guidance of VR marketing methods. So what are the reference methods for VR marketing? We will introduce five methods herein:

1. Abstract perception

If you do not have your own VR device, you may take into consideration the abstract perception, e.g., the use of holographic views.

2. Interactive symptom simulation

In the medical world, VR can aid digital marketing in many ways. For instance, a company manufacturing anti-migraine medication has produced a VR-based interactive symptom simulator that allows the patient's family to feel the pain experienced by the patient himself. This not only promotes their products, but also raises concerns about non-visible chronic diseases.

This technology can render assistance to patients suffering from chronic diseases, such as patients with anxiety disorder and traumatic sequelae. Besides, VR can also show how a treatment or a drug can alleviate the pain of patients, so as to promote related products.

3. Real-time data collection

It is estimated that there are 4 million active VR users today. This number will increase fourfold in the next two years, and real-time data collection can help companies quickly adjust their marketing strategies.

For instance, if a VR marketing project fails to achieve the expected effect, new strategies can be rapidly formulated for the brand based on data feedback to cater to the general public. Nowadays, most consumers are not familiar with VR, not all users accept it, and some of them sometimes even give negative comments on a certain marketing technique.

4. Increasing consumer engagement

There are many factors involved in increasing consumer engagement. When properly used, VR can help consumers better understand the product and the service. Sometimes watching a 3D advertisement with a pair of 3D glasses may make the advertising marketing no longer boring.

For a new company or an old brand, 3D may be a breakthrough point if you want to use VR marketing. You should see if the audience are satisfied with this marketing mode or not, and then let them know about the future VR marketing.

5. Making a blueprint for the future of digital marketing

Facebook's acquisition of Oculus is a start for Facebook to make a blueprint for its future VR digital marketing. VR allows two or more people to interact virtually with each other.

VR has not yet become mainstream, but I believe we do not need to wait too long. The combination of VR and digital marketing will be the future of marketing. Almost every brand can make use of VR to promote its products and services.

Artificial Intelligence – A New Scene for Holistic Marketing

Since 2016, artificial intelligence (AI) has become the new favorite of the capital community at a lightning speed. As scientific research institutions have been working hard on AI for a long time, and emerging entrepreneurs and even tech behemoths represented by Baidu are staging overwhelming strategies continuously, more and more people have become aware of and acquainted with AI and have been itching to try it.

AlphaGo[①]'s triumph over Lee Sedol, which appeared to be the peak of AI development at that time, now seems to be just the beginning of a new age in the development of AI.

AI refers to the intelligent simulation of human consciousness, thinking and behavior with computers. The reasons why AI technology has been developing rapidly are the advancement of algorithm and hardware as well as the mass data generated by PCs and the mobile Internet. There is a good example at the moment: Baidu announced at the 2016 Baidu World Congress that Baidu Brain had gotten hold of one billion user profiles and 10 million levels of tags with vertical portraits showing users' preferences in finance, living, and retail, etc.

Professionals must spontaneously reflect on the value of these data for Internet marketing when they see these data. At this moment when AI becomes the largest outlet, marketing should take advantage of this favorable situation to thrive and continuously adapt to the new age.

With the continuous development of artificial intelligence, the population faced by the marketing will be "smaller" than that in the past when enterprises placed a large number of advertisements on the media and did their utmost to indiscriminately sweep every corner and reach consumers as much as possible. The past marketing model often resulted in high costs and unsatisfactory effects. In the age of the Internet and mobile Internet, the "precision marketing" characterized by keywords predominates. Although a variety of marketing methods are available now, Baidu Promotion is still very popular due to the accuracy of its keyword marketing.

The accuracy of Baidu Promotion is mostly attributed to the keywords directly derived from consumer demands. If the user portraying capability of AI is grafted into Baidu Promotion, billions of user data and ten million levels of tags can directly outline the audience in a precise way, and advertisements will target the audience more accurately and directly satisfy users' needs.

In addition, AI will bring endless possibilities for marketing. In the age of PCs, the so-called marketing methods are nothing more than the purchase of media in the form of text, picture, audio or short video. In the age of mobile Internet, people learn to allow humans to interact with information by means of technology and even make use of social attributes to cause people to spontaneously forward the information. And in the age of AI, AI will inundate various scenes in our life instead of staying at the port, and can send reminders and offer services to people and connect anything they are interested in anytime and anywhere, whether on a computer, a cellphone or a watch.

On this premise, what concerns an enterprise during marketing are identifying its target audience, carrying out the two-way emotional communication and achieving the effective intelligent marketing through these in-depth interactions brought up by technology.

In the future, AI may record the interactions between people and advertisements and report them back to the enterprise. In the next round of marketing activities, a personalized marketing mechanism in which the marketing method varies from customer to customer may be established by virtue of the continuous advertising adjustment by AI based on its learning experience and user profiles. AI will broaden the plastic space for marketing, and thus "advance" the boundaries of marketing.

I. Definition of AI

Artificial intelligence (AI) means computer simulation to human consciousness, thinking process and intelligent behaviors. AI mainly involves the principle for computer intelligence, the manufacturing of human brain intelligent computers and enabling computers to have high-level applications. As a comprehensive technical discipline, AI involves multiple disciplines such as psychology, game theory, information science, biological science and thinking science. Along with the existence of computers, humans began to use computers to simulate human thinking. Now, the computer has replaced humans in many fields and computers are used to work for humans because computers work fast and accurately. AI has always been the frontier discipline in computer science, and both computer programming languages and computer software gained survival and development thanks to AI development. The reason why AI has become popular and rapidly developed lies in the advancement of hardware technology and the development of robots; in addition, the massive amount of data brought about by the popularity of the Internet and mobile terminals.

A popular definition of AI, also the earlier definition in this field, was proposed by John Mccarthy[①] at the 1955 Dartmouth Conference: "AI is to enable the behavior of a machine to look like intelligent human behavior". However, this definition seems to ignore the possibility of strengthening artificial intelligence. Generally speaking, AI definitions can be divided into four classes, i.e., making machine "think like human", "act like human", "think wisely" and "act wisely". For the purpose herein, the word "act" shall be understood broadly as taking action, or stipulating action plan, rather than a body movement.

In the information technology development era, AI also brought about multiple changes to the marketing field, and made business marketing activities more and more intelligent. As a part of intelligent economy, intelligent marketing is a kind of intelligent operation forms. However, differently from virtual marketing or e-marketing, intelligent marketing is an operation model built on a higher technological level. Intelligent expressions in marketing activities are reflected in many aspects.

①

John Mccarthy: the father of artificial intelligence, was born in a communist party family in Boston, USA, on September 4, 1927. Due to the nature of his parents' jobs, his whole family had to relocate from Boston to New York and then to Los Angeles. He received the Turing Award in 1971 for his contributions in the AI field. In fact, he is known as "father of artificial intelligence" for his AI definition proposed in the 1955 Dartmouth Conference. On October 24, 2011, John McCarthy passed away at the age of 84.

II. AI optimizes marketing data collection and processing methods

Take Google Street View for example, which is used in Google Maps and Google Earth to provide users with full views of streets.

Prior to the application of this technique, Google staff had to personally inspect and calibrate the addresses in street views. After the birth of "Google Brain", this time- and labor-consuming work was delivered to machines to complete, and Google employees no longer were necessary to check every street view photo day after day. Google engineers settled image identification difficulties by using AI techniques. Now, Google is able to identify all addresses on the German Street Map within just one hour, which greatly improves work efficiency and optimizes user experience. The application of AI techniques made Google no longer just a search company, but also a machine learning company. In addition to the application in Google Map and Google Earth, Google Brain also can be used in Android voice identification and Google+ image search. AI provides new solutions to Google products related orig-inal data collection and processing, which improved accuracy while lowering down the cost.

III. AI provides personalized marketing strategy

The combination of human and in-telligent techniques/Internet of Things techniques may provide enterprises with a preemptive marketing strategy.

By taking Nike Experience Store for example, merchants may push sales activity information to surrounding con-sumers in real-time by using iBeacon-like technique to solicit consumers to the phys-ical store for trial use. At the same time, merchants may put sensors in the samples in physical stores to record consumer trial use times and experience, and then transmit the experience information to the backend for data analysis. If data quantity is sufficient, user behavior data analysis will be generated. De-pending on real and reliable data, through fast analysis of such data and data model building, the backend AI technique is then able to provide sales personnel with suggestions, and transmit the information to experience store

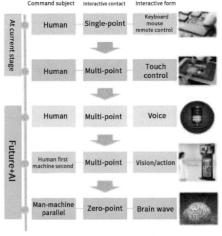

Overview of Human-machine Interaction Evolution and Development. Source: Baidu Wenku

for them to make timely adjustment to their marketing strategy.

AI technique also is able to classify customers with similar features and pref-erence according to customer personal data and preference and through data analysis, based on which it is possible to push targeted ads to customers. This appli-cation is able to provide enterprises with front-end client information at the earliest time, such that it shortens the time spent for transmitting market information to management, and enterprises are enabled to develop preemptive marketing strategy.

AI is now applied in personalized substance planning for interaction with B2B customers. For a period in the near future, text analysis and natural language processing technique will be crucial to market automation revolution. Currently, the most excellent application in using AI in marketing for personalized recom-mendation is e-mail marketing. According to Boomtrain report, personalized e-mail opening rate exceeds 60%. By adding an AI engine for processing e-mails, person-alization increases e-mail opening rate by 228%. This is the working principle of AI driven personalized e-mail.

Following e-mail marketing is AI technique-based personalized video ads. Personalized videos help marketers quickly prepare perfect brand stories.

IV. AI changes advertising methods

The development of the facial recog-nition technique allows a different type of advertising. For example, installing software and webcam devices in digital billboards. Billboards identify viewer's physical characteristics and the ad areas they watch by using the facial recogni-tion technique. Enterprises evaluate the advertising effect according to collected data and information, such that they are allowed to make reasonable choices of tar-geted advertising populations and spaces.

In addition, an AI billboard is able to perceive viewer's preference according to his/her reaction, thereby performing ad screenings and targeted advertising.

Hence, advertisers change one-way ad-vertising to two-way advertising. AI is able to help enterprises have better under-standing of viewers, thus advertising be-comes diversified from viewer to viewer. In addition to image ads, AI also can be applied in voice interactive ads. With the help of interesting accessories such as mi-crophones and gyroscopes on mobile de-vices, companies are able to launch voice interactive advertising to enable ads the ability to listen, speak and think. While listening to ads, users are enabled to inter-act with ads through voice to obtain more detailed product information, thus the ad experience becomes more interesting.

For example, when a user is watching a video, normally there are ads for 10s to 60s before starting the program. Users want to shorten ad time, while advertisers desire to increase ad time length to strengthen users' awareness of advertised brands and improve brand popularity. Dealing with this contradiction, merchants may use AI to launch video interactive ads. During ad playback, merchants may ask voice questions to users, and users answer these questions through voice. If a user's answer is correct, then ads will be skipped free of charge. From a user point of view, interaction saves their time; from a merchant point of view, though ad time is shortened, users have a thinking stage during the interaction, which further addresses a user's awareness to brands. In addition to ad interaction, merchants also can use voice interaction for customer survey for conducting consultation and research on mass users as well as more accurate analysis.

V. New applications of AI marketing

It is unknown when all-people marketing became a new habitus of our lives, from which everyone wanted to have their own chance to seek various means of cashability.

By tracing back to the moment when commodity exchange existed, marketing and selling were related to each other, which provided a series of support to commercial activities. Along with social

 **Case Study** | AI Becomes a New Marketing Engine for TOUTIAO.COM

TOUTIAO.COM has broken down the previous marketing barriers that a brand had in respect of contents, products, interests and other aspects. It has taken the lead in putting into practice the full-chain decision-making path connecting user interests to scenes under the intelligent full-scene marketing model to provide a new dimension of thinking for marketers.

The intelligent full-scene marketing model is based on TOUTIAO.COM's exclusive AI technology, which enables the profile analysis of TOUTIAO.COM's app series including TOUTIAO, IMXIGUA, DOUYIN and HUOSHAN, seeks the target audience for brands and combs their interests and needs in a vertical manner. It also finds out high-quality IPs or good creators for these needs to customize the production contents that will reach scene terminals in the form of pictures, videos, music, quizzes or creative advertisements, and then will be sent to the "right person" under the mode of smart distribution.

The continuously upgraded evolution and application of AI imply that "efficiency/manpower", "knowledge base", "fun" and "creation" are getting closer and closer to the real intelligence. TOUTIAO.COM integrates AI into each phase of the "life cycle of content", namely creation, distribution, interaction and review, which redefines the relation between people and information.

Here we take the newly upgraded PMP product as an example. In the interchange of big data with a brand owner, TOUTIAO.COM effectively analyzes, tracks and selects the "valuable" target population through the combination of intra- and inter-domain data in order to set up a population database dedicated for the brand. On this basis, AI subdivides the target population with

2017 AI Becomes a New Marketing Engine for TOUTIAO.COM In Guangzhou, China

tags, identifies each living person, and displays different advertising materials in front of the audience in a timely way to achieve the customized marketing with everyone served individually.

Additionally, PMP can facilitate the fuse of the advertised brand and the advertising effect in such a manner that both quality and quantity can be guaranteed, monitor the advertising effect in real time, and constantly correct the optimal delivery to the target audience. Traditional advertising forms stop here, but PMP can track user browsing behaviors and emotional changes by virtue of intelligent technologies to feed back to advertising strategies for the brand with periodic market environment insight reports helping the brand make marketing decisions.

TOUTIAO.COM, as a rising star in the age of mobile Internet, has opened up a world of (B: Baidu; A: Alibaba; T: Tencent) BAT with its core algorithm. As leveraging the wave of AI is on the rise, TOUTIAO.COM marketing will make brand owners and itself scale new heights.

Source: TOUTIAO.COM

① SEM stands for search engine marketing. Simply speaking, SEM is a search engine platform based network marketing, which uses people's reliance on search engine and people's habit of using search engine to transmit information to targeted users when people are searching information. SEM's basic idea is to enable users the ability to find out information and access to web pages by clicking for further information. Enterprises carry out paid marketing through search engine, and users are able to communicate directly with company customer service, know the product and realize the transaction.

② Generative Adversarial Networks (GAN) is a deep learning model, and currently one of the most promising unsupervised learning methods in complex distribution in recent years. The model passes at least two modules in the framework: the mutual gaming of generative model and discriminative model, learning generates considerably good output. In original GAN theory, G and D were not required to be neural networks, and it would be OK if they fit the corresponding generated and discriminated functions. However in real practice, deep neural networks are normally used as G and D.

development and advancement of technology, marketing is also escalating. The emerging of the Internet and e-commerce gave the birth to SEM①-based data flow cashability model. However, as the community-based relationship cashability model increasingly matured, it became the symbol of the rise of mobile Internet.

Nowadays, the marketer's toolkit has one more tool called AI. This tool is strong enough comparable to any marketing tools in the past. With this tool, the mass data generated from globalization of Internet-based marketing suddenly had a high-efficient processing method. Enterprises may easily come to the conclusion that is closest to the fact through these data processing results. Decision-making by enterprises no longer rely on the insights developed based on an expert's experience; the blindness and randomness of success have been improved, and some uncontrollable factors have become clear and controllable AI is able to act as customer service, investigator, public sentiment supervisor, competition intelligence analyst, promotion strategist, user profile and user value explorer.

AI completes its mission through its participation in the data acquisition and processing during marketing, by learning and training in this process, and making improvement and playing a role in this process.

Scene I: user profile

In the marketing process, regardless of product positioning, user development, or potential value exploration, user profiles are always indispensable. When we have sales data, it is possible for us to see the gathering of an individual user's biological attributes and social attributes in interaction. How to find out the valuable marketing relevance among data? With increased user scale, the portrait begins to become fuzzy. How to find out the valuable clue in noise? In different marketing stages, we have a different focus on a user's profiles, so how do we define this?

AI is able to learn through GAN②, process mass data quickly and obtain the basic characteristics of related users in current marketing stage, so as to provide marketing and promotion with a focused direction.

Scene II: marketing strategy

Marketing strategy is enterprise guideline for marketing activities. When conducting marketing activities accord-

User Portrait. Source: www.dfic.cn

Marketing Strategy. Source: www.dfic.cn

ing to brands and product positioning, we shall collect industrial information, competitor information and user information, stipulate corresponding small-scale action for testing and obtaining market feedback, and then modify strategy details for realizing marketing objectives.

AI can be used for simulation and feedback training in different fields as well as forecasting of marketing results. For example, in advertising, it is possible to learn data specific to a large number of individuals, then estimate our approximate investment return, rather than knowing the result until actual expenses are spent.

While maintaining quick data analysis, it is possible to build a data model; all of that is far beyond human analytical ability and it is the ideal state of AI.

Programmatic ads have a large scale, as they have been developed to today, which is able to make automatic planning, purchase and optimization, help advertisers locate the specific viewers and their geographic position, and can be used in online advertising, mobile advertising, social media and other activities.

Also, the same principle is also applicable to TV ads and print ads; more than half of online advertisements in the

US are programmatic buying, and Google Ad Exchange and Facebook are two major sources of data flows. Programmatic ads have various advantages including high efficiency and easy operability (no negotiation), as well as perfect combination of automation and related useful data.

However, programmatic ads also have disadvantages, such as the sensitivity to face data flow and multiple hidden agent fees.

As a matter of fact, the wide use of advertising blocking software has imposed a threat to online ads. According to PageFair data, the cost for advertising blocking globally in 2015 reached USD $21.8 billion. However, the popularity of AP and personal intelligent assistant may help programmatic ads out of predicament.

Scene III: customer exploration

Product and service are able to bring value to customers. Different customers have different loyalty and potentials.

When promoting diversified products and services, it is required to explore and classify customer value, evaluate the risk of loss of different types of customers, and most importantly, it is necessary to prepare early plans for the feedback of different users. These could not be known before the existence of big data and AI, and can only be obtained by relying on marketing expert experience and sample customer test; also, long duration, unstable and unreliable test results are the biggest problems.

AI is able to classify users into different levels by consumption ability, consumption tendency and consumption risk according to their consumption data and behavioral habit, and execute different marketing actions to different types of customers. Our customer exploration team is able to achieve double marketing effect with less than half marketing resources.

Marketing evolves along with development of technology: Internet breaks down geographical territory and search costs; mobile Internet explores the commercial value of social relations; AI overrides data, with one end connecting to the use habit of users in different scenes, one end connecting to the feedback of products from different user groups, and one end connecting enterprise marketers; it observes and presents always changing market information.

Though AI now has many restrictions, forward-looking brand owners already paid their best efforts to improve user experience by constructing a real shopping space for users through virtual equipment. Also, users are allowed to construct a virtual scene through five major companies namely: Facebook, Apple, Google, Microsoft, Amazon and Baidu.

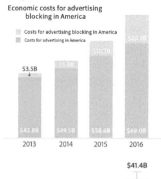

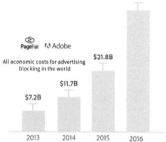

Customer Exploration.
Source: www.dfic.cn

🔆 Case Study | AI Applications by Various Platforms

Facebook

In 2015, Facebook created a virtual assistant "M" for its communication app Messenger, helping users buy products, mail gifts, book hotels and even arrange trips. In addition, "M" could give users weather updates, and even help users buy tickets for hard-to-get movie tickets.

A Virtual assistant "M" for Facebook

Facebook has a team engaged in making neural networks, which also develops applications to help robots think and act like natural men. A good many of these applications have already been used in the virtual assistant "M".

Google

Google's personal intelligent voice assistant "Google Now" is a product which offers services to

Google's personal intelligent voice assistant "Google Now"

users based on data. The more data it accumulates, the better services it will offer.

Google Now can fully understand the user's habits and ongoing actions, and can use the accumulated data to provide the user with relevant information. It is currently available for both Android and IOS devices.

Amazon

Echo is a wireless speaker device with built-in voice control system and virtual assistant "Alexa". It can listen to the user, and can respond to and execute the user's commands at the same time.

Echo for Amazon. Echo is a wireless speaker device with built-in voice control system and virtual assistant "Alexa"

You can start a conversation with Echo and ask it questions about weekly/daily weather forecast, time, alarm setting, shopping list or even simple encyclopedic knowledge, just as if it is your "smart family housekeeper."

Baidu

Baidu is a Chinese company that cannot be underestimated and that can compete with Google. Baidu has also launched its new robotic assistant, Duer.

Embedded in the mobile Baidu app, Duer can provide users with a variety of services, such as restaurant reservation, upon the installation or upgrading by Android users. We can almost predict that in the near future, every user would have his/her own personal intelligent assistant not only to recommend products and services, but also to place orders, make payments and give feedback. In this process, there is

Baidu has also launched its new robotic assistant-Duer

absolutely no need for user involvement, which is of great significance for marketers. Personal intelligent assistants can also be extended to evaluate products and recommend equivalent products based on time. When the sensor is embedded in the product as a part of the IoT, AI will also read a series of data.

For example, when deciding whether to replace a product, the personal intelligent assistant will make the decision for the user based on the data that is previously accumulated, simulated and learned.

BMW

For instance, BMW used iGenius technology at the launch of its first electric automobile Car9 to answer users' questions in text mode.

BMW used iGenius technology at the launch of its first electric automobile Car9 to answer users' questions in text mode

iGenius enhanced BMW's capability to solve multiple problems simultaneously and reduced unnecessary employee training. One of its friendliest features was that iGenius could memorize and store previous problems and then provide more solutions thereto. However, some of these problems still required AI to conduct higher-level learning.

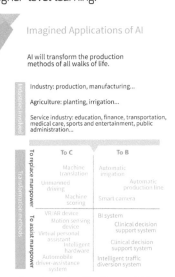

Imagined Applications of AI.

The case source quoted from: pictures and texts from ROBOT-CHINA.COM 2016/04/11
http://www.sohu.com/a/68667589_393482

VI. AI in combination with the IoT[①] to create a smart city[②]

For the Chinese market, the concept of the IoT (Internet of Things) is not new. However, in recent years, the layout of Internet companies, especially the emergence of a large number of smart home products, has been showing such conceptual things to the Chinese people: to control door locks, air conditioners, washing machines, televisions and other electrical appliances with cellphones is today's most fashionable product utilization.

Internet companies like Xiaomi have continuously launched the IoT products of their own brands, such as smart sockets, rice cookers, temperature sensors, and water-testing pens. And with the advertising campaigns staged by a good many similar Internet and home appliance companies, the smart operations enabled by the "IoT" have become increasingly fashionable.

The IoT is the most important link in AI. It is predicted that the proton-like sensors, as described in the Three-Body Problem by Liu Cixin, might spread all over the air to make data collection, calculation and even instruction transmission so ubiquitous that almost all people would have no secret at all. This is not a rumor. At least in the past 50 years, Moore's Law of transistors turned such a hulking computer into the current miniature. Therefore, it is possible to make micro-sensors really invisible with the development of this technology.

The IoT calls for M2M (Machine to Machine) interaction, which means that devices can exchange information autonomously. With the addition of the machine learning of AI, the IoT will break away from the cellphone-based condition and decentralization of the current market and will become a truly advanced intelligence to interconnect all things in the future.

Interaction and intelligent computing of information are not simple byte exchanges, but are made for the ultimate purpose of improving human lifestyle changes. From a micro-perspective, this method is an application based on numerous scenes; and from a macro-perspective, it is the concept of smart city and smart China which prevails today.

The IoT is a key factor and foundation for smart city. With the aid of data collection, network transmission and data analysis, various items such as automobiles and home appliances will be connected to the Internet so that machines can automatically provide humans with more convenient services.

The architecture of the IoT consists of three major components, namely Device and Sensor Domain, Network Domain and Application Domain. Device and Sensor Domain, composed of sensor, video monitoring device, radio frequency identification technology (RFID), bar code and the like, is the foundation for the architecture of the IoT. Network Domain is the connection medium between Application Domain and Device and Sensor Domain. And Application Domain is the IoT solution and application, providing users or enterprises with various services, including different application service middleware as well as data analysis and transmission platforms.

With a wide range of applications, the IoT can meet the needs of different users by integrating the innovative applications of systems and network transmission, such as logistics fleet tracking management, remote medical care and smart energy management. The purpose of the IoT is to take advantage of communication technologies, whether wired or wireless, to achieve a seamless connection among humans, machines and systems and solve various problems in basic necessities of life such as clothing, food, housing and transportation caused by urbanization.

① *Internet of things (IOT) is an important part of the new generation of information technology, and an important development stage for the information age. As its name suggests, IoT is the Internet that connects things.*

② *Smart city means that information and communication technologies are used to sense, analyze and integrate the key information of a city's core operating system so as to make intelligent responses to various needs for welfare, environmental protection, public safety, urban services, industrial and commercial activities, etc. In essence, it makes good use of advanced information technology to carry out smart management and operation for a city so that a better life can be created for people in the city to fuel the harmonious and sustainable development of the city.*

Case Study — Tencent Launches Guangzhou Metro Ride Code to Deploy Smart Transportation

China's mobile payment technology application opens the door to life space. The three-dimensional space of service, consumption and payment creates a new service business form for the next decade. Just as the new retail was a new retail space formed by offline experience, online transaction and rapid delivery, the mobile payment enabled manufacturing and service industries to formally set up a closed-loop space for marketing in 2017. Metro Ride Code, one of Tencent's WeChat Mini Programs, has made the smart city's service space more user-friendly.

2017, Tencent signed a contract with the Guangzhou Metro Group to officially carry out in-depth cooperation in the field of smart transportation

On November 16, 2017, Tencent signed a contract with the Guangzhou Metro Group to officially carry out in-depth cooperation in the field of smart transportation.

As a result, China's first subway ride code was officially put into trial operation in Guangzhou. The passenger might pass through a Shankephone cloud gate machine (orange) by opening the WeChat Mini Program - "Guangzhou Metro Ride Code" and placing the QR code near the gate machine for scanning.

In numerous spotlights, Ma Huateng, founder of Tencent, turned on his cellphone and scanned the code in person to pay for the subway.

With ride codes, the public can "ride first and pay later".

If you leave your wallet at home and your cellphone is out of service or there is not enough money in WeChat, Tencent's Ride Code will send you home still. Even in airplane mode, a ride code can still be generated and used.

This is also the first attempt in China to "ride first and pay later".

Tencent's "Smart Transportation" layout is named "0-1-3-5-7", that is, 0 km for sensor-free payment for parking, 1 km for bike sharing, 3 km for taking a bus with Tencent Ride Code, 5 km for Didi Car Hailing, and 7 km for taking the subway with Tencent Ride Code.

It is worth mentioning that Tencent's sensor-free payment for parking which represents "0 km" has been also officially launched in Guangzhou. With a simple click to bind the plate number with Tencent's Mini Program "Sensor-free Payment for Parking", everyone can experience the convenience of entering without parking card and leaving without scanning QR code.

Almost at the same time, there is a new way to experience the bike sharing which represents "1 km". Tencent has announced that it will further provide those who use Tencent Ride codes with the service to ride Mobikes without any deposit in support of "Green Travel" for the public. More specifically, after successful payment for a ride in the Guangzhou Metro with a ride code, the user can gain seamless access to a Mobike without deposit with the Ride Code Mini Program according to his/her Tencent credit score to finish his/her last one kilometer of travel. This will encourage low-carbon green travel in the city.

According to the data from the Ministry of Transport at the end of 2016, the annual passenger flow of public transport in China exceeded 150 billion person-times. Following peaks and valleys, the public transport has now entered another period of rapid development.

The mobile payment in China has been developing for more than a decade and leading the world, but it has scored fewer achievements in the field of public transportation. So far cellphones have been unable to truly replace transportation cards, which is the last barrier for people to go out without wallets. Pain points and opportunities coexist in the traditional public travel service.

It is very common for public transport companies to receive many broken or counterfeit banknotes which require a lot of manpower to count and manage. And 85% of passengers have ever been out without bus cards or change or had trouble recharging bus cards. In terms of market and user needs, the existing payment methods of transportation cards are still inconvenient, and there is much room for improvement in user needs and convenience, which will provide a market for the generalization of mobile payments.

2017, Tencent signed a contract with the Guangzhou Metro Group to officially carry out in-depth cooperation in the field of smart transportation

Additionally, the bus payment levels up a large market of hundreds of millions of users and high-frequency payments, which will accelerate the cultivation of user habits and facilitate the popularization of mobile payment in all aspects of daily life.

Tencent has been enriching WeChat and its functions in order to bring more convenience to users' daily lives. Tencent has launched WeChat smart transportation solutions to solve the users' travel problems, and will bring out more smart solutions for different vertical fields to better satisfy the social and e-commerce needs of Tencent users and vendors.

With the ride code as a carrier, Tencent will usher in a new situation of industrial cooperation and mutual benefits.

The mobile Internet technology will greatly enhance the level of bus travel services and the ride code will be the solution to the following three key issues: 1) to provide a convenient experience; 2) to serve the smart city transportation, including real-name travel, which may play an active role in strengthening the public transportation safety and may assist in eliminating public safety hazards; and 3) to gradually put into practice the new payment experi- ence and start extensive explorations in various cities for Internet-based transformation and upgrading.

The case source quoted from: China News 2017/11/17
http://tech.ifeng.com/a/20171117/44766419_0.shtml

 # Blockchain – Creating a New Space for Trust

Today's blockchain is just like the Internet in 1993. Ten years from now, you may wonder how society would have been running without it, though most of the users don't even know what it is at the moment.

Some attractive blockchains have already displayed their function; for example, a company is able to make anyone act the role of a bank cashier, while another person is able to tell you the historical owner of a specific diamond - this is a simple way to ensure that your diamond ring has not been used in aiding war. Of course, other blockchain concepts will challenge Uber and Facebook in the near future.

Blockchain is the underlying technology of digital currency: Bitcoin. This is a super complex distributed accounting technology that can store records into thousands or even millions of independent computers; also these computers can work in collaboration, and no single entity can control them. Assuming that the Internet is a military force commanded by generals (General Amazon, General Google), then blockchain is more like ant colonies, each ant is working for collective interests. The ambitious goal of blockchain goes far beyond Bitcoin, just like Internet goal beyond CompuServe.

In 1993, few people had heard the word "Internet", and no one foresaw the birth of Facebook, match.com, wikileaks or pit video. Just think the technology outbreak and collapse that has taken place years later, and think how our life is totally changed by the Internet. Therefore, just imagine what blockchain means.

I. What is blockchain?

Blockchain means the technical solution for maintaining a reliable database collectively through decentralization and trust-free ways.

Simply speaking, blockchain technology refers to a way for all to participate in bookkeeping. There is a database behind all systems, and you may treat this database as a big account book. Then, who shall have the duty of bookkeeping becomes rather important. At present, the bookkeeping is done by the same system, such as, Tencent takes the duty for the bookkeeping of WeChat account book, and Alibaba for Taobao. But, in nowadays' blockchain system, everyone in the system may have the chance to take part in the bookkeeping. If there is any data change within a certain period of time, everyone in the system is allowed to do the bookkeeping, and the system will evaluate who did the best and fastest bookkeeping within this period of time, recorded his/her content into the account book, and sent the account book content within this period to all other persons within the system for backup. In such a way, everyone in the system has a complete account book. This method is referred to as blockchain technology.

The "Blockchain" concept was put forward firstly by Nakamoto Satoshi in 2008; blockchain format, a solution making database secure without credit extension by an administrative agency, was used in Bitcoin for the first time.

In Satoshi's original paper in October 2008, "block" and "chain" these two words were used separately, which was then called block-chain when it was widely used, and then combined into one word in 2016: "Blockchain". In August 2014, Bitcoin blockchain file size reached 20 GB.

In 2014, "Blockchain2.0" became a proper term of decentralized blockchain database. For this second-generation programmable blockchain, its achievement, in the opinion of economists, is that "it is a kind of programmable language which allows users to write more precise and intelligent protocols; therefore, when profit reaches a certain degree, it is possible to make gain from completed shipment orders or dividends of shared certificates". Blockchain2.0 technique skipped over transaction and "intermediary agent acting as money and information arbitration in value exchange". They are used to keep people away from the global economy for protecting privacy, enable people to "convert the information they hold into money", and have the ability to ensure that intellectual property owners can make gains. The second-generation blockchain technology makes possible the storage of personal "permanent digital ID and image", while providing solutions for the imparity of "potential social wealth distribution". From 2014 to 2016, transactions under Blockchain2.0 still needed to pass through Oracle, so that any "time and market conditions based and 'indeed required' external data or events interact with blockchain".

II. Blockchain technology core application advantage

Blockchain technology can construct a robust timestamp system. Without mutual trust among nodes in the system, the system ensures that all data records are true, thus forming a trustworthy and orderly decentralized distributed database, and people are allowed for flexible programming to system internal parameters and exchanged values. When applying these core values into our real life, blockchain can help us settle the following core issues:

1. Decentralized distributed structure: a large amount of agency cost can be saved in real life

Since blockchain technology can be served as a large-scale collaboration tool among people without mutual trust mechanism, it is able to be used in many centralized fields to process those transactions that would be processed by intermediary agents. The biggest impact of blockchain technology in the future is the infrastructure of financial industry, such as securities clearing and registration systems, and cross-border exchange and settlement systems. All these systems now are centralized featured with expensive charge and low efficiency. If blockchain technology can be applied to these fields successfully, the application prospect will be greatly attractive, though only 1% agency cost is saved.

2. Unalterable timestamp: data tracking and information anti–counterfeit problems can be settled

In today's society, a large amount of forged information and data inundate our life, from fake wine, inferior milk, and imitated luxuries, to accounting notes, fake financial data even illegal private bank transactions. At the right time, blockchain technology opens a door for us in data tracking and information anti-counterfeit fields. Since data in blockchain is seamlessly connected to form an immutable timestamp, thus we are able to attach a set of unforgettable real records for all objects, and this would be a great help in our real life in combating counterfeit and shoddy products, and rectifying information disciplines.

3. Secure trust mechanism: IOT technology core defects can be settled

Internet of Things (IOT) is a hot spot now and a trend in the future. However, in the traditional IOT model, all information is collected by a centralized data center, which resulted in severe defects in equipment life cycle and other aspects.

Blockchain technology is able to create a trust consensus for an entire network without coming to trust a single node, such that it settles properly some core IOT defects, enabling things not only to connect each other but also move up accelerating the movement of our life into the era of the Internet of Value.

4. Flexible programmable feature: it helps standardize today's market order

In today's society, the market order is not standardized enough; when we transfer our own assets, it is impossible to ensure that they can produce due value in the future. Now, with blockchain, if we introduce the programmable feature of blockchain technology and write a piece of program with transfer of assets for specifying the future usage and direction of the assets, then we will meet a brand new market and society.

III. Blockchain evolution model

1. Blockchain1.0: digital currency

Blockchain technology was generated along with the birth of Bitcoin, with its initial usage purely based on digital currency. The birth of Bitcoin made blockchain to enter into public view for the first time, following which, Litecoin, ETH, Dogecoin and other emulating digital currencies. The birth of programmable currency makes it possible that values are able to circulate directly in the Internet.

Blockchain forms a brand new decentralized digital payment system, in which monetary transactions anytime and anywhere, block-free cross-border payment, and low-cost operated decentralized system all make this system infinite in charm. The emerging of such digital currency strongly impacts traditional finance system.

2. Blockchain2.0: digital assets/ smart contract

Subject to the impact of digital currency, people began to expand blockchain technology application to other financial fields. Based on the programmable feature of blockchain technology, people attempted to include "smart contract"[①] concept into blockchain to form programmable finance. With the support of contract system, blockchain application scope began to be extended from a single monetary field to other financial fields where contract functionalities are involved.

With the emerging of colored coins, bit-shares, contract coins and other new concepts, blockchain technology began to play its role in multiple fields including stock, liquidation and private equity. At present, more and more financial institutions began to research blockchain technology and attempt use it in real practice; hence the existing traditional financial system is now under overwrite.

3. Blockchain3.0: blockchain big society

Along with the further progress of the blockchain technology, its "decentration" function and "data anti-fake" function received great attention in other fields. People realized that blockchain application is not only restricted in financial fields, but also can be extended to any fields having such demands.

For this reason, in addition to financial fields, blockchain technology has been applied successively in many other fields including notary, arbitration, domain name, logistics, medical, email, authentication and stock, and its scope of application has been expanded to the entire society. In this stage of application, people tried to use blockchain to subvert the lowest-layer protocols of Internet, and apply blockchain technology into IOT to accelerate the entire society to move into intelligent Internet era and form a programmable society.

IV. How does blockchain subvert our life?

1. Hospital decentration

In relation to medical service, blockchain's main application is the storage of personal medical records, which can be understood as electronic medical history on blockchain. Currently, patient medical histories are controlled by hospitals rather than the patients themselves; that's why patients have no way of having their own medical records, which is just like a bank account where you cannot access account transaction records. This causes inconvenience for future medical service. However, if blockchain technology is possible for storing patient medical history, it is a different story where patients are able to access their own medial historical data. One's future medical service or health care planning can be supported by available

data, and nevertheless, this data is controlled by patients rather than a hospital or a third-party agency. Moreover, this data is of high confidential nature, and the use of blockchain technology may help protect patient privacy.

This application is featured with decentration and more openness, and assigns more autonomy to users. What it realizes is a new form of information organization, in which everyone controls his/her private information, rather than that information being in the hand of an agency as was done before.

2. Intelligent lock

Slock.it, a newly established company based in Germany, wants to make a blockchain technology-based intelligent lock, connect such intelligent lock to the

① *Smart contract: this concept can be traced back to 1995, almost coming into existence at the same time as the Internet (world wide web). Nick Szabo, a cryptologist who won great reputation for his contribution to Bitcoin, is the first person who proposed the term "smart contract". In essence, the working principle of these automatic contracts is similar to if-then statement in other computer programs. Smart contracts interact with assets in real life only through this mode. When a pre-defined condition is triggered, smart contract then will execute a corresponding contract term.*

Internet, and control such intelligent lock through a blockchain smart contract. Anyone controlling the lock can be assigned one or multiple private keys, and such private keys are applied with complicated customizing, and set up when the lock is enabled and on which specific time the lock is opened, etc. Through this, sharing economy can be further decentralized, and any locked things can be leased, shared and sold easily. Slock.k concept indeed goes beyond Airbnb user service scope, which wants to further subvert this sharing economy and enables users to make payment directly to one lock, then open it; the lesser also is allowed to replace private key customizing and let the entire experience be more convenient and secure. We may also use this technology for leasing bikes and safes, even allow others to charge vehicles at home, and then collect fees, etc.

3. Decentralized domain name system

Blockchain is able to provide domain name system (DNS)[1] an alternative solution not controlled by companies. It allows anyone in the world to release information freely in the Internet.

4. Digital art: blockchain authentication service

Digital art is another arena where blockchain technology is able to provide disruptive innovations. The main application of digital art in blockchain industry refers to that: use blockchain technology to register intellectual property rights of any forms, or make authentication service more popular, such as contract notarization. Digital art also is able to protect the intellectual properties of online images, photos or digital artistic works and other digital assets through blockchain.

5. Blockchain government

With decentralized, personalized, cheap and high-efficient features, blockchain also is able to provide traditional services and realize brand new and different governmental management models and services. By making full use of blockchain advantages, it makes government work more efficient for winning trust and reliance of the public.

Blockchain is able to use the advantages of its open and permanently stored data (consensus-driven, open audit, globally and permanently) to store all social archives, records and histories available for future use and becoming a global database. This will become the stepping stone of blockchain government services. Through blockchain technology, it is possible to reconfigure public resources, improve government efficiency, save cost, let finance beneficial to more people, increase the basic income level of the public, promote equality, improve public political participation, and eventually transmit to self-governance economic form.

We may sketch the future further: when such mode of thinking is represented by blockchain, such distributed collaboration and decentralized models are not only used in monetary or asset contract transactions, are not only restricted to things that can be set up and programmable, and are not only the interconnection of physical objects, but also they are functioning directly to target our brain, nerve cell and awareness. When human brain and computer interface technology work together with blockchain, when the extraction, transaction and storage of the memory of human and machine can be realized, and when knowledge, inspiration and creation interactive chain is formed in an orderly manner and evolved uninterruptedly, that would come to an explosive growth and magnificent view.

6. Online music

Many musicians are choosing blockchain technology to upgrade the equity in online music sharing. According to Billboard, a US music magazine, so far, two companies are settling license issues by making payment directly to artists and using smart contract. In a blockchain music stream platform, users are allowed to make payment directly to artists without a middleman. In addition to media music, someone imagined it would be possible to apply better classification to artists and authors behind songs by using smart contract as the independent brain of song lists.

7. Automobile lease and sales

Visa and DocuSign announced a cooperation plan for presenting solutions specific to automobile lease by using blockchain technology, and future automobile leases can be done with three steps namely "clicking, signing and driving".

Specific operation: a customer selects an automobile for lease, following which this transaction will be uploaded to a blockchain public account; then, the customer signs a lease agreement and

① DNS: The abbreviation of Domain Name System, a distributed database in the Internet as the mutual mapping of domain name and IP address, enabling users to access the Internet more easily without asking them to remember machine directly read IP string. The process obtaining the IP address corresponding to the host name via the host name is called domain name resolution. DNS protocol is being operated on UDP and the used port number is 53. In RFC documentation, RFC 2181 gives NDS a normative explanation to DNS; RFC 2136 gives explanation to DNS dynamic update; and RFC 2308 gives explanation to DNS inquiry reverse caching.

insurance agreement in the car, and blockchain will upload such information in real-time. Also, as we imagine, this lease model may be used in automobile selling and registration fields.

8. Global public health and charitable donations

Bitcoin is able to provide efficient, direct and specific fund aid for infectious disease crises such as Ebola. The fund flow process of traditional banks may hold the urgent demand for funds during crisis response; however, Bitcoin is able to transfer funds promptly to an address that is open, can be audited and traced. In the future, charitable donation websites are allowed to receive Bitcoin donation transparently for raising a large amount of charitable money for rescue.

9. Blockchain gene sequencing

At present, there are two issues concerning personal gene data acquisition by citizens: (i) the restriction imposed by laws and regulations to gene data acquisition by individuals; and (ii) gene sequencing requires a large amount of computation resources, and high expenses restricted the industrial progress. Blockchain sequencing settled these two issues: through globally located computation resources, complete the sequencing service at low cost, and use private key to save sequencing data, and bypass law issues. With such data, if potential hypertension or Alzheimer's disease is discovered, it is possible to change living habits to reduce the probability of occurrence. It is believed that in the near future the gene sequencing service offered to mass consumers will be popular as blockchain gene sequencing technology becomes mature.

When blockchain is applied to big data fields, it will enter into the next order of magnitude and introduce a genuine big data era; and gene sequencing is just a typical case promoting big data.

10. Blockchain intelligent city

Living in a blockchain-based intelligent city, we are able to pay for any troubles made by us: in case of a traffic jam due to a traffic accident, it is possible to make payment to passing vehicles for delaying them, thus promoting society to develop towards self-discipline and high-efficient self-governance. We also are allowed to openly and transparently make payment to good services and good schools.

11. Network security

Though blockchain system is open, its verification, transmission and other data exchange processes are employed with an advanced encryption technique. This technique ensures not only the correct source of data, but also no interception or modification to data in middle of the process. If blockchain technology is used more widely, its probability of attack by hackers will be decreased; the reason why blockchain system is able to decrease traditional network security risk is because it eliminates the demand for middlemen. Without a middleman, it decreases the potential security risks of hacker attacks; in addition, it reduces possible corruption.

Case Study — Blockchain Chicken-raising? When You Are Talking about Chicken, They Are Thinking about Wide Health

Following the raising of Weyang pigs by Ding Lei and running chicken raising by Jingdong, there is another high-tech company joining this raising farm business. ZhongAn Technology announced it wants to apply blockchain fully to its chick-raising industry in China and give support and aid to China's blockchain venture company "Anlink Technology".

The purpose of launch of the BUBU chicken project, based on blockchain unalterability and IOT equipment automatic acquisition features, is to ensure all data of a chicken generated from baby chick to adult chicken from chick farm to dining table are truthfully recorded for realizing anti-fake and source tracing.

Why are these high-tech companies so fond of agricultural farming? We may find out the answer through our analysis of ZhongAn Technology's blockchain chicken raising.

Why is chicken the object raised by using blockchain?

Currently, Netease, Jingdong and ZhongAn Technology all are focused on chicken and pig raising. Huge market demand is the answer that everyone can perceive. According to third-party statistical data, Chinese people consume nearly five billion chickens a year; chicken is the most common meat on the Chinese dining table, following which is pig.

Obviously, chicken raising of blockchain may contain other considerations. As interpreted by Wu Xiaochuan, Vice Director of ZhongAn Technology-Fudan University United Lab, firstly, chicken is not physically big in size; consumers have the ability and demand to buy a whole piece of chicken, rather than a whole piece of pig, cattle or sheep. If only a part of pig body can be purchased, how does one prove which pig does this part belong to?

Secondly, the body size of baby chicken allows one to attach corresponding blockchain anti-fake device, plus a chicken-raising environment is relatively simple; chicken will not dive into water or fly; if an anti-fake device battery leaks in water, this will cause new food safety issues.

Then, is blockchain able to raise chicken only? As disclosed by Wu Xiaochuan, ZhongAn Technology already paid more attention to animal texture identification, biological gene and other techniques; and these techniques are able to settle whole/part relations in animals and plants which cannot be settled at present, then realize the broader application scope of blockchain to other breeding industries, even plant industry.

Then, will these high-tech companies fond of agricultural farming not be focused on their profession?

Since Netease began to raise pigs, many people have said that the technology sector has been biased by Ding Lei, of course jokingly. Not long ago, ZhongAn Technology announced the transport of financial technologic capability to finance and wide health ecosphere. Nowadays, chick-raising path seems to go far beyond big finance and wide health.

Nevertheless, as believed by ZhongAn Technology, what is important about chicken raising is its important deployment in wide health fields. In traditional understanding, health means seeing a doctor in hospital, having good medical service, and running for physical activity every day; thus, people ignored one thing - food safety is just the source and key to good health.

Therefore, Netease Ding Lei devoted himself to pig raising, while Jingdong launched the "Running Chicken" project, all of which are focusing on green ecological breeding. ZhongAn Technology's blockchain chicken raising project is just aimed at settling this issue from the source.

Chicken shall be raised in wide open fielded, preferably in rural areas with clean water and air by local experienced farmers, together with being fed vegetables, grains as well as natural pollution-free black soldier flies, and ensuring the chicken get a daily amount of exercise. Compared with those chickens fed with feedstock with feed period no more than 45 days sold in the market, BUBU chicken's growth cycle is about 180 days, thus it guarantees the nutrition and meat quality of each chicken.

In order to ensure a chicken purchased by a consumer is indeed a BUBU chicken, BUBU chicken project combines blockchain, IOT and anti-fake technology by assigning every chicken a ID card (ZhongAn Technology's Atsafe Clound provides blockchain technology, and Hangzhou APWL provides IOT intelligent devices and anti-fake technologies) to record automatically in real-time all kinds of information from baby chicken to adult chicken, ensuring the unalterability and being fully true and reliable. As disclosed by Yuan Yongyao, GM of Hangzhou APWL Technology Co., Ltd., blockchain anti-fake label has been incorporated with national classification level algorithm, chaos principle, laser optical, cellphone app intelligent dynamic image scanning, cloud data comparison techniques, thus making it difficult to copy, duplicate and recover, and ensuring the uniqueness of commodities from source points and terminal points. So far, the company has more than 70 patents and many international patents registered in 16 countries, and its partners bearing famous brands amount to over 100.

Each chicken is an eco—system

When we are talking about chicken, high-tech companies all are thinking about deployment and ecosystem. Liu Qiangdong announced the launch of the Running Chicken project in his microblog in early 2016; Jingdong Fresh Food was independent from Jingdong Consumer Goods Division and became an independent business division; after Ding Lei rushed to raise pigs, Netease Yanxuan and Netease Kaola were launched one after another. What is behind blockchain chicken raising?

Chicken raising has developed another demand for big finance and massive health for ZhongAn Technology; moreover, it activated the entire alliance ecology of ZhongAn Technology to serve hundreds of billion rural poverty relief markets. As addressed in "13th Five-year Plan Poverty Relief Plan", 70 million rural poor people shall get rid of poverty as of 2020.

As disclosed by Jiang Long, CBO of ZhongAn Technology Atsafe Cloud, BUBU Chicken is one of ZhongAn Technology's product anti-fake series, and has a public welfare nature for rural poverty relief. According to the planning, BUBU Chicken Project is scheduled to cover more than one thousand poor townships and villages, construct nearly 100,000 mu eco-breeding bases in the coming three years, and it is expected to generate more income to farmers by CNY 2.7 billion.

For achieving this goal, ZhongAn Technology in association with public welfare organizations, logistical companies, slaughter houses and industrial chain partners will provide product sales channels for chickens raised in natural wide open fields, and provide a complete solution to farmers from baby chicken purchase, raising, slaughtering and marketing to realize chicken raising cashability. During this process, entrepreneurial firm Anlink Technology will be responsible for the overall operation of BUBU Chicken Project, ZhongAn Technology provides blockchain technology, Hangzhou APWL provides anti-fake tracing devices and services and tsign.cn will provide blockchain e-signing technology. In addition, certain percentage of BUBU chicken income will be donated to Huodui Public Welfare and other public welfare organizations.

At the beginning, ZhongAn Technology once drew a circle in blockchain field: in association with 24 partners, it established the first cross-industry blockchain business alliance in China - Shanghai Blockchain Enterprise Development Promotion Alliance, and the members of which cover a number of fields including bank, credit reference, consumer finance, data security, communication and scientific research institution.

In this BUBU Chicken Project, we also saw the existence of WPWL, tsign.cn, Huodui Public Welfare and other alliance members.

Source: www.news.cn

The case source quoted from: www.news.cn 2017/06/26
http://news.ifeng.com/a/20170626/51323127_0.shtml

V. Blockchain triggers trust space

Blockchain now is triggering "the Gold Rush" of intelligent IOT era, people from all sectors pour in, some purchase equipment for "mining", and some recruit followers for deployment. Banks use Bitcoin in financial innovation and credit extension transaction, IT companies use blockchain for collection to IOT, idealists use it to build up network with more freedom, and realistic entrepreneurs and venture capitals are expecting to construct another Alibaba or Google.

As predicated by Don Tapscott, a futurist and the author of Blockchain Revolution, the business world in the coming 10 years is defined not by social media, big data, cloud computation, robot or AI, but by blockchain.

Blockchain triggered Bitcoin and Ethereum; in addition, it will trigger "the Internet of Value" and "Trust Economy". Blockchains enabled the digitization and flowability of assets and values, and with the help of intelligent equipment, robot and AI existed everywhere, it forms the Internet of Value. Along with the flowability of assets and value, it is the rise of Trust Economy. Though blockchain is unable to wipe out human dishonesty, it is able to reduce information asymmetry in network transmission with its open and transparency features.

According to Deloitte report "Blockchain: Trust Economy" 2017, Deloitte analysts believe that trust rather than credit is the business value exchange basis. In a digitized world, the public image of a company or an individual is decided no longer by newspaper or TV ads or WeChat Baike advertorials. Our social monetary assets are the stepping stone of the trust economy era.

Blockchain will be the foundation of the trust economy, and it will act the role of a watchdog to make every person and thing's network behaviors and participations transparent and queriable. Blockchain distributed bookkeeping technology ensures data security, and further, with "decentration", let data storage and sharing more quick and transparent.

Due to blockchain open source and "open programming" features, blockchain also is able to help us generate smart contracts. Simply speaking, smart contract means a contract that can be executed automatically in a computer system when certain conditions are satisfied. This business model has remained at a theoretical stage in the past, one reason of which is the lack of a digital system and technology that can support programmable contracts. The birth of blockchain technology solved this problem. Blockchain technology not only supports programmable contracts, but also has the advantages of decentralization, unalterability, transparent and traceable process. It is naturally suitable for smart contracts.

Smart contracts will fundamentally change the relationship between brands and consumers; in addition, they will change brand marketing strategy.

Either party of brand or user may carry out a transaction on an honest and transparent basis. Cheating and dishonesty of either party will trigger a smart contract to punish the defaulting party. For example, brands are not allowed to exaggerate curative effect in ads and text description, and professional commenters who gave malicious negative comment may be cancelled with his/her qualification for comment.

In addition to smart contracts, blockchain based digital identity and trust rating system have played their roll in sharing

①

Black Mirror 3: a mini TV series produced by British TV 4 and US NetFlix. It is screenplayed and produced by British Producer Charlie Bullock, consisting of Season I, Season II, Christmas Special and Season III. This TV series consists of multiple standalone stories under the context of modern science and technology, describing the utilization, re-construction and destruction of modern science and technology to humanity.

the economy field. If you use Alipay "Zhima Credit" or view the social media rating system in movie "Black Mirror 3"① Nosedrive, it is not difficult to understand the digital identity and rating system's working principle.

The biggest difficulty of sharing economy is trust. As the party providing shared services, we have to ensure the "Sharer" is trustworthy. For instance, when you "share" your private car with a stranger, how do you guarantee that he/she will take care of your car and will not maliciously crash and engage in violent driving? As the party receiving shared services, similarly we have to ensure the "Shared" is trustworthy. When traveling alone, it must be ensured that the Airbnb house owner's price is fair and in good faith.

The trust issue contained in two examples above can be cleared through inquiring the digital identity and trust rating of the other party. We further address that, blockchain also will bypass the malicious negative comment that is given to the female figure in "Black Mirror 3" Nosednve, because blockchain cannot be modified at will, and a modification is required to be done under agreed and transparent conditions.

At present, related companies and individuals' rating, comment and other trust information are still stored in "centralized" platforms. Tmall, Airbnb, Didi, Bitbond, UpWork and bazaar are isolated islands without connection to each other.

We can imagine that if blockchain is able to collect the information and save them into a decentralized distributed bookkeeping system, what would happen?

BitTeaser is a blockchain based advertising platform established by a group of teams from Denmark and the US. This advertising system expects to use blockchain technology to construct an IOT era advertising system to challenge Google Adsense's advertising model. BitTeaser cancelled Google Adsense's admittance threshold to enable the participation of low-flow websites or We-media, in addition, it uses Bitcoin for payment and settlement.

The total online ads investment in 2015 amounted to USD $170.5 billion, and this figure is expected to reach USD $252 billion as of 2018, according to Forbes. Google, Facebook oligarchs took the majority part of the ad market, and drew a large amount of fees from this market.

On the other hand, Google and Facebook also are confronted with severe flow cheating and rate-of-click cheating challenges. The "Video Click Scandle" in 2016 made Facebook the subject of suspicion for over-estimation of ad effect.

Blockchain advertising platform like BitTeaser not only cancelled middlemen but also eliminated a large amount of commission of media delivery companies and fees payable to advertising platforms, and enabled brands to cooperate directly with websites and We-media platforms. In addition, blockchain is also able to avoid the maximum extent flow and click cheating, because advertising effect calculation is not based on IP but verified with the digital ID of the viewer and clicker. The technical features of blockchain make difficult for hackers to forge a digital ID, like they do when they produce a fake IP and fake social security numbers in batches.

Phil Gomes, Vice President Global of Edelman Public Relations Worldwide, believes that blockchain's another black tech application is that blockchain will erase information asymmetry by constructing shared and consistent "Digital Truth". He believes that information communication in traditional media and communication field is secure, because advertorials printed in newspaper and ads on TV cannot be changed once published or played out. Therefore communication in the traditional media era is a single-way and unopened communication. Conversely, communication in the Internet era is open but an insecure communication.

In network, information may be processed even tampered, and a same fact may have different versions. However, blockchain is able to guarantee the openness and security of information.

This is extremely important in corporate communications where more and more emphasis is placed on corporate social responsibility and "ethical behavior". Raw material origin and supply chain information service provider Provenance is now cooperating with a U.S.-based fishery company to apply blockchain technology to make guarantees to its retailers and customers that the fishing operation of this company complies with laws and moral conduct as well as the fact that it has no bad records such as use of illegal labor. In addition, Wal-Mart also is cooperating with ffiM and Tsinghua University to ensure the safety and compliance of imported pork from China.

In the customer relationship field, blockchain also will play an important role. Loyyal, a company providing customer award service, is now working out how to use blockchain technology and smart contracts to integrate customer loyalty to improve customer activity and loyalty. As one of the important applications, Loyyal allows customers to accumulate credits of different brands and use them together.

In addition, blockchain also will change our familiar social network. Social media based on blockchain technology such as Your.org will circumvent censorship, and encourage to create better contents through the form of "small bonus". More mature blockchain social platforms such as Steem.io will transform your every view and click into cash and bonus.

Marketing in the digital era is the information and value exchange between consumers and brands, social media and Internet helped us make information transmission online possible, and blockchain will help us make assets and value transmission possible.

 **Case Study** — ## ZF Cooperates With IBM in Offering Mobile Payment Services through Blockchain Technology

ZF Friedrichshafen AG, a German supplier, announced together with IBM in January 2017, that they were jointly developing a future-oriented mobile payment technology called Car eWallet.

This mobile payment system was based on IBM's blockchain technology, allowing mobile operators to create fast and secure automated transactions in various situations. ZF and UBS Financial Services demonstrated a prototype of this system at the CES (Consumer Electronic Show) in Las Vegas in January.

ZF CEO Stefan Sommer said in the cooperation statement at the Frankfurt Motor Show, "Car sharing and driverless cars are the trend of the future, and it is now more than ever necessary to create a trading ecosystem available for everyone."

Automakers and service providers could use the Car eWallet for billing, parking, charging electric cars, car sharing and in-car services. Representatives of these two companies stated that they planned to test this technology in the first quarter of 2018 and might offer it to customers later that year.

Initial pilot projects might be carried out in collaboration with German parking service providers.

A potential blockchain technology application developed by IBM could be used to automatically store transaction records in a separate digital ledger.

These ledgers would be then be copied and stored in different locations on the blockchain to ensure that the data couldn't be tampered with. Blockchain was the underlying technology for digital currencies like Bitcoin, enabling international transactions to be conducted without the participation of any bank or government. It could also be used in the fields such as global transportation, corporate incentive plans and identity tracking.

For automobiles, experts believed that the blockchain technology could safely keep the motion trails of a driverless car in a single ledger to reduce the complexity of management fees and payment methods.

Andreas Kind, an expert in IBM's research department, said, "Car eWallet is like a protective umbrella for cars. Cars need smarter services. We wish to attract more new companies to use this platform and create a new world of cars."

The case source quoted from: AutoNews by Shiraz Ahmed 2017/09/15
http://www.blockvalue.com/app/14097.html

Case Study — ## China's First Blockchain for Medical Scenes

Ali Health announced its cooperation with Changzhou City in the Pilot Project of Health Alliance + Blockchain: to apply the blockchain technology to the underlying technical architecture system of the Changzhou Health Alliance for the purpose of solving the problems about isolated information island and data security that have plagued medical establishments for a long time. At present, data interconnection has been set up among some local medical establishments.

"The Pilot Project of Health Alliance Blockchain in Changzhou is China's first blockchain application based on medical scenes," said Liu Tie, the Head of Ali Health's Blockchain Tech Department.

Changzhou is one of the first 4 pilot cities for "Health and Medical Big Data" designated by the

National Health and Family Planning Commission of the PRC. Tianning District is expediting the construction of Health Alliance and establishing a hierarchical diagnosis and treatment system with focus on mass health management and chronic disease diagnosis and treatment.

Zhang Zigong is the director of Zhenglu Town Health Center in Changzhou which is a community hospital offering primary medical services to 140,000 people in Zhenglu Town with about 30,000 visits every month. Zhang Zhihong said that there was no regional health information platform in Tianning District before, and the huge information of each medical establishment needed to be transmitted to the medical information platform at the municipal level.

However, these medical establishments did not communicate with each other and many business demands could not be heard. At the same time, how to ensure the security of private health information in circulation and storage was also a challenge for existing platforms.

The situation has changed dramatically after the blockchain technology was introduced. Here we take the experience of hierarchical diagnosis and treatment as an example. For those who have undergone physical examinations in the nearest health centers and been diagnosed with cardiovascular and cerebrovascular chronic diseases based on the analysis of physical examination reports on the blockchain, if they need to be transferred to superior hospitals for further treatment, about 5% of them can allow the doctors of these health centers to authorize and submit their medical records to superior hospitals through the blockchain, while the doctors of superior hospitals can quickly know their previous medical records and physical examination reports after being authorized, and they will not need to repeat the unnecessary secondary basic examinations.

The case source quoted from: NetEase Tech 2017/08/18
http://tech.163.com/17/0818/21/CS5BJJCJ00097U7R.html

 # Augmented Reality（AR）Space

Those engaged in marketing are always most interested in applying the latest technology in their work. The emergence of any new communicative and interactive technology may bring great opportunities: to reach audiences more effectively, to make them more effective, and to target more audiences.

Whether or not the new technology should be used in marketing depends on when and how to use it properly. If marketers apply the new technology too early, it may be unacceptable to customers; but if it is applied too late, the competition will be fierce and the effect will be undesirable.

I. What is AR?

Augmented Reality (AR) is a technology that augments the user's perception of the real world with the help of the information provided by a computer system. It applies virtual information to the real world and overlays computer-generated virtual objects, scenes or system prompts onto the real scene so as to augment the reality.

In the visualized AR, a user can see the real world around computer graphics by using a helmet-mounted display to compose the real world and these computer graphics together.

In the field of marketing, there are numerous examples of AR too. However, AR is so unfamiliar to us that we all have been fooled by those suppliers alleging that hyperlinks plus 3D images are ARs.

In 2008, Gartner's famous Hype Cycle of Emerging Technologies first mentioned AR and predicted that this technology would be applied extensively after 10 years.

In 2009, a great number of geotagging-based AR mobile applications began to emerge, and those applications like Wikitude and Layar brought AR into digital marketing for the first time.

Although these mobile AR browsers were criticized as "pseudo-ARs", they showed us the endless possibilities with AR.

In 2011, the new generation of AR applications such as Blippar, Zappar and Aurasma had been freed from the limitations of geotagging and worked directly through image recognition. Blippar officially stated that its brand users had exceeded 1,000 ones, including Coca-Cola, Heineken, Jaguar and other brand players, while Zappar and Aurasma included in their user scenarios the works by big players such as Oreo, Budweiser and Disney.

The development of digital marketing is always following the evolution of technology. Since 2008, AR marketing has gone through the following four major stages:

Stage 1: the stage of QR code. The QR code is a bridge between 2D and 3D. The AR marketing of Nike's Hyperfactory T90 in 2008 is the most representative. During the Euro Cup, Nike posted up QR codes in all sizes on stadiums, subways and stores in Hong Kong. Following the steps described in these QR code posters, everyone could view the 3D details of Nike's new soccer shoes T90 by scanning any of these QR codes with a cellphone. Such AR idea is no longer novel now, but at that time, it was a creative marketing case which shocked the

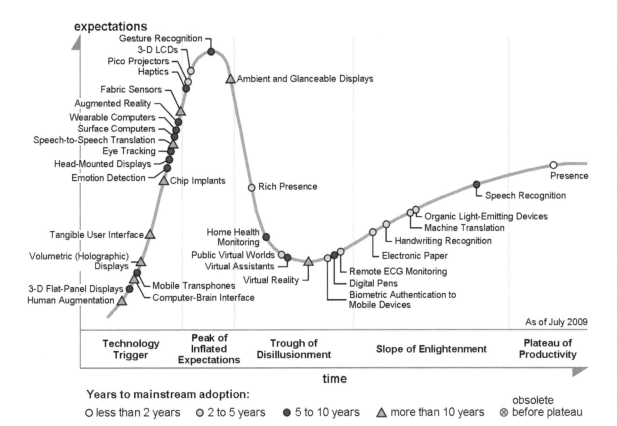

expectations

Gesture Recognition
3-D LCDs
Pico Projectors
Haptics
Ambient and Glanceable Displays
Fabric Sensors
Augmented Reality
Wearable Computers
Surface Computers
Speech-to-Speech Translation
Eye Tracking
Head-Mounted Displays
Emotion Detection
Chip Implants
Rich Presence
Presence
Speech Recognition
Organic Light-Emitting Devices
Machine Translation
Handwriting Recognition
Tangible User Interface
Home Health Monitoring
Public Virtual Worlds
Virtual Assistants
Electronic Paper
Volumetric (Holographic) Displays
Virtual Reality
Remote ECG Monitoring
3-D Flat-Panel Displays
Mobile Transphones
Digital Pens
Human Augmentation
Computer-Brain Interface
Biometric Authentication to Mobile Devices

As of July 2009

| Technology Trigger | Peak of Inflated Expectations | Trough of Disillusionment | Slope of Enlightenment | Plateau of Productivity |

time

Years to mainstream adoption:

○ less than 2 years   ◐ 2 to 5 years   ● 5 to 10 years   △ more than 10 years   obsolete ⊗ before plateau

What is AR? Source: CMO Club

whole industry. However, such AR could not be used unless the related application had been downloaded, which was criticized widely. In addition to production costs, high promotion costs must be paid to make up for extremely low download rates and trial rates.

Stage 2: the stage of PC camera scanning. Compared with cellphones, computers not only provide a richer viewing experience, but also eliminate the need for users to download applications. A typical example of this kind of application is the 3D Wonderland series launched by GE in 2009. Just with a camera, you could log on GE's website of 3D Wonderland, download and print the QR code from the website, and then see cities and wind generators with 3D effects on the computer screen. Another feature of this GE game was the interactive experience. The user could capture the endless wind and transform wind energy into electricity by rotating the printed QR code to manipulate the windmill amongst the 3D images. And this interactive model was used in both contemporary and subsequent similar cases.

Stage 3: the stage of geotagging. The emergence of the application platforms like Wikitude and Layar re-

duced the AR marketing budget for a brand from seven figures to six figures.

A representative example of this kind of application is Le Bar Guide, an AR application launched by Stella Artois. This application was based on geotagging, adding a layer of information templates in real scenes to add extra information to buildings and places. It used to be an example of AR with which we were the most familiar, and a technology extensively applied by chain supermarkets, e-commerce, tourism, hotels, parks, museums as well as other brands and organizations.

Stage 4: the stage of map reading. AR no longer relied on geotagging, but showed 3D scenes on a cellphone screen by scanning directly magazine pictures or other physical objects.

Since 2008, AR marketing has gone through the following four major stages. Source: CMO Club

Stage 4: the stage of map reading. Source: CMO Club

If the user put an IKEA Yearbook of 2004 at a suitable place in his/her house and opened the related AR mobile application, he/she could see a menu and select to view the effect of IKEA's furniture in his/her house. Mobile applications like J.C. Penney's AR dressing mirror and Converse's Converse Sampler were examples of such AR applications.

Now, Hololens and Magic Leap will lead the next stage of AR marketing. AR will directly generate a 3D scene instead of imaging on a cellphone or computer screen. At this stage, AR will "kill" all screens and bring us into the true AR world.

II. Future marketing application of augmented reality

When information is excessive, inattention will take place. In the past 15 years, our attention span has been shortened from 12 seconds in 2000 to 8.25 seconds in 2015. In fact, in the opinion of the scientists from the U.S. National Biotechnology Information Center, human attention concentration is even weaker than goldfish.

In attracting "goldfish", brands always do their best endeavors. If a naked model, pornographic substance and psychedelic chicken soup are sugar-coated bullets contained with smuggled goods, substance marketing and visualized marketing can be taken as perfectly disguised anesthesia javelins. The average reading time for verbal content is 20 seconds, the average viewing time for video substance is 35 seconds, and the average stay time for WeChat H5 game may be longer.

However, all of these are not enough to settle the issue how to attract the attention of consumers. Nevertheless, people are always forgetful and busy. According to Business2Community website survey report, 25% teenagers do not remember much information about their own friends and family members, and 39% people will lose some basic memorized information every day. Meanwhile, our attention also will be interrupted by various influences. We will check email about 30 times per hour, open and check WeChat more than 20 times per day, and receive and dial all kinds of telephone calls and voice more than 1,500 times per week.

And, augmented reality may help brands solve this issue. It is not sugar-coated bullet, nor anesthesia javelin, instead, it is a hypnotic artifact. With richer content, deeper interaction and more direct experience, augmented reality not only triggers a new form of content to combine real world with network world perfectly for the first time, but also constructs a new-type content interactive platform, and enables brands to have the weapon to hypnotize consumers.

Retail industry is the first industry realizing and effectively using this weapon. In 2014, Accenture Consulting listed the five modes of the augmented reality marketing of retail industry in its report entitled "Life on the digital edge: How augmented reality can enhance customer experience and drive growth".

Information inquiry - When you want to know if the milk on the shelf is fresh, you may see the place of origin and date, even a 3D milk producing process just by scanning the packaging box with your cellphone. If you want to find the product you want to buy on many shelves, you may use Google Project Tango app in your cellphone and then find it through a 3D map.

Try-on and try-out - **Topshop**, De Beers and Converse brands are using augmented reality by allowing customers to try on clothes, jewelry or shoes. Shiseido and Burberry further apply augmented reality to cosmetics try-out. As to BMW, Volvo and other automobile brands, augmented reality is also a good choice for new car introduction and virtual trial driving.

Trial play - Building blocks inbox and toy planes on shelves can be tried out through augmented reality

Choosing and purchase. In metro virtual stores of yhd.com, scan then select your wanted products and purchase online.

After-service - From AUDI automobile users' manual to IKEA panel furniture assembly guideline, these augmented reality applications shall give consumers better assistance in installing, using, even repairing automobile and furniture.

Augmented reality may help retail brands choose commodities for consumers, or assist express delivery industry to upgrade their goods distribution service. US based logistics company USPS plans to use augmented reality technology to improve its business flow, after it tried to apply augmented reality to its email marketing. USPS hopes to use augmented reality to improve efficiency and distribution speed in the classification of postal packets, warehousing, distribution and other links.

Augmented reality is moving from a marketing gimmick to a new platform for improving consumer experience. In an augmented reality world, brand and product promotion will gradually decrease, while interaction and services will gradually increase.

Augmented reality opens not only a screen-free age, but also a new era of service, i.e., the era of substance marketing. Now, every company is a media company, and in the future, every company is a public service company, and this would be the most profound impact of augmented reality.

Pepsi: incredible bus station

In order to promote its sugar-free cola, Pepsi made a video ad at the bus stop by using AR techniques to add virtual images to real street view, enabling passengers waiting for a bus to view flying saucers in the sky, monsters in the streets and other incredible scenes. Just due to AR technique which is able to make an impossible visual image possible, it fits well Pepsi Max Series products' "unbelievable" image. Also, the special shots to passengers in the video, from astonishing to participation in, this is just what the advertiser is expecting to receive the audiences' reaction to such sugar-free cola "unbelievable products": from curiosity to deep experience.

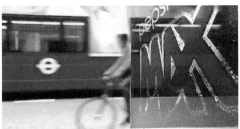

Pepsi: incredible bus station. Source: Tencent Video

IKEA: products come to my house in one second

What consumers worry about is they don't know what it would be like when the purchased furniture is put in their own house. Take a catalog of IKEA products and you can see what it would be like when you put the product at your house in your cellphone screen. AR virtual clothes

IKEA: products come to my house in one second. Source: www. cps.com.cn

fitting is similar to this. The advantages of these virtual clothing try-outs are not necessary to be further explained, naturally many clothing try-out related troubles are eliminated and goods return/replacement costs are saved. If the technology is mature, virtual clothing try-out certainly will receive further development in future e-commerce, and consumers no longer worry that their clothes are not suitable.

McDonald's: world cup in French fries box

It is heard that not eating French fries does not complete a meal of McDonald's. As McDonald's iconic product, the packaging of French fries also has been deeply explored. During the World Cup in 2014, McDonald's changed its French fries' packaging box, enabling consumers to activate a virtual football match game by scanning the new French fries packaging box, all styles of French fries packaging boxes become the goals in the games, and shooting at the goal can be realized by operating a virtual "ball" with one's fingers.

If you bought a piece of McDonald's World Cup package, in addition to a French fries box, you may have received other stage properties, and hamburger box and cola cup all can be used as stage properties in the virtual football field.

McDonald's: world cup in French fries box. Source: www.winshang.com

This McDonald's creativity not only combines the World Cup with this hot spot, but also makes customers feel more involved in virtual games bringing them into this marketing campaign personally and making them full of entertainment spirit. More than ten kinds of different French fry boxes solicit customers to follow and make the sales volume increase. At the same time, since the game has been developed, the exchange between players and game strategy sharing may increase product exposure.

Intel "Ultrabook" innovative experiences create marketing classics

In "Ultrabook" China Release Conference, the innovative marketing carried out based on AR technology by Global chip giant Intel has a larger scale and higher specification, and this just happened around us.

Intel Ultrabook becomes a unique AR interactive experience zone. As long as people who come to shop stand in a designated area before Ultrabook, they will see a famous actress, Wang Luodan, become a cool image of "Agent Luo", and magically coming to one's side from a chip-created flying saucer.

Then, the participant is invited to interact with virtual "Agent Luo", at first, "Agent Luo" wearing black clothes is standing beside you, and after that, "Agent Luo" becomes a pure white "Goddess Luo". When the participant follows the instruction of "Goddess Luo" and touches her palm, she disappears and once again becomes a black "Agent Luo".

This close contact interaction attempt makes the close proximity ever between brands and customers. Moreover, astonishment is not just this, three groups of photos shot by the field camera for the interaction between the participants and "Agent Luo" will promptly be transmitted to Ultrabooks provided by OEM located around the experience zone through wireless technology.

Intel "Ultrabook" innovative experiences create marketing classics. Source: www.hexun.com

This interesting experience shows the features of Ultrabook that are cool, rapid and powerful and so on through interactive means; and users are able to experience AR interactive game similarly experienced in Sanlitun in specialty stores and the Internet. "Three-line Interaction" makes Intel Ultrabook deeply impressed in the consumer's mind, also it highlights "celebrity endorsement" marketing campaign which can be easily "modularized", and opens a new thinking for marketing.

Based on these case studies, everyone may comprehend that the interaction between users and products by using AR technique is the mainstream practice at present, which greatly assigns users more involvement through all kinds of games or try-out of software, thus it transforms passive receiving to active approaching for customers. In this way, it draws products more closely to users; in addition, it decreases the cost for users to know the product by building up more down-to-earth product image. Meanwhile, the contents presented by AR technique also are the stereoscopic extension of print publicities/product packaging, and it has something new compared with commonly used QR code scanning.

🔆 Case Study   IPhone 8 Will Have the World's Biggest AR Platform

IPhone 8 Will Have the World's Biggest AR Platform.
Source: www.winshang.com

Now, it is believed that we are no strangers to the concept of AR augmented reality; particularly after the launch of AR development platform ARkit by Apple in WWDC 2017, where we comprehended the broader future prospect of this technology.

IPhone 8 is designed centered on AR. Even if it is expected that iPhone 8 will release its chip for AR use only, in many iPhone 8 prototypes, it shows that it has vertical double cameras, meaning that AR can be activated even if you are using a camera for landscape shooting. With the arrival of iPhone 8, ARkit functionalities are added in iOS 11 system; owing to many new features and designs, iPhone 8 certainly will be a best-selling device, plus earlier iPhone and iPad devices will be updated to iOS 11, therefore Apple will become "the world biggest AR platform"; in addition, it will attract a large number of AR developers.

These AR applications have displayed the future of iPhone.

IKEA

Function: enable users to place IKEA sofa and armchair copies of same size in their own houses. 2,000 pieces of product are available when its app is released.

How to use: click to enter into a product catalog, then search and select in this catalog.

After one click, the product hovers over your floor; at this time you can rotate it with your fingers; click again, it will be installed in place. The color and texture of the product can be accurately represented, and there are 3D models reproduced based on 3D scans in accordance with IKEA's Home Guide.

IKEA-Function: enable users to place IKEA sofa and armchair copies of same size in their own houses

The Walking Dead: Our World

Function: This is a position-aware shooting game; you have to walk around and use all kinds of weapons to kill zombies.

How to play: the game scene we can see is very three-dimensional. The high-definition zombies will come from all directions toward you, forcing you to dodge, hide and move and use the weapons to resist. You are required to "save" survivors in the game, and they will provide you with unique additional features. The game can also enhance the environment, such as adding a virtual "sewer" that allows zombies to climb out. This gives each scene a unique feel.

The Walking Dead: Our World-A position-aware shooting game

Little Chomp AR Version

Function: turn a widely welcomed children drawing book into an AR App.

Little Chomp AR Version-Turn a widely welcomed children drawing book into an AR App

How to use: after opening the App, click the object in the scene, the story begins. What we can see is just a small part of application scene: apple drops from tree, little chomp moves in the apple and gobbles down, it grows bigger and bigger. Also, this is a "zero control key" AR application.

Arise

Function: this is a game from Climax Studios that can render a devastated 3D world on your desktop, and you are required to use some non-traditional controls to help game characters move through this world.

How to play: you may use your device as an observation hole to align the disconnected paths at a certain angle, allowing the game character to pass through. No screen key is used in the game.

Arise- A game from Climax Studios

AR will change our way of doing things. Since iPhone 8 will bring about AR experience to broad masses, and introduce developers into the platform, it is not long for us to see that AR will become a core application in our daily life. This will change everything.

The case source quoted from: Zhenhua Military Network 2017/09/06

http://pcedu.pconline.com.cn/990/9900570.html

Chapter 18

Mobile Marketing Space Spread

Topics:

1. Field under the Boundary Theory
2. Scene
3. Scene-based Marketing
4. New Retail in the Context of Mobile Internet
5. Application of 4S Theory in New Retail
6. Tool Kit - Mobile Marketing Space Spread

Field under the Boundary Theory

The definition of the Boundary Theory: the boundaries of a country are imaginary borderlines between the territory of the country and that of another country or the unoccupied land or the high seas, or between the territorial airspace of the country and the outer space. In other words, they are borderlines for a sovereign state to exercise its sovereignty. The mobile Internet also has such boundaries. The Internet has experienced the ages of platform portal (1.0), consumer Internet (2.0), social Internet (3.0) and vertical application (4.0). In China, the mobile Internet begins with social networks (such as WeChat, QQ and Microblog) and culminates in vertically segmented small application networks. Although apps are born and die every day, the public is still full of enthusiasm about developing new apps. On the one hand, it is because the huge service industry is waiting for the rescue of apps. On the other hand, it is because the app software that has been developed into a colossus does not activate the commercial application of the closed-loop system despite its opening to connection. As a result, although the service industry may be commercialized, the rules of commercial application are still in the hands of colossuses; and despite the less professional industrial application, the cumbersome programming and the irregular punitive measures of such colossuses, the application boundaries of the mobile Internet have been clearer and clearer since July 2016. This gives birth to an interesting question - is the Internet in the Age 4.0 completely open without boundaries, or incompletely open with boundaries?

WeChat, the biggest mobile social software in the world, is holding high the banner of open connection, which has led the public to a mistaken idea that it be an open age without boundaries. In the past two years, users have increasingly felt the pressure from the open boundaries of WeChat and there are more and more so-called malicious software punished by the WeChat background server while users have no right to request interpretation. The "boundary court" set up by the colossus Wechat has increasingly mighty power to control the life and death of social connection fields of the Internet. People may question how such software

embraced by humans initially due to the Open Theory has so many boundaries. The colossus WeChat gives the answer that the smaller individual is also a brand. The brand is independent, and the independent inclusion is the boundary. For example, you establish a WeChat group in which advertising is strictly prohibited but the group owner is allowed to post an advertisement. This shows that both big and small software have boundaries just as a country is enclosed to be a country. Brexit is supported by the UK citizens in pursuit of a sense of national presence within the national boundaries while those who voted for Brexit are well aware of the economic troubles caused by Brexit. The new age of the mobile Internet presents a confusing dilemma. Are human's pursuits of openness without boundaries and of infinite inclusion not the ultimate goals of all human behaviors? And why is the Internet more like one of the "boundary courts" set up by humans as it evolves? Is it moving forwards or backwards?

When 360 intruded into the boundaries of Baidu to dig up its own search field, and when Baidu made incursions into the boundaries of O2O to activate the online-to-offline mode, Google was standing firmly within its own boundaries and improving the height of technological innovation by the fruitful achievements, such as Google Glass, Google Driverless Car, and Google Maps. Google has never been engaged in "Google Takeaway" or "Google Fresh", and has always adhered to its boundary theory to keep these extremely lucrative commercial fields out of its boundaries. As a result, we all know the fact that Baidu has become notorious but Google has made bold moves toward high-tech. Does the emergence of the boundary theory mean that the cross-boundary theory fails? Does the boundary theory block cross-boundary innovations to extinguish the public's enthusiasm for innovation?

No, it doesn't. The historical evolution of the Internet totally changed by stealth in the summer of 2016, and now is running wildly on the road to the second application of the mobile Internet. If you miss this high-speed train, it'll take you at least three years to wait for the next. However, the boundary theory is so vague that it is extremely difficult to control its usage in the application. These features confuse you in gaining an insight into the Internet. However, the boundary theory did come, just in this hot summer!

Why is the boundary theory the next trend?

1. Bringing truth out of noisy chaos

The mobile Internet that originated in 2014 ushered in a new phase in the Internet Age 4.0. Because of the high mass participation in the mobile Internet, it is inevitable that the cognitive chaos will be brought about and the truth will be covered by the public's voice. Bad money driving out good money is an inevitable process in the initial phase of this age. Don't be surprised by the chaos. Just marvel at the fact that the true knowledge didn't get knocked down but stood up again in the summer of 2016.

In the past three years, the words "openness" and "inclusion" were repeatedly mentioned, of which "openness" was exalted to any place and "inclusion" to no-boundary. Arguably, there is nothing wrong with this. Who can say that the genes of the Internet are not "openness" and "inclusion"? However, there is no doubt that during the three years of the development of mobile Internet, among the numerous entrepreneurs, only a handful of strong performers achieved success in the public memory. Why is that? In the summer of 2016, a small group of people with lofty ideals began to think about why there was such a big gap between mobile Internet idea and mobile application? Was the Internet idea or the Internet application wrong? A cognitive problem should be resolved first. Einstein's theory of relativity theoretically discovered the possibility to make an atomic bomb, but it didn't suggest that Einstein could make an atomic bomb as an engineer. Understanding the difference between theorists and engineers was an important task in the summer of 2016. And even the theory could be classified as pure academic theories and applied theories. This book falls within the range of applied theory. It turns out that "openness" and "inclusion" are correct from the theo-

retical perspective, and should have boundaries from the perspective of application. For an Internet space, no restricted area or boundary should be set up on account of the principle of equality and freedom. But for an Internet organization, whether other-organization or self-organization, the practical application should be taken into consideration and the boundaries should be set up to achieve the "openness and inclusion with boundaries". For individuals, it is reasonable that those specialized in academic learning concentrate on openness and inclusion, while those engaged in application attach importance to boundaries.

2. Applications require boundaries

An indisputable fact is that now it is the Internet Age 4.0 (vertical application) when the characteristics of network applications are niche and verticality.

Niche means the user boundary. It's hard to imagine a plastic drink bottle appearing in an application that sells organic fruits and vegetables. If mobile software dedicated for heart disease also offers treatments for beriberi, it will give the user an unprofessional impression. Therefore, a user application cannot be in line with the Internet spirit of dedicated and focused applications until it has boundaries.

Verticality means the service boundary. Every kind of successful Internet software is an innovation of service mode. For instance, search engines are within Baidu's boundaries, and car-hailing apps are within Didi's boundaries. It would be reasonable for Baidu to go across the boundaries to design a "Baidu Car-hailing" app with the help of Baidu Map. But according to the principle that any application software must have its application boundaries, it is reasonable that Didi make money for car hailing and Baidu for maps.

Niche and verticality predominate the application features of the fourth-generation of the Internet, and also justify the anti-human principle that the greedy never succeeds. We must know that greed is a common humanity trait but the Internet refuses to be greedy.

I. Closed–loop concept

Closed loop (closed-loop structure) is also called the feedback control system that compares the measured value of the system output with the desired given value to generate a deviation signal with which

the output value can be readjusted or controlled to be as close as possible to the desired value. For example, to readjust the tap, set a desired water flow in the brain, then turn on the tap and compare the current flow with the expected value with your eyes, and continuously readjust the flow by hand to form a feedback closed-loop control; the same goes for bicycling - continuously correct the direction and speed to form a closed-loop control.

Feedback link is the major difference between closed loop and open loop. The closed-loop control has a feedback link in which the feedback system improves the accuracy and shortens the response time. It is suitable for those systems with higher requirements for system response time and stability. The open-loop control has no feedback link but with low system stability, relatively long response time and low accuracy. It is suitable for those simple systems with lower requirements for system stability and accuracy.

The closed-loop control is to make use of the difference between the output signal and the input signal to operate the controller so that system errors can be reduced. This is a function that the open-loop system does not have. On the premise that the system input is known and there is no interference, an open-loop system will be sufficient for stable production and the closed-loop control will be unnecessary. However, this premise can hardly be realized. The closed-loop system will function fully when there is unpredictable interference or there is an unpredictable change in the component parameters of the system.

O2O closed loop means the connect-ing and looping from O to O. Online marketing, publicity and promotion should lead the customer flow to offline consumption experiences for consummation of transactions. But this is only an O2O transaction and does not form a closed loop yet. To form a closed loop, we must go back to the online from the offline. A closed loop is formed by feedbacks on offline consumption experiences as well as behaviors to lead offline users to online communications and online experiences, in other words, from the online to the offline and then back to the online.

Closed Loop of O2O

O2O closed loop means the connecting and looping from O to O.

In the field of life services, not all of a user's behaviors are at the online end like the e-commerce. The user's behaviors are divided into two parts: the online and the offline. In terms of the platform, if the user's behaviors cannot be recorded in whole or a substantial part of them are missing, the platform may worry about the threatened loss of control over vendors, that is, the loss of bargaining power, which may decrease the value of the platform. Therefore, closed-loop is a basic attribute of the O2O platform, vitally distinguishing the O2O platform from general information platforms.

II. Circle to field

Circle is a geometric figure which is the set of all points in a plane that are at a given distance from a given point. As stated in the Intention Part of the Guanzi, those who can understand the profound meaning of the circle will be of indomitable spirit. Circle is a very profound theory. As mentioned above, the O2O closed-loop concept is like a circle - online marketing, publicity and promotion to lead the customer flow to offline transactions, and then feedbacks on offline consumption experiences to lead offline users to online communications and online experiences. It loops constantly like this.

In terms of logo shapes, those auto brands like Mercedes-Benz, BMW and Toyota enclose their logos with a circle (see Figure 18-1). And this circle is a field.

"Field" refers to the distribution of objects in a space in physics, and refers to the passages in dramatic works and theatrical performances in literature. When this word is applied to the field of mobile Internet, it usually refers to social, shopping, game and other related behaviors, or the closed-loop application form completed through payment. This is usually called an application scene. A scene where consumer behaviors such as shopping, car hailing and group buying are completed through mobile payment may be considered a payment scene.

With the advent of mobile devices and smart terminals, the Internet has gradually upgraded to the mobile Internet and has become increasingly integrated with

Figure 18-1   Circles in auto logos.
Source: Autohome.

people's daily lives. The mobile Internet and the sharing economy are transforming people's dimensions in whole. The resulting new lifestyle has increasingly epitomized the new environment and new features of social networks. The fragmentation of the WeChat environment is a good example.

Groups in daily life are constantly connected to different individuals from different groups, and the unique value created by this connection forms experience and leads to consumption. On the mobile Internet, this connection is represented as more specific application scenes and payment scenes. The scene has become a way of thinking, advocating that the mobile Internet be regarded as a tool to connect different individual scenes. Meanwhile, it is also a method to achieve high connection efficiency with the use of mobile Internet. It can be summarized as the following four key points:

(1) the scene is the most authentic human-centered experience;

(2) the scene is a connection method;

(3) the scene is a form of value exchange and new lifestyle; and

(4) the appearance of a scene forms the five elements of journalism: time, place, character, event and connection method.

There is no doubt that mobile Internet technology is deeply affecting today's mainstream way of thinking, act and life. WeChat Moment has grown into a trigger scene; Meipai has stood out from the integration of hardware (Meitu smartphone) and software (Meitu Xiuxiu); the NBA Golden State Warriors' three-point line has inspired and brought out UBall; and smart home, 3D printing and VR glasses all are ways to understand the real world.

The experience determines the scene where people are. The experience iteration of a new scene attaches more importance to people's experience and happiness. For comments, people are more concerned about likes in WeChat Moment; and for pricing and payment of a product, people pay more attention to whom to transact with and which scene to get satisfaction from. Since connecting is expressed by scenes, which scene is selected determines which connection method will be used, what kind of community will be set up, and what kind of subculture will eventually be achieved.

The essence of the scene is the possession of time. Having a scene means getting possession of consumers' time, which will make it easier to seize the minds of consumers.

 **Case Study**　**Airbnb**

1.　Experiences

First of all, Airbnb officially launches a new C2C transaction called "Experiences", which is similar to a private tour guide, that is, to experience the local non-traditional tour items under the guide of locals. Individual users can post and offer such experience services that may last several days (called "Immersions") or just a few hours (called "Single Experiences").

Of course, locals charge for such services. For example, one now offers a 2-day guided self-driving tour along California Highway 1 for USD $349.

2.　Places

Airbnb also competes with QYER.COM and MAFENGWO.COM for business. This time, Airbnb launches a new service - the "Places" to help you plan well before travel, acquire knowledge and experience better in travel. Airbnb partners with APPDetour to offer the travel guide service - AudioWalk. For example, when you walk along the street in Los Angeles,

you can hear the electronic tour guide telling the stories behind every corner as long as you open this app.

In addition, you as a traveler can also search by category for the services you are interested in, such as "food tour", before you go to an eating spot. For this purpose, Airbnb specifically partners with Resy, a startup company that provides restaurant reservations, allowing users to make reservations directly on Trips and thoughtfully serving every foodie.

3.　Homes

Airbnb was originally known for its short rental service. Nowadays, Airbnb has three million homes available for you around the world. And the function to find a home has been extended so that you can rent a home and even obtain car rental, takeaway and private chef services through your landlord.

This extended function of Airbnb has helped "landlords" open up new business areas. "Landlords" now not only provide accommodation for tourists, but also lead them to know more about their homes. They build up closer relations with tourists, and of course obtain more income through a good knowledge of their native lands. Tourists also consider Airbnb a travel assistant offering "one-stop" services rather than just providing a place to sleep over.

4. Trips

In addition, you can directly view travel footprints in the Trips tags of the new Airbnb App. This function of Trips helps Airbnb know more about where its users have been or are going to go, what they want to know about this trip, what special services they expect and so on.

At present, the new version of Airbnb is launched with new service function covering 12 cities including New York, San Francisco, Los Angeles, Tokyo and Paris. And Airbnb plans to extend its service function to 50 cities around the world next year.

The case source quoted from: Competing With QYER.COM and MAFENGWO.COM for Business, Airbnb Announces Significant Transformation Today, Airbnb 2016/11/18
http://www.sohu.com/a/119282753_257855

 Scene

I. What is scene?

Scene is a professional term in the film and television industry which refers to the scenes in dramas or movies. When it is extended to the Internet field, it refers to a product or application launched by merchants for meeting the specific demands of a group of users. For example, a user who wants to buy an Apple computer comes to Jingdong Mall; or a user opens WeChat to know gossip news about its circle of friends, and all these are scenes. There is an indispensable element in the scene; and that is people. And, the core performance of the people in a scene is emotion.

In the era of mobile Internet, scene is an integrated experience built on mobile smart devices, social media, big data, sensors and positioning systems. It reconstructs the connection between people and people, people and markets, people and everything in the world. A scene may be a product, a service, or an immersive and ubiquitous experience. It is accompanied with new scene creation, new linkage, new experience and new fashion. While people are still enjoying the convenience of mobile Internet era, a new era of scene has arrived. The ubiquitous scenes allow people to work, learn and live in a way that they can see, remember and experience. By taking Jingdong with strong scene arrangement as the example: a user is fond of an Apple computer, but he/she does not have the necessary funds what shall he/she do? "Dear, just sign your name in IOU, use the computer first, and pay the price little by little", and this is a scenario demand. A user shopping in Jingdong has the desire to buy a real quality product, and IOU removes his worry, and this is a "scenerized" solution.

In the opinion of Robert Scober, a famous reporter in US technology field: the development of the era of scene relies on the joint roles of five forces of scene, which are mobile smart device, social media, big data, sensor and positioning system.

The first is mobile smart device. Mobile smart devices are the key to gain the power of Internet, and they are in various forms, such as smart phones and wearable devices. Mobile devices are the carriers experiencing the era of scenes, which provide a platform for data analysis and aggregate the other four forces.

The second is social media. Social media is the source for obtaining highly personalized contents. Through online conversations in various media, make clear people's preferences, where they are and the goals they seek, and make technology understand people's personal demands, what they are doing, what they are going to do and other scenes.

The third is big data. Nowadays, data exists everywhere; people's basic necessities of life all exist in the form of data; the whole world is recorded with data through equipment and network, then, through data, customers' consumption tendencies are mastered, and customers' demands are explored.

The fourth is sensor. Simple and compact sensors are generally mounted on moving or fixed objects for detecting data collection and connection as well as reporting changes. For example, a common smartphone is equipped with seven sensors, by and through which increasing cellphone apps acquires customer's location through sensor and knows their movements.

The fifth is positioning system. The core mechanism behind positioning system actually is to collect related data; different from traditional location service, positioning service in scene requires high precision; for example, it is required to know in which building the targeted user is, which floor, and being able to use the collected position data and other information data to provide customers with forecast service.

The popularity of mobile Internet and smart terminal devices pushes human towards the era of scenes, where people will have more options. Nowadays, people no longer have worry for buying a piece of commodity because similar commodity is countless in quantity online and offline. The oversupplied market environment causes escalation of people's consumption

desire or rigid demand; and the one whose products or services are closer to people's desired real scenes will win more loyalty of customers and become the winner in market share.

At present, among those who take leading positions in China's mobile Internet field, all of them are masters in terms of scene construction. Why MOMO is able to enter into Wall Street under the siege built by WeChat is that it helps users construct a brand new scene for making friends with strangers that is totally different from WeChat. Nowadays all popular apps such as MeiTu, Meilishuo, Dayima, Babytree and Headlines Today, behind which are all vivid and lively scenes.

Alibaba, Baidu, even 360 and MI, etc., also are working hard to improve their own ecosystems by constructing various scenes, such as shopping, water/electricity/gas payment, car-hailing, super market, finance management, borrowing, medical treatment and travelling, and so forth. Obviously, scene construction-based brand new commercial ecology has become the consensus of industrial bosses.

II. Characteristics of Scene

1. Fastness and convenience

In traditional marketing mode, touch points are limited and generally presented on media like TV, Internet, magazines, ads, and outdoor billboards through advertising channels; however, from the perspective of scene, consumer demands exist in the entire process of discovery, exploration, purchase and use, and in-depth analysis and exploration are conducted according to consumer demands; therefore, the touch points are unlimited. The reason for the mobile Internet marketing mode to replace the traditional marketing mode to become the main scene in people's lives is because of the fast access of network information anytime anywhere, fast access of the preferential content in the surroundings, and satisfaction of personalized services needed in consumers' lives.

2. Personalized recommendations based on scene

Data are an important reference for information delivery. Only the huge and accurate data can enable the precise deliv-

ery of information, to thus reduce waste. The big data function of the scene-based mobile marketing platform of Hives World can subdivide the population, establish detailed user portraits, and help merchants achieve precise delivery of preferential content by analyzing shopping habits and characteristics of consumers.

3. Liveliness and interaction of scene

Before the mobile Internet, the marketing mode was divided into online and offline modes, with the former having big traffic but small conversion, and the latter having small traffic but high cost. With the development of mobile Internet, the scene-based mobile marketing has broken the deadlock of the difficulty in combining online and offline modes, making the most of the "broadness" advantage of online marketing and sense of participation of offline marketing. For example, consumers can win store discounts via online mini-games, which will not only make it more interesting, but also enhance consumers' sense of participation, to thus make the scene-based mobile marketing more lively and interesting.

4. Virtualization of scene

As mobile smart terminal devices achieve seamless access anytime anywhere to meet the demand for accessing any network from any device at any time, it becomes possible to make the scenes objectively existing in realities into VR or AR models and display them on screen by simulating the point of view of people. The essence of virtualization of scene is online and offline connection, and networking and virtualization of objective scenes in realities.

Virtualization of scene can provide a realistic simulation of real world and environment, to make the virtual scene more realistic and attractive, letting users consciously enter the scene, as if they were personally there, to increase the sense of substitution. Scenes can be used as the solution if problems in real life cannot be solved with measures of real life, for example, regarding the problem of difficulty in hailing a taxi in some cities, apps like Didi Chuxing have solved such problem in the real world by scene building.

III. Basic Elements of Scene

The scene in the mobile Internet context includes three elements.

1. Space element

Mobile scene is always a variable to users and means the fast switch between time-space and environment scenes, with each scene bringing different feelings and demands to users. Mobile Internet makes boundaries of work, life, and leisure increasingly blurred. Smartphones distract people's attention, which breaks people's full time, fills up their time, and also increases their interaction.

2. Time element

In the age of the mobile scene, people's time becomes increasingly fragmented, consumers can socialize, play games, watch videos, and even work anytime anywhere on their cellphones. Then how to choose the time nodes for marketing in those time nodes? This is worth studying.

The map navigation app Waze is doing great in this regard. Waze does not only provide users with strong and convenient navigation function, but also guides users' consumption. For example, when a user is driving to work in the morning, Waze will help the user avoid the most congested section, and when the user is waiting for the traffic light, an ad will pop up reminding the user to buy a cup of refreshing latte when passing by Starbucks; for another example, when a user wants to go shopping at Walmart, Waze will thoughtfully pop up ATM locations. The time nodes are well grasped.

3. Relationship element

Source: 360doc.com

Social media are an important element in the age of scene, and people are clear about their preferences, positions, and targets through relationship interaction. The relationship element has great influences on activities of the participating users, and such influences become increasingly clear. Shopping in the mobile age is not as fixed and complete as in a physical store, or as formal and serious as on the PC end; shopping becomes a fragmented scene in the mobile life scene, with "simple, quick, and impulsive" being the main characteristics of the new shopping age. With such background, the effect of word-of-mouth or friend recommendation is much higher than ever before: a word from a friend may be the direct reason for you to touch the "Buy" button.

The underwear brand Victoria's Secret launched a lightweight app in order to warm up Qixi Festival (Chinese Valentine's Day), and the cool product form soon became hot in WeChat Moments: starting from the movement of "wiping screen to see sexy models", users could browse the brand introduction of Victoria's Secret page by page, to eventually reach the underwear price pages.

Compared to the independent mobile client, such form is relatively "lighter", and

The underwear brand Victoria's Secret. Source: 360doc.com

quicker in obtaining information. "Scene" is spread via social relationships and shared to like-minded people.

The three elements of scene always center on users, which is the subtlety of scene. Mobile Internet greatly unlocks individual value, and users return to the center of market, become the center of everything, and constitute the very heart of scene. Strictly speaking, scene is an interaction and trust chain formed based on human relation. In the scene age, the product is only a start, of which the function improvement and iteration need user participation. The ability to define scene has become an important measurement of whether an enterprise can gain market.

IV. Profound Influences of Scene on Mobile Internet

1. Causing the focus of competition of mobile Internet economy to change from traffic to scene users

According to the latest financial report of Tencent, the users of WeChat Chinese and English versions totaled over 400 million, with almost every one of them being an active user; while among the 500 million users of Microblog, the monthly active users are only 160 million and daily active users are only over 70 million, far less than those of WeChat. The success of WeChat lies in the strongly connected and strongly interactive "scene-based" lives created by it. The emergence of scene causes the previous scramble of Internet enterprises for traffic users and traffic entrances to change to scramble for scene users. In the future, the information portals will no longer be the information centers on PC, but will be based on scene for access of information "anytime, anywhere, and as one wishes". Pushed by scene, the Internet pattern will be changed, scene will weaken the traditional search, people's time spent on mobile Internet will be far past the total time spent on computer webpages, interpersonal communication will tend to be digitalized and mobile, and the mobile Internet will become the main portals of information in the future to gain the value of a new round of user migration.

2. Promoting the physicalization process of the mobile Internet to accelerate development in both depth and breadth

The essence of scene is connection: human-machine connection, human-object connection, and human-human connection. As scene is created on a broader scale, it upgrades the past human-informa-tion connection to human-service connection, and connects everything by the force of five core technologies, to enable mobile Internet to gradually integrate with business of each industry and enter aspects of production and life through the constantly physicalized form to optimize people's ways of life and communication. For example, in a specific scene, people can learn the traffic condition by using intelligent navigation and optimize route according to the congestion situation; they can process information by using sensors and intelligent chips of smart home devices, and obtain suggestions for optimizing life quality.

3. Realizing tracking of online and offline behaviors to deepen the understanding of users

Scene enables manufacturers and service providers to get closer to consumers than ever before, break the past online tracking mode of traditional PC, solve the problem of offline tracking of data through sensors, realize online + offline tracking mode, and collect detailed data like consumers' preferences and attributes, so as to understand customers more deeply, and develop personalized product services according to individual demands. For example, sensor technology is added to the Nike+ running shoes and wearable devices, to connect to network, app, training program and social network site, and not only record running path and time, but also connect the user with other runners with common interests. The user will receive the customized training program. Every bit of progress will be recorded, and different guiding opinions will be offered according to the personal realities.

V. Mobile Internet Relying More on Scene Rather than Portal

In the era of traditional Internet, Internet giants represented by Alibaba, Baidu, and Tencent won the favor of users and achieved their own business models upon satisfaction of the "people and commodities", "people and information", and "people and people" user demands, being the real Internet giants in the era of PC Internet. With the development of the mobile Internet, the "people and scene" business model has also started to emerge more and more, and giants based on mobile Internet have started to see the enormous business opportunities in this regard.

The mobile Internet is a new interface for merchants and users to establish communication and service. Mobile terminals are emotional and sentimental media. How to build an interface for the deeper relationships with users is what the mobile Internet should pay attention to.

The biggest difference between mobile Internet and PC Internet lies in that the portal is no longer important, and what's important is the application scene.

The really effective marketing must be based on specific scenes—pushing product services of brands according to the correlations between mobile devices and consumers. Good marketing is accompanying and scene-triggered marketing. Nowadays, many ads have no scene, which are difficult to resonate with consumers without scene matching.

Scene applications are closer to users' using habits. The difference between scene and portal can in fact be deemed as that scene starts from user habits and is closer to user habits, while portal starts from perspective of business, and relies more on resources.

 **Case Study** | **Momo**

Momo is a mobile social tool based on geographic location. Via Momo, users can get to know people around them, and send text messages, voice messages, photos, and precise geographic locations free of charge, to better communicate with people around; they can create and join the nearby interest groups, message boards, and nearby activities and Momo Bars by using Momo. Momo was officially listed on NASDAQ on December 12, 2014, with a closing price 20.5% higher than the IPO price on the first day of listing, showing the rise of the fourth largest social app of China. Momo's registered users grew from the initial 0 in August 2011 to 180.3 million in September 2014, in the three years from founding in 2011 to listing in 2014.

Listed on NASDAQ with market value exceeding USD $2 billion just in the third year after founding, Momo's rise is inextricably linked to its seizing of opportunities to create new scenes during product iteration, to thus keep user growth and activity.

Then what are the typical usage scenes of Momo groups?

1. Communication of owners

Via Momo, neighbors in a community who don't know each other can conveniently gather, talking about the community property, child education, or other life information, and conveniently organize offline gatherings.

2. Interest group

Remain indoors at ordinary times, and can't find people with the same hobby? Various game groups, sports groups, and board game groups can be created on Momo, and people interested nearby can easily see and join, for offline activities or online communication.

3. Chatting with colleagues

Employees of a company can create their own group on Momo. Advantages of Momo groups over WeChat groups are that the Momo group has the concept of administrator, group members can instantly see the distance between each other, and colleagues can easily communicate with each other.

4. Communication of peers

Nowadays, the nature of companies in the same office buildings might be similar, but people there are unlikely to know each other. Momo groups can organize white collars in buildings, to exchange, expand connections, or even recruit or hunt talents.

5. Merchant information

There have been some merchants, restaurants, and bars, etc. gathering their own users or potential users and posting discount and promotion information via Momo groups, and users can offer relevant suggestions and make reservations, etc. in the groups, which provides a new O2O thought.

The success of Momo is a result of breaking social barriers, improving social scenes, and enriching social experiences.

The case source quoted from: 360doc.com 2014/08/12
http://www.360doc.com/content/14/0812/06/6474625_401192434.shtml

Scene–based Marketing

For most of our lives, we live under a scene. If we follow the past brand theory, the scene is a kind of mental influence. An enterprise or a brand attracts people's attention by promoting its "value" through advertising, public relations and even promotions, to maintain the consumption as much as possible. This is well known to most entrepreneurs and consumers. In the age of mobile Internet, it is nothing new that people keep refreshing their ideas and thinking about new things.

1. Scene marketing depends on "mind influence"

The consumer behavior itself has some scene suggestion; for example, when you fall in love and want to get the one you love a special creative gift, and after others remind and inform you, you then "choose" a certain commodity or service to express your love via the different sources of information; you are controlled by a certain mind, emotionally or intellectually.

Both consumption rationality and emotion are inducements of consumption decision; however, such cognition of people has changed in the fragmented mobile scene age. Traditional ads, recommendations from offline malls to online acquaintances, and even the touching of certain information provide you with the chance to choose once again, so that you change your decision: not choosing commodity or service according to the established route, but choosing the consumption according to the shopping guide provided by the mobile scene.

2. Scene marketing crystallizes consumers' buying habits

Many consumers have got used to online shopping and waiting for express,

which is not wrong; however, when they are to carry out consumption next time, they will have the desire and impulse for second consumption only for those that specially impress them or where they have formed buying habits (address). Such crystallized consumption behavior is equal to brand loyalty, and with such, merchants can mark relevant consumers as repeat customers.

"One-shot deal" is the last thing all merchants want to see or accept, because attracting customers requires much energy and even money. The continuous buying can have consumers truly "stuck" on your brands. This brings the "customer accumulation" issue all merchants are confronted with, besides the "conversion rate" issue that prevails in the e-commerce circle.

If it wasn't for those needs to "crystallize" user habits, people would not need to spend much effort thinking about how to realize the real O2O in a market where the offline channel continues to collapse and a market where the online communication continues to be fragmented.

Communicating or opening store online is an interface for you to reach users, while the offline interface is more direct but falls behind user's thinking. What we need to do is online and offline connection to rebuild the scene, which can be a scene that forms a resonance effect or a coupling system for mutual transmission of information and commodities. People will become the medium and carrier, and also the biggest scene experiencer and consumption decision maker.

To crystallize user habits, a sustained, convenient consumption crystallization portal is required, which may be store, online shop, public account, or WeChat Moments.

I. Current Situation and Strategy of Scene Marketing

In the Internet age, scene marketing was based on the online behaviors of netizens and was always about one of three scenes: entry scene, search scene, and browse scene. In the era of mobile Internet, scene marketing can be independent of content and operated according to the time and place attributes of users, for example, restaurant information push based on lo-

cation, and news and weather information push based on time, etc.

Stage I: User network behaviors

Browsers and search engines extensively serve network behaviors of most netizens like data search, information acquisition, network entertainment, and online shopping. Scene marketing is an online marketing mode that targets the entry, search, and browse scenes, pays full respect to user's web experience first, centers on netizens' behavior paths and Internet surfing scenes of entering, searching, and acquiring information, and takes "interest guiding + massive exposure + portal marketing" as the clue. The "user network behavior" is overall centered on as the core.

Stage II: Exploration of user demands with data

Time, place, and user browsing and using behaviors can be further taken into overall consideration to recognize and judge user scenes in a more detailed and accurate manner, to enable information and help provided by brands to more naturally and directly meet user demands, for example, during the flight ticket booking, reservation information of hotels and sce-

nic spots around the corresponding destination may be provided to the consumer.

A certain famous home furnishing retailer can be called a model of scene marketing (see Figure 18-2). We can see from customers "disorderly and unscrupulously lying" in the mall that this retailer knows well the way of scene marketing. The brand has changed the metro station and cars of Chongqing passing by the mall into its own product exhibition area that is bright-colored, comfortable and cozy, creating a new marketing scene.

Figure 18-2   A Model of Scene Marketing.
Source: 360doc.com

II. Scene Marketing Interaction under the Mobile Internet Background

Under the background of mobile Internet industry, consumers stop paying for one-way information dissemination due to changes of their consuming behaviors and more diversified information sources, making the interaction between marketing and consumers more important. The essence of scene marketing is establishing connection between brands and consumers' lives, and getting marketing into the real environment; therefore, the effective interaction with consumers is one of the core elements of scene marketing. Interactive creativity can enable consumers to gain personalized feelings in the scene.

Layout of IKEA store.
Source: 360doc.com

Eternal love occupying Beijing subway.
Source: 360doc.com

Case Study   "Blood Sucking Building with People Working Overtime" Creative H5 Page Ad

To build up the momentum for the launch of the Premier business, Didi seized the scene of working overtime late at night of the target users and launched the creative H5 page ad: "Blood Sucking Building with People Working Overtime" on April 15, 2015, which generated constant discussion and spread among white collars on social media, became a common topic, and even caused the momentum borrowing

marketing of other brands and media discussion (see Figure 18-3).

Value creation. By walking into the life scenes of consumers and stimulating the interaction between consumers, and between consumers and brands, scene marketing enables brands to form viral communication via social networks, and have long-lasting effects. How to sense, discover, track, and respond to every "individual" in the fragmented era of mobile Internet, listen to their voice, understand their problem, have a heart-to-heart talk with them, and create value for them becomes another core element of scene marketing.

Integrated communication. Merchants need not only the integration of new media and traditional media, but also the integration between new media, and the integration of marketing means and resources, to reach tight connections between users and marketing creativity content. The key to the integration does not lie in how many resources are utilized, but in whether effective resources are appropriately utilized and whether maximum benefits are gained at minimum cost.

Entertainment. The brand and consumers will be closer in an entertaining atmosphere. By exploring consumer behaviors and consumption itself, we find out that what people ultimately demand is not merely material needs, but more the feeling of the entertaining virtual space. Scene marketing precisely explores how to make marketing more interesting and attractive to consumers, to have them gain fun and pleasure during the participation.

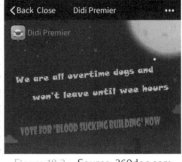

Figure 18-3   Source: 360doc.com

The case source quoted from: Successful Marketing 2017/03/21
http://www.360doc.com/content/17/0321/21/32150962_638869080.shtml

III. Scene Breakdown under the Mobile Internet Background

2013 Nike +Ipod:"when they are exercising, Nike always accompanies.
Source: 360doc.com

Under the background of the mobile industry, mobile terminal technology continues to develop, consumers' life consumption patterns become more diversified, and "situational variables" in users' information interaction with the outside world are largely enriched, such as before/during/after shopping, dynamic state/static state, solitude/gathering, indoors/outdoors, concentrated/distracted state, single-screen tasks/multi-screen tasks, with more variable indicators to emerge with technological progress and industrial form change. Breakdown of those variable indicators can help design and build marketing scenes, to more accurately lock in target customers and improve the accuracy of communication with users.

Exploring existing scenes. An important function of marketing is to boost consumer demands, and some consumer demands will be effectively boosted only with the help of specific scenes; therefore, it's very important to find the scenes. Finding the right scene means finding the opportunity. Many existing scenes in our lives can be explored and used. The key is to really go into consumers' lives, and accurately judge consumers' living habits and psychology.

For example, according to consumers' habit of recording sports data in the sport scene, Nike launched Nike + iPod in 2013, for users to duly see their own speed and distance, etc. during the sports, to thus establish constant connection with them: when they are exercising, Nike always accompanies.

Creating new scenes. If there are no existing scenes, new scenes can be created according to the excitement or pain spot of customers in the era of mobile Internet. Creation of new scene should be based on the profound insight into consumer demands and pay attention to the heart-to-heart talk with consumers, not on purpose, otherwise, it would be easily seen through by clever consumers.

Source: 360doc.com

For example, the Nike laser-projected pop-up soccer field: Nike implemented a campaign called "anytime, anywhere" in Madrid, Spain, in which it created the fields for young people with laser projection; users might call "Nike bus" with app, and then this bus would bring soccer field (laser-projected) and gates, etc., and even free Nike shoes, for young people to have fun in the laser-projected field.

IV. Scene Marketing Strategies in the Context of Mobile Internet

1. Accurate Identification of a Target User

Any scene can be an opportunity to seek a target group because it always has real or potential consumers. The term "scene" indicates the positioning technology plays a very key role in the scene marking. Technologies vary in positioning accuracy and application range. For example, for a large target area of interest, GPS technology is used; for a shopping center, WiFi technology is needed. However, iBeacon[①] technology is appropriate if marketing activities are carried out according to consumer behaviors.

2. Precise Push of Brand Information

Positioning a target group based on the scenes of the consumer's life is only the first step of the scene marketing, which brings a large inlet flow for the entire purchase process, and the key to successful marketing is the deep insight into consumer demands and the precise push of brand information. Insight is to discover the deeper reasons that are more related to consumer psychology behind their behaviors and it is, therefore, to mine the deep psychological needs of consumers.

3. Closed Loop System

The crucial step in the scene marketing is to turn potential consumers into real ones and to finalize the sales. According to the 4C Marketing Model proposed by Prof. Robert Lauterborn, vendors should consider the customer cost, render convenience to the customer and well communicate with them, which is also applicable to the scene marketing. Reasonable consumption guide is the way to render convenience to customers. It is very easy for consumers to make the purchase decision if they are provided with such convenience.

V. Design Principles for Scene Marketing Strategies

Scene-based strategy, as our customers transition from eating to live, to eating healthy when the differentiation of society is gradually formed, the gap between urban and rural areas began widening, consumer attitudes began to appear different, and inter-brand competition began deteriorating. In order to better promote competition in the industry, the brand began a category of competition between industries. Category of competition is the best way to make this category become synonymous with the brand.

The scene strategy is the important way to quickly establish the category leader. Drinking Wong Lo Kat herbal tea for example, when the demands of 'fear of internal heat' scene is highlighted, consumers began to think that this scene would have a relation with them, and they will naturally think to drink Wong Lo Kat when they have a "hot pot". The scene strategy must be the future development direction of the enterprise, whatever the industry is inevitable.

The scene marketing strategies should start with the product, which is to construct the scene of sales channels and the scene of promotions, so that consumers associate products with themselves and finally complete the purchase. Specifically, we can base it on the following methods to implement:

Firstly, it is the scene-based product, including scene-based packaging. You must make people "love" the packaging at a glance. Novel packaging not only attracts the attention of consumers, but also clearly reveals the appeal of the product itself. The scene-based naming is adopted. The name must be catchy and easy to remember. For example, to use the purpose of a product as the name is one method, such as fresh noodles, and steamed bread sauce.

Secondly, it is the scene-based marketing, including: (1) simulating the most realistic usage scene at the site, which should be explicitly suggestive. This requires a good understanding of the product, its features and whether it

① *iBeacon is a new feature on IOS for mobile devices released by Apple in September 2013. A device equipped with a low-power Bluetooth function can send its own unique ID to the surroundings, and the application that receives the ID will take some actions based on the ID. For example, if an old iBeacon communication module is installed in a store, an information notification server can be run on the iPhone and iPad, or the server sends discount coupons and points to customers. In addition, iBeacon can also be used to send information to application when the appliance fails or stops working.*

Case Study Cebu Pacific's "Rain Code"

Cebu Pacific's "Rain Code"

Some of the needs of people will only be stimulated under a specific scene. Therefore, the scene will be an opportunity. Hong Kong has a monsoon-influenced climate, with rainy days much more than sunny days. This is depressing. But this "rainy" scene is an opportunity for Cebu Pacific to attract people to sunny places. The rain code used by Cebu Pacific is a QR code that is applied on the street with waterproof paint for the purpose of advertising, and is only visible when it rains – "IT'S SUNNY IN THE PHILIPPINES".

Scan the QR code and come to the Philippines to play in the sun!

Math Paper Press – The Offline Book

In the digital age, people spend a lot of time in the virtual world. In addition to the "three important factors" of online marketing, i.e., the blog, forum and online shop, every pain point on the Internet can be used as a scene. On the subway and bus, young people reading information with mobile phones are everywhere and they can do nothing when the phone constantly has a weak signal. Math Paper Press, a Singapore-based book publisher, used this scene to embed passages from books into these offline pages. Users will see them and see the address of a bookstore when the network is broken, which can help them to kill time and bring business to bookstores.

THE OFFLINE BOOK

The case source quoted from: 360 Personal Library 2017/03/21
http://www.360doc.com/content/17/0321/21/32150962_638869080.shtml

can meet customers' real needs; whether customers really need the product and are in urgent need, and so on. (2) Making a scene-based price. Specifically, when consumers see products and prices, they believe the product is worth the price, and simply put, it is their expected price or meets the needs of their social status. Of course, the price should be marked in such a way that consumers can easily identify it.

Thirdly, it is the scene-based spread. A good product and its publicity are inseparable. For example, herbal tea drinks have been available in the market for several decades, but why has the explosive growth been in recent years? That is the previous advertising fails to set root in people's mind. Wong Lo Kat's advertising slogan "FEAR OF INTERNAL HEAT? DRINK WONG LO KAT!" directly and effectively expresses their demands.

Moreover, why does only Wahaha Nutrition Express have the annual sales of over 20 billion even though there are so many milk-containing beverages? That is because they use the right scene of "A BOTTLE IN THE MORNING TO MAKE YOU REFRESHED ALL DAY", making consumers think of their own lives. Another example is Six Walnuts. Its promotional slogan, "THINK MORE, DRINK SIX WALNUTS MORE", clearly defines the scene and is easy for consumers to accept. It is not hard to see that the first half is about a scene, and the last half cuts into products or benefits.

Fourthly, it is the scene-based channel. That is to make the distribution channels an important venue for delivering the product information. After distributing products at all levels, scenes shall be created from product posters and pages to workplace layout and final promotions. In short, the scene-based channel is essential for a successful product.

In other words, the scene-based channel strategy is to let channel providers know both the scene in which our products are sold, and the scene in which consumers use.

Systematic implementation, however, is the most important thing of the scene marketing strategy. The scene-based product is like the foundation, the scene-based spread like the leaves, and the scene-based channel like the branches of a tree. Only when they are closely complementary with each other, the big tree of scene marketing strategy will thrive.

In the design of a scene, especially in a relatively closed environment, it is necessary to make full use of psychological cues, and to exploit customers' herd mentality with some details to receive the unexpected gains.

The environment suggestion that should not be neglected in the scene marketing design: the broken windows theory is a criminological theory introduced by James Q. Wilson and George L. Kelling after observation and says that the environment can be strongly suggestive and inducible to a person.

Broken windows theory: when a window glass in a building is shattered but is not timely repaired, others may get some kind of hint and then break more windows.

Human behavior is affected by the environment, and many things in our daily lives are results of actions suggested and induced by the environment. For example, we would subconsciously keep quiet and lower our voices instead of speaking loudly in a quiet library; on the contrary, in a vegetable market with a noisy environment, people speak loudly and litter.

Therefore, when conducting a marketing activity and setting up the scene, we can guide user behavior by making the best of environment construction, thus reaching the marketing purpose. For example, in a parent-kid place where there is happy music, colorful setting, sweet and kid-friendly food, and various toys, people will immediately behave like children to go with the scene atmosphere.

We can be said to live in an era in which the information is seriously excessive, with the most saturated and numbing stimuli; people always feel they don't have enough time and are always in a hurry, with different matters grabbing their attention, and they have no more energy to fully think about every piece of information to make a decision; most of the time, it is not information itself that makes people make decisions, but the background and situation thereof. This is why it has become difficult to persuade users by presenting the facts and reasoning things out.

Therefore, one-sided emphasis on how good the product is should be avoided during scene design, because only user recognition makes the product really good.

Presenting the facts and reasoning things out is now quite a blunt promotion method and a method that tends to impose ideas, but people now reject compulsory and didactic methods.

Laozi said in the Tao Te Ching, "A person of great virtue is like the flowing water. Water benefits all things and contends not with them. It puts itself in a place that no one wishes to be and thus is closest to Tao", which stresses that "a person of great virtue is like the flowing water" and gentleness overcomes strength. According to Laozi, water acts according to the natural way; therefore, there is nothing that it will not accomplish; it has no shape, but goes everywhere; it performs effortlessly according to the natural way without its desire, and practices the wordless teaching through its deeds. This does not only stress the way of conducting oneself in society, but also can be used in our marketing activities and scene design.

I want to mention two things here: social proof theory and psychological suggestion.

Social proof: it is the conformity (following the crowd) and one of the basic principles of human behavior; it means that people's behavior is largely shaped by the behaviors of others around them, especially those with whom they strongly identify. This is the root of the word-of-mouth marketing that is popular at present. The strength of social proof often trumps rational cognition. The conformity comes from the human motivations: the motivation to make accurate decisions as efficiently as possible, the motivation to affiliate with and to gain the approval of others, and the motivation to see oneself in a positive light.

Some behaviors in daily lives: users see how many people have bought an item and how the reviews are during online shopping as the reference for their own buying; and read reviews and ratings of movie or restaurant when they see a movie or go to a restaurant. In this society overloaded with information, looking at "what others do" is often a correct and efficient shortcut.

Next, let's see some methods used consciously or unconsciously in enterprise marketing at present. For example, a charity organization would immediately mark the donation amount and donator's name; a street performer would put some changes in the box; a training institution would say how many people have signed up when attracting new students, and show you the thick pile of registration forms; those people who are enjoying the lighting and music of a bar would affect the late-comers.

Psychological suggestion: means subtly impressing and inducing personal subconscious through various media; indirectly instilling anything into the minds of others without starting a controversy; impressing or inducing minds via gesture, symbol, language, speech, body movement, or environment, etc. Both broken window theory and conformity are outward expressions of psychological suggestion.

In the environment design of a scene, suggestions can fully start from eyes, ears, nose, tongue, body, or mind of people: both external sense organs and internal psychology guide user behavior. Psychological suggestion should be fully used in the scene design, especially in a relatively closed environment, to grasp the conformity of users from design of some details, which would often achieve unexpected effects.

Fifthly, "providing consumers with correct information at the right time and in the right place" is the ideal state marketers have been pursuing and has become the ultimate goal the scene marketing needs to achieve in the post-mobile Internet era. In a word, there has been a more advanced play of the scene marketing promoted at present, with mobile Internet development and data and technology upgrading: actively providing consumers with solutions by deeply exploring user

demands and pain spots; reconstructing new usage scenes online and offline, to eliminate disadvantages of the traditional communication mode, create new marketing opportunities from nothing, and open broad space for later development.

Then the way to get closest to this ideal state is to build a scene marketing ecosystem that is based on the mobile Internet social platform, to digitalize offline marketing scenes and intelligently link online mobile marketing scenes, to eventually gather users to the marketing automation cloud service platform, and to form a complete marketing ecosystem that is physically closed.

Under the entire ecosystem, the marketing, based on the judgment of demands of consumers in the current environment, will deeply explore user demands and pain sports; get through different channels, and conduct labeling, data analysis, and portrait of population in the scene, with online and offline mobile socializing separately working and connecting each other, to eventually complete marketing interaction.

To be clear, what scene marketing pursues is win-win cooperation instead of monopoly, meaning that the scene marketing should be shaped together by traditional enterprises, e-commerce enterprises, and consumers, to not only continue to deepen advantages and value of scene marketing, but also connect upstream and downstream to promote interconnection development of scene marketing, and drive the entire ecosystem.

New Retail in the Context of Mobile Internet

New Retail: Innovative Marketing Channels and Scenes

In essence, the retail is to meet the needs of consumers anytime and anywhere, while the new retail, with the customer as the center, is to improve transaction efficiency by combining online and offline platforms. As a new model, the new retail is a reconstruction from "goods-field-people" to "people-goods-field", with the logistics as a link. The online retail and offline retail now are complementing instead of competing, producing bidirectional closed-loop traffic.

Before introducing the new retail, let me give you a history. In 1588, the British

fleet defeated the Spanish Armada and opened the era of British maritime hegemony. This is a famous naval battle. In the battle, the Spaniards though they had an absolute advantage in military strength and had managed to win, for they had 30,000 soldiers while the British fleet had 15,000 soldiers.

However, this figure cannot be scrutinized because the ratio of the army to the navy in the Spanish fleet was 3:1 and the British fleet was just the opposite, i.e., 1:3. So, most soldiers of the Spanish fleet were the army, and the rest of them were the navy who were only responsible for paddling. It is easy to see that the so-called

Spanish Armada was actually only a means of transport. It is essentially an army. However, most of the soldiers of the British fleet were highly skilled in sailing.

Therefore, they had different behaviors in the war. The Spaniards always wanted to hook the British ships over so that their soldiers could jump to the ship to kill them. But for the British, they maneuvered the ship in the waves to repeatedly row through and to kill the Spaniards with artilleries on board.

Witnesses said that the Spanish ships were full of blood and that many Spaniards who had gathered on the deck waiting to rush onto the British ship had become live targets. Of course, casualties were heavy.

It is known from the destruction of the Spanish Armada that the navy did not mean soldiers on board, and a new mode of the naval battle had already formed. Later, the British troops also relied on this new naval battle concept to defeat France, a land power, and won France's colonies in North America.

This history is quoted here to describe the changes that the new retail may bring. New retail is like the evolution of British naval thinking in the 16th century. Different from any retail revolution in the past, it really integrates data and business logic to truly provide consumers with more than expected "acquisition". The new retail will bring the Internet technology to traditional retail modes, reshape the value chain and create companies that are efficient and have zero-inventory and real-time access to user needs, resulting in new service providers and forming new retail mode.

New Retail

I. New Retail from Online to Offline

What is "New Retail"?

The term "new retail" was first coined by Ma Yun at the Cloud Habitat Conference 2016. He said that pure e-commerce would become a traditional business and would be replaced by the new retail in the next one or two decades. In other words, only combination of the online and the offline and logistics can create truly new retail. Specifically, the enterprises which have physical stores must start online businesses and the enterprises which deal with online shops must open up physical stores to create a truly new retail by fully using modern logistics.

Since then, Zhang Yong, CEO of Alibaba, has enriched this concept – "the new retail cannot be narrowly understood as interactions between and integrations of the online and the offline, and other than the omnichannel that is a part of the new retail, the cyberstar economy, user interaction behavior based on personalized recommendation, changes in customer movement and other elements should be included in the new retail concept. In marketing, it is necessary to explore the Uni-marketing and entertainment marketing for the purpose of effective branding; in logistics, we must not only pursue fast delivery, but also consider using big data to make the transport of goods more efficient."

In addition, the Opinions on Promoting the Transformation of Physical Retail Innovation released by the General Office of the State Council of the People's Republic of China at the end of 2016 provides, "Promote online and offline integration, encourage online and offline businesses to integrate market resources through various forms such as strategic cooperation, cross-shareholdings, mergers and acquisitions and restructuring, and cultivate new types of market players that integrate online and offline development.... establish socialized and market-oriented data application mechanism, encourage e-commerce platforms to conditionally open data resources to physical retail enterprises, and improve resource allocation efficiency and operational decision-making."

Therefore, as a relatively large concept, the new retail involves a lot, including sales, supply chain, logistics, warehousing, marketing, membership, distribution, payment, data and other links.

JD Logistics Group was set up by JD Group to provide the following services and authorized with more independent management and decision-making power:

(1) Supply chain services including warehousing, transportation, distribution, customer service, and integrated supply chain solutions for reverse logistics;

(2) Cloud + logistics technology services, including logistics cloud, logistics technology, and vendor data services;

(3) Cross-border logistics services; and

(4) Express and delivery service.

JD Logistics Group, however, focuses on its customers of convenience stores.

B2B mode in FMCG has become a hot spot for investment institutions. JD announced the formation of JD New Path in 2015. In March this year, it announced increased investments in B2B businesses.

In addition, Ali also launched the Ali retail platform in 2016 and JinHuoBao, Huimin, etc. also attempted the B2B mode in FMCG.

In 2016, the Be & Cheery, a business with sales value up to CNY 2.7 billion, decided to return to the offline market, and it was announced that the sales value would reach CNY 10 billion within three years, largely depending on continuing the distribution of supermarket channels and officially launching the "one city and one shop" plan in the future. For a long time, the Be & Cheery, together with the Liang-pin Shop and the Three Squirrels, have

been regarded as the three major brands of casual snacks e-commerce.

In 2016, Xiaomi began to conduct offline retail businesses and announced that it plans to extend its channels to offline by 2020 and open at least 1,000 retail stores.

So far this year, Dangdang has opened 143 offline bookstores and it plans to open 1000 stores in the next three years.

In 2016, the "Three Squirrels" also opened the "Three Squirrels Feeding Store", a physical store. It plans to open 1,000 offline stores because offline store is actually more profitable than online ones.

GOME officially renamed as Gome Retail according to its announcement released on May 15, 2017. The Announcement said that Gome will be transformed from an electrical appliance retailer to an appliance-led solution provider, depending on the supply chain, new scenes and post-services to upgrade new retail strategies.

Wanda, which has the largest physical business resources in the country, takes Feifan.com as a strategic project of the Group and has spent CNY 5 billion to build the world's largest O2O platform.

 **Case Study**

Full Disclosure of Hema Fresh Store: How Does Alibaba's New Retail Example Come Into Being?

2017 was a year of transition in the retail industry. As one of the industries hit hardest by the Internet, retailers know that only the "Internet Plus" can make them survive. Traditional retailers have tried new ways such as self-media, mobile shopping malls, and experiential consumption to advance new retail businesses.

The first store in Shanghai has made profits.
Source: Hema Fresh Store Official Website

Driven by this tidal wave, Internet giants have rushed around and took actions. The Millennials are also becoming the target of retailers and mobile payment providers.

Specifically, Alibaba incubated the Hema Fresh Store, operated under a new business mode; JD has

cooperated with the giants Wal-Mart and Yonghui, and Tencent led two rounds of investment in Miss Fresh…

Of which, the Hema Fresh Store, with a good consumer reputation and an innovative business mode, has expanded rapidly over the past one and a half year since its opening. Sounding like "hippo" in Chinese, it is indeed merging with the surrounding fresh markets like a hippo.

According to the data, as the forefront explorer in this field, the Hema Fresh Store has achieved initial success in the complex model of Internet-driven and offline experience. The first store in Shanghai has made profits, exploring a road to maximize advantages for retail industries with trillions of output value in the course of the Internet-fueled transformation.

For Alibaba, incubation of the Hema Fresh Store is the first step in its goal of new retail. In the age of SOLOMO in the future, social + local + mobile will be indispensable.

Consumer fragmented shopping decisions, accordingly, should be WYSIWYG, and goods should also be received in a fragmented way after shopping. If the traditional method of picking products in the physical supermarket is regarded as the age of one-dimensional shopping, the online selection and logistics delivery model is the age of two-dimensional shopping and

Hema Fresh Store is an experience store for Alipay membership.

Hema provides the freshest products of the day of vegetables, meat and milk.

Source: Hema Fresh Store Official Website

Alibaba's Hema Fresh Store + Amoy a new dimensional exploration mode of the new retail.

The study of Hema Fresh Store cannot only facilitate fundamentally analyzing the current new retail benchmarking companies, but also understanding the meaning of the new retail as an example.

Creation

The Hema Fresh Store was initially launched by Hou Yi, head of JD Logistics, in Shanghai as a fresh supermarket. After Alibaba's full involvement, Hou Yi developed a supermarket distribution system and called out "traditional supermarkets + takeaways + Hema App". He put forward a new concept of retail delivery service within half an hour in the range of 5 km (current distribution range of Hema Fresh Store is 3 km around the store), and from then on, the coverage radius and sales efficiency of a single store have been improved several times.

With a rapid iterative upgrade of the new retail mode, the expansion of Hema Fresh Store is also accelerating. According to the plan, Hema Fresh Store will adopt a model of self-operation + joint ventures. In the future, more than 2,000 stores will be opened in more than 30 cities in China.

As of now, a total of 13 Hema Fresh stores have already been launched in three cities, namely Shanghai, Beijing and Ningbo, with ten ones in Shanghai, two in Beijing, and one in Ningbo.

Layout

Hema Fresh Store is positioned as a supermarket integrating the online and offline worlds with big data, specifically:

Offline experience store to pull online sales;

Targeting 80s and 90s young consumers;

Provision of a 30-minute delivery service within a radius of 3 km of the store.

Quality

Unlike ordinary supermarkets, as a boutique supermarket mainly selling fresh products, Hema Fresh Store:

Provides the freshest products of the day of vegetables, meat and milk;

Adopts the "Raw-Cooked Food Linkage" and "Cooked-Raw Food Linkage" modes;

Guarantees all foods are traceable for the purpose of food safety;

Guarantees an unconditional refund.

Membership

In order to cultivate the customer mobile payment habits, Hema Fresh Store accepts the Hema Fresh Store App as the only payment portal. Consumers must download and register Hema app membership to complete the payment before they use Alipay.

In this sense, Hema Fresh Store is actually an experience store for Alipay membership, and the "membership card" is a Hema app that is bound to Alipay. Therefore, although the use of Hema app brings Hema Fresh Store criticism, for Hema Fresh Store, the app is the basis for its establishment.

Hema app has such features as screening users (who are accustomed to using mobile payment), access (the payment cannot be made without the app), payment (binds the Alipay account), and binding users (post-sale and coupon exchange), driving offline users to make online shopping.

This will not only help users get used to using Hema app and Alipay, but also obtain their data and conduct definite marketing based on preferences and spending habits.

In addition, with the app, the delivery services can be extended to customers within a radius of 3 km. After all, for Hema Fresh Store, the physical store is only for the experience, and online sales are the main business.

However, since the media and retail counterparts questioned the illegality of not accepting cash, after a TV station reported on that, Hema Fresh Store set up a cash checkout desk, but the salespersons still promote the payment with Hema app by using coupons and other methods.

The case source quoted from: Huxiu.com 2017/07/31
https://www.huxiu.com/article/207761.html

II. New Retail from Offline to Online

1. How to play New Retail offline?

Ye Guofu at MINISO can be taken as a representative of offline retail. According to him, New Retail centers on products and improves customer experience and operation efficiency by using new technology. Currently, the annual sales of Uniqlo are CNY 120 billion, that of IKEA are CNY 275 billion, and that of MINISO are CNY 10 billion upon only three years of development.

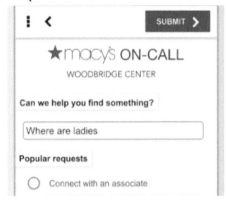

Figure 18-4　Macy's On-Call in-store intelligent shopping guide-"Macy's ON-CALL Woodbridge Center". Source: Baidu Baike

Online sales of those enterprises are insignificant. According to some entrepreneurs, New Retail is not simply "online + offline" combination, but centers on products, provides customers with shopping experiences with high user experience and high cost performance using new technologies like Internet and artificial intelligence, and vertically integrates the value chain from R&D, design, production, logistics, to terminal, to create bigger value and increase operation efficiency. As people's demands become increasingly simple, rational, and efficient, only well-chosen, quality, and low-priced commodities will satisfy most people.

Memory Mirror In Uniqlo. Source: Baidu Baike

Then, what does centering on products mean? According to Ye Guofu, most enterprises should build extremely cost-effective products in the future. Then how to build such products? His method is "three-high" and "three-low": high physical attractiveness, high quality, and high efficiency; low cost, low gross margin, and low price.

2. Trend of New Retail: Self-transformation of traditional commerce

Compared to the rapidly changing innovative business format, the traditional commerce has very tenacious vitality. Traditional commerce still has great competitiveness no matter in commercial layout, technical strength, or staffing, after brand battle, channel competition, and resource scramble.

Since the development of e-commerce, traditional commerce has long lost its past glory, with wave after wave of store closures making people sigh; however, traditional commerce has started to spend efforts in many channels to timely stop loss and transform, in the boom of New Retail.

Take the U.S. traditional commerce for instance, in order to optimize the in-store shopping experience of consumers, Macy's, after closing nearly 200 stores, cooperated with IBM's Watson AI assistant in 2016 to launch the Macy's On-Call in-store intelligent shopping guide service based on AI technology (see Figure 18-4).

Such in-store service, the intelligent shopping guide, by analysis of geographic location accurate to the counter location, could answer consumers' frequently asked questions on commodity stock and navigation, etc., and match and recommend commodities according to consumers' preferences. On-call system will also become smarter and more intelligent with use.

Uniqlo and high-end department store Neiman Marcus have worked with the AR startup MemoMi to install AR dressing mirror: Memory Mirror in the store.

This "magic mirror" will help build user profiles according to customers' body shape data. Customers don't need to pick and try clothes in a flurry, as the mirror will display color suggestion, style, and collocation suggestion in real time; if a customer is unable to decide on the purchase, he/she can send his/her own trying video to mailbox via Memory Mirror, and then decide whether to place an order online after watching it at home.

III. Drivers of the Birth of New Retail

1.　Technology foundation

On the one hand, the infrastructure that includes information platform, payment platform, logistics platform, and cloud computing has been preliminarily built; on the other hand, the popularity of smartphones, upgrading of mobile communication network, and mature application of mobile payment technology have also provided the foundation of development of New Retail.

In the future, data analysis technology, map technology, and indoor and outdoor location technology, etc. will help B-end and C-end to mutually understand supply and demand, thus to make C2B flexible manufacturing possible; machine vision technology will provide solutions for unmanned retail; AR/VR technology can provide offline consumption experience with online and offline integration; the IoT and WT will electronize information of any commodities in the circulation, to truly integrate logistics, information flow, and fund flow; the block chain technology can solve the basic business issues like B-end or C-end identity authentication, credit guarantee, contracts, and settlement.

On the "Double Eleven" in 2017, according to the data provided by Ant Financial, the payment peak of Alipay reached 256,000 amounts per second at 00:05:22 on November 11, 2.1 times that in 2016, and the database processing peak reached 42 million times per second. At 00:12:00 on November 11, a buyer in Jiading District, Shanghai received the snacks he just bought, which were delivered from the nearest smart warehouse, preliminarily realizing "goods go ahead of orders".

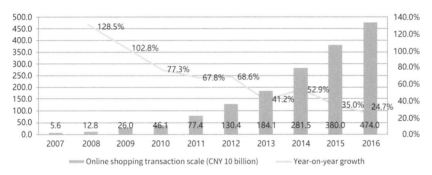

The payment peak of Alipay On the "Double Eleven" in 2017.
Source: Sohu.com

2.　Bottoming out of online traffic dividend

As growth of the e-commerce industry slows down, the online traffic dividend of e-commerce enterprises gradually bottoms out, and the pure e-commerce income hits the ceiling; with the gradual increase of online shopping user penetration, the online customer acquisition cost largely increases. Therefore, exploiting new profit growth point requires going offline, and achieving online and offline omnichannel integration.

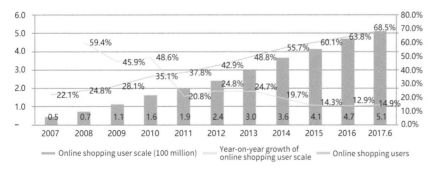

The e-commerce industry slows down.
Source: Sohu.com

3. Sluggish brick–and–mortar retail industry

It is now a critical period for brick-and-mortar retail to decide "store closure to stop loss" or "upgrading and transformation". Wanda Department Store, Parkson, and Central Department Store, etc. have begun to reduce physical stores, and the department store giant Wangfujing has said goodbye to department store and announced shifting focus to shopping centers and outlets; Guangzhou Friendship based on high-end imported commodities has changed its main business to "department store + finance".

A portion of operating costs increased in retail enterprises could be passed on to consumers by price increase in the past; however, in the Internet age, commodity prices are more transparent, making it more difficult to pass on such portion. Therefore, price increase of some offline stores is held back, and some physical stores with lagged management have to close stores to stop loss, or conduct upgrading and transformation, to seek process optimization.

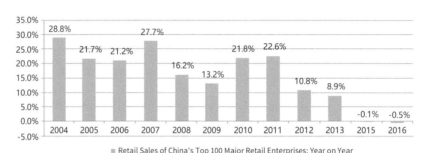

■ Retail Sales of China's Top 100 Major Retail Enterprises: Year on Year

Sluggish brick-and-mortar retail industry.
Source: Sohu.com

4. Consumption upgrade at the cru–cial moment of real implementation

People's demand for consumption upgrade has been rising in recent years with improvement of their consumption level. Since the development, e-commerce has seen great dividends while bringing convenience to people's lives. The appetite of consumers has become increasingly picky after experiencing the impact of offline shopping and convenience of online shopping.

According to the statistical data of the Ministry of Commerce of China, the online retail sales declined year by year since 2010. Many e-commerce platforms including Taobao discovered that pure e-commerce has become difficult to continue to convince consumers to make purchases since 2014.

At this time, the only thing that can stimulate consumers is the consumption experience improvement, which requires merchants to put in time and energy on architecture of sales logic, and consumption experience transformation, utilize current online and offline resources, and make consumption upgrade own advantage and competitiveness.

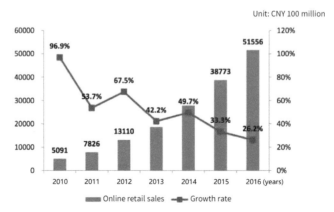

The online retail sales has declined since 2010.
Source: Baidu Baike

IV. New retail brings revolution

1. Consumption revolution

The age of consumer sovereignty has arrived.

With the development of science and technology and the continuous improvement of production and transaction efficiency, the consumption form in China has been changing from Consumption 1.0 to Consumption 4.0.

(1) Consumption 1.0 - Planned consumption.

Under the planned economic system, both market supply and demand are strictly controlled, and a large number of articles for daily use are subject to the quota system, which are exchanged through food coupon, clothing coupon, kerosene coupon and other media. Consumers are passive in the planned consumption. The commodities are scarce in category and narrow in selection scope, so the demands of consumers are difficult to be satisfied. The retail channel is mainly in the form of supply and marketing cooperatives based on counter sales.

(2) Consumption 1.0 - Free to purchase.

With the reform of the economic system and the continuous development of the productive forces, the disposable income of people and the production capacity have been continuing to increase. The consumption model of supply and marketing cooperatives has been increasingly unable to meet people's daily consumption life. China has learned from western developed countries to build such retail formats as department stores, supermarkets and convenience stores. As commodities have become diversified in sales and purchase channels, and the supply and demand have been gradually balanced, the basic consumer demand has been met, consumers are basically free to purchase, and shopping is much more convenient.

(3) Consumption 3.0 - Quality consumption.

The society has entered an era of abundant economy with excessive production and increasingly enriched commodities, so the supply has begun to exceed demand.

As the material civilization and life are greatly enriched, people's consumption concepts have changed to pursue the quality of consumption and focus on service and experience. There are large numbers of retail formats emerging to meet the diverse quality consumption demands, such as franchised stores, membership stores and shopping centers.

(4) Consumption 4.0 - Personalized consumption.

In the Internet age, the post-1980, 1990 and even 2000 generations have become the main consumption groups. With the rise of individuals and the diversifying of user demands, a long tail trend shows up, and the consumption upgrading prompts more consumers to pursue commodities with added value. Quality, aesthetics and even personal identity have all become the driving forces of consumption. More and more people are purchasing products or services for preferences rather than needs. Nowadays, consumers are paying more attention to personalization, emotionalization and socialization. With the change of consumer motives, the standardized but "cold" products are gradually being replaced by the "warm" customized and nonstandard products. Consumers are more likely to "waste time on good things". As an online saying goes, "In terms of tea, users are no longer paying for daily necessities but for entertainment and luxury."

New features of new consumption.

(1) The consumption demand has changed from a 20/80 Principle to Long Tail Effect[①].

In the economic society of shortage, the distribution of commodity sales follows the 20/80 Principle, that is, 20% of commodities dominate 80% of the market shares, so standardized products with good reputation and quality can dictate the market. For example, Kelon

> ①
>
> *Long Tail Effect: "Head" and "tail" are two statistical terms. The protruding part in the middle of the normal curve is called "head", while the relatively gentle parts on both sides are called "tails". From the perspective of people's demand, most of the demand will be concentrated in the head which is called "popular", while the demand distributed in the tails are personalized and fragmented small demand. These differentiated and small demands will form a long "tail" in the demand curve. Long Tail Effect lies in its quantity, which will accumulate all non-popular markets into a market larger than the popular market.*

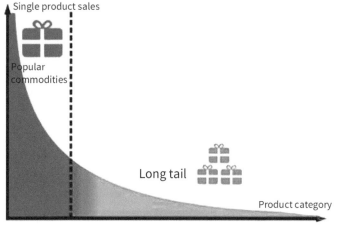

Long Tail Effect.
Source: Baidu Library

air-conditioner, Haier refrigerator and Santana car occupied half of the segment market, and almost became synonymous with their categories.

In the economic society of abundance, commodity sales are presenting the trend of Long Tail Effect. There are popular commodities as shown on the Head as well as massive commodities as shown on the long Tail which are segmented into different profit-based markets. Commodities on the Head and those on the Tail almost occupy equal market shares, and Commodities on the Tail may even cover more market share. For example, the current market of smart phones is a typical long tail market. In 2016, 74 kinds of mobile phones launched in offline channels of Chinese Mainland. Top selling models, such as iPhone7 and Mate8, became the Head of the market, while other mobile phone brands, including Gionee, Letv, Coolpad, ZTE and

DOOV, are the Tail, which forms a typical Long Tail shape.

Although the dominating Haier refrigerator is still No.1 in market share, its market share has gradually declined to 16.9% in 2016. Apparently, the 20/80 Principle is gradually out of date.

From the perspective of consumption, the demand will be concentrated on the Head and form popular commodities, while on the Tail are personalized and fragmented demand. These differentiated and small demands will form a long "tail" in the demand curve, which will accumulate all markets into a market larger than the popular market. This is the so-called Long Tail Effect. The Long Tail Effect is a phenomenon in the society of abundance, where the Head alone cannot satisfy user needs, while the Tail alone will lead users into a completely strange world with no way to start. 20/80 Principle and Long Tail Effect are compared as follows in Figure 18-5.

Product features	20/80 Principle	Long Tail Effect
Development period	Consumption 1.0/2.0	Consumption 3.0/4.0
Economic background	Scarce in resources	Abundant economy
Market-oriented	Seller market	Buyer market
Customer service	Popular demand	Personalized requirements

Figure 18-5   20/80 Principle and Long Tail Effect are compared. Source: Baidu Library

(2) Consumption scene: Channel revolution.

Channels are the carrier of retail, the medium between consumers and commodities, and the last mile of the supply chain. With the development of economy, advancement of productivity, innovation of science and technology, and upgrading of consumption, the reform of the retail industry and retail channels has been continuously promoted. Up to now, the evolution process can be divided into five stages: department store stage, chain store stage, supermarket stage, shopping center stage and non-store operation stage.

From the perspective of evolution process, there are two development trends in retail channels: the first trend is fragmentation with the sinking of channels and the continual dispersal and reconstruction of consumption scenes, which have greatly improved the convenience of shopping. In recent years, small business formats, such as convenience stores, boutiques and membership and experience stores, have experienced rapid development, which are

evidenced by the expansion of Meiyijia, Family Mart and SEVEn-ELEVEn. The second trend is centralization. With the further concentration of channels, continual aggregation of consumption scenes and diversification of shopping experience, large business formats (including shopping malls and commercial streets) continue to grow and expand, which contribute to the vigorously growing trend of Wanda Plaza and other large commercial complexes.

(3) Consumption connection: From "price" to "taste"

In the age of consumer 1.0, it was still the planned economy rather than the market economy. Generally, commodities had value but not market prices, and products were mostly based on distribution rather than trading. In the age of consumer 2.0, "price" was the most important consideration in purchase decision. The market was fully in line with the supply and demand curve in western economics, that is, demand decreases as price increases, and supply increases as price increases. Therefore, cheap and high-quality commodities were most popular, and cheap commodities will prevail. In the age of consumer 3.0, "quality" became a key factor in decision-making. The improvement of material civilization and life has driven the consumption upgrading. High-quality and excellent service became the selling point of commodities. Users were no longer blindly pursuing low prices, and high quality surpassed cheap prices. In the age of consumer 4.0, "personality" became the contact point of transaction. As the massive consumption turned to be more and more personalized, the Ford practice of "any color so long as it is black" in the era of industrialization is no longer feasible. Consumers need personalized products that are not only functionally satisfying a certain pain point, but also emotionally connecting to them.

IP-based products have become the transformation direction for retail objects, which shall include the following three levels: In the physical level, the product must be useful and have at least three differences in function. In the chemical level, it should be able to interact with the users joyfully. In the social level, it shall be sentient (i.e., have feelings), so as to create the cultural and emotional resonance points and form a community of common value.

2. Supply chain revolution

In the past 10 years, great changes have taken place in the Chinese market. On the supply side, the prosperity of large-scale manufacturing has promoted material progress. The commodity shortage era with high demand has evolved into a commodity excess era with fierce competition. On the demand side, the rapid development of the Internet has broken the information barriers, and has turned the world into a global village. With a wide range of experience and knowledge, consumers become more rational and mature in face of bombing products, and generate higher demand.

Under such circumstances, most suppliers and channel providers are still resting on the past practices and try to maintain the "high rate" business model, which obviously cannot keep pace with the market.

However, MINISO has taken a quite different practice. On one hand, from the perspective of qualitative analysis, the buyers of commodity centers are mainly young women in first consumption tier, so it is easier to develop products from the perspective of consumers. On the other hand, the big data platform based on Internet technology has made it possible to quantitatively analyze consumer demand. The data feedback on the sales volume and best-selling products can be generated the next day, which means the store can at least begin to analyze consumer demand with scientific methods. More accurate development means fewer deviations and investment errors as well as more effective profitability.

The traditional supply chain relationship has been burdened with complex intermediate links and high logistics cost, but the manufacturers, channel distributors and brand owners lack the motivation to change. As shown in the following flow chart:

The traditional supply chain relationship.
Source: Linkshop

MINISO has invested a lot of money to build its own distribution centers and storage logistics systems, so as to achieve direct access from factory to shop.

The supply relationship of new retail can provide timely replenishment, reduce losses, reuse package materials, control costs and lower prices. As shown in the following flow chart:

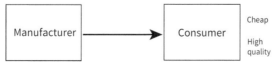

The supply relationship of new retail.
Source: Linkshop

The importance of warehousing for retail companies is reflected in the smoothness and bearing capacity of logistics. In a word, "After putting commodities in storage, how to get them on and off from the shelves as soon as possible and deliver them immediately? If not, the process will be blocked." The logistics process carries too much cash flow and information. In the process of loading, commodities will be sorted and shipped to the cargo container piece by piece according to the planning and coordination data and the order demand of each store. When delivering, commodities will be unloaded at each and every store according to the amount in the shipment order. In the areas with geographically concentrated stores, special vehicles will be arranged for distribution, and each vehicle is responsible for distributing to several stores. In the areas with scattered stores, commodities will be distributed with social logistics and carpool distribution channels to reduce costs.

Stores can work efficiently, but require high delivery frequency. On average, MINISO will arrange a delivery every two days, while daily delivery may be arranged for popular stores. Because the commodities sell well, the warehouse of the store is very small with average inventory only for two days. In some cases, the store may have no warehouse, and completely rely on the supply chain. The goods in the distribution center and in transit can support 15-day sales of the store; it is capable of delivering multiple times every day.

V. New logistics for new retail

Intelligent logistics[①]: Big data and AI lead to high speed of logistics, and multi-parties cooperation makes the transportation process more stable. The realization of Lightning Transport is based on sound storage layout. With the further development of e-commerce, especially the rapid rise of fresh e-commerce, the storage layout has become essential to many e-commerce platforms and logistics companies. Big data + AI have become the "Magic Key" to inventory problems of many related companies. For example, during the Tmall Double Eleven Day in 2017, Cainiao Logistics adopted the smart warehousing technology with big data. Based on the predictive information, popular commodities are deposited near consumers in advance, so the online shoppers can receive commodities from courier as soon as possible.

In simple terms, it can "foresee" things. As an official from Cainiao Logistics said, "according to the pre-sale data of Tmall Double Eleven Day and Cainiao Logistics, the top 10 commodities on Double Eleven Day were predicted to be sanitary napkins, laundry detergents, facial masks, biscuits, puffed food, drag tissues, roll tissues, pure milk and switch socket set, mainly concentrated on FMCG household items. These predicted popular products have been stored at the front warehouses of Cainiao Logistics in advance." As a technology expert from Cainiao Logistics said, "These front warehouses are spread across multiple cities in China, and are the closest warehouses to consumers. When the consumer places an order, the front warehouse will begin to deliver immediately, so the delivery efficiency is greatly improved."

With the speeding-up of delivery, how to improve the freight quality has also become a hot topic for many logistics companies. With the increasing types of online shopping products, there is no doubt that the universal express delivery cannot meet diversified logistics needs. Therefore, many logistics companies began to cooperate with third-party platforms to create refined logistics with their special advantages.

On Double Eleven Day in 2017, SF Express cooperated with Gooday, a long-established company in large-scale logistics, to provide safe delivery service for furniture and home appliances that are bulky, heavy and easily damaged. In terms of end distribution, SF Express cooperated with Gome and other platforms to provide users with such end services as delivery and installation. SF Express announced in its official website that it will strive to achieve unlimited delivery for shipments under 100KG. The occurrences of parcel accumulation, product mismatches and unattended installations have been greatly reduced.

Smart warehousing: logistics robots are playing significant roles, and unmanned warehousing has grown from small-scale application to full bloom.

① Intelligent logistics (ILS): It was first proposed by IBM. In December 2009, it was jointly proposed by the Information Center of China Logistics Technology Association, China Internet of Things and the editorial office of Logistics & Material Handling. Logistics is a dynamic state of material goods (such as commodities) in the change of space and time.

On every Double Eleven Day, there have emerged various "black technologies" in warehousing and logistics, and now the most popular AI technology will also be used in the logistics industry. Logistic robots can autonomously sort and pick up products, and even build warehouses. The former single application will be expanded to large-scale application.

Green Logistics[1]: Shared Express Box and Decomposable Express Box are put into centralized application for the first time.

For logistics companies, the rising packaging cost has undoubtedly brought tremendous pressure. On the Double Eleven Day in 2018, many logistics companies began to focus on green logistics. They are trying to reduce transportation costs as well as ease the increasing environmental pressure.

During the Double Eleven Day, JD.com has launched recyclable packaging bags that were sealed with drawstrings. After the consumer has taken the goods from Jingdong self-pick-up site, the delivery staff would collect the bag and return it to the warehouse for another packaging. JD.com currently has put into use thousands of recyclable bags in the distribution link, and plans to invest millions in the future.

Cainiao Logistics, an affiliated company of Alibaba, plans to enable 20 green warehouses in the world, which will use tape-free delivery boxes and 100% biodegradable delivery bags. In addition, during the Double Eleven Day, Cainiao Logistics will also initiate a full carton recycling plan at the Cainiao sites in key cities. "As an official from Cainiao Logistics said, at the Cainiao sites in Jinan, Beijing, Shanghai, Guangzhou, Shenzhen and other cities, consumers can choose to leave the boxes at site after unpacking."

Since 2016, Cainiao Logistics has cooperated with 32 logistics partners in the world to explore green logistics. Cainiao Logistics set up the first environmental fund in the logistics industry in cooperation with the Ministry of Environmental Protection, which officially includes green logistics into national action. The high integration of online and offline stores and logistics is the core of new retail, and the Double Eleven Day has also become the actual practice of new retail.

At present, the new retail is the iteration of service quality and methods, and also the change of consumption patterns brought about by the scientific and technological means. The AI, robotics and big data are just a microcosm of business intelligence, which will not just be used in e-commerce. In the future, these technologies will be used and developed in our lives in a broader and more in-depth manner, and the Double Eleven Day will also become the science and technology competition between giant corporations.

① *Green Logistics: From the perspective of management, green logistics refers to the green economy management activities for effective and fast green goods and services that overcome the constraints of space and time, so as to achieve customer satisfaction and connect green demand subjects with green supply subjects. The word "green" in Green Logistics is a specific metaphorical word. It refers to the embodiment of activities, behaviors, plans, ideas and concepts that are to protect the ecological environment in logistics and its management activities.*

A Supply Chain Ecosystem - the New Retail Mode of Home Apparel Created by Dangxiapin

As the traditional apparel industry is facing varied challenges including constant impact of mobile Internet and consumption upgrade, how the emerging apparel industry uses the scientific concept of industrial development to explore innovative strategies and balance the growth of the brand production and the decline in market operations and how the industry uses the Internet and attracts consumers through communities will be the key to future marketing.

Dangxiapin, for example, has grown into the most influential brand in China's home apparel industry, by creating a new retail mode in which a supply chain ecosystem is built through integrating entrepreneurs, vendors, and consumer values, and has love and happiness as the core concepts.

For this purpose, Dangxiapin integrated the original basic systems with respect to production, business, customer, supplier, and supplier's resource through an innovative business model, linked the upstream and downstream industry chains and all its extended resources to build a new supply chain ecosystem and achieved online and offline integration with B2B2C2O (Internet + industry) model, in order to build a new business system between vendors and consumers, and this undermines the original simple relationship between them. Using the supply chain ecosystem to provide consumers with better value and experience is the key to the success of Dangxiapin.

1.   Model of Sharing Economy

In the age of Internet+, an increasing number of people use social networking tools to build social relations with other people via mobile terminals, and the distribution model, a kind of marketing, therefore, comes into being, in which product information is effectively spread through a large communication network between people, resulting in fission sales. In the sharing economy, vendors, buyers, and consumers have a closer relationship in which they may be the owner and the buyer.

Under the ecosystem built by Dangxiapin, vendors may quickly build and manage online distribution platforms in a way that allows each consumer to benefit from their own purchases and start a zero-cost venture.

With the big data analysis, Dangxiapin makes the business data flow completely traceable by each customer and for each order, and in addition, the fact that all goods are directly delivered to consumers puts an end to fake supplies.

2. Social Marketing

Under the ecosystem, each vendor can develop innovative and creative designs based on behavioral characteristics of different people in different communities by using the characteristics of social media (such as Microblog, BBS, public number, news, Weitao, and video), so as to brand the product, increase user loyalty and promote sales.

3. Overall Layout to Create a Supply Chain Ecosystem

Dangxiapin has made an overall layout, combining physical stores, platforms and self-media, with physical stores to provide customers with the best experience, the platforms to provide inlet flow and self-media and community interaction to improve user's stickiness, repurchase rate and entering rate. Through standardized technical services and Internet-based operation programs, vendors are provided with wide and extensive marketing strategies to create a new lifestyle for consumers.

Taking the establishment of the shared platform of supply chain ecosystem as its goal and main strategy, Dangxiapin has made all efforts to construct a unique and distinctive brand and eventually develop into an innovative business that leads the industry.

Application of 4S Theory in New Retail

Retail involves all details.

Four Formulas of New Retail: Once you understand MINISO, you will understand New Retail in China

2017 was termed as the first year of New Retail. In 2016, there was still no standard methodology for reference after the reforms of convenience stores, unmanned shelves, and offline supermarkets; knowing that the New Retail would revolutionize the structure and efficiency of the retail industry, enterprises still didn't know where to start; new projects were trapped in the supply chain and product creation, while traditional enterprises were constrained by marketing and operation bottlenecks.

In this chapter, four formulas of New Retail are summarized in combination with MINISO and other excellent New Retail cases to provide new thinking dimensions for the fission of New Retail enterprises from the perspectives of marketing, service, substance, and enterprise value, etc.

According to the law of the retail industry, once the rent is 15% higher than the performance, it will lead to loss.

Land is scarce and expensive in Hong Kong. Therefore, most people believe that opening a store in Hong Kong will definitely lose money with the monthly rent as high as CNY 300,000. However, the performance of MINISO reached over CNY 3 million in the first month after opening the store in Hong Kong, with the rent only accounting for 10% of the performance, showing very high profits.

Thereafter, MINISO opened 20 stores in Hong Kong within one year, and gradually went abroad. Presently, MINISO has become a brand with high popularity worldwide and expanded to over 170 countries and almost occupied the best locations of malls.

Compared with the overseas marketing environment, China is more expensive in every aspect, except that the labor is cheaper. Therefore, a store only might earn on average CNY 960,000 a year in Mainland China, but on average CNY 1.72 million a year overseas. And there are few changes in overseas commerce: the store brands in many malls in Europe, America, and Southeast Asia may stay the same for 10 years.

Retail Involves Details

Retail involves all details, including weight and cost of every shelf, and packaging and place of origin of every product. The more details are focused on, the higher the success rate will be. Many people cannot tell the differences of the shelves of ZARA, H&M, Walmart, and Watsons and don't know the most reasonable height of unmanned shelves. Actually, even the shelf heights and aisle widths of stores near schools and near office buildings are worth studying, which are the details many Internet people pay no attention to.

Is unmanned retail becoming the next battlefield of giants?

The key for the bucking the trend of MINISO and other excellent New Retail enterprises lies in the application of the following four New Retail formulas.

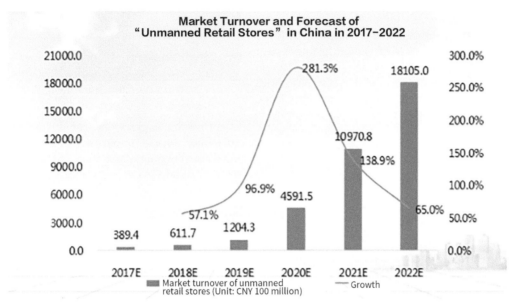

Market Turnover and Forecast of "Unmanned Retail Stores" in China in 2017–2022.
Source: Linkshop

I. Marketing performance formula: E (Earnings) = M (Merchandise)C² (Customer)

The first formula applies Einstein's mass-energy equation in marketing.

The marketing in the era of mobile Internet only needs to focus on two indicators: product and user, instead of price and channel.

According to the 4S Marketing Theory, service = product + user. The motivation for innovation is consumer demands. Only by introducing service into product can lead to the supreme product, and only by introducing service into users can result in the ultimate user experiences.

To build the supreme products, what consumers need and what are problems of consumers when using those products should be addressed. To solve consumers' problems, product innovation should be explored from users' consumer psychology and even deeply into their spirit. Your product will be popular around the world and loved by all consumers if it can move consumers' souls and have consumers find inner peace. Therefore, all products involve services.

1. Product is marketing: With the supreme product, marketing happens without extra effort

① Durex "only" won in ads while Okamoto won in products.

The performance of Okamoto was 1/10 of that of Durex in 2012, with profits as 1/3 of that of the latter; the performance of Okamoto was 1/3 of that of Durex in 2016, with profits flat with the latter; and Okamoto fully surpassed Durex in 2017.

In the era of consumption upgrade, Okamoto has upgraded user services and built supreme products with the idea of user service. The difference between supreme products and common products lies in that the former contain the idea and behavior of serving users. Therefore, all products involve services.

Okamoto 003. Source: Linkshop

Okamoto 003 achieved sales of CNY 1.7 billion in China, while Durex's sales in the same period were less than CNY 1 billion. Products of Okamoto underwent substantial changes since the introduction of 003 series, and the 002 and 001 series enjoyed hot sales after entering China, even causing the shortage of the products in Japan, whereas Durex had no revolutionary product in the last decade.

Durex has phenomenal marketing cases, with almost all gold and silver awards for the relevant ads won; however, no one makes money by marketing cases; everyone makes money by selling products.

People are not so impulsive to buy Durex, although its marketing is really good. For the same 10-piece pack, Okamoto costs CNY 98 while Durex costs CNY 50. People don't care much about the price difference in the era of consumption upgrade when they really like the products.

Therefore, enterprises should put products first in their operation. If products are not good enough, marketing will only be futile, no matter how much.

② Heytea: Most people want to copy how to become hot instead of how to do products

Heytea store. Source: Linkshop

"Inspiration of tea". Nie Yunchen, born in 1991, the founder of Heytea, has been adhering to innovation and making the supreme milk tea for over five years.

Heytea "seckilled" other beverage shops after its emergence, because it uses Starbucks model for the cashier, instead of McDonald's model. Heytea has built the user experiences into an interactive experience space that promotes the consumer engagement and loyalty.

In a Starbucks store, the customers queue horizontally to pay. Source: Linkshop

In a Starbucks store, the customers queue horizontally to pay, which can optimize the shopping experiences, reduce the labor cost, and make full use of the space to market the products.

In a McDonald's store, the customers queue vertically to pay. Source: Linkshop

In a McDonald's store, the customers queue vertically to pay, which can prompt the customers to make their decision ASAP, reduce the movement of service personnel, and increase the efficiency of both sides.

It's reported that the monthly sales of each store of Heytea has now exceeded CNY 1.50 million. Source: Linkshop

The customers can sit and wait after ordering, and the store offers some space and comfort, pays attention to customer experiences, combines with the traditional tea culture, and integrates Zen, minimalism, and aesthetics, etc.

It's reported that the monthly sales of each store of Heytea has now exceeded CNY 1.50 million. The sales per square meter per day of many stores of Heytea have now exceeded CNY 300, surpassing most restaurant stores. Heytea has relatively less investment. Therefore, its gross margin could reach above 50%.

Milk tea has a market that is worth hundreds of billions of CNY. Lipton and Xiangpiaopiao had taken much share; Starbucks wanted to copy its own success in coffee commercialization by spending heavily to acquire the tea brand Teavana but failed. The success of Heytea in fact lies in its product and system capacity that is far exceeding those of other milk tea and tea enterprises, with the high popularity being the premium and word-of-mouth effect brought by the height of quality. It took three years for Heytea to hone its products, with a dozen SKUs and three SPUs in total. So long as the products of Heytea are good enough, it will be unnecessary to worry about how many imitators there are, because most people do not put their hearts in products but think about marketing and promotion.

③ MINISO never did promotion, but the in-store purchase rate is up to 70%.

MINISO store. Source: Linkshop

MINOSO achieves the ultimate in products; for the same products, their prices are lower than those in other stores, and for the same prices, the quality is better. Suppliers of MINISO are all source factories, with perfume supplied by Chanel's factory Givaudan, eyeliner supplied by Dior's factory Intercos, and even the laundry detergent supplied by Blue Moon's factory.

In terms of product prices, MINISO achieves the overwhelming advantages. A characteristic about MINISO is that the users will not consider whether the goods of MINISO are too expensive.

In its overseas stores, the customers will get a basket from shop assistants when entering, and almost nobody leaves with the basket empty, with the in-store purchase rate achieving over 70%.

MINISO firmly grasps 200 suppliers which make money depending on stable orders, and orders of MINISO account for above 1/3 of many factories.

MINISO has never done promotion, but directly puts expenses for promotion in products to make prices a part of products.

2.   Principle of super user—users are channels: how to make users want to share on WeChat Moments?

Users are media and channels. A product that cannot make the users share on their WeChat Moments is definitely not a good product. Many people question whether some products of MINISO are losing money. Indeed, not all categories of MINISO make money; however, those that lose money will make users scream and share on WeChat Moments.

The shopping bag of MINISO is also one of its characteristics. In almost all malls, we can see people shopping with MINISO shopping bags. The 500 million shopping bags given away a year amount to 500 million mobile ads.

Hutaoli Music Restaurant & Bar has never done promotion, because Hutaoli provides screen occupation and has live music and wine worth only CNY 100, making users want to share on WeChat Moments.

Hutaoli Music Restaurant & Bar. Source: Linkshop

In Hutaoli, you can listen to live music free of charge, drink wine at hundreds of CNY, and spend only CNY 88 to occupy the big screen for 60 seconds. There is almost no item more than CNY on the menu of Hutaoli. With no pressure put on consumption, beautiful decoration, wine and music as the stimulant, and less than CNY 100 to watch a big screen and express love, the users are definitely willing to take photos and share on WeChat Moments.

Marketing should consider the perspective of users. You should reflect on yourself if your product fails to make users take photos and share on WeChat Moments.

II. Super product formula: S (Super Products) = NE (New Experiences) – OE (Old Experiences) – CC (Conversion Costs)

1. Hot sale item strategy of MINISO

Eyeliner is a hot sale item fostered from the side category market, with annual sales of 100 million pieces.

Firstly, about the new experiences: eyeliners are easy to lose and damage; therefore, MINISO produces eyeliners as consumable to minimize users' use cost. The common eyeliner produced by Intercos costs over CNY 100/piece, but it only costs CNY 9.9/piece with MINISO, leading to the 100 million pieces sold per year. One among every 20 people going to MINISO will buy an eyeliner.

The products are produced by the same factory. Therefore, the feelings of use do not vary much; however, MINISO has made the product originally worth CNY 99 and easy to lose or damage possibly during the use into consumable and priced it only CNY 9.9. Getting rid of the old experience that was bad is equal to the provision of an apparent new experience.

Secondly, about conversion cost: why does MINISO only make eyeliner but not other cosmetics? A woman who uses Estee Lauder would not suddenly change to MINISO because she might not trust such a low-priced product would cause allergy and whether the conversion cost would be too high. But eyeliner will not cause the above problem.

MINISO Natural Water: With three years' efforts, the annual sales reached up to 60 million bottles.

About new experiences: MINISO Natural Water is a kind of drinking water on which MINISO has spent three years and invested in over CNY 100 million. Why does MINISO sell water? Because no merchants sell water in malls: no merchants dare to sell water under the pressure of the high mall rent.

However, users have the demand for water when they are in malls. The price of CNY 3.5/bottle is more expensive than that in street convenience stores, but it is relatively cheaper than that in mall cinemas, and users will not be so sensitive to the price when they are tired and thirsty during shopping.

About conversion cost: MINISO sold 60 million bottles of water in 2016, and the water cost is calculated by ton with very high profits, so there was barely conversion cost.

2. To have opportunities, the latecomers should have new experiences that are 10 times better than competitors

Meituan entered the mobile travel business in 2018. Does it succeed as observed according to the above formula?

Firstly, about new experience: mobile travel project has very high technical barriers. Didi has been doing this and honing drivers for quite a long time, with the technology gradually maturing. It is very difficult for the new experience of Meituan to exceed Didi. Latecomers find it difficult to have opportunities when their new products and services are not 10 times better than those of their competitors.

Secondly, about conversion cost: drivers and users have using habits; the conversion cost will be very high unless Didi caused big problems.

Any product can be observed using this logic. For example, unmanned shelves have no noticeable differences from convenience stores like 7-Eleven in terms of new and old experiences; unmanned shelves enterprises fail to consider the perspective of users: users covet little advantages, but they would feel guilty if they didn't pay. Unmanned shelves make users hesitate too much and experience pain. Therefore, the conversion cost is very high.

Internet enterprises don't understand users because they don't spend efforts on understanding users' thoughts and emotions, but only regard them as traffic.

III. Substance fission formula: S (Substance) = KOL2 (Key Opinion Leaders) *E1.5 (Emotion) *C1.2 (Coupon)

Any communication needs the participation of key opinion leaders (KOLs). We studied an underwear case with two choices at that time: Lin Chi-Ling and Aoi Sora, and we eventually chose the latter.

1. Mimeng & Uncle Tongdao: communication will be meaningless without emotion

Substance and communication will be meaningless without emotion, because people will not care about it at all.

Many people know constellations, but no one can be as good as Uncle Tongdao with the twelve zodiac signs, because he does not regard them only as zodiac signs, but as emotions and socializing. The basic features of a zodiac sign are in fact quite boring and are a conclusion like blood type and Chinese zodiac; however, his description of zodiac signs is emotional: quite good or quite bad.

Tongdao made Rankings of Zodiac Signs Playing the Field. According to him, if Aquarius ranked first, the girlfriend of an Aquarius man would be correlated therewith and would give trouble to her boyfriend. This is the so-called emotion.

Mimeng is also good at provoking emotions. All titles and content of her articles display emotion. "Her To a Bastard" was reposted by many women as they've met bastards. She wrote Mao Kankan from the perspective of an entrepreneur, which

soothed souls of many entrepreneurs, and what she showed was not her own emotion but the emotion of entrepreneurs.

Mimeng: Real name: Ma Ling, We-media operator, writer, and scriptwriter. She's been operating her official account "Mimeng" since the end of 2015. By 2017, fans of her WeChat official account exceeded 10 million, views exceeded 624,692,036, reposts exceeded one billion, average views per article exceeded one million, and total views of articles reached 218,692,036 with reposts exceeding 600 million.

2. Coupon: Low but effective

The reason that Didi could rapidly occupy the market is because it made full use of users' psychology of coveting little advantages—subsidies. Users would certainly choose Didi if it took CNY 12 for them to take a taxi home, but it was free.

Sephora would give away a sample to users after they check out, which exceeds their expectations. The additional gift would make users feel that they are taking advantage.

Hutaoli would use 5% of the turnover every day to buy certain customers fruit or a cup of cocktail fruit. The shopping bags of MINISO are in fact also coupons: MINISO gives them away to customers when other supermarkets charge for them, which is another reason that it attracts customers.

IV. Enterprise value formula: E (Enterprise value) = {(U User Growth + S Sales Growth + P Profit Growth)/4.5}3

The fourth formula is about how enterprises profit from the perspective of physical industry. Internet companies do not necessarily put profit first, but focus more on market value.

"Growth" follows user, sales, and profit in the formula. Why is growth emphasized?

Dezhou Braised Chicken is still selling the traditional braised chicken, and is difficult to achieve growth by selling a chicken after another, whereas Zhouheiya is different: it sells duck necks as snack, so it has stood out.

Zhouheiya's "fight" against Juewei Food in terms of "number one stock of duck necks" turned white-hot for a time. The total

market value of Zhouheiya reached CNY 17.3 billion, and that of Juewei Food reached CNY 14.3 billion, with a difference of CNY 3 billion by the closing on May 23, 2017.

In fact, the "chasing each other" of Zhouheiya and Juewei Food in market value is only a reflection of both companies' state of operation in the capital market. The "fight" of both companies is also fierce in physical operation.

The performance in 2016 separately showed characteristics of Zhouheiya and Juewei Food: the former profited the most, while the latter sold the most. According to the financial data of both companies last year, in 2016, Zhouheiya and Juewei Food separately achieved operating income of

CNY 2.82 billion and CNY 3.27 billion; in terms of revenue, Juewei Food was ahead of Zhouheiya by CNY 400 million, to become the enterprise that sold the most in the duck neck industry that year; however, the CNY 720 million net profit attributable of Zhouheiya in that period was far above Juewei Food. According to the financial data, the gross margin of Zhouheiya was 62.3% last year, twice that of Juewei Food; its net profit margin was 25.4% in that period, 2.2 times that of Juewei Food.

The comparison of revenue of the two companies last year apportioned to the stores may be more visual. By the end of 2016, the offline stores of Zhouheiya and Juewei Food separately reached 778 and 7,924, with the latter more than 10 times the former. In terms of the revenue of the two companies apportioned to the stores, revenue of single store of Zhouheiya was up to CNY 3.62 million, while that of Juewei Food was only CNY 410,000, with the former nearly nine times the latter.

Zhouheiya: Founded in 1997, a Hubei Famous Trademark, a chain operation enterprise specialized in production of braised products like duck-related/goose-related/duck by-products/vegan products. "More entertainment, more fun" is the brand concept of Zhouheiya. Zhouheiya believes that the delicious, healthy, and convenient products can bring bigger fun and better experiences to consumers.

Zhouheiya uses the sales model of full self-operation, and generally opens stores at airports and high-speed rail stations, etc. where there is huge pedestrian flow, with nationwide transportation hubs still the strategic focus in its store network expansion. By the end of 2017, about 300 stores were opened at transportation hubs, and brought revenue accounting for 40.7% of all its revenue. Zhouheiya Model shows the principle of space in the 4S Marketing Theory. People at a station know that they would be on the plane or high-speed train for several hours and food there would cost extra and be very expensive. Therefore, those features cause Zhouheiya leisure food to upgrade to necessities, and customers will not pay too much attention to product prices when they are in a hurry.

While Juewei adopts the sales model of "guided by regular chain, and based on franchising", with franchised stores accounting for up to 98% of the stores. Juewei Model shows the principle of super user in the 4S Marketing Theory. Customers upgrade to consumer business and franchisee on the basis of consumption and purchase. It has opened over 7,000 stores in eight years, what a speed!

Zhouheiya has the profitability out of reach of enterprises in the same industry—thanks to its business strategy based on direct marketing mode; however, while seeking high profits, Zhouheiya gives up some market shares, giving Juewei Food, which explosively increases the store quantity by franchising, a head start.

Comparison of Business Models of Both

Comparison	Zhouheiya	Juewei
Income, CNY 100 million	28.2	32.7
Gross profit, CNY 100 million	17.6	10.4
Net profit, CNY 100 million	7.2	3.8
Sales volume, ton	32,830	83,879
Income per ton, CNY	85,800	33,400
Gross profit per ton, CNY	53,500	10,000
Net profit per ton, CNY	21,800	3,900
Product	Vacuum+MAP Duck neck, clavicle and bone + vegetables	Mail in bulk Duck, chicken and pork + edamame, radish and peanut, etc.
Sales	Based on direct marketing 778 stores	Guided by regular chain 115 stores Based on franchise chain: 7,600+ stores
Production	2 factories in the country MAP+vacuum products	21 production bases in the country Fresh and in bulk, basing production on sales prospects, distributed every day

Comparison of Business Models of Both. Source: Linkshop

Comparison of Gross Margin and Net Profit Margin

Zhouheiya	2,016	2016H	2,015	2,014	2,013
Gross margin (%)	62.3	62.7	56.5	54.7	57.2
Net profit margin	25.4%	27.42%	22.75%	22.72%	21.34%
Juewei	2,016	2016Q3	2,015	2,014	2,013
Gross margin (%)	31.8	31.1	28.6	26.9	27.5
Gross margin of direct-sale stores	51.9	60.5	54.4	68.6	
Gross margin of franchised stores	24.9	23.0	24.8	27.9	
Net profit margin	11.62%	12.02%	10.30%	8.99%	8.49%

Comparison of Gross Margin and Net Profit Margin. Source: Linkshop

Comparison of Single-store Revenue

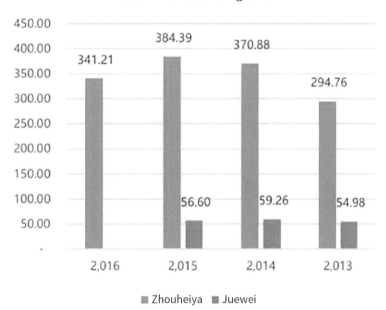

Standard of Retail-Comparison of Average
Retail Revenue of Single Store

- 2,016 — Zhouheiya: 341.21
- 2,015 — Zhouheiya: 384.39, Juewei: 56.60
- 2,014 — Zhouheiya: 370.88, Juewei: 59.26
- 2,013 — Zhouheiya: 294.76, Juewei: 54.98

■ Zhouheiya ■ Juewei

Standard of Retail-Comparison of Average Retail Revenue of Single-store. Source: Linkshop

The above differences show that Zhouheiya and Juewei are totally different in terms of company type, although they are both selling duck products. The model differences of the two companies lead to differences in sales growth and profit growth, to thus affect the enterprise value.

1. User growth

Didi car wash: earn CNY 1 per wash, and CNY 36 million a year.

Didi Chuxing has no profit, but Didi can develop other businesses to achieve profits. The 300,000 Premier and 10 million Express drivers of Didi all need to wash cars. Didi requires Premier cars to

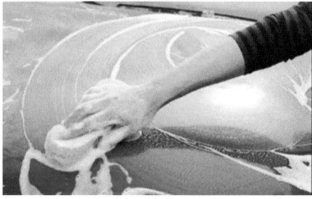

Didi car wash: earn CNY 1 per wash, and CNY 36 million a year.
Source: Linkshop

be washed once every three days to offer better Premier experiences, namely, Didi could earn CNY 36 million even it only earns CNY 1 per wash.

Didi will implement the automatic car washing machine program at gas stations in Beijing in 2018, with personnel able to wash 50 cars per day and machines able to wash 120 cars per 12 hours. The growth of users, sales, and profits will show geometric growth.

Only the high growth can support high enterprise value.

2. Sales growth

Fenda Education Company under Shenzhen Fenda Technology was originally a vocational training department, and later, it was upgraded to a product, achieving CNY 90 million profit per month in two years.

Fenda Education sends workers to OPPO, VIVO, Foxconn, and Huawei.

Worker recruitment had been a problem for factories of those brands, but now Fenda Education guarantees the workers sent by it to be able to operate immediately after taking up the post, without the need for training or interview. And many factories are willing to take students from it, because interview and training require time cost.

There are eight teams of Fenda Education that especially go to vocational secondary schools and junior colleges in the country to make speeches, to attract people who want to work at Huawei, etc. They will be guaranteed to enter the enterprises they want after joining the training.

Users of Fenda Education are from schools. So many graduates every year have become the deterministic source of users and orders of it, leading to deterministic revenue and growth.

V. New Retail has arrived, and all retail fields are confronted with reshaping of business models. It is the feature of the great era – growing or dying out in the reshaping.

Brick-and-mortar retail that does e-commerce does not necessarily mean New Retail, and a department store that adds the life experience service does not necessarily mean New Retail either. The four formulas summarized in this chapter by analysis of development of MINISO represent a law; however, to really walk out the business dilemma, traditional retail should trace to the source and find out the cause, not only at level of method and technique, but also the level of business philosophy, so as to become possible to stride forward New Retail. Enterprise business model is the implementation of business philosophy. Traditional retail

and New Retail are different in terms of business thinking: the business model of traditional retail centers on enterprise efficiency, while that of New Retail centers on user experiences.

The business model of traditional retail centers on enterprise efficiency and focuses more on enterprises themselves, showing the "personal state".

The business model of New Retail centers on user experiences and focuses more on others, showing the "impersonal state".

The differences in business model decide the differences in value orientation and in method and technique implementation.

Tool Kit – Mobile Marketing Space Spread

1. Definition

Events and Experiences: a thing that is happening or has occurred and makes people have a vivid and immersive feel to face the features and causes of the thing itself.

Public Relation: a series of public activities aimed at improving the relationship between some people and the public in the hope the public shows understanding and support, establishing a good image and finally promoting the selling.

Publicity Propaganda: activities to use the third-party media to spread relevant positive information about the organization or business to the public so as to build a positive image of the organization or business.

Advertising	Promotions	Events and Experience	PR & Public Propaganda	Online & Social Media Marketing	PC-side Propagation	Direct Marketing & Database Marketing	Personnel Selling
Printed ads & radio advertising (TV, radio, newspapers)	Contests, games, sweepstakes, lotteries	PE	Press conference	Baidu keyword search, and other search ads	Online shop	Product list	Sales statement
External packaging	Discounts and premiums	Entertainment	Speeches	E-mail	Shop decoration	E-mail	Sales meeting
Instructions	Samples	Festivals	Lectures		PC-side advertising	Telemarketing	Incentive plan
Cinema	Trade fairs and trade shows	Arts	Annual report	Display report	Online flow acquisition	E-shopping	Samples
Brochure	Exhibitions	Art crafts	Charity donation	Company blog & Company website		TV shopping, shopping guide	Trade fairs and trade shows
Posters and flyers	Demonstration	Visit factory	Publications	Third-party chat room, Microblog, blog		Fax	Premiums
TV drama ads	Offline scanning	Big things	Gifts	Facebook and twitter updates			
Table of contents	Coupons	Corporate museum	Community relations	Potato, Youku Video			
Advertorial reprint	Rebate	Street activities	Lobbies				
Billboards	Low interest financing		Identity media				
Display logo	Trade-in allowance		Company magazines				
Focus display	Periodic order agreement						
DVD	Tying						

Common communication platforms.

TV Drama Ad: implanting of some advertisements in hit TV dramas to deepen the impression of the public.

Exhibition: the display of a selection of products to the public at certain occasions, so that the public can understand the products.

Big Thing: an event at a certain period of time that is shocking, very attractive and causes heated discussion, also known as a network term.

Street Activities: activities in the street to facilitate the spread of the products by attracting people to participate.

Obtain: gains from some efforts.

Sales Statement: a well-established sales statement that may give the public a fresh look and feel, and also allows salespersons to more confidently demonstrate the products to the public.

Incentive Plan: any plan to improve people's enthusiasm and competitiveness.

Direct Marketing: direct sales of goods or services by manufacturers to customers, with no middlemen and retailers.

Database Marketing: activities by using the marketing database, in which a large amount of information is collected and managed and can be used by salespersons to conduct consumer analysis, determine the target market and manage sales activities.

Focus Display: activities in which the focus of the products is directly demonstrated to the public, so that the public can understand whether such product is what they need.

Rebate: also called sales rebate, a strategy where after the consumer buys things, the vendor gives a certain amount of cash back. It is also used by the vendor to attract consumers, with the amount depending on the profits.

Tying: refers to a marketing practice of selling, by which one product is sold as a mandatory addition to the purchase of a different product. Consumers can only purchase the mandatorily added product from the store rather than from another manufacturer.

Missing one player.

Visit Factory: allows the public to understand the company's corporate culture and production process.

Community Relations: refers to local relationships, interests, and partnerships, etc. in the circles in which they are.

Periodic Order Agreement: is an inventory management practice in which orders are placed at predetermined interval.

Trade-in Allowance: is the amount of money taken off the sale price in exchange for the item being traded in by the customer. A promotional discount is an amount deducted from the price given to a dealer cooperative in the company's product promotions.

Social Media Marketing: refers to the use of virtual communities and online platforms that people use to create, share, exchange views, opinions, and experiences to market a product. It is known for its obvious effect of promotion and large amount of reprint.

LBS (Location Based Services): is a software-level service that uses telecommunication mobile operator's radio communication network (such as GSM, CDMA) or global positioning systems (such as GPS) to acquire the location data (geographic coordinates or geodetic coordinates) of the mobile end user and finally to provide users with value-added services, by using the geographic information system platform. In the age of mobile Internet, it is very important to know the whereabouts of others, which may make it easier for you to do something for them or cooperate with them better. For vendors, knowing the location allows them to target customers more precisely so that they can provide customers with a better optimized online experience, or provide them with relevant information.

2. The Logic of Marketing Success

Assume that the marketing success is based on the following logics: customers' participation is absolutely necessary for all successful marketing activities; the barrier to successful marketing is that you do not try in the window period, but follow in the growth period; and the logic of marketing is fundamentally the logic of the user.

Then, in the age of mobile marketing, users' demand for marketing spread is totally different. Good spread should allow users to participate. Assuming that the content of the spread remains unchanged, curiosity encourages users to turn to new ways of spread. The risk of spread is that users are fond of innovation, but you failed to achieve it.

From the point of view of cost estimation, the costs of products, substance and super users, which is, together with space connections, regarded as the four elements of mobile marketing, is definite, and the uncertainty lies in the user experience and connection between space and user. If it is necessary to use a traditional marketing term, it should be "where users complete the product experience and transactions, and how to spread the product to the user."

3. Connections Between Users and Products

On the mobile side, the user and product connect through:

WeChat Moment: WeChat Moment is a social function of the Tencent App WeChat that users can post texts and pictures in WeChat Moment, and share articles or music with friends in WeChat Moment through other software.

WeChat Official Account: It is an application account that a developer or a vendor applies for on the WeChat official platform and is connected with the QQ account. Through the public number, the vendor can realize powerful communication and interaction via text, pictures, and voice with specific groups on the WeChat platform. WeChat official account includes subscription number, service number and enterprise number.

Tencent QQ: It supports online chat, video calls, point-to-point resuming, shared files, network drives, custom panels, QQ mailboxes and other functions, and can be connected to a variety of communication terminals.

Micro Blog: As a sharing and communication platform, it focuses on timeliness and randomness. With Micro Blog, users can better express their thoughts of every moment and latest developments, while blogs are more focused on sorting out what they have seen, heard and felt in a period of time. A tiny genre was born out of Micro Blog.

Live: It is the activity to record and play videos to the public through a live streaming platform and the public may interact with the anchor in real time.

Social Networking Platform: It provides a social platform to connect people who have common interests or are like-minded or people in particular areas. It facilitates the spread of information by relevant people in the community and people use the platform to share information.

App (Application): It refers to a third-party application installed in a smartphone.

Mini Program: It is an application that can be used by scanning the QR code and there is no need to install additional applications on mobile devices.

Bulletin Board System: It is an electronic information service system on the Internet. It provides a public electronic whiteboard, where each user can write, publish information, or submit ideas. It is a service system that is interactive, rich and instant.

Mini Video: it is a video that is pushed through a mobile terminal and displays products to the public in a more vivid form.

4. Mobile Marketing Toolkit

According to the 4S Theory of mobile marketing, if a company has three elements, i.e., good products, human resources of super users and rich cultural content for sharing, the fourth element must be added for the mobile marketing to form a closed loop. The fourth element can be called a "field", which is a mobile network space to display products, interact and share contents, spread brands, conduct transactions and provide after-sales services. The mobile network space with the above five functions is called "field spread" (as shown in Figures 18-6).

Field spread is a basic concept of the interconnection of mobile marketing space functions integrating display, sharing, transac-

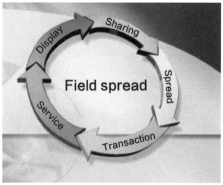

Figure 18-6　Field spread.

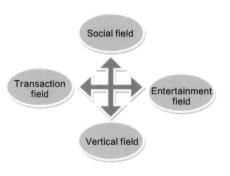

Figure 18-7　Four fields.

tion, communication and service. On the current mobile network technology development platform, only apps developed by enterprises themselves have the five functions of field spread. This is also the internal reason why a large number of business owners invested large sums of money in developing apps from 2012 to 2016. However, since 2017, business owners' enthusiasm to develop independent app has been fading, because apps are too difficult to promote. This requires mobile marketing researchers to find alternative solutions. Based on the application experience of successful cases in the past five years and an in-depth study of mobile network technologies, this book finds that there are four kinds of mobile network technologies and platform applications that can replace all the functions of apps. The application characteristics of these four directions can provide a toolkit for the portfolio strategy of mobile marketing spread (as shown in Figure 18-7).

(1) The social networking platforms, represented by Twitter, Facebook and WeChat, can support the substance sharing and product display functions of mobile marketing.

(2) The entertainment network platforms, represented by microfilm and mobile video broadcast platform, can support the ad spread and embedded ads functions of mobile marketing.

(3) The vertical network application platforms, represented by Microblog and WeChat public account, can support the content spread and the acquisition and accumulation of super users.

(4) The online payment platforms, represented by Alipay and WeChat Pay, can support the transaction and service functions of mobile marketing.

5. Features of Social Platforms

Social and contact are two basic functions of mobile Internet and also the most frequent used function. We will discuss the features of various social platforms in the following.

KaKaoTalk: It is a free chat software from South Korea. This application can be used to manage friends with actual phone numbers. With push notification service, the user can quickly send and receive messages, pictures, videos and voice intercoms with friends, family and colleagues. Similar to QQ, your KaKaoTalk message can

be received by an offline friend, just like sending a text message.

GaGa: It is a social mobile application based on international translation and the mobile application software of GaGaHi International Dating Platform. You can chat with everyone in the world without any language barriers through eight languages and nine writings. You can make friends in the world, and walk into each other's spiritual world through real-time multilingual translation.

Skype: It is a kind of instant messaging software with all IM functions, such as video chat, multi-user voice conference, multi-user chat, and file transfer and text chat.

Tencent QQ: It is a kind of Internet-based instant messaging (IM) software developed by Tencent. Tencent QQ can support online chat, video calls, point-to-point file resuming, files sharing, online hard disk, custom panels and QQ mailbox, and it can also connect to a variety of communication terminals.

Twitter: It is an American social network (Social Network Service) and microblog service website, which is one of the ten most visited websites on the Internet. It is a typical application of microblog. Users can update messages with no more than 140 characters, which are also called Tweets.

WeChat: It is a free application launched by Tencent to provide instant messaging services for smart terminals. WeChat can support quickly sending free (consuming a small amount of network traffic) voice message videos, pictures and texts through cross-communications operators and cross-operating system platforms. At the same time, it also provides location-based social plug-ins through sharing streaming content, such as Shake, Message in a Bottle, Moments, Official Accounts and Voice Input.

Line: It was launched by South Korean Internet Group NHN and its subsidiary NHN Japan. Although as a late starter that was officially launched into the market in June 2011, its registered users worldwide have exceeded 400 million.

Facebook: It is an American social network service website and a leading photo sharing website in the world. As of November 2013, there were about 350 million photos uploaded every day. As of May 2012, Facebook had about 900 million users.

The Cooperation between Microfilm Marketing and Microblog Marketing Is Becoming a New Favorite of Mobile Marketing.

DeRucci was awarded the 2013 China Entertainment Marketing Forum and China Entertainment Marketing Effectiveness Award. As an internal review pointed out, as an integrator of global healthy sleep resources, DeRucci has always insisted on spreading healthy sleep concepts. Its microfilm "Romantic Adventure" has got great success in spreading healthy sleep culture, which made DeRucci the worthy winner of the 2013 China Entertainment Marketing Effectiveness Award.

Facts have proved that the microfilm "Romantic Adventure" really lives up to expectations. It got more than 12 million hits in two days, and more than 100 million hits in one month, making it a popular video in microblog, WeChat and other major mainstream video sites. The healthy sleep culture of DeRucci has also aroused the concern of the entire public and caused fierce discussions. DeRucci has successfully passed its healthy sleep culture to every consumer through such emerging media as microblog and WeChat.

According to analysis by professionals, "Romantic Adventure" has created a miracle in the amount of play, and its healthy sleep culture is deeply rooted in people's mind and has drawn the public attention to healthy sleep. According to statistics, DeRucci has experienced a market growth of more than 50% in 2013, and more and more consumers agree with the healthy sleep culture of DeRucci. As the public's concern about their own healthy sleep reached a new high, it is of great significance to the DeRucci brand, the bedding industry and social welfare.

It is reported that "Romantic Adventure" is the third microfilm produced by DeRucci. Before that, "Bed Relationship" and "A Sleeping Fame" have all achieved quite good results. The significant entertainment marketing of "Romantic Adventure" has been highly recognized by industry experts as a new benchmark for entertainment marketing in the bedding industry.

The case source quoted from: BMLINR.COM 2014/05/12
https://tieba.baidu.com/p/3038830571?red_tag=0792553960

6. WeChat Marketing and Microblog Marketing

What is the difference between WeChat marketing and vertical microblog marketing?

In the era of social media marketing, business owners are all trying to gain consumer attention through microblog and WeChat. However, most people simply do not know the difference between WeChat marketing and microblog marketing. This is also the reason why the invested funds cannot achieve expected results. Both WeChat marketing and microblog marketing seem to be social media marketing, but there are actually a lot of differences, which are mainly reflected in the following three aspects:

(1) Spread range. From the perspective of forwarding, WeChat mainly relies on Moments (Circle of Friends), which can build a highly reliable relationship. While microblog mainly takes advantage of rapid spread (within few seconds) and openness, but users can hardly believe in strangers on the Internet. At the same time, there is too much information on microblog, and what you post is likely to be ignored. In comparison, WeChat marketing is more likely to gain the trust of users, but its spread speed is slightly inferior to that of microblog.

(2) Marketing methods. WeChat marketing is more suitable for some middle- and small-sized enterprises and business owners. WeChat marketing mainly relies on the substance posted in Moments, which will encourage friends to help forward and spread out. To some extent, the microblog is easier to form a hot topic, so business owners often can conduct marketing with hot topics. When microblog users browse topics, they will see advertisements at the same time. Business owners will also cooperate with some users with large numbers of fans to forward their recommended products. In comparison, microblog marketing is more effective but costly.

(3) Interactivity. As social tools, WeChat and microblog are different in nature. Most WeChat contacts are familiar acquaintances that are easy to communicate. Therefore, simple interaction may generate feelings and sell products. While most microblog contacts are strangers, it is hard for business owners to establish a sound interaction process.

7. WeChat Pay and Alipay

Mobile payment is critical to the closed loop of mobile marketing. In China, WeChat Pay and Alipay are the most common mobile payments. We will discuss their differences in the following content. It can be roughly divided into four aspects:

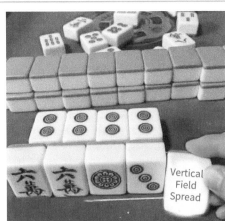

The vertical field paves the
road for Chinese Mahjong.

After a few years of entrepreneurship, Logic Talkshow is more aware of its real business mode.

Dangdang can hardly make money in selling books, while Logic Talkshow can make considerable money in doing so. E-commerce companies need to pay high cost for traffic, while the WeChat official account of Logic Talkshow has 10 million followers. Luo Zhenyu proposed a smart positioning in the early stage: readers around you. The daily 1-minute voice

input can spread contents and maintain high frequent interaction with users. Therefore, selling books becomes a natural course for Logic Talkshow: readers around you recommend books for you. This is a best match for content and e-commerce.

Especially after the launch of Dedao app, Logic Talkshow has a more profound understanding of the paid content mode. From the cash realization through e-commerce mode at the very beginning to the introduction of paid reading mode through Dedao app, Logic Talkshow has been pursuing to build a platform for high-quality content. Moreover, users can clearly know the products of Logic Talkshow. When Logic Talkshow sells book, Luo Zhenyu is a best bookseller who tells the public what is worth buying.

When doing the paid content, Luo Zhenyu has become a column seller who tells the public why you should subscribe to a column. In many cases, the public are more willing to buy books in Logic Talkshow, although they know that these books are more expensive than those on Jingdong and Taobao. Because these books are selected by Luo Zhenyu, and he has provided a kind of service through quality content and saves time for the public.

Source: Content differences between TouTiao.com and Logic Talkshow.

(1) Accepting institution. In WeChat Pay, each business manager corresponds to multiple authorized service providers, while in Alipay each authorized service provider corresponds to business managers for different industries and different regions.

(2) Access threshold. The threshold of WeChat Pay is much higher than the national standard. Business owners must apply for WeChat service account and provide a lot of license data to prove themselves. The threshold of Alipay is based on national standards or the bottom line. Business owners just need to reach a low threshold, which basically means to provide a business license.

(3) Relationship with the service provider. The ecology of WeChat Pay supports different accepting institutions which serve one business owner, specifically on the identification number of business owner and third-party authorization (Since 2015, the third-party authorization was launched to solve the competition for in-

terface resources between service providers). Different service providers can also provide different "bank cards" (ID No. of business owner), and the business owner can choose which and how to use. Alipay adopts a single method that allows a service provider to provide full service windows and payment services for a business owner.

(4) Operational behavior. WeChat Pay is based on large numbers of accepting institutions in its ecology, which depends on WeChat's technical cooperation with the close or estranged partners. While Alipay pays little attention to various tricks, it tries to win the favor of high-frequent consumption industries and high-profile companies through heavy subsidies.

Well-known payment systems around the world are as follows:

(1) PayPal: It allows the money transfer between users who use e-mail as identity, and avoids the traditional bank check mailing and remittance. PayPal also cooperates with some e-commerce websites

and becomes one of their payment methods, but it will charge a certain amount of processing fees for money transfers.

(2) WorldPay: It is a leading global independent payment service operator. This supports a variety of credit cards, including Mastercard, Visa, Visa Purchasing, Visa Delta, Visa Electron, JCB, Solo and Switch. The payment will not enter the account immediately after the payment is made. The payment cannot actually be received until the order is confirmed. For geographical reasons, some regions may charge foreign transaction fees.

(3) PayDollar: It is an online payment method that supports multiple currencies, languages, cards and payment modes (such as telephone transactions, fax transactions and mail orders) as well as multi-channel payments.

(4) Amazon Payment: It is a payment method that Amazon payment system provides for its trading platform, similar to the relationship between PayPal and eBay. It provides no active payment function, that is, customers can only purchase through the shopping cart provided by business owners.

We will take WeChat Pay and Alipay as the example to discuss the payment scenes.

WeChat Pay can be divided into three aspects: offline QR code scanning, i.e., users scan an offline static QR code to generate a WeChat Pay transaction page and complete the transaction process; Web QR code scanning, i.e., users scan a PC QR code to jump to a WeChat Pay transaction page and complete the transaction process; and WeChat public account payment, i.e., users follow the WeChat public account of a business owner, and purchase and pay for goods and services on the public account.

In a sense, Alipay acts as an online fund safe. Nowadays, many people are accustomed to depositing money in Yu Ebao which at least provides higher interest rates than banks. Many people believe that the safe shall be lying quietly, except for the necessity to put important assets in occasionally. The less it moves, the less risk it will bear.

In some micropayment scenes, users may directly pay with WeChat Pay, and there is no need to use Alipay. But for macropayment scenes, Alipay may

be safer. From this perspective, Alipay is more suitable for large consumption scenes and financial management scenes, so it can avoid the direct conflict with WeChat Pay and maintain its own advantages. But there is also a paradox because the vast majority of consumption scenes are micropayments. If Alipay shifts its strategic focus away from these aspects, it is very unfavorable to itself, and may be attacked by WeChat Pay in the rear. Moreover, in macropayment scenes, people are more willing to pay directly with bank cards rather than use Alipay.

According to the current circumstances, people may think Alipay is more confusing, because it is trying to cover every aspect, which in turn makes users feel at a loss. Therefore, in the case that the micropayment scenes are indispensable, while macropayment scenes are too small, we can predict that entering micropayment scenes is an inevitable choice for Alipay.

Although there are differences in the layer of payment scenes between WeChat Pay and Alipay, both of them are much faster and more convenient than foreign payment systems.

8. WeChat Mini Programs

WeChat Mini Program is a small application that can be used without downloading it. It makes applications at hand, and user can open an application just by scanning or searching it. It also embodies the concept of "Closing after Using", and users do not have to worry about whether they have installed too many applications.

The introduction of mini-programs does not mean that WeChat will act as an application distribution market, but to "provide an open platform for some quality services". On the one hand, users can log in mini-programs with WeChat, and the developers can connect the user data of existing apps to mini-programs.

With the official launch of mini-programs, users can experience the mini-programs of developers through scanning QR code or by searching. Mini-programs provide the top display function. This means that users can quickly return to the chat interface in the process of using a mini-program, and they can also quickly enter the mini-program through the chat interface, so the mini-program and the chat interface can switch conveniently. Android users can also add shortcuts for mini-programs.

The mini-program of self-select stock has relatively reserved more app functions, which only left "Information" as an independent section and reserved three main functional sections, i.e., self-selection, quotation and setting. It also provides the same stock price reminder and other functions with the app. When sharing specific stock pages with friends, the real-time stock price information will be shown after click, so the experience is very complete. The link function of WeChat public accounts referred to by the WeChat team has already been reflected in the current page of public account. On the public account page with mini-programs, users can see the mini-programs developed by the public account, click to enter the mini-program. Since mini-programs and public accounts are under the same account, account followers can be transferred as mini-program users with lower costs.

 **Case Study   Alipay Wallet**

Alipay Wallet is a leading mobile payment platform in China. It has a built-in civilian financial management tool Yu Ebao which sweeps around China as well as such free services as Credit Card, Transfer, Phone Top-up and Utilities. The public can also use Alipay Wallet to call a taxi, go shopping at a convenience store and buy drinks at a vending machine. Users can quickly complete the payment process through mobile phones. Based on the linked bank card, Alipay provides safe, fast and efficient payment services to users.

Alipay Wallet

Alipay Wallet

Payment environment: Alipay public payment platform, app payment (third-party application store), QR code payment and card payment. Presently, Hangzhou has launched a face payment.

Users only need to link a bank card with Alipay and complete the real name authentication, and the Alipay app can be turned into a universal wallet. Users can also deposit money in Yu Ebao which will generate interest every day. Afterwards, users can purchase goods and services from business owners with cooperation relationships. Users only need to enter the password or verify fingerprint a on the smart phone to complete the payment, and the whole process is simple and smooth without any card-related steps.

The case source quoted from: Baidu Baike

https://baike.baidu.com/item/%E6%94%AF%E4%BB%98%E5%AE%9D%E9%92%B1%E5%8C%85/3881052?fr=aladdin

Part 6

Global Marketing

Chapter 19

Global Marketing – A Viewpoint from China

Topics:

1. Reinterpreting Four Industrial Revolutions
2. Age of Conflict 4.0

Industrial Revolution1.0 -Age of steam

Although we are living in a great technological period, many Chinese companies are trapped by immense operation changes and market challenges when the Industrial Revolution 4.0 and Age of Conflict 4.0 meet in the era of mobile Internet, and the market environment evolves to an era of information economy featured by longitudinal development. In the meantime, there are companies across the globe facing a similar situation.

Behind the scenes of rapid market change are iteration, competition and transformation of marketing and market ideas. Knowing this is helpful for enterprises to find the right spot more accurately.

Reinterpreting Four Industrial Revolutions

I. The First Industrial Revolution

The three industrial revolutions in the western world are known to all[①]. When asked about the origin of the First Industrial Revolution, many people would probably say "England".

It's not.

The criterion to identify the First Industrial Revolution should be the release of human from the restrictions of agriculture, i.e., the First Industrial Revolution should be marked by the evolution of human civilization from weather-dependent cultivation to handicraft industry-based production.

Obviously, the British Industrial Revolution of England having started in the 18th century does not meet this requirement. Principally, it drove people from scattered manual production mills to large mechanized factories for mass production. Hence, although it has been recorded as a big stroke in human history, the Industrial Revolution taking place in England is not the first.

Actually, the First Industrial Revolution started in China some 1,000 years ago and reached its peak around the Tang and Song Dynasties. The drastic growth turned the ancient silk road into a crowded passage. Moreover, the deep impact of the Four Great Inventions on the world has remained till today.

Francis Bacon, the English philosopher known as the "Good Heart of the Western Countries", wrote in 1620 that "we should notice the forces, effects, and consequences of the inventions, which are nowhere more conspicuous than in those three which were unknown to the ancients; namely, printing, gunpowder, and the compass. These three inventions have changed the appearance and state of the whole world; firstly in literature, and then in warfare, and lastly in navigation; innumerable changes have been thence derived, so no empire, sect, or star, appears to have exercised a greater power and influence on human affairs than these mechanical discoveries".

Mr. Bacon reviewed correctly the historic significance of the three great inventions, which originated from China. Woodblock printing, as the name implies, is a process where the text of a page is carved on wooden blocks. The oldest work in existence is a piece of Buddhist scriptures printed in 868 AD. Also invented first by the Chinese, movable type printing was actually tested successfully by an ordinary Chinese craftsman, who made baked-clay types during 1041-1049. Over the following centuries, Chinese people substituted clay for wood and metals. These inventions were introduced to the Middle East and then to Europe. The woodblock printing was first used in Europe in 1423 and the Gutenberg Bible was first printed by the European with movable types in 1455.

①
The three industrial revolutions in the western world:
The First Industrial Revolution: 1760s.
It is marked by invention of steam engine by Watt.
The Second Industrial Revolution: 1860s.
It is marked by wide application of electrical power; invention of generator by Siemens, light bulb by Edison, and phone by Bell.
The Third Industrial Revolution: 1940s-1950s. It is marked by and is mainly represented by application of atomic energy, aerospace, electronic computer technologies; other hi-techs include artificially synthesized material, molecular biology and genetic engineering.

The Chinese made fireworks from gunpowder early in the Tang dynasty (618-907 AD). In 1120, the Chinese invented "fire-spitting lance", which consists of a thick bamboo pipe and gunpowder stuffed in it. This was basically the predecessor of metal-barrel guns, which were believed to be made around 1280. As to whether they were invented firstly by Chinese, Arabian or European, no one knows exactly.

Although magnetic force was clearly mentioned in some books around 240 AD, compasses were used merely in wizardry over several centuries followed, and for marine navigation only from 1125. It was obviously Arab merchants who learned how to use them and carried them to Europe.

A lot of things, apart from the three great inventions, spread from China to its neighbors on the Eurasia continent. Invented also by the Chinese in 105 AD, papermaking laid the ground work necessary for germination of printing technology. In 751 AD, Arabs learned papermaking technique from Chinese prisoners taken to Samarkand, and spread it to Syria, Egypt and Morocco. The technique spread to Spain in 1150 and further to France and other European countries, replacing parchment everywhere it had passed. Papermaking has proven values: it saves at least 300 pieces of parchment required to make a Bible.

Among other things, rudder, stirrup and chest harness are also far-reaching inventions that swept the Eurasia continent. Rudders were taken together with compasses to Europe around 1180; stirrups enabled knights in medieval Europe to be heavily armored; and chest harness, different from its defective neck-mounted predecessors, protected horses from being suffocated when pulling heavy loads. At last, the Chinese also cultivated a variety of fruit and vegetables, including chrysanthemum, camellia, azalea, tea rose, China aster, lemon, and citrus, which were spread by Arabs to every corner of the Eurasia continent. Citrus is generally called "Chinese apple" today in Holland and Germany.

Great thinkers or scientists with landmark achievements, world-changing technical inventions and transformations in global trade are three solid standards we applied to define an industrial revolution. Meeting all three standard (the formation of groups of thinkers, represented by Confucianism advocates, the four world-changing inventions and the transformations brought about by the trans-Eurasia Silk Road), the Tang and Song dynasties were meant to initiate the First Industrial Revolution.

Nevertheless, China has not been able to keep the momentum since the invasion from the north ceased the progress of industrial revolution in Central China around 1206 on the eve of the founding of Yuan dynasty. As China stopped and took breaks, the steam engine of the United Kingdom across the English Channel boomed at the other end of the Eurasia continent to declare the beginning of the Second Industrial Revolution.

II. The Second Industrial Revolution

The Second Industrial Revolution began in Britain in the 18th century when thinkers/scientists, inventors and global traders, the three essential drivers of industrial revolutions, stepped up to the stage center.

Relationship among the three drivers is similar to a football game, where the fullback passes the ball to the midfielder, who passes it further to the striker, who takes the decisive kick.

Specifically, thinkers release restrictions on the social environment, which is necessary for scientific inventions. In a more open and free humanistic atmosphere, inventors turn their creative ideas into tangible technical inventions, which push forward global trade further to enable global-wise reallocation of resources. As a result, the Second Industrial Revolution brought prosperity to the British Empire.

Although science and thought cannot generate cash, they do function as a powerful blower capable of inspiring technologies covered with dust and cutting chains put on scientific invention.

Isaac Newton (1642-1727) and C. R. Darwin were two pioneers before the advent of the Second Industrial Revolution. As the most prominent figure of his time, Newton discovered the law of universal gravitation: a particle attracts every other particle in the universe with a force which is directly proportional to the product of their masses and inversely proportional to the square of the distance between their centers.

The law of universal gravitation is a splendid and revolutionary interpretation of the rule of the physical world. In fact, nature is more like a mighty machine and we can discover some natural rules by observing, carrying out experiments, measuring and calculating to provide theoretical support for mechanization.

Well, how influential is Newton? Invention of steam engine is a manifest proof. In 1769, James Watt modified steam engine and a range of new inventions emerged for its improvement.

John Kay's flying shuttle (1733) which speeds up spinning, Richard Arkwright's water-powered spinning frame (1769), James Hargreaves' 'Spinning Jenny' (1770), and Samuel Crompton's spinning mule (1779) were also excellent examples. Using the 'Spinning Jenny', a man was able to spin eight yarns simultaneously, the number then increased to 16 and further to above 100.

The historical significance of steam engine cannot be overstated. It provided means to control and use thermal power to drive machinery and thereby put an end to human's continuing dependence on animal, wind and hydraulic power. The acquisition of this new powerful energy source ushered in another new era.

You may want to ask what China was doing at that time. So, when the Second Industrial Revolution raised mountainous waves, what did China do across the ocean?

In 1709, the 48th year of his reign, Kangxi Emperor granted the new built Old Summer Palace in Beijing to his fourth son In-Jen[①], who ordered numerous skillful craftsmen across the country to expand it and took 50 years to build it into the Garden of Gardens. Stepping up after his father, Qianlong Emperor further expanded the garden. Millions of gardeners were drafted from southern China to decorate this artistic royal palace. The century-long construction exhausted the Qing dynasty but it did not result in a happy ending. The garden was burnt by British and French armies in 1860, the 10th year of Xianfeng Emperor's reign.

What an incredible comparison of history. When the banner of freedom and science was flapping above the Atlantic Ocean, when the British people spared no effort to engage in the Second Industrial Revolution for a hundred years, the Qing Empire extracted the power of the whole nation and spent the same amount of time to build a royal garden doomed to be ruined.

Let's look at Britain's many achievements at that time. Invention of new spinning frames and steam engines inevitably boosted demand for iron, steel and coal; and the demand was satisfied via advancement in mining and metallurgical technologies. Henry Cort invented "puddling" to remove debris from melted iron; and Watt's steam engine was widely applied to manufacture blower and jackdrill, as well as in turning and cracking technology.

The result of the Second Industrial Revolution is that Britain had produced more coal and iron than the total of the rest of the world by 1800. Society, except for the isolated Qing dynasty, moved into the age of steam and iron.

In its early days, the impact of the Second Industrial Revolution on China might not have been so noticeable that Empress Dowager Cixi continued building the Old Summer Palace until the end of the 19th century, unaware of the approaching threat.

In 1840, Samuel Cunard founded a trans-Atlantic regular shipping line. The alteration of transportation and emergence of a new trade mode released the real power of the Second Industrial Revolution. Long-distance sailing of steamships brought about the thorough change in the way of asset allocation, which led to an affluent Britain and left China in poverty.

Moreover, ships can be used both for commercial and military purposes. Missing out on the Second Industrial Revolution, China was humiliated in three destructive wars: the First Opium War with Britain (1840-1842), the Second Opium War with Britain and France (1856-1860), and the First Sino-Japanese War which ended in 1895.

During the First Opium War in 1840, it was literally impossible for the Chinese with outdated weapons to defeat the British armed with steamed artillery and ships. "Arthur David Waley, an English historian, described a tragicomic scene of Ningbo naval battle: the signal for the general attack was to be the setting alight of the fire-rafts which were to be sent to drift against the English ships, setting fire to them before they could weigh anchor... The English ships' boats put out long before the blazing

①

Aisin-Gioro In-Jen, the 5th emperor of the Qing dynasty and the 3rd emperor after Beijing was chosen as the national capital. He was the 4th son of Kangxi Emperor. His mother, Lady Uya, was Consort De and reputed as Empress Xiaogongren. After Kangxi died at Changchun Palace on November 13, 1722, the 61st year of reign, In-Jen ascended to the throne and changed the tile of reign to Yongzheng the following year.

rafts arrived, took them in pieces... and the Chinese fled".

Someone suggested that fire-crackers should be tied to the back of a number of monkeys, who would then be flung on board the English ships. The flames would spread rapidly in every direction with these jumping monkeys and might with luck reach the powder magazine, in which case the whole ship would blow up. Nineteen monkeys were bought, and at the time of the advance and were brought to the frontline before the assault...You probably know the result.

The lesson learned from being marginalized in an industrial revolution is that old-fogies lag behind, and laggards are beaten. During the 2014 conference of APEC, President Xi Jinping had a 4-hour conversation with President Barack Obama at Zhongnanhai. The press report highlighted that President Xi introduced modern history of China to President Obama, and explained the underlying reason China should implement a reform policy.

China has to reform for the lessons learned from history. Although China missed the Second Industrial Revolution 200 years ago, it grasped the last chance of the Third Industrial Revolution some 30 years ago.

III. The Third Industrial Revolution

The flame of the Third Industrial Revolution was ignited in the persisting ardor of Britain's industrial revolution.

Like its predecessor, scientists, inventors and global traders are necessary also for the Third Industrial Revolution. The difference is the legend of a great scientist. In 1905, as a staff member of a Swiss patent office, Albert Einstein published his paper on the theory of relativity, raising the curtain of a brand new realm and leading the world to the Atomic Age.

Einstein must be the best choice to unveil the Third Industrial Revolution. Newton laid the ground for the Second Industrial Revolution, and his law of universal gravitation nurtured so many amazing achievements. However, it was not completely correct. Einstein had made thorough corrections with his theory of relativity.

Gravitational effect, in Newton's opinion, was something instantaneous by which we could transmit signals at an infinitely fast speed. Einstein held that it was impossible for us to do that faster than light. The law of universal gravitation was therefore defective.

Newton personified the gentleman scientist—well connected with the privileged class, devoutly religious, unhurried, and methodical in his work. His style of doing science set the standard. Eccentric, disheveled, absent-minded, utterly absorbed in his work, and an archetypal abstract thinker, Einstein's story, in comparison, was like a big win of an underdog.

In his theory, Einstein introduced the well-known mass-energy equation, which led to the generation of atomic bomb, the most powerful, and horrific, weapon of the Third Industrial Revolution.

All the four typical industrial products of this revolution – automobiles, aircraft, telephone, and computer, are connected to Einstein's mass-energy equation ($E=MC^2$).

Each industrial revolution came after a scientific revolution. Scientists are a lighthouse for inventors exploring in the dark. We have no reason to look down on physicists, biologists and other experts of fundamental disciplines, or even theorists. They are forerunners of the industrial civilization. In 1752, Benjamin Franklin discovered electricity, driving the coal-powered door industrial civilization into the era of electric power. The Wright Brothers responsible for inventing the first plane in 1900, which led to the birth of Boeing. So far, 80% of long-range wide-body planes are manufactured by Boeing. Combining "electric power", "rubber" and "gas engine", Ford created Model T. In addition to this classic automobile, Ford also made significant contributions to the Third Industrial Revolution by offering new modes of mass-production management.

Electronic engineering and information technology joined the chorus of industrialization after the 1970s. The delicate melody of automation and industrial civilization was being played on the arena of the Third Industrial Revolution for a hundred years. The Third Industrial Revolution has created more wealth than the sum over the past 1,000 years. It is not exaggerative to say that we have "excess capacity" today.

The century-long history of industrialization was accompanied by American enthusiasm for invention. In 1946, the world's first computer was born in the US. From that point on, evolutions have been made from hardware and software. We are now living in a well-connected world where the Internet technology reaches every corner.

The statement that Internet technology is omnipotent in the world will probably receive no objection. Although Einstein's mass-energy equation marked the start of the Third Industrial Revolution, he might not have expected that the energy of the Internet is, before achieving full potential, beyond a nuclear explosion.

Let us ask: what would China look like if the Third Industrial Revolution started in China? Or we may rephrase the question like this: what did China do a hundred years ago? Why did this country miss an opportunity of an industrial revolution again?

In 1895, at the dawn of the US Third Industrial Revolution, China was engaged in a war with Japan and compelled to sign the Treaty of Maguan. During 1937-1945, when the Third Industrial Revolution was in its most crucial period, China had to fight against Japan's invasion and set aside industrial development. In the early years of the 20th century, China's spark to ignite industrial revolution was suffocated by its neighbor across the sea. Fortunately, China grasped the last chance by implementing the reform and opening up policy, and wowed the world with its fast but small-stepped industrialization over the lucky 30 years.

In spite of the emergence of railways, trans-Atlantic vessels and electronic information, the revolution continues till today with inventions coming out unceasingly. When an invention causes imbalance in a sector, it drives more invention in other sectors to correct such imbalance. The United States stands in the center of this revolution, although Germany and Japan have made many inventions during the Third Industrial Revolution.

So, what has the US done in this revolution to make it the only super-power on the planet today? In addition to science and technical inventions, the result of industrial revolution is solidified more by the change of trade mode. Americans designed a US-oriented system of global trade – the World Trade Organization (WTO)- and invented the International Monetary Fund. What matters the most is that it invented the Bretton Woods system, by which the international trade is primarily settled in the US dollar.

IV. The Fourth Industrial Revolution

Representing industrial innovation and advancement, "Industry 4.0[①]" signifies the Fourth Industrial Revolution in human history. The concept shocked the world in 2013 when it was first introduced by the Federal Ministry for Economic Affairs and Energy (BMWi) and the Federal Ministry of Education and Research (BMBF) of Germany.

"Industry 4.0" tells us an incredible story about the future. Starting from the transformation of the manufacturing industry, human society will embrace the Fourth Industrial Revolution featuring highly digitalized production, network and self-organizing machines, following the previous three industrial revolutions (application of steam engine, mass industrial production, and electronic and information technology).

However, it also sparked debates. Is it sufficiently justified to use the term "revolution"? or is "evolution" a more appropriate word? The question has a point. In the "Industry 4.0" initiative, the technical factors to change the future world are software, sensors, actuators and other electronics, which have been in existence in the Third Industrial Revolution, not something new.

In fact, we are at the intersection of diversified new technologies and inventions, where the quantitative change is about to trigger the qualitative change. Any one industrial revolution spans decades. From this point of view, time span may not have a ground to deny the concept of the Fourth Industrial Revolution. What's more, technical changes since the beginning of the 21st century trend

① As one of the ten major programs scheduled in the High-tech Strategy 2020 for Germany, "Industry 4.0" is to receive EUR200 million sponsored by BMBF and BMWi. It aims at building smarter factories characterized by adaptability, resource efficiency, ergonomics, and integration of customers and business partners in business and value processes. Its technical bases are cyber-physical systems and Internet of Things.

①

Quantum Mechanics is a branch of physics studying motion laws of microscopic particles of the material world. It focuses on research of atoms, molecules, and condensed matters, as well as fundamental theories concerning structures and properties of atomic nuclei and elementary particles, and forms the theoretical basis of modern physics together with the theory of relativity. Quantum mechanics is not only one of the fundamental theories of modern physics, but also is applied extensively in chemistry and many other modern technologies.

reversely to the practice and theories of the previous industrial revolutions. For this reason, more people tend to agree that it is a revolution rather than a patch-it-up evolution.

Given the trilogy of progress (science – technology - trade) as we pointed out for the three previous industrial revolutions, it is reasonable to assume that revolutionary scientific results or thoughts should come at first if "Industry 4.0" prefigures a real revolution.

The truth is, the signs have been there for long, and theoretical physics still played a pioneering role.

People used to believe that Einstein's theory of relativity was flawless and no one would ever expect that it would be challenged by quantum mechanics, the most advanced and fantastic science in the modern world. Quantum mechanics has been recognized for the last three decades as the milestone of a new era.

Quantum mechanics refreshed people's perspectives on atoms.

What if all science and knowledge were destroyed in a catastrophe, and we had only one chance to leave our last words to new humans in the future, how could we convey the most information with the least amount of words?

It must be the atomic theory, i.e., matter is made up of atoms, tiny and restless particles that attract and reject each other at the same time.

Just thinking about it, you may understand that this sentence included a tremendous amount of information necessary to reconstruct the world view of man. So, men are merely piles of atoms, like stones, steel bars and trees. The only difference is the specific combination and sequence of atoms. In this case, if inter-personal network is made possible, why not to build man-stone and tree-stone networks?

From Internet to IOT, the atomic theory has reshaped the world view in the Fourth Industrial Revolution.

Sometimes, we think about truth and feel scared, though it is true. Physics is so complicated but interesting: the "movable thing" walking and talking in front of you is actually a huge pile of complicatedly arranged atoms; the "sweetheart" lying beside you every night is an atomic sequence

in sleep mode; and a "baby" delivered by a woman is a pile of atoms arranged together by her and her husband.

In classical physics, matters are believed to have definite motion laws; while from the perspective of quantum physics, it is impossible to know the position of an object and how fast it moves at the same time. The momentum and position uncertainties are complementary and the law is $\Delta x \Delta p \geq h/2\pi$.

An interesting conclusion drawn from quantum mechanics① on scientific concept and philosophy is that it is impossible to precisely predict anything in the future under any circumstances, i.e., the famous Uncertainty Principle. This principle has been a guardian angel of all inventors before the dawn of the Fourth Industrial Revolution, protecting their passion from being stifled by traditionalists. The reason is simple: since success comes randomly, why bother to have doubt about creativity of small potatoes? Unintentionally, quantum mechanics has opened a door to the microscopic world, where tons of innovations are made possible.

1. Don't understand Industry 4.0? Go to the future factory of Siemens.

We were so amazed by the automatic production of industrial robots at Tesla's super factories.

You will definitely be shocked to see the data below, with all your previous cognition about automation being overwhelmed by this master of automation: delivery time of 24 hours; one product per second, acceptance rate of 99.9985%; 3 billion elements; 75% of processes handled by automatic equipment and computers; and underground magnetic element conveyor belt 5 km long.

Established in Nuremberg, a small city in the east of Bavaria, Electronics Works Amberg (EWA) is among the most advanced factories in Europe and even the world. No one would notice its inconspicuous appearance but it is Siemens' factory of the future, one of the best models of Industry 4.0, and the world's first digital factory.

Founded in 1989, EWA focuses on SIMATIC (Siemens' brand for automatic product series), and PLCs (something like the CPU in a computer and is used for

Don't understand Industry 4.0? Go to the future factory of Siemens. Source: Official website of Tesla

EWA focuses on SIMATIC and PLCs. Source: Siemens publication

automation of machinery systems), covering fields from automotive fabrication to pharmaceutical manufacturing.

Generally speaking, an automotive manufacturer needs 50-100 SIMATIC control systems, and an oil platform needs 5-20. At EWA, there are more than 1,000 types of products.

From production line and product delivery, and from warehouses to production buildings, all processes installed on 108,000 sq ft (10,033 sq m) floor area of EWA are automatic.

Since its founding, EWA has, without expanding the plant or recruiting more employees, increased production capacity by eight times, and product quality by 40 times, and the numbers keep increasing.

We should not think that these advanced technologies are beyond common people like us. In fact, every penny of our everyday life is closely related to the manufacturing industry, and EWA represents the trend of manufacturing in the coming years.

EWA is designed with a strict assessment control system. Authorized visitors should wear white overalls after dust removing and static discharge to distinguish them from in-house employees, who wear blue. So far, Angela Dorothea Merkel, Chancellor of Germany, is the only exception who wore a blue overall like other employees.

Industry 4.0 was introduced first by Germany[①]. Unlike other countries, Ms. Merkel was under great pressure. But after her visit to EWA, she might probably have been much less stressed.

EWA is sterilized and the interior is so clean that looking for a piece of dust here is comparable to searching for a needle in a haystack. Walking on the light-colored flooring made of marble-like PVC, you can ignore the stepping sound. Machine cabinets stand in a row, and between them are monitors displaying floods of data that scroll downwards like waterfalls.

Siemens is a world-leading PLC provider. As its showcase plant, EWA manufactures more than 12 million SIMATIC products and processes nearly 3 billion elements per year in 230 working days per year, which means that the EWA produces one control unit every second at an acceptance rate of 99.99885%.

2. Super factory EWA changed the production mode

At EWA, 75% of processes are automatically controlled by equipment and computers. Humans are required only at the early stage of production, where they load initial parts to the production line. After that, it all goes automatically.

Every element is designated with a unique barcode containing "identification information" such as respective destination for scheduling of production process in a virtual environment. By using the barcode, 'direct communication' between elements and production equipment is made possible. An element can 'tell' the equipment where and when it should be used as well as requirements and steps of operation. Elements will be held for 1-2 seconds at the joints of magnetic conveyor belts and, upon selection of the right direction, sent to the processing center, where they are scanned and identified. Production equipment can extract all processing information in a real-time manner and adjust production parameters automatically.

① Germany's Industry 4.0 initiative denotes that IOT systems are utilized to enable digitized and intelligent information of supply, manufacturing, and marketing in order to realize fast, effective and customized product supply. This initiative has evolved to a new stage of Sino-German cooperation. In Sino-German Cooperation Action Plan, four articles are related to cooperation in Industry 4.0 and it is indicated in the first article that digitization of industrial production is "Industry 4.0".

Production of SIMATIC unit is controlled by SIMATIC unit. About 1,000 SIMATIC controls. Source: Siemens publication

It should be noted that production of SIMATIC unit is controlled by SIMATIC unit. About 1,000 SIMATIC controls are designed for each production line, which embeds at most 250,000 elements (such as resistors, capacitors and micro-chips) per hour. Once the welding process is done, PCBs are transported to an optical inspection system for quality inspection, including the check for correctness of element positions and quality of welding points. Defective products are identified and rejected, and qualified PCBs are installed in cabinets. Finished products are then inspected and sent to the distribution center in Nuremberg, where they are delivered to more than 60,000 clients across the globe.

Computer-based automatic system has been established for internal transportation of raw materials inside EWA. When a certain type of material is required for production, related information is displayed on the monitoring screen. Human workers then scan the barcode of a sample and the barcode information is sent to automatic warehouse. The ERP system then gives command and orders the internal automatic logistic system to take the material stored at a specific position in the underground warehouse. The material is transported to a specified position via the 5,000 m underground conveyer belt and moved to the vicinity of the production line with an automatic elevator.

3. Big data + IOT

At EWA, more than 50 million pieces of process information are handled each day and stored in the SIMATIC IOT manufacturing execution system. It can observe every product's entire lifecycle down to the last detail. In other words, every product's lifecycle is traceable. Software defines all of the manufacturing processes and commands so that production can be recorded and controlled from start to finish. More than 1,000 scanners document all of the manufacturing steps in real time and record product details such as soldering temperature, placement data, and test results. The system is also closely networked with the R&D department in order to ensure orderly production of a thousand different products at EWA. Based on data of this big volume, the factory not only tracks lifecycle of all products, but also optimizes and adjusts all processes to ensure the lowest possible defect rate. Quality has increased substantially as well. Whereas the production facility had 500 defects per million (dpm) in the early days, it now has a mere 12 dpm.

When machines are about to add materials or need maintenance, they send signals to the system in advance. The system records the amount of resources consumed and updates inventory data timely.

4. Bricks of Industry 4.0

In addition to building digital factories of its own, Siemens also outputs complete solutions for traditional enterprises interested in transformation towards 'digitization'. For example, Siemens has deployed Braumat integrated control system for the old brand Spaten-Brewery, one of the top 10 beer manufacturers, to reduce cost, increase production efficiency and improve constancy in flavor. The whole production process is traceable.

EWA also manufactures smart equipment for production lines of German manufacturers, such as Daimler and BMW.

EWA is the fruit of Siemens' decades of digitization efforts. Siemens Electronic Works Chengdu (SEWC), the world's second largest digital factory and EWA's sister, opened and started operation in September 2013. Every part of the plant replicates its Amberg counterpart.

The key to success of EWA lies in that three major technologies (product lifecycle management (PLM), manufacturing execution system (MES) and industrial automation) are integrated by controlling communication and IOT system of product and production equipment.

At present, about 1,100 employees work at EWA to a three-shift schedule, roughly 300 per shift. Intelligent does not mean workerless, not at least in the near future.

"We're not planning to create a workerless factory," says Karl-Heinz Büttner, who heads the EWA. After all, humans play a crucial and decisive role. The employees' suggested improvements account for 40 percent of annual productivity increases. The remaining 60 percent is a result of infrastructure investments. "We still need ten years to design a fully automatic Internet-based smart production line. Now we have a brick to build a great mansion," said Siegfried Russwurm, Managing Board member of Siemens.

What an awesome brick of Siemens!

Innovation is the keynote of an industrial revolution. The Fourth Industrial revolution features five innovations: ① smart manufacturing; ② gene and bioengineering; ③ IOT; ④ bid data and ⑤ mobile Internet. Each one of them is innovative enough to change the landscape of the world. What's more, they can be combined to further activate enormous commercial and revolutionary potential.

5. Intelligent manufacturing

Personalized requirements are the driving force bringing about the era of Industry 4.0. The traditional repetitive mode of mass production has been overwhelmed by diversified individual demands. Creative and customized products manufactured efficiently in batches are what we need next. Intelligent manufacturing is the tool that directly eliminates the mass-customized production contradiction, i.e., mobile Internet serves as a highly efficient mediator that coordinates rigid production and customized requirement of the industrial chain.

Although the real Industry 4.0 has not arrived yet, a soft transition is taking place in automatic production and intelligent virtual space. Industrial software engineers have also joined to make contributions in adding humanistic service to the cold manufacturing. The significant progress of big data is made possible with open industrial networks, convenient operation, and integration of hard (technologies) and soft (service) elements.

As the world's factory, whose industrial products account for 20% of the global market, China is now at the turn point from intensive streamline production to intelligent manufacturing. Whether it can grow into an intelligent factory of the world depends on how fast it moves steps towards transformation in the next five years. In fact, China possesses unparallel merits for such transformation: it has the world's greatest manufacturing base; the most extensive ground for application of smart machines; and the smart city program advancing in its 180 major cities.

The only question is if the Chinese government has the courage, like when it executed the export tax refund policy some 20 years ago, to implement ambitious incentives amid sluggish economy when enterprises are not so interested in transformation in front of high financing cost, and create glorious achievements in intelligent manufacturing in this country. The good news is that China has become the fourth largest manufacturer of robots following the US, Japan, and Germany.

6. Gene and bioengineering①

In 2012, more than 500 scientists from 22 labs across the globe discovered in their unprecedented cooperation that insignificant DNA fragments, which were misunderstood as 'junk DNA', actually contained millions of 'switches' embedded in an extreme network. These switches played a key role in gene function regulation and interaction.

Only 1% of the phenomenon was described by scientists, but that was exciting enough. The network-based 'biological elements' refer to DNA sequences with known properties and definite functions. Synthetic biologists may acquire them at considerably low costs.

The fancy genetic engineering has inspired synthetic biologists who are now wondering if they can create an artificial life form like manufacturing a robot.

As 3D printing becomes more mature, synthetic biologists are convinced that they can print out at least an organ, if not a real man.

It really is a bold vision that someday humans will be able to design their life to

①
Bioengineering is an emerging technology that integrates chemistry, mechanics, computer, and other modern engineering technologies on the ground of theories and technologies of biology (particularly molecular biology, microbiology, genetics, biochemistry, and cell biology), in which latest achievements of molecular biology are applied to manipulate genetic material consciously and modify organisms or their functions in a targeted manner, so as to create new species with ultra remote characteristics in a short period. These engineered bacteria or strains are then proliferated massively in proper bioreactors to produce tons of useful metabolites or give play to their unique biological effect.

celebrate their 300th and even 500th birthday. Once a certain part catches diseases, the only things to do are printing a new one with a 3D printer and putting it into the body.

Will hospitals be changed into factories? No doctors or nurses are needed except for smart organ manufacturing plants where a sick body part can be replaced, and people buy new hearts like they are buying pig hearts on the market today.

This is not groundless talk any more. Genetic engineering, 3D printing and synthetic biological products are moving out of labs. Synthetic biology will make 15%-20% products of chemical industry being replaced in the following five years. Chemical products, the pride of the Third Industrial Revolution, are going to be replaced by synthetic biological products, which are more affordable and environmentally friendly.

China has virtually been among world leaders in the field of bioengineering and advanced further especially in genetics and analytic application of life science. Beijing Genomics Institute, the pilot of China's genome analysis program, has finished plotting complete genetic maps of 50 animals and plants (panda, honey bee, rice, and bean, etc.) and more than 1,000 bacteria. China's life science is now steering in a new direction to research one of the key body parts – the human brain.

Breakthroughs achieved in genetics and bioengineering will be the most valuable gifts for human beings from the Fourth Industrial Revolution, only if the progress is not interrupted manually.

7. Internet of Things

The concept of Internet of Things (IOT) was initially introduced to China some ten years ago. By adding 'services', it forms Internet of Things & Services (IOTS).

The Internet which emerged in the Third Industrial Revolution enabled extensive interpersonal connection, and Web2.0 opened the door to human interaction. The Fourth Industrial Revolution not only expands the Internet down to mobile terminals, but also makes thing-to-thing and thing-to-human connections possible.

All of the previous three industrial revolutions in human history have a core of technical innovations with the glory of

wisdom, which triggered marvelous social evolutions. Industrial revolutions are essentially endogenous and active. Looking back, China was an awkward performer in the last two revolutions. While its pace was interrupted by the Japanese during the Second Industrial Revolution, China only won the status of the world's factory in the Third Industrial Revolution at the cost of excessive energy consumption and serious environmental pollution.

The resource-exhausting production and consumption modes in the second and Third Industrial Revolutions are bound to be terminated by the combination of distributed energy and mobile Internet, plus IOTS. It is possible that buildings, structures and even individuals are energy users and providers at the same time.

8. Big data

Big data is a new piece of land to nourish human civilization. It will lead humans to an intelligent society. The so-called "big data" is a generic name of numbers, texts, images and videos. People tend to connect 'big data' to the era of intelligence because operation of any smart devices and software rests on the capacities for calculating and digging big data. That is, an intelligent society is the fruit grown from the soil of big data.

Human-machine interaction is the key for opening the door to an Intelligence Era. In the age of Internet, intelligence is studied to figure out how humans can communicate with computers; while in the era of mobile Internet, as the smart phone screen keeps shrinking, it's not easy for people to click icons with fingers, even if they are much simpler. How humans can interact with smart phones turns out to be the new topic.

With big data technology, human-machine communication in the future will be easier, at some level, than human-human communication. From the perspective of human-machine interaction, we are able to better understand why the concept of intelligence in the era of mobile Internet is essentially different from that in the past. Back in the old days, it was people who tried hard to reach machines, master their temperament, and make use of them. In an era of intelligence supported by big

① *Cloud data is a generic designation of technologies and platforms for data collection, analysis, integration, distribution and alarm applied on the basis of commercial modes of cloud computing.*

data today, machines are driven actively to approach people, understand people and serve people.

What drives machines? The big data of objects stored in them. Machines are intelligentized by setting operation programs.

Human-machine interaction is not the only field of big data. Cloud healthcare, cloud city, cloud transportation, cloud computing and building of smart cities are all grounded on big data technology.

The truth is, mobile Internet is the technology that really enlivens big data.

9. Mobile Internet

Without a doubt, the mobile Internet is the most significant invention of the 21st century because:

(1) It is the only Internet for all in any real sense.

(2) Instead of being a lone star, it paves the way for connection among all key technologies that underpin the Fourth Industrial Revolution, including smart manufacturing, genetic and biological engineering, IoT and big data. By connecting notes in the symphony, mobile Internet orchestrates the shake-up of the world. In other words, if it wasn't for the mobile Internet, technologies of the budding Fourth Industrial Revolution would be isolated from one another, falling short of their expected roles.

(3) Once commercialized, it releases energy greater than that of the previous three industrial revolutions combined. In the Second Industrial Revolution, Britain changed the methods of conducting trade with steam-powered ships and established a preferential global trade rules with the help of gunboats. America dominated the trade in the Third Industrial Revolution with the bully pulpit of its strong dollars

and overthrew the hegemony of Britain. In the Fourth Industrial Revolution, whoever owns the commercialized mobile Internet will be the rule-maker of international trade.

10. Tevatron

Scientists who study nucleon already know that there's a particle smaller than proton, electron and neutron. So often discussed, the family of particle is given many names such as Postine Kaon, Y (3940), Sinma-Minus, lambda-C-plus and Charm-Quark (C). The scientists now refer to a standard model somewhat resembling the periodic table[1] that helps chemists predict the existence of atom unseen in the natural world. Similarly, scientists use the nucleonic model to shed light on smaller particles, including the mysterious meson and the much-expected Higgs boson.

11. Wet vs. Dry Nanotechnology

Nanotechnology is manipulation of matter on an atomic, molecular, and supramolecular scale. It is often seen in the manufacturing of superconducting component of microchip and material of particular properties, such as the artificial blood cell that functions one million times better than its natural counterpart. Dry nanotechnology uses inorganic materials, including metals and semiconductors, to create items used by electrical and mechanical engineers to promote development in manufacturing techniques. Wet nanotechnology, on the other hand, studies nanoscale materials on a biological level, including cell parts. Wet nanotechnology, compared with dry nanotechnology, has great advantages because Mother Nature gifts us an enormous codebase and the ability of exponentially replicating a certain design at an alarming rate.

①

Periodic table: short for the Periodic Table of Elements. It also refers to cycles in Bernstein theory, as well as in theories of economy and foreign exchange market

 ## Age of Conflict 4.0

What does history mean to us today? In the eve of a new era that heralds mobile Internet and Industry 4.0, a retrospect on what we have done right and wrong over the past thousands of years could help us

find the key to bringing human civilization to the next level and steer clear of the same mistakes.

Sadly, the history of mankind is a book full of mutual conflicts. It seems mankind has achieved above and beyond any imagination. Possibly coming out of Africa, the first ancestors of mankind were few in number and defenseless. Without any superiority in physique, agility or self-defense, mankind has lived to prevail over other species. Instead of submitting to adversities, they took fate into their own hands and overcame unbelievable odds.

Their ability of wielding technology has given them dominance over the nature and animals, yet it wasn't enough for them to triumph over themselves. As mankind evolves, their technology and culture advance and bloom ceaselessly between war and peace. Technology bridges the gap between the rich and the poor while driving them further apart. Now it has developed to a point that gives rise to overproduction. Science and technology are used to cater for the needs of mankind as well as wage wars among countries. Why is the progress of science and technology unable to stop wars and collision among men? Why are we repeatedly subject to social conflicts and stagnation now that we have access to limitless scientific and technological expertise?

The reason is simple: transformations brought by technology are usually accepted and welcomed since they can directly improve the livelihood of people. Cultural changeovers, however, are terrifying and boycotted, because they threaten traditional and comfortable social standards and practices. For every nation, culture is a control mechanism established to keep its social members in line. It is the wisdom born of survival and enclosed in nature. In the case of an extraordinary people, social class or group, its culture shines with unique characteristics and grows on its own instead of converging with its external counterparts, resulting in an inherent exclusiveness; hence the collision of various cultures.

According to the technology/culture dichotomy, all the conflicts and wars are disastrous results of cultural exclusiveness. Throughout the history of man, the four major conflicts are class conflict, faith conflict, religious war and psychological illness.

All clashes before World War II fall into the category of class conflict where one class topples another. Before WWII, there were hundreds of lower class-led uprisings in recorded history, in addition to tens of thousands of unrecorded ones, including the peasant uprisings in China. These conflicts in the cold weapon era are attributed to the rebellion of oppressed classes. In most cases, aristocrat and proletariat are culturally divided. Theoretical researches show that the possibility of conflicts increases in direct proportion to the width of cultural gaps. As the poor becomes poorer and the rich richer, class conflict is pending.

The advancing science and technology didn't stop conflicts. On the contrary, they serve cultural conflict as long as it exists. In World War I, defense based on trenches and machine guns proved to outmatch offensive; In World War II, assailment with tanks and aircrafts destroyed fortifications. These wars led to constant shifts of power in countries and even continents. Historical studies show that the root of World War II is the collision of beliefs between Adolf Hitler's "statism" and Aryan supremacism and the basic values of western democracies, and also between Japanese militarism and Chinese pacifism. The differences in belief and values have contributed to the largest world-scale conflict in the history of human warfare.

The faith conflict didn't end with the closure of World War II. It took the form of the Cold War between powers in the Eastern Bloc (the Soviet Union and its states) and powers in the Western Bloc (the United States, its NATO allies and others), lasting for 50 years and causing harm greater than that of World War II that came to an end in the early 1990s. Between 1944 and 1985, a total of 96 countries declared independence, accounting for about 1/3 of the world's population. Aside from the development of the two sides' nuclear arsenals, and their deployment of conventional military forces, the struggle for dominance was expressed via proxy wars around the globe, psychological warfare, massive propaganda campaigns and espionage, rivalry at sports events, and technological competitions such as the Space Race. Among them, the Non-Cooperation Movement was a significant phase of the Indian independence movement from British rule led by Mohandas Karamchand Gandhi. For the leaders rising to the waves of time, Nelson Rolihlahla Mandela, who had once been imprisoned for 27 years, was probably the brightest star during the Cold War. On May 10, 1944, he took the office of President of

South Africa which was the last country abolishing racial segregation in the world. In the Constitution of the Republic of South Africa, the Preamble spurred optimism – "WHEREAS there is a need to create a new order in which all South Africans will be entitled to a common South African citizenship in a sovereign and democratic constitutional state in which there is equality between men and women and people of all races so that all citizens shall be able to enjoy and exercise their fundamental rights and freedoms".

These hopeful words sparked questions among the public. Will the faith conflict come to an end? Can all human races join hands and usher in a future with no conflict? A police officer's acquittal triggered riots in South Central, Los Angeles. On the third day of the riots, Rodney Glen King, the man brutally battered by the police officer, made a public appearance, making his now famous plea: "People, I just want to say, can't we all get along? Can't we all get along?"

With the advent of the 21st century, all human races held their hopes high. People of all ages and all occupations seemed to be for peace. However, with terrorists crashing airliners into the World Trade Center in 2001, the third round of human conflict came. Different from the previous two conflicts, it was deemed the war against terrorism with a focus on the Middle East. The western countries flexed their muscles of high-tech weaponry on the battleground of Iraq and Lybia, bringing more chaos to the picture.

Despite the way America sees it, the third wave of conflict was cultural in nature, religious more precisely, between Islamic extremism and Christianity. It's time for humans to wake up to the fact that scientific and technological development alone cannot settle the conflicts all at once. On the contrary, it could heighten the collision if science and technology falls into the wrong hands. The only way of settling conflict is cultural identification in an all-inclusive world.

Culture, mostly intangible, is enclosed and thus exclusive in nature. Its existence is aggressive like conditioned reflex. It is so dominant that it could intensively oppress another. Its entrenchment dictates that it's not easy to achieve cultural identification.

As the study of human conflicts draws near to the end, we as survivors of unprecedented dilemma and chaos, whose energy has been consumed up by endless large-scale conflicts, have lost interest in further development of any science and technology. Can't humans draw a lesson or two from past mistakes? We have conquered nature, outraced the fastest animal on earth, why can't we triumph over ourselves? Do we have to expel all foreign cultures and end conflicts with wars and deaths? Over our heads hangs the mystery of the era: we've conquered Everest and ironically we falter over cultural conflicts – not because of the fear of dying on a mountaintop, but of dying on the way up there. Is culture as hateful as it is desirable?

Optimism is no stranger to people on earth. As Industry 4.0 sounded the trumpet in 2012 and mobile Internet came to light in 2014, the optimists firmly believed that a new era has come: science and technology will no longer be kidnapped by cultural extremists and their development from then on should help settle conflicts, and mobile Internet has opened a door to cultural tolerance and identification. It's time for the nightmare of human races to end.

Sadly, we found ourselves soon enough in the midst of the fourth wave of conflicts, heralded by November 2015 Paris attacks and March 2016 Brussels bombings. The most incomprehensible incident took place on July 14, 2016. In that evening, a white cargo truck was deliberately driven into crowds of people celebrating Bastille Day on the Promenade des Anglais in Nice, France. Although it is believed that the attack bore the hallmarks of jihadist terrorism, the author sees it differently. An investigation shows that all attackers are citizens of the countries under attack, unlike those in the September 11 attacks who have been intensively trained for a long time. Their attacks seemed more likely to be an act of impulsive abreaction.

From a broader perspective, conflicts in the new world since 2012 prove to be more than terrorist attacks. According to the Index of Social Health, Fordham University, the rates of suicide, unemployment, drug abuse and dropout in middle schools among American teenagers doubled in nearly five years. A random survey by an international team targeting 30,000 Americans, Canadians, Germans, French, Lebanese and New Zealanders suggested that the number of severe depression-inflicted respondents is three times greater than that of their grandparents with the same condition. In China, families of patients tangled up in patient-doctor disputes lashed out at hospitals and sent the number of fatal incidents soaring. Suicide news paraded down China's front pages and social-media feeds. Sociopathic individuals taking it out on the innocent public sprouted across the country. Such incidents that happen on a daily basis are more than simple words can describe. The world has entered the era of psychological illness – a mentallyill person can vent to anyone, anytime, and in any way.

The mentallyill in fact is extremists but not necessarily religious believers who follow the doctrine of religion. They are more like pessimists whose psychological illness is caused by various reasons, such as business failure, frustrated by romantic relationship, mockery, deception, family break-up, long-standing malady, lack of sense of accomplishment and rejection. From the view of cultural study, the mentallyill is similar to cultural defeatists who are jealous of successful people and take pleasure in going to the lengths to drag those people down. Extremism rhetoric, enormous desire of controlling and night-time motivation is often seen among the mentallyill.

As physicist Werner Heisenberg points out: "For the first time in the course of history, man on earth faces only himself, he finds no longer any other partner or foe." It is hardly too dramatic to insist that we are finally face to face with ourselves. No longer can we avoid asking why this age of unprecedented human dominance and achievement is also the age when the possibility of species extinction for the first time is a sober possibility.

Biologist Marie Clark argued that the roots of human conflict lie in the prevalence of mental depression. After studying "Human Needs Theory", she found that "when conflict arises within a society, it is almost always because this biologically-based need for bonding among its members is being thwarted by one or another social arrangement."

The belief that cooperation, rather than conflict, is one of the human natures that sparked the inception of Woosii[1]. It is Woosii's mission to heal the wounds of society with education, rid the mentallyill of extremism and return to them the inner peace, and resolve cultural conflicts with tolerance. Of course, education is not the solution to all issues. It cannot heal the extremists among the mentallyill. And another definition of tolerance is protecting the majority with intolerance of a revolutionist.

At the emergence of science and technology, Francis Bacon warned that they were not something omnipotent, but tools for creating value and benefit for life. Similarly, universities, in addition to imparting knowledge, should teach students moral ethics. "Belief in goodness and harmony", the creed of Woosii, dictates that humans, in their pursuit of cooperation rather than conflict, should do so with modesty and benevolence. Such endeavor should be rooted in aspiration to the interests and values of all human races, instead of taking pleasure in harming their fellow men, being superior to them, or seeking inferior cultural by-products like profits, fame and privileges.

①

Woosii Mobile Internet University: A new O2O mobile education platform based on online education services. With a focus on start-ups, failed corporate transformation and business-related conundrum, Woosii creates a business model that incorporates online education, offline training and incubation of mass entrepreneurship and innovation to advise small and medium enterprises (SMEs) in corporate transformation, entrepreneurial training and incubation.

Spiral Economics

Chapter 20

Topics:

1. Spiral Economics

Spiral Economics

National marketing emerges in the era of free global trade. Obviously, the strategy of national marketing is national economics. The transformation and growth of China's economy since 2012 has demonstrated a set of unique economic principles behind the Chinese Model, which is neither a copy of western economics nor a plagiarism of the Former Soviet Union's socialist economics, but an original model created by China for the underdeveloped countries to catch up. President Xi Jinping refers to it as 'community of shared future'; and some people call it 'Chinese experience' or 'Chinese model'. In this book, we would like to give it a new name – Spiral Economics.

I. About spirals

A spiral is a curve that resembles the pattern of a snail.

Spirals are also seen on a screw, a simple tool of deformed slope. The spirals on the surface of its cylindrical body, like those on a snail shell, are male spirals, and those inside the body are female spirals. The two sets of spirals are mated so that you can turn any one of them to rotate both sets. The tighter the threads and the larger the diameter, the less force required. Spirals are widely applied in machinery, such as screw nails, bolts, presses, and jacks.

According to the principle of work, by rotating the screw for a turn with force F, the work done by F on the screw equals $F2\pi L$. By rotating a turn, the load is raised by a pitch (the axial distance between the screw threads), the work done on the load by the screw equals Gh. Therefore, $F=(h/2\pi L)/G$. since the pitch h is always far less than $2\pi L$, the load can be lifted up merely by applying a weak force on the screw handle. Although efficiency of the screw is low due to presence of friction force, the G/F ratio is considerably high while distance ratio is determined by $2\pi L/h$. Screws are generally used for tightening, force transmission and driving.

Something about nature loves a helix, the ubiquitous spiral shape taken on by DNA and many other molecules found in the cells of living creatures.

Then why has the helix formed its shape today? "The classic answer is that because the shape is dictated by bonds between molecules. But that only answers how a helix is formed and not why they are that shape," said Randall Kamien, a professor in the University of Pennsylvania's Department of Astronomy and Physics. "It turns out that a helix, essentially, is a great way to bunch up a very long molecule, such as DNA, in a crowded place, such as a cell."

In the dense environment of the cell, long molecular chains frequently adopt ordered helical conformations. Not only does this enable information to be tightly packed, as in DNA, but it also forms a surface that allows molecules, such as the machines that enable DNA transcription and repair, to grab onto it at regular intervals.

To picture how space matters to the formation of helices, Kamien built a model where a flexible, unbreakable tube was immersed in a mixture of hard spheres, analogous to a molecule in a very crowded cell. Kamien and his colleagues find that the best shape for the short flexible tube, the conformation that takes the least amount of energy and takes up the least space is that of a helix with a geometry close to that found in natural helices.

Let's now look back on the development history of western economics.

A spiral is a curve that resembles the pattern of a snail

Adam Smith, a Scottish economist, philosopher and author, argued that it was natural for humans to pursue maximum self-interest, which was a commonly accepted perception. Under the restriction of fundamentalism on human nature, individualism and hedonism were brought into being.

People believe that, comparing with religionists who repress their humanity and restrain desires, it's not wrong to pursue the human nature. This had encouraged the prevalence of individualism and hedonism. It was true that hedonism drove people to become slaves of money and promoted the generation of Marxism①. But that is another story to tell. Adam Smith is usually thought to argue that the result of everyone pursuing their own interests will be the maximization of the interests of society. This was because the invisible hand of the free market, which automatically adjusts the supply-demand relation to maximize the general interest. Smith himself was a representative of liberalism.

Guided by liberalism, people were keen to pursue their maximum self-interest, which eventually resulted in excess capacity and triggered the world-shaking economic crisis. The General Theory of Employment, Interest and Money, a Keynesian② masterpiece, was published at that time and become enormously popular worldwide. Respected as a prescription to save the world, the General Theory indicated that the root of an economic crisis lies in decrease of demand. Why does demand decrease? Keynes pointed out that people who purchased the maximization of their self-interest would rather deposit more assets gained instead of, as expected by liberalists, transferring their fortune to consuming market or investment. A huge amount of fortune was held from consumption and investment would lead to demand

decrease and excess capacity. Therefore, Keynes believed that a country is made rich by consumption, which is stimulated to boost demand, which drives investment, which then creates jobs. However, liberalists have always been advocates of saving who assume that capitals should be accumulated to expand production. Keynes argued that as individuals tended to save, it was the national government's job to stimulate consumption and increase demand by rising money supply, which led to inflation and price increase. As a result, enterprises would expand production to maintain the profit, and people would consume as the value of their money declined. That is, inflation is favorable to a nation's wealth.

Keynes's theory pulled the western countries out of crisis and brought about an economic boom. Nevertheless, as they tasted the bitter fruit of inflation, Keynesian theories were in doubt. Today, the liberalism has been modified and evolved to neoliberalism and Keynesian theories also have their new versions among numerous other insightful but imperfect opinions. Looking at all the economic theories we are familiar with, we may notice that they were effective only for a period of time: Adam Smith's theory brought prosperity and then excess capacity, and Keynes's theory facilitated boom and then inflation. Does this remind you of Marx's words that 'all truth is relative'?

Human society has evolved from the times of real economy and currency economy to the virtual economy today. New challenges will emerge for sure. In front of many crises of the world's economy, people are so anxious about economic bubbles, worrying about the catastrophe once the bubbles break. At that time, another updated magical economic theory is needed to solve the problem.

II. Momentum of the double helix: high–speed railway + mobile Internet

"China has made marvelous achievements in poverty alleviation. High-speed railway and mobile Internet have been two powerful engines in this regard. It sets a good example for Chile," said Jorge Heine, Chilean Ambassador to China on February 10, 2017.

Being the country that has the world's longest mileage of high-speed railway (HSR) in operation, China has built an HSR system of more than 20,000 km long, that's about 60% of the world's total

and the number is increasing. In addition, China has also increased the number of regular-speed trains running between medium and small cities in the mid-west and remote regions.

According to CNNIC, the number of Internet users in China reached 731 million by December 31, 2016, representing 53.2% of the Chinese population; and 695 million of them, i.e., 95%, access Internet via cellphone. China now has the most number of mobile apps in the world, with

① *Marxism is short for Marxist Theory System, which covers Karl Marx's opinions and doctrines on the social formation in the future – scientific socialism.*

② *Keynesian economics, or Keynesianism, includes theories built on ideas of the General Theory of Employment, Interest and Money, a masterpiece by economist Keynes, who argued that national government should increase demand to facilitate economic growth by implementing aggressive economic policies, i.e., the government should spend more, at the cost of fiscal deficit, to stimulate the economy and maintain prosperity. In Keynesian theory, macro-level economic trends can outweigh the behaviors of individuals. While all theories of political economics or economics since the 18th century had been based on the opinion that the increase of economic output sourced from unceasing production development, Keynes believed that the decline in aggregate demand was the predominant contributor of an economic downturn. On that ground, he pointed out that measures maintaining the general balance in data of economic activities could reach macro-level equilibrium between supply and demand. Keynes's opinions, as well as other Keynesian economic theories are therefore referred to as macro-economics, distinguishing from micro-economics, which stresses research of individual behaviors.*

increasingly close connection between mobile Internet and off-line economy.

The influence of HSR development on the growth of the national economy has been fundamental, structural and strategic. By facilitating circulation of people and goods, HSR has stimulated consumption and improved the economic mix of areas along the railway. The mobile Internet has played a decisive role in driving the national economic growth. Circulation of people and goods is possible only with the support of information and cash flows.

The 'Internet+' strategy introduced by the Chinese government in 2013 has been a direct driving force pushing forward the progress of many sectors, such as entrepreneurship and innovation, collaborative manufacturing, modern agriculture, smart energy, inclusive finance, public service, efficient logistics, e-commerce, convenient transport, green ecology, AI, and government transparency. In 2006, each percentage point of increase in GDP corresponded to 800,000 jobs created; while in 2016, it corresponded to 2 million. This means that instead of being an instrumental, temporary and local drive, mobile Internet has been boosting the national economy in a strategic, sustainable and global way. in 2016, each 1% increment of GDP was equivalent to a value of CNY 1 trillion, 4 times that of ten years ago.

China has started an unprecedented double-helix development mode of national economy.

According to the Spiral Dynamics [1] concept, each time the spiral turns to rise, it signifies an update of human consciousness and interpretation on the current existence. As the spiral of human society keeps turning and rising, it also brings along the systems of values and thoughts of every existence environment at every stage.

① Spiral Dynamics: in their book Spiral Dynamics published in 1996, Beck and Cowan illustrated the 8-level model of human and organization evolution, and demonstrated that the mature human mentality is in an extending progress.

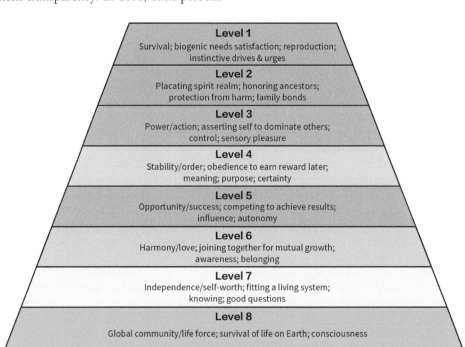

However, the spiral does not turn automatically. It needs a prime force to start turning and it gains the rotational acceleration only under cyclic drive. In China's case, the first prime movers are HSR and mobile apps, and the spiral is kept turning by the energy from favorable net population growth rate and the consequential consumption increase.

The increasing rate of income has been slow for lower-middle income groups (about 1.06 billion people) since 2016, lower than the average rate of national residents' income. However, urban upper-middle groups (316 million) have seen a faster income increase, resulting in wider income gap.

China's population of upper-middle income has reached 316 million, roughly the population of the entire United States, and the per capita annual disposable income was CNY 56,000 in 2016.

When the consumption upgrade is driven by 300 million quasi-high-end consumers, it is easy to explain why the high-speed trains are crowded, occupancy rate of five-star hotels is higher, and per capita overseas spending of Chinese tourists leads the world.

The 'Godfather of Silicon Valley', Sequoia Capital partner Michael Moritz, believes that China has surpassed or is surpassing the US in many technical sectors. "The most impressive example of Chinese global leadership is in electronic payments thanks to Alipay and WeChat Pay, the payment systems of the country's two largest Internet companies, Alibaba and Tencent," said Moritz in his article for the *Financial Times*, stating that China has outpaced the US with regard to HSR and mobile payment.

Mentioning the two countries' attitude toward robots, Moritz said: "While Mr. Trump barks about wanting to restore the manufacturing jobs of the 1950s, the Chinese are taking the opposite track. Instead of placing more people on assembly lines, the government wants to install mil-

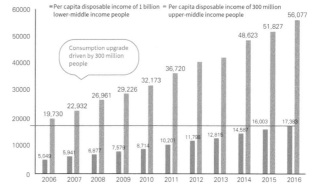

Consumption Upgrade Driven by 300 Million people.
Source: CEIC and Zhongtai Securities

lions of robots over the coming decade. It has set itself the more audacious challenge of raising literacy levels rather than pretending it is possible to return to the past."

Internet-based mobile apps are the national economy's factory of new businesses, catalyst of new consumption, incubator of new models, connector of new economies, and generator of new technologies.

III. Mobile payment: the jewel in the crown of China's spiral economy

Along with the development of Internet technology and spread of personal electronic devices, mobile market size has seen an increasingly faster expansion. In China, the market value of mobile Internet industry from 2012 to 2015 was CNY 183.5 billion, CNY 473.42 billion, CNY 1343.77 billion, and CNY 3079.46 billion, corresponding to the increasing rate of 158%, 183.8%, and 129.2%, respectively from 2013 to 2015. Population of China's mobile Internet users from 2012 to 2015 was 570 million, 650 million, 730 million, and 790 million, corresponding to the increasing rate of 14%, 12.3%, and 8.2%, respectively from 2013 to 2015.

The mobile Internet market is classified into five segments: traffic fee, mobile entertainment, mobile shopping, mobile marketing and mobile life service. From 2012 to 2015, shares of the traffic fee were 49.1%, 30.6%, 15.6% and 8.8%; that of mobile entertainment were 6.3%, 4.9%, 3.1% and 2.3%; that of mobile shopping were 37.4%, 55.3%, 64.10% and 67.40%; that of mobile marketing were 3.6%, 2.8%, 3.5% and 2.9%; and that of mobile life service were 3.6%, 6.4%, 13.7% and 18.6%.

The boom of mobile shopping nourished the third-party payment technolo-gy. The third-party payment is realized in three ways: Internet-based, mobile and prepaid card-based payment. From 2011 to 2015, shares of Internet-based third-party payment were 73%, 77%, 72%, 54% and 55%; that of mobile third-party payment were 3%, 4%, 16%, 40% and 42%; and shares of prepaid card sales were 23%, 19%, 12%, 5% and 4%. As indicated, the mobile third-party payment overwhelmingly prevailed over the past five years and its shares increased annually. It is expected that mobile payment will keep gaining ground in the years to come.

Mobile payment has enjoyed rapid growth in 2018. As the demand hikes up, methods of mobile payment become diversified, such as payment by QR code, NFC, password, fingerprint, voice and iris, to name a few.

Scenarios of mobile payment are categorized into online and offline payment. Among numerous online payment scenarios, the top five are shopping, bill charging, ticket reservation, travel cost payment, and credit card repayment. Proportions of consumers paying via mobile Internet are 81.87%, 77.8%, 58.36%, 58.22%, and 57.40%, respectively.

Industrial deployment of Alibaba and Tencent. Source: Research and Development Department, China Securities Co., Ltd.

IV. Global application of spiral economics

The double-helix development model has enabled China to overtake many developed countries in a short period. Is this model also applicable for other underdeveloped countries to transform their sluggish economic models?

The gap is only manifested under comparison. Let's unfold two maps, one for HSR and the other for the world before and after the development of the Internet industry.

1. Railways and economy of Argentina

Argentina's Western Railway inaugurated in 1857, stretching from Buenos Aires all the way to the Pampa Plain. We may notice that the development of railways was closely connected with the booming times of Argentina's economy, i.e., 1882-1889 and 1904-1912: in 1870,

railway mileage of Argentina was 740 km. The number increased to 2,500 km in 1880 and exceeded 12,500 km in 1891.

Argentina's economic growth had been progressed along with development of its railway network, which provided efficient service for freight transportation from places of origin to ports (mainly Buenos Aires and Rosario) and further destinations (mainly the UK). During these times, Argentina gained its development under a 'going out' strategy: most communication and transportation facilities were sponsored by foreign investors, who intended to facilitate their access to raw materials in this country.

2. Update of Cuban economy

Cuba was once the 'Sugar Bowl of the World' for its output of sugar represented nearly 10% of the world's total.

The Communist Party of Cuba decided to update the 'Economic Model' at its Sixth Congress. Under this framework, Cuba's economy would be governed by planning, while taking into account the market trends. While basing the economy on the public ownership, other forms of non-state ownership were encouraged. From 2011-2016, Cuba maintained the annual economic growth rate at 2.8%, higher than the average of other Latin American countries over the same period. The update of economic model since 2008 had influenced Cuban society profoundly.

In its special session on June 1, 2017, the National Assembly of the People's Power decided that Cuba would continue

World map of high-speed railways.

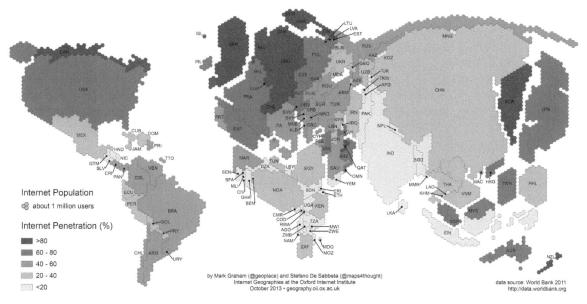

Internet population and penetration. Source: Internet Map of Oxford Internet Institute

Internet Population
about 1 million users

Internet Penetration (%)
>80
60 - 80
40 - 60
20 - 40
<20

by Mark Graham (@geoplace) and Stefano De Sabbata (@maps4thought)
Internet Geographies at the Oxford Internet Institute
October 2013 · geography.oii.ox.ac.uk

data source: World Bank 2011
http://data.worldbank.org

its socialist road map and specified that the socio-economic model of Cuba should be put under ongoing 'update'.

The Cuban government started provision of free WIFI hot spots in public places since 2015. At present, 240 hot spots have been put into operation across the country. 'I want to continue to live in Cuba, but I want to live with Internet' has been a shared appeal of the young generation.

3. Opportunities of spiral economics in Africa

As the African economy is closely tied with the rest of world, the opportunities can be identified more clearly by putting Africa against a global background. Generally speaking, African countries would deliver neat economic data when the bulk price rose in a booming global economy. This is because most African economies see their growth relying on export of raw materials, and the pressing challenge for them is that their feeble industrial bases have trapped them to the end of the world's industrial chain. Some of them, such as Tanzania, Kenya, and Ethiopia, have access to few chances. But it would be extremely hard for most of the rest to crawl out from the pit of resource dependence.

Nigeria and Egypt have merits. They hold not only the largest and second largest populations among African countries, but also abundant oil and gas resources. Nigeria is the largest oil producer on this continent. Advantageous population and resource conditions mean that its consumption market is supported by a huge consumer base.

The hardest nut to crack for African countries is education – they are in a grave shortage of well-educated talents, most of whom have left and settled in developed countries. India enjoys conditions way better than them in this regard. Despite its intermediate education quality, India has educated a large number of high-level talents far more than African countries thanks to its gigantic population base. After all, man-power is an indispensable element to drive the progress of national development and social modernization.

A possible way for African countries to change their talent mix is investing in the mobile Internet to access MOOC[①] and other free mobile education platforms, thereby gaining quality education resources and opportunities.

4. The way leading to liberty of Mexico's economy

The weekly trade volume between Mexico and the US nearly equals the annual trade volume between Mexico and China. Since the country's accession to the North American Free Trade Agreement (NAFTA) in 1994, the annual increase rate of income per capita has been limited to 1%. Half of its people are trapped in poverty, 1/4 are at the risk of falling into poverty again. The situation may only become worse without the labor market provided by the US.

①

MOOC (Massive Open Online Courses) was launched in the US. It provides Internet-based free education resources and complete learning experience, with the aim of building an educational ecology that involves platforms, colleges, teachers, students and enterprises, and establishing an online education management system that fits personalized study and life time education. MOOC has made it possible that ordinary people in every corner on this planet are able to receive quality education and make their dreams come true.

So far, Mexico has concluded free trade agreements with around 50 countries, mostly after NAFTA. Benefited from NAFTA, intellectual property is protected strictly in Mexico, with undertakings to enforcement of copyrights, patents, trademarks, and trade secrets. As a result, supply chains in this region are more appealing to many large companies which would like to return and run factories. Brookings Institute believes that complete industrial chains of the so-called 'advanced manufacturing', covering aerospace, computer and medicine, will be developed in this country. As Mexico is introducing the production of information devices, mainly smartphones, it will soon present a brand new look.

V. Is the Chinese model worth learning?

"It sets a good example for Chile," said Jorge Heine, Chilean Ambassador to China. Chile is the slenderest country in the world. Its territory stretches 4,352 km from north to south but the average east-west span is merely 180 km. "This unique terrain drives Chile to build convenient railway network and fast Internet. I believe that we have cooperation opportunities in this regard."

Bibliography

［1］中国互联网络信息中心．中国互联网络发展状况统计报告［R］.2009.

［2］李旭，徐永式．关键人和关键意见领袖［J］.企业管理，2005（2）.

［3］王丽．虚拟社群中意见领袖的传播角色［J］.新闻界，2006（3）.

［4］陶文昭．重视互联网的意见领袖［J］.中国党政干部论坛，2007（10）.

［5］白海滨．网络舆论及其调控研究［D］.西南大学硕士学位论文，2008.

［6］陶东风．粉丝文化读本［M］.北京：北京大学出版社，2009.

［7］刘建明．舆论传播［M］.北京：清华大学出版社，2001.

［8］许纪霖．中国知识分子十论［M］.上海：复旦大学出版社，2015.

［9］刘军．社会网络分析导论［M］.北京：社会科学文献出版社，2004.

［10］陆扬，王毅．文化研究导论［M］.上海：复旦大学出版社，2015.

［11］［美］沃尔特·李普曼著．阎克文，江红译．公众舆论［M］.
　　　上海：上海世纪出版集团，2006.

［12］［美］曼纽尔·卡斯特著．夏铸九等译．网络社会的崛起［M］.
　　　北京：社会科学文献出版社，2006.

［13］［美］艾尔·巴比著．邱泽奇译．社会研究方法基础［M］.北京：华夏出版社，2010.

［14］［美］理查德·谢弗著．赵旭东等译．社会学与生活［M］.
　　　北京：世界图书出版公司，2014.

［15］刘锐．微博意见领袖初探［J］.新闻记者，2011（3）：57-60.

［16］陈然，莫茜．网络意见领袖的来源、类型及其特征［J］，新闻爱好者，2011（24）.

［17］杜绮．网络传播中意见领袖的角色分析．东南传播，2009（05）.

［18］薛可.BBS中的"舆论领袖"影响力传播模型研究［J］.新闻大学，2010（4）.

［19］刘果．微博意见领袖的角色分析与引导策略［J］.武汉大学学报（人文科学版），2014（2）

［20］彭琳．网络意见领袖的培养机理［J］.学校党建与思想教育，2010（32）.

［21］肖蜀．开始介入现实的新意见群体［J］.南风窗，2009（22）.

［22］李路路．社会变迁：风险与社会控制［J］.中国人民大学学报，2001（2）.

［23］成伯清."风险社会"视角下的社会问题［J］.
　　　南京大学学报（哲学·人文科学·社会科学版），2007（2）.

［24］Rogers，E F. Shoemaker，Communication of Innovations. New York：Free Press，1971.

［25］Ragers，E. Cartano D. Methods of Measuring Opinion Leadership. Public Opinion Quarterly，
　　　1962，（26）.

［26］ZHENG，YN. Technological Empowerment；The Internet Starte，and Society in China［M］.
　　　Stanford，CA：Stanford University Press 2008.

［27］马化腾．分享经济［M］.北京：中信出版社，2016.

［28］刘建军，邢燕飞．共享经济：内涵嬗变、运行机制及我国的政策选择［J］.
　　　中共济南市委党校学报，2013（5）.

［29］海天电商金融研究中心.APP营销与运营完全攻略［M］.北京：清华大学出版社，2015.

［30］阿里巴巴（中国）网络技术有限公司．从0开始跨境电商实训［M］.
　　　北京：电子工业出版社，2016.

［31］吴声．场景革命：重构人与商业的连接［M］.北京：机械工业出版社，2015.

［32］杰克·特劳特，史蒂夫·里夫金著．谢伟山，苑爱东译．重新定位［M］.
　　　北京：机械工业出版社，2011.

［33］斯科特·戴维斯，迈克尔·邓恩著．李哲译．品牌驱动力［M］.
　　　北京：中国财政经济出版社，2007.

［34］维克托·迈尔-舍恩伯格，肯尼思·库克耶著．周涛，等译．大数据时代［M］.
　　　杭州：浙江人民出版社，2012.

［35］八八众筹．风口：把握传统互联网带来的创业转型新机遇［M］.
　　　北京：机械工业出版社，2015.

［36］菲利普·科特勒著．梅清豪译．营销管理（第12版）［M］.上海：上海人民出版社，2003.

［37］薛娜．经典品牌故事全集［M］.北京：金城出版社，2006.

［38］李光斗．故事营销：世界最流行的品牌模式［M］.北京：机械工业出版社，2009.

［39］柴先生.用你的故事感动你［M］.上海：东方出版社，2014.

［40］黎万强.参与感［M］.北京：中信出版社，2014.

［41］庞晓龙，黄颖.一本书读懂互联网思维［M］.长春：吉林出版集团有限责任公司，2014.

［42］安杰.一本书读懂24种互联网思维［M］.北京：台海出版社，2015.

［43］周禹，白洁，李晓冬.宝洁：日化帝国百年传奇［M］.北京：机械工业出版社，2010.

［44］汤马斯·鲍加特纳（Thomas Baumgartner），霍玛耶·哈塔米（Homayoun Hatami），
琼·范德·亚克（Jon Vander Ark）.大数据时代创造大业绩［M］.蓝狮子文化创意有限公司，2013.

［45］孙国强.微商是怎样炼成的［M］.华文出版社，2015.

［46］黄铁鹰.海底捞你学不会［M］.中信出版社，2015.

［47］陈光锋.互联网思维 —— 商业颠覆与重构［M］.机械工业出版社，第1版，2014.

［48］胡迪.利普森.3D打印［M］.中信出版社，2015年.

［49］曼昆.经济学原理.北京大学出版社.2014年.

［50］华红兵.一度战略［M］.中国财政经济出版社，2008.

［51］华红兵.依滴集［M］.中国作家出版社，2007.

［52］华红兵.顶层设计［M］.清华大学出版社，2013.

［53］华红兵.移动互联网全景思想［M］.华南大学出版社，2014.

［54］江小娟.中国的外资经济［M］.北京：中国人民大学出版社，2002.

［55］麦肯锡.大数据：创新、竞争和生产力的下一个前沿［R］.（James，2011）.

［56］尹松平.出版社图书直销探析［J］.企业家天地下半月刊（理论版）.2008（12）.

［57］梁建.浅议团购营销［J］.市场周刊：理论研究.2006（10）.

［58］赵亮.出版社图书营销的综合思考［J］.中国出版，2006（08）.

［59］张卫国，章卫兵.浅谈特种专业图书的营销思路［J］.中国出版，2005（02）.

［60］常秀.移动互联网虚拟社群图书营销模式研究［D］.北京印刷学院，2015.

［61］王丽.社会化媒体视角下的图书微信营销研究［D］.北京印刷学院，2015.

［62］王斯爽.透视当下数字杂志的第三方平台［D］.北京印刷学院，2015.

［63］周怡玲.全媒体时代图书网络营销策略分析［D］.北京印刷学院，2015.

［64］周莹.餐饮类网络团购口碑对消费者团购意愿的影响研究［D］.重庆工商大学，2014.

［65］郝玉敏.论我国出版企业的品牌营销策略［D］.北京印刷学院，2013.

［66］孙梦莹.全球化背景下我国少儿出版企业"走出去"策略研究［D］.北京印刷学院，2011.

［67］鲁慧.渠道关系破坏性行为原因分析［J］.现代商贸工业.2013（04）.

［68］董维维，庄贵军.营销渠道中人际关系到跨组织合作关系：人情的调节作用［J］.预测，2013（01）.

［69］蒋兆年.关系型营销渠道模式对于营销效率的贡献［J］.现代营销（学苑版），2012（07）.

［70］杨富贵.复合渠道模式的构建及其优化［J］.商业时代.2012（17）.

［71］叶松林.保险营销渠道团队管理研究［J］.对外经贸，2012（05）.

［72］张秀云.谈营销渠道冲突管理［J］.企业家天地，2012（02）.

［73］郭海沙.营销渠道中间商价格竞争博弈分析［J］.科技创业月刊，2012（01）.

［74］肖康.企业营销团队管理的问题探讨［J］.东方企业文化，2011（24）.

［75］邵昶，蒋青云.营销渠道理论的演进与渠道学习范式的提出［J］，外国经济与管理，2011（01）.

［76］易正伟.客户关系管理理论体系的三大基石［J］.经营与管理，2011（01）.

［77］曾力，赵宏.渠道冲突理论综述［J］.企业家天地（理论版），2010（10）.

［78］路十.超级二合一［J］.中国汽车画报，2007年第10期.

［79］王佳佳.营销渠道理论综述［J］.现代商贸工业.2010（21）.

［80］李薇.现代营销渠道的整合与创新［J］.新西部（下半月）.2010（04）.

［81］唐鸿.营销渠道权力对渠道关系质量影响的实证分析［J］.软科学，2009（11）.

［82］陈文江.营销渠道发展趋势分析和管理策略［J］.市场论坛，2009（03）.

［83］唐胜辉，陈海波.论家电行业营销渠道创新［J］.企业家天地，2009（01）.

［84］于志成.太阳能热水器行业营销渠道建设简析［J］.家电科技，2008（22）.

［85］周理民，刘伟.新营销时代太阳能热水器渠道和经销商的嬗变［J］.太阳能.2008（06）.

［86］庄贵军，徐文，周筱莲.关系营销导向对企业使用渠道权力的影响［J］.管理科学学报，2008（03）.

［87］范小军，陈宏民.关系视角的营销渠道治理机制研究［J］.软科学，2007（03）.

［88］姚振纲.产品生命周期发展中和产品间的渠道模式研究［D］.安徽大学，2004.

［89］陈青.猎豹汽车分销渠道模式的探讨［D］.湖南大学，2003.

［90］李彦民.我国手机市场现状与渠道模式研究［D］.北京邮电大学，2010.

［91］马文君.我国国际货代企业网络渠道模式研究［D］.山东大学，2009.

［92］李新华.格力空调的分销渠道模式研究［D］.西北大学，2004.

［93］叶庞.三星的成功与不足［J］.招商周刊，2005（7）.

［94］左仁淑.关系营销：服务营销的理论基础［J］.四川大学学报，2004（4）.

［95］何海英.三星 GSM 手机营销渠道新模式创新研究［J］.东方企业文化，2010（08）.

［96］崔景波.论我国手机市场营销渠道发展［J］，经济研究导刊，2010（35）.

［97］Ken Burke. Channel to Channel［J］. Target Marketing，2004（4）.

［98］Michael Porter. Competitive Strategy. Harvard Business Review. 1998.

［99］Heide J B，George J. Do Norms Matter in Marketing Relationships?
Journal of Marketing，1992，56（2）：32-44.

［100］Frank H，Andreas H，Robert E M. Gaining Competitive Advantage through Customer Value
Oriented Management. Journal of Consumer Marketing，2005，22（6）：23-24.

［101］Christian Gronroos. Strategic Management and Marketing in the Service Sector. Cambridge.
Mass：Marketing Science Institute，1983，85-88.

［102］Parasuraman A，Valarie A Zeithaml，Leonard L Berry. SERVQUAL：A Multiple-Item
Scale for Measuring Customer Perceptions of Service Quality，Cambridge.
Mass：Marketing Science Institute，1986，30-32.

［103］Liljander Veronica. Comparison Standards in Perceived Service Quality.
Helsingfors：Svenska Handelsho gskolan，1995.

［104］Strandvik，Tore. Tolerance Zones in Perceived Service Quality.
Helsingfors：Svenska Handelsh gskolan，1994.

［105］张诚.中投公司启航：一出生，就跻身世界前五［N］.新京报，2007-10-10.

［106］邵芳卿.利朗男装背后的金融推手［N］.第一财经日报.2007 -10 -8.

［107］何欣荣.德国拜尔斯道夫成功入主欣丝宝 双管齐下再站宝洁［N］.
第一财经日报，2007 -10 -8.

［108］李萌.车险进入电销直销时代［N］.参考消息，2007 -10 -8.

［109］艾·里斯，杰克·特劳特著.谢伟山，苑爱东，等译.
定位：有史以来对美国营销影响最大的观念［M］.北京：机械工业出版社，2013.

［110］迈克尔·波特著.陈小悦译.竞争战略［M］.北京：华夏出版社，2005.

［111］哈维·汤普森著.赵占波译.创造顾客价值［M］.北京：华夏出版社，2003.

［112］王则柯.经济学拓扑方法［M］.北京：北京大学出版社，2002.

［113］阿马蒂亚·森.以自由看待发展［M］.北京：中国人民大学出版社，2002.

［114］亚德里安·斯莱沃斯著.吴春雷译.发现利润区［M］.北京：中信出版社，2003.

［115］张世贸.现代品牌战略［M］.北京：经济管理出版社，2007.

［116］原研哉.设计中的设计［M］.桂林：广西师范大学出版社，2010.

［117］克里斯·安德森著.乔江涛，石晓燕译.长尾理论［M］.中信出版社，2006.

［118］Liljander Veronica. Comparison Standards in Perceived Service Quality.
Helsingfors：Svenska Handelsho Gskolan，1995.

［119］Strandvik，Tore. Tolerance Zones In Perceived Service Quality.
Helsingfors：Svenska Handelsh Gskolan，1994.

［120］Gronroos C. Internal Marketing-Theory and Practice，in American 1999 Marketing
Association Services Marketing Conference Proceedings，1981，41-47

［121］年小山.品牌学［M］.北京：清华大学出版社，2003.

［122］余鑫炎.品牌战略与决策［M］.吉林：东北财经大学出版社，2001.

［123］叶海名.品牌创新与品牌营销［M］.石家庄：河北人民出版社，2001.

［124］刘威.品牌战略管理实战手册［M］.广州：广东经济出版社，2004.

［125］宋永高.品牌战略与管理［M］.浙江大学出版社，2003，73-75.

［126］巨天中.品牌战略［M］.北京：中国经济出版社，2004，231.

［127］Hart.C.W.L，Heskett，J.L & Sasser，W.E.JR. The Profitable Art of Service
Recovery.M. Harvard Business Preview［J］.1990：1，48-56.

［128］Kate Bertrand，Marketers Discover What Quality Pearly Mean
［M］.Business Marketing，1987，4：58-72.

［129］符国群.消费者行为学［M］.武汉：武汉大学出版社，2000.

［130］理查德.L.霍德霍森.市场营销学［M］.上海：上海人民出版社，2004.

［131］卫海英，王贵明.品牌资产构成的关键因素及其类型探讨［J］.预测，2003.

［132］范秀成.基于顾客的品牌权益测评：品牌联想结构分析法［EB/OL］.南开管理评论，2000.

［133］丁家永.整合营销观念与锻造核心竞争力［EB/OL］.商业研究，2004.

［134］马瑞华.城市品牌定位与品牌溢价［EB/OL］.商业研究，2006.

［135］何志毅，赵占波.品牌资产评估的公共因子分析［EB/OL］.财经科学，2005.

［136］李倩如，李培亮 . 品牌营销实务［M］. 广州：广东经济出版社，2002.

［137］石涛 . 基于品牌的核心竞争力打造［EB/OL］. 中国安防，2006.

［138］［美］戴维·阿克著 . 奚卫华，董春海译 . 管理品牌资产［M］. 北京：机械工业出版社，2006.

［139］陈春花 . 品牌战略管理［M］. 广州：华南理工大学出版社，2008.

［140］胡泳 . 众生喧哗：网络时代的个人表达与公共讨论［M］. 桂林：广西师范大学出版社，2013.

［141］中国新闻出版研究院 . 第一次全国国民阅读行为调查报告［R］. 2013.

［142］高丽华，徐天霖 . 都市报全媒体转型思路探析［J］. 中国出版，2013.

［143］IBM 中国商业价值研究院 . IBM 中国商业价值报告［M］. 东方出版社，2007.

［144］W. 钱·金，勒妮·莫博涅著 . 蓝海战略［M］. 商务印书馆，2005.

［145］托马斯·弗里德曼著 . 何帆，肖莹莹，郝正非，等译 . 世界是平的
　　　　［M］. 湖南科技出版社，2008.

［146］曹峰 . 都市报全媒体运营模式的管理与完善［J］. 新闻界，2013（20）.

［147］蔡恩泽 . 移动互联网生态竞争："新三国"鼎立大一统难成［N］. 人民邮电报，2013-08-09.

［148］刘佳 . 谷歌的野心包揽衣食住行［N］. 第一财经日报，2014-01-15.

［149］洪黎明 . 2014，互联网还将"消灭谁"？［N］. 人民邮电报，2013-01-13.

［150］王瑜 . 化数据为价值：中兴通讯助力行业掘金大数据［N］. 通讯产业报，201-01-16.

［151］吴高莉 . 移动互联网背景下的无线旅游市场发展策略研究［J］. 电子世界，2013（21）.

［152］张高军，李君轶，毕丽芳等，旅游同步虚拟社区信息交互特征探析 —— 以 QQ 群为例
　　　　［J］. 旅游学刊，2013（02）.

［153］王业祥 . 移动互联网在我国旅游业中应用发展分析［J］. 价值工程，2012（28）.

［154］孙晓莹，李大展，王水 . 国内微博研究的发展与机遇［J］. 情报杂志，2012（07）.

［155］王正军 . 上海下一代广播电视网建设和运营经验交流［J］. 电视技术，2012，36（22）.

［156］黄升民，马涛 . 在挑战中奋起，在竞争中转型：2012 报业盘点 . ［J］中国报业，2013（01）.

［157］张东明 . 从报网互动到报网融合：从《南方日报》第九次改版看全媒体转型探索之路
　　　　［J］. 中国记者，2013（02）.

［158］牟丰京 . 向全媒体发展不可逆转［J］. 新闻研究导刊 2013（02）.

［159］张向东 . 深化体制改革，促进传媒发展［J］. 中国报业，2013（05）.

［160］孙源，陈靖 . 智能手机的移动增强现实技术研究［J］. 计算机科学，2012（01）.

［161］王文东，胡延楠 . 软件定义网络：正在进行的网络变革［J］. 中兴通讯技术，2013（01）.

［162］中国通信标准化协会 . 面向移动互联网的新型定义 —— 人机交换技术研究报告［R］. 2013.

［163］中国通信标准化协会 . 移动增强现实课题研究报告［R］. 2012.

［164］中国互联网络信息中心 . 中国互联网络发展状况统计报告［R］. 2013.

［165］汪志晓 . 浅谈移动互联网及其商务模式研究［J］. 科技信息，2012（31）.

［166］卢彰诚 . 浙江中小商贸流通企业的商业模式创新研究 —— 基于电子商务的视角
　　　　［J］. 中国商贸，2012（17）.

［167］宋明艳 . 移动互联网应用及其发展分析［J］. 网络与通信，2012（10）.

［168］胡坚波 . 3G 环境下的移动互联网发展［J］. 数学通讯，2010（05）.

［169］陈进勇 . 大象起舞：发展移动互联网的九大撒手锏［J］. 信息网络，2009（02）.

［170］山石 . MSDP 让运营商自由驾驭移动互联网［J］. 通讯世界，2009（04）.

［171］朱凯，姜伟，刘童 . 基于物联网的智能家居实训方案［J］. 科技视界，2013（19）.

［172］金错刀 . YY 李学凌 . 颠覆新东方俞敏洪在线教育的三大招：免费，用贪嗔痴变现，
　　　　让老师变老板［DB/OL］. 2014.

［173］俞敏洪 . 新东方会被新的教育模式所取代［DB/OL］. 2014.

［174］丁蕊 . 俞敏洪的互联网焦虑：无法防止颠覆者［DB/OL］. 2014.

［175］朱亚萍 . 中国零售业面临第三次挑战及其应对思路［J］. 经济理论与经济管理，2011（07）.

［176］布伦诺·S. 弗雷，阿洛伊斯·斯塔特勒著 . 静也译 . 幸福与经济学：经济和制度对人类福祉的影响
　　　　［M］. 北京：北京大学出版社，2006.

［177］王易，蓝尧 . 微信这么玩才赚钱［M］. 北京：机械工业出版社，2013.

［178］高尔 . 齐若兰译 . 驱动大未来：牵动全球变迁的六个革命性巨变
　　　　［M］. 台北：远见天下文化出版股份有限公司，2013.

［179］王建秀 . 移动互联网之 CDMA 发展策略探讨［J］. 信息网络，2009（04）.

［180］阿呆 . 移动互联网时代渐行渐近［J］. 通讯世界，2010（01）.

［181］叶惠 . 移动互联网：加速变革和创新［J］. 通讯世界，2010（12）.

［182］徐子沛 . 数据之巅：大数据革命，历史、现实与未来［M］. 北京：中信出版社，2014.

［183］杰伦·拉尼尔著 . 祝朝伟译 . 互联网冲击：互联网思维与我们的未来
　　　　［M］. 李龙泉，北京：中信出版社，2014.

［184］史蒂文斯著 . 曾文斌译 . APP 创富创奇［M］. 北京：人民邮电出版社，2013.

［185］猫咖，兔酱，毛豆茶 . APP 故事：从来没有这样爱［M］. 北京：机械工业出版社，2012.

［186］克里斯·安德森著 . 连育德译 . 自造者时代：启动人人制造的第三次工业革命
　　　［M］. 台北：天下远见出版股份有限公司，2013.

［187］曾航，刘羽，陶旭骏 . 移动的帝国：日本移动互联网兴衰启示录
　　　［M］. 杭州：浙江大学出版社，2014.

［188］池田信夫 . 失去的 20 年［M］. 北京：机械工业出版社，2012.

［189］井上笃夫著 . 王健波译 . 远见：孙正义眼中的新未来［M］. 南京：凤凰出版社，2012.

［190］日本总务省 . 平成 17 年（2005）情报通信白皮书［R］，2005.

［191］马克·安尼尔斯基著 . 林琼译 . 幸福经济学［M］. 北京：社会科学文献出版社，2010.

［192］吉本佳生 . 快乐上班的经济学［M］. 北京：华文出版社，2009.

［193］朱晓维，何晓晓 . 用于 W-CDMA 移动终端的开槽微带双频贴片天线设计
　　　［J］. 无线电工程，2002（12）.

［194］姜吕良，李春安，马建 . 移动终端上的 IPv6［J］. 电信工程技术与标准化，2004（08）.

［195］李树秋，郑万波，夏亮 . 基于 SOAP 协议移动终端的实现和应用
　　　［J］. 吉林大学学报（信息科学版），2005（05）.

［196］徐秀 . 基于泛网中移动终端的应用［J］. 微机发展，2005（12）.

［197］北京星河亮点通信软件有限责任公司 . SP6010/TD-SCDMA 终端综合测试仪
　　　［J］. 现代电信科技，2005（12）.

［198］官宗琪，金超 . 移动终端 GPRS 嵌入式协议栈的实现［J］. 现代电子技术，2006（06）.

［199］邱翔鸥 . IPv4 向 IPv6 的过渡策略［J］. 移动通信，2006（02）.

［200］王硕，侯义斌，黄樟钦 . 环绕智能系统中移动终端软件设计与实现［J］. 电子产品世界，2006(15).

［201］何训，王俊陶 . 运营商移动互联网发展四大策略［J］. 通信企业管理，2009（04）.

［202］陈建峡，张杰，范欢 . 无线应用协议 WAP 及其在移动终端的开发
　　　［J］. 湖北工业大学学报，2006（04）.

［203］王旷铭 . 移动终端技术简介［J］. 电子与电脑，2006（12）.

［204］于志文，于志勇，周兴社 . 社会感知计算：概念、问题及其研究进展
　　　［J］. 计算机学报，2012（01）.

［205］林闯，李寅，万剑雄 . 计算机网络服务质量优化方法研究综述［J］. 计算机学报，2011（01）.

［206］林闯 . 物联网关键理论与技术专题前言［J］. 计算机学报，2011（05）.

［207］周傲英，杨彬，金澈清，等 . 基于位置的服务 . 架构与进展［J］. 计算机学报，2011（07）.

［208］霍峥，孟小峰 . 轨迹隐私保护技术研究［J］. 计算机学报，2011（10）.

［209］张海粟，陈桂生，马于涛等 . 基于在线百科全书的群体兴趣及其关联性挖掘
　　　［J］. 计算机学报，2011（11）.

［210］李韬，孙志刚，陈一骄，等 . 面向下一代互联网实验平台的新型报文处理模型 ——EasySwith
　　　［J］. 计算机学报，2011（11）.

［211］黄汝维，桂小林，余思，等 . 云环境中支持隐私保护的可计算加密方法
　　　［J］. 计算机学报，2011（12）.

［212］乔秀全，杨春，李晓峰等 . 社交网络服务中一种基于用户上下文的信任度计算方法
　　　［J］. 计算机学报，2011（12）.

［213］周傲英，杨彬，金澈清，等 . 基于位置的服务：架构与进展［J］. 计算机学报，2011（07）.

［214］王玉祥，乔秀全，李晓峰，等 . 上下文感知的移动社交网络服务选择机制研究
　　　［J］. 计算机学报，2010（11）.

［215］潘晓，郝兴，孟小峰 . 基于位置服务中的连续查询隐私保护研究
　　　［J］. 计算机研究与发展，2010（01）.

［216］刘东明 . 移动互联网发展分析［J］. 信息通信技术，2010（04）.

［217］郭靖，郭晨峰 . 中国移动互联网应用市场分析［J］. 通讯世界，2010（08）.

［218］胡坚波 . 3G 环境下的移动互联网发展［J］. 数字通信世界，2010（05）.

［219］赵慧玲 . 移动互联网的现状与发展方向探索［J］. 移动通信，2009（01）.

［220］李正豪 ."移动互联网国际研讨会"之业务分会场 2Mashup 将丰富移动互联网业务品种
　　　［J］. 通信世界，2007（47）.

［221］付亮 . 从全新的视角理解移动互联网［J］. 信息网络，2009（08）.

［222］David Bregman，Arik Korman. A Universal Implementation Model of the Smart Home
　　　［J］. International Journal of Smart Home，2009（03）.

［223］Acemoglu Daron，James Robinson. Why Nations Fail：The Origins of Power，Prosperity，
　　　and Poverty［M］. NewYork：Crown Business，2012.

［224］Brzezinski，Zbigniew. Strategic Vision：America and the Crisis of Global Power
　　　［M］. New York：Bisic Books，2012.

［225］Buchanan，Allen. Better than Human：The Promise and Perils of Enhancing Our Selves
　　　［M］. New York：Oxford University Press，2010.

［226］Steve Coll. Private Empire：Exxon Mobil and American Power［M］. New York：Penguin Press. 2012.

［227］Soliman H，Castelluccia C，El-Malkik，et al. Hierarchical Mobile IPv6 Mobility Management
　　　（HMIPv6）［P］. IETFRFC4140，2005.

［228］Koodlig. Fast Handovers for Mobile IPv6［R］.IETFRFC4068，2005. Gundavellis，Leungk，
　　　Devarapalliv，et al，Proxy mobileIpv6［P］. RFC5213，2008.

［229］Calhoun，Harab.，Suri R.，et al. Lighg Weight Access Point Protocol［P］. RFC5412，2007.

［230］Narasimhan P，Harkins D.，Ponnuswamy S. SLAPP：Secure Light Access Point Protocol
　　　［P］. RFC5413，2005.

［231］Calhoun P，Montemurro M.，Stanley D. Control and Provisioning of
　　　Wireless Access Point（CAPWAP）Protocol Specification［P］. RFC5415，2009.

［232］Calgoun P.，Montemurro M.，Stanley D. Control and Provisioning of
　　　Wirless Access Points（CAPWAP）Protol Binding for IEEE80211［P］. RFC5416，2009.

［233］Bernaschi M.，Cacace.，Davoli A.，et al. ACAPWAP Based Solution for Frequency
　　　Planning in Largrs Calene Tworks of WiFi Hot spots［J］. Computer Communications，2011（11）.

［234］Morgan Stanley. Mobile Internet Research Report［R］. 2009.
　　　KPCB，Mobile Internet Trends Report［R］. 2011.

［235］Carr，Nicholas. The Shallows：What the Internet Is Doing to Our Brains
　　　［M］. New York：Norton，2012.

［236］［日］井上笃夫著. 孙律译. 信仰 —— 孙正义传［M］. 南京：凤凰出版社，2012.

［237］［日］三木雄信著. 薄锦译. 孙正义的头脑［M］. 北京：中信出版社，2012.

［238］［日］池田信夫著. 胡文静译. 失去的二十年［M］. 北京：机械工业出版社，2012.

［239］［日］野口悠纪雄著. 贾成中，黄金峰译. 日本的反省依赖美国的罪与罚
　　　［M］. 北京：东方出版社，2013.

［240］连玉明，武建忠. 景气中国［M］. 北京：中国时代经济出版社，2007.

［241］连玉明，武建忠. 中国国策报告［M］. 北京：中国时代经济出版社，2007.

［242］张世贤. 现代品牌战略［M］. 北京：经济管理出版社，2007.

［243］高建华.2.0 时代的赢利模式：从过剩经济到丰饶经济［M］. 北京：京华出版社，2007.

［244］傅和彦. 中小企业经营之道［M］. 厦门大学出版社，2007.

［245］王茵. 品牌营销中国［M］. 北京：北京大学出版社，2007.

［246］张明立. 顾客价值：21 世纪企业竞争优势的来源［M］. 北京：电子工业出版社，2007.

［247］冯英健. 网络营销基础与实践（第 3 版）［M］. 北京：清华大学出版社，2007.

［248］赫尔普曼著. 王世华，吴筱译. 经济增长的秘密［M］. 北京：人民大学出版社，2007.

［249］杜新. 关联经济：一种新的财富视角［M］. 北京：新华出版社，2007.

［250］李善峰. 长三角经济增长的新引擎［M］. 济南：山东人民出版社，2007.

［251］吴敬琏. 中国增长模式抉择［M］. 上海：上海远东出版社，2006.

［252］冯飞、杨建龙.2006·中国产业发展报告［M］. 北京：华夏出版社，2006.

［253］中国产业地图编委会，中国经济景气监测中心. 中国产业地图
　　　［M］. 社会科学文献出版社，2006.

［254］黄铁鹰. 谁能成为领导羊［M］. 北京：机械工业出版社，2006.

［255］周莹玉. 营销渠道与客户关系策划［M］. 北京：中国经济出版社，2005.

［256］黄静. 品牌管理［M］. 武汉：武汉大学出版社，2005.

［257］吴泗宗. 市场营销学［M］. 北京：清华大学出版社，2005.

［258］陈小悦. 竞争优势［M］. 北京：华夏出版社，2005.

［259］戚津东. 中国经济运行的垄断与竞争［M］. 北京：人民出版社，2004.

［260］林成滔. 科学简史［M］. 北京：中国友谊出版公司，2004.

［261］李玉海. 经济学的本质 —— 价值动力学［M］. 北京：中国经济出版社，2004.

［262］胡鞍钢. 世界经济中的中国［M］. 北京：清华大学出版社，2004.

［263］中国市场总监业务资格培训考试指定教材编委会. 市场营销学原理
　　　［M］. 北京：电子工业出版社，2004.

［264］中国营销总监职业培训指定教材. 消费者行为［M］. 北京：朝华出版社，2004.

［265］黄恒学. 公共经济学［M］. 北京：北京大学出版社，2003.

［266］杨小凯. 发展经济学：超边际与边际分析［M］. 北京：社会科学文献出版社，2003.

［267］杨小凯.经济学：新古典与新古典框架［M］.北京：社会科学文献出版社，2003.

［268］樊纲、张晓晶.全球视野下的中国信息经济［M］.北京：中国人民大学出版社，2003.

［269］卢希悦.当代中国经济学［M］.北京：经济科学出版社，2003.

［270］陈秀心、张可云.区域经济理论［M］.北京：商务印书馆，2003.

［271］王文举.博弈论应用与经济学发展［M］.北京：首都经贸大学出版社，2003.

［272］卢峰.商业世界的经济学观察［M］.北京：北京大学出版社，2003.

［273］中国市场总监业务资格培训考试指定教材编委会.战略营销
　　　　［M］.北京：电子工业出版社，2003.

［274］屈云波.销售通路管理［M］.北京：企业管理出版社，2003.

［275］杨保军.中国原创营销企划实战范本解读［M］.广州：广东经济出版社2002.

［276］陈放.品牌与营销策划［M］.北京：中国国际广播音像出版社，2002.

［277］陈则孚.知识资本：理论、运行与知识产业化［M］.北京：经济管理出版社，2002.

［278］薛兆丰.经济学的争议［M］.北京：经济科学出版社，2002.

［279］龚天堂.动态经济学方法［M］.北京：北京大学出版社，2002.

［280］王志伟.现代经济学流派［M］.北京：北京大学出版社，2002.

［281］晏智杰.西方经济学说史教程［M］.北京：北京大学出版社，2002.

［282］韩德强.萨缪尔森《经济学》批判［M］.北京：经济科学出版社，2002.

［283］何训，邱玮.ZARA：平民的时尚［J］.销售与市场，2007年总第275期.

［284］刘焕然，郭俊.PPG：平面直销2.0的先行者［J］.销售与市场，2007年总第278期.

［285］黄河.诺基亚成规模之王［J］.环球企业家，2007年总第137期.

［286］汪若菡，仇勇.告别低价时代［J］.环球企业家，2007年总第137.

［287］骆轶航.迷你K线［J］.环球企业家，2007年总第138.

［288］袭祥德.北京现代抛锚［J］.环球企业家，2007年总第138.

［289］刘涛.谁在威胁中国制造［J］.中国企业家，2007年第9期.

［290］刘建强.背影李宁［J］.中国企业家，2007年第18期.

［291］董晓常.混沌的未来之路［J］.中国企业家，2007年第17期.

［292］瑜瑜.Multipurpose Necklace奢华配饰还是数码新宠［J］.瑞之魅，2007年8月号.

［293］于是.杨岷：假如只有音乐美的人生将不充分［J］.瑞之魅，2007年8月号.

［294］成远.涂料业的橙色未来［J］.IT经理世界，2007年第9期.

［295］周应，李娜.网络购物回潮［J］.IT经理世界，2007年总第227期.

［296］高永.打造手机上的"第五媒体"［J］.全球商业经典，2007年总第60期.

［297］黄宥宁.改造服务流程 —— 客舱服务做到全球第一［J］.全球商业经典，2007年第9期.

［298］高永钰.远程教育产业化的领头羊［J］.全球商业经典，2007年总第61期.

［299］曾如莹.当科技碰撞时尚［J］.全球商业经典，2007年第10期.

［300］王露.瑞安航空：插上了翅膀的沃尔玛［J］.快公司2.0，2007年第8期.

［301］张放."黄鹤楼"成功七要素［J］.快公司2.0，2007年第8期.

［302］周中庚.中国企业超速度的基因［J］.中国商业评论，2006年第7期.

［303］路疗.狗与孩子的消费比较［J］.中国民航，2007年第8期.

［304］常伟.欧米茄也疯狂［J］.Thirty plus，2007年总第19期.

［305］泰戈·佟.中国的知识经济道路［J］.曼谷邮报，2007年9月29日.

［306］陈磊，李欣宇，王新胜.中端饭店：谋求突围［J］.饭店现代化，2007年第4期.

［307］中国将迎来新一轮"消费大爆炸"［J］.参考消息，2007-10-8.

［308］邹宇晴.争夺1％客户［J］.环球企业家，2007年第7期.

［309］王育琨.乔布斯打造"苹果联盟"的启示［J］.快公司2.0，2002年第8期.

［310］宴子.愉悦餐桌的水晶盛装［J］.瑞之魅，2007年8月号.

［311］葡雷，吴家喜.内创业革命［M］.北京：机械工业出版社，2017.

［312］康至军.事业合伙人：知识时代的企业经营之道［M］.北京：机械工业出版社，2016.

［313］布莱恩·罗伯逊.重新定义管理：合弄制改变世界［M］.北京：中信出版社，2017.

［314］韩叙.超级运营术［M］.北京：中信出版社，2017.

［315］奥利弗·加斯曼，卡洛琳·弗兰肯伯格，米凯·拉奇克.商业模式创新设计大全
　　　　［M］.北京：中国人民大学出版社，

［316］中国互联网络中心(CNNIC).第29次中国互联网络发展状况统计报告［R］.2012年1月.

［317］淘宝网.淘宝公告，http://bbs.taobao.com.

［318］百度百科.http://baike.baidu.com/view/5052997.htm.

［319］魏宏.我国B2C电子商务现状及问题分析［J］.标准科学，2004（8）：52-54.

［320］黎军，李琼.基于顾客忠诚度B2C的网络营销探讨［J］.中国商贸，2011（5）：34-35.

［321］沃德・汉森.网络营销原理［M］.北京：华夏出版社，2001.
［322］戴夫・查菲.网络营销战略、实施与实践
　　　　［M］.北京：机械工业出版社，2006.
［323］王耀球，万晓.网络营销［M］.北京：清华大学出版社，2004.
［324］凌守兴，王利锋.网络营销实务［M］.北京：北京大学出版社，2009.
［325］黄深.趋向web3.0：网络营销的变革及可能［D］.浙江大学，2009:9.
［326］罗汉洋.B2C电子商务模式分析与策略建议
　　　　［J］.情报杂志，2004，23(2)：10-12.
［327］中华人民共和国国家统计局.2011年国民经济和社会发展统计公报
　　　　［R］.2012年2月.
［328］艾瑞网.http://ec.iresearch.cn/17/20120112/161325.shtml.
［329］向世康.场景式营销：移动互联网时代的营销方法论
　　　　［M］.北京：北京时代华文书局，2017.
［330］肖帆.江西农产品网络营销研究［D］.南昌大学，2014.
［331］杨婷.中小企业移动互联网营销模式研究［D］.安徽大学，2014.
［332］叶丽雅.移动营销的真挑战［J］.IT经理世界，2013(22).
［333］龚恺.智慧城市评价指标体系研究［D］.杭州电子科技大学，2015.
［334］于瀚强.基于微信的企业网络营销模式探讨［D］.大连海事大学，2014.
［335］赵越.微信平台商业模式研究［D］.北京印刷学院，2015.

Definition and Interpretation

Woosii Research: the mobile marketing laboratory established by Woosii Mobile Internet University, constituted by the partners led by Hongbing Hua and the content center of the university.

Mobile Service Mode: the way the mobile commerce service provider provides service for the user, including the interrelations between the service provider, service receiver, and the service content. Based on the subject-object relationship of the service, the mobile commerce service mode can be divided into three types: push to the user, self-service by the user, and user interaction. Based on the service channel, the mobile commerce service can be divided into pure online mode, online and offline combination, and pure offline mode. The permeation of mobile internet into the life service field has made O2O of this field a popular investment spot; a large number of O2O enterprises have emerged in the fields of community service, take-out service, automobile, education, medical care, cosmetology, fresh food, wedding celebration, real estate, etc.

Constitution of Mobile Commerce Service Industry Chain: the mobile commerce service industry chain is mainly constituted by the infrastructure provider, the mobile internet operator, the software and system integrator, the application and service provider, and the end user.

Software and System Integrator: the APP developer, the operating system (iOS and Android), the mobile middleman, the database, the security software, etc.

Mobile Internet Operator: the mobile communication network operator and the broadband network operator.

Infrastructure and Equipment Provider: the wireless network infrastructure provider, the mobile terminal equipment manufacturer, and the virtual reality equipment manufacturer.

End User: individuals, partnerships, enterprises, governments, and other organizations.

Mobile Payment Service: mobile payment means the user pays for the commodity or service he consumes by the mobile terminal (usually the cellphone). The mobile payment integrates the terminal equipment, the internet, the APP provider, and the financial organization to provide financial services like monetary payment for the users.

Mobile Securities Service: mobile securities service is a service mode providing the investors with the access to real-time market browsing, online transaction, and stock market information via mobile terminals like the cellphone based on the online trading channel.

Mobile Banking Service: a service mode for the user to handle bank-related businesses such as inquiry, transfer, and payment via mobile terminals like the cellphone based on the mobile communication network. Safety and credibility are great concerns of the users when they resort to such service.

Mobile Information Service: the mobile information service means the user subscribes to news, weather information, finance and economics information, entertainment information, information based on location, etc. via the mobile equipment.

Mobile Shopping: the user conducts product and service transactions via the mobile equipment.

Mobile Internet Community: a special social relationship established by a group of people with the same interests and benefits via the mobile internet, which includes community spirit and community feelings.

Sharing Economy of Mobile Internet Age: the individuals, organizations or enterprises share their idle physical resources or cognitive surplus via the mobile internet platform and provide services and obtain incomes at a marginal cost lower than that of professional organizers in order to "make the best use of everyone and everything", forming an economic ecosystem.

Consumer Merchant: a brand-new risk-free key business subject of selling, as well as a new opportunity marketing principle. It is the consumer and the shareholder at the same time.

PC Internet Structure Hole Defect: the influence produced under the impact of "information super flow" and "capital super flow" of the traditional PC internet. The existence of this defect in the PC internet is the reason for the PC internet to be replaced by the mobile internet.

Mobile Virus Theory: APPs based on endogenous mechanism have an operation principle like the virus under the guidance of uncertainty principle.

Three Ways of Living for the Mobile Mode: only three kinds of mobile companies can survive: high-frequency super APP, vertical rigid demand APP, and super APP plugin.

Zero Kilometer of Mobile Internet: the birthplace of the basic theory of the first panoramic scanning mobile Internet in the world.

Seven Elements of the Mobile Internet Business Mode: the beginner's mind, demand, team evolution, product, value, profit model, and contribution.

Triple Linking of Mobile Internet: linking the age, commerce, and individuals.

Four Standards for Mobile Winners: the founder, good model, executive ability, and the external environment.

Mobile Methodology: constituted by the four parts of agile management, mobile finance, new 4C marketing theory, and 4M marketing system.

Mobile Marketing: a marketing mode that makes contacts with the customers and delivers the product or service to them through direct channels without any middleman.

Efficiency Revolution: the reason why the mobile Internet will over-set all the industries is that it has a high efficiency. All the high-efficiency productive relations will replace those low-efficiency productive relations.

Peaceful Sharing: different from the e-commerce age which claims to be the subverter, the mobile internet is more like a pacifist chanting a poem of sharing with others.

WeChat Payment: WeChat payment is an innovative mobile payment product jointly promoted by the famous mobile social communication APP of Tencent, WeChat, and the third-party payment platform, Tenpay, in the purpose of providing better payment service for the large number of WeChat users and merchants. The payment and safety system of WeChat is supported by Tenpay which is a third-party payment platform with the Internet payment license and a complete security system.

Fuzzy Wisdom: in the "Internet Plus" age, only two kinds of people will succeed: "the crazy" and "the foolish". You should be either "crazy" enough with outstanding ability or "foolish" enough with inadequate ability; otherwise, you'll only be "Internetized". This is a kind of fuzzy wisdom.

Micro-commerce: there hasn't been a uniform definition for micro-commerce. Informally, micro-commerce refers to the small merchants selling commodities on mobile terminals. Micro-commerce began to get popular from the goods selling in WeChat moments. In the beginning, some beauty-loving girls might post some facial masks or cosmetics, and then they found the underlying business opportunity; af-

terwards, various unknown cosmetics and facial mask manufacturers began to enter the WeChat moments. Currently, the WeChat moments, QQ space, WeChat official platform, and Microblog can all be the selling platforms for micro-commerce, as well as many vertical mobile communities.

Credit Money: anything in the credit money supermarket can be exchanged as per a certain ratio; for the buyer, it is the trade-in currency for high-quality discount, and for the seller, it is a marketing platform tool of accurate shopping guide. The credit money has replaced the discounts.

Crowd Funding: a foreign term; it means public funding or financing from the public.

We Media: one of the ten annual Internet terms in 2013. There have been endless network operation platforms such as WeChat official platform, Tencent Great Masters, Zhihu, Guokr.com, and huxiu.com. We Media has created its own world by combining various forms like Microblog, WeChat, light blogging, news client side, and video website through such ways as texts, voice messages, and videos. According to incomplete statistics, there have been over 8 million WeChat official accounts and over 150,000 Chinese We Media writers, and the WeChat moments are read nearly 30 billion times every day.

O2O: "Online to Offline", meaning to combine offline business opportunities with the Internet and make the Internet the foreground of offline transactions. This concept derived from the US in the beginning. It is broad concept; anything related to both online and offline operations in the industry chain can be called O2O. Mainstream business administration courses have all introduced and paid attention to this new business mode. O2O entered the rapid development stage in 2013 and began the localization and mobile equipment integration; then appeared the O2P business mode, which is a localized branch of the O2O mode.

Coexistence of Fire and Water: the relationship between animals and between plants and animals is syncretic. In the mobile Internet age, the world view of business people has turned from "incompatible as fire and water" to "compatible and coexisting".

Integrate Everything: in the mobile Internet age, "To connect everything" is the external world view of enterprises, and "To integrate everything" is their internal world view. To integrate the three powers that seem irrelevant, i.e., marketing, technology, and innovation; is a kind of super power.

Consistent Experience: the mode of omni-channel experience consistency advocated by the mobile Internet.

Point-to-point: the ultimate business objective of the mobile Internet is to eliminate all intermediate links and realize point-to-point connection between manufacturing and consumption.

Opening to the Inside: the bonus age of opening to the outside has ended; the mobile Internet has produced the idea of opening to the inside, which includes the system, mechanism, management, and technology, as well as resource links, equity investment, and decision-making power.

Intranet: a closed network system for the internal use of a company.

Association Pattern: the multi-industry e-commerce platform established by relevant industries by combining the B2B mode and vertical B2B mode in order to improve the extensiveness and accuracy of the information on existing e-commerce transaction platforms.

B2C: the abbreviation of "Business to Consumer", known as "Merchant to Client" in Chinese. It is a mode of e-commerce, generally known as commercial retail, i.e., selling the product and service directly to the consumer. This mode of e-commerce is mainly online retail business, carrying out online selling activities via the Internet. B2C means that the enterprise provides a new shopping environment for the consumer via the Internet—the online store where the consumer can shop and pay online. This mode saves time and space for the customer and the enterprise and largely increases the transaction efficiency, saving precious time especially for the busy office workers.

B2B: the abbreviation of "Business to Business". It is a kind of Internet market, an enterprise-to-enterprise marketing relationship. It closely connects the intranet of the enterprise with the customer via B2B website and provides better service for the customer through the quick response of the network, so as to promote the business development of the enterprise.

C2C (Consumer to Consumer): the e-commerce between individuals in a user-to-user mode.

B2M (Business to Manager): the e-commerce enterprises oriented to marketing.

M2C (Manager to Consumer): the business mode based on the complementary advantages of the Internet and the offline channels, where the terminal promotion channels and after-sales service outlets of various places are shared to activate the terminals and reduce the commodity circulation links and make the manufacturers directly deliver the product to the consumers and provide M2C deliver service as well as M2C after-sales service for the consumers.

Cross-border E-commerce: the buyers, mainly individuals, buy products from overseas via the Internet platform and pay through third-party payment mode, and the sellers deliver the goods through expressage.

Virtual Reality Product: the software products and hardware products related to the virtual reality technology field.

Virtual Reality Software Product: generally including the VR editor, WEB3D application platform, digital city platform, physical simulation system, industrial simulation platform, virtual tourism platform, and virtual pavilion platform.

Virtual Reality Hardware Product: generally including the digital cinema system, cylindrical screen stereoscopic projection system, urban planning exhibition hall, cylindrical screen guide training classroom, virtual vehicle driving system, virtual bicycle and sailboard, interactive physical touch screen, helmet-mounted display, data gloves, dynamic cinema system, and object VR panorama system.

VR (Virtual Reality): VR means to simulate and produce a 3D virtual world with computer equipment to provide the user with visual, auditory and other sensory simulations, giving the users a sense of "immersion" and "presence".

AR (Augmented Reality): it literally means here's the "reality", but augmented.

Big Data: the data set that cannot be captured, managed or processed with conventional software tools in a certain time range. They are massive and diversified information assets with high growth rate that can only have stronger decision-making power, insight, and process optimization ability with new processing modes.

QR Code: specific black and white patterns distributed on the (two-dimensional) plane according to certain rules. It is a key to all the information data. The QR code can be widely applied in modern commercial activities, such as product anti-fake/tracing, ad pushing, web linking, data download, commodity transaction, positioning/navigation, electronic certificate, vehicle management, information passing, business card exchange, and WiFi sharing. Nowadays, the "Scan the QR Code" function ("313" for short) of smartphones has made the QR code more and more popular.

Geek: originated from the American slang "Geek". With the rise of Internet culture, this term has the meaning of superior intelligence and hard work, used to describe the people who are enthusiastic about and who spend a lot of time studying the computer and network. Now Geek is more often used to describe those people who create brand-new business modes, cutting-edge technology, and fashions in the Internet age and who regard innovation, technology, and fashion as their meaning of life. Despite gender and age, these people are fighting at the frontline of new economy, cutting-edge technology, and global fashions, making their contributions to the modern electronic social culture.

Fragmentation: "fragmentation" is a picturesque term describing the current social dissemination of China. The word "fragmentation" originally means a complete object is broken into pieces. We can also understand "fragmentation" as a kind of "diversification". The fragmentation in the nature of dissemination embodies the fragmentation or diversification of the entire society.

One for All: "One for All" may not be necessarily result from "All for One"; even if the "One for All" situation exists, there may not necessarily be "All for One". That reflects the uncertainty of the mobile Internet.

Microblog Marketing: a kind of marketing mode that creates value for the merchants, individuals, etc. via the Microblog platform.

Break-even Point: the sales volume in which the operating margin of the enterprise just compensates for the fixed cost and the variable cost, also known as zero-profit point. The break-even point sales volume = fixed cost ÷ sales margin.

Market Share: the percentage of the sales volume of a certain enterprise in the total market sales volume, measured by the same unit: Market share = enterprise sales volume ÷ total market sales volume × 100%.

Relative Market Share: the market share of an enterprise compared with its major competitors. Relative market share = enterprise market share ÷ market share of leading brands of the industry × 100%.

Brand Development Index: the ratio of per capita sales volume of a certain brand in the consumer group in a specific market to the per capita sales volume of the brand in all the markets.

Category Development Index: the ratio of per capita sales volume of a certain category in a specific market to the per capita sales volume of the category in all the markets. The market may refer to a certain region or a certain group of people.

Product: anything that can be provided for the market, used and consumed by people, and can satisfy a certain need of people, including tangible goods, intangible services, organizations, concepts or the combination of them. This is only the definition of product in the industrial age.

Product Story: also known as "brand story". Simply speaking, it is the cultural connotation given to the product in addition to its functions. The purpose is to increase the decorous feeling of the brand, arousing the empathy of the consumers mainly by vivid, interesting, and affecting means of expression.

New Product Trial Rate: the ratio of consumers that buy the product for the first time to the total consumers in a certain period. New product trial rate = the number of consumers buying the product for the first time in period N ÷ total consumers × 100%.

Product Erosion Rate: the ratio of the sales volume of the existing product reduced due to the promotion of the new product to the sales volume of the new product. Product erosion rate = reduced sales volume of the existing product ÷ sales volume of the new product × 100%.

User Experience: the purely subjective feeling established during the user's usage of the product. However, for a specifically defined user group, the similarity of the user experience can be recognized through fine design experiments. The new competitiveness once mentioned the development of computer technology and Internet in the network marketing basics and practice, changing the form of technical innovation at present. User-centered and people-oriented features are more and more emphasized, and thus the user experience has been regarded as the essence of the innovation 2.0 mode.

Social Thinking: social thinking actually provides the enterprises with an open platform to promptly establish massive connections with the audience. For any product, to open an enterprise account in a social medium, post some product-related contents therein, and interact with people interested in your product on the social medium is the process of social thinking.

Word-of-mouth Marketing: the whole process of applying the word-of-mouth concept to the marketing field, that is, to attract the spontaneous attention of the consumers, media and public and make them actively disseminate your brand or product. The dissemination should be a positive reflection displaying the features or advantages of the brand or product and can be accepted by the general public, thus turning the public into consumers.

Craftsmanship: the synonym of industrious, dedicated, dignified, capable, rules observing, scrupulous, faithful, meticulous, perfection seeking, etc.

Extreme Thinking: to perfect the product and service as well as the user experience to surpass the user expectation. The competition in the mobile Internet age only applauds for No. 1, not for No. 2. Only extremity can win the consumers and the public.

Simple: it means to strive for concentration and simplicity on product planning and brand orientation, and for conciseness on product design.

Cross-border Marketing: a new marketing mode where some irrelevant elements are integrated and extended to show a distinctive life attitude, aesthetic taste, or value based on the similarity and connection between consumers of different industries, products, and preferences, so as to leave a favorable impression to the target consumers and maximize the market and profits of the cross-border combined enterprises.

Product Life Cycle: PLC for short, the market life of the product, i.e., the whole process of a new product from entering the market to being eliminated by the market.

Subversive Innovation: the process from quantitative change to qualitative change based on traditional innovation, disruptive innovation, and micro innovation, from gradual change to overturn. It turns the original mode into a brand-new mode and a brand-new value chain.

Studio: a space for creative production and working. It's not just an office, but usually refers to some like-minded entrepreneurs working together in a small space.

Venture Studio: an emerging group constituted by one or several innovative individuals with the same dream, bonded by interest and operating in the unit of the team of "partners"; relying on the resource of skills, it undertakes and independently completes corresponding businesses as required by the customer, and thus gain corresponding remuneration. It is a new type of "micro" enterprise.

Personalized customization: means that the user gets involved in the production process to make designated patterns and characters printed on the product, and then gets a commodity with strong personal attributes.

Flexible manufacturing system: FMS for short, it is the entirety that organically combines a group of CNC machines and other automatic process equipment through computer information control system and automatic material handling system, consisting of processing, logistics, and information flow subsystems.

Gearing production to demand: organizing production according to the market demand, namely, arranging production according to the market demand for commodity quantity, variety, pattern, specification, quality, and packaging, etc. on the one hand, and looking ahead into the future and back into the past, making overall arrangements, and planning for the long term to enable production to adapt to the development and change of market demand on the other hand.

Product development: the creative development of new products or the improvement of original products by individuals, research institutions, enterprises, schools or financial institutions, etc. through invention, combination, deduction, technological innovation, or business model innovation or reform, etc.

User participation R&D: the users have excellent opportunities to participate in innovation before, during and after sales in which the user comes into contact with the enterprise product, and the enterprise adopts the innovation idea proposed by the user and improves the product.

3D printing (3DP): a kind of rapid prototyping technology, constructing objects by layered printing with such adhesive materials as powdered metal or plastic based on digital model files.

3D model: the polygon presentation of an object, usually displayed by the computer or other video equipment. The object displayed can be an entity of the real world or an imaginary object. Any object existing in the physical nature can be presented by 3D model.

Cloud manufacturing: the product of the combination of advanced information technology, manufacturing technology and emerging technology of the Internet of Things, reflecting the idea of "Manufacturing is service". With the cutting-edge IT concepts including cloud computing, it supports the manufacturing industry to provide service of high added value, low cost and global manufacturing for the products under the background of extensive network resources.

Inter-Micro: a new highly efficient, green, and high-accuracy technology used for processing various 3D micro-parts.

Microfinance: a financial service system built specially for poor and low-income people and micro-enterprises, including small-sum credit, savings, remittances, microinsurance, etc.

Agile manufacturing: the manufacturer effectively and collaboratively responds to user demand by rapidly allocating various resources (including technology, management, and people) via modern communication means to realize the agility of manufacturing.

Price skimming: sometimes referred to as a "market-plus" approach because the price is higher relative to prices of competitive products.

Penetration pricing: Penetration pricing strategy is the very opposite of the price skimming strategy; it is a strategy where the price of a product is set relatively low in order for it to reach the huge market. The low price is set to capture a large share of the market, thus to lower the production costs.

FOB origin pricing: also known as FOB factory or FOB shipping point; is a price strategy that requires the buyer to pay the shipping cost from the shipping point ("free on board"). The farther the buyer is from the seller, the more the buyer pays, because shipping cost normally increases as shipping distances increase. It is also called "freight collect" pricing method.

Flexible pricing: also known as variable pricing, referring to a price strategy where different customers pay different prices for the same quantity of products of the same nature.

Leader pricing: also known as loss-leader pricing, is an attempt by the marketing manager to attract customers by selling a product near or even below cost in the hope that they will buy other items once they are in the store. Such pricing type appears weekly in the advertisements of supermarkets, special sale stores, and department stores.

Bait pricing: tries to attract consumers to a store with false or misleading price advertising and then persuades consumers to buy more expensive products through hard selling.

Odd-even pricing: also known as psychological pricing, meaning pricing at an odd-numbered price to indicate the cheapness and at even-numbered price to imply the quality.

Price bundling: sells two or more products in bundle at a special price.

Two-part pricing: charging two separate prices when selling a single commodity or service.

Brand community: a specialized, non-geographically bound community, based on a structured set of social relations among consumers of a brand, with consumers' emotions and interests toward the brand as the tie. The experience value and image value publicized by the brand fit their outlook on life and values, to thus produce psychological resonance. To strengthen the sense of belonging for the brand in terms of manifestation, consumers in a community will organize to form totemic worship and loyalty to the brand logo through a rite recognized inside the organization. It is an extension of the consumption community and will develop into a community awareness jointly held by community members.

Community commerce: a business form in which people gather based on same hobbies and interests via social tool or certain carrier, and enterprises meet certain products or services of the community via such carrier.

Opinion leaders: refer to those people who play an influential intermediate role in the transmission of media messages to social groups.

Sharing economy: a new form that gathers, reuses, and matches with supply and demand the massive, scattered and idle resources of the society on a platform and in a coordinated manner, to thus realize economic and social value innovation.

Involvement: a person's perceived relevance of the object based on his/her inherent needs, values, and interests.

The Marketing Theory of 4Cs: also called 4C Marketing Theory, proposed by the U.S. marketing expert Professor Robert F. Lauterborn in 1990, corresponds to the 4P of traditional marketing, and redefines the four basic elements of marketing mix as oriented by consumer demand, namely, consumer, cost, convenience, and communication. It emphasizes that the enterprise should firstly pursue the satisfaction of customers before trying to reduce the purchase cost, and should fully consider the convenience for the customers during the purchase, instead of deciding the selling channel strategy from the angle of the enterprise, and finally carry out effective consumer-centered marketing communication.

STP strategy: the S, T, and P in the STP theory separately corresponding to the three words segmenting, targeting, and positioning.

Roseonly: a luxury rose brand that focuses on building love tokens in China and lays down the bizarre rule of "only love one person for life"; it advocates "a believer obtains love and love is the only thing that matters", and makes the eternal love tokens with luxury roses and shimmering jewel.

4P Theory: a marketing theory; 4P refers to product, price, place, and promotion. This theory was first put forward by Professor Edmond Jerome McCarthy in his textbook: Basic Marketing: a Managerial Approach (1960).

4X Marketing Combination Theory: includes 4P, 4C, 4R, 4V, and 4E marketing theories, etc., and requires acting with 4P, thinking with 4C, developing with 4R, competing with 4V, and breaking through with 4E.

Network economy and network marketing: The core of the traditional economic marketing theories is to study how enterprises can better satisfy customers' needs than competitors, which is a simple linear relationship, however, we've entered the network economy featured by information, knowledge, and culture as the era progresses and economy develops.

Place: i.e., placement, meaning the commodity selling route and circulation route by extension, and referring to the fact that the manufacturer's commodities are sold to different areas via a certain social network or agent, to reach the selling purpose.

Channel distributor: the numerous intermediaries that connect manufacturers and consumers, including wholesalers, distributors, retailers, agents, and commission merchants, etc.

Agents: also known as commercial agents, refer to general agents that accept entrustment of others within the scope of their industry practices to facilitate or conclude transactions for others; agents run business on behalf of enterprises, and agency is a kind of operating behavior for which the manufacturers offer commissions to the agents, with the goods agented belonging to the manufacturers instead of the agents.

Added value: the product value that is newly created by the economic entity.

Profitability: the ability of an enterprise to gain profits, is also called the fund or capital appreciation ability of enterprise, and usually manifests as the amount and level of revenue of an enterprise within a certain period.

Profit margin: profit is the difference between income and cost, while the profit margin is the relative index that reflects the profit level of an enterprise within a certain period. Profit-to-cost ratio = Profit ÷ Cost × 100%, Return on sales = Profit ÷ Sales × 100%.

Main business income: Main business income = Total sales of a month - Sales return.

Main business profit: Main business profit = Main business income - Main business cost - Taxes and surcharges.

Operating profit: operating profit = main business profit + other business profits - Three expenses (operating expenses, overhead expenses and financial expenses).

Net profit (income): the retained profit of a company after paying the income tax as specified from the total profit, and is generally called after-tax profit.

Gross margin: Gross margin = Gross profit / Business income × 100% = (Main business income - Main business cost) / Main business income × 100%.

Return on equity: the percentage between net profit and average stockholders' equity, and the percentage obtained by dividing a company's after-tax profit by net assets, reflects the income level of stockholders' equity, and is used to measure the efficiency of a company in utilizing own capital.

Price-earnings ratio: i.e., P/E Ratio, is also called "price-to-earnings ratio" or "PER" (PE for short).

Customer value: the benefits brought by the supplier to its customers through participating in their production and operation activities in a certain manner.

Product value: the value generated from a product's functions, characteristics, quality, varieties, and styles, etc.

Broken-window theory: also known as "broken-window fallacy", stems from a parable of a scholar called Hazlitt in a pamphlet (others argue that this theory was summarized by the French economist Bastiat in the 19th century as a target to criticize; see his well-known essay "What Is Seen and What Is Not Seen"). According to Hazlitt, if a kid breaks a window, this will cause the glass to be replaced, to enable the glazier and glass producer to work, to thus promote social employment.

Spinning: (bike) initiated by the U.S. personal trainer and extreme athlete Johnny G in the 1980s, is a unique and dynamic indoor bike training course that combines music, visual effects, etc.

OEM: or Original Equipment Manufacturer, the brand producer does not produce directly but takes charge of design and development of new products by utilizing own key core technology and controls the selling channel, with the specific processing tasks entrusted to other manufacturers of similar products for production through contract ordering, and then buys out the products ordered and directly labels own brand trademark. Such cooperative way to entrust others for production is referred to as OEM.

Marketing space 4.0: country fair (1.0), exclusive shop (2.0), online store (3.0), and VR space (4.0).

Temple fair: also known as "temple market" or "outside festival"; is one of the forms of country fair trade in China.

Exclusive shop: a retail format that specifically operates or is authorized to operate commodities of a major brand.

Brand positioning: a name, term, sign, symbol or design, or a combination of them intended to identify the goods and services of one seller or group of sellers and to differentiate them from those of other sellers (from the American Marketing Association).

Online store: a form of e-commerce; a website that enables people to conduct actual purchase while browsing and pay via various online payment means, to complete the whole transaction process.

Marketing channel: a set of interdependent organizations involved in the process of making a product or service available for use or consumption. Marketing channels are the set of pathways a product or service follows after production, culminating in purchase and consumption by the final end user.

Intermediaries: they buy, take title to, and resell products, and are called merchants.

Facilitators: they assist in distribution process, neither taking title to products nor negotiating purchases or sales.

Marketing channel system: the particular part of distribution channel of a company.

Promotion strategy: uses the manufacturer's sales force, promotion money, or other means to induce intermediaries to buy, promote, and sell the product to end users.

Pull strategy: the manufacturer uses advertising, promotion, and other forms of communication to persuade consumers to buy the product from intermediaries, thus inducing the intermediaries to order it.

Hybrid channels: the manufacturer delivers the same product to markets at difference places via several channels.

Multi-channel marketing: roughly in two forms, one is that the manufacturer sells products with the same trademark via more than two competitive distribution channels, and the other is that the manufacturer sells different products with different trademarks via multiple distribution channels.

Zero-level channel: also known as direct marketing channel, consisting of a manufacturer selling directly to the final customer.

One-level channel: contains one selling intermediary, such as a retailer.

Two-level channel: contains two intermediaries. In consumer markets, these are typically a wholesaler and a retailer.

Three-level channel: contains three intermediaries. For example, in the meat packing industry, the jobber (turnover function) buys from wholesalers and sells to retailers.

Exclusive distribution: strictly limits the number of intermediaries.

Selective distribution: relies on only some of the intermediaries willing to sell a particular product.

Intensive distribution: the manufacturer sells products or services in as many stores as possible.

Integrated marketing communications (IMC): a planning process designed to assure that all brand contacts received by a customer or prospect for a product, service or organization are relevant to that person and consistent over time (from the American Marketing Association).

MR (mixed reality): also called hybrid reality.

E-commerce: a new commercial operation model that enables buyers and sellers to conduct various commercial and trade activities without meeting each other, realizes consumers' online shopping, and online transactions and online e-payment between merchants, as well as various commercial activities, trading activities, financial activities and relevant integrated service activities, among the extensive commercial and trade activities across the globe, under the open Internet environment, and based on browser/server application mode.

ABC mode (Agents to Business to Consumer): an e-commerce platform integrating production, operation, and consumption set up by agents, businesses, and consumers, with the three convertible into each other and mutually serving and supporting, to truly form a highly interdependent community of shared interests.

Vertical mode: the vertical B2B that faces the manufacturing industry or commerce.

Integrated mode: the B2B that faces the intermediate trading market.

Self-building mode: setting up the industrial e-commerce platform with own product supply chain as the core, based on own information construction degree.

Multi-channel Circular-screen (3D) Projection System: a multi-channel big screen display system formed through the combination of multiple projectors, which has bigger display size, wider field of view, more display content, higher display resolution, and more shocking and immersive visual effects than the common standard projection systems, and can be applied in teaching, video playback, and film playback (now many cinemas use such system), etc.

Linking: the process of passing parameters and control commands among modules of the electronic computer program and combining modules into an executable entirety.

Expenditure share: the proportion between consumption of commodity of a brand by consumers and their consumption of similar commodities. Expenditure share = Brand consumption ÷ Category consumption of consumers of the brand × 100%.

Frequent-use index: the ratio between the average consumption of consumers of a brand on a category and the average consumption of all consumers of the category within a certain period. Frequent-use index = Average consumption of consumers of a brand on a category ÷ Average consumption of all consumers of the category × 100%.

Market penetration: the proportion of the number of consumers buying certain category for at least once in the entire population within a certain period. Market penetration = Number of consumers having bought commodities of a category ÷ Total population × 100%.

Brand penetration: the proportion of the number of consumers buying certain brand for at least once in the entire population within a certain period. Brand penetration = Number of consumers having bought commodities of a category ÷ Market share of the industry leading brand × 100%.

Workload: the amount of work of each person calculated by time. Workload = (Number of existing customers × Service time needed by each customer) + (Number of potential customers × Service time needed to convert potential customers into customers).

Determination through expected sales growth: Sales growth (use the absolute value if it is negative) refers to the proportion between the expected sales or sales volume of next year (quarter) and sales or sales volume of this year (quarter). Sales growth = Sales volume of next year ÷ Sales volume of this year × 100% - 1.

Determination through expected target market share: Market share refers to the proportion between the sales or sales volume of the product of an enterprise in the market and the total sales or total sales volume of similar products within a certain period. Expected market share = Sales volume of certain product of an enterprise for the current period ÷ Total market sales volume of the product for the current period × 100%.

Sales Contribution of Individual Customer: the average sales volume of each customer of or in a specific business region of an enterprise. Sales contribution of individual customer = total sales volume ÷ number of customer.

Distribution Rate: the proportion of the number of POS terminals selling a product in total POS of the same category of product. Distribution Rate = number of POS terminals ÷ total POS of the same category of product × 100%.

Category Distribution rate: the proportion of the sales volume of a retail store selling a product of the enterprise in a specific product category in the sales volume of all retail stores selling said product in this specific product category. Category Distribution rate = category sales volume of a retail store selling a product of the enterprise ÷ category sales volume of all retail stores selling said product × 100%.

Premium: the proportion of a certain product exceeding the market price of similar products in the market. Premium = (product price of the enterprise - average market price of similar products) ÷ average market price of similar products × 100%.

Worth-buying Rate: the rate of customers having the willingness of purchase against all customers in the target market for a specific product sold at a certain price. Worth-buying Rate = number of customers having the willingness of purchasing a certain product at a certain price ÷ total customers in the target market × 100%.

Price Elasticity of Demand: an indicator evaluating the extent of reaction of product demand to price change with other factors influencing demand unchanged. Price Elasticity = (variation amplitude of sales volume ÷ variation amplitude of price).

Impression: the number of times of disseminating an advertisement to potential customers; also called the "exposure or publicity frequency". Impression = arrival × average frequency.

Cost per mille: the cost for achieving 1,000 impressions of an advertisement. Cost per mille = advertising cost ÷ impression produced (unit: thousand people).

Market Share of Advertisement: it refers to the percentage of advertisements of an enterprise in the total advertisements for similar products in the market within a certain period of time. Market Share of Advertisement = advertising input of enterprise ÷ total advertising input on similar products in the market × 100%.

CTR (click-through rate): the proportion of the number of clicks on a certain online advertisement in total impression of the advertisement. CTR = number of clicks on advertisement ÷ impression × 100%.

Customer Retention Rate: the rate of maintaining the relationship with existing customers by an enterprise, which may be an absolute or a relative number. Customer Retention Rate = (current-period business volume of enterprise - volume of new business in current period) ÷ customer scale of prior period × 100%.

Customer Acquisition Rate: an indicator evaluating the rate of acquiring new customers or businesses by an enterprise, which may be an absolute or a relative number. Customer Acquisition Rate = new customers of current period ÷ customer scale of prior period × 100%.

Unmarketable Inventory Rate: the rate of unmarketable products against all inventory products, usually expressed as a percentage. Unmarketable Inventory Rate = unmarketable inventory ÷ total inventory × 100%.

Timeliness Rate of Delivery: the rate of timely finalization of orders and deliveries or amount against total orders of a specific customer. Timeliness Rate of Delivery = number of timely deliveries ÷ total orders × 100%.

Customer Profitability: the rate of the net profit produced by the enterprise in cooperating with a certain customer against the actual amount of transaction with said customer. Customer Profitability = net profit produced from cooperation ÷ total achievement produced from cooperation × 100%.

New Customer Growth Rate: the rate of business volume from a new customer against the rate of business volume from said customer in the prior period. New Customer Growth Rate = (current sales volume of customer - sales volume of customer in prior period) ÷ sales volume of customer in prior period × 100%.

Per Customer Transaction: the ratio of sales volume against actual number of transactions. Per Customer Transaction = daily sales volume ÷ daily number of transactions.

Cross Ratio: the product of retail gross profit margin and stock turnover. Cross Ratio indicates the profitability of a retail enterprise within a certain period of time as well as the profitability of a certain brand or product within a certain period of time. Cross Ratio = gross profit margin × stock turnover.

Gross Margin Percentage of Key Categories: the percentage of categories making greater gross margin contributions among several categories of commodities in sales in total gross margin. Gross Margin Percentage of Key Categories = gross margin of key categories ÷ total gross margin.

Monthly Promotion Collaboration Rate: the rate of the number of promotions collaborating with customers by a manufacturer in a month against total promotions. Monthly Promotion Collaboration Rate = monthly number of promotions in collaboration by the retailer and the manufacturer ÷ total number of promotions by the retailer × 100%.

Promotion Frequency: the number of promotions of an enterprise performed for all of its retailing customers within a certain period of time, usually counted by month, or year for low-frequency industries.

Sales Growth Rate of Promoted Product: the increase in sales of a promoted product in a promotion activity in comparison with that of the prior period. Sales Growth Rate of Promoted Product = (sales volume of promoted product in the promotion period - sales volume of the product in prior period) ÷ sales volume of the product in prior period × 100%.

Unmarketable Product Rate: the percentage of unmarketable products in total inventory products. Unmarketable Product Rate = number of unmarketable product ÷ total number of inventory product × 100%.

Per Capita Sales: the contribution of each employee to sales within a certain period of sales. Per Capita Sales = total sales volume of current period ÷ total number of employees of current period.

Per Capita Gross Margin Contribution: the gross margin realized by each employee in a certain stage of sales. Per Capita Gross Margin Contribution = current-period gross margin ÷ total number of employees of current period.

ROS (return on sales): an efficiency indicator evaluating the profit obtained from sales volume by a company, calculated based on total after-tax profit and total sale volume. ROS helps to determine the efficiency of profiting from sales volume. In addition, it is also an indicator used to evaluate management efficiency. Calculation Formula: annual profit or annual average profit ÷ total investment × 100%.

Order Processing Cycle: the average time required from the issuance of an order from a customer or a subordinate sales organization to the actual receipt of goods.

Regional Sales Structure: a method of adding up and tabulating sales from pre-determined segments and calculating their percentages in total sales from the perspective of a wider sales region. Sales proportion of segment region = sales volume of a segment region ÷ overall sales of the region × 100%.

Product Sales Structure: the percentage of all products in sales of an enterprise in its sales volume, requiring the calculation of the percentage of individual product in total sales volume and tabulating the sales percentages of all products to present the product sales structure of the enterprise. Sales percentage of individual product = sales volume of individual product ÷ total sales volume of corresponding period × 100%.

Product Inventory Structure: the percentage of each category of product in total inventory, requiring the calculation of the percentage of each individual product in total inventory and tabulating the results. Individual product inventory percentage = averaged inventory of individual product ÷ average inventory of corresponding period × 100%.

Cost Structure: the summary of the percentage of each category of cost in total costs. Individual cost percentage = individual cost ÷ total cost of corresponding period × 100%.

Year-on-year Growth Rate: the growth (in sales, profit, etc.) in comparison from a year ago. Year-on-year Growth Rate = (current-year data - data from a year ago) ÷ data from a year ago × 100%.

Year-on-year Chain Growth Rate: the growth (in sales, profit, etc.) in comparison from the prior period of last year. Year-on-year Chain Growth Rate = current-year data - data from the prior period of last year) ÷ data from a year ago × 100%.

Sales Achievement Rate: the percentage of actual sales achieved in a certain period of time in total planned sales. Sales Achievement Rate = actually achieved sales volume ÷ planned sales volume × 100%.

Time Cost: the time, as a cost, required for achieving a certain agreement. In the category of economics, time cost not only means the lapse of time itself, but also refers to the loss of opportunity or economic benefit during a certain period of time. In One Degree Strategy, time cost is defined as the evaluation of economic comparison strength in time value by adopting the theory on comparative economics.

New-arrival Loading Rate: the proportion of customers (stores) already purchasing new-arrival products and providing samples for some time after the arrival of new products in total customers (stores) of an enterprise. New-arrival Loading Rate = customers purchasing new products and providing samples ÷ total number of customers dealt with by marketing personnel × 100%.

Stock-out Rate: the proportion of stock-out orders in total amount of orders received by the enterprise within a certain period of time. Stock-out Rate = amount of stock-out order ÷ total amount of order × 100%.

Man-hour Productivity: the hourly sales revenue per employee. Man-hour Productivity = sales revenue ÷ total working hours of employees × 100%.

Personnel Fielding Percentage: the average area of shopping place taken charge of by each operating person. Personnel Fielding Percentage = total area of shopping place ÷ number of operating personnel.

Utilization Rate of Shopping Place: also called the utilization area of shopping place, the ration of the actual area used for product sales against the total area of the shopping place. Utilization Rate of Shopping Place = area of shopping place ÷ total field area × 100%.

The First Industrial Revolution: applying a brand-new historical view to push the First Industrial Revolution back to the Tang and Song Dynasties of China (about 1,000 years ago) so as to prove that it was the Chinese people that had led the first industrial revolution in human history.

Revolution 4.0: to find out the corresponding relationship of the first to fourth industrial revolutions in physical theories. The Second Industrial Revolution corresponds to Newtonian mechanics; the Third Industrial Revolution corresponds to the Einstein theory of relativity, and the Fourth Industrial Revolution corresponds to quantum mechanics.

Minority is Majority: the core idea of fans economics is to cultivate a minority of highly loyal and adhesive fans to lead the majority.

1℃ Principle: to obtain returns from investment by taking advantage of the time lag between advanced and lagged areas based on time machine and proper judgment on trend.

Human beings have three longings: possession, association and existence.

Substitution Mode: similar to the substitution in mathematics, the virtual-physical conversion in the era of mobile Internet is a mode of substitution that results in an energy conversion each time.

Payment Mode: different from the PC Internet era when free services dominated, the mode of "payment to customers" is expected in the era of mobile Internet.

Uncertainty Principle: both success and failure are uncertain in entrepreneurship of this era.

Elephant, Nuclear Explosion and Virus: elephants, nuclear explosion and virus are separately the core principle of the industrial economy, information economy and the era of mobile Internet.

Customer Lifetime Value: the sum of discounted value creating profit for the enterprise by a customer in the future.

Lifetime Value of Potential Customer: the value obtained from each potential customer minus the cost for acquiring such customer. Lifetime Value of Potential Customer = customer acquisition rate × (initial gross margin + Customer Lifetime Value) - acquisition cost.

Customer Acquisition Cost: the average cost of acquiring a customer, being the total cost divided by the number of acquired customer. Customer acquisition cost = acquisition cost ÷ number of new customer.

Customer Retention Cost: the cost for retaining existing customers, being the total cost divided by the number of customer retained. Customer Retention

Cost = cost for retaining customers ÷ number of customers retained.

Attention: PC Internet focused on "traffic thinking" while mobile Internet focuses on "attention thinking".

Brand Focus: it refers to the brand association of a customer for product extremity.

New 4C Marketing Theory: Charm, Crash, Commit and Conclude.

Demand Mining: the essence of mobile marketing is to escalate from finding demands to creating and then mining demands, as customers' demands are being hidden deeper and deeper.

Everyone Principle: everyone is a We Media, a customer, an investor, a designer, an innovator and a brand.

Petty Gain: what customers do is not to take advantage, but to take petty gains.

Trot: make continuous and timely updating. Accommodation to circumstances: give up and move onto another road once errors are tried and found. Avoid hesitation.

4M Marketing System: it may be the most perfect marketing experience in today's world, consisting of four systems: APP, We Media, micro-distribution and micro-community.

Seed user: core fan users exhibiting strong relations in mobile marketing.

Vertical User: information-priority user acquired through micro-communities. Priority: mobile micro-distribution replaces conventional hierarchical structure in offline product distribution with an interest relation chain-based priority system according to the sequence of information exposure.

First Renaissance: to define the First Renaissance with a brand-new historical view, that the First Renaissance was jointly initiated by China and Greece 2,000 years ago and China had dominated Asia.

Third Renaissance: the Third Renaissance started one hundred years ago led by China. Today, we are just on the eve of the highest tide of the Third Renaissance.

Agile Management: agile management originates in software development. In this book, it is adapted to enterprise management in the era of mobile Internet.

Chief Market Technology Integration Officer: a chief technology and marketing integration officer masters both technologies and business.

Dualism: a theory arguing that good and evil are two opposite forces existing in the world, and the world is the battle field of the forces.

Universal Connection: viewing biology from the perspective of quantum mechanics that each living being is the connection of numerous cells via a specific program. That is why we say connection is the composition code of a living being.

Cubicles: a feeling like being a shaft. A company full of cubicles usually finds it hard to adapt to the rapidly changing mobile Internet.

Creative Economy: if Newton hastened the industrial economy and Einstein incubated the knowledge economy, then quantum mechanics advocates the creation economy.

For modernization measures: organic cellphone, flattened time, fragmented interest and personalized product.

Design Innovation: a method of designing the relationship among human beings, products and the environment on the basis of scenario analysis and focusing on user experiences in the era of customization, a unique mode of product presentation in the era of mobile Internet.

Human-oriented Economics: in information economy, mobile Internet urges economics to transform from the non-human oriented mode to the human-oriented research system. Attributed to experiments and demonstrations, human-oriented economics has questioned and criticized the "hypothesis of rational man" adopted in economics in the past five hundred years.

Information Literate: an "economic man" living on information in the era of mobile Internet. There are two possibilities for information literate as information can be certain or uncertain: "hypothesis of rational man" and "hypothesis of non-rational man".

Time Schedule: the proportion of total time lapsed till a certain time node within a period of time in total time span. Time schedule = total time lapsed till a certain time node ÷ total time span of a period of time × 100%.

Sales Progress: the percentage of staged sales achievements in overall sales objective. Sales progress is closely related to time. When speaking of sales progress, it clearly reveals the correlation between a certain time node and a certain period of time.

Employee Turnover Rate: the percentage of separated employees in the average employee scale during a period of time. Employee turnover rate = number of separated employees ÷ average employee scale during the period × 100%.

Turnover Rate of Key Employee: the percentage of separated employees of special value to an enterprise in total employee scale. Turnover rate of key employee = number of separated key employees ÷ average key employee scale during the period × 100%.

Monthly Visit Rate: the average times of visit by a salesman to a certain customer on a monthly basis. Monthly visit rate = number of visit to a certain customer within a certain period of time ÷ number of natural months within the period × 100%.

Recommendation Rate: the percentage of featured products recommended to the customers in total products in customers' warehouses, or the percentage of sales volumes of featured products in current sales volume. Recommendation Rate = number of featured product ÷ total number of product in customer's warehouse × 100%.

First Economic Revolution: taking place in Ancient Greece and China about 2,000 years ago, focusing on "land allocation and monetary transaction" and mainly studied the project of wealth management.

Second Economic Revolution: taking place featured by the classic economics prevailing from the mid-18th century to the early 20th century, mainly studying the project of wealth production with the representative figure being Adam Smith.

Third Economic Revolution: a macroscopic analysis mode taking national economy as the object of study, represented by Keynes.

Fourth Economic Revolution: the "information literate"-based humanism economics for the era of mobile Internet coming.

Sharing Economy: people share all social resources in a compensated manner and contribute and share benefits in different ways to enjoy economic dividends; such share will more and more apply mobile Internet as the media during its evolution.

New 4S Marketing Model: composed of four major factors: Super Product, Substance, Super User and Space.

4P Theory: Product, Price, Place and Promotion.

4C Theory: the redefinition of four elements for marketing based on consumer demands: Consumer, Cost, Convenience and Communication.

4R: Relevance, Reaction, Relationship and Return.

4V Strategy: according to the strategy, the success of an enterprise must be based on differentiated orientation, that is, you need to provide unique products and services, and your products shall have added values so as to arouse resonance from the consumers toward your services and products.

Six-strength Theory: the problem is not "who to buy", but "who to sell". Distributors need to have a higher status in the market system than terminal consumers.

2G: second-generation cellphone communication technical specification. 2G is usually defined as a cellphone communication technical specification that is incapable of sending Emails, software, etc. The only functions available are calling, date and time transmission, etc.

3G: third-generation mobile communication technology, a kind of cellular mobile communication technology that supports high-speed data transmission. 3G technology realizes simultaneous transmission of vocal information and data at a speed usually exceeding hundreds of Kbps. 3G is a new-generation mobile communication system that combines wireless communication with Internet and other means of multi-media communication. Currently there are four standards adopted for 3G: CDMA2000, WCDMA, TD-SCDMA and WiMAX.

4G: fourth-generation mobile communication standard, i.e., fourth-generation mobile communication technology, 4G in short. There are two 4G systems: TD-LET and FDD-LET. (Technically, LET belongs to 3G. Although promoted as a 4G wireless standard, it is actually not accepted by 3GPP as the next-generation wireless communication standard (IMT-Advanced) by International Telecommunications Union, thus, in the strictest sense, it does not meet the 4G standard. Only upgraded LTE Advanced can meet the 4G standard of International Telecommunications Union.) 4G combines 3G and WLAN technologies and is capable of rapidly transmitting data, high-quality audios, videos and images. 4G network allows downloading at a speed over 100MBps, 25 times faster than existing household ADSL (4M) and can meet the requirements for wireless services of nearly all users. 4G network is deployable where there is no DSL and cable TV coverage and expandable to the entire region.

ADSL: ADSL is a type of DSL technology fully described as Asymmetric Digital Subscriber Line, also Asymmetric Digital Subscriber Loop, being an emerging form of data transmission. ADSL provides asymmetric up and down bandwidths, which is the origin of its name. ADSL divides an ordinary telephone line into three relatively independent communication channels—telephone, up and down—via the frequency division multiplexing technology so as to avoid mutual interference. The users may surf the Internet while on the phone without worry about surfing speed and poor connection.

ARPU: short for Average Revenue Per User. It is an indicator used to measure business revenue of a telecommunication operator. ARPU focuses on the revenue obtained by the operator from each user within a specific period of time.

B2B2C: short for Business-to-Business-to-Consumer; an E-business-based online shopping mode - the first B refers to the supplier of product or service; the second B refers to the enterprise engaged in E business; C refers to the consumers.

BBS: short for Bulletin Board System, which allows the users to connect to the Internet through terminal programs, executed downloaded data or programs, upload data, read news and exchange opinions with other users by running service software on a computer. Many BBSs are managed by webmasters. For the moment, BBS sometimes refer to online forums or communities.

CP: short for Content Provider; also ICP (Internet Content Provider), meaning the telecommunication operator providing Internet information services and value-added services for the users.

CPA: short for Cost per Action. CPA is a pricing mode applied in the field of online advertising, i.e., to charge each visitor for actions taken against online advertisements.

CPC: short for Cost Per Click, i.e., the cost for each click on an online advertisement. CPC is a key parameter for evaluating the effect of injecting online advertisements, also a commonly adopted pricing method in the society of online advertising.

Facebook: a social service network established in the U.S., officially put into operation on February 4, 2004, mainly founded by Mark Zuckerberg, an American. At present, Facebook is the number one photo sharing platform in the world, nearly 8.5 million photos uploaded every day. As of May 2012, Facebook had registered nearly 900 million users, being the largest social platform worldwide.

Google Play: formerly known as And Roid Market, being an online application store developed by Google for Android devices. An application named "Play-store" is pre-installed in cellphones where Google Play allows the users to view, download and purchase third-party applications on Google Play. On March 7, 2012, Android Market was integrated with Google Music and Google Play Movie and changed its name to Google Play.

NFC: short for Near Field Communication. It is a non-contact identification and interconnection technology jointly developed by Philips and Sony for near field wireless communication between mobile devices, consumer electronics, PCs and smart control tools.

OTT: short for Over The Top, a word very popular in the communication circle which originates in basketball and other sports activities, meaning "players passing balls over the head repeatedly and finally to the destination". It means that Internet companies develop Internet-based video and data service business bypassing the operators and emphasizes the irrelevance between service and physical network.

P2C: short for Production to Consumer, a process of delivering products for the manufacturer to the consumer without any intermediary transaction, another new E-business concept after B2B, B2C and C2C, usually called "life service platform" at home.

P2P: short for Peer to Peer, i.e., individual to individual. P2P loaning is a financial mode that an individual provides small-amount loans for others through a third-party platform (a P2P company) with a certain amount of fees charged.

PE: short for Private Equity, an investment act that raises funds through private placement and conducts equity investment on private (i.e., unlisted) companies so as to increase value of said companies and ultimately sell the shares held, cash out and exit the investment by way of listing, merger, management buyout and equity replacement.

SNS: short for Social Network in Services, referring to network services aiming to help people to set up social networks, also existing mature and popular information carriers such as SMS. Another definition for SNS is Social Network Site.

Twitter: in Chinese, a foreign social network and micro-blog service platform. Twitter realizes instant communication via wireless network, wired network and varied communication technologies, being a typical application of micro-blog. It allows the users to text their updated statuses and ideas to cellphones and customized web farms, not only just to individuals.

UI: short for User Interface. UI design means the overall design for man-machine interaction, operation logic and interface aesthetics of software. A good UI design not only highlights the uniqueness and taste of software, but also makes software operation more comfortable, easy and free, completely reflecting the purpose and feature of software.

VC: short for Venture Capital. In China, VC is a long-established concept assigned with specific connotation. Maybe it's better to translate it as "entrepreneurship investment" in Chinese. Generalized risk investment includes all investment behaviors featured in high risks and high potential returns, while narrow risk investment refers to investment behaviors based on high and new technologies and producing and operating technology-intensive products. According to definition of National Venture Capital Association (NVCA), risk investment is a sort of equity capital that is invested by professional financiers into emerging, rapidly growing and having great potential enterprises.

WAP: short for Wireless Application Protocol, a global network communication protocol. WAP establishes a common standard for mobile Internet and aims to introduce abundant information and advanced business of Internet into cellphones and other wireless terminals.

WiFi: a technology that interconnects PCs, hand-held devices (e.g., Pads, cellphones) and other terminals in a wireless manner and aims to improve interconnectivity of wireless products based on IEEE802·11. Any local network using IEEE802·11 series protocols can be a WiFi.

WiMAX: short for World Wide Interoperability for Microwave Access. WiMAX is also called 802·16 WMAN or 802·16. It is an emerging broadband wireless access technology that allows high-speed connection to Internet, with a maximum data transmission range of 50km.

Service Provider (SP): the direct provider of mobile Internet service content and application service, usually the provider of value-added telecommunication services who develops and provides services for cellphone users based on user demands.

Google: an American-listed company founded on September 7, 1998 as a private holding company, designing and managing an Internet-based search engine. Google Plex, the headquarters, is located in Mountain View, California. Google is widely recognized as the largest search engine in the world which provides the users with simple free services.

Community: by definition, community is a small circle of people surrounding a "leader", who have the same "belief" or objective and learn with and help each other so as to achieve win-win.

Angel Investment: a form of equity capital investment featured by wealthy individuals making contributions to original projects with patent technologies or unique concepts or small-sized start-up enterprises as a one-time upfront investment.

Special supply: products, either natural or artificial, exclusively supplied for special classes or higher leadership. For instance, since the ancient times, there had been special supplies for nobilities, including extremely high-quality tea, honey, wine, fruits, rice, vegetables, etc.

WEB: literally, "web" means the spider web or network. In webpage designing, we call it a web page. There are three forms of webs: hypertext, hypermedia and HTTP.

LINE: a communication application launched by NHN Japan, a Japanese subsidiary of NHN—a South Korean Internet company—starting in June 2011 and has already had more than 300 million registered users around the world.

APP STORE: a part of Itunes Store, functioning as the service software for iPhone, iPod Touch, iPad and Mac, allowing the users to view and download certain applications developed for iPhone SDK or MAC from Itunes Store or Mac APP Store. The users can purchase pay applications and use free applications by downloading them to their iPhone, iPod Touch, iPad or Mac. Such applications may include games, calendars, translation formals, galleries and other useful packages. The APP Store in Mac is called Mac APP Store. Different from IOS applications, APP Store provides massive mobile APPs which are customized by Apple and third-party developers for iPhone. The more APPs you download, the greater power will iPhone bring you, which is completely beyond imagination. It will be a joyful experience to download APPs from APP Store. The users can easily find what they are looking for and be surprised by those they have never imagined.

BAT: three Chinese Internet giants, separately: Baidu, Alibaba and Tencent.

MIXI: the largest social network of Japan, currently representing a fashion culture of the country. For many Japanese, especially young people, Mixi has become a part of their lives; some people even get dependent on Mixi by an obsession with Mixi's community activities. These Mixi fans care much about their performances in communities, worrying about others' opinions of their photos and diaries, browse number and whether there is a decline in visitors. From another point of view, it reflects the significance of Mixi for Japanese users.

NFC Payment: consumers make payments using their cellphones or other hand-held devices adopting the NFC (Near Field Communication) technology when buying products or services, an emerging mobile payment mode. Payments are handled on the spot and off the line. No mobile network is required. Local communication with a POS, vending machine or other equipment is realized via the NFC RF channel. NFC is the mainstream technology for near-field payment, a short-distance high-frequency wireless communication technology that allows the non-contact point-to-point data transmission and exchange between electronic devices. NFC evolves from and combines the RFID technology, mainly promoted by Philips,

Nokia, Sony, Samsung, China UnionPay, China Mobile, JePower, etc. for the application by cellphones and other hand-held devices.

Standard Play (SP) mode: tape runs at standard speed in this mode and images recorded meet the standard requirement for definition, i.e., VHS reaches around 240 lines and Mini DV reaches over 520 lines.

Diaosi (loser): someone who is short, poor, bad-looking, clumsy, fat, etc. You may be described as a "loser" when fitting several aforesaid features. "Diaosi" is an ironic term born during the blossom of China's network culture. At first, people fitting these features were called "the short, clumsy and poor", opposite to "the tall, rich and good-looking". Poverty is the signature of "Diaosi", for whom houses and cars are merely distant dreams. The term "Diaosi" became popular in mainland China since the beginning of 2012, widely used among the young group. In comparison to its original definition, "Diaosi" has become more like a kind of self-mockery these days. Everyone calls themselves "Diaosi", whether they fit the apparent definition and internal attributes of "Diaosi" or not. To figure out the reason, "Diaosi" perfectly matches the realistic characteristics of modern society. On the other hand, some people practice self-deprecation by lowering their self-expectations and thus relieving the overwhelming social stress. Most of them are self-conscious and self-awakening, voluntarily categorizing themselves as "Diaosi". Meanwhile, "the tall, rich and good-looking" is more and more used for irony and mocking instead of admiration. Some argues that the "Diaosi" culture is nothing but the rise of an Internet-based sub-culture, meaning that Chinese have gained more rights of interpreting their lives.

Fans: bearing the meaning of enthusiasm, fondness, etc., later extended as someone who enthusiastically follows a movie star and other celebrities, etc. In modern western countries, the term "fans" has also been extended to the meaning of "gay".

Scream: verb, synonym for screak, screech, shriek, etc., a sudden sharp crying indicating fear.

Beverly Hillbillies: originally meaning the villain in a village. The term becomes popular with Chinese people because of the Movement of Cracking down Land Owners and Dividing the Land during the Land Reform and the Cultural Revolution. During that period, land owners were the object of dictatorship and crack-down, who used to be rich and cruel, usurious to the poor and sabotage the revolution. Nowadays, "Beverly Hillbillies" usually refers to those wealthy but not purposely showing their riches (different from "upstart"). They may refer to impulsive consumers on line or those in other fields (online games, electronics, cartoon ACG, etc.) For instance, some RMB players in online games are called "Beverly Hillbillies", sometimes called short for "壕" ("hao", the combination of the two Chinese characters for "Beverly Hillbillies"). Later, "Beverly Hillbillies" were gradually used to mock RMB players playing money without thinking in online games, e.g., those rich and showy, especially who are poor and pretending to be rich. Cyber sentences, such as "Beverly Hillbilly, let us be friends", became popular since then. Some even call all those willing to spend money "Beverly Hillbillies". In games, players use the word "Beverly Hillbillies" very often, meaning that someone's equipment is gorgeous and showing no derogatory sense.

Closed Loop: also closed loop structure (feedback control system), comparing measured system output with expected preset value to produce a deviation signal, based on which adjustment and control are made so that the outputted value is as close to the expected value as possible.

Acquisition: when an enterprise is acquired by another enterprise, its brand will be combined, retained or put aside by the dominating enterprise.

Agencies: companies that provide professional brand services for their customers, usually including marketing companies, brand agencies, digital agencies, design agencies or public relation agencies.

Best Practice: the selection of the optimal method for brand naming by an enterprise.

Brand: the public image designed based on strict conception for a proper commodity, service and even individual, consisting of belief, presentation and strategy.

Brand Architecture: it refers to the way adopted by an enterprise to establish brand name and mutual relationship in its business units.

Brand Mark: a mark that carries the image of a brand, also called identification. Brand mark constitutes the intellectual property of an enterprise.

Brand Perception: it refers to the audiences' perception, cognition and subjective opinion of a brand.

Brand Producer: brand producer is usually the enterprise founder.

Brand Spend: the total capital invested in marketing and promoting a brand.

Brand Values: it refers to the measurable value or feature of a brand that can be converted into monetary assets.

Channel: terminal medias or publications utilized for brand marketing, including agencies, distributors, TV, broadcast, billboards, newspaper, etc.

Co-branding: it refers to the simultaneous marketing of more than two brands in a marketing campaign.

Communications: in the science of brand, communications means a series of activities in brand promotion aiming to transmit information to both enterprise employees and the public audiences.

Concessions: stores set up for particular brands. Concessions are a popular mean for brands to enter into a new market, which allows the consumers to positively attach the new brand to existing and more famous brands.

Consumer: people investing money on a brand by way of purchase.

Consumer-Facing Brands: brands aiming to meet consumer demands instead of production demands.

Corporate Branding: the synonym for enterprise image, including brand creation, brand upgrading and enterprise name application, usually referring to the parent brand. Co-branding sometimes may be applied to sub-critical products of an enterprise to exhibit enterprise image and support ancillary brands of the enterprise.

Creativity of the Brand: the creation process in branding, including graphic design and literal expression of the brand.

Brand Demerger: a brand demerges from another brand, which usually requires a new name and a new and independent image.

Brand Equity: it refers to brand valuation and the value of assets represented by it. Brand equity allows the consumers to identify all brand features and relevant brand interest sharers, i.e., the cognition of the consumers, which not only constitutes the brand value by itself, but also makes the brand measurable for valuation.

Flagship Store: among chain stores, a flagship store is the one with the most complete exhibition, largest size and the latest products issued so as to present the brand to the customers in a comprehensive manner.

Franchises: an operation mode under which a company owns and controls a brand and retailing stores take charge of daily operations.

Global/Local: a marketing term meaning the adaptation of a global brand to local culture when marketing in a specific country.

Brand Licensing: it refers to an individual or a company purchasing a brand or a part of it so as to obtain the operational rights under self-owned brand.

Loss Leader: stores selling products at below-cost prices so as to obtain the opportunity of guiding the customers to spend more on other products. For example, a bookstore sells its most popular book at a below-cost price, hopefully to attract the consumers and thus increase the sales of other books.

Mindshare: the emotional and cultural identity of targeted consumers towards a brand.

Narrative: an original story working as the foundation of a brand concept.

Parent Brand: it refers to an owner or company who has the ownership of the main brand. Prospects: potential new customers. Reposition: re-design conducted to attract new targeted groups when the target market of a brand shifts.

Roll-out: a popular marketing tool for launching new products, usually including the phase between pre-sales and official sales.

Spin off: a brand first being launched in a market and then handed over to another enterprise for further promotion.

Stakeholder: the massive audiences influenced by a brand, including investors, news media, consumers, banks, shareholders, employees and communities.

Strapline of Tagline: a word or phrase related to a brand and defines the core spirit of the brand as a conclusion.

Strategy: a word often misused and misunderstood. Strategy usually refers to the overall consideration for the market and the market theories applied in brand marketing.

Sub-Brand: a sub-brand of any brand, e.g., Sony Play Station of Sony.

The Law of Horse's Ass: The law reflects a narrow view of the market by most people in current days. Modern enterprises have insensibly fallen into the Law of Horse's Ass in their channel strategies. We often asked the question when designing channel strategies whether to establish our own branches or to develop agencies? We never thought about a third path.

One Degree Strategy: a new enterprise strategy determined to rewrite western theories. Traditional marketing philosophy looks at the 2D strategic dimension, while One Degree Strategy extends the view to a 3D space. Mostly important, One Degree Strategy localizes western marketing theories and makes analyses based on marketing research methods and value inclination perspectives of Chinese scholars, instead of merely interpreting western theories in Chinese (On this level, we borrow classic theories from the west and root them deeply in China's soil and optimize them with Chinese practices). One Degree Strategy starts the localized innovation of western theories, which, in nature, is to thoroughly understand and master western theories and methods and deeply interpret the local market. It is fundamentally different from the former two paths in that the interpretation of the Chinese market is not only to verify western theories, but also to rewrite the latter so as to ultimately establish Chinese marketing theory architecture. One Degree Strategy consists of four spaces: the first space means strategic design: Commanding Strategy; the second to fourth spaces are the Strategy Implementation level that consists of Model Innovation, Value of Innovation and Innovation Strategy.

The essence of One Degree Strategy is the customer-centered Six-strength Model. Many medium and small Chinese enterprises have satisfied 99% conditions for brand creation, including product R&D, manufacture, quality and technology. What they lack is "99% + 1%". The rest 1% is to plot a brand route map based on enterprise situation, adopting third-party strategies to increase value and creating brand. One Degree Strategy establishes a basic business model, which is the innovation of 4P, 4C, 4R and 4V theoretical models in multilayer economy, a rethinking of new marketing strategies in reality. We can simply understand this business mode as three kinds of hardware and three kinds of software. Customer, product and channel are the hardware we need. We must guarantee products of the best quality, channels for optimal operation and customers of the highest loyalty. Value, communication and brand are the software we need. Altogether, they constitute the Six-strength Model for One Degree Strategy: Customer, Product, Brand, Price, Place and Communication.

One Degree Theory offers some "special" opinions based on a mass of practical strategies for enterprise, for instance, it believes that there is no necessary correlation between brand value and product quality, that the building of brand value is much more important than product quality, and that the setbacks in selling product functionality are much more than those encountered in selling brand value.

Wealth Addition: in the wealth addition mode, wealth is accumulated through market expansion by copying successful cases, for example, Wal-Mart, KFC, Ford, McDonald's, etc. First, a specialty store is set up, then comes the second, the third... by borrowing experiences from the first one, and thus wealth is added. It is always product. Product is the pillar of the mansion of wealth addition, and the most basic competition method is price. In the era of wealth addition, enterprises' competition is more like a one-match game. The first half highlights the speed of product innovation, while the second half focuses on the advertising effect.

Wealth Subtraction: not all enterprises are allowed to follow the path of wealth addition. For large numbers of medium and small enterprises who lack funds, technologies and knowledge, the only way of survival is wealth subtraction. By definition, wealth subtraction means to lower the costs by acquiring cheaper resources and manpower and obtaining a relatively friendly taxation policy, for which the most basic competition method is price.

Information Game: there are complete information games and incomplete information games. The former includes the strategic space of the participant and the payment under specific strategic portfolio, being the game of "public knowledge" among all participants. In incomplete information games, the participants make every effort to maximize their anticipated payment or utility.

Wealth Multiplication: the foundation of the mansion of wealth multiplication is value, that is, wealth multiplication = (customer + product + brand + channel + communication) × value. Value herein contains the returns from brand building, product design and value creation for third parties.

Six-strength Model and Six-strength Theory: the core theoretical basis of One Degree Strategy. It shall be pointed out that the Six-strength Model is not a traditional operational mode, i.e., the simple combination of product, price, channel and promotion. It is customer-oriented and aims to expand and reposition the six operation factors—customer, product, brand, value, channel and communication— and completely overturns the tradition. The correlation among these factors forms a brand-new operation system with replicable system innovation capability.

The Third Angle Innovation Thought: the idea inspiration of One Degree Strategy. In our life, we usually apply certain dialectics to explain the world. For example, we analyze the two sides of one coin utilizing the contradiction theory and view things from opposite perspectives. As a matter of fact, the greatest impact of the dualism operational and life philosophy on enterprise innovation is that it denies the third and fourth possibilities. The Third Angle Innovation Thought is a new thinking mode that breaks away from the dualism, "either-or" and other traditional thinking modes and views the world from a third angle, aiming to establish a new order. Guided by the Third Angle Innovation Thought, in the new world described in One Degree Strategies are derived "third-party customer", "third space" of product, "third-party" payment, "third value" of brand, "third design" for channel, "third choice" for communication, "third-party value creation" and other "third-party strategies".

The Sixth Media: a new media different from existing film and television media, print media, broadcast media, outdoor media and network media that transforms intangible products provided as services, e.g., EMS and letters, into tangible products carrying the function of media spreading. That is, it is a new media providing information spreading for enterprises based on mail services.

Commanding Strategy: One Degree Strategy proposes to, based on the comparative economics, establish a Chinese characteristic commanding field by applying the basic concepts of the Blue Sea Strategy and experiences in the Red Sea Strategy between the latter two. The Commanding Strategy emphasizes the "commanding power", no matter it is a "red sea" or a "blue sea".

Comparative Economics: in One Degree Strategy, comparative economics means a value creation mode that, with both shortage and abundance conditions existing, creates a day-to-day level by way of horizontal comparison and correlation so as to achieve differentiation-based comparative advantage. Comparative economics is a daily-updating and dynamic balance instead of a rigid and static comparison.

Shortage Economy: according to this theory, all commodities are in shortage and, in a restricted and under-developed market, commodities can be sold out anyway, regardless of consumer willingness. The research on traditional economics is based on shortage economy, arguing that the shortage in the market is the cause of accelerated industrialization. The traditional economy takes the side of the supplier, featured in massive production of a single variety, which necessarily leads to the shortage in choice. In One Degree Strategy, it carries the meaning of the shortage in choice.

Abundant Economy: as long as there are sufficiently large storage and distribution channels, the total market shares of those poorly demanded or sold can match and even exceed the market shares of the smaller quantities of commodities in hot sales. According to One Degree Strategy, the abundant economy exists relatively to the shortage economy, being the foundation to widen and flatten the space of choice of the entire society based on highly developed information technology.

Three Rivers Affluxes: the confluence of three major rivers from America, Asia and Europe: the Mississippi, the Yellow River and the Danube. The Mississippi of the United States means that we are in the information technology era; the Yellow River of China means that we are in the "made-in-China" industrial age; while the Danube of Europe means that we are in the European brand concept era. Three Rivers Affluxes indicates the convergence and integration of different time characteristics and cultural features at the same time and in the same place.

Premium Profit Margin: the exceedance in normal profit of an enterprise in current period, i.e., the ratio of additional money willingly paid by a consumer for a certain brand or product against the normal profit.

Premium Profit: the sense of value of a customer towards a brand decides his consumption confidence and the willingness of recommending the product to potential customers. Enterprises do not need to pay marketing costs for customers' word-of-mouth spreading and thus such return needs no additional cost.

Relevance Customer: people who are unaware of product quality but can produce major influence on consumption choice. Customer value consists of the opinion of the relevance customer on the brand and the opinion of the consumer himself. Network economy has broadened the customer boundary and activated those who were originally not the target group or the potential consumer group, making them relevance customers and further target customers.

Chinese Type Marketing: a Chinese characteristic marketing route proposed by Hongbing Hua in 1995. The plain and core principle is to create differentiated competitive edge and thus improve market performance and realized enterprise growth based on China's actual situation. It is a multi-dimensional marketing that explores and studies marketing from multiple perspectives, in multiple spaces and at multiple levels. In its early days, Chinese Type Marketing advocated the 123 Principle, that is, enterprises need one momentum (resources advantage), two advantages (in both cost and brand) and three objectives (accelerated sales increase, market share and product innovation). In the maturity, Chinese Type Marketing proposed the New 123 Principle: one center (centered on customer value), two bases (brand marketing and product design upgrading) and three accelerations (accelerated sales increase, net profit increase and gross margin increase).

Third Party Payment: engaging third parties to pay for the manufacturing, communication or channel costs of enterprise by creating values for them.

The Third Space: people are requiring diversified experiences in products and services with their consumption behavior continuously upgrading, which brings along third space for innovating experiences in high quality products and services.

Channel Timing Expansion: traditional channel terminals realize point-to-point instantaneous consumption, while channels in the network economy are capable of realizing non-point-to-point instantaneous consumption, that is, point-to-plane, plane-to-plane or plane-to-point delayed consumption in different spaces.

Customer Value: a sense of identity of a customer for a product or service in a manner exceeding the value of said product and service, which is expressed in money, because the attribute or core value of the product or service matches the customer's core value.

The Funnel Effect: enterprises continuously obtain new customers, but also lose existing customers at a quicker pace, leading to faster increase in marketing cost than revenue and thus showing a funnel-like descending trend in enterprise profit due to high customer loss rate and low technical research and development capability.

Customer Marginal Cost: marginal cost represents the variation in total cost due to the increase or decrease of a unit production at a certain productivity level, which is usually applied to evaluate the economic practicality of increasing or decreasing production. According to One Degree Strategy, customers holding same ideals form an alliance in the network economy. Such alliance realizes spreading communication through modern communication tools so as to enlarge the actual cost or profit of the customer and generate polymerizing or cracking effects that cannot be underrated.

Third-Party Strategy: a marketing strategy that entails taking view from a third party, creating values for a third party and winning profits from a third party by way of third-party innovation for the six elements for marketing: customer, product, value, communication, channel and brand.

Customer Lifetime Value: the sum of the current and future profit brought along by a customer in all his life dealing with the enterprise.

Time Value: the difference in value of an amount of capital at different time nodes. For an enterprise, the effect of monetary income varies by time.

Customer Satisfaction: customer satisfaction depends on the gap between the customer's anticipation for product and service values and the actual effect. Continual customer satisfaction requires continuous provision of high values for the customers. However, customer satisfaction cannot foresee future consumption behaviors of the customers and high customer satisfaction does not necessarily guarantee high profit.

News Public Relation: enterprises properly manipulate the media to spread information to consumers through news and thus promote brand value.

Postscript

I have researched nearly 300 cases in the fastest-developing field of mobile marketing in China since 2012 and summarized a set of "4S mobile marketing" theories over seven years, which was verified by some enterprises' practical results when tutoring marketing practice for enterprise in China. Therefore, I generated the idea to write a tutorial for the business college. I have published eight books such as *Panorama of Mobile Marketing* since 2012 and have received positive comments from the marketing circles in China.

Actually, as many famous Internet enterprises, Alibaba and Tencent as representatives, are rising successfully, mobile marketing in China develops rapidly and occupies the leading position in the industries of the world. Are the mobile marketing practice and related theory in China beneficial to the mobile marketing industry in the world? Or could they become the extracurricular reading material for students from business colleges around the world? I have always been interested in these questions. Therefore, I had the idea to publish, in the US, the English version of *Mobile Marketing Management* which was published in China in April 2017 for the first time and modified in May 2018 for the second version.

Certainly, I soon found that it was not easy to translate theoretical works of Chinese scholars into English and get officially published in the US. Fortunately, I got Bright Power (Beijing) Culture Media Co., Ltd. as the general agent for publishing and distribution of the book all over the world. With great help from the company, publishing confirmation from the famous Taylor & Francis Group publisher was obtained in half a year after the completion of the English translation. People who provided efficient assistance for publishing of the English version are as follows: Ms. Helen Zhang, Copyright Manager of China Publishing Group Corporation Research Press; Rene Yang, a professor from Claremont University; Vincent G. Xie, an associate professor of Marketing in University of Massachusetts Boston; Zhou Qiang, a doctoral student of Management in Texas State University; Virginia Cheung, a doctoral student in Drucker Academy; Jenny Darroch, dean and a professor in Drucker School of Management; and Issam A. Ghazzawi, a professor of Management at the University of Laverne, who wrote the pertinent recommendation letter for the book. Ying Wang, an associate professor from Youngstown State University, not only helped review the manuscript and proposed modification opinions, but also wrote an ardent recommendation letter.

Thomas Qin, General Manager of Bright Power (Beijing), visited some prestigious universities in the US twice for advice on the manuscript, and communicated with multiple presses in the US. In August 2018, he attended AMA Summer Academic

Conference and exchanged ideas on the book with multiple professors from universities in the US in Boston. He went to the headquarter of NACS (National Association of College Stores) in Cleveland, Ohio, visited Robert A. Walton, Chief Executive Officer of NACS, and discussed the corresponding university marketing plan with Jessica Hickman, Senior Director of Course Materials Services. And, finally, Ms. Kristine Mednansky, Senior Editor from Taylor & Francis Group, provided guidance on relevant matters. As a result, a publishing approval from Taylor & Francis Group was obtained under her patient guidance.

Hereby, I would like to extend my sincere thanks solemnly to the persons who assisted in publishing the book in the US.

The date of publishing the book is also a start for me to think about the next question. When mobile marketing is popularized around the world, I, as a marketing scholar with an open mind in China, would like to invite more intelligent scholars in marketing circles around the world to compile a general textbook of Mobile Marketing together. My ideas are as follows:

Is 4S theory of mobile marketing verifiable or empirical?

Are there more international cases added in the book?

Can algorithm, as a kind of computer language originally, be inherent operating logic of mobile marketing?

Shall we discuss the ethics and sustainable marketing of mobile marketing?

Can the macroeconomics be proposed in the micro view?

Is the solution Spiral Economics? And I would like to invite coauthors to enrich the connotation together.

If the above hypotheses are true, I hope to find like-minded coauthors to work together and provide a brand-new textbook of *Mobile Marketing* for the business colleges in the world. My email address is 1439458335@qq.com. Marketing professors from the US or around the world are welcome to contact me and join in discussing the academic topic.

-Hongbing Hua on September 3rd, 2018 in Guangzhou, China